AGENT STORM

AGENT STORM

My Life inside al-Qaeda

MORTEN STORM WITH PAUL CRUICKSHANK AND TIM LISTER

VIKING

an imprint of

PENGUIN BOOKS

VIKING

Published by the Penguin Group

Penguin Books Ltd, 80 Strand, London WC2R ORL, England

Penguin Group (USA) Inc., 375 Hudson Street, New York, New York 10014, USA

Penguin Group (Canada), 90 Eglinton Avenue East, Suite 700, Toronto, Ontario, Canada M4P 2Y3
(a division of Pearson Penguin Canada Inc.)

Penguin Ireland, 25 St Stephen's Green, Dublin 2, Ireland (a division of Penguin Books Ltd)

Penguin Group (Australia), 707 Collins Street, Melbourne, Victoria 3008, Australia
(a division of Pearson Australia Group Pty Ltd)

Penguin Books India Pvt Ltd, 11 Community Centre, Panchsheel Park, New Delhi – 110 017, India

Penguin Group (NZ), 67 Apollo Drive, Rosedale, Auckland 0632, New Zealand
(a division of Pearson New Zealand Ltd)

Penguin Books (South Africa) (Pty) Ltd, Block D, Rosebank Office Park,
181 Jan Smuts Avenue, Parktown North, Gauteng 2193, South Africa

Penguin Books Ltd, Registered Offices: 80 Strand, London WC2R ORL, England

www.penguin.com

First published 2014
002

Copyright © Morten Storm, Paul Cruickshank, Tim Lister, 2014

The moral right of the author has been asserted

Set in 11.5/14.75 pt Dante MT Std
Typeset by Jouve (UK), Milton Keynes
Printed in Great Britain by Clays Ltd, St Ives plc

A CIP catalogue record for this book is available from the British Library

HARDBACK ISBN: 978–0–241–00377–0
TRADE PAPERBACK ISBN: 978–0–241–00378–7

www.greenpenguin.co.uk

CONTENTS

Contents

Contents

Map of Yemen

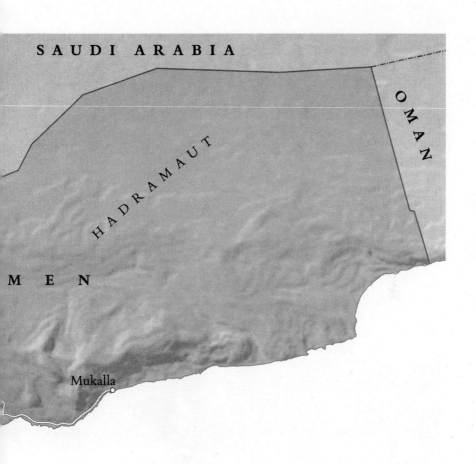

SAUDI ARABIA

OMAN

HADRAMAUT

MEN

Mukalla

Arabian Sea

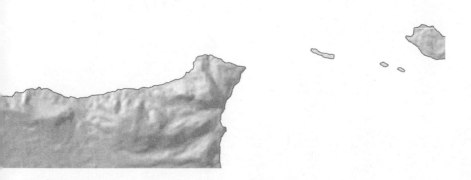

AUTHORS' NOTE

Any spy who goes public will inevitably face scrutiny, especially one claiming to have worked as a double agent for four Western intelligence services on some of their most sensitive counter-terrorism operations after 9/11.

What makes Morten Storm's story unique is the extraordinary amount of audiovisual evidence and electronic communications he collected during his time as a spy, which both corroborate his story and enrich his account.

This material, to which he gave us unfettered access, includes:

- emails exchanged with the influential cleric Anwar al-Awlaki;
- videos recorded by Awlaki and the Croatian woman who travels to Yemen to marry the cleric, a marriage arranged by Storm even as Awlaki was being hunted by the US;
- dozens of encrypted emails between Storm and terrorist operatives in Arabia and Africa that are still on the hard drives of his computers;
- records of money transfers to a terrorist in Somalia;
- text messages with Danish intelligence officers still stored on his mobile phones;
- secret recordings made by Storm of conversations with his Danish and US intelligence handlers, including a thirty-minute recording of a meeting with a CIA agent in Denmark in 2011 during which several of Storm's missions targeting terrorists were discussed;
- handwritten mission notes;
- video and photographs of Storm driving through Yemen's tribal areas just after meeting Awlaki in 2008;
- video of Storm with British and Danish intelligence agents in northern Sweden in 2010.

Unless otherwise stated in the endnotes all emails, letters, Facebook exchanges, text messages and recordings of conversations quoted in the book are reproduced verbatim, including spelling and grammatical mistakes. Some have been translated into English from Danish.

Storm also provided photographs taken with several of his Danish intelligence handlers in Iceland. Reporters at the Danish newspaper *Jyllands-Posten* were able to confirm the identity of the agents through their sources.

Several individuals mentioned in the book corroborated essential elements of Storm's story. We have not disclosed the full identity of some of them for their own safety. No Western intelligence official was willing to go on the record.

Storm provided us with his passports, which include entry and exit visas for every trip outside Europe described in the book from the year 2000 onwards. He also shared hotel invoices paid by 'Mola Consult', a front company used by Danish intelligence, which according to Denmark's business registry was dissolved just before he went public. Additionally he provided dozens of Western Union receipts cataloguing payments by Danish intelligence (PET). His PET handlers listed Søborg – the district in which PET is located in Copenhagen – on the paperwork.

We used pseudonyms for three people in the book to protect their safety or identity, which we make clear at first reference. We have used only the first name of several others for security or legal reasons. A *dramatis personae* is attached at the end of the book. The book includes Arabic phrases and greetings; a translation is given at first reference.

We have added a number of photographs and other visual testimonies of Storm's work in an archive at the end of the book and a colour picture section. These include a photograph of a briefcase containing a $250,000 reward from the CIA, handwritten notes from a meeting with Awlaki, decrypted emails, money transfer receipts, and video images and pictures taken in Yemen's Shabwa province on trips to meet the cleric.

Paul Cruickshank and Tim Lister, April 2014

CHAPTER ONE
DESERT ROAD

Mid-September 2009

I sat in my grey Hyundai peering into the liquid darkness, exhausted and apprehensive. Exhausted because my day had started before dawn in Sana'a, Yemen's capital, some 200 miles to the north-west. Apprehensive because I had no idea who was coming to meet me or when they would arrive. Would they greet me as a comrade or seize me as a traitor?

The desert night had an intensity I had never seen in Europe. There were no lights on the road that led from the coast into the mountains of Shabwa province, a lawless part of Yemen. At times there hadn't been much of a road either. A fine coating of sand had drifted on to the baking tarmac. Long after sunset, a humid breeze wafted in from the Arabian Sea.

My apprehension was fed by guilt: I had only been able to drive into this no-man's-land, where al-Qaeda's presence was growing as the government's authority waned, because my young Yemeni wife, Fadia, was beside me.[1] On the pretext of visiting her brother we had negotiated one checkpoint after another on a dangerous route south.

In my quest to reconnect with Anwar al-Awlaki, an American-Yemeni cleric who had become one of al-Qaeda's most influential and charismatic figures, I knew I was risking my life. Yemen's military and intelligence services had recently stepped up their attempts to combat al-Qaeda in the Arabian Peninsula (AQAP), one of the most active and

---

1 Fadia is not her real name. For her safety and that of her family, I have given her a pseudonym.

dangerous franchises of Osama bin Laden's group. There was the risk of an ambush, a shoot-out at a checkpoint or just a lethal misunderstanding.

There was also the danger that Awlaki – now dubbed 'al-Qaeda's rock star' by Western newspapers – might no longer trust me. My trip had been at his request. In an email he had saved in the draft folder of an anonymous email account we shared, he had told me:

'Come to Yemen. I need to see you.'

It had been nearly a year since I had seen Awlaki and in that time he had continued a remorseless and fateful journey. The radical preacher sympathetic to al-Qaeda had become an influential figure within its leadership, aware of and involved in its plans to export terror.

I had already missed one rendezvous. Awlaki had invited me to come out to a meeting of Yemen's leading jihadis in a remote part of Marib, a desert province that had reputedly been the home of the Queen of Sheba centuries earlier. Awlaki's younger brother, Omar, was meant to organize my travel to Marib, but had insisted I dress as a woman in a full veil, or niqab, so that we could get through the checkpoints. At 6 foot 1 inch tall and weighing nearly eighteen stone, I was dubious. I had declined the offer, even though the driver who would take me to meet these wanted men was a police officer. Such were the contradictions of Yemen. My absence from such an important gathering of al-Qaeda's leaders in Yemen had gnawed at me. So a few days later my wife and I undertook this odyssey to Shabwa.

After a few minutes I heard the muffled growl of a distant engine, then saw headlights and the approach of a Toyota Land Cruiser packed with serious young men brandishing AK-47s. The escort party had arrived. I grasped my wife's hand. If things were about to go very wrong, we would know in the next few moments.

All day we had followed curt directions texted from Awlaki, as if they were clues in some bizarre treasure hunt. 'Take this road, turn left, pretend to the police that you are going to Mukalla along the coast.'

I could hardly blend in with the locals. As a heavy-set Dane with a shock of ginger hair and a long beard, I might as well have been an alien life form in a country of wiry, dark-skinned Arabs. In a land where kidnapping and tribal rivalries, trigger-happy police and militant jihadis made travelling an unpredictable venture, the sight of someone like me, with a petite Yemeni woman at my side, crammed into a hired car heading towards the rebellious south was – to say the least – an unusual one.

The day had started well enough. The morning cool before the intense heat took hold was invigorating. There had been a hold-up at the first checkpoint outside Sana'a, always the most troublesome. Why would anyone want to leave the relative security of the capital for the badlands of the south? I chatted in Arabic, which always impressed my inquisitors, while my wife – her face and hair covered in the black niqab – sat mutely in the passenger seat. It was no accident that a CD in the car was playing verses from the Koran. I told them we were going to see my wife's brother and join a wedding party on the coast and would be travelling via Aden – Yemen's main port on the Arabian Sea and the hub of commercial life.

The police at the roadblock had difficulty deciphering my passport. Few of them were likely to read Arabic well, let alone be able to understand the Roman alphabet. They seemed to think I was Turkish – perhaps because the very idea of a European travelling across Yemen was so unfathomable. My broad smile and apparent ease with my surroundings were enough for them. It probably helped that it was not only September – a scorching month in Arabia – but also the middle of Ramadan. The men were tired from fasting.

Once we were clear of that first checkpoint, the challenge was to stay on the road, or at least to prevent others from driving us off it. Several times I caught a glimpse down sheer cliffs of the rusting carcass of a truck or bus. Roads in Yemen seemed to attract pedestrians with a death wish, whether camels, dogs, cows or kids. As vehicles hurtled towards them they would wander into the middle.

The colours of the morning gave way to the white heat of the mid-afternoon, and I struggled to stay focused on the road and on the risks of our journey. At last the mountains began to give way to the coastal lowlands – the Tehama. In the distance lay the port of Aden. The city had suffered since the collapse of South Yemen and the ruthless military campaign of the North's President, Ali Abdullah Saleh, to unify the two halves of Yemen in the 1990s. The people of the south saw themselves as neglected. A separatist movement was gaining strength, compounding the challenge to the Yemeni government from al-Qaeda militants.

In my rear-view mirror, the mountains were swallowing the glowering sun. I tried to navigate my way around Aden's chaotic fringe – to join the long coastal road that I had been instructed to take by another of Awlaki's text messages.

Anwar al-Awlaki was from a powerful clan in the mountainous Shabwa province. His father had been a respected academic and a minister in Yemen's government who had gone to America on a Fulbright fellowship and had a Ph.D. from the University of Nebraska. The younger Awlaki had himself been a university lecturer in Sana'a after abandoning the United States in the wake of 9/11, worried (with justification) he was being targeted by the FBI. He had met two of the hijackers in California months before the attack, though there was no evidence that he knew their plans.

Seven years on, the landscape – and Awlaki – had changed. President Saleh was ever more desperate for US aid and was under growing pressure to take a harder line against al-Qaeda sympathizers. There had already been a suicide bomb attack on the US embassy in September 2008, which killed ten, and mass breakouts of al-Qaeda inmates from supposedly top-security prisons. Yemen was al-Qaeda's favourite recruiting ground – it had provided a pipeline of young men with little education who were dispatched to Osama bin Laden's training camps before 9/11. Some of them had become bin Laden's bodyguards before being caught escaping from the Tora Bora mountains of Afghanistan and sent to Guantanamo Bay.

Now Yemen was the base for al-Qaeda's affiliate in Yemen, AQAP, and a top destination for European and American militants dreaming of jihad. And Awlaki's militancy had hardened. His sermons – carried around the world on YouTube – were a guiding light for would-be jihadis. In rural townships in Pennsylvania, cramped flats in England, the suburbs of Toronto, young men were consuming his every word.

For the CIA and MI6, Awlaki represented the future of al-Qaeda. His knowledge of Western societies, his fluent English and his command of social media posed a new and more lethal threat than grainy videos and arcane statements from bin Laden.

In 2006 he had been arrested and charged with being involved in a vague kidnapping conspiracy. He had spent eighteen months in jail in Sana'a and had even received a visit from FBI agents wanting to know more about his meetings with the 9/11 hijackers. And then he had vanished into Yemen's vast and unforgiving interior.

And so I found myself heading east out of Aden, on the last leg of my mystery tour of Yemen. We arrived at another rudimentary checkpoint, a couple of battered 'STOP' signs either side of a shed of corrugated metal that only concentrated the searing heat. In some ways this shed was a frontier, marking the effective limit of the state's authority. Beyond was a road that foreigners could only travel if escorted by soldiers, forbidding lands roamed by al-Qaeda fighters and bandits.

We repeated the wedding story; how I knew the route to Mukalla along the coast and could converse in Arabic. Should we decline protection, we were told, we would have to return to Aden and sign a document absolving the authorities of all responsibility for our safety.

An hour later the sun had gone but its red rays still illuminated the dusk. We returned to the checkpoint, document in hand. By then, the guards were about to break their Ramadan fast with the meal known as *iftar*. They couldn't care less what happened to this crazy European and his silent Yemeni bride.

The southern coast of Yemen could be the perfect vacation destination: endless beaches of soft sand, warm waters, superb fishing. It was untouched but sadly untouchable, the fringe of a failing state – interrupted only by scruffy coastal towns like Zinjibar, where scattered breeze blocks spoke of projects unfinished or not yet begun.

As we drove, now free of the last barrier, our spirits lifted. Adrenalin coursed through me.

The final text instruction from Awlaki arrived. I should tell the police I needed petrol and then head north.

Shaqra was little more than a fishing village. On this steamy night it was deserted, the occasional dog hobbling across the main street. If anything it was more dilapidated than when we had passed through a year before on our previous voyage to meet Awlaki.

Outside the town, a grandiose junction with signs showing a

smiling President marked the point at which the road divided, one branch going inland and up into the rebellious interior, the other continuing along the coast. I knew I would never be allowed to head inland, so my instructions were to tell the police checkpoint that I was going along the coast but needed fuel from the petrol station a couple of miles in the other direction. It was a ruse that had clearly worked before. The police, rendered dozy by *iftar*, waved us on. They would not see us return.

Now I sat with Fadia – our pulses racing on a lonely desert road – dazzled by the headlights of a vehicle packed with armed men.

A bearded man in his mid-thirties with sharp, dark eyes, and a red-chequered scarf around his head, emerged from a cloud of dust drifting across the beam of the Land Cruiser's headlights. The way the rest of the group fell in behind him made it clear that Abdullah Mehdar was their leader. He was known as being fearless, and having militant leanings. I scrutinized his face as he walked towards us.

'*As salaam aleikum* [Peace be with you],' he said at last, greeting me in Arabic and breaking into a broad smile. The tension left my body as if a fever had broken. In my relief I hugged every one of Mehdar's companions. They had brought food – bananas, bread – and we broke the Ramadan fast together. I felt safe for the first time that day. I was with some of Yemen's most wanted, a group of armed men I did not know, in the dead of night, heading towards the wilderness of Shabwa. But it was as if I were in a cocoon, admitted to a brotherhood of simple beliefs and unquestioned loyalties.

Mehdar was Awlaki's personal emissary, like him a member of the Awalik tribe – and Yemen was a country where tribal loyalties trumped all others. Knowing that I had been invited here by Awlaki and was the cleric's friend, he was deeply respectful and courteous.

After a few minutes, he said we should move. This was an area where highway robbery was all too common, and where criminals were as well armed as militants. It must have been gone 9 p.m. by the time the convoy arrived at its destination: the Land Cruiser followed my little Hyundai – surely the first hire car ever to have puttered through this remote corner of Shabwa. The vehicles threw up a cloud of dust as we sped down a track outside an unlit hamlet. Mountains loomed beyond, though on this moonless night there was no telling where the land ended and the vast sky began.

I could not know it then but I was in the vicinity of al-Hota, a settlement nestled in the shadow of a towering rocky plateau in the Mayfa'a district of Shabwa – the heart of al-Qaeda country.

We arrived at an imposing two-storey house inside a compound with high walls. The gates were opened and swiftly closed by two men with AK-47s slung over their shoulders. I felt a surge of panic. My journey to meet Anwar al-Awlaki was complete, but what if Yemen's security services knew of my plans and had let me make this journey, or Awlaki himself no longer trusted me? And then there was Fadia. She knew Awlaki, and knew we were friends, but had no inkling of my true purpose.

I glanced up at the constellations before climbing the steps. My feet were made of lead; the few paces up to the house felt like an eternity. There was no way out now. Images of Nick Berg and Daniel Pearl, two Americans who had met gruesome deaths at the hands of al-Qaeda, beheaded on video, flashed through my mind.

Fadia was escorted to the back, where the tribesmen's womenfolk were waiting. In this part of Yemen the sexes would never mix socially. Later she told me about the stoicism of the women, many of whose husbands had been killed in the cause of jihad. It was common for the widows to marry another jihadi – but hardly a recipe for domestic tranquillity.

The large unfurnished hall led to an even larger reception room, and the first thing I noticed was a line of weapons neatly propped against the wall – more AK-47s, vintage rifles, even a rocket-propelled-grenade launcher. This was a group ready to fight at a moment's notice, but its enemy was as likely a rival tribe as the Yemeni security services.

A dozen men were gathered around a big silver bowl laid on the floor and piled high with chicken and saffron rice. They were young; some had been village boys just a few years ago. And in the middle of them was Anwar al-Awlaki, slim, elegant, with those intelligent eyes that had already seduced so many restless souls in Europe and America. He rose with a warm smile and embraced me.

'*As salaam aleikum,*' he said with affection. He exuded natural authority, gesturing at the room as if to underline that he was master of this
place and these people.

Awlaki was wearing his trademark white robes, immaculate despite
the dust and heat, and the glasses that seemed to confirm his intellect.
I was struck by the contrast between the simple and uneducated country boys gathered here and this scholar of Islam, a philosopher turned
spiritual guide of jihad. After his greeting, the entire party rose to welcome me. They were all in awe of 'the Sheikh', whose magnetism was
undimmed despite his seclusion.

'Come, eat,' Awlaki said, his American accent tinged by several
years back in his Arab homeland.

He seemed delighted to have my company, a welcome interruption
to his intellectual solitude. But first he must see to his guest's needs.
After introducing me to the men sitting on the floor, Awlaki found me
space among them as the communal meal began. The guests were
devouring the chicken and rice with their hands – and for all my familiarity with Yemeni ways I could not help but ask for a spoon. This was
a source of huge amusement. I found that a couple of self-deprecating
remarks and my Arabic – honed over more than a decade visiting and
living in Yemen – set them at ease.

Scrutinizing Awlaki, I saw a detachment, a melancholy about him –
as if his isolation in Shabwa and the American-led pressure on him
were beginning to take a toll. It had been almost two years since his
release from prison, thanks to the intervention of his powerful family.
In the early months of 2008 he had left Sana'a and taken refuge in his
ancestral homeland. The motto of the Awalik tribe was reputed to be:
'We are the sparks of Hell; whoever interferes with us will be burned.'

In the year since I had last seen him, Awlaki's movements had
become more furtive – hence my odyssey for the sake of this brief
encounter. The Sheikh was constantly on the move from one safe
house to the next, occasionally retreating to mountain hideouts around
the fringes of the 'Empty Quarter' – the ocean of sand that stretched
into Saudi Arabia.

Despite the preacher's seclusion, he continued to deliver online sermons and communicate with followers through email accounts and

texts. His messages had grown more strident – perhaps because of his months in detention, where he was held in solitary confinement most of the time, perhaps because his reading of Islamist scholarship had led him to a more radical outlook. And maybe his banishment to the mountain wilderness had fed a growing hostility to the world.

When the meal was done, Awlaki stood and asked me to accompany him to a smaller room.

I studied his face.

'How are you?' I asked, at a loss for anything more substantial.

'I am here,' Awlaki said, with a hint of fatalism. 'But I miss my family, my wives, my children. I cannot go to Sana'a, and it is too dangerous for them to come here. The Americans want me dead. They are putting pressure on the government all the time.'

Drones wandered the skies, he said, but he was not scared of them.

'This is the path of the Prophets and the pious men: jihad.'

He said the 'brothers' were disappointed that I had not made it to Marib; they had heard much about me. As we talked it became clear that Awlaki felt little threat from the Yemeni government, which would rather box the al-Qaeda problem into Shabwa and hope it went away than try to tackle the tribal feuds that had allowed militants space to settle and organize.

Awlaki told me he wanted to see the end of the Saleh government, regarding it as secular and a pawn of America. With relish he described how a recent ambush of government forces had netted heavy weapons, including anti-tank rockets, and inflicted severe casualties. Perhaps they could be transferred to Islamists in Somalia, who were badly in need of such weapons, he mused.

The spiritual guide had become the quartermaster.

A few months earlier, Awlaki had sent a message to al-Shabaab, the militant Islamist group that had brought Sharia to much of Somalia. They were, he said, setting Muslims an example on how to fight back.

'The ballot has failed us, but the bullet has not,' Awlaki had written. 'If my circumstances had allowed, I would not have hesitated in joining you and being a soldier in your ranks.'

The man who had once condemned the 9/11 attacks as un-Islamic when he lived in America had recently written on his blog, 'I pray that

Allah destroys America and all its allies . . . We will implement the rule of Allah on Earth by the tip of the sword whether the masses like it or not.'

He had also begun to convey this message to Muslims living in the West, likening their situation to that faced by the Prophet Mohammed and his followers in pre-Islamic Mecca, where they were persecuted and forced to make the journey – the *hijra* – north to Medina.

And just weeks before my visit, writing from his Shabwa oupost, Awlaki had attacked the cooperation of Muslim countries with the US military, saying 'the blame should be placed on the soldier who is willing to follow orders . . . who sells his religion for a few dollars.'

It was an argument that would have a deep impact on an officer in the United States army, Major Nidal Hasan, who had already exchanged emails with Awlaki.

Awlaki told me that in jihad it was acceptable that civilians would suffer and die. The cause justified the means. I swiftly disagreed, knowing that my plain-spoken views were part of my appeal to Awlaki, who was prepared to argue the point based on his reading of the Koran and *Hadith*.

Several months before, a young man who had attached himself to Mehdar had travelled to a neighbouring province and killed himself and four South Korean tourists in a suicide attack.

'He is now in paradise,' one of his friends had told me over dinner. It wasn't clear to me whether Mehdar himself had any role in the attack or even condoned it – but the commitment of these fighters went far beyond the rhetorical.

I told Awlaki I supported attacks on military targets, but informed him flatly that I could not and would not help him obtain anything that would be used against civilians. I did not want to be scouring Europe for bomb-making equipment that would ultimately result in civilian deaths.

'So you disagree with the mujahideen?' Awlaki asked.

'On this, we will have to disagree.'

I also detected a more toxic animosity towards America, as if Awlaki felt he had been victimized there as a Muslim. He had been arrested in San Diego – though never charged – for soliciting prostitutes. The humiliation still gnawed at him: the way the FBI had 'let it be known' that Awlaki's personal conduct was sometimes not that expected of an imam, a nod and a wink aimed at besmirching his character.

The subject of women was very much on Awlaki's mind as we conversed into the small hours. Awlaki's self-imposed exile meant that he no longer had any personal contact with his two wives. One he had known since childhood; they had married in their teens. More recently he had taken a second wife, not yet twenty when they were married. But, he told me, he needed the company of a woman who understood and would share the sacrifices of a jihadi's life, someone who would be married to the cause.

'Perhaps you can look out for someone in the West, a white convert sister,' he suggested.

It was the second time he had broached marrying a woman from Europe and I knew he was now serious. It would not be easy and there would be risks. But I knew there were plenty of women who saw Awlaki as a gift from Allah.

There were other requests. He asked me 'to find brothers to work for the cause and to get money from Europe and some equipment'.

He also wanted me to recruit militants to come to Yemen for training and 'then return home – ready to wage jihad in Europe or America'. He did not specify the training – nor what they would be expected to do. But in our two-hour conversation I was left with the impression that Awlaki wanted to begin a campaign of terror attacks in Europe and the US.

The next morning, Awlaki was gone – whether for his own security or because of some meeting I was not told. Instead I spent some time with Abdullah Mehdar, the tribal leader who had met me the previous night. I could not help but admire this apparently honourable man, his unquestioning loyalty to Awlaki. He seemed to have no interest in attacking the West, but wanted Yemen to become an Islamic state with Sharia law. His commitment was so intense that he wept as one of the young fighters leading prayers spoke of the promise of paradise.

They might have a warped world-view, I thought, but these people were not hypocrites. Their loyalty was simple, intense.

I was in a hurry to get away: our flight was due to leave Sana'a for Europe the next evening, and who knew how long the journey back would take? Fadia emerged from the women's quarters and we prepared to leave.

As those forbidding gates swung open, I discovered our car had a puncture – which was perhaps not surprising after the high-speed drive through the mountains.

Abdullah ran out and helped me change the tyre. There were again tears in his eyes: he seemed to sense an incipient danger.

'If we don't meet again, we will see each other in paradise,' he said, the tears now running down his cheeks.

The mujahideen escorted us to the main road and bid us goodbye. We had left the cocoon.

I knew that in three Western capitals there were people waiting to hear every detail of the hours that I had spent with Anwar al-Awlaki. I needed to get to Sana'a – and then out of Yemen, fast.

CHAPTER TWO

GANGS, GIRLS, GOD

1976–1997

The path to my meeting with Anwar al-Awlaki in the mountains of Yemen was – to put it mildly – an unlikely one. I was born on the second day of 1976 in a windswept town on the coast of Denmark. Korsør, with its neat red-brick bungalows, could not be more different from the outer reaches of Yemen. At the edge of undulating farmland on Zeeland, it looks westwards across the grey waters of the Great Belt towards the island of Funen.

Korsør belies the conventional image of Scandinavian tolerance and progressiveness. It's a gritty, working-class town of 25,000 people, including a sprinkling of immigrants from Yugoslavia, Turkey and the Arab world.

My family was lower middle class – but we were not really a family at all. My alcoholic father left home when I was four. In fact he vanished. There were no weekend visits, no fishing trips or days out. My mother, Lisbeth, seemed to have a weakness for flawed men. She remarried, and my stepfather was a brooding, menacing presence, exploding into fits of violence. It might be the way I was holding my fork or just a word. There was no warning, just a fist delivered with force. My mother did not escape the violence, and a few times left home only to return when promised that things would change. They never did, yet she stayed with him for nearly twenty years.

'I'm not proud of the childhood you got,' she would say with sadness years later. 'I actually feel that it is my fault that you became what you did.'

As a child I roamed the shoreline, woods and fields around Korsør. I had plenty of time to myself and wanted to be away from home from dawn till dusk. I would build camps with friends, swing ropes over the frigid waters and drop in, yelling.

The few photographs I have from those days show a face full of uncertainty. There is a wariness about my eyes that brings back a host of unwelcome memories. But I also had a manic energy – energy that seemed to invite trouble.

I celebrated turning thirteen by attempting my first armed robbery with two friends, Benjamin and Junior. It was not a triumph of planning or execution. We chose a small store run by an elderly man renowned for his meanness and his cheap cigars. Clad in balaclavas, we waited in the gloom for the shop to close and then tried to burst in as the shopkeeper began to lock up. Benjamin brandished a .22 revolver that belonged to his father.

The man's strength belied his age as he tried to force the door shut. Perhaps it was the fear of losing the contents of the till that inspired his resistance. Somehow he managed to lock us out.

Humiliated, we turned to a takeaway restaurant nearby. This time I was sent in with the gun.

My heart sank the moment I pulled out the weapon. I recognized the young woman behind the counter, a family friend. I tried to sound older than I was, lowering my voice in a way that must have come across like a record playing at the wrong speed.

'This is a robbery.'

It did not sound convincing.

The woman peered over the counter, more puzzled than alarmed.

'Morten, is that you?'

I turned and fled. We took out our frustrations on an elderly woman in the street by snatching her bag. But she fell and broke her hip, and the police soon beat a path to my home.

It was the start of a spiral. In school I enjoyed history, music and the discussion of religion and cultures but was bored by the demands of classwork. None of my teachers really connected with me – or even seemed to notice me – and I would taunt them. They would respond by throwing chalkboard dusters at me – or by breaking down in tears – as the classroom was reduced to chaos.

I was sent to a 'special school' – one for wayward, hyperactive boys – which concentrated on sports and activities, and where students were confined to the classroom for just two hours a day. I was entrusted with a chainsaw in the woodlands and allowed to wear myself out on the football field. There was no shortage of adventure. The school organized trips abroad for the children they were trying to mould into citizens. The intention was well-meaning but the results were less rewarding. A visit to Tunisia triggered my love of travel and adventure, but we reduced the teachers to emotional wrecks, even stealing their clothes and selling them to some locals.

By fourteen I was an unstoppable force. An immigrant from the former Yugoslavia called Jalal and I unravelled water hoses in the school corridors and fired hundreds of gallons into every corner of the building. The school from which it was supposedly impossible to get expelled could take no more.

I had one last chance – at a high school near Korsør, where a maths teacher who saw my sports potential took me under his wing. I was soon playing junior football at a high level. There were mutterings that scouts for professional teams were checking my progress. But my school record, bulging with disciplinary notices, preceded me. One teacher in particular wanted me out of the school. When I was selected to play for a Danish schools' football team at a tournament in Germany, she took me to one side. Her eyes narrowed and with an expression of grim satisfaction she told me I would not be going because my academic record was not good enough. She knew that going to the tournament was the one thing I craved. I kicked a cup of coffee out of her hand.

It was the last thing I would ever do inside a school. At sixteen, just weeks before my final exams, my formal education was finished. But my street education was just beginning. I joined up with a group branded the 'Raiders' by local police because we roamed the town wearing Oakland Raiders baseball hats and baggy trousers.

The Raiders were mainly Palestinians, Turks and Iranian Muslims.

We made an unlikely group: the young Dane with red hair and thick biceps (looking like a Norse raider) and his Muslim friends. I gravitated to the Raiders because like many of the immigrant kids I felt like an outsider in Korsør, and I always identified with the underdog. We had few prospects and a lot of time on our hands; most of our energy was devoted to drinking as much cheap beer as we could afford and scoring with as many girls as would let us. My teenage Muslim friends wore their faith lightly. They drank and partied like the rest of us. They would defend Islam in the face of a growing anti-Muslim mood, but did not feel bound by its more demanding restrictions.

Their families had come to settle in Denmark – escaping violence or poverty in their homelands. By 1990, Denmark, like other Scandinavian countries, had a sizeable immigrant population. It had granted refugee or guest-worker status to thousands of families from Turkey, Yugoslavia, Iran and Pakistan. In the first dozen years of my life, Denmark's immigrant population from 'non-Western' countries more than doubled. The influx had begun to test Denmark's reputation as a liberal and progressive society. Skinhead gangs would descend on Korsør with sticks and bats but the Raiders were ready for them. I was never far from the action and found the rush addictive.

It helped that I had a talent for boxing and spent plenty of time in the gym. One of Korsør's few claims to fame was that it had been the point of departure for Viking raids on England a millennium ago. So it seemed appropriate that one of its more recent sons was Denmark's best-known boxer, Brian Nielsen, who would fight Evander Holyfield and Mike Tyson.

Nielsen was involved with a thriving amateur boxing club in Korsør, where the youth programme was run by a professional boxer named Mark Hulstrøm. A heavyweight in his late twenties, Hulstrøm was still fighting. Built like an ox, balding with a goatee, he was a man of few emotions. But he was excited by my potential as a young welterweight. I was quick on my feet, with a fast jab, a solid right-hook and a strong jaw. And I loved the physical exertion. Boxing – as well as jujitsu – was a release for the anger I felt, towards my brutal stepfather and against every attempt to make me conform.

I went to the gym – an anonymous grey building on the edge of Korsør – for three years. One day, soon after my sixteenth birthday, Mark took me aside.

'You have real class,' he said – his dark-brown eyes gleaming. 'You could make the Olympic squad, even turn pro.'

Mark visited my mother to explain why I should get more boxing training. Young enough to remember how chaotic a teenager's life could be, he was also old enough to be a figure of authority. He was as close to a surrogate father as I would get.

My talent took me to tournaments in Czechoslovakia and Holland. Denmark's national coach came to watch me and I was selected for the national school sports squad. The Korsør club had provided several of Denmark's Olympic boxers; there seemed every possibility that I could join that elite.

For a while I dreamt of making it as a boxer. But, to Hulstrøm's disappointment, the discipline demanded was beyond me and I spent as much time using my boxing training in brawls as I did in the ring.

My mother, the essence of lower-middle-class Danish propriety, had long given up on me, and by the age of sixteen I was rarely at home. Rather than face her disapproving looks I bunked down at the homes of my Raider friends. I was never quite sure where I would lay my head the next night. Frequently it was long after midnight, because by now I had discovered the down-at-heel pubs and clubs of Korsør.

Shortly before my seventeenth birthday, there was a big street festival in Korsør. A thug confronted me and accused me of trying to take his girlfriend. With one blow I floored him, knocking him nearly unconscious. It would prove a busy weekend. Another girl's boyfriend threatened me with a carving knife. With the blade against my throat, my welterweight training kicked in. I stepped back quickly and delivered a right-hook. Two punches; two knockouts. Maybe the Olympics were not such a pipedream after all.

On weekdays I would visit Hulstrøm's boxing club. At weekends the action would continue, but without gloves. I was rarely hurt, thanks to my speed and a sense of when I was about to be hit. To combine partying, drinking and fighting was far more fun than nine minutes in the ring. And I could look after my friends whenever racist baiting erupted at the clubs. 'Paki', 'black pig' . . . the insults would fly. And I would step forward and put the assailant on the deck with a couple of punches.

Hulstrøm was a man of many parts. Beside the boxing club, he ran a Korsør disco called Underground. I could be found there several nights a week, even though my musical tastes were more Metallica and death metal than Abba. It was at Underground that I met my first love – a slim, red-haired girl called Vibeke.

Vibeke was a postal worker but her passion was dance and she took ballet lessons in Copenhagen with the sort of dedication that I lacked. She was a calming influence. I found work as an apprentice in a furniture workshop, and with time Vibeke might have tamed my wilder side.

But trouble seemed to follow me. One evening, after plenty of beer, I made out with another girl at a Korsør youth club. Unfortunately her boyfriend heard about our connection. He threatened me with a Danish army assault rifle and was subsequently picked up by the police. Incredibly, they released him without charge after a few hours. Perhaps they reasoned that such a threat was understandable if the target was Morten Storm.

I decided to take matters into my own hands. The boyfriend had supposedly turned up at a party in a grim apartment block on the outskirts of Korsør. When I arrived with three friends the host insisted he had not been there. Convinced he was lying, we beat him with pots and pans we found in the kitchen.

I never found the boyfriend, but the Korsør police found me. I was convicted of aggravated assault and sentenced to four months in a juvenile remand centre.

My prospects were not exactly blossoming. I had been kicked out of five schools and my mother had washed her hands of me. I also had a criminal record. The chances of my choosing the 'straight and narrow' were diminishing by the day. And far from leading me away from crime, my apprenticeship inside the remand centre made me harder.

My eighteenth birthday – spent in jail – offered little to celebrate. But at least when I came out I was eligible to drive, and that proved a passport to easy money. Mark Hulstrøm was supplementing his income from the gym with a thriving business smuggling cigarettes from Poland through Germany and into Denmark. We called it the 'Nicotine Triangle'.

By the mid-1990s cigarette smuggling had become the third-largest illegal business in Germany behind drugs and gambling. The business model was simple. Low taxes and no custom duty meant that a carton of cigarettes in Poland was one third the price of a carton in Germany or Denmark.

Our cover story was that we were buying spare car parts in Germany, where they were cheaper, and bringing them to Denmark. Hulstrøm saw me as a loyal, fearless operator. I spoke some German and was trusted to exchange currencies. We used hired cars – to minimize losses in case the driver was stopped and the vehicle impounded. The cars picked up a few dents – but it was a lucrative circuit.

The distribution centre was a remote farmhouse near the Polish border. At the gates of the farm, an unkempt guard who smelt of sour cabbage would wave me in. I would place a pile of Deutschmarks on the table, and a few minutes later an entire toilet would be moved to one side, revealing a cellar crammed with cartons of cigarettes.

On the drive back, I would look out for foreigners – preferably dark-skinned ones – approaching the Danish border and then follow them. The Danish border police were usually far more interested in questioning them and examining their passports than stopping a young Dane in a van. Occasionally I would cross from Germany into Denmark on tracks or unmarked roads. It was tradecraft that would prove useful when I moved on.

Sometimes I was making the trip two or three times a week and earning the equivalent of $1,000 each time. Not only was the money good: I loved feeling like an apprentice gangster, alert for the police, hiding the contraband, keeping my nerve at border crossings, handling large piles of crisp banknotes.

Just months after emerging from a remand centre penniless and homeless, I had wads of cash, wore smart clothes and was living the high life. Mark Hulstrøm entrusted me with the keys to Underground – now frequented by escorts from Copenhagen who had smelt the money. For the first time in my life I felt important, part of something big. I may have given up making it as a boxer, but I still enjoyed sparring and wanted to stay in shape. I continued to train in Hulstrøm's gym, and as I bulked up I moved into the light-heavyweight bracket.

My biological father had moved across the Great Belt to Nyborg. I had not seen him in well over a decade but now I was an adult and felt obliged to try to reconnect with him, even if not wildly enthusiastic about what would at best be an awkward encounter. My cousin Lars agreed to come with me and we took the ferry one slate-grey morning from Korsør across to Nyborg.

My apprehension was justified. My father was gruff and unrepentant about abandoning me and my mother. His breath, at midday, reeked of alcohol. We left him after less than an hour; I felt deeply depressed and angry.

Lars and I dropped by a bar in Nyborg to recover. A mistake. A drunk man disrupted our game of pool and then tried to pick a fight. I did my best to ignore him, but when he shaped up to strike me, I responded with a sharp upper cut. The bartender said he was calling the police and closing the place, and Lars and I left. We split up but Lars was arrested almost immediately, and so was I soon after returning to Korsør.

Convicted of assault, I was sentenced to my second spell behind bars – this time six months in Helsingør. The fact that I was provoked made no difference. By now I had what they call 'form' – a record of violence. From jail I wrote a confession to Vibeke. This was the person I was, I wrote, suggesting trouble followed me like a dog. But we could still make a life together, I added. Casting us as American gangsters, I imagined Vibeke as my 'Bonnie' and signed my letters 'Your Clyde'.

I could not see much alternative to a life of crime, with jail time an occupational hazard and violence never far away. I rarely derived pleasure from hitting anyone; none of my friends would have ever called me vicious. But I was loyal to a fault and would defend others and myself if threatened. I was not the sort who would walk away from a confrontation.

I did have one score to settle, one that had been a long time waiting.

At a family birthday party soon after my release from jail in April

1995, tensions flared between my mother and stepfather. He had a venomous tongue and knew how to wound her. I saw tears well in her eyes. I warned him to back off but the sniping continued. Without thinking, I stepped forward and struck him hard in the face. He looked stunned, as if suddenly realizing the boy he had so long abused was now a man – and much stronger than him. His glasses shattered and he fell backwards across a table. I watched him go, a tablecloth wrapping itself like a shroud around him.

There was stunned silence. My mother looked at me with a mixture of horror and gratitude; it was perhaps the strangest expression I have ever seen. I walked out of the hall, my knuckles throbbing but my eyes gleaming with pride.

It wasn't easy to find work after my release from prison. I had two convictions, no qualifications, few skills – but I also had some useful contacts. During my time inside I had met a senior member of the Bandidos biker gang, Michael Rosenvold. I think he liked me because I was the only inmate who wasn't scared of him.

Denmark had thriving motorbike gangs, and the Bandidos were locked in a violent struggle with the Hell's Angels. The Bandido motto was: 'We are the people our parents warned us about.' I would surely fit in perfectly.

Across Scandinavia, the 'Great Nordic Biker War' had been raging for more than a year. At least ten people had been murdered and many more seriously injured. In Sweden an anti-tank rocket was fired at a Hell's Angels clubhouse. The conflict was fuelled by the trade in drugs coming from southern Europe.

Rosenvold introduced me to other gang members as 'Denmark's youngest psychopath'. It was meant in jest but I certainly cut a formidable figure, tall with broad shoulders and thick biceps. I quickly warmed to the camaraderie, the supply of drugs and girls. By then I had got my first tattoo, on my right bicep: 'STORM'. It did not take me long to become accepted: reliable in a fight, ready to party. The Bandidos were the Raiders on steroids.

Despite my time inside, Vibeke had stuck with me. In a town where thrills were few and far between, she found my links to the underworld exciting and liked how I mimicked the life of a high-roller. Even so she was taken aback by some aspects of the lifestyle. At one party in Korsør she turned up in a black turtleneck with her hair neatly tied back. Most Bandidos women were pneumatic (if not natural) blondes, who wore minimalist outfits of tiger and leopard prints.

When Vibeke found a sports bag full of guns, explosives, hashish and speed that I had hidden under her bed, she erupted in anger. She threw the bag out of the window and yelled at me to get out of her apartment and never come back.

In March 1996, Hell's Angels gang members opened fire on a group of Bandidos outside Copenhagen airport with machine guns and other weapons, killing one.

Rosenvold called me.

'I want you to organize a group in Korsør, people we can rely on, who can hold territory,' he said. 'And I'm going to need you as one of the guys around me. I'm a target now.'

At twenty I was the youngest chapter leader for the Bandidos in Denmark. It was like I had found a family. Loyalty to the cause was everything.

For the next few months I was Rosenvold's bodyguard and we 'held' Korsør and its surroundings. There were street battles, nightclub brawls. An evening would not be complete without a fight and we knew how to pick them, whether the Angels were down the street or nowhere to be seen.

To begin with, I relished the adrenalin rush and the sense of importance. But as 1996 drew to a close, I worried that the lifestyle was making me an addict – to a cycle of drugs, gratuitous violence and hardcore partying. There was no space left for relationships, for peace of mind.

Two episodes crystallized my unease. On a freezing night shortly before New Year's Eve, a fight broke out between two big guys and some Bandidos at a Korsør dive. It was normal enough. But this time a bouncer intervened, dragged one of the Bandidos out on to the street and pummelled him. We were not about to let it pass.

The next morning, along with another member of the gang, I paid a visit to the bouncer. The icy grey was giving way to darker gloom when we arrived. I had a baseball bat hidden in my jacket. We donned balaclavas and knocked at his door, pushing him to the floor as he answered. Wielding the bat I swung it at his hips and knees.

In the days after the beating I couldn't get the sound of his moaning out of my head. I could still hear the crack of his knee fracturing and see his limp broken arm. I began to feel ashamed. Perhaps Rosenvold was right and I was a psychopath.

Occasionally I would look at other young men turning twenty-one, studying for a degree, starting a job, owning a car, going steady. I knew I couldn't handle routine, but I was beginning to worry that the constant fixes of violence and drugs could kill me. And that made me start questioning the purpose of my life and what might come after it. Deep down I didn't like the person I was turning into. Was I becoming an even more vicious version of my stepfather?

The second thing to feed my doubts was a meeting in one of Korsør's clubs with a twenty-year-old woman called Samar. After being evicted by Vibeke I badly needed a lover. I soon imagined a relationship with Samar, and not only because she had the exotic looks of a gypsy with wild, dark eyes, full lips and raven-dark hair, and a presence that I found irresistible.

A Palestinian-Christian, Samar came from a large immigrant family. Her mother soon treated me as a son. I felt wanted, and not just because I could tip the balance in a brawl.

It wasn't long before I proposed, and her family threw an engagement party. It began as a polite affair at a local hall until some Bandidos turned up. Samar's grandmother looked on as the guys leapt about to Arabic pop songs in their leather jackets and snorted lines of coke among the couscous and baklava.

Samar's family remained fond of me. The possibility of having her as a partner made me reconsider the Bandidos. Exhaustion had seeped into my soul. For all the highs my life in the gang had become meaningless.

We spent the night of my twenty-first birthday together, and I was happy: a feeling so rare that it almost shocked me. I was frightened of losing it. In the following weeks, when I wasn't with Samar, I would lie awake at night. I imagined getting into another fight that would land me behind bars again, or overdosing or getting stabbed. There were plenty of ways to be taken out of circulation. And then Samar would be gone.

On an unusually bright morning a few weeks after my birthday, I found myself in the town's library. I felt empty and needed sanctuary.

The library, a two-storey building of corrugated steel and concrete, was close to the water's edge. That morning it provided warmth from the chill breeze that found every corner of Korsør. For a while I stared at the choppy waters and the span of the Great Belt Bridge. I browsed aimlessly among the shelves, vaguely aware of the chatter from the children's section, but gravitated towards history and religion, subjects that had always fascinated me despite my wasted school days.

I had never felt religious – I had even been expelled from confirmation classes. The priest had told my mother that I was too much of a troublemaker, even for God. But I thought there must be some sort of afterlife. I had had some contact with Islam through my immigrant friends – Palestinians, Iranians and Turks – and had always envied the strength of their families, the way they always had dinner together, the bonds that united them while facing poverty and discrimination.

Perhaps that was why I sat down in an alcove with a book about the life of the Prophet Mohammed. Within minutes I was so absorbed in the story that the world outside evaporated.

The book laid out the tenets of Islam and the life of its founder with seductive simplicity. Mohammed's father had died before he was born. As his mother, Aminah, gazed at her first son, she heard a voice. 'The best of mankind has been born, so name him Mohammed.'

She had sent him into the desert to learn self-reliance and to master Arabic as spoken by the Bedouin. But Aminah had died when Mohammed was just seven, and he was passed into the care first of his grandfather and then of his uncle.

What immediately appealed about his life was its dignity and simplicity. As a young man, Mohammed would be called 'al-Saadiq' (the Truthful One) and 'al-Amin' (the Trustworthy One). He had granted freedom to a slave who had been given to him and declared him his own son.

I learned Mohammed was a successful trader who travelled through Arabia and as far as Syria. But he was also a deeply spiritual man, and in his thirties he would retreat to meditate in a cave on Mount Hira near Mecca. It was there that the Archangel Gabriel visited him and declared he was God's messenger.

'Proclaim in the name of your Lord who created! / Created man from a clot of blood.'

As the sun slanted across the Scandinavian sky, I became immersed in the events of the seventh century. I imagined Mohammed taking refuge in a cave as his enemies, the Quraish of Mecca, searched for him. By a divine miracle, it was said, a spider had spun its web over the mouth of the cave and a bird had laid eggs nearby, so the place looked undisturbed and was not searched. The episode was recounted in the Koran. 'When Disbelievers drove him out, he had no more than one companion; they were two in the cave and he said to his companion, "Have no fear, (for) Allah is with us."'

I did not notice the approach of dusk. Mohammed's story was one of battling the odds, as he sought to propagate Islam in the face of persecution. Here was a man – with his small band of followers – prepared to fight for his beliefs. In the words of the Koran:

'Permission to fight is granted to those against whom war is made, because they have been wronged, and God indeed has the power to help them. They are those who have been driven out of their homes unjustly only because they affirmed: Our Lord is God.'

Fighting for a cause appealed to me; it brought a sense of solidarity and loyalty.

I pictured the migration from Mecca to Medina, the desert battles that Mohammed and his few hundred followers waged and his triumphant return to the holy city, where he showed clemency to the Quraish despite their many attempts to stifle the young religion.

I felt I could relate to Mohammed's struggles as a man better than to some vague deity with a beard. As Allah's messenger he seemed a more plausible historical figure than Jesus. It seemed ludicrous to me that God should have a son. I was also struck that Mohammed's words provided for every aspect of life, from marriage to conflict to obligation. Good intentions were recognized and rewarded. The book cited the Prophet: 'Certainly, Allah does not look at your shapes [appearance] or wealth. But He only looks at your hearts and deeds.'

Here was a prescription that was both merciful and compassionate and offered absolution for sins. A pathway to a more fulfilling life. Islam could help me rein in my instincts and gain some self-discipline.

I was still reading when a librarian approached me to announce that the library was about to close. I had been sitting in that same alcove for six hours and had read some 300 pages about the life of the Prophet.

The chill wind took my breath away as I stepped out of the library into the cobblestoned streets. Nearby the beacon of a lighthouse rotated. After being steeped in the Arabian desert and consumed by divine revelations, I found it disorientating to be back in the Scandinavian winter. But my mind and my soul were still far away.

CHAPTER THREE
THE CONVERT

Early 1997–Summer 1997

I was far from the only young man in Europe or America at the end of the twentieth century to find meaning in a different way of life and code of conduct, to find faith and fellowship where there had been none.

In the weeks after reading about Mohammed I engaged several of my Muslim friends in debates about Islam, and I read more about the religion and its founding generations. I borrowed another of the library's few books on Islam and bought a copy of the Koran. At first I found it difficult to understand the Holy Book and felt overwhelmed by the demands of Islamic culture. But I was encouraged by a Turkish friend, Ymit, who was thrilled that for once a Dane wanted to embrace rather than sneer at his religion.

Ymit had been one of the 'Raiders' and we had remained friends despite my encounters with the Danish criminal-justice system and graduation to the Bandidos. He had a sharp wit and was intelligent, genuinely interested in the world beyond Korsør. He was knowledge-able about Islam and took it seriously, even if he was also familiar with alcohol and cocaine. Ymit told me that Mohammed's illiteracy was a blessing and made the faith purer.

'It meant that everything he said was a revelation from God, untainted by man. It meant the Koran was a miracle.'

'But if you are a real Muslim, Ymit, how come you drink and do drugs like me?'

'Because I can still repent if I go to Friday prayers and seek forgiveness for my sins.'

Others tried to dissuade me. A Christian Lebanese friend called Milad, who owned a small grocery across from the library, was stunned.

Morten Storm – biker, boozer and boxer – had found religion, and the wrong religion at that.

'Why do you want to follow that ignorant pervert? Mohammed was a fool, a Bedouin who could not read or write.'

'At least he was a human being, someone who really existed and received messages from God. No one pretended he was the Son of God,' I shot back.

A couple of weeks after my epiphany in Korsør library, Ymit asked me to come to the mosque in a nearby town for Friday prayers. The building was not what I expected – there was no golden dome, nor a minaret from which the muezzin would call the faithful. It was a nondescript bungalow in a side street. But the intensity of the congregation and the warmth of their welcome to me, a stranger, a pale European, was moving.

The imam was an elderly man with watery eyes and a thick, powder-white beard. He spoke in a low soft voice that trailed into a whisper as he asked me about the Prophets and the Pillars of Islam. He had little Danish and Ymit translated for me. Did I accept the Five Pillars of Islam – that there is no God but God and Mohammed is His messenger, performing prayer, paying the *Zakat* (charity to the poor), fasting in the month of Ramadan and performing *Hajj* (the pilgrimage to Mecca)?

Did I accept that Jesus was not the Son of God?

I answered yes, even though the finer points of theology and doctrine were beyond my understanding.

At the end of this series of questions, I had to recite the Declaration of Faith, the *shahada*.

'There is no God but God, and Mohammed is the messenger of God.'

There was a pause. And then the imam said, 'You are now a Muslim. Your sins are forgiven.'

Ymit translated and then embraced me.

'Now you are truly my brother,' he said, his eyes glistening. 'But you are not really a convert, more a revert. In Islam, we believe that every person is born a Muslim because we are all created by God and there is only one God.

'You should be circumcised,' he said with a grin, 'but it's not compulsory. It's more important that you now take a Muslim name.'

My life had undergone a momentous change. It was uplifting; I had been purged. Guilt evaporated, a fresh start beckoned.

'I think you should be "Murad",' Ymit said. 'It means "goal" or "achievement".'

It seemed appropriate.

I did not become a strictly observant Muslim immediately. In fact, my friends had an unconventional way of celebrating. We converged on an apartment to consume several six-packs of beer. It was my first communion – Korsør style. I could always repent later, they laughed.

To begin with, the forgiving of sins, absolution through prayer, was a large part of Islam's appeal to me. I soon learned and would cite a saying of the Prophet:

'Suppose there is a river that flows in front of your house and you take a wash five times in it. Then would there remain any dirt and filth on you after that? Performing daily prayers five times a day is similar to that which washes away sins.'

The Koran and the sayings attributed to the Prophet were especially generous to the dedicated 'revert' who took his religion seriously. In the words of one such saying – or *hadith*: 'If a servant accepts Islam and completes his Islam, Allah will record for him every good deed that he performed before [adopting Islam]; and will erase for him every evil deed that he did before.'

I did not leave the Bandidos immediately and even took several members along with me to the mosque. This did not go down well with senior members of the gang, who called me to a meeting to tell me to keep my beliefs to myself.

Samar, even though she was from a Christian family, was more accepting. She thought my conversion showed a maturity that was a welcome departure from my gang lifestyle. She did not seem to harbour any anti-Muslim feelings and we continued to make plans together.

It was – of all people – the Korsør police who inadvertently pushed me towards a much stricter adherence to my new religion.

On a glorious June evening, days after the summer solstice and with the sun still high in the sky, I joined some friends at a Kurdish restaurant in Korsør to watch the world heavyweight title fight – the bizarre bout in Las Vegas between Mike Tyson and Evander Holyfield.

A police car passed and then came back to the restaurant. Two officers got out.

'Morten Storm,' one said, with a look of smugness, 'you are under arrest in connection with the attempted robbery of a bank.'

I had nothing to do with the break-in and thought they were just trying to annoy me. Expecting that I would be back at the restaurant in a matter of minutes, I shouted to my friends: 'Keep the beers cold.'

I was wrong. I never tasted the beer and never saw Tyson bite off part of Holyfield's ear.

Instead I spent the night in a police waiting room, studying the bare walls and reflecting on my situation. Once again, just as I seemed to be getting ahead, sensing progress and even stability, my past and my reputation had pulled me back.

It's never going to end, I thought. They're just going to keep coming after me. So long as I am in Korsør I'll be a marked man, rotating between life in a gang on the outside to life in a much worse gang inside. I don't want to spend half my life in prison.

The next morning, waiting for yet another court appearance, I said to myself, very simply: 'It's over.'

It was time to change my life, not just its trappings, before I was dragged into a never-ending cycle of court appearances, jail sentences and attempts at rehabilitation. I was remanded in custody for ten days. I knew several Bandidos who had been involved in the bank job but refused to give names. Loyalty still mattered. But my brief stay in Køge prison was a landmark because it reinforced the values and self-discipline I was beginning to learn as a new Muslim.

My first act was symbolic. I declared myself a Muslim to the prison authorities and refused to eat pork. Then I met a fellow convert, Suleiman, who had a profound and immediate impact on me. Suleiman, with his shaven head, looked like Bruce Willis. He was inside on weapons charges, but that did not prevent him from lecturing me about Islam and membership of the Bandidos being irreconcilable.

'You have to choose,' he said one afternoon as we wandered through the exercise yard. 'Allah cannot accept you as a true Muslim if you are going to drink and do drugs and go through your life without good intentions. The heart is the sanctuary of Allah; so do not allow anyone to dwell therein except Allah.'

Suleiman's words rang true. It was time to put the Bandidos behind me. Islam was already beginning to change me, not as a weekly or even daily rite but as a belief system that would influence and soon dictate my every action.

A Palestinian friend had given me a key ring with 'Allah' inscribed on it; I treasured it. I began keeping the Koran in the highest place in the room, out of respect.

Another inmate I met in Køge was a Palestinian Dane named Mustapha Darwich Ramadan. His trade was armed robbery in the cause of jihad. He was in solitary confinement and I could hear him praying. I managed to slip him some fruit and we were able to talk briefly. He would later resurface in one of the most brutal videos to emerge in Iraq.

No charges were brought against me over the robbery and I walked out of Køge determined to leave Denmark as soon as possible – and to avoid Bandidos members. Some could not accept that I had left the gang and even suspected that I was planning to join the Hell's Angels. I felt like I was on the run; I kept a loaded gun on me at all times, moving from place to place.

Suleiman was released from jail soon after. His wife's family were Pakistanis and had settled in central England. He was planning to join them – and his old van represented my escape route to a new life.

On an overcast early summer day we set off for Calais and then crossed the English Channel. The white cliffs of Dover – more a dirty eggshell – invited me towards a new adventure. I was leaving behind some angry bikers and a chaotic love life. I had discovered that Samar, whose sex drive was apparently insatiable, had been less than angelic while I was behind bars. I had even begun seeing Vibeke again but had soon realized that I wanted Samar back. She had visited me during my brief stay in Køge jail and we had talked about Islam. She even said that she was ready to become a Muslim.

A job, somewhere to live, new horizons – and then I would call her. She had promised she would join me.

My new home was in Milton Keynes in England. A town created on an architect's master plan, it was a bland collection of housing estates surrounded by countryside. Suleiman's in-laws helped me find accommodation and a warehouse job. For the first time in my life – guided by Islam – I saved a little money. I hoped Samar would see that I'd turned a corner and come to live with me.

Every day Suleiman prodded me towards being a conscientious Muslim. I was a project; he was the proselytizer. He encouraged me to pray five times a day and wear an Islamic cap.

'The companions of the Prophet Mohammed were never seen without their heads covered,' he explained to me one day as we drove to one of the mosques that were popping up across the English Midlands.

Soon I was praying on my own. I had the zeal of a convert, soaking up the customs and prescriptions of Islam. I felt a sense of stability I had never had before.

Several weeks after arriving I plucked up the courage to call Samar and ask her to come over. I hoped I could sell my new setting, a fresh start.

I was not normally given to nerves, but as I jammed pound coins into a public phone I realized my palms were sweating and my stomach turning.

After a few tones she picked up.

'Darling, it's Murad, er, Morten. How are you?'

She was subdued. I pressed on.

'I have a good job. I'm making some money. And I've got a decent place to live. Milton Keynes isn't very exciting, but it's not far from London.'

I sounded like a telemarketer. There was silence at the other end. I soldiered on.

'I have enough to plan a good wedding for us, and a honeymoon. I know people here who can help organize a proper Muslim wedding ceremony.'

She cut me off and poured pure venom down the line.

'Fuck you and fuck Islam. I don't want to live in England and I don't want to live with you.'

I reeled.

'Samar . . .'

'Don't call me again.' The line went dead.

I stared through the grimy glass panes. Without any explanation the engagement was over – for good. I stumbled into the street. My first attempt to build something with someone had crumbled to dust. I was on my own.

There was a call from across the street.

'*As salaam aleikum.*'

A middle-aged Pakistani recognized me as a fellow Muslim, thanks to my cap. His name was G. M. Butt and he owned a kiosk near a cinema complex called The Point.

We had exchanged greetings on my occasional visits to his little shop. He was a man of good intentions, who saw pleasing Allah as one of his duties on earth.

I told him a bit about the phone call. He was sympathetic.

'Brother! Come and help me and I will try to help you. I am not the young man I used to be – I need help with all the boxes and deliveries.'

So my fianceé had rejected me because of my religion, but a man who scarcely knew me had embraced me for it.

G.M. was a good man. Soon I told him how I cried at night, my longing for Samar. One day I asked him for a day off so that I could go to London and pray.

London's most famous mosque is on the edge of Regent's Park, set among the rose gardens and graceful Edwardian terraces. Since its construction in the 1970s, largely with Saudi money, it has somehow blended into this leafy corner of London. The gold of its dome flickers through the plane trees; the call to prayer wafts across the traffic.

I went to the mosque's bookshop. Perhaps if I sent Samar some books about Islam she would understand better. The attendant directed me towards the office, or *dawa*, where a tall and venerable Saudi with dark skin and a long salt-and-pepper beard greeted me.

'*Masha'Allah* [God has willed it],' he exclaimed, delighted that a European convert had come to his mosque.

He introduced himself as Mahmud al-Tayyib.

'Where are you from?' he asked.

I told him that I had recently arrived from Denmark and had converted to Islam just a few months earlier.

'Are you married?'

I launched into my sad tale about Samar, how she had promised to join me, my plans for a Muslim wedding.

Tayyib was sympathetic. In his gentle way he was also persuasive. Like Suleiman he had a passion for conveying his faith. He was a man of deep learning.

'Would you like to study Islam? Why not travel to a Muslim country?'

It was a soft but earnest sell.

'I can get you to Yemen. It's the easiest Muslim country to get a visa to study – do you have a passport?'

I did. But I had never heard of Yemen. And I had little notion of what Tayyib regarded as the authentic expression of Islam. He was one of the many well-funded envoys sent around the world by wealthy Saudi interests to bring Muslims into the Wahhabi fold. Ever since the Islamic Revolution in Iran, the Saudis had spent lavishly promoting their 'authentic' brand of Islam in the face of the challenge posed by Ayatollah Khomeini. To the puritanical Wahhabis – Sunni fundamentalists – the Shia were heretics guilty of polluting Islam.

Of this battle for the soul of Islam, being waged in mosques around the world, I knew little. But I was about to become one of its foot soldiers.

'There is a seminary in Yemen. It is remote and it is primitive by European standards,' Tayyib continued. 'But it is pure. Many foreigners seeking truth in Islam go there. It is called Dammaj. I can organize a plane ticket for you and people to look after you when you arrive.'

His eyes were sparkling.

'The imam at Dammaj is a great scholar, Sheikh Muqbil. He is returning Yemen to the true path of the Sunnah. But you should know that the day is long and you will have to get a grasp of Arabic.'

I was excited. I loved to travel and the thought of visiting Arabia had been beyond my wildest imagination. Now I was being offered a return ticket, a place to stay and a chance to become immersed in my new faith.

I accepted Tayyib's offer and said it would take me a couple of weeks to wrap up my affairs in England. He was delighted.

'But don't become a Sufi or a Shia,' he said with a wry grin, 'and don't shave any more.'

CHAPTER FOUR
ARABIA

Late Summer 1997–Summer 1998

For a 21-year-old Dane, the searing heat of Sana'a was an assault on the senses. Before I flew into Yemen's capital in the late summer of 1997 I had no sense of my destination. I had vaguely imagined that Sana'a was actually in Oman, where Western oil companies were established and a moderate Sultan ruled a peaceful kingdom. I could not have been more wrong.

I was shocked by the ramshackle building that passed for Yemen's welcome to the world. Flies drifted in the arrivals hall as wiry Yemeni men jostled for position at passport control.

Tayyib had organized for me to be picked up. I was greeted by a couple of young men of Somali background (a lot of Somalis had crossed the Gulf of Aden to settle in Yemen). I was overwhelmed by the noise and chaos, the mountains rising above the city.

Sana'a filled the senses: the medieval buildings of mud brick in Sana'a's old quarter decorated like outsize marzipan confections, the air full of dust but also of the scent of herbs and spices, the shabby appearance of the men, the women shrouded in black, the call of the muezzin and the guttural Arabic. I was taken aback at the sight of men holding hands. Above all I was amazed by the Kalashnikovs; people even carried them while visiting the supermarket.

My first two weeks were spent in a poor district of Sana'a, living in a house without furniture, sitting cross-legged on the floor, eating Somali food. It was a halfway house as well as a half-built house. Tayyib had warned me that it might take some time to reach Dammaj, which was in a valley some 100 miles north from Sana'a. Depending on the political climate, the Yemeni government frequently put up roadblocks to prevent foreigners from travelling there, concerned that it was becoming a magnet for militants.

Within days I realized that Yemen was the destination of choice for a growing number of Western converts to Islam – including several Americans in search of what they imagined was the authentic (and austere) Salafi interpretation of Islam. Among those I encountered in Sana'a was a Vietnam veteran close to the firebrand preacher Louis Farrakhan. There were also British, French and Canadian converts.

Salafism was capturing the imagination of a generation of Muslims and converts. It derived from the Arabic *'al-salaaf al-salih'* – meaning the pious forefathers, the first three generations of Muslims. As such, it represented a return to the pure and original core of Islam, free of interpretation or revisionism. But Salafism was far from coherent; its adherents derived different messages from those forefathers. Some eschewed politics and loathed the Muslim Brotherhood for its political activism; only God could legislate through the application of Sharia law. Others reviled 'non-believers' and non-Salafi Muslims (especially the Shia), and disavowed rulers who allied themselves with the hated West.

I was not prepared for this ferment among Muslims. In my naivety I had imagined a religion whose followers were united in obedience to Allah. The books I had read in Denmark said nothing of the schisms and hatreds that ran through Islam like faultlines. And I was not familiar with the one concept that would come to dominate the next decade of my life: jihad.

Getting to Dammaj would be the first trial of my faith and dedication. I decided to travel with one of the Americans I had met – Rashid Barbi, an African-American convert from North Carolina – and a Tunisian.

After an hour in a battered Peugeot, Rashid, the Tunisian and I – along with a Yemeni guide – had to climb out to avoid a military checkpoint. This was an area of tribal rivalries and frequent clashes between Sunni and Shi'ite groups.

We began walking through the mountains in the blazing sun, but were ill-prepared. We had no water and no protection, either from the heat or later from the cold as night fell. I was wearing cheap sandals and soon my feet were a forest of blisters.

At dusk we stopped to pray at the edge of a cliff, but it was too dark to make any further progress. A burst of monsoon rain further damp-ened our spirits. I began to feel feverish and more than once I asked myself what on earth I had done. I had left Milton Keynes just two weeks ago, but its bland comforts suddenly seemed very appealing.

It would be a night and half a day before we finally traipsed into the valley of mud houses and date-palm trees, which were overlooked by a massive escarpment. The whitewashed-brick complex of the Dam-maj Institute was snuggled into an oasis of greenery. The chugging of diesel water-pumps in the surrounding fields was the only sound in the torpid afternoon heat.

Sheikh Muqbil thought our little group must have been arrested and was relieved to hear of our arrival. He approached us with a whole chicken, exclaiming that the man from 'Benimark' had finally made it. He had little sense of European geography. Rashid and I devoured the food while the Sheikh and his bodyguards laughed at our sunburned and bedraggled appearance.

I was taken aback by the Sheikh's appearance; it was the first time I had seen a man with a long, straggly hennaed beard, a custom among distinguished preachers and tribal figures in Yemen.[2]

---

2 Sheikh Muqbil bin Haadi was a local preacher from the Wadi'a tribe who had stud-ied for two decades in Saudi Arabia before being imprisoned and then expelled from the country. He had been suspected of links to the jihadist group that had briefly and violently occupied the Grand Mosque in Mecca in 1979. Despite his persistent criti-cism of the relatively secularist government of President Ali Abdullah Saleh in Yemen, Muqbil continued teaching unhindered. This was in part because he taught that rebel-lion against rulers was only permissible if they acted as disbelievers. Muqbil had rejected the overtures of Osama bin Laden, who was recruiting many of al-Qaeda's foot soldiers from Yemen, frequently poor and illiterate young men who were easily persuaded to travel for jihad. He had asked Muqbil to provide shelter and guns for his fighters, but Muqbil had refused, wary that too close an embrace of bin Laden could provoke unwelcome consequences. Muqbil wrote polemics against aspects of popu-lar culture such as television and against other Islamic sects. He saw equality of the

I was entrusted to the care of Abu Bilal, a bookish Swedish-Ghanaian student in his mid-twenties, who gave me a tour of the complex. He spoke fluent English as well as Arabic. During my first weeks in Dammaj, he or Rashid was almost always at my side translating for me.

The intensity of the place was difficult to take in. Like a new boy at a big school I felt intimidated by the collective emotion of Dammaj and its size. On the tour Abu Bilal told me the Institute – or Masjid – had started as a small collection of mud-brick buildings, but had expanded as its reputation spread. Now it had a library and a mosque capable of accommodating several hundred worshippers. Loudspeakers blared to announce the start of classes and lectures. The complex was surrounded by intensively cultivated and irrigated plots.

Abu Bilal explained to me the rules: single male students were strictly prohibited from going into areas of the complex reserved for married men. The five daily prayers were compulsory: each student was required to arrive on time and in silence. In between, students were required to attend lessons on the Koran and lessons from the life of the Prophet Mohammed. The mosque was the only one in the Muslim world in which students were required to keep their shoes on. A *hadith* viewed as authoritative by Sheikh Muqbil stated the Prophet had prayed in this way, and he was not about to let a practice built up over the centuries get in the way of his students following the true path.

Dammaj was a place of religious ferment. There were perhaps 300 young men there when I arrived, almost every one of them bearded, with the ardent expression of those convinced they had found righteousness. They came from many places but were united by a rejection of the modern world.

Despite my lack of Arabic, I soon found out what was driving these young men – and most were under thirty. They felt Muslims – and especially Arab Muslims – had been betrayed by their own leaders and exploited by the West. Dictators had robbed the people in a sea of

---

sexes and democracy as un-Islamic. And the enemies of Islam included both communists and America.

corruption but done nothing to help the Palestinians. The original religion had been corrupted by Western modes of thinking. And so it was time to return to the purest and most authentic expression of Islam.

Dammaj was a place of few comforts. I was given a bare room made of breeze blocks as my quarters, which I shared with Abu Bilal. We slept on blankets on the concrete floor, which was a luxury because most students were sleeping on mud floors. Food was frequently rice, beans and ginger tea. An egg was an extravagance. The toilet was a hole in the ground in the washroom. I had to learn how to clean myself with water with my left hand. The drainage system had not kept pace with the expansion of the Institute and a whiff of raw sewage would often interrupt our studying. But for all the discomforts, it was a haven of calm, self-discipline and devotion after my biker years.

The great question of the day was when and how Muslims should take up jihad in defence of their religion. Sheikh Muqbil refused to support violence against rulers and most Salafis saw education as the way to restore Islam. But some of his students would later criticize him for not speaking out against the presence of US troops on Saudi soil. This had been a cataclysm for Salafis: how could the infidel be allowed to set foot in the kingdom that protected Islam's holiest sites?

Under a date-palm one autumn afternoon one student – an Egyptian – spoke for most when we discussed the evils that Islam must grapple with.

'How can it be that the Custodian of the Two Holy Sites allows American troops to defile our lands? How can it be that our governments spend billions on American planes and tanks? They turn their back on Islam, allow alcohol, allow women to dress as prostitutes. Muslims have lost their way and it is up to us to re-educate them in Allah's way.'

Many of Dammaj's students had already returned home to set up similar institutes and schools across the Muslim world. Part of the appeal of this radical philosophy was that it bypassed the religious establishment and went directly to the fount of Islam. In that sense it empowered the poor and the persecuted and allowed them to spread the word, even if they had not benefited from decades of religious learning in the schools of Islamic law.

Sheikh Muqbil regarded the *Hadith*, accounts of the actions and sayings of the Prophet recorded by his early followers, as the core of his teaching. The crisis of Islam, he held, could only be addressed by returning to the original texts and rejecting 'innovators' – mere mortals who had the temerity to interpret God's word: 'There is no God except God and Mohammed is His messenger.' The spirit of Dammaj could be summed up by a *hadith*: 'The most evil matter is novelty, and every novelty is an innovation, and every innovation is an error, and every error leads to hellfire.' It did not leave much room for argument.

It was a bare but liberating message. And for someone like me who hated elites and establishments, it was intoxicating. I was now a witness to the multiple and overlapping struggles within Islam: between Salafis and others, among the Salafis themselves. And I was soon a willing participant in these struggles, soaking up scholarly texts, plunging into debates with other students.

It was in Dammaj that I began to get a sense at first hand of the violent rivalry between Sunni and Shia Muslims. The day I arrived, I saw rows of AK-47 rifles neatly lined against the walls of the Institute; and a number of students were on security duty, with weapons slung over their shoulders. The Institute was in a part of Yemen dominated by a Shia sect known as the Houthis.[3] The Sheikh made no attempt to hide his loathing of the Shia, and there were frequent clashes between his tribe and the Houthis.

The students at Dammaj did everything together – learning, eating, praying. Life revolved around the mosque. The day began before dawn with the first prayers of the day, and we received hours of Koranic instruction in the shade of the palms. We would spend long periods memorizing the Koran.

---

3 Some Houthis in northern Yemen subscribe to a form of Shi'ism that is close to that of Iranian Shia. Others subscribe to a Zaydi Shia revivalist movement that is strongest around Saa'da. Until the 1962 revolution Zaydi imams – who claimed they were directly descended from the Prophet Mohammed – ruled North Yemen. Despite the fact that the Zaydi creed is closer to Sunni Islam than any other branch of Shia Islam, hardline Sunnis in Yemen regarded them as apostates.

We never received anything amounting to paramilitary training but like many young Yemenis we did learn to fire guns, including AK-47s, at makeshift targets in the hills. A couple of Americans with military backgrounds played a leading part in the training, among them Rashid Barbi, who had been in the US army in Kuwait.

The Sheikh said such training was commanded by a *hadith* that stressed a strong believer was of greater value than a weak one and that all Muslims had to be prepared for jihad. Several students approached him to ask for permission to travel to Chechnya or Somalia to fight; but he only granted permission to those less than whole-hearted in their studies. It was a way to winnow out the thinkers from the men of action.

I embraced the purity of the lifestyle, the absence of mobile phones or music, drugs and alcohol. I began teaching boxing to some of my fellow students and took them running. In return I sensed their respect. It felt far more satisfying than any knockout I had delivered on the streets of Korsør. By night, as I gazed up at the stars, I felt I belonged.

Occasionally I would write to Samar, but I never mailed any of the letters. As I became submerged in the rituals of Dammaj there seemed less and less point. One day, sorting through the few belongings I had brought, I was surprised to find photographs of our engagement party. Without much feeling I shredded them one by one. When I wanted a wife, she would have to be a good Muslim.

The Sheikh, for all his learning, had a mischievous sense of humour, and for some reason I became one of his favourite students. He would take me by the hand and walk through the oasis, talking to me in Arabic. I would grasp only one word in every ten, but he went on talking.

He would also single me out during his lectures.

'Beni-marki,' he would exclaim, grinning broadly, before commanding me to stand up and read *hadith*. I had begun to learn a few phrases of Yemeni Arabic but was unable to recite *hadith*, and would mumble apologies. A Libyan student took pity on me and taught me one *hadith* in Arabic. When I stood and recited it, Sheikh Muqbil was delighted – and began pounding the desk. He told the several hundred assembled students that my diligence showed Islam would spread throughout the world.

'This is the sign that Allah promised us,' he said. 'We must take care of our new Muslim brothers and teach them Islam and be patient with them.'

Despite the best efforts of the Yemeni government, there were plenty of foreign students at Dammaj, among them British Pakistanis from Birmingham and Manchester, Tunisians, Malaysians and Indonesians. There was also a second African-American called Khalid Green. A few had been in Bosnia, fighting with its Muslim population against the Serbs and Croats in the mid-1990s. Some would later become prominent militants in their own countries.

To begin with I was the only fair-skinned Caucasian at Dammaj. That made me an object of curiosity for many of the students and the local tribes. Yet I never felt excluded or ostracized because of my ethnicity.

I was later joined by a soft-spoken American convert from Ohio, called Clifford Allen Newman, and his four-year-old son, Abdullah. Newman went by the name Amin. He looked and sounded like what some Americans would call a 'redneck', but he spoke Arabic well and had spent time in Pakistan before moving to Yemen. We struck up a friendship. Like me he seemed to be fleeing a bad relationship. US authorities had a warrant for his arrest on international kidnapping charges because he had brought Abdullah with him to Yemen after a judge awarded custody to his ex-wife in their divorce the year before. Newman had wanted his son to have a strict Muslim upbringing.

I spent four months in Dammaj. In early 1998 I left the isolation of the seminary and travelled back to the capital, where I found myself a basic apartment. Newman and his son moved in with me briefly, while they looked for a place of their own.

I was serious about my faith; it was my compass and I planned to return to Dammaj. By the time I travelled back to Sana'a I was a hard-core Salafi. I could argue against the accursed 'innovators'.

In Sana'a I was introduced to some radical preachers, including one Mohammed al-Hazmi – who three years later would take to the pulpit and welcome the events of 9/11 as 'justified revenge' against America.

Another was Sheikh Abdul Majid al-Zindani, one of the most powerful religious figures in Yemen and prominent in the main opposition party, which he had co-founded. Al-Zindani, who was in his late fifties, had thousands of followers. He ran a university in Sana'a – al-Iman – whose mosque was crammed with several thousand worshippers every Friday.[4]

When my first experience of Ramadan as a devout Muslim came about, I was invited to break the fast with him one evening. Al-Zindani wanted me to enrol in al-Iman University.

A man of great wealth, he had a fabulous library at his house in Sana'a.

'What can I do to help you?' he asked.

He was not expecting my answer.

'Is it true you are with the Muslim Brotherhood?' I asked. 'If that is so, you will lead me to hellfire.'

We had been taught at Dammaj that the Muslim Brotherhood, a political movement that was one of the few sources of dissent in Arab countries, had abandoned true Sharia and were innovators where it suited their political ends, in some countries supporting the concept of democratic elections. This was anathema to true Salafis, because it pretended that mere mortals could make laws.

I did not ask the question with any animosity but al-Zindani looked stunned. Despite his radical profile, the Sheikh was not sufficiently militant for my taste. And as a strident Salafist and no respecter of status, I was not afraid to tell him as much.

He was clearly not used to being challenged by a novice but recovered his composure.

'It seems that if you come to al-Iman, we will have many interesting debates. But you must not believe everything you are told. Even good Muslims are sometimes confused or misguided,' he said, smiling.

To show he had no hard feelings about my insolence, al-Zindani let

---

4 Al-Zindani would later be described by some as the spiritual leader of al-Qaeda in Yemen. In 2004 the US designated him as a 'global terrorist', noting his long-standing connection to Osama bin Laden. In reality he was his own man, sympathetic to bin Laden's world-view but jealous of his status – and freedom. For example, in the early 1990s he had refused to support a plan by bin Laden to overthrow the Saleh regime.

me see some of his most precious volumes, and we talked more about the early days of Islam. I was learning fast.

A friend from Dammaj introduced me to a network of young Salafis in the city. Some were veterans of jihad who had fought the Soviets in Afghanistan in the 1980s and more recently had been in the Balkans. Of the growing pool of militants in Yemen, some were beginning to see the West, and especially America, as the enemy of Islam. There had already been bomb attacks against US interests in Saudi Arabia; and more were being planned. One of this circle was an Egyptian named Hussein al-Masri. Although he did not acknowledge it directly he was very likely a member of the Egyptian group Islamic Jihad. Al-Masri was a wanted man in his homeland. In his mid-thirties, he had a diffident manner and soft voice that belied his experience as a militant with extensive contacts. He was also the first person I heard utter the name Osama bin Laden.

At that time – in early 1998 – bin Laden was building al-Qaeda's presence in south and eastern Afghanistan, in Kandahar and around Jalalabad. Welcomed by the Taliban, his organization was already plotting attacks against Western targets, including a deadly bombing it would carry out months later on US embassies in Nairobi and Dar es Salaam.[5] Al-Masri told me of the training camps al-Qaeda had established in Afghanistan and how to travel there via Pakistan. He said he could arrange passage if I ever wanted to go.

I was in two minds: the adventurer in me was tempted, but as a Salafi I had not yet accepted that waging such a jihad was legitimate. Pure Salafis also looked down on groups like the Taliban, whose practices we saw as unorthodox.

To Western eyes, such differences might seem like semantics, but to teachers at Dammaj or in Riyadh, the Taliban's philosophy bordered on heresy. They encouraged 'excessive' praying beyond the five times a day mandated by the Prophet. Sheikh Muqbil had taught that one should not even countenance sitting down with such men. While they might be Muslims, they could lead you to damnation.

---

5 The near simultaneous 7 August 1998 bombings of the US embassies in Nairobi and Dar es Salaam killed over 200, including twelve Americans.

In making this point he liked to quote a famous *hadith* of the Prophet: 'My Ummah [nation] will break into seventy-three sects – only one will be in paradise and the rest will be in hell.'

For now, my sense of ideological purity won out.

Among my companions in Sana'a was a dark-skinned seventeen-year-old Yemeni with a generous smile and a shy courtesy. Abdul had curly, short-cropped hair and the beginnings of a beard. He can't have weighed more than seven stone; his legs were like stalks. But even at his age he was well connected with militants in Sana'a – men who had fought the communists in Afghanistan, the Serbs in Bosnia. Abdul and I often talked late into the night at his home, fuelled by endless glasses of sugary mint tea. I loved his natural enthusiasm and curiosity. He was full of questions about Europe, amazed and delighted that Islam had gained a foothold in these northern heathen lands. He yearned to travel and enjoyed practising his rudimentary English on me. I was impressed by his deep religious commitment. He was not unusual in knowing the Koran by heart but his voice was so melodic that he was often asked to recite prayers in the mosque.

My time in Yemen had deepened my faith. It had been little more than a year since I had entered a mosque for the first time and mumbled my Declaration of Faith. Now I knew the Koran, could recite *hadith* and discuss Islamic law. The man who had sent me, Mahmud al-Tayyib, had probably expected I would return home within weeks, unable to cope with the hardships of the poorest country in the Arab world.

But after the best part of a year in Yemen I was ready for a change. I had endured two bouts of dysentery, had no money and was beginning to tire of being stared at in the streets of Sana'a. I dug out my return ticket to London.

CHAPTER FIVE
LONDONISTAN

Summer 1998–Early 2000

I arrived at Heathrow airport on a muggy late summer's day in
1998, relieved to be free of the dust and heat of Sana'a and faintly
amused by the orderly appearance of suburban London. I was soon
reunited with Mahmud al-Tayyib at the Regent's Park mosque and
regaled him with stories of Dammaj and Sana'a.

I helped teach Muslims who came to the mosque and began accompanying an elderly Iraqi preacher and several converts to Speakers'
Corner in Hyde Park, where we would try to spread the word of Islam.
We must have been a strange sight in our long Islamic *thawbs*, the
ankle-length robe. Sometimes we would get into heated debates with
evangelical Christians.

'The Koran is the pure word of God,' I would shout, remembering
to quote a famous verse from the Koran. 'Had it issued from any but
God, they would surely have found in it many a contradiction.'

We were usually greeted by a mixture of indifference and suspicion,
which only reinforced our determination to continue proselytizing.

For radical Muslims London had become a cauldron of debate and
rivalry. There were many echoes of the discussions that had occupied
our afternoons under the date-palms of Dammaj. And the gritty district of Brixton, south of the River Thames, had become the centre of
this tussle for the soul of Islam.

Brixton had seen riots in the early 1980s, pitching Afro-Caribbean
youth against the Metropolitan Police. Disturbances had then spread to
a dozen cities. The area had since become somewhat gentrified, but its

housing was rundown and there was still plenty of poverty. Even on a bright summer's day in 1998 the high street was gloomy – a collection of down-at-heel stores and roads strewn with escaped plastic bags. But Brixton mosque was thriving and its reputation for Salafism was attracting devotees from across Europe. I had first heard about the mosque from British Muslims who had come to Yemen.

Most of my friends and flatmates were of a similar outlook. My experiences in Yemen and especially my time at Dammaj fascinated them. I even met the singer Cat Stevens several times. He had changed his name to Yusuf Islam and become a Sufi Muslim; I had some animated conversations with him about the true path of Islam. Salafis scorned Sufi Muslims for their veneration of saints and other perceived distortions of the faith.

I picked up temporary jobs, mostly driving, which helped me find radical mosques throughout London: in Hounslow, Shepherd's Bush and Finchley. None was as grand as Regent's Park; some were no more than shabby basements. But they were energized by a fervour which was by then challenging – and worrying – more moderate preachers, as well as the British security services.

The new circle I had entered included plenty of angry young men looking to inflict revenge on the West for its persecution of Muslims. A few clearly had emotional or psychological issues, displaying wild mood swings or budding paranoia, but most were driven by an unshakable belief that they had found the true way to obey Allah and that obedience called for waging jihad. A surprising number of French converts had come to Brixton, including one called Mukhtar. We talked about everything, shared a passion for martial arts and attended the mosque together.

Mukhtar was a French convert in his thirties, with a lean physique and close-set dark eyes. He reminded me a little of the French footballer Zinedine Zidane. We had met at Brixton mosque and he told me he had come to London to get away from police brutality in the rundown suburb of Paris where he had lived.

I soon met his French-Moroccan flatmate, one Zacarias Moussaoui. They lived in a decrepit 1960s council tower block that reeked of decay.

Their apartment was bare: no beds or sofas, just a couple of mattresses and rough hessian mats on the floor. It was a typical Salafists' pad.

Moussaoui had just turned thirty. He was well-built but beginning to put on weight. A thin black beard ran from his sideburns down his jaw and petered out at his chin. His receding hair was swept back. He would often cook tagine and couscous for everyone.

Moussaoui was clearly intelligent and had recently received a Master's degree at London's South Bank University, which was not far from Brixton. Most of the time he was quiet and unassuming, but brooding. He rarely talked about himself and never about his family. He did, however, have a passion for martial arts, especially Filipino knife-fighting.

Occasionally he would talk in general terms about jihad in Afghanistan and especially in Chechnya, which was at that time the cause célèbre of jihadis. Islamist rebels were battling the might of the Russian army. We all agreed that there was an obligation to support the rebels, through prayer, money or even waging jihad ourselves.

'It would be sinful if we don't at least raise money,' Moussaoui once said in his soft French-accented voice, as we sat cross-legged on the floor.

The age of online videos had dawned and we would watch stuttering, blurry images on websites which championed the Chechen struggle: ambushes of Russian troops, but more often human rights atrocities by the Russians against Chechen civilians in the Chechen capital, Grozny. Moussaoui would stare at the screen, his eyes glistening and his head shaking.

'*Kuffar* [infidel] Russians,' he muttered one day. 'I would happily die in Grozny if I could take a platoon of them with me.'

What he never told us was that he had already been to Chechnya and worked for the rebels – helping tell the world of their cause with his IT skills. He had also helped recruit others from abroad to join the Chechen war. Nor did he tell us he had spent time in one of al-Qaeda's camps in Afghanistan in the spring of 1998. While the rest of us debated jihad, Moussaoui had already lived it.

In October 1999 the Russians began a ground offensive against

Grozny. Television coverage and videos posted online revealed the true horror of what amounted to a scorched-earth campaign, with tens of thousands of civilians forced to flee their homes.

Thousands of miles away, my small Salafist circle in Brixton could not contain its anger. One bright autumn morning we emerged from the Brixton mosque furious that the preachers had never called for prayers let alone action in support of the Chechen resistance. Their battle against overwhelming odds made them heroes to us. We also knew that hundreds of foreign fighters, including graduates from Dammaj, had made their way to the Russian Caucasus.

'You see,' I said to Moussaoui and others, 'once again the establishment has deserted us, allowing the atheists to murder and maim our people without even raising a murmur. Our preachers are terrified they will fall foul of the police; they are so comfortable with their London life.'

We picketed the mosque, appealing for money and support for the Chechen resistance.

On 21 October Russian rockets rained down on a market in Grozny, killing dozens of women and children. I was instantly reminded of the Bosnian Serbs' shelling of the Sarajevo market, which had killed dozens of Muslims in 1995. The television footage was heartbreaking and enraging – and we redoubled our efforts to shame the mosque establishment into acknowledging the Chechens' suffering. Sometimes we would register our anger by attending a nearby mosque run by Nigerians that openly supported jihad in Chechnya.

In autumn 1999 Moussaoui's demeanour changed. The brooding became anger. He began to turn up at the Brixton mosque wearing combat fatigues and embraced the more militant environment at the Finsbury Park mosque in North London. Among those who trailed in his wake was a tall Jamaican-Englishman called Richard Reid, who had a long, thin face, a straggly beard and unkempt, curly hair held together in a ponytail. In another era he might have been a hippy. Reid was a petty criminal and Muslim convert, and he always looked like he needed a decent meal.

It was clear that Reid was in awe of Moussaoui. He attached himself to our group but said little; he seemed lonely. I lost contact with both men late in 1999 and thought little more of them, especially Reid – who seemed weak, impressionable. There were rumours that they had gone to Afghanistan – and I wondered whether the two of them had trained with al-Qaeda. Even so, I was stunned when their names and faces were splashed on television and newspapers two years later.

Moussaoui would be arrested shortly before 9/11 in Minnesota. He had entered the United States to get flying lessons, and would soon become known as the 'twentieth hijacker'. Reid would board a flight from Paris to Miami on 22 December 2001 with explosive powder hidden in his shoes. Restrained by flight attendants and passengers as he tried to light fuses hidden in his shoes, he would become known as the 'shoe-bomber'.

As my associations with radical Islamists expanded, I was often surprised by who among them crossed the Rubicon from talk to terror. They were rarely the obvious ones. But it was clear even in 1999 that London – and especially the mosque at Finsbury Park – was becoming the clearing-house for dozens of militants intent on acts of terrorism. And they often had similar backgrounds: with difficult or violent childhoods, little education and few prospects; unemployed, unmarried and seething with resentments.

Aware of the militant rhetoric emerging from places like the Finsbury Park mosque, the British security services were beginning to pay more attention to London's jihadist scene. But like many Western agencies they seemed to be playing catch-up, trying to grasp the extent of the problem, find out more about the leading lights, travel and funding, the rivalries among radical circles. Brixton and Finsbury Park became the battlegrounds for Londonistan, pitching the pro-Saudi Salafis like old Tayyib against a generation of angry jihadis that wanted to bring down the Saudi royal family, fight the Russians in Chechnya and purify the Muslim world of Western influences.

For my own part, books, lectures and conversations late into the night all helped prod me towards support for jihad, for taking up arms to defend the faith. I could not understand why the imams of most London mosques, including Abdul Baker at Brixton, studiously avoided mention of jihad let alone issue fatwas, commands to action. In Dammaj the duty of jihad as part of our religion had been our daily fare.

In the dying days of 1999 I went to a lecture in Luton, a town north of London, by Shaikh Yahya al-Hajuri, one of the teachers at Dammaj. He was surprised to see me.

'What are you doing here?' he asked me as I greeted him afterwards. 'You are supposed to be back in Yemen.'

I was taken aback by his tone. Had I abandoned the true path? Was my faith being adulterated in Europe? I went home and prayed for guidance, for a sign from Allah that I should return to what in many ways was the cradle of my devotion.

It came on a Friday morning just weeks later. I had dropped into the basement kitchen at the Regent's Park mosque for a cheap meal. A dark-skinned woman approached me, looking anxious.

'Brother, please can you come to help my husband. He wants to pray but he can't walk from the car.'

I went upstairs with her. The couple were from Mauritius. Her elderly husband looked so fragile that I thought to move him might break him. He was sitting in the driver's seat of an ancient Mercedes.

'I'm all right, brother,' he said. 'I just need to rest and get my breath back.'

I picked up an inhaler from the floor of the car. But he only became paler; it was almost as if he were vanishing before my eyes. His breathing became laboured, a quiet heaving scarcely audible amid the rush of traffic. His eyes closed and he fell back in the seat. There was a faint gurgling in his throat and his eyes reopened, staring vacantly through the front window.

I thought for a moment that he had recovered from some sort of spasm but soon found myself muttering in Arabic 'There is no God but Allah' to aid his passage to paradise. He coughed weakly and was gone.

As his wife screamed hysterically, I lifted the man out of the car and was struck for an instant by how surreal the scene must seem: a large Viking carrying a sliver of an African across lanes of London traffic. A park warden ran over to tell me that he had radioed for an ambulance. But it was too late.

It shook me. How we all hang by a thread. I helped prepare the man's corpse for burial at the Wembley mosque in keeping with Islamic practice. As I washed the grey skin I thought about how I had seen him leave this world – and how fortunate he had been that a fellow Muslim had been on hand to pray for him as he passed.

It was a sign. I could not die here among the *kuffar*. I had to be surrounded by people of my faith. Allah had prescribed it. If you died among disbelievers it was a sin. In the words of one *hadith*: 'Whoever settles among the disbelievers, celebrates their feasts and joins in their revelry and dies in their midst will likewise be raised to stand with them on the Day of Resurrection.'

The world was divided into believers and non-believers, and the worst Muslim was better than the best Christian.

But to return to the Muslim world would require a passport. Mine had been ruined during my travels. I went to the Danish embassy in London to try to get a replacement. But they had other business with me – an outstanding criminal conviction. Back in 1996 I had been involved in a scrap in a bar over a spilt drink. I had head-butted one of my assailants and then punched another. I was arrested on the way home and later sentenced to a six-month term, to be served in typically Danish fashion when cell space became available. Before it did, I had left Denmark, and under the date-palms in Dammaj I had forgotten the whole episode. Now the sentence was overdue – and I would only get a new passport if I returned to Denmark to face the music.

I would spend the first months of the new millennium behind bars.

CHAPTER SIX

DEATH TO AMERICA

Early 2000–Spring 2002

After negotiation with the Danish authorities, I returned home to serve my delayed sentence in early 2000. I had only one condition: I would not return to a prison where any Bandidos were held. The prison service ignored the agreement and I thought I would have to fight for my life – but discovered that other Muslims in the prison in Nyborg had formed a gang for mutual protection.

I served my penance, spending the time weightlifting and running, but it was a time of frustration. I was desperate to return to Yemen but I had to make money. And to make money I had to gain some sort of qualification. With the help of counsellors who worked with released prisoners, I signed up for business studies at a college in Odense (which included a monthly stipend for living expenses from the Danish state) and began worshipping at the Wakf mosque. It was a lively place full of Somalis, Palestinians and Syrians that would degenerate into violence over theological disputes. During one Friday prayers I grabbed the microphone from a preacher whom I thought misguided – he had the temerity to wear his trousers below the ankles, a practice scorned by Salafis.

'Don't listen to him. He's an innovator who belongs to one of the seventy-two sects destined for hellfire!' I yelled.

Odense is the home-town of Hans Christian Andersen, and its old streets and quaint gabled houses would fit neatly into a children's story.

It is a model of Danish progressiveness – bicycle paths, pedestrianized streets, green spaces. But its outskirts are less evocative. Many Muslims – first- and second-generation immigrants – had moved into its less salubrious social housing in the suburb of Vollsmose, and as in London there was a drumbeat of jihadism.

After I was released from prison I learned that Sheikh Muqbil, my mentor at Dammaj, had issued a fatwa calling for Holy War against Christians and Jews in the Moluccan Islands of Indonesia, where sectarian fighting was raging. He urged non-Indonesian Muslims to help establish Islamic law there.

The leader of Laskar Jihad, the al-Qaeda-affiliated group at the centre of the fighting, was Ja'far Umar Thalib. He had been a fellow student at Dammaj. And some of my friends there – including the former American soldier Rashid Barbi – had gone to Indonesia to join the battle.[1]

I made a trip over to England with a Pakistani friend, Shiraz Tariq[2] – to raise money in mosques for the mujahideen in the Moluccas. Once again I was angered by the feeble response of many Salafist imams to this gross assault on our faith.

To me, jihad was still a defensive duty rather than a right to wage offensive warfare against disbelievers. I took the words of the Koran as my guide: 'Fight in the cause of Allah those who fight you, but do not transgress, for Allah loves not the transgressor. Fight in the way of Allah against those who fight against you, but begin not hostilities. Lo! Allah loves not aggressors.'

These words brought an obligation to fight or support the fight – whether in the Balkans, Chechnya or the Moluccan Islands of Indonesia. But jihad without such a foundation was illegitimate.

The boundaries between defensive and offensive jihad were not

---

1 Barbi eventually returned to North Carolina. The last time I heard from him was around 2009. He had married a Somali woman and was working in a factory.

2 Tariq claimed he had connections to the Pakistani terrorist group Lashkar e Taiba and that he had taken several young men to train in Pakistan. He was killed fighting with al-Qaeda-linked jihadists in Syria in late 2013.

always clear and would blur further as al-Qaeda began its campaign of global jihad. They were at the heart of animated debates I had with friends in Odense such as Mohammad Zaher, a Syrian-Palestinian immigrant who had a strong Middle Eastern nose, a close-cropped beard and deep-set, solemn eyes.

Zaher like me was unemployed and with time on our hands we often went fishing together. He would bombard me with questions about Dammaj and Sheikh Muqbil. I explained the fatwas he and other imams had issued making jihad lawful in Indonesia, but also stressed that random acts to 'terrorize the disbelievers' were not allowed. In evidence I summoned the words of an eminent Saudi cleric who had said that the obligation of jihad 'must be fulfilled by Muslims at different levels in accordance with their different abilities. Some must help with their bodies, others with their property and others with their minds.'

Zaher seemed ordinary, sympathetic to the idea of jihad but not as extreme as some I knew. Yet again I would be dumbfounded when the ordinary did the extraordinary. In September 2006 he would be arrested for what Danish authorities at the time called the 'most serious' plot ever discovered in the country.

I had not forsaken my goal of returning to the Muslim world but as usual was short of cash, trying to complete my studies on a modest stipend. My talents as an enforcer would once more come to the rescue.

Odense had a substantial and volatile Somali community. One afternoon I received a call from a Somali friend asking me to intervene at a local wedding where a row had broken out.

When I reached the venue, I saw what was becoming an all too familiar dispute playing out. Against the wishes of the presiding imam, the sexes were mixing and music was blaring from speakers. Such Western practices were anathema to Salafis.

The argument escalated as I intervened and a wedding guest lunged at the imam with a knife. Thankfully, reflexes honed in the clubs of Korsør did not desert me and I knocked the knife out of his hand. What I did not see was his accomplice, who struck me on the back of the head with a bottle. As blood streamed down my neck, the man was dragged away.

Anxious that the disturbance not be reported to the police, community leaders assured me that they would apply Sharia law to my assailant. I was given the options of breaking a bottle over his head, forgiving him or taking blood money of nearly $3,000. I wasn't inclined to forgive him and did not want to return to prison for breaking a bottle over someone's head. But the blood money meant that suddenly I could travel again.

I had recently taken to browsing Muslim 'matrimonial' sites on the internet, hopeful of finding a suitably religious but also suitably attractive partner. They would never be referred to as dating sites and were rather more prim than their American counterparts. The women who had posted their details had little to say of their personal likes and dislikes, more often promising to be good, obedient and faithful wives. Every one of them wore the hijab and a meek expression. Even so, one living in the Moroccan capital had attracted my attention. Karima spoke English, was well-educated and religiously observant, and had approached me with a simple online question: would I like to marry her?[3]

Flush with cash thanks to a broken bottle, with a clean Danish passport and my debt to society paid in full, I was soon airborne.

I was met by her brother in Rabat – the vetting committee. Even before I met Karima I went to a couple of the more radical mosques in Salat, a poorer neighbourhood of Rabat. Here too Salafism was thriving: the fact that I had been to Yemen and knew Sheikh Muqbil opened doors. It also impressed Karima's family.

Karima was petite with olive skin, almond eyes and a demure manner that complemented her deep faith. I found her both attractive and intelligent. She was already thinking about emigrating to Yemen or Afghanistan with me to seek a purer existence. Within days we were married at her family's house. It may seem ridiculous that two people

---

3 Karima is a pseudonym. I am not using her real name to protect her identity for security reasons.

could marry days after meeting each other, but it was the way dictated by our faith. There was no question of dating, of discreet dinners to explore each other's thoughts and emotions. Allah would take care of everything.

And the Danish state would take care of relocating me to Yemen. Youth education grants were just one aspect of its overarching social welfare system. I applied to learn Arabic at the CALES language institute in Sana'a and received a grant – no questions asked. Karima remained in Morocco while I set about preparing for our new life in Yemen.

In April 2001 I flew into Sana'a again. It felt strangely like I belonged there. What had been an assault on the senses on my first visit was now pleasantly familiar. The chaos of the streets was welcoming rather than overwhelming; I was excited to catch up with my acquaintances there and spend long evenings on roof terraces talking about faith and the world. And I felt a real affinity for this poor corner of the Arabian Peninsula. This was where the struggle for the soul of my religion was being waged.

The neighbourhood of Sana'a where I settled seemed much more spontaneous than the bland, well-ordered suburbs of Denmark. I smiled to see the battered carts of fruit and vegetables being hauled through the streets by thin young men, the tiny kiosks selling gum and cigarettes, the old men gathered on corners with their prayer beads.

Yemen's bureaucracy meant it would be several months before Karima could join me in Sana'a. That same bureaucracy was also having trouble keeping up with my former Salafist comrades, who had become even more active and radical in my absence. And it was by now beyond doubt that al-Qaeda saw Yemen as a 'space' in which to attack Western interests. A few months before my return, terrorists aboard a skiff had approached the visiting USS *Cole* in Aden harbour. They saluted the sailors on board before detonating hundreds of pounds of C4 explosives against the *Cole*'s hull. Seventeen US sailors lost their lives and the ship nearly sank.

Young Abdul, a skinny teenager when I had left, was now a confident young man with a growing jihadist network and much-improved English. He often visited the house I had rented and we fell back into long conversations about religion. He urged me not to read books by Salafis who did not support jihad and we devoured websites that reported on the conflicts in Indonesia and Chechnya.

One evening I went to visit him at his mother's home – a plain breeze-block house on an unpaved street in Sana'a. Emaciated cats wandered among the piles of garbage as children played football or ran with hoops. Hussein al-Masri, the Egyptian jihadi who had previously offered to get me to bin Laden's camps, was there when I arrived.

As we sat on the floor, drinking tea, it became clear Abdul had been busy while I'd been in London. He told me in hushed tones but with unmistakable pride that he had travelled to Afghanistan, spent time in al-Qaeda's camps and even – he claimed – met Osama bin Laden.

'He is doing Allah's work,' Abdul said. 'The attack on the American warship and on the embassies is just the beginning,' he continued, referring to al-Qaeda's bombing of US embassies in Nairobi and Dar es Salaam in 1998. 'There are good Muslims from all over the world who are now in Kandahar and Jalalabad.' He and al-Masri told me they could get me to Afghanistan to help build the promised land. I sometimes wondered whether Abdul was embellishing his exploits and encounters, but he certainly displayed first-hand knowledge of Afghanistan and none of the al-Qaeda members I subsequently met contradicted his account.

I was tempted to go myself. My religious views were certainly no longer an obstacle. Once back in Yemen, encouraged by Abdul, I had devoured books by pro-jihadist Islamic scholars – even translating some into Danish. I had forsaken my Salafi purism to view preparation for jihad as a necessity.

It was not religious fervour alone that tempted me to head to Afghanistan. One of my circle in London – a half-Barbadian, half-Englishman – had told stories of training in Afghanistan, stimulating the sense of adventure that always itched within me. He spoke of roaming the majestic mountains, weapons training and an intense fellowship among the fighters.

'I might be going back soon,' Abdul said. 'The Sheikh said that people like you should come,' he added, referring to bin Laden. He showed me a video from Afghanistan with scenes of al-Qaeda recruits training on monkey bars and firing rockets, footage which later became iconic.

'I would like to go,' I said. I could not restrain my excitement about being with the mujahideen in the mountains of Afghanistan. My new wife was soon to join me in Sana'a, but training for jihad was all I could think about.

'We can arrange a plane ticket to Karachi, from where you'll be picked up and driven over to Afghanistan,' Abdul said.

Karima arrived in the height of summer, but I was now in a quandary. I felt I could not just leave her in Sana'a while I disappeared to the Hindu Kush – even though she accepted it was my religious duty to prepare for jihad. She knew nobody in Sana'a.

I sought an audience with Mohammed al-Hazmi, one of the radical clerics I had encountered during my previous stay in Sana'a.

'I want to train with the mujahideen in Afghanistan,' I told him.

'*Masha'Allah*, this is good. According to Sharia you can't leave your wife unless she is with a responsible family member: a father, brother or uncle. But for jihad there is an exception. Your wife can stay in your residence in Sana'a and the landlord can take her as family.'

There seemed a lot of flexibility in the rules as applied to Holy War.

Abdul, just back from Afghanistan, had different advice, telling me that if I travelled there I should take my wife with me, so that we could make *hijra* – emigrate to a Muslim land. He was relaying Osama bin Laden's appeal for jihadis to bring their families. Many did: when al-Qaeda's last redoubt at Tora Bora was cleared later that year, women and children were among those killed or put to flight.

I decided against taking Karima, a decision that seemed all the more realistic when she told me she was pregnant in August. Despite this, she still agreed to my imminent departure.

One morning after returning from prayers, I caught a glimpse of her as she struggled down the stairs. She was suffering in the heat – debilitated with morning sickness and back pain. She looked pale and tired and my instinct to protect her – and my unborn child – smothered my dream of becoming a trained warrior for Allah, at least for the time being.

'I am staying here with you,' I told her. 'You can't remain alone here – pregnant and penniless in a strange city, supposedly under the protection of a landlord.'

She began to weep. I felt less than chivalrous for even contemplating leaving her. And the prospect of fatherhood dulled the disappointment of not being able to travel to Afghanistan.

Instead of going there I returned to Dammaj for a short visit. Sheikh Muqbil, the great Salafi religious guide, had passed away in July while receiving treatment for liver disease in Saudi Arabia. His funeral took place in Mecca, but the seminary was holding a memorial. Hundreds of his former pupils gathered from around the Arab world, many of them weeping during prayers. There seemed to be a vacuum without him. My friend the American convert Clifford Newman and his son, Abdullah, were among the mourners. Clifford showed me an Uzi machine gun he had acquired for their protection from the Shia tribes in the area.

My drift towards full-blooded militancy was brought into focus on 11 September 2001. Late in the afternoon I went to a barber's shop in Sana'a. The Arabic news channel, Al Jazeera, was blaring in the corner. Soon after I arrived, it began airing live footage from New York. Smoke was drifting from the upper storeys of the World Trade Center. The breathless commentary soon made clear that a terrorist attack had occurred.

I rushed home and turned on the radio as further details of the attacks came in. Until that day, the name Osama bin Laden had meant little to the average Salafi. He was respected for giving up the trappings of wealth and fighting in Afghanistan to establish an Islamic state there. But of al-Qaeda's growing capabilities and ambitions little was known. Despite the attacks on the US embassies in East Africa and the USS *Cole*, no one I knew had expected al-Qaeda to take its war to the US homeland. Some regarded it as misguided, others as wrong because it targeted civilians. But among most of my acquaintances in Sana'a – especially those who flocked to Sheikh Mohammed al-Hazmi's mosque that evening – euphoria drowned out any more sober perspective on the attacks.

Al-Hazmi was popular among young militant Muslims in Sana'a. Addressing an overflowing congregation in the stifling heat that evening, he was unequivocal.

'What has happened is just retribution for American oppression of Muslims and the occupation of Muslim lands,' he said – a reference to the continuing presence of US forces in Saudi Arabia and elsewhere in the Gulf.

The congregation prostrated themselves in gratitude to Allah. At that point I was unsure who had committed the attacks and had heard that as many as 20,000 people might have died. I had seen few pictures and was unsure how to respond to such an act – even if it had been carried out by fellow Muslims as an act of jihad. I had so many questions. Did Islam permit a suicide attack? Was targeting civilians in a far-off country justifiable?

Many Salafis, even in Sana'a, were critical of the 9/11 attacks – saying they had no justification in Islam. But for me the theological answer came a few days later and helped cement a sense of obligation to make jihad. A Saudi cleric, Sheikh Humud bin Uqla, published a long fatwa in support of 9/11, saying it was permissible to kill civilians when they were 'mixed up' with fighters and drawing a comparison with a US military strike in 1998 on an alleged al-Qaeda facility in the Sudanese capital, Khartoum.

'When America attacked a pharmaceutical firm in Sudan, using its planes and bombs, destroying it and killing everybody in it, staff and labourers, what was this called? Shouldn't the action of America in the Sudanese firm be considered as an act of terrorism?' the Sheikh asked.

I devoured the fatwa, even as Sheikh bin Uqla was condemned by other clerics. A prominent supporter of the Taliban before 9/11, he was constantly under attack by the Saudi religious establishment. But his arguments, in those feverish days after 9/11, were what I wanted to hear.

Ultimately I accepted that in this clash of civilizations I was a Muslim. Weeks after 9/11, as the United States embarked on its invasion of Afghanistan, President George W. Bush would say, 'You are either with us or with the terrorists.' That left me no option; I could not side with the *kuffar*. Osama bin Laden was pure; he was a hero. President Bush did not believe in Allah or accept Mohammed as His messenger. His was a crusade against Islam; he had even used the word – and that pushed many doubters into the camp of the mujahideen.

In the debate over how Muslims should respond I lost a lot of friends who were Salafis. To me they were cowards; they had turned their backs on fellow Muslims. But I gained many other friends and they were jihadis. Many of them left for Afghanistan. Some militants I knew expected a US invasion of Yemen any day; I even told Karima that she would be safer back in Morocco.

Abdul and I had many discussions about the way forward.

'I have something to tell you, Murad,' he said one evening. 'I have been travelling around for Sheikh Osama. I've been delivering messages for him. You know the training video I showed you? I myself smuggled that out of Afghanistan.'

'*Masha'Allah!*' I replied. It was frowned upon to praise someone directly. Everything had to come from God.

'You can see one of the hijackers in the video – he's the guy filmed from behind firing the anti-aircraft gun. I met him while I was over there. But nobody told me what was being planned.'

I was impressed. Abdul, scarcely out of his teens, was moving in rarefied jihadist circles.

On 7 October – the day US cruise missiles were launched against Afghanistan, I was with friends at a house in Sana'a. We saw the battle for Afghanistan in very distinct colours. On one side the Taliban, who for all their faults represented Islam; on the other an unholy alliance of America, communists, Tajik warlords and Shi'ites.

I hated the Salafi scholars who refrained from depicting the conflict with the US as a Holy War of defensive jihad. One of the *hadith* became popular in our circle at the time: 'When you see that black flags have appeared from Khorasan [Afghanistan] then join them.' It was as if the Prophet had predicted Operation Enduring Freedom as a war for the future of Islam.

Clifford Newman, my American Salafi friend, felt the same way. In early December he came to my house in an excited state.

'Murad – have you seen the news?' he blurted out. 'The American they captured in Afghanistan who's all over TV. I was the guy who sent him.'

He was referring to John Walker Lindh, the so-called 'American Taliban' who had just been interviewed by CNN in Afghanistan after being captured. Lindh had studied at the CALES language institute in Sana'a the previous year, and flown from there to Pakistan, before travelling into Afghanistan. Newman told me he'd helped Lindh travel.

As far as I was concerned the attack on our Muslim brothers meant that jihad was now obligatory for every Muslim. To play my part I had begun collecting money for the Taliban and fighters hoping to join them, which attracted the attention of the Yemeni intelligence services. I was summoned to meet the committee that ran the mosque I usually attended in Sana'a.

'Murad,' said a frail, elderly man, 'this is a mosque that welcomes all Muslims, and we have a duty to all our congregation. Some are concerned, as we are, that this holy place is receiving the wrong sort of attention. You may have noticed that there are men standing across the street, watching. And they are watching you. We cannot have members of the congregation using this place to raise money for foreign wars.'

He paused and glanced at the rest of the committee.

'We have been told it would not be good for you to come here any more, for our sake and for your own sake. I hope you understand.'

I began to glance over my shoulder when walking through the streets. More than once I was sure a man had stopped to study a shop window or turned in a different direction. I even started checking my car, in case someone had tampered with the brakes or planted a device. I imagined strange clicks or interference on my phone. Things were becoming unpleasant. It was time to get out of the capital, so in the dying days of 2001 I took Karima south.

The city of Taiz is one of the most historic in Yemen – sitting amid towering mountain ranges halfway between Sana'a and Aden. In the rainy season electric storms illuminate the peaks. Its inhabitants see Sana'a as lazy and backward, and there is certainly a greater sense of industry in Taiz – none of it very picturesque. The outskirts are scarred with hideous cement plants and ramshackle factories that would be condemned in an instant if sited in the West. But its mosques are glorious. Not a few of its young men had embraced the militancy that I had also seen in Sana'a. I attended a mosque that welcomed combat veterans of Bosnia and Chechnya as well as several who had trained in bin Laden's Afghan camps. When they learned that I was being watched by the Yemeni security services they embraced me straight away. Soon I was criss-crossing the city, meeting at the homes of bright-eyed young militants, many of whom were looking for ways to join in the new war.

Among the young men I knew in Taiz were several who would be involved in a suicide attack in October 2002 on a French tanker, the MV *Limburg*, in the Gulf of Aden.

Karima gave birth a few months after we arrived, in the first week of May 2002; we called our son Osama. When I told my mother of the name she yelled down the phone.

'No, you cannot give him that name. Are you mad?'

'Mum,' I replied, 'if that's the case no Western families can call their sons George or Tony. They are the ones who have declared war on Islam.'

We were talking different languages.

CHAPTER SEVEN

FAMILY FEUDS

Summer 2002–Spring 2005

Even if my first-born was called Osama, his grandmother had a right to meet him. It was also a good moment to leave Yemen for a while. The security services, no doubt encouraged by the Americans, seemed much more intent on monitoring foreign 'activists'.

On a balmy late-summer's day in 2002, a neat suburban house near my home-town of Korsør was decked out incongruously in Moroccan and Danish flags. It was the welcome that my family had prepared for an unlikely couple: the Danish jihadi and his Moroccan bride. Aunts, uncles and new great-grandparents – all were there to greet the first of a new generation, a three-month-old boy with a shock of black hair named Osama.

My stepfather brooded in the background; he had not forgotten that I had put him in hospital. My mother tried to conceal her anger at the choice of Osama as her grandson's name, just as I tried to suppress my disdain for her as a non-Muslim. I tried (as was my duty) but inevitably failed to persuade her to convert to Islam, and she could never bring herself to call me Murad. But she found some solace in my faith – at least I was now not going to become a criminal. She may not have felt so confident had she known some of the people I counted as friends in Sana'a and Taiz. She had no idea how radical I had become. I think it was partly because she was in denial. She simply didn't want to know.

The atmosphere in Denmark after 9/11 hardened towards Muslims. Karima wore a niqab in the streets, so only her eyes could be seen. She wore gloves even on a summer's day. I wore a traditional, long, flowing *thawb*. Between us we drew plenty of suspicious glances.

After a couple of months my mother's welcome began to wear out and I found the primness of our surroundings too much to bear. In the wake of the attack on the MV *Limburg*, I had been advised by contacts in Taiz not to return to Yemen yet; the 'brothers' were being rounded up in dozens. If I had to stay in Denmark I would rather it be among 'my own' – among the grey apartment buildings of the Odense suburb of Vollsmose, where Muslims outnumbered native Danes. Many were Somali, Bosnian and Palestinian immigrants. Stories were beginning to appear in the Danish media about the crime rate in Vollsmose, stories that were meat and drink to the far-right parties.

We moved into a bare three-bedroom apartment. While Karima felt more comfortable to hear Arabic on the streets and see other veiled women, she did not appreciate our modest surroundings, nor my preference for debating jihad rather than clocking on for some menial job. Vollsmose had plenty of gang-related trouble and occasionally we would be woken by the sound of gunfire.

I soon reconnected with old associates such as Mohammad Zaher, my fishing partner from a couple of years previously. I noticed Zaher had become more militant and now had a recent convert to Islam trailing around as his sidekick.

Abdallah Andersen, who worked as a teaching assistant, was clean-shaven with a mop of dark hair and a fleshy round face. He was insecure and timid, easily led, and looked up to Zaher.

Nothing suggested they would soon plan to bring terror to the streets of Denmark.

In September 2006 Zaher, Andersen and several others would be arrested in Vollsmose after a sting operation by the Danish intelligence agency, PET, involving an informant. Angered by the publication of controversial cartoons in Denmark that lampooned the Prophet, the group had discussed attacking the Danish parliament, Copenhagen town hall square and the Danish newspaper *Jyllands-Posten*. Police found fifty grams of detonating explosive in a glass flask in Zaher's bathroom. He was convicted and sentenced to eleven years. Andersen received a four-year sentence.

I found that I was something of a celebrity among the more radical in Vollsmose thanks to an interview I had done with a Danish newspaper in which I refused to condemn the 9/11 attacks so long as people in the West declined to condemn the sanctions that had caused the premature deaths of so many Iraqi children. It was a glib comparison, but one that made me plenty of friends in the more radical mosques.[1]

I had no work but was still receiving an allowance from the Danish government for studying in Yemen, even though I was now in my mid-twenties, living in Denmark and not even attending college courses. The income allowed me to spend my days in prayer. I posted on Islamist chat forums and watched the growing archive of jihadist videos. I began to adopt a *takfiri* viewpoint, seeing some other Muslims as *kuffar* – no better than disbelievers because of their views. One of them was Naser Khader, a Syrian-born immigrant and Denmark's first Muslim MP, who took to the airwaves to argue that Islam and democracy were compatible. Then he began criticizing Sharia law. Seething with anger I wrote on an online Islamic forum: 'He is a murtad [apostate]. You don't need a fatwa to kill him.'

My commitment to the cause went beyond words. I joined other would-be jihadis, including Zaher and my Pakistani friend Shiraz Tariq, for training at paintball sites. To us it was not a game; we declined protective gear so that when we were hit by a pellet it hurt. One drill involved a team member charging out in a suicide-style attack to draw fire from the other team. Although I did not know it at the time, my activities, especially online, were being monitored by Danish intelligence. My situation was faintly ridiculous – funded by one Danish ministry, housed by another, watched by a third.

---

1 Among my circle was a Moroccan called Said Mansour who had married a Danish woman. He often came to my home and spent much of his time producing CDs and DVDs of sermons and speeches by al-Qaeda figures. He was also alleged to have been in contact with Omar Abdel Rahman, the blind Egyptian cleric convicted of conspiracy in the first attack on the World Trade Center in 1993. After three police raids on his home, Mansour would eventually become the first person in Denmark to be prosecuted and convicted under new legislation that criminalized incitement to terrorism. But by 2009 he was freed and disappeared underground. After spending time in jail he was arrested again for 'incitement' in February 2014.

Everywhere I went, militant groups were growing and coalescing – and the intelligence services were struggling to identify those who would cross the line from talk to terrorism.

Karima did not like Odense, nor Denmark, and by early 2003 was pregnant with our second child. I hoped that she might settle better in Britain. For the second time I set off for England to find work and a place to live so that the woman in my life could follow me. And for the second time, the woman had other ideas. When I called home, day after day, there was no answer. I called hospitals, the police, my family; no one had seen Karima. Eventually I found out by calling her brother in Rabat that she had returned to Morocco with Osama.

Our relationship had been struggling. She was still pious but she also seemed to hanker after a life of comfort in Europe. A rundown apartment did not match her expectations, and she had begun berating me for not providing sufficiently. I began to think that her humility and deference years earlier in Rabat had been a well-acted play.

Angry and frustrated, I flew to Morocco. It took a month and a good deal of money to be allowed to see Osama, and Karima also insisted on a private hospital to give birth. With help from friends, I scraped the money together. Our daughter, Sarah, was born in early August.

It was a time of upheaval. The US invasion of Iraq – its 'shock and awe' resembling some Hollywood script – had begun in March. I watched videos of US soldiers crossing into Iraq carrying bibles as if to bait Muslims. Neither I nor anyone I knew had any sympathy for a tyrant such as Saddam Hussein, whom we regarded as an atheist. But none of us believed the claims made by President Bush that Saddam's regime had worked with al-Qaeda or was hiding weapons of mass destruction. We saw the invasion as another declaration of war against Muslims and another reason to embrace jihad.

The humiliation of another Muslim country seemed complete. It had taken days for US tanks to advance on Baghdad. The Iraqi army had crumbled; its leadership surrendered or fled. The Stars and Stripes fluttered across the country. There was an arrogance to the Americans' war aims. They would make Iraq a beacon of democracy and the rest of the Arab world would follow gratefully. Islam could take a running jump.

For now I had more immediate and personal issues to deal with. If I wanted to repair my marriage, I needed to find work and improve our standard of living. In Denmark my criminal record stalked me, preventing me from getting a job. In England I had a better chance of finding work and someone to stay with – the former prison inmate Suleiman with whom I had arrived on the ferry six years earlier. Karima and I made a pact: if I could find a job in England she would bring the children over.

Suleiman had moved from Milton Keynes to a small ground floor flat in Luton, just north of London. On my return there from Morocco I got work driving a forklift truck in a warehouse in nearby Hemel Hempstead. It was hardly the goal of an aspiring jihadi. But if I wanted to see my children again, it would have to do.

If Vollsmose had been simmering with militancy, Luton was ready to boil over. It had a high concentration of Kashmiri immigrants from Pakistan, and unemployment and discrimination were pervasive. Many of their children had grown disaffected with mainstream British society and rejected their parents' efforts at assimilation. They had turned to radical Islam and the war in Iraq had added fuel to the fire.

I saved enough cash to begin renting a nondescript terraced house; by the end of 2003 my rare bout of self-discipline had paid off. Karima, Osama and Sarah arrived and settled into an anonymous existence on Connaught Road among the backstreets of Luton. It was a tightly packed street of post-war homes crammed with cars and vans. None had any sort of front garden; just a few paving slabs decorated with dustbins. Karima, to start with, was happier. Dressed in the full veil she was like hundreds of women in Luton. But, for that very reason, the town was also beginning to attract far-right parties, and racial assaults were not uncommon.

In Luton I quickly fell in with like-minded brothers. We would hang out, eat chicken and chips and talk jihad. I developed a following because I had met some of the best-known radical figures in the Arab world. The Islamist insurgency in Iraq had emboldened us and provided a platform for a radical preacher called Omar Bakri Mohammed – a man who could whip up a crowd.

I first heard him speak in the spring of 2004 at a small community centre on Woodland Avenue, where some of the most militant Muslims in Luton congregated.

It was packed for the occasion – rows of young bearded men wearing Taliban-style salwar kameez. Women shrouded completely in black stood in a segregated section at the back of the hall.

A hush went around the room when the cleric, a large and portly figure, climbed up on stage, supporting his girth with a walking stick. He had oversized spectacles and a thick beard.

'Brothers, I carry important news. The mujahideen in Iraq are fighting back and they are winning. They are striking fear into the Americans,' he roared in an accent that was a cross between his native Syria and East London.

The resistance of one city had given jihadis cause for hope. Fallujah, fifty miles west of Baghdad, was a Sunni stronghold whose people had never welcomed the Americans. Within days of their arriving and commandeering a school there were protests which turned violent. US forces opened fire on rioters, killing several. The Americans had just launched an offensive in the city after the charred bodies of four US security contractors were strung up on a bridge by insurgents. But the Americans had run into stiff resistance, and around the world jihadis were looking to Fallujah as the defining battle to save Iraq from the apostates. Emboldened by the failure of the Americans to capture the city, the jihadists had declared an Islamic emirate, and started implementing Sharia law.

'*Subhan'Allah, Allahu Akbar* [Glory be to God, God is Great]!' Bakri Mohammed bellowed. 'I just received greetings from brothers in Iraq from Fallujah saying the fight is going well. They ask us to keep on working for our Deen. Sheikh Abu Musab al-Zarqawi himself gives us his greetings,' he thundered.

Zarqawi, a Jordanian building a new al-Qaeda franchise, was winning growing fame in extremist circles as the standard bearer for resistance against the American occupation.

The audience lapped up Omar Bakri's remarks. He was not a man wracked by self-doubt. While his Arabic rendition of the Koran left something to be desired, he had charisma and answers to the questions of the day and remarkable contacts. What particularly appealed to me was the way he marshalled the Koran, *Hadith* and centuries-old Islamic law to justify bin Laden's war.

Omar Bakri led the group al-Muhajiroun, a radical UK outfit that was the cheerleader for al-Qaeda, and walked a thin line between freedom of speech and incitement to terrorism. He had called the 9/11 hijackers the 'magnificent nineteen' and his online sermons – followed by hundreds of young militants – justified jihad against those he called the 'crusaders' in Iraq and Afghanistan.

At the next few lectures I attended his message was inflammatory. Omar Bakri said the United States was massacring Muslims and it was the duty of all Muslims to fight back. He was fond of quoting one verse from the Koran:

'The punishment of those who wage war against Allah and His Prophet and strive to make mischief in the land is only this: that they should be murdered or crucified or their hands and their feet should be cut off on opposite sides, or they should be imprisoned.'

His acolytes would sometimes set up a projector, flashing images of Iraqis allegedly killed by the Americans. There were also photos of the prisoner abuse at Abu Ghraib prison near Baghdad, which had just been made public. Such humiliation of Muslims made me seethe with anger.

Omar Bakri also told us that in this war there was no distinction between civilians and non-civilians, innocents and non-innocents. The only real distinction was between Muslims and disbelievers and the life of a disbeliever was worthless. Bakri had formed al-Muhajiroun in Britain in 1996 and had steadily become more radical, especially after 9/11. Though he was dismissed by many as a loudmouth, his followers, many of whom only had a superficial knowledge of Islam, hung on his every word and sometimes gravitated towards violence. Several of his acolytes had become involved in terrorist plots – including one sponsored by al-Qaeda to set off large fertilizer-based bombs in crowded spaces, such as the Ministry of Sound nightclub in London. He had a remarkable record of mentoring and teaching young militants who subsequently plotted violence – but of never being involved in, nor aware of, their plans.

After two British men carried out a suicide attack against a bar in Tel Aviv, he boasted that one of them had taken a course he had run on

Islamic law, but insisted he was unaware of their plot. He also spoke of a 'Covenant of Security' – which held that Muslims living in Britain should not commit acts of jihad there, but could wage jihad overseas. He told a story about the companions of the Prophet Mohammed who were given protection and hospitality in Christian-ruled Abyssinia. This had brought about the concept in the Koran of a covenant, whereby Muslims are not allowed to attack the inhabitants of a country where they find refuge. It was a cunning way to avoid getting into trouble with the UK's tough terrorism legislation.

At Omar Bakri's lectures a quiet British-Pakistani called Abdul Waheed Majeed sat at the back, taking the official minutes of the proceedings. He lived in Crawley, a sleepy market town south of London, but drove up for the talks. He had been one of a group of young men mentored by Omar Bakri in Crawley, several of whom had planned to blow up the Ministry of Sound nightclub in London. Majeed was not implicated in the plot but years later would himself make the ultimate sacrifice for al-Qaeda.

Soon I was attending Omar Bakri's 'VIP' lectures, which were open to only a few of his closest followers like Abdul Majeed. Omar Bakri was impressed by the fact I had spent time in Yemen and by the name I had given my son. He liked to call me Abu Osama (the father of Osama).

These sessions were held at least once a week in followers' houses in Luton with six to ten of us. They were followed by a large dinner of lamb or chicken offered by the host. Omar Bakri liked his food.

Behind closed doors his message was very different. On one occasion he said he was issuing a fatwa that allowed for the killing of the disbelievers – the *kuffar* – in England because in his view they were part of a larger conflict. Asked by one of the group – a red-bearded optician of Pakistani origin from Birmingham – whether it was permissible to stab *kuffar* on the street, he confirmed that it was.

Omar Bakri had come to the UK to escape prosecution in Saudi Arabia, but was quietly giving his blessing to followers to kill people on the streets of the country he now called home.

I was among a small group of his followers who tore down advertising posters showing scantily clad women and maintained a stall in

Luton town centre to distribute leaflets and proselytize with mega-phones. For me, it was belonging to another gang. But the fractious atmosphere – including a growing number of assaults on Muslim women – gave us a real sense of purpose in defending our community. It was not Fallujah, but it was a much smaller part of the same struggle.

We would beat up drunkards who were harassing veiled women. On one occasion a fellow al-Muhajiroun member and I chased two men through the Arndale Shopping Centre after they had abused Muslim women. I caught up with one in a Boots chemist's store and dragged him to the ground among the shelves of cosmetics, punching him repeatedly before escaping as the police arrived. When Luton Town football club played home matches, which attracted groups of neo-Nazi skinheads, I would carry a baseball bat or hammer with me. And my little circle rejected attempts by other Muslims to engage politically in England, regarding such efforts as useless and against Islam.

I felt Islamophobia at first hand, especially when subjected to 'additional screening' at airports on a regular basis. On one trip from Denmark, I was held up for two hours at customs at Luton airport while they checked through my luggage and asked me the usual questions.

'Are you doing this because you hate Muslims? That's the reason, isn't it?' I asked accusingly. They looked offended. One went to fetch a colleague, a British-Pakistani woman wearing a hijab.

'I'm a Muslim too and I can assure you this is nothing to do with our religion,' she said.

'You're not a Muslim. You're just pretending to be one. What you actually are is a hypocrite,' I snapped.

Jihadi-Salafism was not exactly an inclusive creed.

Omar Bakri designated me the 'Emir of training' for the group because of my boxing background. I instructed a small group of al-Muhajiroun in boxing in the gym. And I began leading expeditions of young British extremists to Barton Hills, a nature reserve north of Luton, where we conducted paramilitary exercises without weapons.

I made the drills up as I went along, using al-Qaeda training videos I had seen online as inspiration. Getting my trainees to crawl through an icy stream and then run up a steep bank was a staple. I loved being outdoors and so did my students. They got to play at being mujahideen for the day; shouts of '*Allahu Akbar!*' resounded through the forested hills.

Soon there was so much demand for the training that I was leading groups of a dozen into the hills twice a week. They came from as far away as Birmingham to join in.

Among those I encountered in Luton was Taimour Abdulwahab al-Abdaly, a young man of Iraqi descent who had spent much of his childhood in Sweden. We bumped into each other in the men's clothing department at a large store where he worked. Al-Abdaly had deep-brown eyes and luxuriant black hair; he could have been a matinee idol. But he was in Luton, a place that did not scream opportunity. We played football and went to the gym together, and met at Friday prayers.

Occasionally Taimour came along to al-Muhajiroun's open meetings, more out of curiosity than conviction. He was a quiet character who rarely expressed any views. From time to time we did get into theological debates, and he would gently challenge me on my uncompromising embrace of the *takfiri* position. Like my Danish friends in Vollsmose, he seemed an unlikely candidate for terrorism. His wife did not wear the full veil, or *niqab*, but a modern loose hijab. Years later Taimour would be another to confound my expectations.

For extremists like me, the imprisonment without trial of alleged al-Qaeda members at Guantanamo Bay and the scandal at Abu Ghraib infuriated us. My Luton fraternity would mockingly describe the US President as Sheikh Bush because the Saudi religious establishment was so deferential to the Americans, condemning terrorist attacks in Iraq but never mentioning the deaths of ordinary Iraqis at the hands of US forces.

On 7 May 2004 the American civilian Nick Berg was executed in Iraq by Abu Musab al-Zarqawi, the Jordanian jihadi for whom no level of violence or brutality seemed excessive. Zarqawi ensured that Berg's beheading was filmed.

At that time Zarqawi was something of a hero to us; he was on the frontline and not cowed by vastly superior forces. He was ready to use the sword himself and was developing even more of a following than Osama bin Laden among my Luton circle.

The video of Berg's killing, and others of attacks on US forces in Iraq, became popular among jihadis in Luton and elsewhere in the UK, turning up on DVDs distributed by al-Muhajiroun.

I too watched the video of Berg's murder, but had no idea until later that the man to his right, restraining him as Zarqawi prepared for the fatal blow, was Mustapha Darwich Ramadan, whom I had spoken with in a Danish prison in 1997. After his release Ramadan had got into more trouble and fled to Lebanon and then Iraq, where he had adopted a *nom de guerre*, Abu Mohammed Lubnani, and joined the militant Islamist group Ansar al-Islam.

Lubnani and his sixteen-year-old son were killed in Fallujah, fighting with al-Qaeda against US forces.

I was not alienated by the brutality of the videos emerging from Iraq because they represented justifiable retribution for the invasion of Muslim lands. They would instil terror in the enemy. Allah had told Mohammed that in war slaughter was preferable to taking many captives. In the words of the Koran: 'It is not for any prophet to have captives until he has made slaughter in the land. You desire the lure of this world and Allah desires (for you) the Hereafter, and Allah is Mighty, Wise.'

I could separate these remote acts of war from my everyday surroundings in a way that many of Omar Bakri's followers could not. To young men like the optician who attended his private lectures, the enemy was everywhere, in uniform and out of uniform, in Baghdad and Birmingham. They had bought into a very simple distinction: it was the disciples of Allah against the disbelievers.

I found it difficult to accept that simplistic formula. Perhaps my basic humanity held me back from seeing the world as a struggle between good and evil, where the evil included ordinary people trying to raise families and hold down jobs. Despite the fatwas that justified the 9/11 attacks, I had begun to feel nagging doubts about the targeting of civilians. Jihad to me was still a defensive action to protect the faith. And on a personal level, I simply liked to be liked – by Muslims and non-Muslims. Whether it was a brief chat with a supermarket cashier or a bus driver, a conversation about football at the warehouse or help-ing someone struggling with their shopping, I saw non-Muslims I knew as fellow human beings, albeit misguided ones.

I became adept at distinguishing between my commitment to the cause – and to al-Muhajiroun – and the rapport I developed with ordin-ary people I encountered.

I was proving less adept at keeping my marriage alive. I had given up my job as a forklift driver and was working as an occasional nightclub bouncer. I certainly had the build to qualify, and made more money than when I had a regular job. Being paid in cash at the clubs and pubs of Luton and nearby towns had one additional benefit: tax on my income would not directly go into the British government's coffers for its war against Muslims overseas.

But Karima was unhappy, prone to mood swings, intolerant of my lifestyle as the 'Muslim bouncer'. She felt alone and struggled to cope with the children. Osama had become a boisterous toddler. At one point – during a row about my lengthy absences from Connaught Road – she spat in my face.

On a grim evening of drizzle in the autumn of 2004 she came to me with a simple request.

'Can you leave?' she asked. 'I don't want you here any more.'

Karima asked me for a 'divorce in Islam' and even wanted me to help find her a new husband. Rather than allow a man I did not know to move into the house where my young children lived, I went as far as introducing her to a Turkish friend of mine. He became her new husband – at least in Islam if not according to the law of the land – and moved in with Karima. But three days later he moved out again.

'I couldn't take her,' he sighed. We laughed.

With nowhere to live and a sense of failure, I hit a low that recalled my trip to jail in Denmark. Then my response had been very different: no more crime, find discipline and self-respect through becoming a good Muslim. As 2005 began, turmoil produced the opposite effect: it was like a relapse to my Bandido days. There was nothing in the Koran to guide the conduct of a nightclub bouncer. When I found club-goers with cocaine, I gave them the option of handing it to me or handing it to the police. Soon I had a lot of cocaine and began using it again after seven years of self-denial. I also had a wild partner, a blonde called Cindy[2] who worked for a car dealership and filled the rest of her waking hours with hardcore partying.

Within about three minutes of meeting her and a friend outside one of the clubs where I was working, Cindy had leered at me.

'I love spanking,' she said.

'What do you want me to spank you with?' I shot back.

She named a certain whip apparently well known in S&M circles and gave me her phone number.

Whether I was still technically married to Karima or not, the Koran promised severe punishment for sex outside marriage.

'The woman and the man who fornicate scourge each of them a hundred whips; and in the matter of God's religion, let no tenderness for them seize you if you believe in God and the Last Day.'

It was the sort of punishment that Cindy might appreciate. But I spent the next few months living a life of contradictions, giving in to every sort of temptation but then trying to repent through prayer. I was hopelessly adrift, in a maelstrom of sex, drugs and brawls, interrupted by occasional reconnections to the faith.

One of the clubs where I worked was in the town of Leighton Buzzard. Shades was a pitiful place: a scar on what had once been a pretty street in a country town. It saw plenty of fights and I earned my keep. Tony, the head doorman, was an affable guy in his early forties and smarter than your average bouncer. He could be thoughtful and inquisitive, unlike the louts that we threw out of Shades most nights. I was the first Muslim convert he had worked with and he was curious about why I had chosen Islam.

On a bitterly cold evening in February 2005 Tony picked me up at Leighton Buzzard station in his ageing Honda Accord. Normally we would talk about boxing, work or the weather. But on that evening, as we sat at traffic lights, he turned to me and asked simply:

'Why does Allah want people to kill other people? Don't you think, Murad, Allah would prefer you to teach people to read?'

I stumbled, before offering up stock answers about the need for

2 Cindy is not her real name. I have used a pseudonym.

jihad to protect my religion in the face of Western oppression. But the nakedness of Tony's question troubled me. Since becoming a Muslim seven years before, I had learned to cultivate or imagine enemies – Shi'ites, the Muslim Brotherhood, racists in Luton, more recently the US government. Somehow I had become identified by whom or what I loathed; enemies provided an outlet for my anger. But they also camouflaged the real reasons for embracing hatred. Anger and frustration had been part of me since childhood; how much easier it was to hate than to reconcile.

My reflex reaction when confronted with painful questions was to blame the Devil for trying to undermine my faith. Since becoming a Muslim I had been constantly reminded by imams and scholars that Satan was always looking to sow doubt. As it was written in the Koran: 'Satan said: "O my Lord! Because You misled me, I shall indeed adorn the path of error for mankind on earth, and I shall mislead them all. Except Your chosen slaves among them."'

Amid the hedonism of life with Cindy, I felt weak – as if slipping back towards my clubbing days in Korsør. I had to escape before the quicksand enveloped me. And it was my estranged wife who would – at least for a while – rescue me.

'Would you come back?' was Karima's simple question when I picked up the phone. It was the early spring of 2005. She sounded exhausted rather than desperate for my company. Even so I was elated at the chance to be reunited with my children. I would miss the sex with Cindy but not the unhinged lifestyle – nor the lack of any purpose.

Repentance is a formidable force, and helped me to put the wild interlude behind me. Walking through the backstreets of Luton, I would recite to myself the words of Allah.

'Those are the true believers who, when they commit an evil deed, or wrong their souls, remember Allah, and seek forgiveness for their sins – and who but Allah forgives sins?'

CHAPTER EIGHT

MI5 COMES
TO LUTON

Spring–Autumn 2005

On 30 April 2005, *Newsweek* went to print with an incendiary story. US military personnel at Guantanamo Bay had defiled the Koran and humiliated prisoners.

The magazine reported that 'Interrogators, in an attempt to rattle suspects, flushed a Qur'an down a toilet and led a detainee around with a collar and dog leash. An army spokesman confirms that 10 Gitmo interrogators have already been disciplined for mistreating prisoners, including one woman who took off her top, rubbed her finger through a detainee's hair and sat on the detainee's lap.'

Newsweek retracted part of the story, but by then Muslims around the world were outraged. There were deadly riots in Afghanistan, and in Pakistan the opposition politician Imran Khan used the story to undermine the country's military leader, General Pervez Musharraf. Jihadist communities everywhere thirsted for revenge, among them our band of brothers in Luton.

Omar Bakri helped organize a protest outside the US embassy in London on Grosvenor Square in mid-May, and I drove down from Luton in a convoy of his followers.[1]

---

1 Omar Bakri announced the dissolution of al-Muhajiroun in October 2004, citing the need for Muslims to 'merge together as one global sect against the crusaders and occupiers of Muslim land', but in practice the disbandment was a ruse to confuse

A video of the event is still available online, and among the Pakistani and Arab men yelling abuse there is a tall, broad-shouldered Dane, stamping on the Stars and Stripes as it smouldered on the London pavement, smiling and chanting.

'Bomb, bomb USA.' 'Remember, remember, eleventh September.' The chants were as provocative as possible. Then we knelt to pray, before, to my astonishment, the 200 or so protesters drifted away, as if a few slogans had restored Islam's self-respect and caused the diplomats of the Big Satan to quiver behind the bullet-proof glass of their embassy.

I was furious. Just as my adrenalin was beginning to run, the protest was over. These so-called militants were pussies. Surely we had a duty to take on the police cordon and try to enter the embassy. So we would most likely be hurt and arrested, but that would be a pin-prick compared to the injury done to our faith. I was frustrated, disappointed by Omar Bakri. He had delivered a fiery speech and then retired to his comfortable car. It was all talk. I also began to doubt whether he really had contacts in Iraq and other jihadist battlegrounds.

I returned to Luton that evening determined to expose the blow-hards who proclaimed jihad but did not want to miss lunch. With the passion of a man recently redeemed from straying into the wilderness, I threw myself into research on Salafism and jihad. As an ordinary Muslim I could not pretend that I could compose a fatwa, but I planned to publish a booklet, 'Exposing the Fake Salafis'.

Over the next few weeks, working day and night, I wrote a pamphlet that became a paper and then a treatise – more than 140 pages of closely argued rhetoric, crammed with quotations from the Koran and the ancient scholars. The fake Salafis liked to talk but were secretly in league with the *kuffar* who had invaded Muslim lands.

'The Fake Salafis in our time use thousand and one excuses to deny the obligation of Jihad Fard Ayn in Iraq and other Muslim lands, also denying that those who assist the Kuffar (disbelievers) in this crusade against Islam are apostates,' I wrote.

---

those investigating his activities. The group's operations continued and have done ever since. Al-Muhajiroun has periodically changed its name to avoid being banned. For example, recently it operated under the name 'Shariah4UK'.

My conclusion was a call to arms:

'Your duty as a true Muslim, is to support your Muslim brothers and sisters, who right now are being killed by the neo-crusaders and Jews, I ask you kindly to at least make Dua [prayers] for them, collect finance for them, and try your best to reach the frontline where your brothers are striving or at least help someone to go there.'

Intellectually at least I was already on the battlefield.

My studying was interrupted one morning in June 2005 when there was a knock on the door at our semi-detached house. (By then, we had moved to Pomfret Avenue, another nondescript street in Luton.) I looked through the bedroom window and saw a policeman. There was another knock. I whispered to Karima to tell them I was not home.

From the landing I listened.

'What do you want?' Karima asked.

'It's the police. We'd like to speak to Mr Storm.'

'He's not here.'

'Yes, he's here – we know he's here.'

I put on my clothes and went down to the door.

The officer was soft-spoken but did not give me his name.

'Can you come with me, Mr Storm? We have some questions we'd like to ask you.'

It seemed like this was a routine he had performed a hundred times before.

'No,' I replied. 'I can't come with you but if you want you can come into my house.'

He declined, and I asked what the problem was.

'Your car has been seen filling up at a petrol station. Thirty pounds of fuel and then whoever was driving left without paying.'

I knew it was a fabrication. Surely they could do better than this.

'Here, take the key. Go look at the gauge. No one put thirty pounds of fuel in.'

I accompanied him outside and unlocked the car. As soon as I turned on the ignition, the police officer melted away. In his place, opening the passenger door, was a dapper young man in a suit.

'Mr Storm – my name is Robert. I'm with British intelligence.'

His words went straight to the pit of my stomach.

'All right,' I said weakly, getting out of the car. 'What do you want to speak to me about?'

'This is dangerous,' Robert said, 'very, very dangerous. It's very important that we speak.'

It was far from clear to me what was dangerous. I invited him to come inside, but insisted I had nothing to tell him.

He declined and we stood beside the car. As I began to recover my composure I was struck by how young he was. He must have just graduated. This was probably one of his first jobs in the field.

Perhaps, I thought, the security services were aware of my relapse into drugs and believed it might make me vulnerable.

'Can I ask you a few questions?' he resumed. Across the street I noticed glances from neighbours leaving for work.

'Morten,' he said, trying to be familiar and informal, 'there's a very dangerous situation in the UK with terrorism.'

'First, my name is Murad,' I replied. 'Second, you don't have anything to fear from Muslims. There have been IRA attacks, by Catholics, so why don't you go to search for Catholics, or the Spanish ETA? Why are you harassing Muslims? There's never been a terrorist attack by Muslims in the UK.'

Warming to my theme, I raised Iraq. 'How many hundreds of thousands of children have you killed? You don't expect Muslims to be angry? You expect to be able to hit people but for them not to retaliate? I am not scared of you. If you want I will pack a bag of clothes and you can take me to prison.'

Robert smiled and shook his head.

'We don't want to arrest you. We just want to ask you some things.'

Here we were – the Danish Muslim and the man from MI5 – engaged in debate on Pomfret Avenue, just around the corner from Treetop Close, in Luton.

Then the generalities ended.

'What do you think of Abu Hamza?' he asked.

Abu Hamza al-Masri was a militant Egyptian cleric known in the racy English tabloids as 'Captain Hook' because of his prosthetic hand. He claimed he had sustained the injury while on a de-mining project in Afghanistan. He had been the imam of the Finsbury Park mosque in North London.[2]

'I don't know much about him,' I replied, which was the truth. Our paths had never crossed and I had never read his lectures. 'And I am not going to backbite him just to please you. You are a non-believer and he is a brother Muslim.'

We talked for about two hours, standing by the car outside my house. All the time, I asked myself whether I would be charged with one of the many anti-terrorism charges already on the books. Perhaps MI5 were somehow aware of the diatribe I had drafted to justify jihad, or had identified me from the protest at the US embassy. Or perhaps I had been grassed up by the Islamic Centre in Luton, which saw me and my friends as dangerously radical.

Robert took his leave. We shook hands, both aware that I was now part of the game. What I did not know is that two officers from Danish intelligence had seen everything from a car parked nearby. MI5 and their friends clearly thought I was worth spending time with and were angling for me to share my contacts.

Just three weeks after that conversation, on 6 July 2005, the world's leaders converged on a Scottish golf resort for the G8 summit, hosted by Tony Blair. After nearly eight years in office, Blair seemed unassailable. He had tied Britain closely to Bush by his support for the wars in Afghanistan and Iraq, where a large chunk of the UK's armed forces were now deployed. But at home public opinion had turned decisively against the war. The rationale for the invasion had been undermined by allegations that evidence of Saddam Hussein's weapons of mass destruction had – at the very least – been embellished.

The wars had also enraged many British Muslims. A few had travelled to Pakistan with the aim of joining al-Qaeda, the Taliban and

---

2 Abu Hamza had been charged in 2004 with encouraging the murder of non-Muslims and incitement to racial hatred. At the time of my meeting with Robert the beginning of Hamza's trial was just days away. After being convicted and serving jail time he was extradited in 2012 to face trial on terrorism charges in the US.

other groups. Some had stayed and been killed – or disappeared into the tribal territories, their fate unknown. A few had come home.

On the morning of 7 July Blair and his senior ministers were presenting an ambitious agenda to the summit. An aide passed the British Prime Minister a note. Three suicide bombers had attacked the London Underground system; there were casualties and the capital was paralysed. Shortly afterwards a fourth suicide bomber blew up a London bus.

Blair emerged from the conference looking shaken.

'It is reasonably clear that there have been a series of terrorist attacks in London,' he said, before hurrying to a helicopter.

That morning I was oblivious to the carnage some thirty miles to the south; and I had no idea that the bombers had caught a train from Luton on their way to the capital. But my insistence to the MI5 man Robert weeks earlier – that Britain had nothing to worry about from Muslims – was suddenly null and void. And as news spread of the bombings and speculation spiked, I got hostile stares as I walked through Luton in my Muslim garb, still unaware of events in London.

A friend called me to tell me of the attacks and we all hurried to meet at the Woodland Avenue community centre. Everyone was wary of a backlash. By now we knew that some fifty people had been killed and several hundred injured.

Despite the casualties, all of them civilians, I found a way to justify the attack. Brothers in Islam had struck fear into the hearts of the *kuffar* and a blow at the financial heart of a state committed to war against Muslims. The attack would surely cost the British economy tens of millions, money that could not be spent on war.

My adrenalin was pumping. We had all talked about jihad; we had cheered on the brothers in Iraq. Now it was on our doorstep. Was England the next frontline in this war of religions? Anything seemed possible.

As we travelled to London the following day for a Muslim wedding, the tension was palpable. A young white man on the pavement saw us pass and raised his hand as if to take aim with a pistol. I stopped the car and called him over. He saw I was white and may have thought he had an ally in his provocation.

I spat at him and he ran to his car to grab a crowbar. I jumped out, ready for a fight, but others held me back. The last thing this wedding party needed was a brawl on a London street.

There was a spate of assaults on Muslims in Luton; Karima was harassed. Community meetings brought together Muslim sects that usually avoided each other, to discuss a common threat.

Omar Bakri Mohammed saw a dividend out of the 7/7 bombings. He summoned close followers to a meeting in Leyton in East London days later. The situation had changed, he said. The 'Covenant of Security' – that British jihadis should not consider attacking targets in Britain – was dead.

'Now,' he told us, 'jihad has come to the UK. You can do whatever you wish.'

Perhaps he knew he was on safe ground. Most of his acolytes were not ready to follow the path of the 7/7 bombers. But it was not for want of permission.

Had it not been for an old Danish associate and a mislaid mobile phone, I would probably have continued listening to Omar Bakri's bombast and training in the English countryside for the day that jihad would inevitably call.

I had met Nagieb in 2000 – he was a Danish journalism graduate of Afghan descent. He knew of my time in Yemen and wanted to make a film about the mujahideen there. And he wanted me to go with him to open doors.

I was excited by the prospect; my spirit was beginning to stir again and I still wanted to return to a truly Muslim land as Allah had ordained. I felt more in common with my friends there than with the radical blowhards in the UK. The rush that immediately followed the London bombings had worn off and I was worried that MI5 might come calling again as they stepped up their efforts to discover more about UK-based jihadist cells in the wake of the London attack.

I even began to indoctrinate my son, Osama, who was now three. We would play a game of call and response.

'What do you want to be?'

'I want to be mujahid.'

'What do you want to do?'

'I want to kill *kuffar*.'

I argued to myself that if Western children could kill dark-skinned turbaned figures in computer games, I could teach my son about retribution. Hatred again.

My relationship with Karima had never really recovered. When Karima asked me back, Cindy had come looking for me in my family home in Luton, not realizing Karima would be there. It was the second time I witnessed the full force of Karima's volcanic temper, as she shouted abuse – angered not so much by the fact that Cindy had slept with me but because she represented the decadence and permissiveness of Western women.

When I told Karima of my plans to return to Yemen, she shrugged and turned away. There was no discussion, just resignation. She felt abandoned, unwanted.

So perhaps it should not have come as a surprise when one afternoon I picked up her mobile phone as it buzzed – Karima had gone out – and read the following text: 'Meet me in the hotel. I love you.'

It was not the fact that she had found someone else that bothered me. We had long ceased to love each other; our relationship was more a pact for the sake of the children. It was the fact that she still sheltered in the house I was paying for, still used my name to keep her European residency, and while happy to take another man in Islamic law would not divorce me in civil law.

When she returned home, she was nervous. Had I seen her phone?

I lied. It was in my pocket.

'I want you out of the house while I look for it.'

She was not very good at keeping her nerve.

I called the number from which the suggestive text had come. A man answered. I found out later that he was a Palestinian living in Luton, whose Moroccan wife was Karima's best friend. He and Karima had had a secret Islamic wedding.

I went back inside and confronted her.

'I know exactly what you are up to,' I told her quietly. 'I know where you are going and everything. I am just asking you to give me my children.'

She looked at me with spite.

'You will never see your children again,' she said. 'Never.'

She grabbed Osama and Sarah and made for the front door. I held her back and she swung round and hit me in the face. She pulled Osama by the hood of his jacket, nearly throttling him. He was crying.

'Osama is staying with me,' I told Karima as he cowered on the floor.

Shortly afterwards I left the house with my three-year-old son, only to find out the following day that the police were looking for me. Karima had told them that I had abducted him. I felt as if I were on the run for a crime I had never committed.

Before any sort of mediation could begin, Karima left for Morocco with Sarah – without telling me or seeing Osama.

Eventually the police tracked me down to a friend's house in Luton. His mother had been caring for Osama while I was out. Her eyes were red and swollen when I returned.

'They took Osama,' she sobbed. 'They said they were taking him to the police station.'

I summoned fellow militants and nearly a dozen of us converged on the police station. The waiting room was full of beards and robes.

I was blind with anger.

'Where is my son?' I demanded loudly. 'Give me my son back.'

By then Osama was in the care of the social services department and I was redirected to an adjacent building while the rest of the unlikely delegation sat in the police waiting room.

I looked out of a featureless waiting room at a thousand shades of grey. Luton in the approaching British winter was not cheering. There was a knock and a woman brought Osama in.

To my relief, he didn't say, 'Kill Bush and the *kuffar*; victory to the mujahideen.' I might have lost custody of him there and then. Instead he ran to me and wrapped his arms tightly around my neck.

'Why did you take him?' I asked the woman.

'We were told you had kidnapped him,' she replied.

'Where is his mum?' I asked.

'We don't know.'

'Exactly,' I replied – unable to hide my sense of triumph. 'That's because she is in Morocco, with my daughter. I should report her for kidnapping.'

I walked out of the building, clutching my son's hand tightly and leading a group of bearded Salafis with angry faces who had come to rescue a child called Osama from Bedfordshire Social Services.

The drizzle began to seep into our clothes.

CHAPTER NINE

MEETING THE SHEIKH

Late 2005–Late Summer 2006

There is a popular joke in the Arab world. There are different versions but its essence is this. Millennia after creating the earth, God returns to see how things have changed. First He looks down at Egypt. 'Ah, the industry, the cities, the beautiful buildings; I would never have recognized it,' He marvels. Then He surveys Syria. 'The architectural splendour, the sophistication of society,' He says. Moving south, He then sees something more familiar. 'Ah, Yemen – same as ever.'

I had that same feeling in the dying days of 2005, when I arrived at Sana'a airport. Yemen was a country that kept drawing me back – despite its poverty, its almost medieval treatment of women and the growing dossier held by the Yemeni security services on one Murad Storm.

I had good reasons for returning – to help Nagieb make his film and reconnect with old friends, or those who were not languishing at the pleasure of the Yemeni state. I felt like a different person this time. I was about to turn thirty and I had my son, Osama, with me. Now he would grow up to be a God-fearing Muslim.

A fresh start: I seemed to need one every eighteen months. Was it boredom? The hope of one day finding the perfect wife? A compulsion to be on the road?

I was still serious about Islam. I enrolled at the al-Iman Islamic

University in Sana'a, which was still being run by Sheikh Abdul Majid al-Zindani. Since our previous encounter seven years before, when I had insolently questioned his Salafist credentials, the Sheikh had attracted the attention of the US government. He was now designated a 'global terrorist' for fundraising on behalf of al-Qaeda. Despite that dubious honour, he was still a public presence at al-Iman. And he welcomed me back, assigning me a special room to study in at the university. Al-Zindani became particularly fond of Osama, who used to tag along with me.

I also caught up with Abdul, the young Yemeni courier who was so proud of his association with Osama bin Laden. His English was more polished and he had recently married. He now had a much bigger home in Sana'a and a relatively new car parked in front of it. Being an al-Qaeda courier clearly had not prevented him from embarking on some promising business ventures.

It was refreshing to be away from the endless circular chatter of *faux*-jihadis in England, and instead in a place where imprisonment and even death were daily risks, a place at the centre of a web that spread to Pakistan and Indonesia in the east, and Somalia to the south. I found out that the jihadist presence had become more intense in my absence, despite the growing scrutiny of the security services.

Word spread that the big European was back in Sana'a, the one with the red hair and tattoos. And one man was intrigued to meet me. He had heard that I had spent time in Taiz back in 2002 and knew that I had attended Dammaj.

His name was Anwar al-Awlaki. He taught at al-Iman University, and he too had recently returned to Yemen.

Awlaki's father was an eminent member of Yemen's establishment and a grandee of the Awalik tribe. He had studied in the United States, where Anwar had been born, and been Minister for Agriculture in his home country. Early in 2006 I was invited to a banquet at the Awlaki family home.

Awlaki had asked an Australian-Polish convert studying at the Sana'a Institute of Languages who called himself Abdul Malik to gather together some of the young foreign Muslims living in Sana'a and bring them to dinner. Malik's real name was Marek Samulski. In his mid-thirties, he was tall and well-built, and like so many Western Salafists had been radicalized by the events that followed 9/11. He had been persuaded by his South African wife to come to Yemen so their sons could be brought up as good Muslims.

Awlaki by then had developed quite a reputation as a preacher in militant circles in the West. I was only dimly aware of his English-language sermons because I had preferred listening to Arabic clerics, but I knew he was a rising star in Salafi circles.

The Awlakis' home was an imposing three-floor building of grey stone not far from Sana'a's old university – a house that was laid out in traditional Yemeni style, with large windows. The younger Awlaki occupied the middle floor, which he shared with his first wife, a woman from a well-connected Sana'a family, who had lived with him in the United States.

I took my son with me to the dinner. It was a cool evening in January, one of the few months of the year in Sana'a when the weather is familiar to a north European. I made sure Osama looked his best, and bought a new *thawb* for the occasion.

We were ushered into Awlaki's apartment, which was furnished with impeccable but not ostentatious taste. Books lined the walls, most of them Islamic texts. Samulski introduced me to the preacher, and I warmed to him immediately. He was urbane and well-informed, with a scholarly air and an undeniable presence. He exuded self-assurance without coming across as arrogant. But he also had a sly sense of humour. Awlaki was well-groomed, with a neat beard and gentle brown eyes behind wire-rimmed glasses. Like most Yemenis, he was slight; unlike them he was very nearly six feet tall. He conversed easily in English and Arabic and was a generous host.

'How did you like Dammaj?' he asked me.

'It opened my eyes. And Sheikh Muqbil had such deep knowledge and understanding. I just wish my Arabic had been better then.'

'And now?'

'Oh, it's much better. But my religious Arabic is stronger than my street Arabic.'

Awlaki was interested in finding out more about my contacts – in Sana'a and Taiz. He asked me about the other foreigners in my circle and some of the Yemenis – like Abdul – that I had got to know. It seemed that he was looking to tap into a wider pool of radicals in the Yemeni capital and beyond.

I asked Awlaki how long he had been back in Yemen.

'On and off about three years. Sometimes I find it a little dull, but life in the West was not easy after 9/11.'

'It wasn't very easy here either,' I laughed.

Our exchanges were little more than pleasantries, but afterwards I thought he had been gently trying to get the measure of me, find out the depth of my commitment and the circles in which I moved.

At one point Awlaki's son, Abdulrahman, came in to show him some homework. He was about ten, tall for his age, with his father's eyes. There was clearly a close bond between them. Abdulrahman seemed to be in awe of his father, who in turn was much more affectionate and attentive than many Yemeni fathers I had met. A gentle and polite boy, Abdulrahman helped entertain Osama despite the difference in their ages.

Samulski, probably by prior arrangement with Awlaki, suggested we start a study circle to learn more about Islam – a weekly occasion for an honoured group of students to discuss the issues of the day and their implications for Islam. Awlaki agreed and I offered to host some of the meetings.

Awlaki started coming to my home to give his lectures to our small group of English-speaking militants. It was a beautiful old house with whitewashed walls and I had decked it out with dark-blue Arabic furniture and a thick Yemeni carpet. It was a privilege for me, but he clearly enjoyed our company. We were more worldly than most of his students, and he loved being our mentor, seeing his every word absorbed. Sitting cross-legged on the floor with notes in front of him, poised and eloquent, he liked to show off his intellect and learning, peering occasionally over his glasses at us.

He focused a great deal on Islamic jurisprudence related to jihad, marshalling verses from the Koran and *Hadith* to make his case. One of his most popular online tracts, '44 Ways of Supporting Jihad', grew out of these lectures on my carpet.

He reserved much of his ire for the Yemeni government for its cooperation with the United States. A favourite phrase of his was: 'We should clean the dirt in front of our doorsteps.'

After the study sessions he never lingered for lunch or dinner with the rest of us, perhaps because he wanted his relationship with the group to remain formal. He'd politely accept a biscuit and take his leave. If Omar Bakri was the gourmand, he was the ascetic.

But as I got to know him our relationship became more informal. He had a good sense of humour and liked a candid discussion. Some of the attendees at his lectures were deferential to the point of fawning. There was no danger of that with me, and he probably warmed to me because I could be his intellectual foil.

Awlaki had a rare ability to combine his learning with a talent to communicate and a broad understanding of the world. So many Islamic scholars I had met could talk endlessly about the nuances of the Koran but were unable to connect with a wider audience, and especially a younger audience.

I began to do some background reading on him and asked him about his time overseas, to get beyond the reputation that preceded him and to try to discover what made him tick. He was five years older than me. He had been born in New Mexico in 1971 while his father was studying there and had returned to Yemen when he was seven. He had clearly been a brilliant student across the board and had won a full scholarship to study in the United States.

He had chosen to attend Colorado State University at Fort Collins to study civil engineering and told me he enjoyed fishing in the nearby Rockies. Then he had come home for a short period to get married, before returning to the US. A popular preacher at Denver-area mosques, he came to feel that education and propagating Islam were his vocation. One of the reasons, he later told me, was the US-led campaign to oust Saddam Hussein's forces from Kuwait in 1991, which had prompted him to take his religion 'more seriously'.[1]

---

1 Awlaki later claimed to have made a trip to Afghanistan to wage jihad in this period, but said he abandoned attempts to fight after the Mujahideen 'opened' Kabul. While there is little evidence that he had already become radicalized in the mid-1990s, Awlaki even then had connections that were unusual and unexplained. In 1999 the FBI had

In 1996 – at the age of just twenty-five – he was appointed as an imam at the Rabat mosque in San Diego, a small bungalow squeezed among ranch homes in La Mesa. He said he liked the climate in southern California, and stayed there nearly five years. Awlaki was justifiably proud of his academic record in the US. After leaving the west coast, he began preaching at the al-Hijrah Islamic Center in north Virginia and attended graduate school at George Washington University, intending to complete a doctorate in Human Resource Development. In his first term, he scored a 3.85 GPA (Grade Point Average).

The young cleric appeared to have a glittering future: he was bright, well-connected and very well-educated. The University of Sana'a expected him to return home and head a newly created Faculty of Education to help raise the standard of education in his poor and largely illiterate homeland.

And then, after 9/11, everything changed.

Among a large number of articles I found that featured him, I was drawn to one published the day after the 9/11 attacks. A *Washington Post* photographer, Andrea Bruce Woodall, went to the al-Hijrah Center, which had called an interfaith prayer meeting. One photograph was of Awlaki from above, showing his cap and clasped hands. 'It shows the grief that Muslims felt but also their fear that people might think they were responsible for this tragedy,' wrote Woodall.

Soon after the attack Awlaki gave an interview to *National Geographic*.

'There is no way that the people who did this could be Muslim, and if they claim to be Muslim, then they have perverted their religion,' he said. 'I would also add that we have been pushed to the forefront because of these events. There has been huge media attention towards us, in addition to FBI scrutiny.'

But there was also this warning:

'Osama bin Laden, who was considered to be an extremist, radical in his views, could end up becoming mainstream. That's a very

---

opened but not pursued an investigation into Awlaki's association with one of the men in the entourage of Omar Abdel Rahman, the so-called Blind Sheikh convicted of conspiracy in the 1993 bombing of the World Trade Center.

frightening thing, so the US needs to be very careful and not have itself perceived as an enemy of Islam.'

Vast resources – money, agents, technical surveillance – were poured into the 9/11 investigation and thousands of leads followed. In the immediate aftermath of such an outrage, civil liberties took a back seat to the need to know. Who had helped the hijackers? Who had they met? Were other attacks planned?

Awlaki was just one of those caught in the dragnet and was interviewed four times in the weeks after the attacks.[2] By early 2002 he felt intimidated and harassed. He always insisted he had nothing to hide, and in conversations we had in Sana'a he made no attempt to conceal his feeling that the Muslim community in America had been targeted by a deeply intrusive investigation.

2 Handwritten notes by Special Agents – released in 2013 under the Freedom of Information Act and posted by Judicial Watch – show Awlaki was frequently under surveillance between November 2001 and January 2002. Comings and goings at his suburban Falls Church home were noted, as were his travels in his white Dodge Caravan, the times of his mobile-phone calls, and his visits to the mosque and the Islamic Society at Woodlawn, Maryland.

On 15 November 2001 he was tailed on his way to National Public Radio in Washington DC, where he took part in a panel discussion for the show *Talk of the Nation*.

The surveillance of Awlaki revealed no contacts that might have had consequences for US national security, but did uncover an almost compulsive appetite for sex. Agents found that Awlaki was making visits to area hotels but staying just an hour or so, and they began contacting escorts known to have worked out of those hotels.

On 9 November an escort met FBI officers at the Loews Hotel in Washington. She showed them notes about a customer who had paid her $400 in cash four days previously for oral sex. The listed name was Anwar Aulaqi, with an address in Falls Church. Another escort working out of the Washington Suites Hotel told agents that on 23 November she had met a client who 'was tall and thin with a full beard, and polite. He claimed to be from India and employed as a computer engineer', according to the agents' notes of an interview with the woman. She recognized Awlaki from a photograph and said he had paid $400 for an hour with her.

The documents show that Awlaki had several more encounters with different escorts at a number of Washington-area hotels in the winter of 2001. He paid between $220 and $400 for a variety of acts. One escort who met him at the Melrose Hotel told agents that he looked very much like Osama bin Laden. Altogether, the FBI interviewed seven women about their appointments with Awlaki, but he was never charged.

Awlaki decided to quit his doctoral programme and return to Yemen, and by March 2002 he was gone, his wife and child following a month later. He returned only briefly in October to settle his affairs in the US. He was detained when he arrived at New York's JFK because a warrant for his arrest on suspicion of passport fraud had been signed by a Denver judge. But the US attorney in Denver had cancelled it the day before he arrived.

The manner of his departure from the US, the premature end to his studies, the aura of suspicion, still rankled with him when we got to know each other four years later. And the sense of grievance had been deepened by the publication of the 9/11 Commission's report in 2004.

I found the Commission's report online and devoured it, reading great chunks late into the night.

Tracing the hijackers' movements in the United States, the Commission had noted that two of them had known Awlaki while staying in San Diego, and one of them had visited his mosque after he had moved to Virginia early in 2001, which the Commission said 'may have not been coincidental'.

One of the Commission's staff reports had said: 'There is reporting that [Awlaki] has extremist ties, and the circumstances surrounding his relationship with the hijackers remain suspicious. However, we have not uncovered evidence that he associated with the hijackers knowing that they were terrorists.'

To Awlaki, this was accusation by innuendo. The Commission noted several times it had been unable to interview the cleric, suggesting he was on the run.

There was more in the footnotes of the report. 'The FBI investigated Aulaqi in 1999 and 2000 after learning that he may have been contacted by a possible procurement agent for Osama bin Laden. During this investigation, the FBI learned that Aulaqi knew individuals from the Holy Land Foundation and others involved in raising money for the Palestinian terrorist group Hamas.'

Worse still for a Muslim preacher were leaks to the media about his arrests in San Diego in 1996 and 1997 for soliciting prostitutes – and allegations of similar misconduct after he moved to the Washington DC area. One article written around the same time as the 9/11

Commission report was published said: 'FBI sources say agents observed the imam allegedly taking Washington-area prostitutes into Virginia and contemplated using a federal statute usually reserved for nabbing pimps who transport prostitutes across state lines.'

It was all, in Awlaki's view, the dark art of character assassination.

'They did everything they could to humiliate me, to make me a laughing stock among Muslims,' he told me.

I also began to watch some of his online sermons, which had been viewed by tens of thousands on YouTube. Awlaki had begun recording video sermons in English after leaving the US, refining and sharpening a narrative that depicted the West as hostile to Islam. His gift was breaking down the complexity of the Koran into language readily understood by young English-speaking Muslims. His eloquent and authoritative tone was pitch-perfect; and he made the radical sound reasonable.

He made several visits to the UK between 2002 and 2004, staying for the most part in East London. His celebrity meant that when he gave sermons, the rooms were packed. Sales of box sets of his CDs and later DVDs did brisk business. Among the avid consumers were some of the suicide bombers who attacked London in July 2005.

While he whipped up anger against the oppression of Muslims, Awlaki was careful not to be too specific lest he attract the attention of British security services. Even so, Muslim community leaders became concerned that he was luring at least some of his audience towards what they called 'rejectionism'. As one East London imam later put it, 'he left the congregations all revved up with nowhere to go.'

Behind closed doors, as with Omar Bakri, it was a different story. In small study circles Awlaki spoke out in favour of suicide bombings in the West. One such meeting was attended by undercover MI5 inform-ants, prompting the British authorities to ban him from travelling to the UK.

In 2005 Awlaki recorded 'Constants on the Path of Jihad', a six-hour online audio lecture series. Building on the work of a Saudi al-Qaeda ideologue, Awlaki argued that Muslims needed to fight continually against their enemies until the Day of Judgement. It was an intricate yet eloquent exposition that drew on Islamic texts, history and current events. Gently, without hectoring, he dwelt on the plight of Muslims in the West, identifying their situation with that of the Prophet and his followers.

'[The Prophet Mohammed] did not customize Islam based on his location . . . he customized the location based on Islam,' Awlaki said.

Efforts by moderate Muslim groups in the West to interpret jihad as a non-violent struggle were just one element of the drive to destroy Islam, he said. Muslims should reject non-Muslim practices and avoid relationships with disbelievers.

The lecture was a tour de force – widely disseminated online, expanding his following in extremist circles in the West.

I got to know Awlaki in Sana'a shortly after the lecture began to get traction online. During long, all-encompassing conversations we talked about Salafism, al-Qaeda, the legitimacy of jihad and the civilian casualties it so often caused. And we talked about bin Laden.

One evening in the late spring of 2006, after we had met about half a dozen times in the study group, he lingered after the others left.

He fixed me with those dark eyes and said simply: '9/11 was justified.'

To his mind, a global struggle between Muslims and disbelievers was underway, and the 9/11 attacks – despite the civilian victims – were a legitimate episode in that battle. Soon after we spoke, he recorded a lecture entitled 'Allah is Preparing Us for Victory', in which he said America had declared war on Muslims.

It is impossible to be sure whether his outlook stemmed from his treatment in the US, and was now fed by a vendetta because of the leaks about his visits to escorts, or whether like me he saw the waging of jihad as the logical and obligatory response to the Muslim predicament. It was probably both. He may also have been swayed by the fact that as his sermons became more militant and as his criticism of the US grew more strident, so his online following around the world grew.

While the cleric was openly sympathetic to al-Qaeda, I did not detect any ambition in him to join the group – nor signs that he had any influence over the rising numbers of al-Qaeda fighters in Yemen. But within days of our first meeting al-Qaeda became a much more potent force.

At morning prayers one cool day in early February, the congregation was abuzz at the news of a major prison break in Sana'a. Two dozen of al-Qaeda's most dangerous men had crawled through a tunnel they had dug from a basement in a political prison to an adjoining mosque. Among the escapees were a number of those involved in the attack on the MV *Limburg* in the Gulf of Aden, and a slight man in his late twenties called Nasir al-Wuhayshi, who had been bin Laden's private secretary in Afghanistan.

The prison escape breathed fresh life into al-Qaeda in Yemen. In the years after 9/11 US and Yemeni counter-terrorism operations had arrested and killed dozens of operatives, bringing the group to the brink of defeat. Wuhayshi would spend the next several years building a new and highly effective al-Qaeda franchise in Yemen.

The sessions with Awlaki soon became a weekly fixture. Anwar's study group, as we began to call ourselves, was a diverse collection of about a dozen English-speakers from the four corners of the earth, including from as far afield as Mexico and Mauritius. I would cook huge meals, and some of the group would stay over in the several spare bedrooms I had. Most of the circle were in Sana'a to learn Arabic or study Islam, but some had other agendas. My neighbour – a Yemeni general who prayed at the same mosque I attended – saw the comings and goings and warned me about some of my visitors. I was being watched, he told me.

One of those visitors was Jehad Serwan Mostafa, a lanky, bearded young man from San Diego with distant blue eyes. His lips seemed perpetually curled into a scowl of disdain, the only exception being when he listened spellbound to Awlaki. His father was Kurdish and his mother an American convert. Once upon a time he had worked in a car repair shop on El Cajon Boulevard. Now he was studying at al-Iman – and applying for a Somali visa. The Somali embassy had told him to go to the US embassy to collect the right paperwork to apply to enter Somalia. I was amazed to find out that the US embassy had given him the necessary documents, no questions asked. Within three years, Mostafa would graduate to the FBI's Rewards for Justice list, accused of aiding and fighting with the Somali terror group al-Shabaab.

Another regular at the study sessions was a Danish convert with auburn hair I knew from extremist circles in Copenhagen. He came from a wealthy family and even I was unnerved by his wild-eyed radicalism. He called himself Ali.[3]

Through the circle I got to know many other militants in Sana'a.[4] One of them – Abdullah Misri, a dark-skinned tribesman from Marib with a neatly trimmed beard – was already al-Qaeda in Yemen's senior money man. He would buy cars in Dubai and smuggle them into Yemen, using the proceeds to bankroll the group's growing capabilities. It occurred to me I was probably by now under surveillance by Western counter-terrorism agencies. After all, I knew a lot of interesting people.

In Sana'a I was also reunited with a Danish convert called Kenneth Sorensen. He had gravitated to Sana'a partly because of what I had told him about my time in Yemen when we met in 2002 in Odense. He had read about me in the Danish newspapers and had sought me out.

Sorensen was younger than me, broad-shouldered and burly, the product of a harsh upbringing. His mother, he told me, was a drug addict, he had little education, and in Denmark he had scraped by as a part-time dustman.

Sorensen had arrived in Sana'a ostensibly to study Arabic, but craved action on the frontline. Awlaki had not invited him to his study sessions because he had a reputation as a loudmouth and loose cannon, dressing up as a jihadi and brandishing guns on the streets of Sana'a.

But I enjoyed his company. He was one of several friends who accompanied me to a rally in Tahrir Square in the centre of Sana'a early in 2006 to protest against cartoons published in Denmark and other European countries which we saw as insulting the Prophet Mohammed. The cartoons had originally been published the previous year by a Danish newspaper, setting off a firestorm across the Muslim world, because of

3 Ali's last name is omitted for legal reasons.
4 Another member of the study circle was Abdullah Mustafa Ayub, an Australian militant whose father was allegedly a leading figure in the terrorist group Jamaat al-Islamiyya. Ayub's convert mother – Rabiah Hutchison, an ex-surfer girl, dubbed the 'the matriarch of radical Islam' in Australia – was even more notorious; rumour had it Osama bin Laden had once courted her in Afghanistan.

a taboo in Islam against the physical representation of the Prophet. One by the Danish cartoonist Kurt Westergaard depicted the Prophet Mohammed with a bomb in his turban, and a Norwegian newspaper had just poured fuel on that fire by republishing them.

'Death to Denmark!' I shouted with the others till I was hoarse. Unlike the feeble crew that had protested in Grosvenor Square the previous year I felt those around me had the courage of their convictions, and that felt intoxicating.

The film-maker Nagieb and I had not given up on his project to make a documentary about the mujahideen, and Abdul said he would try to introduce us to one of the al-Qaeda figures who had escaped from jail in Sana'a. His name was Sheikh Adil al-Abab; Abdul said he had spent time with him in Afghanistan. He would later become the religious Emir of al-Qaeda in the Arabian Peninsula and among the top half-dozen in its leadership.

Abdul drove us to a residence in a rough part of town. He stopped the car but kept the engine running. Within minutes the cleric jumped into the car. He was a young but portly figure with a handlebar moustache.

I became friendly with al-Abab and fascinated by his command of religious texts and his views on jihad. Getting to know him would pay a significant dividend in years to come.

It never ceased to amaze me that the Yemeni security services failed to arrest al-Abab. We met several times without great secrecy in Sana'a. Al-Abab was clearly on the same journey as Awlaki, moving towards a declaration of war against the US and bitterly critical of the Yemeni government for its submissive attitude towards the US.

I had no doubts about the loyalty and principles of the militants I knew. So I was disturbed by what Awlaki told me in the spring of 2006 about Abdul, by then my closest friend in Sana'a.

'Abdul lost $25,000 while on a mission for the brothers in Djibouti,' he said, with more than a hint of disbelief about 'lost'. 'He disappeared off the map for six months and the money has never been recovered, but, as you know, Abdul now has a new house here which seems to be beyond his means. Just be careful,' Awlaki said. 'I don't think Abdul is trustworthy.'

I was taken aback, but also intrigued that Awlaki had spoken about 'the brothers'. He could only mean al-Qaeda; perhaps he was closer to the group than I had imagined.

Without naming my source, I broached the subject with Abdul.

'I swear by Allah that I did not steal the money and what they accuse me of is unjust,' he said. He said he had been arrested in Djibouti, and the intelligence services had confiscated the cash. He showed me passport entry and exit stamps that were some six months apart.

'That's how long I was detained,' he said.

'What were you doing there?'

'I was a courier. I was working for Abu Talha al-Sudani.'

He watched closely for my reaction.

I was taken aback. Abdul, if he was speaking the truth, was clearly moving in rarified and perilous circles. Abu Talha was one of al-Qaeda's leading operatives in East Africa and near the top of the US most-wanted list.[5]

'*Masha'Allah*. That's amazing,' I blurted out. I wondered, did Awlaki know this? Or did he not believe it?

By now I had managed to get my son into a local school and he was beginning to learn Arabic. But both of us missed female company; Awlaki had told me I should find a new wife to look after Osama, and even offered – with a wry laugh – to set me up. But his matchmaking services were not required. After picking Osama up from school one afternoon, I had told him to run ahead and find me a sweet woman to marry. Never a shy boy, he ran into the offices of a driving school for women and when I caught up with him he was talking to a young Yemeni woman. Petite, very pretty and with a winning smile and infectious laugh, she won me over within minutes.

I asked her where she had gone to school and what she did – the usual introductions. Within minutes I told her that I was divorced and living in Sana'a alone with my son. I tried to sound helpless and a little lost; it must have seemed an obvious ploy.

5 Abu Talha al-Sudani was suspected of involvement in al-Qaeda's bombing of US embassies in Nairobi and Dar es Salaam in 1998. In 2003 he ordered the casing of a US military base in Djibouti. He was killed in an air strike in Somalia in 2007.

A week later I returned to the driving school in the hope of seeing her again. I sent Osama in.

'My dad wants to speak with you,' he told her in Arabic.

Her co-workers looked on with a mixture of curiosity and amusement. This was not how introductions between the sexes were usually handled in Yemen. We agreed to meet at the Libyan Centre in Sana'a, a place where many foreigners gathered.

I turned up with Osama. She said her name was Fadia and she peppered me with questions, about my divorce, why I was staying in Yemen, what I wanted from a wife.

'I want someone who doesn't pretend to be something she isn't,' I said. 'I was married to a woman who pretended to be a pious Muslim but she wasn't.'

I followed up with an unusual question for what might be described as a first date, Yemeni-style.

'What do you think about Sheikh Osama bin Laden?'

Fadia looked taken aback and hesitated. But then she surprised me.

'I think he has given honour to the Muslims,' she said. 'But I don't like that he killed innocent civilians. If he had attacked the military it would have been better.'

I was delighted and impressed: a Yemeni woman who was not only attractive but spoke English, and was thoughtful. But I also had the arrogance of a true Salafi and believed I could mould her to become a better Muslim. I gave her a CD, embossed with a heart. She probably expected it to be full of romantic music, but it contained nothing but jihadist chants.

I had other questions, most of them to do with religion. As a genuine Salafi, that was what mattered, not her tastes in music or family background. How much of the Koran had she memorized? (My first wife, Karima, knew the entire Koran by heart in two dialects.)

Fadia's parents were both dead, so within a few days she asked her uncle, with whom she was very close, to meet me and to find out whether I was the genuine article or some chancer. The interview was held in Sana'a's only Pizza Hut, which looked exactly like its US counterparts and could have been dropped into the Yemeni capital from Arizona. Apparently I performed adequately. The uncle reported back that I was very likeable and had a sense of humour, but had some dangerous ideas.

'He also has a temper,' the uncle told her, 'but I believe any woman can change her husband.'

Others in her family, a well-respected Sana'a household, were less enthusiastic. Some even checked with contacts in the intelligence services, who said that I should be avoided at all costs because I associated with militants.

That changed the uncle's outlook.

'You can marry him,' he said, 'but we want to see all his papers: residency, health, everything.'

The confident expectation was that I would be unable to trawl Yemen's byzantine bureaucracy for the documents. Then she could be steered towards another suitor preferred by her family, a wealthy surgeon who did not have my baggage of divorce, a young son and the wrong friends.

Somehow I gathered all the papers, even one from the Ministry of the Interior that granted me residency. I could sense the animosity among some of the officials; I was an unwelcome guest.

The new love of my life chose me rather than the wealthy surgeon. One Friday in the late spring of 2006, our marriage contract was sealed at her uncle's house. While he had grudgingly accepted the match, other family members had not. Her brother refused to attend the wedding.

I didn't tell any of them that the paperwork for my divorce to Karima had not been completed: as far as I was concerned the man-made laws of the UK had no jurisdiction over such matters.

I went to the tailor to order a sumptuous new *thawb* for the ceremony and asked a Yemeni friend to lend me the equivalent of $2,000, as a dowry to the bride's family. The only hitch was that my friend forgot to bring the cash – and Fadia's uncle had to intervene and find the money, to give to himself.

Her family looked askance at some of the guests – most of whom were from my immediate circle. Abdul, Jehad Mostafa, Samulski and Ali – the red-haired Danish convert – were there; so was Rasheed Laskar, a British convert from Aylesbury, with a long thick beard and glasses, who went by the name Abu Mu'aadh and often stayed at my house.

And then, as is customary in Yemen and much of the Muslim world, the party divided into men and women. My new wife wanted me to join her so photographs could be taken. To me that was wholly un-Islamic, a form of idolatry. She also insisted on music at the post-wedding celebrations. Mindful of the Odense fight, I ensured my jihadist friends were gone by then.

At the end of a long day, my bride was brought to my large rented home by her female relatives. So many women dressed in black and wearing the full niqab descended on the house that I had no idea who among them I had married.

When the rest of the party were gone, I realized Fadia was anxious to the point of panic. She stood with all her possessions in a suitcase, in a large house she didn't know, with a hulking north European who was a militant jihadi – and now her husband. Like me when I was on the road to Dammaj, she must have wondered what she was doing.

I recited a few words from the Koran and said a prayer and then carefully lifted the veil from her face. In true Yemeni tradition, she had been caked in heavy Arabic make-up and henna tattoos for the ceremony.

'Darling,' I said, 'why don't you go and wash your face?'

Fadia looked crestfallen, thinking that the hours of beautification would bring me to my knees. But to me she was beautiful without make-up, with her caramel skin and dark almond eyes.

I helped her take off her elaborate wedding dress. It was astonishingly weighty.

'I can't believe it,' I said. 'How did you manage to carry this all day and not die of heat exhaustion?'

What she did not expect was a European sense of romance and seduction. I had prepared her a bath with candles, rose petals and herbs – even a hardcore jihadi can turn on the charm.

Unfortunately, after bathing, she applied a liberal dose of a heavy sweet Yemeni perfume that I could not abide. I asked her to take another shower.

She soon realized she had married a man for whom Islam was ever-present and whose interpretation of the Koran was unyielding. My home had no television; the computer was overflowing with jihadist videos; a cassette recorder played and replayed Islamic lectures. She was surprised to be woken at 4 a.m. on her first day of married life. For me it was a routine occurrence to prepare for *fajr* – the first prayers of the new day. I immediately rose to wash and walk in the pre-dawn cool to the mosque, while my drowsy wife eventually rose from her slumbers to pray at home.

I asked after our first breakfast together whether she would help me read the Koran in Arabic, just as Karima had. I also showed her several of the more gory jihadist videos on my computer. This was completely natural as I was so immersed in this holy battle. She winced and gently reminded me that as this was our first full day of married life, we should treat it as a honeymoon and try to relax together. So we took Osama to Fun City, Sana'a's answer to Disney World. Its gates were a feeble multicoloured reproduction of a castle's turrets, and inside girls clad in black niqabs rode merry-go-rounds, like witches flying through the air.

Fadia was not very religiously observant; I thought it would take me a few weeks to educate her to the path of the true Muslim. She had other ideas and was reluctant to wear the niqab, while also harbouring designs to loosen my religious straitjacket.

Before we had been married a week, I asked her to sit with me one afternoon so I could tell her something very serious. She looked apprehensive: perhaps I was HIV-positive or had some disease.

'I have to go to jihad and I have to go to Somalia,' I told her. 'So you have to prepare yourself.'

Plenty of would-be jihadis – in the West and from Arab countries – were excited by events in Somalia. A militia called the Islamic Courts Union had put an end to years of warlordism and anarchy across much of that benighted country. It had brought calm to Mogadishu, a city that had turned into a quagmire for international peacekeepers. For militant Islamists like me, Somalia was a rare victory to be celebrated, where authentic Islamic principles had brought stability.

'You have to be proud of me and support me,' I told her.

Fadia was taken aback, but said nothing. It was not customary for a young Yemeni wife to challenge her husband on such issues.

'Jihad in these times is obligatory. Islam is not only about peace, and if they suggested that when you went to school they were wrong.'

My determination to travel to Somalia grew when Ethiopia – with the encouragement of the Bush administration – sent troops into Somalia in July 2006 to prop up the feeble transitional government, which was at risk of being overrun by the Islamic Courts. To any self-respecting jihadi, the invasion of a Muslim country by Christian soldiers was the ultimate provocation. If I wanted to be the true jihadi I would have to return home to Denmark to raise the necessary cash – thousands of dollars – so that I could help expel the Ethiopians.

As I was preparing to leave Yemen, Anwar al-Awlaki disappeared. On a boiling day that summer, he failed to turn up at my house to continue his lecture series. I was irritated: they were a highlight of my week.

A few days later I learned from al-Qaeda's money man in Yemen, Abdullah Misri, that Awlaki had been arrested. He faced a vague and almost certainly fabricated charge of being involved in plots to kidnap a Shi'ite and a US official. The case never went to trial and his followers were convinced the charges were the result of pressure on Yemeni authorities from the Americans.[6]

---

6 Documents obtained by the group Judicial Watch under the US Freedom of Information Act – and posted in July 2013 – showed that the FBI's interest in Awlaki had certainly grown in the years since he had left America. A memo marked 'Secret' and written by the Bureau's San Diego office on 1 December 2006 requested access to Awlaki while in jail.

'Aulaqi left the United States in the early part of 2002. Significant information regarding Aulaqi has developed since this time and since the time he was interviewed in September 2001,' it said. 'It is unknown at this time whether the interview will take one or two days or if a polygraph will be conducted. Specific requests from San Diego will be made after approval for access to Aulaqi from Yemen officials,' the memo continued.

The same document recalled an FBI interview with a man called Eyad al-Rarabah, who had helped some of the 9/11 hijackers find accommodation in Virginia as well as

The FBI would get its way and obtain access to Awlaki while he was held in a Sana'a jail, most of the time in solitary confinement. His family's prominence meant that he was not mistreated, nor were his conditions as deplorable as those of most inmates. But he was not allowed any contact with the outside world and his study circle evaporated, none of us knowing if or when we would see our mentor again.

It was time to leave Yemen for a while. With the words of Awlaki and al-Abab still fresh in my mind, I wanted to start preparing to make my own contribution to the cause of global jihad – and my heart was set on Somalia.

---

illegal driving licences. Al-Rababah 'later stated that he met [9/11 hijackers] Hani Hanjour and Nawaf Alhamzi [sic] at the Dar al-Hijrah mosque with Anwar Aulaqi'.

There were a host of other topics the Bureau wanted to discuss with Awlaki, including 'his overseas travel in 2000 and 2001; his association with San Diego individuals believed to be involved with international terrorism; his involvement in fund raising in the United States for known terrorist organizations; and his involvement in criminal activity in an effort to support terrorist organizations'.

CHAPTER TEN

THE FALL

Late Summer 2006–Spring 2007

My plan was to return to Denmark and work for a building company run by a Muslim friend so I could save money to go to Somalia. I had initially wanted to help the Islamic Courts Union by starting a dairy farm in southern Somalia, using the skills I had gained during a few months at an agricultural college in Denmark. But as Ethiopian forces advanced towards the capital, Mogadishu, I knew I would be drawn into the battle for the future of Somalia. Even if it brought martyrdom I had no option but to fight for my religion. Only then would my son grow up being proud of his father.

Fadia, however, persuaded me that she and Osama should follow me to Denmark. On arrival she would need to apply for an EU 'Schengen visa' rather than come in as my spouse – because I was not technically yet divorced from Karima.

Fadia had never flown before and was more than a little anxious. When she passed through Frankfurt airport, a security officer demanded she take off her long jacket. She refused, saying it was traditional dress, and was nearly detained. All the same, when she arrived in Copenhagen, I was less than happy to see she was wearing nothing more than a scarf on her head, far less the niqab I had bought her in Sana'a.

'It doesn't matter that you are in Europe; you have to dress like a Muslim woman,' I told her. 'Did you marry me just so you could come to Europe and get a passport here?' I asked bitterly. Perhaps I was haunted by previous relationships. Within days she found a Yemeni woman who supplied her with all the garments she needed to appear respectable.

We moved into a rented apartment in a neighbourhood of Aarhus heavily populated by immigrant families. My network of extremist contacts continued to grow. My strident views and exotic travel had made me something of a celebrity in Danish Islamist circles.

I was happy with Fadia. She was gentle, intelligent and kind to Osama, who adored her. But I knew that at some point my son had to be with his mother and so I came to an agreement with Karima. She had left Morocco to resettle in Birmingham and said that if I brought Osama home I could have regular access to both children.

The arrangement meant that I would be shuttling between Denmark and Birmingham, but I was overjoyed to be reconnected with my daughter, Sarah, and was capable of keeping the peace with Karima. I wanted to see as much of my children as I could before the next chapter of my march towards jihad.

Commuting between Aarhus and Birmingham also extended my contacts with supporters of the Islamic Courts in Somalia, of whom there were a surprising number in the English Midlands. They had a significant presence at a large mosque in the rundown Small Heath district of Birmingham. The Ethiopian incursion had enraged the Somali community and dramatically boosted the popularity of the Islamic Courts, fusing their cause with Somali nationalism.

I went to a crowded event at the mosque with a Danish-Somali friend, who had travelled with me from Aarhus. He also had family in Birmingham – a cousin called Ahmed Abdulkadir Warsame.

Warsame was a wiry teenager, with drooping eyelids that gave him the appearance of being half asleep. He had protruding front teeth.

He had evidently been inspired by the speeches from representatives of the Islamic courts.

'I'm going. I'm definitely going.'

'*Masha'Allah*. That makes two of us,' I replied. It would be the beginning of a long and momentous relationship. I was keener to get to Somalia than ever. I was being regaled with stories via email about the killing of 'disbelievers'; mainly Ethiopian troops. Two of my Sana'a study circle had already travelled to fight in Somalia – Ali, the Danish convert, and the American, Jehad Serwan Mostafa. Mostafa had emailed me, urging me to join the fight. 'We are winning!' he had exclaimed.

Warsame invited me to a dinner at a Somali-Yemeni restaurant for the Islamic Courts representatives who had attended the conference. He had come to the UK three years before as a refugee and was desperate to return home to fight the Ethiopians but lacked the funds to travel.

I quickly befriended this kid. His ardour for the cause impressed me. I would drop by his small council flat near the Small Heath mosque. An ancient leather sofa, piled high with lecture notes, dominated the room. He was taking a course in electronic engineering. But all he could talk about was confronting the Ethiopians and liberating his country. In October 2006 the Ethiopians began to push eastwards from the town where they had been protecting Somalia's hapless government. As we followed news reports and received messages from friends it seemed obvious the troops were intent on attacking the capital.

At the same time, authorities in Yemen, a short journey by sea across the Gulf of Aden, moved against militants they suspected of helping the Islamic Courts.

Early on the morning of 17 October I had a frantic call from the wife of Kenneth Sorensen, one of my Sana'a study circle. He had been arrested along with Samulski, two young Australians and my British friend, Rasheed Laskar. They were allegedly involved in a plot to smuggle weapons from tribes in lawless eastern Yemen to the Islamic Courts Union, a transaction organized on the Yemeni side by Abdullah Misri, the car-dealer and al-Qaeda financier.

I knew the reputation of the Yemeni security services and worried that Sorensen and the others would be tortured in jail. I told Sorensen's wife I would try to publicize the case in Denmark. I asked my friend Nagieb to put me in touch with a television station and the next day recorded an interview with Denmark's TV2.

The crew met me in a shopping arcade in Aarhus. I knew the interview would be heavily edited so tried to get across my appeal as succinctly as possible. Sorensen was innocent, I insisted. He was a friend who was studying Arabic and had no involvement with militants.

The Danish government should be working for his release or at least ensuring it had consular access to him.

In reality, I suspected he was involved in the scheme, though I had no idea how far it had evolved. My suspicions were deepened by the arrest in Yemen of another associate of mine from radical circles in Denmark, Abu Musab al-Somali. He had come to Denmark as a refugee when he was a child, but returned to Somalia and joined with foreign fighters affiliated with the Islamic Courts Union – shuttling between Mogadishu and Yemen. He received a two-year jail sentence for his part in the weapons plot.

Sorensen and the others were luckier – they were released and deported in December. But my television interview had made me an even greater 'person of interest' to the Danish authorities.

On a grim afternoon of drizzle and mist, I received a call at my apartment in Aarhus.

'This is Martin Jensen. I am with PET,' a voice said flatly.[1]

PET is the Danish security and intelligence service, and in the state apparatus a branch of the police.

'We need to speak with you. Can we arrange a meeting?'

'No,' I said. 'There's nothing to talk about. You are fighting against Islam and we are protecting ourselves. In any case, you could be Mossad, the CIA. I could be just "rendered" somewhere. It's all the fashion.'

I tried to sound relaxed but my mind was racing. Were my travel plans known? Were my phone and internet monitored? Had one of the Sana'a group identified me as some sort of ringleader? Had the Yemenis given MI6 or the CIA access to their new crop of detainees?

In the end we agreed that I would come to a local police station. But first I called my mother. I had to tell somebody and I didn't want to alarm my wife.

'Mum, I can't go into this on the phone but PET have asked me to go and meet them. I just want to let you know in case anything happens to me.'

She let out a sigh. I imagined her raising her eyebrows and gently

---

1 He was not using his real name.

shaking her head, resigned to yet another twist in her wayward son's life. 'Okay. Be careful,' she said.

There were two agents waiting for me in a conference room, including a tall well-built man who introduced himself as Jensen. The other, a paunchy bald guy, was looking out of the window and smoking. Barely forty, he moved with difficulty.

Jensen pushed an open Coke bottle towards me.

'I don't drink anything you give me that's already open. You could have put anything in it,' I said, being deliberately melodramatic.

He shrugged and went to fetch me a sealed bottle.

So what did I know about Sorensen and the rest of the group detained in Sana'a? I repeated what I had said on television.

Then they turned the screw. Jensen leaned forward across the table. He was handsome, in his late thirties with a carefully maintained suntan and perfectly groomed hair. He could have passed for a Danish George Clooney. And he had the self-assurance of a man who knew he looked the part.

'We know your wife has outstayed her visa. But that's fine. We just want to be sure that neither you nor your friends have any violent intentions towards Denmark. Perhaps you could even help us.'

'I would never help you,' I shot back. 'To help the *kuffar* against a Muslim brother is apostasy.'

'By the way,' I added as I got up to leave, 'I want to go to Somalia. Can you check if that is against Danish law?'

They looked taken aback by my chutzpah. In fact it was perfectly legal for me to travel there as the Islamic Courts Union had not been declared a terrorist organization by Denmark or other Western governments.

My connections in Yemen had clearly placed me under suspicion. One of the Sana'a group who had been arrested told me later that he'd been questioned by a Western intelligence agent while he was in prison.

'They were trying to find out more about you,' he told me. 'They said, "We know Storm is behind this."'

As I left the police station it dawned on me I was a marked man. I realized that very soon I would have to make a choice – to go to

Somalia and invite even greater scrutiny or to retreat from wearing my commitment so plainly on my sleeve. But if anything my encounter with the agents had made me more determined to leave. They knew they were making no progress. Jensen left me his number just in case. For some reason I did not tear up his card in front of him, but tucked it in my pocket as I left.

Soon my mission had a godfather – Abdelghani, a Somali friend from Denmark who had already travelled to join the Islamic Courts militia. On 19 December he emailed me formal permission from the Islamic Courts' 'Foreign Affairs Office' to enter the country.

I felt a surge of adrenalin. It was a religious duty beyond debate – the sort of decisive action that the pitiful preachers in Denmark, the blathering Omar Bakri Mohammed, would talk about endlessly but never carry out.

I bought a plane ticket – one-way to Mogadishu. I would be travelling solo. My Birmingham sidekick Warsame still did not have the funds to travel. I emailed him to tell him I hoped he could join me soon.

A new chapter was about to begin with new comrades, on the newest frontline of a global conflict. But my wife would burst into tears whenever the subject arose.

'What's going to happen to me? I will be left here alone in a country I don't know, with no rights, no money.'

'Allah will provide and take care of you. And when we've pushed out the Ethiopians you'll be able to join me,' I told her. It was not exactly reassuring, and at the time less than convincing even for me. But that was the answer for everything.

She told me she would return to Yemen if I was gone for long.

As the first snowflakes of an early winter storm drifted down, I drove to a military surplus store in Copenhagen to buy the supplies Abdelghani had requested: camouflage gear, water bottles and Swiss army knives. Hardly lethal weapons, and easy enough to take without raising suspicion.

Getting to the frontline in Somalia seemed more necessary than ever. Ethiopian forces were closing in on Mogadishu. Some of my friends had already retreated with other fighters south towards Kismayo, a port city south of Mogadishu. In a few days I was due to leave.

As I went around the shop, I had a call from Somalia. It was from Ali, the Danish member of the Sana'a study circle. He told me excitedly that he had just beheaded a Somali spy the group had discovered near Kismayo.

Setting aside his naivety in calling me on a mobile phone, I congratulated him loudly in Arabic. The shopkeeper looked at me with a hint of suspicion.

On the drive back from the store Abdelghani called. I started telling him about all the supplies I had bought, but he cut me off.

'You must not fly down here now. It's too dangerous. Ethiopians have surrounded the airport and are arresting all holy warriors who have come to the country to fight alongside the Islamic Courts. Stay away!'

I was stunned, and infuriated by Abdelghani's defeatism.

A question started ringing in my ears, one directed to Allah: 'Why won't You let me go? Why am I being prevented from serving You?'

It was – after all – His decision. Allah was all-knowing; as mere mortals we had no influence over our destinies.

And then another question: 'Why have You let the mujahideen lose – yet again?'

My wife was waiting for me when I returned home.

'They lost,' I mumbled, my eyes averting her gaze. 'They lost the fight.'

I dragged the equipment up the stairs and discarded it in the bedroom. I was quiet, brooding, defeated – and reminded of the time I sat in the police car on my way to prison in Denmark, vowing somehow to change course. I needed answers.

Dejection soon became anger, and anger began to ask some difficult questions. At every turn I had been stopped; every plan had disintegrated. I had spent a decade – what should have been the best years of my life – devoted to a cause, sacrificing my relationships and any potential I might have had as a boxer. And that cause now seemed so distant.

I sat in the darkened bedroom, the silence interrupted only by the purr of cars passing through the snow. I was days away from my thirty-first birthday, but my future seemed empty. My children were in a

Me aged seven.

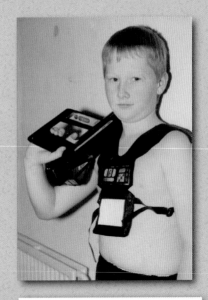

The 'king' of laser tag.

Vibeke and me in the summer
of 1993. I was seventeen.

Vikings do housework too.

The Korsør Library in Denmark,
in which I found a book about Islam
and began reading.

Returning to the bookshelf many
years later.

A meal with my mother in 1999.

In Yemen, 2006.

Holding my son, Osama, in Denmark during my radical years. (Credit: Politiken)

In 2006 after arrest of Kenneth Sorensen. (Credit: TV2 Denmark)

Protesting outside the US embassy in London in 2005.

Omar Bakri Mohammed led the protests outside the embassy.

Taimour Abdulwahab al-Abdaly, my friend from Luton who carried out a suicide bombing in Stockholm in 2010.

Zacarias Moussaoui, my one-time friend in Brixton and the so-called 'twentieth hijacker' of 9/11.

Sana'a, Yemen.
(Credit: Cityskylines.org)

Dammaj, Yemen. (Credit: Wikipedia)

Taiz, Yemeni highlands.
(Credit: Supportyemen.org)

On the misty mountain
road to deliver
supplies to Awlaki,
October 2008.

Shabwa province.

Ataq, Yemen. (Credit: Panoramio.com)

Yemen visa stamp, 2001.

Yemen driving licence.

Awlaki with RPG.
(Credit: AQAP)

Awlaki while living in the
US. (Credit: *Washington Post*)

Re: From Viking land   Tue, 8 Apr 2008 at 12:06

From   Anwar Awlaki   +

To   Murad Storm

No it is not allowed because even though all of the alchohol evaporates it is najasah (impure) and that najasah
has mixed with the chocolate.

Murad Storm wrote:
> Waleikum Salaam Warahmatullah
> Sheikh, regarding the chocolate, is it permissible to eat it when it has got like alcohol flavour in it. I asked one
who makes it, and they use real vine or wisky, however they burn up the alcohol before using it for the chocolate,
otherwise the chocolate would melt, so only they wisky flavour stays.
> What is the ruling regarding this?
> May Allah reward you
> Assalamu AleikuM Warahmatullah
> Abu Osama
>
> */Anwar Awlaki <al_aulaqi@yahoo.com>/* wrote:
>
> Asslamu alaykum Murad,
> Jazak Allahu khairan. I use xl in shirts. Forget about shoes since I
> only use sandles.
> Cheese and chocolates please:)
> AA
> Anwar

Email chain with Awlaki
in the weeks before I
met him in Aden in May
2008. The cleric had
requested cheese and
chocolate.

Shaykh Anwar with the mujahideen's leader in the Arabian Peninsula, Shaykh Abu Baseer al-Wuhaishi.

Awlaki with AQAP emir Wuhayshi, taken from AQAP's *Inspire* magazine.

Awlaki in video sermon to supporters in the West.

Awlaki DVD box set.

Irena Horak, who changed her name to Aminah (from her public social media page).

Awlaki's video proposal to Aminah.

Aminah Muslimah Fisabilillah

I would go with him anywhere, I am 32 years old and I am ready for dangerous things, I am not afraid of death or to die in the sake of Allah subhane we te'alla. I didn't know he has 2 wife already. But I do not mind at all. I want to help him in his work and make dawa to other non-muslims or Muslims. I am good in housekeeping jobs. As he already have 2 wifes and kids I am sure it would be a problem to have a wife with him all the time, without kids, inshaalllah.

I do not know what I will see but I am willing to be a very hardworking and active wife, J support wife and if it is requires I can go inshaallah.

Aminah's Facebook message affirming her desire to marry Awlaki.

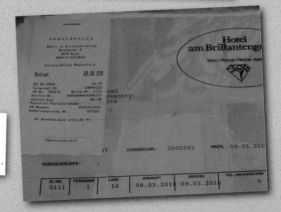

The hotel receipt from my first trip to Vienna to meet Aminah, March 2010.

different country, my friends in Sana'a scattered, my wife baffled by my mood swings. I had spent the last of what I had earned working at the construction site on supplies that now sat unopened beside me, mocking my failure.

I had been driven on in my quest to fight for the underdog. Years earlier I had come to the aid of my Muslim friends on the streets of Korsør when they were picked on by bullies. I had sat in the library, transfixed by the story of the Prophet's battles against far greater forces in Mecca. I had dreamt of going to Afghanistan to join the mujahideen, and of helping build a beacon of true Islam in Somalia. Everything had turned to dust.

I thought of the bluster of Omar Bakri Mohammed, of the mealy-mouthed preachers in Brixton, the fair-weather protesters outside the US embassy, the cowardice of the Sheikhs all too ready to send ignorant, gullible men to their deaths. Perhaps my devotion to the cause had stifled all sorts of unresolved questions. Perhaps my embrace of Islam was only a way of lashing out at the world and my real inspiration – even if I did not fully understand it – was not doctrinaire Salafism but to fight injustice.

And then the unthinkable began to seep into my mind. Was my understanding of Islam flawed? Was the faith being distorted by men like Awlaki? Or was Islam itself riddled with inconsistencies to which I had been blind?

I had already begun questioning the concept of predestination – *Qadar* – one of the articles of the faith. I had been taught that it held that Allah had decided everything, both in the past and in the future.

In the words of the Koran, 'Allah is the Creator of all things, and He is the Guardian over all things . . . He has created everything, and has measured it exactly according to its due measurements.'

So what was the place of free will, where was the capacity to make a difference? It seemed that none of the scholars I had talked to could explain how *Qadar* fitted with the obligation of jihad, nor why Allah would create a man He had already condemned to hellfire. Even Anwar al-Awlaki had skirted around the subject.

One *hadith* seemed to me to render the individual as a helpless puppet: 'Allah, the Exalted and Glorious, has ordained for every servant amongst His creation five things: his death, his action, his abode, the places of his moving about and his means of sustenance.'

Eventually I roused myself and went downstairs to the kitchen. Fadia looked worried.

'What has happened to you?' she asked.

'I don't know. I just feel that there is no point to anything any more.'

I made myself a coffee and sat down in front of my laptop at the kitchen table. Impulsively my fingers typed: 'Contradictions in the Koran.'

There were more than a million hits. Plenty of entries were just anti-Islamic diatribes, frequently on Christian Evangelical websites that were less than coherent. But in other places I read commentaries that revived long-held but suppressed questions in my head. The words I had once shouted in Hyde Park came back to me: 'Had it issued from any but God, they would surely have found in it many a contradiction.'

The whole construction of my faith was a house of cards built one layer upon the next. Remove one, and all the others would collapse. It had relied on a sense of momentum – a journey from finding Islam to becoming a Salafi to taking up jihad in spirit and action. My reading of the holy texts had been clear. Waging jihad to protect the faith was ordained. But somehow I had been prevented from carrying out my religious duty, while other Muslims evaded or denied it.

I also began to reconsider some of the justifications made for the murder and maiming of civilians. I had accepted such prescriptions in my obedience to the Salafist creed. I had lapped up the words of scholars who had found vindication for the events of 9/11 in scripture. But now I thought of the Twin Towers, the Bali bombings, Madrid in 2004, London in 2005. These were acts of violence targeting ordinary people. If they were part of Allah's preordained plan, I now wanted no part of it.

The words of my bouncer friend Tony replayed in my mind: 'Why does Allah want people to kill other people? Don't you think, Murad, Allah would prefer you to teach people to read?'

My loss of faith was as frightening as it was sudden. I was staring into a void, and knew that should I desert the faith I would soon be a target for many of my former 'brothers'. I knew so much about them and their plans. At least half the Sana'a circle alone had joined terror groups. To them I would be the worst of all: the convert who had given up and become an atheist, the foulest of hypocrites. Just as the convert had been promised a double reward in paradise, so the convert who recanted must be doubly punished.

The questions that crowded in on me made me withdrawn at home and prone to anger. My wife seemed worried that I was slipping away from her. Her EU entry visa had expired and, now living in Denmark illegally, she was afraid of being marooned. The atmosphere at home was toxic.

I had to get out, to find time and space to think. On a bitter March morning, I set out to do some fishing in Braband Lake on the outskirts of Aarhus. Winter was clinging on. The reeds along the fringe of the lake were brown and crackled in the breeze, and there were still patches of ice in inlets. The path around the lake was deserted.

I sat down and cast my line, but my mind was elsewhere. For nearly three months, I had prayed without conviction. I had read the Koran again but kept seeing new inconsistencies and contradictions. I had listened to preachers in Aarhus mosques but none had revived my spirits. And all the while the drumbeat of jihadism was intensifying, moving on from the defence of Muslim lands towards a declaration of war against all disbelievers, the meek as well as the mighty.

Out of nowhere, the volcano inside me erupted. Throwing my fishing rod into the lake, I shouted into the water.

'Fuck Allah, and fuck the Prophet Mohammed. Why should my family go to hellfire just because they are not Muslims?'

I thought of my mother and grandparents. We had had our issues but they were decent people who had no malice.

'What if Zaher and Andersen had not been uncovered and my mum or Vibeke had been in the way when they detonated their bomb?'

There were more men in Denmark with their mindset – perhaps dozens within 100 miles of where I lived. Some of them had the potential to bring terror to my country; but how could I help prevent them from taking the lives of innocents?

I reached the car.

'I wasted ten years of my life,' I said, as I gripped the steering wheel and stared through the mist at the outline of pine trees. 'I gave myself to Allah. I believed in the justice of the struggle. But I deceived myself, and I allowed others to deceive me. I could have been a sportsman, I could have enjoyed life, kept my children, made something of myself.'

The rebel in me had rekindled my free will, but I knew how dangerous that would be. Suddenly I was walking in the shadow of Kurt Westergaard, the cartoonist who had drawn the Prophet Mohammed and had his life threatened for doing so. Not so long ago, I had wanted him dead.

Now, I am my friends' enemy, I thought one night as I lay in bed, restless. My wife lay peacefully at my side. What danger might she be in if I abandoned my 'brothers'? For now, the less she knew the better.

The next morning I tried to busy myself with chores, washing-up and laundry. As I threw a shirt into the washing machine, a card fell out. I picked it up. Frayed and crumpled, it was still legible. It was the business card of the so-called Martin Jensen at PET.

The card had a phone number. I tucked it in my pocket and left the house, wandering the streets of suburban Aarhus. If I called him there would be no turning back, no middle ground. I would have to lead a double life, one in which a single mistake could cost me my life. But the alternative seemed worse. Would I stand by as people I knew, people I could stop, brought carnage to my homeland and the rest of Europe?

That same evening I called the number.

Not for a moment did I think his real name was Martin Jensen, and I was doubtful he would even answer. But he did.

'This is Murad Storm. I need to meet you, soon,' I said. 'I have something I want to tell you.'

I could sense him struggling to stay calm.

'Okay, how about the Radisson Hotel in Aarhus?'

CHAPTER ELEVEN
SWITCHING SIDES

Spring 2007

The Radisson looks like a slab of ice, eight storeys high, with glass that reflects the clouds drifting above. The view from the Presidential Suite took in the canals and old cobbled streets of Aarhus, a spacious room of leather sofas, cool Scandinavian fixtures in birch and ash.

The same PET officers who had been at the police station late the previous year were there.

'Martin Jensen', the Clooney lookalike, clearly had a penchant for designer clothes: that day he was sporting a Hugo Boss shirt, expensive loafers and an even more expensive watch.

'Murad, it's good to see you again,' he said, shaking my hand. He had a crisp Copenhagen accent and exuded confidence. This was his show.

'You remember my colleague?' he said, introducing the bald over-weight smoker. 'We call him Buddha,' he said with a smile. 'And you can call me Klang.' He gave no explanation for the code name.

I sat down opposite the two agents on the leather sofas. They perched on the edge of their seats, attentively. This could be a career-defining moment for them – they knew I would be a treasure trove of information about jihadis. Buddha thrust a menu into my hand. 'Should it be halal? Chicken? Fish? Something vegetarian?' he asked, sensitive to my Muslim diet. 'Some bottled water? Coffee?'

His politeness amused me. It was time to make a statement.

'No, I will have a bacon sandwich, and a beer, a Carlsberg Classic,' I replied.

There was a stunned silence.

'That's what I want, guys.' It was my way of saying: 'I'm on your side.' I felt like a weight had been lifted from me.

'I've decided I'm no longer a Muslim,' I said. 'I am ready to help you in the fight against terrorism. For me, the religion that became my life has lost its meaning.'

'This is going to be the biggest,' Klang said, barely able to contain himself. They had a high estimation of my jihadist Rolodex.

The food arrived.

'Skol,' I said – raising my glass and savouring my first taste of alcohol in years. And then I set about a substantial bacon roll. I was a Dane again.

'Let's get started,' I said, and I began to tell my story.

I was the convert unconverted; the scales fell from my eyes. Having been so rigid, I had swung to the other end of the pendulum. While I could do nothing to change the past, my embrace of 9/11, my delusions about jihad and my admiration for Awlaki, I could atone for it. I knew the murderous world-view of al-Qaeda and I wanted to play a part in stopping them.

The agents could hardly take notes fast enough. They kept stopping me – staring in disbelief that I could know so many militants in so many places. The meeting went on for three hours, but it was no more than a prologue.

To share my story was liberating, and the more I told the more I felt myself distanced from my former life. When I walked out of the lobby into the late-afternoon sunshine, I felt at peace. This was the right thing to do.

Klang and Buddha asked me to meet them again in a few days.

'This work is going to take up a lot of your time so we can pay you 10,000 kroner a month,' Klang said after we exchanged greetings in the follow-up meeting.

It was $1,800 – hardly a sum to make me blush but I had not expected to be paid anything at all. Given how cash-strapped I was it would be welcome. 'That sounds good.' Klang handed me a Nokia mobile phone.

'You'll need this to contact us. We'll pay the bill,' he said.

'And it'll make it easier for you to keep tabs on me,' I replied. It was meant as a joke.

'No, no – we wouldn't do that. We trust you,' Buddha replied, protesting too much.

They had my first homework assignment. From a manila folder, Buddha produced two photographs and sheets with short biographies of two of my Islamist contacts in Aarhus.

'We want to know if we need to worry about them,' Klang explained.

The first was Abu Hamza, an overweight Moroccan cleric who liked to preach the merits of jihad, but whom I had always thought to be a blowhard. As I sipped tea in the sitting room of his mosque, listening to him sound off on the oppression of Muslims overseas while he devoured biscuit after biscuit, a suspicion that I had felt for some time hardened. Maybe Hamza was an informant on the payroll of PET. Was I testing him or was he testing me?

While I wasn't sure where he stood, I felt increasingly confident about the decision I had made. It felt surreal but empowering. As I listened to the cleric rant on I nodded my head occasionally. But it was as if I was listening with a different part of the brain. No longer was I seeking religious truth, guidance on what Allah demanded. Instead I was filing away every last detail to take back to my handlers.

The second target was Ibrahim, an Algerian I knew from the mosque in Aarhus. I knew I would meet him at Friday prayers. Afterwards Ibrahim offered me some tea and I walked with him to his shabby apartment nearby.

'Murad, I've found where Kurt Westergaard lives and I know where we can get weapons,' he blurted out once we were inside.

I looked into his excited eyes. Why was he telling me this now? Was he working for PET too? Was this another test? Or did he mean every word?

'Will you join me?' he asked.

'Let me think about it,' I replied.

As soon as I left I punched Klang's number into the mobile phone he had given me.

'We need to meet as soon as possible,' I said.

That evening I met him and Buddha in a hotel room in the city centre and relayed everything I had been told. They didn't seem that alarmed, which made me think my instincts had been right all along: these first targets had been a test. PET had needed to know if they could trust me.

Just to be sure, I went to see Ibrahim again. We met outside the mosque.

'So is it on?' I asked. He looked startled.

'I'm not interested any more,' he replied, cutting off the conversation and walking away quickly.

In the weeks that followed I had frequent meetings with Klang and Buddha. Soon I seemed to know every hotel in Aarhus. We also spoke often on the phone, sometimes several times a day. I was being developed into a regular informant.

I warmed to Klang, who had become my main point of contact. Despite acting as the dandy, he came from a modest background like me. He had worked in the drugs squad before being redeployed to counter-terrorism after 9/11. He knew how life on the streets worked – even if he had little interest in the religious side of jihadism or the places that were breeding militancy. I gradually laid out my web of connections in Denmark. I came up with a colour-coding system: green for harmless, orange for those with potential for violence, and red for dangerous. There were some 150 names.

My task was to keep my eyes and ears open, and report back to my handlers on any potential threat.

'Follow where your nose takes you but keep us informed each step of the way,' Klang said.

The agents told me that occasionally they would ask me to visit radicals on their radar screen. They also gave me a USB stick specially configured to quickly suck out the contents of a hard drive when inserted into a target's computer.

My cash flow steadily improved. The PET agents gave me a further 15,000 DKK so that I could pay the deposit on a new apartment. The payments were masked – either arriving as Western Union cash transfers or deposits to my bank account via a PET front company called 'Mola Consult'. PET would use the company to pay expenses relating to my work, including hotel bookings. To process invoices the company had a registered address in Lyngby, a Copenhagen suburb just a couple of miles from PET headquarters.

Fadia had no idea of my new source of income, nor of my contacts with PET. I told her I had received a bonus from the building firm. As a young Muslim woman in a foreign country she asked few questions about her husband's activities. I also did my best to put on a show of recovering my religious faith. It was a necessary deceit – to protect us both. If she knew about my real work and let it slip, her life could be in danger, as could her family back in Yemen. Instead I tried to make her believe my sudden collapse in December had been an aberration brought on by depression.

Every Friday I left the house as usual to go to *Jumma* (Friday prayers). More often than not I did go to the mosque, but not to pray. The gatherings of 'like-minded' young men in fast-food joints or tea shops afterwards were always rich sources of information.

While my wife was safer knowing nothing, I needed to share the sea-change in my life with someone. And there was only one person in the world who could begin to fathom what had happened and would tell no one.

'Mum, you can't tell anybody this. And you're the only person in the world who knows. I'm not a Muslim any more and I've started to work for Danish intelligence.'

There was silence for a few moments.

'There's never a dull moment with you,' she finally replied.

I wasn't even sure that she believed me but telling her was a relief. For the first time my work as a PET agent felt real. On the few occasions we met in the following years she never brought it up.

The first few months of 2007 had been traumatic for Fadia. I had not been a predictable companion and she seemed to expect that at any moment I would announce my departure for some foreign battlefield. She missed her family and had overstayed her visitor's visa. PET told me that if she returned to Yemen they could enrol her in a Danish university and then arrange a student visa, so she could quickly return to Europe.

But leaving Denmark would prove another trial for her. The immigration officer at Copenhagen airport noticed her lapsed status and began berating her. Fearful that she might be arrested, she called me – and I called my new friends at PET. Within a few minutes, the officer's demeanour changed. He saluted my wife smartly and wished her *bon voyage*. She had no idea why.

I remembered my hostile encounter with officers at Luton airport a couple of years before. Being on the side of the 'disbelievers' had its advantages.

Now on my own, I found myself in great demand with Klang and Buddha. One of the Islamists I had coded red was Ali, the Danish convert who had called me up from Somalia to boast that he had beheaded a Somali spy. He had fled advancing Ethiopian troops but was captured shortly afterwards in Kismayo and held for two months before being deported to Denmark.

PET wanted to build a criminal case against Ali so enlisted my help in a sting operation.

'Invite him to your home and get him talking,' Klang instructed me.

He handed me a small black battery-operated electronic recording device, disguised to look like a pager, and showed me how to activate it. A couple of days later, I called Ali. I had carefully rehearsed what I wanted to say.

'Ali, it's Murad. I'm still in Denmark. I heard you came back. What happened? Can you come and see me in Aarhus? I want to hear everything about Somalia. I still want to go, *Insha'Allah* [God willing].'

Ali came to my apartment with several friends from Copenhagen. As they knocked at the door, I turned on the recording device and slipped it into my pocket.

I greeted them with Islamic salutations. It was like being in a film or a play. I had simply reverted to being Murad Storm. I could assume the role as easily as flicking on a light switch.

Ali looked thinner than when I had last seen him in Sana'a, but had that same fierce intensity in his eyes. After we prayed I made them glasses of tea and we sat down cross-legged on the carpet to talk.

'Tell me about the fighting,' I said. 'I can't believe what happened to you.'

This was gathering intelligence, in its purest form.

As he began describing his time in Somalia I looked around the room. His friends were listening with rapt attention. So was I, for rather different reasons. Ali clearly loved the attention. He needed little encouragement to describe the beheading of the Somali spy.

'He had been pretending to be one of the mujahideen. But there was something about him that made us suspicious, and when he was interrogated he admitted he had been sent by the Ethiopians to find out our plans.

'He begged for mercy and said he would join us as a fighter but he was sentenced to death by the Islamic Courts. I volunteered to carry out the sentence. Praise be to Allah for letting me serve Him,' he said.

'*Alhamdulillah* [praise be to God],' I replied. He had just told me everything I needed. I decided not to wash the tea glasses. If the courts needed proof he had been in my apartment they could match his fingerprints.

Klang had disappointing news for me the next time I saw him.

'The recording didn't work.'

'I did everything exactly as you told me.'

'Don't worry about it. It was a glitch. We'll find another way.'

The Danish authorities never charged Ali. I began to suspect that the recording had worked but that PET did not want to compromise me as a source by handing it over to prosecutors. When I later asked Klang whether a case was being prepared against Ali he claimed that as the Somali spy had not been identified there was as a matter of law no victim. Ali remains free to this day and still lives in Denmark.

There were plenty of equally dangerous targets to pursue, and I was given great latitude to follow my instincts. On a breezy spring day in 2007, I was wandering through an immigrant neighbourhood in Copenhagen, hoping I might come across an old associate. I did. His name was Abdelghani Tokhi, a Danish resident of Afghan descent. His appearance made me suspicious. Gone was the long beard – he was now clean-shaven. It was a telltale sign. Jihadis in Western societies frequently shave off their beards to blend in better as they prepare to go operational.

I told PET it might be a good idea to take a closer look at him. It transpired Tokhi was an associate of a Danish-born Pakistani called Hammad Khurshid who had just returned from Pakistan's tribal areas. At that time, before the drone campaign ravaged jihadist ranks in Pakistan, the mountainous tribal areas were still the wellspring of international jihad. Khurshid had received bomb-making training from a senior Egyptian al-Qaeda operative who had supervised the explosives training of the bombers involved in the 2005 London attacks.

Unbeknown to him, Khurshid's notes on how to make explosives were discovered in his luggage by security at Copenhagen airport. PET had subsequently used a front company to offer a cheap apartment for rent close to where Khurshid lived. The apartment was equipped with secret cameras and bugs. The agency turned away several prospective renters, before Khurshid and Abdelghani came calling. A short while later they would film Khurshid making ten grams of the powerful detonating explosive TATP in the apartment, and in September 2007 Danish police would arrest Khurshid and Abdelghani. They were convicted of terrorism offences and remain in prison.

My bona fides – and value as an informant – were growing with every tip. And PET wanted to show me off to their allies in the intelligence world.

CHAPTER TWELVE
LONDON CALLING

Spring 2007

My Luton mentor, Omar Bakri Mohammed, had left Britain in 2005, weeks after the London attacks, amid hostility from the media and growing scrutiny from the security services. 'Send him Bak!' screamed the front page of the tabloid *Sun*.

Omar Bakri insisted he was going to see his mother in Lebanon for a holiday and planned to return to the UK. Britain's Deputy Prime Minister had commented: 'Enjoy your holiday – make it a long one.'

The preacher had taken refuge in the city of Tripoli on the coast of northern Lebanon and soon developed ties to Salafist militants. PET were interested that my former comrade and fellow Danish citizen Kenneth Sorensen was also there.

'How about a visit to Lebanon?' Klang had asked me. 'See what Omar Bakri might be planning, who he's hanging out with.'

I couldn't wait.

Staring out at the twinkling lights on the hills as the plane began its final descent into Beirut on 25 April 2007, I felt a rush. The city had not so long ago been torn apart by religious conflict. How appropriate that this place of sectarian rivalry should be the first destination in my new mission.

The Danes planned to share my findings with the British intelligence agencies MI5 and MI6, part of the back-and-forth trade that is the lifeblood of intelligence services the world over. The Danes had nothing like the resources of the CIA or the British, but they were keen to show they could punch above their weight. They also calculated that reconnecting with the preacher would further enhance my reputation in radical circles in the UK, something that one day might be useful to their British friends.

Omar Bakri and a couple of men with long beards and the look of enforcers were waiting for me in the Beirut airport arrivals hall. The preacher locked me in a bear hug.

'How are you, Murad, my brother – it is good to see you,' he exclaimed. I could not help but notice that his girth had expanded further.

We stepped out into the balmy April night and climbed into his gleaming black four-wheel-drive GMC. As he collapsed into the seat, the vehicle shook. He was clearly getting money from somewhere, probably from those young extremists that I'd sat with in Luton, listening to his bluster. We drove through the Christian suburbs of north Beirut and two hours later were in Tripoli.

On my first day in Tripoli, Omar Bakri took me to the mosque packed with worshippers by the old market. After prayers he bellowed out, 'This is brother Abu Osama al-Denmarki – he studied in Yemen and knows all the brothers there and he would like to say a few words.'

That caught me by surprise. It seemed the cleric wanted to bathe in the reflected light of my jihadist connections. I managed to wing it – recycling all the old lines on the religious obligation of jihad – and it seemed to do the trick because many of the eager-eyed young men came up to embrace me afterwards. It was a moment I would have relished if I had still been on their side.

After a week in the cleric's company, I tired of Omar Bakri's outlandish claims. The preacher may have radicalized a generation of young British Muslims, but he was clearly out of his depth among the hardened militants of Tripoli. They had had to survive real war in the streets. Omar Bakri by comparison was a vacuous windbag.

Keen to impress my handlers, I decided to go after bigger prey. I would not have long to wait. One day when I was in Omar Bakri's company, I met a young man with an impressive beard at a tailor's in the old market in Tripoli. My Nordic complexion clearly took him aback.

'*Masha'Allah!* Where are you from, brother?' he asked me in Arabic.
'Denmark,' I replied.

'Me too,' he said, in Danish, laughing, introducing himself as Abu
Arab. He was a Palestinian who had moved to Denmark as a young
refugee; his real name was Ali al-Hajdib.

Abu Arab invited me to his house a few days later. Soon after I
arrived he received a telephone call. 'Come with me!' Abu Arab said.

He led me down an alley. A black BMW with its engine running was
waiting for us.

'Get in!' Abu Arab said, his eyes flashing.

We clambered into the back of the car. In the front were two fighters wearing military fatigues and headscarves. A Kalashnikov assault
rifle was thrust into my hands and I was offered a pistol. After I declined,
the man riding shotgun held up a hand grenade.

'Perhaps you would like this?' he asked. He seemed to be a
commander.

'Or maybe one of these?' he said, opening his camouflage jacket to
reveal an explosive belt around his waist. As the car accelerated down
the narrow streets, the commander confided that if they were stopped
by the security forces or a rival militia it was better to die than suffer
the horrors of interrogation.

I tried not to wince whenever the car hit a pothole; explosive belts
have an awkward tendency to detonate when jolted.

I did not immediately realize it but I had just been given a backstage
pass to Fatah al-Islam, a hardline Sunni group with ties to al-Qaeda
which was then sprouting in the Palestinian refugee camps of northern Lebanon.

The commander in the car was Abu Arab's younger brother, Saddam
al-Hajdib, a senior member of the group and one of several al-Hajdib
brothers in a budding terror dynasty. Saddam was in his late twenties,
had fought with al-Qaeda in Iraq and knew its top leadership.[1] Another
brother, Youssef, had been arrested in Germany the previous year – at

---

1 Saddam al-Hajdib knew al-Qaeda in Iraq's then newly installed Egyptian operations' chief, Abu Hamza al-Muhajir, who, along with an Iraqi, took over after Abu
Musab al-Zarqawi's death in a US strike in June 2006. Al-Hajdib had recently brought

the age of just twenty-one – after leaving two suitcases full of explo-sives on trains near Cologne in a failed attack.[2]

Over the next several weeks I was given a tour of the Tripoli refugee camps, where preparations seemed to be afoot for the 'next war' in Leba-non. Abu Arab told me they would stop at nothing in their quest to bring Sharia law to the camps, then to the north of Lebanon, and one day to the whole country. Given the resources of the rival Shi'ite militia Hez-bollah, and Lebanon's raw sectarian divides, that seemed a pipedream. But their ambition was irrepressible, they had powerful allies that saw Fatah as a useful counterweight to Hezbollah – and their willingness to make common cause with international terrorism was unquestionable.

I left Lebanon early in May and flew to London, to be debriefed by Klang and Buddha. This time, their immediate boss, whose given name was Soren, was also present. He was in his late thirties and in good shape – his athletic appearance let down by his regular fumbling for cigarettes. Like Klang, he had switched to counter-terrorism after working in the drugs squad, a unit I once had particular reason to hate during my days with the Bandidos. Now he and Klang were partners in the fight against terrorism. The Danes ordered beers for the debrief-ing. They seemed to want to make me as relaxed as possible.

Soren told me with a smile that half a decade previously he had once been part of the team that had me under surveillance, following my communications with fellow radicals as far apart as Odense and Indonesia. It was Soren and Klang who had witnessed my pavement meeting with Robert from MI5 in the UK.

'He looked like a schoolboy trying to scare you,' Soren laughed. As we swapped stories Klang revealed to me that he and Buddha had worked on the Vollsmose terrorism case – the investigation that led to the arrest and conviction of Mohammad Zaher and Abdallah Andersen – once my friends – for a bomb plot the previous year.

---

funds back from Iraq to Lebanon with him and had killed a Syrian soldier on his return across the border.

2 Youssef al-Hajdib – caught as he tried to escape to Denmark – would receive a life sentence without parole, a punishment he would greet in court by raising both middle fingers in defiance.

'The informant we used testified in the trial. And we then had to arrange for him to change his identity and leave Denmark – it's been pretty tough for him because he rarely sees his kids.'

His words weighed on me for a while. Would that be my fate?

The Danes seemed impressed with the information I had gathered about the convoluted alliances and shadowy leaders behind the Tripoli violence. Would I care to meet their British colleagues?

The Churchill Hotel – close to Hyde Park – is one of London's finest. Behind the elegant facade, the lobby boasted marble floors and columns and mellow walnut furniture. If this was the typical venue for intelligence debriefings, then I was in the right business. The further I travelled from the spartan demands of Salafism the more I was seduced by the trappings of the espionage business.

As I crossed the threshold of the Churchill with my Danish handlers on a glorious spring evening, I had to restrain myself; it was just too easy to replay the Bond theme in my head. It became even more tempting when I set eyes on the MI6 officer who was waiting for us in the hotel suite.

He introduced himself as Matt. He knew how to wear a suit, had a cut-glass accent and impeccable manners, and was ruggedly handsome. He was the epitome of the British intelligence officer, with his oversize, fleshy ears the only part that seemed incongruous.

I imagined his background: one of England's finest boarding schools, where he no doubt excelled at both rugby and Latin, followed by Oxford or Cambridge. And then perhaps someone at the careers department had casually inquired whether intelligence work for Her Majesty's Government would be of any interest.

While I had developed a laddish repartee with my Danish handlers, Matt was all business and polish. In contrast to the sometimes crude Danes and the demanding Americans, the British spies I dealt with were polite and formal, almost to the point of being apologetic.

Even so, Matt laughed out loud when I called room service for some pork scratchings. It was not what he expected from a former jihadi.

I told him that Fatah al-Islam would try to ignite a war inside Lebanon, but he seemed more interested in what I had to say about Omar

Bakri, who had developed a network of supporters in the UK and was probably using them as a source of revenue.

Since the July 2005 bombings, MI5 was intensely focused on uncovering jihadist networks in places like Luton and Birmingham, networks and places I knew well. Since Karima had moved to Birmingham I had spent plenty of time there, renting temporary accommodation so that I could see my children whenever possible.

Not long after my meeting with MI6 my warning about events in Lebanon was borne out. Saddam al-Hajdib, the Fatah al-Islam commander I had met, robbed a bank near Tripoli and made off with $125,000. Lebanese security forces tracked him to an apartment block in the city. Al-Hajdib was true to his pledge: he blew himself up as the security services stormed the building. But the raid triggered days of clashes between Fatah and the security forces around the Nahr al-Barid refugee camp. More than twenty Lebanese soldiers and a similar number of Fatah fighters were killed.

Soon afterwards the Danes told me the British wanted to meet again. 'You impressed them on Lebanon: they didn't really see that coming,' Klang said.

At my second meeting with the British, Matt was accompanied by an MI5 officer called Andy. He was from the English Midlands, in his late forties and not wearing a suit. He seemed harder – more operational than a handler, someone used to being on the streets. I later found out he had previously been a police officer targeting drug traffickers. He and the patrician Matt made an odd couple, but Andy had a very specific mandate – the extremist scene in Birmingham.

'Can you keep your eyes open for us?' he asked.

The initial arrangement was for me to report to the Danes, who would pass on my information to the British, and for me to travel back to Denmark whenever needed. PET were happy with the arrangement because it improved their standing with the British. Soon, however, it was agreed I should also report directly to MI5.

At the behest of MI5 I moved into a modest terraced house in the Alum Rock area of Birmingham. They paid me £400 each month to cover the rent. Like Luton, Birmingham epitomized Britain's industrial decline, its poorer neighbourhoods of rundown terraces and drab tower blocks home to a large South Asian immigrant community, and a hotspot for Islamist radicals. Weather aside, Alum Rock could be mistaken for the rough-and-tumble streets of Karachi.

In the early summer of 2007, as a new season of cricket games began in Birmingham's parks, I immersed myself in the extremist scene. Most mornings I got up before dawn for the first prayer of the day at local mosques. As much as I was used to it, it was harder now that I was only a Muslim on the outside. Afterwards I'd often go to breakfast with 'like-minded' brothers at a halal restaurant. Then we might visit someone else's home to read the Koran together or discuss the latest news from Pakistan or Iraq. And so the sequence would continue: cheap meals on polystyrene plates in cafés with Formica tables, invariably followed by a talk from a radical preacher. One of the most popular was Anjem Choudary, a British-Pakistani lawyer who had been Omar Bakri's deputy in al-Muhajiroun and had taken over his mantle as the most controversial militant in the UK. I was not impressed by him, but noticed how many young men lapped up his every word.

Not all my time was spent in Birmingham. With Fadia away in Yemen and only occasional custody of my children, I had time on my hands. I returned periodically to Luton to keep tabs on the radical circle I had frequented two years before.

Getting 'fellow' extremists to open up was not difficult. Most loved nothing better than to talk. Sometimes I mentioned a new video sermon by Awlaki to get the conversation started. As in Denmark, I colour-coded UK-based radicals for MI5, according to the potential danger they posed. At the Small Heath mosque in Birmingham I rekindled my friendship with the young Somali, Ahmed Abdulkadir Warsame. He was still desperate to return home to fight the Ethiopians but had yet to raise the funds to travel.

If I could help him to Somalia, we could gain valuable intelligence from a region where there was precious little. Andy liked the idea and with his approval I began fundraising in mosques for Warsame's travel. A bureaucratic idiosyncrasy meant that MI5 rather than its sister service would run the operation because the intelligence would be collected through my email account.

The stories of rivalry between the domestic and overseas branches of the UK intelligence services are legendary. But I found that the MI5 and MI6 officers I dealt with cooperated and respected each other's needs. They were fighting different fronts of the same battle – MI6 in Somalia, Yemen and Pakistan, MI5 in Luton and Alum Rock. The suicide bomb attacks in London had given that collaboration new urgency.

It did not take me long to raise the money for Warsame's travel in the mosques and from my militant contacts in Birmingham. He was overcome with emotion when I handed him £600 in cash. 'May Allah reward you,' he said as he embraced me.

We agreed to keep in touch by leaving messages in the draft inbox of a shared email account. Warsame left the UK to join the fight in Somalia, and before very long had a shopping list for me and a request for funds.

One man impressed by my fundraising – and by my friendship with Anwar al-Awlaki – was a Syrian in his mid-thirties called Hassan Tabbakh. He also knew me by reputation from my days with al-Muhajiroun. And we found we had several mutual acquaintances, including Hamid Elasmar, a British-Moroccan, convicted in connection with a plot to behead a British Muslim soldier in Birmingham. It seemed I was not short of links to extremists across the UK.

Tabbakh was a balding chemistry graduate in his late thirties with a beard just beginning to show flecks of grey. I was struck by the sneer that seemed never to leave his lips and by his rather dispirited eyes. He was not a man that radiated enthusiasm. But we were among the few non-Somalis at the Small Heath mosque so it was inevitable that our paths would cross.

I had my son with me the first time we met. 'This is Osama,' I told him.

'*Masha'Allah*, this is a good name,' he replied unsmilingly. He told me he had been granted political asylum in the UK after fleeing for his life from Syria. He said he had been detained for possessing anti-government literature. His constant anxiety suggested that his interrogation by the secret police of the Assad regime had been vicious.

Tabbakh invited me to his home, a small dark ground-floor apartment in a decaying terraced house around the corner from the mosque.

It suited his morose temperament. But he was not short of ideas, and he was desperate to share them.

'I've been busy,' he said.

He had been learning how to build bombs and showed me sketches of targets in London. They included Oxford Street, packed every day with shoppers and tourists, and the area around Parliament.

On the sketches he showed me where exactly he planned to set off his bombs. I noticed his hands were trembling.

'Brother, what do you think? Will it work?' he asked. He wanted me to join the plot. I was stunned that he should share so many details with someone he hardly knew.

With his background as a physics and maths graduate, I had little doubt he would be able to build the bombs, but what was his timetable?

I looked him in the eye. *'Insha'Allah.'*

'You need to be careful, brother,' I added, trying to coax him into slowing down. Anything to buy time.

I alerted MI5. Tabbakh had until then not been on their radar. He was the archetypal 'lone-wolf terrorist', the sort that are most difficult to detect for their lack of contact – by any means – with others. And I had stumbled into his plans.

'We need you to stick very close to him in the coming weeks,' Andy told me.

At another meeting soon afterwards, Andy asked me about the keys Tabbakh used to open his door.

'Big keys, small keys, double keys?' he asked. They were clearly planning to break in. I was told later that in the course of a break-in agents had found the sketches, photographed and carefully replaced them. They would be prima facie evidence of Tabbakh's plans.

As part of the operation MI5 even staged detaining me at Gatwick airport to bolster Tabbakh's trust in me. To set this up I asked Idriss, a well-connected British-Pakistani extremist from Walsall, to drive me to the airport to catch a flight to Yemen. When I tried to pass through security, a police officer made a big show of detaining me, knowing that my driver would tell all and sundry.

I was frogmarched to a small room near the security screening area where an MI5 officer was awaiting me. The police officer was – to say the least – surprised when the agent jumped up and gave me a bear hug. We chatted for a while and then I was escorted back to the departure lounge, where I made a plaintive call to Idriss, complaining about the brutal British security service and asking him to come back to Gatwick to collect me. The incident burnished my credentials among the militants in Birmingham.

Tabbakh hadn't settled on a date to launch his attack but sketched out a diagram of the electronics of the bomb design and told me which chemical ingredients he planned to mix. He said he would use large soda bottles to hold the charge. I wished I had paid more attention during science classes at school, but I told MI5 he seemed to know what he was doing.

The police did not move in immediately because MI5 was wary of blowing my cover. After all, I was the only one in whom Tabbakh had confided. In the following weeks, MI5 took elaborate steps to mask my role by shifting suspicion on to one of his radical associates.

Tabbakh was arrested in December 2007 and later convicted of making bombs to launch a terrorist attack. Police found bottles containing acetone and nitrocellulose in his dingy flat and instructions for converting the ingredients into bombs. They would have been crude and basic, but the judge at his trial said they had 'great potential for destruction, injury and death'.

My street-by-street knowledge of the militant scene in the UK and my Rolodex of jihadis abroad were generating results. Islamist terrorism posed a multitude of problems for agencies which not so long ago had concentrated the lion's share of their resources on the Soviet bloc. It was young, difficult to penetrate and spreading quickly. Inside information was hard to come by; a Dane with good Arabic and nearly a decade of militancy behind him was the ideal informant.

No wonder the Americans came calling.

CHAPTER THIRTEEN
FROM LANGLEY WITH LOVE

Summer 2007–Early 2008

My handlers at PET always talked of the British as 'the cousins'. The CIA were 'Big Brother'. Klang and Buddha found it difficult to contain their excitement when word reached them that the Americans would like to meet Mr Storm.

The Danes set up a meeting at the Scandic Hotel on the waterfront in Copenhagen. Eighteen storeys of steel and glass, it looked like a functional American office building from the outside. But inside it was all pale woods, minimalist Scandinavian furniture and peculiar white perspex trees climbing through the lobby.

Klang and Buddha fussed over me when I arrived. Even Klang's familiar mask was slipping with the Americans sitting upstairs.

'Joshua' and 'Amanda' must have been in their early thirties, both neatly attired in business suits. Joshua was tall with dark hair, good-looking in that preppy, north-eastern way. He had clearly never done a day's manual labour in his life. Amanda made an altogether different impression. I was drawn to her eyes. They were cornflower blue and had a searching, almost beseeching aspect. She had full lips and high cheekbones; honey-coloured hair fell from her shoulders.

For the CIA, the Scandic meeting was a fishing expedition. How much had I learned about Fatah al-Islam, al-Qaeda, and the militants I had met in Yemen? They were especially interested in two topics: Anwar al-Awlaki – still held in solitary confinement in a Sana'a prison but not charged – and the Yemeni connection to Somalia. At that time, the militant Islamist group al-Shabaab, a spinoff of the Islamic Courts Union, was emerging to challenge the Ethiopian troops that had intervened to save the Somali government, and it was beginning to attract fighters from the Somali diaspora in Europe and North America.

Amanda had a way of asking questions which was disarming. Perhaps it was her enthusiasm, her ability to find the same wavelength, or those eyes. For several hours I held court, laying out a spider diagram of my jihadist militant contacts on three continents.

Amanda said the CIA might be interested in having me travel to Somalia, whose anarchy had haunted US policymakers since the disastrous intervention of 1992–4 and 'Blackhawk Down'. Should militants seize large tracts of the coastline or bog down the Ethiopians in urban warfare, it could become much more dangerous than Yemen.

Throughout the meeting Joshua and Amanda took notes. I watched Amanda's manicured hand moving gracefully across the pages of her notebook, her neat script soon filling twenty pages. At the end they had a simple question: 'How would you feel about working for us?'

'I would feel very good about that.'

'We'll be in touch,' Amanda said, that smile finally escaping the corners of her mouth. I could only hope so.

I wanted to keep my options open. I could probably keep both the British and the Americans happy with some agile footwork, but their methods and priorities were different. The British seemed methodical to the point of pedestrian, cautious but well-informed. They had an almost academic approach to developing expertise overseas, relishing discussion of tribal rivalries and geographic oddities. But they were preoccupied by an enemy at home whose strength and determination they could not gauge.

The Americans by contrast wanted to use their formidable technical resources to take the battle overseas – to Yemen, Somalia and Pakistan. The homeland had been hit once; never again. They would prove impatient for results – ready to throw money at problems. They had been seared by 9/11 and were prepared to pursue targets with little consideration for legal niceties. The British could not countenance assassination. Their resources, I fast discovered, were very different too. PET and now MI6 flew economy, even on long-haul flights. So much for the James Bond lifestyle. CIA agents still turned left when they boarded. The Danes used to joke with their CIA counterparts that if they ever flew together, the Americans ought to send their leftovers back to them.

I was also fast discovering that PET wanted everyone to share the adventures I might provide, just so long as they were taken along on the magic carpet. And the next stop would be exotic enough. Klang at PET had a strange request.

'Send me a draft email requesting a meeting in Bangkok.' We had a practice of leaving draft emails in an account to which we both had access, the same trick that al-Qaeda used. The fewer emails that actually travelled the better.

For my PET handlers I was the passport to places they would otherwise never see on their government salaries. They appeared to be able to justify top-class hotels for meetings with Morten (aka Murad) Storm.

A three-day visit to Bangkok at the beginning of December to plan a mission to Kenya seemed ludicrous, but I soon found out why Klang was so enthusiastic about the Orient. Within hours of touching down he was in the red-light district with the rest of the Danish team, including team leader Soren, drinking beer after beer and negotiating terms for the services of a shy teenage girl.

And so it was that the taxpayers of Denmark subsidized the varied appetites of a government servant. Once he had found a girl, I left. The next few days would be arduous and I did not need to start with a monstrous hangover.

'I guess I'll see you later,' he said with a leer.

At least one of Klang's escapades ended in his humiliation. After he had spent some hours canoodling with another woman at a lap-dancing club, he brought her along to a restaurant. The waitress whispered that the woman was not all she seemed; in fact she was a very well-made-up 'lady-boy'. As Klang's face turned pale, the rest of us were bent double with laughter.

The Danes were taking a risk going out drinking with me. American and British agents never socialized with me in this way. But the Danes were more cavalier. There was always the possibility that I might be recognized by someone, blowing my cover and endangering my life. But I was happy to let my hair down. I needed the release and assumed it was unlikely that any of my extremist acquaintances would be frequenting Bangkok nightclubs.

The weakness of several of my Danish handlers for escorts, exotic locales and expensive booze may have begun when they were working in the drugs squad, which had a reputation for hard partying and sampling the powder they confiscated. Now equipped with diplomatic passports, my squad were reaching horizons they had only dreamt about. As we logged more and more 'debriefings' in foreign fleshpots it would become all too easy to forget the PET agents were meant to be my professional partners.

Matt was as usual much more restrained, his only concession to this unusual field trip being an unbuttoned business shirt and neatly pressed jeans.

'Hello, Morten. Beats damp, grey old London, doesn't it?' he said with a glint in his eye when we met in my luxurious hotel suite high above the thronging city.

'We want you to go to Kenya; we have some presents for your Somali friends,' he said to me.

By now, in the dying days of 2007, al-Shabaab was winning territory in large swathes of Somalia. The Transitional Government was confined to a few blocks of Mogadishu, propped up by the Ethiopian troops that had brought down the Islamic Courts Union and an African Union peacekeeping force.

Among al-Shabaab's youthful ranks there were a growing number of foreign fighters. Within weeks, the US State Department would designate the group as a foreign terrorist organization. Somalia – once just written off as a failed state – was a source of increasing alarm in Western capitals.

One young man climbing the ranks of al-Shabaab was Ahmed Abdulkadir Warsame, whom I had helped to travel to Somalia earlier that year. Since then, he had left several messages in our shared draft email folder asking me to find and deliver equipment such as a laptop, camcorder and portable water filtration equipment.

For MI6 such a mission would open the door to the group's inner workings and senior personnel. A laptop – suitably fitted out – could convey valuable information when connected to the internet or when seeking a WiFi connection, and Matt had made arrangements to provide one. He introduced me to an earnest young man in thick-rimmed glasses who looked like he had not seen sunshine for weeks.

'You look a bit young to be Q,' I said, referencing the boffin made famous in the Bond films.

He carefully placed the laptop into a sports bag containing the other supplies: a camcorder, portable filtration equipment, a PowerMonkey solar mobile-phone charger, a Suunto GPS watch (useful for tracking a terrorist if suitably adulterated), run-of-the-mill night-vision goggles and a few hundred dollars in cash.

I wrote a draft email in the account I shared with Warsame to let him know I had what he needed.

As I left Bangkok for Nairobi, I was sharply focused. I rehearsed scenarios exhaustively, devised answers for any questions. I needed to rest but could not sleep, instead gazing out of the window at huge formations of clouds below. This was my first mission for MI6 and I felt I was at the centre of a global battle. Both they and Danish intelligence were assembling teams in Nairobi to support the mission.

I landed in Nairobi on 7 December 2007. I couldn't stay at a luxury hotel. I was in jihadist mode, and that meant the modest Pan Afrique Hotel. At a nearby internet café, I logged on to the shared email account and found Warsame had left me a Nairobi phone number to arrange the drop.

In my room, I inserted a local SIM card into my mobile phone and called.

The voice that answered had a thick Kenyan accent. He was expecting to hear from me.

'I have the equipment,' I told him. 'I'll meet you tomorrow in the car park at the Intercontinental Hotel – three o'clock.'

The Danes had set the location and time of the pick-up; they and the British wanted to monitor it. To my surprise the contact did not argue.

My first field operation was going too smoothly. I kicked back in my room and watched Floyd Mayweather slug it out with Ricky Hatton for the world light welterweight title. It took me back a decade to the

Tyson–Holyfield bout, when I was bundled into that police car in Korsør. A lot had happened in the intervening years, but the Pan Afrique Hotel was surely better than a Danish prison cell.

I was early for the handover. A lanky Somali with large ears loped into the car park and spotted me. There were times when being a large Dane with flame-red hair could be useful. I felt my heartbeat accelerate as he walked towards me. Without a word, he took the bag and was gone. We had an audience – MI6 and a Danish agent had been watching.

There was another quick dividend to getting inside al-Shabaab. Kenyan intelligence trailed the man who collected the equipment to a Shabaab safe house in the Eastleigh neighbourhood of Nairobi. Several days later – on 13 December – the police raided the house, seizing a large quantity of weapons and fake identity papers, and arresting more than twenty men alleged to have been planning attacks on Western targets in Kenya.[1]

By the time those arrests had been made, I had been debriefed by the triad of PET, CIA and MI6 in faraway Amsterdam. It would be my last encounter with the elegant Amanda. As always she took copious notes about my travels, though I left out some of the interludes in Bangkok.

As we said goodbye, I expected we would see each other again. But Amanda was soon back at CIA headquarters, being trained for a mission to Afghanistan. It would be her last overseas assignment. She was killed with six of her colleagues in a suicide bombing at a CIA base in Khost, Afghanistan, in December 2009. It was a tragic day for the Agency, later brought to the screen in the film *Zero Dark Thirty*. I recognized her from pictures published in newspapers; her real name was Elizabeth Hanson. She was from suburban Chicago and was widely regarded as one of the CIA's most talented young analysts.

Exhausted but elated that I had completed my first real overseas mission, I left Amsterdam to return to Yemen. The Americans and Danes wanted me back in Sana'a to work the Yemeni and Somali networks, and the British, who I sensed would have preferred me to

1 One of the Danish agents subsequently told me my operation led to the arrests.

continue countering terrorist plots in the UK, had agreed. And I badly needed to be reunited with Fadia; we had not seen each other for months. She had no idea that in the last few days alone I had been on three continents working with three intelligence agencies. She thought I had been living off UK benefits in Birmingham.

As I presented my boarding pass at Amsterdam airport, I suddenly realized it was almost exactly a year since I had trawled through a camping store collecting supplies for the Islamic Courts in Somalia. Now I had finally delivered supplies to the group that had risen from its ashes, but how different were the circumstances. I shuddered to think what might have been.

The arrivals hall at Sana'a airport was the usual mixture of shouting, half-formed queues and surly immigration officers. It was so familiar, but now I observed it from the opposite end of the spectrum. I had first passed through this building as a wide-eyed convert. Now my work was to find, track and inform on people whose beliefs were those I had shared not so long ago.

Fadia was much more buoyant than during my crisis of faith in Denmark, happy to be around her family and showing greater self-assurance and maturity. She had rented and furnished a home on 40th Street, a pleasant area of the city, and her family was impressed that she seemed prosperous, though of course neither they nor she had any idea that Danish intelligence was the source of much of our income.

Days after I returned, Anwar al-Awlaki was released after more than eighteen months in detention. He had never been brought to trial. A week or so later, I visited him at his home, the same place where he had entertained a group of us nearly two years earlier. He looked pale and thin.

'I was in solitary confinement for the first nine months,' he told me. 'The only contact I had with humanity was my guards, and the cell was three metres long. It was underground. There were times when I thought the isolation and the claustrophobia would drive me insane . . . I had no paper to write on. I got no exercise.'

Awlaki was bitter and angry, but also thankful.

'I survived thanks to the will of Allah and the suffering has deepened my faith. And although it was very difficult to get books, I was able to read Qutb again.'

The Egyptian religious scholar Sayyid Qutb was widely regarded by many as having provided the intellectual cornerstone of al-Qaeda's global jihad. One of his devoted students was Ayman al-Zawahiri, Osama bin Laden's second-in-command.

'Because of the flowing style of Sayyid I would read between 100 and 150 pages a day,' Awlaki wrote later of his time in jail. 'I would be so immersed with the author I would feel Sayyid was with me in my cell speaking to me directly.'

I knew my handlers would be interested in information on Awlaki's state of mind. Prison had hardened him. I could see it in his eyes. They'd danced before; now there was steel. There was also a hint of paranoia. He saw spies everywhere.

He recounted being visited by FBI agents wanting to know more about his meetings with two of the 9/11 hijackers. He said that he had refused to speak English to them, insisting on communicating through a translator. At one point he said he had pushed a CIA officer down into a chair in protest at being questioned by the Americans. He said his only consolation was that unlike other prisoners he had never been harmed in jail. The guards were well aware that his father knew President Saleh.

His anger was directed as much towards the government that had imprisoned him as the Americans. He told me that jihad was necessary to overthrow President Saleh, who he said paid lip service to Islam but was a puppet of the Americans.

'The mujahideen need to establish an Islamic State in Abyan, as the *hadith* have foretold,' he told me. The *hadith* said, 'An army of twelve thousand will come out of Aden-Abyan. They will give victory to Allah and His messenger; they are the best between myself and them.'

Awlaki believed God had given him a mission to carry the banner of jihad, and to start in southern Yemen.

By the time Anwar left prison, al-Qaeda was regenerating itself in ungoverned tribal areas east and south of Sana'a.

Wuhayshi, the bin Laden protégé who had broken out of prison in 2006, was leading a newly formed group: al-Qaeda in the Land of

Yemen. Suicide bombers in cars packed with explosives had recently attacked two oil facilities in Marib and Hadramaut provinces. Attacks on Yemeni security forces and Westerners followed. For Wuhayshi it was the first chapter in a rapid ascent towards the upper echelons of al-Qaeda.

The group built up a network of safe houses, including in the capital, Sana'a. But its main haven was in the mountains and rugged terrain of the southern and eastern provinces of the country – Marib, Abyan and Shabwa, where Awlaki's family was influential. These areas were still dominated by local tribes who were suspicious of the central government in Sana'a. Keen to keep their autonomy, some tribal factions provided sanctuary and support to al-Qaeda fighters.

This was the militant environment into which Awlaki emerged, even if he was not yet an active figure in al-Qaeda.

In late January 2008, Awlaki came to lunch at our home on 40th Street. A few other friends from the lecture days (those not arrested or deported) came along too.[2] Sana'a was quite the jihadist melting pot. My wife cooked a huge array of dishes – including chicken, rice and a pot of *selta* – a traditional Yemeni dish of ground beef, eggs, okra and fenugreek. The food was laid on the floor, which was protected by a large plastic sheet as the assembled company ate.

After the plates had been cleared away, I lit a *bakhoor*, an incense smoke pile which filled the room with its herbal scent. We reclined on cushions against the walls and talked about the state of jihad, including al-Qaeda's progress in the south of Yemen and how best to topple the Saleh regime. It was treasonable talk.

The conversation then turned to Somalia, and progress made by al-Shabaab in extending its reach across the country.

I had a mischievous idea.

---

2 Among the other guests was a young black South African and a nineteen-year-old Somali called Issa Hussein Barre. The latter would soon take advantage of my connection to Warsame to join the struggle in Somalia. The usually cautious MI5 even approved cash transfers to him to finance his wedding so that I could nourish my connection for information. Unfortunately he was killed while fighting for al-Shabaab – a young husband sacrificed in an ever more brutal cause.

'Sheikh, why don't we call up the brothers in Somalia and ask them how it's going?' I asked with a provocative grin.

They were sceptical: how could I just place a call like that?

The reason was Ahmed Warsame, now rising through the ranks of al-Shabaab.

'*Masha'Allah*, it's Murad, how are you? I have someone here who wants to talk to you,' I said, handing the phone to Awlaki.

When Warsame recovered from the surprise of speaking to the famous cleric, he told him how the fight was going. Awlaki seemed elated, pleased to be talking to the mujahideen in Somalia. The two exchanged email addresses and mobile-phone numbers.

I had just brokered a connection between Somali and Yemeni militants. As Awlaki gravitated towards al-Qaeda's inner circle in Yemen, his connection to Warsame would prove useful to both sides, but even more useful to Western intelligence services, now furnished with email addresses and phone numbers.

Before Awlaki took his leave that evening, we agreed on a new mode of communication, the tested technique of writing draft emails in a shared email account. I explained to him how it worked. In the wake of his incarceration, and amid the persistent attention of Yemen's security services, he was more cautious about his links to the outside world.

A few weeks later, he abruptly left Sana'a – perhaps under pressure from his family, as his father had pleaded with him to soft-pedal his fundamentalist views. But equally he may have felt that he could not relaunch himself as a spiritual guide under the eye of Yemen's intelligence services.

The city of Ataq sits on the fringe of the Empty Quarter, the endless expanse of desert that straddles the Yemeni–Saudi border. Some 200 miles south-east of Sana'a, Ataq is overlooked by dun-coloured mountains on three sides. Its skyline is dominated by functional government buildings, but several medieval jewels in and around the town have survived, elaborate mud-brick buildings baked into towering rock-faces. Ataq is also the provincial capital of Shabwa, where Awlaki's family has influence. And so it was in Ataq that Anwar resettled and was spending time with his second, very young, wife.

Awlaki's first wife had shared his life in the United States. She was from a prominent family in the Yemeni capital, was well-educated and spoke good English. She also had a strong personality, driving herself around Sana'a and frequently putting Anwar in his place. So she had not reacted positively when he had told her in 2006 that he planned to take a second wife, especially when she found out that the new bride was a teenager.

Awlaki had been offered the girl in marriage by her two brothers (this was, after all, Yemen), who were great admirers of his. Instead of declining this generous gesture, Awlaki had accepted enthusiastically. The wedding ceremony was not a triumph. The family of the first wife were offended by this young *arriviste* and felt her social standing was inferior.

At first Anwar had installed his new teenage bride in an apartment near the Air Force Academy in Sana'a. Now she had accompanied him – apparently with little enthusiasm – to the wilds of Shabwa.

In Ataq, Awlaki spent much of his time online. The cleric's incarceration had seen his fame in Islamist circles in the West grow. Weeks after emerging from prison, Anwar created a website – anwar-alawlaki.com – and a Facebook page. From the town's internet cafés with their crawling connection speeds, he began railing against the United States and its allies, including the Saleh government, for 'waging a war on Islam'. He started exchanging messages with dozens among his legion of followers through more than sixty email accounts he registered.

My wife and I made the journey from Sana'a to Ataq in February 2008 to catch up with Awlaki. It was the first time we ventured into Yemen's deep interior to seek out the cleric, but would not be the last. The trip was on my own initiative but approved by both PET and the CIA. To begin with, the security forces blocked us from the route because of tribal fighting in Marib (no unusual occurrence) – forcing us to try again the following day. For my wife, it was a social visit; she had no idea of my real intent in seeing Anwar again.

The nine-hour road trip passed along the fringes of the Ramlat al-Saba'tayn, where the wind had corrugated the sand into immense dunes. Once in a while, an adobe house of three or four storeys would emerge from the haze, defying the ages, the winds and the swirling

sands. The edge of the desert was defined by black granite domes –
like giant loaves of pumpkin bread – rising hundreds of feet above the
desert.

It was important that I stayed in character, even in the privacy of the
car. I played CDs of *nashids* – Islamic songs – and my wife remained
fully veiled. When we finally reached Ataq at sunset, Anwar was waiting for us in a new Toyota Land Cruiser. He was not short of cash. He
wore tribal dress and the Yemeni sword, or *janbiya*, on his hip.

We found a curious domestic arrangement for the emerging star of
Islamic fundamentalism. Awlaki and his young wife had rented a modest third-floor apartment in the middle of the town. I was struck by the
simple furnishings – a far cry from the grand living quarters of clerics
like Sheikh Abdul Majid al-Zindani. Awlaki lived almost ascetically, his
only luxury being the best honey available, which he insisted on every
morning.[3]

A ceiling fan whirred above – it was already warm outside, even in
February. The street below sent up the muffled sound of cars and the
shouts of traders.

I never interacted with his new wife because of strict segregation of
the sexes in conservative Yemeni circles. But my wife spent a lot of
time with her, and soon found out she was hardly the obvious partner
for a scholar of Anwar's standing. By this time, she was nineteen –
petite, very pretty and still with the bubby personality of a teenager.
Anwar had been out of prison just three months but she was already
pregnant – and prone to bouts of morning sickness.

She found Ataq tedious and hot, a remote and conservative corner
of a remote and conservative country. She told my wife that the early
days with Anwar had been tough. The wedding had felt like a funeral
because of the first wife's hostility. The two did not speak for months,
but eventually they reached an accommodation. Now they took turns
spending time with their husband in Ataq.

The younger wife could not wait to escape the stifling apartment
and return to Sana'a to see her family. She seemed to love Anwar but

3 Perhaps it wasn't just the taste. Control of stores selling top-grade Yemeni honey
had once been used by Osama bin Laden to fund al-Qaeda.

told my wife that all he did was read. His study was crammed with books from floor to ceiling, on Koranic law and Islamic jurisprudence.

He studied Islamic teachings compulsively. But he was selective about how he applied them at home. He had installed a TV in the bedroom so that his wife could watch Turkish soaps dubbed into Arabic – to which she was addicted. It was a surprising concession: many militants within al-Qaeda considered television *haram* – strictly forbidden by Islamic law. Her viewing schedule also appeared to have taken priority over housework. The maids had taken care of that in Sana'a, but not in this backwater. More than once Anwar indulged her and went into the kitchen to prepare a meal for the two of us.

The teenage wife had little education and not much to say – it seemed to my wife that she was little more than a plaything for Anwar. But even as she carried his child, Anwar broached with me the possibility of finding him yet another wife – a convert from the West.

Most of the time we talked about Islam. He was an ocean of knowledge and a tower of authority. But he also talked about his days in America and told me more about his fishing trips in Colorado.

Then he paused and went back to 9/11. 'The Americans had it coming. We need to drive them out of Muslim lands!' His rhetoric was sharper than before.

Word had reached him that he should not return to Sana'a if he wanted to avoid another spell in detention. The message from Yemen's intelligence services was blunt: 'Don't call for jihad and don't meet with foreigners, or you'll be in more trouble.' At this I felt a pang of anxiety. If he was being watched constantly, I might find myself back on the authorities' radar, and that would be awkward for both me and my handlers.

I was careful not to probe too far with Anwar. His words were deliberate; I had the sense he was being more cautious than before and was not ready to trust me with his plans. But I suspected those plans would be fed by the visceral hostility he now felt towards America and its client in the Presidential Palace in Sana'a.

CHAPTER FOURTEEN
COCAINE
AND ALLAH

Early 2008

The traffic thundered down London's Euston Road. It was a sunny afternoon in March 2008 – one of those days that dare hint spring is not too far away. Carpets of purple-blue and golden crocus illuminated the city's squares and parks. Overhead the airliners drifted towards Heathrow. I had just flown in after four months in Yemen.

As I crossed the road, I glanced towards King's Cross, the station that had been at the heart of the carnage in 2005 when suicide bombers struck London. Nearly three years later the British security services were still under pressure over intelligence failures in the run-up to the attacks. They did not want to be caught out again and were keen to exploit my familiarity with the jihadis of Luton, Birmingham and Manchester. But the CIA wanted to use my knowledge of the militant fraternity in Yemen and Somalia.

At an anonymous hotel near Euston station, the three agencies had gathered to debrief me and I gave them a detailed account of my recent stay with Awlaki in Ataq.

The CIA team was now headed by an officer in his late thirties whom I guessed to be the Agency's number two in Copenhagen. Jed was balding with ginger stubble on his chin, a man whose plain looks were at odds with his iceberg-blue eyes. And he used them to great effect, impaling me with an intense stare. He spoke with precision and took detailed notes. Jed was all business, with the occasional flair of laconic humour. He was ambitious and wanted results. On the rare occasions that he lost his temper, his left eye would begin to twitch as if sending Morse code.

Jed clearly had the authority to make a pitch for my services, once he was persuaded that I had a direct path to Awlaki.

The rest of the meeting focused on gathering more intelligence on al-Shabaab in Somalia. PET was interested in developing a line to Shabaab by sending equipment to them: water purifiers, tents, sleeping mats, but nothing combat-related. Curiously the British drew the line at hammocks, perhaps on the grounds that no terrorist should get a good night's sleep. I witnessed the strange spectacle of three intelligence services arguing about hammocks – the first obvious dissent among them.

Matt from MI6 was at the Euston meeting, and it was clear that Her Majesty's Government was worried that a valuable source who had made his home in England was about to be coaxed away by all the Americans' baubles. So the British met and raised the Americans' offer with a series of team-building exercises which were smartly calculated to appeal to my love of the outdoors but were also a serious bid for my services.

The first card they played was a day of fly-fishing in north Wales. As always there was also a Danish presence. I was first and foremost their man, and they weren't about to let me spend time alone with MI6, to be dispatched to far-flung corners of the world.

Klang, my Danish handler, turned up looking like a mail-order catalogue model in a Barbour jacket, hunting trousers and a tartan cap. He was in love with the idea of playing the country gentleman for a day, even if he was in the wrong part of Britain for tartan. It took all Matt's self-restraint not to laugh.

Klang was accompanied by a PET agent I called Trailer because he had grown up on a farm. He had replaced Buddha, who had been incapacitated with a bad back. There was nothing designer about Trailer's grimy jacket. He was as unpretentious as Klang was sophisticated – very tall, from rural Jutland, and once an accomplished handball player. He had been the agent who observed the handover of equipment to the al-Shabaab courier at the Intercontinental in Nairobi.

It was a cloudless spring day. As the Danish pair tried unsuccessfully to hook a trout out of the River Dee with the help of an instructor, Matt sidled up to me on the bank, out of their hearing.

'We don't want you to go to Somalia for the Americans,' he said. 'I think you should stay here a little bit more: we need you.' The British wanted me to develop leads in England's inner cities as well as focus on the Somali contacts I had established.

Not long afterwards there was another exercise at an imposing country house near Aviemore in Scotland. MI6 had sent a car to pick me up at Inverness airport and the forty-minute drive took us past Loch Ness to the property, nestled in hilly woodland.

Matt was waiting for me on the steps, standing next to a striking brunette who was about thirty years old. Emma would be my new MI6 handler as Matt was being moved to other duties. Tall and athletic with high cheekbones and an immaculate complexion, she spoke in an unforced upper-class tone and seemed imperturbable. Her chiselled features and wide smile reminded me of Julia Roberts.

'It's good to finally meet you,' she said, flashing me a smile.

During the retreat, Emma revealed that her grandmother was Swedish and she could speak the language. I tried out some Danish on her, and she laughed, answering back in Swedish, which Danes can more or less understand. It helped break the ice.

Again the Danes came along; and Andy was there from MI5, but the Americans were not invited. They must have resented that. The two-day course featured training by a UK Special Forces (SAS) specialist in mountain navigation, abseiling and survival skills. His name was Rob and he had just come back from undisclosed duties in Iraq.

There was also a psychologist on hand, who introduced himself as Luke. A dapper, well-educated Scot in his mid-forties, he was softly spoken and had grey-blue eyes. He had a neatly trimmed beard that made him look older than he probably was. His mission was to see how resilient and suitable I was for life as an informant on the front-line. I felt I was being fast-tracked by the British.

Luke presented me with some difficult hypothetical choices.

'What would you do if you were with al-Qaeda and ordered to execute a prisoner?' he asked.

As I pondered, he leaned forward and said quietly: 'You'd execute him to avoid attracting any suspicion or provoking any doubts among your comrades.'

We talked through the burden of living a double life, and my break-up with Karima. He understood better than I could imagine the pressure I was going to face.

The evening was more light-hearted. We played bingo, and the Danes cheated. They also thought it hysterical to point the beam of a laser pointer on to the faces of my British handlers as we tried to talk business, focusing on Matt's outsize ears. At times their antics were embarrassing and I felt they had become much too familiar with me.

To add to my discomfort, Klang made a none too subtle play for the attention of Emma. Matt, it seemed, had more luck. I noticed, as they cooked a Scottish breakfast for the house guests, that there seemed to be a special chemistry between the two.

The British were subtle about their entreaties, but quietly insistent. I would be better off working with them; it would be a genuine commitment on both sides. I would be properly trained and supported. The unspoken implication was that at some point the CIA would hang me out to dry.

As the tension between the British and American agencies grew more palpable I sought the advice of my PET handlers. It was the wrong thing to do. They smelt money and opportunity with the CIA.

'You'll get to do more with the Yanks,' Klang told me, 'and they pay more.'

I was conflicted. Matt, Andy, Emma and the others from the two UK agencies had been good companions, straightforward and intelligent. They were trapped by bureaucracy and regulation, but they were professionals.

The American riposte to the special treatment by the British took place in the Danish coastal resort of Helsingør, sometimes called the capital of the Danish riviera. Its most famous landmark was Kronberg Castle, a Renaissance pile that Shakespeare used in inventing Elsinore for *Hamlet*. It was an appropriate place to plot against Awlaki, the future prince of jihad.

At the end of our meeting, Jed took me aside.

'You never took your wife on a honeymoon, right?' he asked, the iceberg eyes melting just for an instant.

'No. I've not exactly had much time over the last two years.'

'Well, consider it a gift from us. Just let us know where you'd like to go and we can make the arrangements,' Jed said.

I was flattered. They were taking me seriously. Perhaps it was standard practice to win the loyalty of an impressionable source. And given the treats showered on me by the British it was a well-timed gesture. I began to make plans for another visit to Thailand, hopefully one that would be more relaxing.

My work for PET and the British was becoming more demanding, and more perilous. I needed cover stories. My cover, or 'legend', in Denmark came courtesy of a garrulous, dim-witted Danish Bosnian called Adnan Avdic, whom I knew from my extremist days. He had been held in jail before being acquitted in a terrorism case.[1]

One afternoon I picked him up on the outskirts of Copenhagen in a brand-new Toyota. It was rented by PET as part of the ruse but Adnan thought it was mine.

'Nice wheels, Murad! That must have cost you a packet,' he said. As we drove, our conversation soon turned to jihad.

'I have to drop something off so need to take a bit of a detour.'

His curiosity got the better of him, as I knew it would.

'What?'

'It's to help the cause. Don't tell anybody this.'

I paused and made a show of looking in every direction furtively.

'Open the glove compartment, but don't touch what you see because you'll leave fingerprints.'

He stared in amazement at a small bag of white powder.

'Wow – Murad – are you sure this is permissible?'

'I have a fatwa,' I replied.

Little did he know that it was a mixture of flour and crumbled candle wax.

I pulled up just before the meeting point.

'You need to get out and wait for me here,' I told him.

---

1 Avdic was arrested in 2005 in connection with a terror plot uncovered in Bosnia. A jury ruled there was sufficient evidence to convict him, but he was acquitted a few days later by a three-judge panel who disagreed.

A man in a brown bomber jacket was standing at the street corner. I handed him the bag and walked back to the car, knowing that Adnan would have seen the deal go down.

There was the glint of a smile on my senior handler Soren's face as he walked off in the other direction with the bag. He had apparently enjoyed his brief cameo as a street dealer.

In England MI5 also arranged a cover for me to allay any suspicions about the cash I was receiving: fully licensed Birmingham cab driver. Her Majesty's Government even bought me a Mercedes minivan with leather-trim seats.

I started work for an Alum Rock cab company owned by a Pakistani businessman. His son, Salim, whom I had first met in al-Muhajiroun meetings in Luton, was on MI5's radar screen. They hoped that if we worked together I would gain greater access to his British-Pakistani extremist contacts in the city. The security service was especially concerned about this demographic because several plots in the UK had involved young men of Pakistani descent, some of whom had received bomb-making training in al-Qaeda camps in their ancestral country.

But radicalized British-Pakistanis were proving hard for me to infiltrate. They tended to be wary of Muslims from other ethnic and national groups and were especially distrustful of converts. After trekking across the deserts of Yemen, driving my cab around Birmingham was exceptionally dull. Eventually I told MI5 taxi driving was not for me.

I did not adapt well to domestic life in Birmingham. Fadia had returned with me and we had moved into a council house on Watson Road, a drab street in Alum Rock. Our new digs could not have been more depressing, but it was the price of living my cover. Discarded needles and trash littered the street. Young gangs of British-Pakistanis roamed the area, sometimes getting into knife fights. Fadia complained that the rats were bigger than the cats. I was desperate to tell her that she deserved better and I could provide it; our diminished circumstances had put up a wall between us. But, for her safety and mine, I couldn't let her know the real reason why we were living there.

Fadia had no idea her return to Europe had been engineered by the intelligence services. PET had been true to their promise by providing her with a student visa to return to Denmark and she had then been provided with a five-year European residence permit at the British embassy in Copenhagen, courtesy of Her Majesty's Secret Service.

My lifeline was the mobile phone with which I communicated with my handlers. They alone knew my secret purpose. Klang and I spoke several times each day, running information and ideas past each other but always being careful with our language. My MI5 handlers called several times a week, usually to arrange meetings.

Even when things were slow I found it difficult to switch off. Often Fadia would have to ask the same question several times before I responded. My mind was elsewhere, thinking of the next email I needed to write or plotting ways I could enhance my jihadist network. I found it difficult even to fully focus on my kids on the weekends I had custody. The espionage business was all-consuming.

One evening Fadia and I sat down to watch the George Clooney movie *Syriana*, a thriller set in the Middle East. I was soon absorbed in the film, recognizing both the implausible parts and the efforts to re-create the tradecraft of espionage. But the sense of mistrust among some of its characters resonated. I was desperate to tell Fadia, to point to the screen and say, 'That's how I feel.' But I knew it was impossible.

Occasionally I took long drives deep into the British countryside. I'd put on a Metallica CD, turn up the volume and breathe deeply. Sometimes after a walk I would drop into a country pub for a pint of bitter and a chat with the regulars. It was unlikely that Muslims would hang out in such places. For a few precious minutes I just needed to drop the mask.

Not all the extremists in Birmingham were blowhards. I soon encountered one of the most volatile figures in the city, a British-Pakistani I knew only as Saheer. He was in his late twenties, muscular and always wearing a tracksuit. He was clean-shaven and good-looking with a buzz-cut hairstyle, but his eyes seemed to be on the lookout for trouble and his hands itching for a fight. He already had a criminal record, having gone inside for armed robbery while still a teenager, and had only recently been released.

I met Saheer through one of the most active extremists in Birmingham at a Moroccan cake shop in Alum Rock. Like a growing number of young Muslims, Saheer had been radicalized while in prison. Perhaps like others he also sought redemption. Saheer was a man of few words but had a craving for action. When I revealed I knew Awlaki and told him of my recent meeting with him in Yemen, he started opening up.

'Brother, we need to fight back against the *kuffar*,' he said, as we shared *meskouta*, a Moroccan yoghurt cake.

As we walked out into the evening drizzle, Saheer looked at me with intense almond eyes.

'Murad, I'd like to do a martyrdom operation, *Insha'Allah*.'

His words hung in the air. Had he really just said that? Was he testing me? I told myself to go slowly, let this play out. I would be neither dismissive nor overly eager to help. I tried to remember the advice of MI5's psychologist, Luke.

'Do you have any ideas? You know the Danish newspaper that drew the pictures of the Prophet Mohammed, peace be upon him. Do you know anything about its security?' he asked me.[2]

'I can try to find out,' I replied.

'Do you know how to get weapons in Denmark?' he asked.

'Oh, that can be done,' I said. I dropped in my background with the Bandidos.

'You must understand that what I want is to die in this attack. I want to get shot and I want to be killed "*fee sabeel Allah* [for the sake of Allah]",' he said.

Time to call Sunshine, I thought.

Sunshine worked with my senior MI5 handler, Andy, and had become my principal point of contact in the agency. Klang and the Danes had given her that name because she was irrepressibly cheerful. She was in her mid- to late twenties, clearly learning the trade but with an instinct that would carry her a long way. She also had a no-nonsense attitude.

---

2 The Danish newspaper in question was *Jyllands-Posten*, which had published controversial cartoons of the Prophet Mohammed in September 2005.

Klang had placed his hand on her leg once during an after-hours drink and she'd shouted so loudly that he recoiled like a scalded cat.

Sunshine might not be able to recite Latin poetry like Matt, but she was good at reading faces. She dyed her hair blonde and was pretty in a girl-next-door kind of way. Perhaps, I thought, she cultivated ordinariness because it set people at ease and led them to drop their guard.

'I need to set up a meeting,' I told her on the phone later that night.

'Roger that – eleven a.m.,' she said, hanging up the phone. She liked the military clichés.

The next morning I waited in the car park of a Sainsbury's supermarket on the outskirts of Birmingham, our rendezvous. I sat in my car and watched harried mothers deal with carts of shopping and rebellious kids.

My phone started buzzing.

'Walk to the far end of the car park. You'll see a red Volvo. Keep going. We'll pick you up.'

On cue a white van with a ventilation unit on its roof skidded to a stop beside me. Sunshine was there, with the trademark smile.

'Jump in the back.'

There were no windows in the back so I had no idea where we were going. Forty minutes later we arrived. It could have been round the corner for all I knew.

I heard a chain and then a mechanical grind – perhaps a garage door being raised. The driver, hidden from me, gunned the engine and we drove in. The door rattled down behind us.

'Clear!' I heard Sunshine say on her walkie-talkie up front. A man opened the door. It was Kevin, another of Andy's MI5 team. Kevin looked like he was in his twenties and might have been a presenter on one of those outdoor adventure shows, building fires out of dung and coaxing deadly snakes out of holes in trees. I would not have messed with him.

We seemed to be in a large warehouse – one of MI5's operations centres.

It looked like a printing press that had been turned into an architect's office. There were posters on the wall and rows of workshop tables lit by lamps hanging from the high ceiling. It was hardly high tech. There was an internet connection, and a few PCs, and that was about it.

In the corner was a small glass-walled office with chairs set around a table. Andy was waiting for me. Sunshine and Kevin let him take the lead. I told him about my encounter with Saheer.

'You need to keep talking to him,' Andy said, after hearing me out. It was the first of several debriefing sessions as Saheer's intent became clearer.

Saheer was extremely security-conscious. In many ways he was MI5's worst nightmare: a savvy career criminal who was morphing into a jihadi with a death wish. He only spoke to me about his plans when we were alone and outdoors. We used to take long walks in a park in Alum Rock. He insisted that I not carry my mobile, and each time we went out he patted me down for any devices.

'Just a precaution, brother,' he said.

'He's really dangerous, a total psycho,' I told Andy at my next debriefing. 'What the hell am I supposed to do? I'm the only one he's telling this stuff to.'

'Just keep talking to him,' Andy replied, with concern in his voice.

Given Saheer's intended target, I was not surprised to see my Danish handlers make an appearance.

'The Minister has been briefed on this,' Klang told me. 'The bosses really appreciate what you are doing.'

For once, Klang was being serious.

But as I saw it we still had a problem. There was no evidence beyond Saheer's less than coherent plan to take out the Danish newspaper, a plan that he had confided only to me and of which there was no record. There was certainly nothing to warrant his arrest or charges. It was all hearsay and I might be accused of entrapment. So I improvised, taking advantage of his doubts about raising money for the guns and planning.

'You know Sheikh Anwar agrees to the selling of drugs as long as we support the brothers for jihad,' I said to him during our next walk in the park. 'First of all you're destroying the *kuffar*, you're ruining their society. Secondly you're getting money you can send to the mujahideen.'

Saheer looked interested.

'And you get to keep a fifth of the proceeds yourself as war booty, *Inshallah.*'

'Murad, are you sure about this?' he said, his eyes widening.

'Yes. He gave me a fatwa,' I replied, knowing a similar story was now most likely circulating in extremist Danish circles if he should ever check.

My attempt to have Saheer return to the world of crime was not well received by Andy at MI5.

'We can't encourage people to commit crimes. What the hell were you thinking? You can't just do this sort of thing without checking with us,' he said.

'I was improvising – how else are we going to arrest this guy?' I replied.

Andy disappeared into the glass office with Kevin and Sunshine and made several phone calls.

When he came out his mood had brightened. He was still irritated, but seemed to recognize the opportunity.

'All right, all right, you said it so it's too late now. There's not much we can do about it.'

Not long afterwards, Saheer came calling – in a silver Lexus. Drugs money, I thought: he must be wanting to enjoy his last days on earth.

We reached the park. As we walked in the rain towards the duck pond, I realized that we must make for a strange sight.

'I've got hold of the money – can you make sure about the weapons,' he said.

I looked around as casually as I could to see if we were being followed. I knew MI5 were now trying to monitor his every step, but it just seemed to be me and him. The ducks were quacking urgently. It was surreal.

'Brother, let's go, just me and you, and do this mission. I need you to be there with me in Denmark.'

'I'm with you, brother,' I replied, feeling the words sounded less than convincing.

He embraced me. 'This is the best, Murad, the best. We get to be *shuhada* [martyrs]. There's nothing better than this, remember that.'

If anyone was looking at us at that moment, they might get the wrong impression.

'I know. This is paradise. We are mujahideen and this is what we fight for,' I replied, summoning all the conviction I could manage.

He wants me to die with him, I thought. How am I going to get out of this?

Klang was at the next debrief. He made clear the Danes wanted the plot stopped well before Saheer could get to Denmark.

'We'll kill him if he comes to Denmark. We'll shoot him.'

It was bravado. Danish law would not permit a summary execution.

'We've been following him,' Kevin from MI5 told me. 'He's selling drugs all right. But he isn't touching the stuff himself.'

'This is where you're going to have to trust us,' Andy said.

'I want to go to Denmark in two weeks,' Saheer told me at our next meeting. He asked me to reconnect with my underworld contacts there so that we could buy guns and ammunition.

The day of our departure loomed, but my handlers kept me in the dark.

I had travelled through the wilder reaches of Yemen and driven around with heavily armed fighters in Lebanon, but the idea of travelling to my homeland with this psychopath was giving me sleepless nights.

British police arrested Saheer a week before we were meant to travel, as he sold drugs on the streets of Birmingham. It was not his first offence so he received a lengthy prison sentence. The beauty of the operation was that even after he was jailed he never suspected I was working for intelligence. But even inside he appeared to exercise a chilling effect on other jihadis in Birmingham; none would dare talk about the mysterious Saheer, and I never found out his real name.

With Saheer safely behind bars, my handlers and I could plot my next trip to see Awlaki.

CHAPTER FIFTEEN

CLERICAL TERROR

Spring–Autumn 2008

In April 2008, I wrote an email to Anwar al-Awlaki, telling him I'd presently be making a short trip to Yemen.

The cleric soon replied and had a special request.

'Cheese and chocolates please:)'

I knew he liked pralines but I needed to get some guidance first: 'Sheikh, regarding the chocolate, is it permissible to eat it when it has got like alcohol flavour in it[?]'

The answer came back. 'No it is not allowed because even though all of the alchohol evaporates it is najasah [impure] and that najasah has mixed with the chocolate.'

The Holy Book had an answer for liqueur chocolates.

I assured him I would bring the non-alcoholic variety and added a little flattery.

'Went into a shop yesterday in Birmingham, the owner was listening to one of your lectures . . . he told me, that he only listen to your lectures, as he couldn't trust anyone else anymore hahahahaha Masha'Allah, I was laughing and so happy, the people here in uk and denmark, really loves you sheikh, you have done a great job and won their hearts, masha'Allah, may Allah reward you.'

On 13 May 2008 Fadia and I landed in Sana'a. Leaving the plane, I inhaled the warm moist air, happy to have escaped the chill dullness of Birmingham. Fadia too was pleased to be away from Alum Rock and looking forward to seeing her beloved uncle. She also knew I was an admirer of Awlaki and perhaps saw my relationship with him as a stabilizing influence after witnessing my crisis of conscience in Denmark.

Awlaki told us to come down to Aden to meet him. He had decamped to the southern port city from Ataq for a few weeks with his pregnant wife. We met them for lunch in a restaurant near the fish market. I embraced him at the entrance and handed him the chocolates.

He thanked me profusely.

'Our wives can eat separately. We'll order for them,' he said. It was standard procedure.

Fadia and Awlaki's wife disappeared into the 'family section'. She was six months pregnant by now.

Anwar and I were digging into grilled white fish when I almost choked. His wife had wandered brazenly into the men's section.

'Where's my fish?' she demanded, through her niqab.

Awlaki smiled knowingly at me.

Throughout lunch I kept the conversation away from his plans. I saw the encounter as a confidence-building measure. He seemed more relaxed than when he had emerged from prison. He was careful to be discreet, but not exactly in hiding. It seemed typical of the way Yemen worked: there were understandings, coded warnings, limits. In Aden, Anwar was being protected and housed by a wealthy businessman.

'Brother, I have been doing a lot of writing, a lot of thinking,' he offered, leaning back and looking across the very harbour where the USS *Cole* had been attacked.

That writing and thinking were coming to fruition. As the boiling summer approached, Awlaki recorded a brace of lectures for followers in the West.

In one, 'Battle of the Hearts and Minds', he railed against attempts by the US government to empower 'moderate' Islam.

The other, 'The Dust Will Never Settle Down', was given live over Paltalk, an online voice chat forum, and directly addressed the continuing cartoons controversy. Awlaki challenged Muslims the world over:

'How concerned are you? How concerned are we when it comes to the honor of the Rasool [the messenger], when it comes to the honor of Islam, when it comes to the book of Allah? How seriously do we take it?' he asked.

'We are not followers of Gandhi . . . [as] Ibn Taymiyah says it is mandatory to kill the one who curses the Messenger of Allah,' he said.

The cleric could not have chosen a more hot-button issue. A Swedish artist had poured fuel on the fire by depicting the Prophet as a dog. Awlaki's calmly articulated outrage struck a deep chord with extremists in the West. The talk was widely circulated online.

Anwar al-Awlaki had reached the Islamist stratosphere. And Western intelligence services were beginning to notice just how often his lectures were cropping up in terrorism trials in Europe and North America.[1]

For those seeking to contribute financially to the cause, looking for moral justification for their actions or the terrorists' equivalent of a changing-room pep-talk, Awlaki's online output had become essential reading. Awlaki could harness the power of ideas. But it was soon apparent that he wanted to do more to restore the honour of the Rasool.

In the early autumn of 2008, I was back in Birmingham, helping MI5 keep tabs on the burgeoning militant scene in England's second city, when Awlaki left a draft email in our shared account. After the customary greetings and praise to Allah, he got down to business. He wanted supplies for the mujahideen: solar panels, night-vision goggles, water purification equipment and more. And he wanted money. He suggested I collect funds from mosques in Europe and said $20,000 would be greatly appreciated. Awlaki was smart enough not to ask for anything that could be obviously used in combat, but was evidently aware of what al-Qaeda lacked in infrastructure. I wondered who had helped compile the shopping list. My handlers were surprised and alarmed by the request. Awlaki was then regarded by the more

---

1 Avid consumers of Awlaki's videos included the so-called Toronto 18, who plotted to launch attacks across Canada in 2006, and the British al-Qaeda cell that plotted to blow up transatlantic airliners the same year. Several of those who conspired to attack the Fort Dix military base in New Jersey in 2007 were also devotees of the cleric's sermons.

complacent analysts as a blowhard, and few if any of the intelligence officers I knew imagined him becoming more than a rhetorical outlet for jihad.

'Didn't I warn you he was dangerous?' I reminded Jed when we met to discuss the request.

Jed was clear about what needed to be done. Deliver some $5,000 in cash and several items of the equipment requested. My Danish handlers told me this had caused further friction between Big Brother and the British. Senior UK intelligence officials had baulked at such a large cash handover, nervous they would later be accused of funding terrorism should the media find out. Solar panels were all very well; cash (and hammocks) were not. MI6 made clear their limit would be £500.

Jed was intolerant of such finer points. At a meeting in Copenhagen which the British did not attend, he handed me the money in $100 notes.

'Just take it.'

Once the supplies were organized I contacted Awlaki by writing a draft email.

'I have gifts.'

On 23 October 2008 Fadia and I waited in line at customs and immigration at Sana'a airport. I was apprehensive. Inside my large suitcase, which was sealed with a rigid, heavy-duty plastic strap, was a sports bag. And inside the bag were the small solar panels, night-vision goggles, portable water purification units and a laptop.

Try to sound confident, I thought, as I approached the customs desk and a weathered middle-aged man perspiring through his worn uniform. He looked listless in the stifling heat, dealing with another plane-load of Yemenis returning with whatever goods they could afford to bring back from wealthier places.

Yemeni customs officials are not renowned for their dedication or perceptiveness. We had hoped that even if the equipment was discovered it would not be regarded as suspicious. I was about to find out.

'Open it,' the official said – pointing at the plastic belt.

'I'm going to need a knife or something,' I told him in Arabic.

Annoyed to have to get off his chair he shuffled off to a side room. I tried hard to remain nonchalant.

The protocol was for me to stonewall. Jed's orders were simple.

'On no account tell them you are working for Western intelligence. If that makes you look like you're working for the bad guys then so be it. Leave it to us to sort out through diplomatic channels.'

The customs man returned empty-handed.

'Go,' he said.

It was a lucky break and, I hoped, an omen for the mission.

The Nairobi operation the previous year had shown that al-Qaeda affiliates always wanted more equipment, things that were difficult to obtain locally and expensive. My supplying that equipment was a promising way to find out more about their members and plans. By now, AQAP had become the most effective of all al-Qaeda's franchises. The month before we arrived with supplies for Awlaki, it had carried out a coordinated gun and car attack on the US embassy in Sana'a. Ten Yemenis had been killed. The attack had induced a state of high anxiety among Yemen's security services.

I decided to lie low for a few days before contacting Awlaki. I would have to take Fadia with me. Driving down solo into Yemen's southern badlands alone as a white European was not an option. I had told her I was taking supplies to Anwar and left her with the impression that they were to help his pastoral work.

'And then on the way back, why don't we see your relatives in Taiz?' I said.

She was quietly pleased that I wanted to see her family.

Less than a week after we arrived, I received a text message from Awlaki. He told me to set out south towards Aden and to text him once we got to the port city so that he could provide further directions. He was more conscious of security than before and would only specify the meeting place once I was through the final checkpoint. And he didn't want to use the phone because he was concerned that American voice recognition software might identify him. He clearly saw himself as more of a target than the Americans did.

We set off shortly after dawn. As we navigated the checkpoints on the road out of Sana'a I was nervous about the equipment hidden in the trunk. Now we were heading towards areas where al-Qaeda was active, the discovery of night-vision goggles by some over-zealous police officer would require some explaining.

The journey south towards Taiz is dramatic. The road descends from the Sana'a plateau for a while until the Yemeni Highlands come into view. October marks the end of the rainy season in Taiz, and the mountains were shrouded in morning mist.

We found lodgings that evening in Aden, and I texted Awlaki again. He told me to take the road up the coast. We were essentially driving an exaggerated U-shaped route to avoid the more serious checkpoints. Fadia accepted the convoluted journey as a typically Yemeni inconvenience. If we were stopped and questioned, she would explain that we were going to see friends in Ataq. But for some reason – perhaps because Aden was more secular than Sana'a – vehicles tended to get less scrutiny along the coast road.

The next morning we passed through lush oases close to the ocean. Camels loped beside the road, telegraph poles bent by the onshore wind stood like matchsticks against the emptiness of the coastal plain. My final instructions were to leave the coast and climb towards the mountains. Just one look at the impenetrable ranges ahead was evidence enough of why al-Qaeda had made this area home.

The rendezvous point was near an isolated hamlet in Shabwa province. Seas of boulder-strewn shale stretched towards the horizon, to be met by steep, craggy mountains. Even at the end of October, the midday heat would generate a rippling haze. I marvelled at the survival of the few plants and bushes that dotted the lunar landscape.

I was especially nervous around a town called Lawdar, which had seen tribal violence and abductions, and was – even by Yemeni standards – an area where the word of the central government had little impact.

After several hours in the car, Fadia and I finally approached the rendezvous point in a flat, parched valley surrounded by mountains. There was an eerie beauty in the desolate landscape.

I was relieved to see the concrete structure that Anwar had told me to look for. A dusty vehicle with a canvas roof was parked a short distance away. Inside was Anwar with a young bodyguard who had a thick pitch-black beard and was clutching a Kalashnikov. I parked the car, leaving Fadia inside, and walked up to them. The cleric got out and embraced me.

'*As salaam aleikum akhi* [brother], finally!' he said. 'This is my nephew, Saddam,' he added.

Anwar was wearing a green military camouflage jacket, bin Laden style, over his robe. He had a Yemeni ceremonial dagger and a revolver in his belt and a Kalashnikov was slung over his shoulder.

I tried not to look surprised. The preacher had become a fighter.

I fetched the sports bag with the supplies: the laptop, night-vision goggles, headlamps, matches, sandals for the mujahideen and solar panels, and we walked to the shade of a solitary tree beside the road. It was the first tree I had seen for many miles. But it provided more than shade. Al-Qaeda leaders had begun instructing fighters to use the shelter of trees in case drones, now being used by the US in Pakistan's tribal areas, should also be deployed to Yemen.

British agents had asked me to purchase the solar panels at a Maplin's electronics store and had shown me how they worked. The laptop had a backstory to it. At the MI5 warehouse in Birmingham a technician had provided me with the computer and told me that some of the components had been switched for identical but 'modified' parts. Even experts would not find the programs they had installed. I assumed their modifications were designed to locate Awlaki through the laptop's WiFi signal as well as upload data if he ever connected to the internet.

But at the final meeting before the mission, my Danish handlers told me they were exchanging the British laptop for one supplied by the Americans. Now that I had told the CIA of Awlaki's 'operational status' tracking him down had become a priority for the Americans. Big Brother was pulling rank.

I handed Awlaki the laptop and the other equipment and explained how the solar panels functioned. I also gave him the $5,000.

He put it in his breast pocket without uttering a word. He looked disappointed I had not brought more. But it somehow seemed judicious not to provide his every need all at once. After all, I was a struggling jihadi.

'*Alhamdulillah*, that's all I could raise so far, brother,' I told him.

After fifteen minutes sitting under the shade of the tree by the roadside, I returned to the car.

'Anwar says we should eat,' I told Fadia. 'Come, follow us.' We walked towards the building nearby. It was a restaurant, but only half built, and I wondered how it stayed upright.

Two men in the doorway looked suspiciously at my red hair and beard. This was bandit territory. Even Yemenis not from the area were kidnapped for ransom. But we were under Awlaki's protection and therefore safe. Or so I hoped.

The owner greeted Awlaki warmly and asked his wife to escort Fadia to the women's section. He then took the cleric and me up to the roof, where we sat on the concrete and ate platters of lamb and rice on tin plates. A merciful breeze had begun to drift through the valley. When Awlaki finished eating he tapped on the wad of dollars in his breast pocket, and looked me straight in the eye.

'The money from the brothers – can it be used to buy weapons?' he asked.

For a fraction of a second, I considered how to reply.

'You can buy anything you like with this money.'

We did not stay long. I wanted to reach the coast again before dusk. Even then we would have a long, arduous trek to Taiz and Fadia's relatives. So immediately after we finished eating, I told Awlaki we had to go. He seemed disappointed. Although we would stay in touch, I would not see him again for nearly a year.

As the restaurant disappeared in a haze of dust and heat behind us, I handed Fadia my phone.

'Could you shoot some video of the scenery? It's so spectacular and I doubt we will ever see this part of Yemen again.'

But I had other reasons for wanting the footage. I knew Jed would be interested to see the area where I had met the Sheikh. It might also give him and his colleagues pause, I thought. Winning a war in this sort of territory would not come easily.

We weaved through the ravines, the hairpin bends apparently never-ending. At the top of the climb a vast barren panorama opened up below us, like a lunar sea, and we began driving downhill towards the sea.[2]

---

2 I have a saved copy of this video and dozens of pictures during the journey.

Two weeks later I was in a luxurious Bangkok hotel suite being debriefed by my intelligence handlers. Fadia and I had flown in for our CIA-sponsored honeymoon, although I led her to believe that I'd been saving some money from construction and driving jobs to pay for the trip.

I had slipped away to meet my handlers on the pretence that I wanted to do some shopping.

I recounted every detail of the meeting in Shabwa and our conversation about the money.

'You just passed the test, brother,' Jed told me. 'He was testing you to see if you were genuine. If you were working for an intelligence agency, you'd have to say no, this is for food or something like that.'

Jed handed me an envelope with a $6,000 bonus in cash after the meeting. 'This is for a helluva good job – enjoy your honeymoon,' he told me. He was not so subtly delivering a message: when it came down to choosing between the CIA and the British, it literally paid to be their guy.

Awlaki never tested me again.

CHAPTER SIXTEEN

KILLING MR JOHN

Autumn 2008–Spring 2009

Through 2008 I kept in contact via draft emails with Ahmed Abdulkadir Warsame, the stringy Somali youth I had first met in Birmingham. What he lacked in ability he had made up for in dedication. He was now one of al-Shabaab's senior operatives, his CV no doubt burnished by my connecting him with Awlaki.

To keep the communications going MI5 authorized my sending the first in a series of cash transfers to Warsame via Dahabshiil, an African money transfer company with a branch in Birmingham.[1] In another email he requested I supply him with chemical suits and rubber gloves so al-Shabaab could experiment with explosives. I purchased this equipment with funds from the British but was never greenlighted to deliver it.

During the second week of November – just before my delayed honeymoon in Thailand – I returned to Nairobi to deliver new supplies Warsame had requested. He wanted another laptop and some cash. My Western intelligence handlers had welcomed the opportunity for me to enhance my credentials with the group, and had no doubt planted another tracking device in the laptop they supplied me.

---

1 I have receipts for the Dahabshiil transfers made to Warsame: $100 in March 2008, $200 in July 2008, $400 in September 2008, $138 in January 2009 and $500 in January 2010.

Warsame sent a Kenyan al-Shabaab operative who had lived in Norway to meet me. He called himself Ikrimah al-Muhajir.[2]

'You'll recognize him because of his long hair,' Warsame had told me.

We met at a Somali restaurant in Nairobi. He walked in with a confident stride and sat down at the corner booth I had chosen. Ikrimah did indeed have long, flowing locks and from that day my nickname for him was 'Long Hair'. Trailing behind him was his driver, Mohammed, a Kenyan of Somali ethnicity.

Ikrimah was built like one of Kenya's long-distance runners, and had a trimmed beard and gleaming white teeth. He was of Somali and Yemeni descent – on his father's side he belonged to the Ansi tribe in Yemen. He would later start changing his appearance to evade detection, at one point wearing a thick Saddam Hussein-style moustache.

We bonded over our shared Scandinavian background. He spoke Norwegian, as well as English, French, Arabic, Somali and Swahili. He had been brought up in Kenya and his family were middle class. Ikrimah spent his early years in Mombasa on the Indian Ocean coast, before the family moved to Nairobi. He told me he had moved to Norway four years previously to look for work and had sought refugee status.

'They never let me settle there,' he said. 'I never really felt accepted. I began to spend more time in the mosque.'

I found Ikrimah cheerful and sharp – smarter than Warsame, who had sent him. There was an intense ambition about him and an unshakable commitment to Holy War. Over goat meat and *canjeero* – a Somali-style pancake bread – he revealed he had been in Mogadishu, fighting for the Islamic Courts Union, when Ethiopian troops invaded in 2006.

'Do you know a Danish convert called Ali?' he asked me.

'Of course!' I exclaimed. 'He called me during the fighting. He cut the head off one of the Somali *kuffar*.'

'*Subhan'Allah*,' Ikrimah replied, incredulous. 'I was with him: I filmed this blessed act on my phone.' He went on to cheerfully describe

2 Al-Muhajir means 'the foreigner' in Arabic. His real name was Mohamed Abdikadir Mohamed.

the execution: how Ali had kicked the spy's legs from under him, and then pinned him down as he struggled for life, and slowly sawn off his head.

After Ethiopian forces finally expelled the Islamic Courts Union from the capital and much of central Somalia, Ikrimah said he had returned to Norway but failed to gain political asylum. He had spent about a year in London and then in 2008 returned to East Africa. Now he was working as a messenger for Warsame and other Shabaab leaders, splitting his time between Somalia and Kenya.

I feared he might mention the arrests in Nairobi that had followed the handover at the Intercontinental Hotel the previous year. But he didn't and it seemed no one in al-Shabaab had made the link. I had to remind myself to be careful, to be sure my handlers never put me in a situation where someone might begin to turn apparent coincidences into related events.

After dinner Ikrimah picked up the laptop for Warsame from my hotel room.

For the next several days I travelled around Nairobi with Ikrimah in Mohammed's white Toyota estate. Mohammed was irrepressibly cheerful and spoke Swahili and a decent smattering of English. He lived in the Eastleigh district of Nairobi and like me moonlighted as a taxi driver, but much of his time was spent helping al-Shabaab with their logistics. If you needed someone to drive you to a secret rendezvous in Nairobi, or into Somalia, Mohammed was your man. He also housed Shabaab operatives.

As we hurtled through the chaotic traffic of Nairobi, Mohammed made elaborate manoeuvres to make sure we were not being followed. He'd accelerate quickly when the traffic light went green, then a mile later screech to a halt, and take a random turn. Sometimes he ran red lights to put distance between him and the cars behind.

We stopped off at some of Ikrimah's favourite haunts in Nairobi, including some of its shopping malls. It was a city he knew very well; I could see how useful he would be to al-Shabaab.

My time with Ikrimah fascinated and alarmed my handlers during my debriefing in Bangkok. He was not on their radar, but was evidence of al-Shabaab's growing reach and support network in Kenya. Western intelligence was already stretched trying to deal with al-Qaeda as it metastasized, as well as home-grown radical cells. Now al-Shabaab and its legion of foreign followers had joined the club.

In the spring of 2009, Warsame, now in command of hundreds of Shabaab fighters, asked for more equipment, but made the mistake of telling me – via a saved draft email – that the equipment was for a Kenyan called 'Mr John'. He said once I sent word I was in Nairobi he would arrange for me to be smuggled across the border into Somalia to deliver the equipment and meet 'Mr John'.

'Mr John', it transpired, was Saleh Ali Nabhan – an individual of great interest to Western intelligence. Even though he was only in his late twenties, Nabhan was suspected of involvement in the bombing of the US embassy in Nairobi in 1998, as well as a bomb attack on a resort in Mombasa in 2002, and on the same day a failed missile attack on an Israeli airliner taking off from Mombasa's airport. He was now regarded as al-Qaeda's most dangerous operative in East Africa – and Warsame and Ikrimah were his protégés.

Al-Shabaab might espouse a medieval view of the world and oppose television and sport, but Nabhan apparently needed a BlackBerry and a laptop. (It is a strange fact of Somali life that amid all the anarchy it had a viable mobile-phone network.)

Jed, now my chief point of contact in the CIA, asked me to come to the Hotel Ascot in Copenhagen to discuss the mission they had in mind.

Among the Danes at the meeting was a new agent, Anders. Ginger-haired, tall and burly, Anders was as informal as his colleagues, but his intelligence and background set him apart. He had studied Arabic in Syria and Lebanon, and understood the mindset of the region. He had served in the military and then studied the rise of Islamist militancy. I took to him immediately, because alone among my handlers he had worked hard to understand what made al-Qaeda and its sympathizers tick. He was principally an analyst, which led the others to tease him as a bookish nerd. They also called him 'the puppy' because of his relative youth. But he did his homework and provided me with invaluable details about al-Shabaab's structure and leading lights.

Jed was even more intense than usual. He scented blood: the chance to take out one of al-Qaeda's most dangerous. He slid a BlackBerry and laptop to me across the conference table in the penthouse suite. 'This is for Mr Nahban with our compliments,' he said.

I had no doubt the CIA had played around with the hardware. I was learning that mobile phones and laptops have a unique digital signature that allows their location to be pinpointed. Even a phone not being used to make calls can be located, because – when connected to a power source – it continuously transmits a weak signal to seek out the nearest base station. The same principle applies to WiFi-enabled laptops, which seek an internet connection.

By the time Nabhan came into our sights, advances in technology were already making it easier for security services. Manufacturers had started rolling out GPS-enabled phones, making it possible for security services to track targets even more precisely. The beauty for the agencies was that even if a phone was turned on in an area completely off the grid, or a laptop was powered up hundreds of miles from the nearest WiFi-hotspot, spy satellites could still lock on to the signal.

Jed said he would fly to Nairobi and link up with CIA agents there to manage the operation. He explained the protocol for getting in touch with him.

'You'll need to take a bunch of jabs for Somalia,' he said with his laconic drawl.

'Malaria will be the least of my worries,' I laughed.

Before I departed, PET ran some weapons training at the military firing range in Jægerspris on the northern shore of Zealand. A short, stocky former special-forces soldier taught me to fire a Kalashnikov. Klang and Trailer looked on as I learned to fire at fixed and moving targets. The power of the weapon was overwhelming, but gradually my accuracy improved. I had carried a handgun during my Bandidos days, done target practice at Dammaj and had a Kalashnikov thrust into my hands in Tripoli, but this was my first real training in handling and firing a weapon. It was a humbling but invaluable experience.

It was pouring with rain when I flew into Nairobi on 12 May 2009.

'It's been like this for a week now,' the cab driver told me on the drive from the airport. I booked into the Jamia Hotel, a modest travellers' hostel squeezed into a shabby shopping mall near Nairobi's largest mosque. It was just the sort of place that an international jihadi might pick to stay under the radar.

The rains persisted, sheets of steamy tropical water cascading from the sky.

I sent an email to Warsame to tell him I had arrived. A day later he replied: 'Bad news: border closed because of flooding: working on new plan.' The few roads across the Kenya–Somali border were not in the best repair.

My handlers were across town at the Holiday Inn. We met in a private room on the ground floor overlooking a lush tropical garden. Only a lazy ceiling fan provided relief from the steamy humidity. Jed was clearly not enjoying the monsoon conditions, and even the ever cool Klang looked overheated. Perspiration glistened on his brow and he dabbed his forehead with a monogrammed handkerchief. Despite his discomfort Klang could not help but steal furtive glances at his MI6 counterpart. Emma seemed unaffected by the heat. She was wearing a green safari shirt and beige shorts which showed off her long tanned legs.

She turned to me.

'Morten: as you seem to have a bit of spare time on your hands, we'd like you to do something for us. There's somebody in the Eastleigh district that we'd rather like you to meet.'

She started explaining the mission.

Jed exploded. 'You Brits always fucking do this,' he shouted. His eyes were bulging. He threw his papers and stormed out, slamming the door. The room went silent. Klang and I exchanged looks.

Through the window I could see Jed light a cigarette and pace around in his cowboy boots.

After he finished he came back into the room.

'All right, let's continue,' he said.

Emma said nothing – I had to admire her cool. I guessed Jed was furious because the CIA had funded this mission and he felt the British were trying to take advantage. An intelligence coup that could advance his career seemed to be slipping from his grasp.

The next day another email came in from Warsame. 'New Plan: Longhair will come to you tomorrow.'

It was a risky enterprise for Ikrimah, who may by now have felt that the Kenyan security services were aware of him. When he came to my room at the Jamia, it was clear we would not be having dinner together again.

'I can't hang around, brother,' he told me. I handed over the phone and computer; he checked them out and looked pleased. This Murad delivers, he seemed to be thinking.

Before he left, he mentioned other equipment al-Shabaab wanted: model aeroplanes with live transmission cameras for surveillance and remote-controlled model cars to which they could attach explosives to attack government checkpoints. I resisted the temptation to raise an eyebrow and promised to look into the possibilities. He hurried away.

A week later I received a coded email from Warsame, which said very simply: 'Mr John says thanks.'

On 14 September, about three months after the equipment was delivered, Nabhan was travelling along the coastal road that linked Mogadishu with al-Shabaab's heartland in the south of Somalia. Four dots appeared on the horizon. They were US assault helicopters. Unnoticed by Nabhan, they raced towards the coast above the waters of the Indian Ocean. As they crossed the sandy coastline, a volley of rockets destroyed the two-car convoy. US Navy SEALs descended from the helicopters and dragged the bodies out of the cars to try to identify them. They later positively identified Nabhan. President Obama, who had authorized the kill mission, was immediately notified. The Americans buried Nabhan's body at sea.

The Danes later told me my equipment had allowed the SEALs to zero in on their target.[3]

---

3 Klang, Trailer and Soren were later honoured at a ceremony in Washington DC for their role in the mission that led to the successful targeting of Nabhan. Klang told me each of them had received gold coins from the Americans. He said the equipment had indeed allowed the Navy SEALs to zero in on their target. I neither requested nor was offered any reward for helping track down Nabhan.

A week later, I received an email from Ikrimah. 'Mr John was killed in a US helicopter attack,' it said flatly. My other al-Shabaab contact, Ahmed Abdulkadir Warsame, told me that Nabhan's entourage suspected the Americans had located him by tracking the BlackBerry and computer. He said the group blamed a Somali courier used by Ikrimah to deliver them. Al-Shabaab believed the courier was in Kenya and was trying to track him down and eliminate him.

My connection to Awlaki seemed to put me beyond suspicion.

CHAPTER SEVENTEEN
MUJAHIDEEN SECRETS

Autumn 2009

As Saleh Ali Nabhan's body was being lowered into the Indian Ocean, I was preparing to reconnect with Awlaki – a man the Americans had been less successful in tracking. Nearly a year had passed since I had taken him supplies deep in Shabwa province. We had remained in regular touch via our shared draft email folder, but he wanted to meet, and Western intelligence very much wanted me to meet him.

Once again I had to follow his drip-by-drip directions into Shabwa, for the encounter in the compound of the tribal leader Abdullah Mehdar which begins this story. Not only had I found Awlaki (when the CIA seemed to have no idea where he was) but I gained a much clearer idea of his evolution from intellectual guide to organizational brain. Western intelligence agencies were struggling to get a handle on the strength and intentions of AQAP (al-Qaeda in Yemen's new name after an influx of Saudi fighters) – and on what specific role Awlaki might be playing. Drones could show pick-ups moving, camps and compounds – but not who was in them. 'Humint' – raw, first-hand reporting from ground level – was precious.

My meeting with Awlaki that September night provided me with not only a window into his evolution from thinker into planner, but also some hard evidence of that transition.

'I need to show you something,' he said – reaching for his laptop and a thumb drive as we sat together after dinner. 'This is how we need to communicate from now on.'

The thumb drive had encryption software called – appropriately – 'Mujahideen Secrets 2.0'. Awlaki had already begun using it in his contacts with followers in the West and it was based on a 256-bit key 'advanced encryption standard' algorithm. He believed our draft inbox method was no longer secure.[1]

I was fascinated as he demonstrated the software. The programmers had created a few flourishes – an image of an AK-47 flashed up with a muzzle in the shape of a key as the software loaded.

I began taking notes.

'You can find the software online. Never download the program to your hard drive and never load it when you are connected to the internet,' he told me. He explained that authentic copies of the software had a particular digital fingerprint displayed in a pixilated pattern on the screen which I would need to check.

'To communicate with me you need to create a private key,' he said, showing me how to generate it. The private key was in essence a unique secret digital code which I could use to lock and unlock messages sent to me, protected by a personal password and saved inside the program on the thumb drive. It seemed that Awlaki had delivered this tutorial before.

'Now you need to create a public key,' he said, showing me how to navigate the program. 'We can exchange our public keys through email and then start sending each other encrypted communications. When you receive an encrypted email click on the text and copy it, then open up the program. The software will prompt you to enter both our public keys and the password for your private key. Then paste the text into the program and hit decrypt.'

---

1 Awlaki reiterated his concern over the draft message technique in a February 2010 encrypted email to me: 'some brs have advised me that the draft system is suspicious because the enemy know that the brs use it.' In the same email he also revealed that he was not now opening emails himself. He had presumably switched to using a courier to open and send emails for him.

I was amazed how a random assortment of letters, numbers and symbols turned within fifteen seconds into clear prose. To encrypt messages I would carry out the same steps in reverse. It was possible to encode just about any file using this method, including images and video. Anwar told me to send the actual scrambled message via an anonymous email account, but I found out later that an encoded message could equally be copied on to a thumb drive.

'We believe this method to be secure but obviously be cautious what you say on it all the same,' he said.

Awlaki had become very aware of security. As I was about to retire, exhausted at the end of a nerve-wracking day, he stopped me.

'There's one other thing. You know Mohammed Usman?'

'Yes,' I said. 'He stayed with us in Sana'a for a while.'

'He came down here – he said he was suspicious of you.'

'Really?'

I was stunned, and anxious.

'Yes, he said he suspected you were working for British intelligence. Of course, he had nothing to back up such a ridiculous accusation. I thought he was a strange guy.'

'When was he here?' I asked.

'A few days ago. I don't know where he went.'

'Well, he won't be staying with us again,' I laughed – trying to make light of an awkward moment. Awlaki seemed to be studying my expression intently.

I had met Usman by accident, or so I had thought. On my way to Yemen from Europe, I had been politely but firmly detained by two security officers at Dubai airport and taken to a detention room. My retinas were scanned, I was fingerprinted and held for eight hours. There were few questions, and only a cursory check of my documents and belongings. Before dawn the following morning, bleary-eyed and irritable, I was escorted to the gate of the Yemenia flight to Sana'a. It was half empty, but I was given a seat next to a man in his thirties who looked as if he were Pakistani.

Halfway through the flight he introduced himself as Mohammed Usman; he was from Leyton in East London. He knew some of the 'brothers' in Luton and wanted to meet some like-minded radicals in Yemen. But he had no entrance visa. Would that be a problem?

I suggested that he tell the Yemenis that he had come for a wedding. It had worked before – and it worked for him. I offered him a place to stay for a few nights and he began asking about Awlaki; he wanted to meet him. I had not even told him that I knew the cleric, but replied cautiously that it might be possible.

'But how do I know you are not a spy?' Usman asked.

He was smiling but there was an intent in his question that I found troubling.

'I could ask the same about you,' I retorted.

Despite my misgivings I had connected him with some jihadist contacts and through them he had reached Shabwa – and Awlaki, only to repay my hospitality with scurrilous allegations.

I replayed in my mind time and again the way Awlaki had raised the issue and then dismissed it. I was as sure as I could be that he gave Usman's claims no credence, and on the drive back to Sana'a I began to think more optimistically about what the trip had achieved, and especially about how the CIA would salivate over the Mujahideen Secrets software.

As Fadia dozed beside me, I sent the briefest text message to Klang. 'Fucking good,' it read.

As soon as I landed in London the following day, I was summoned to a debriefing. Andy and Kevin were there from MI5, Jed from the CIA, and two Danish agents. The British Foreign Intelligence Service, MI6, was represented by Emma.

I recounted every detail of the journey and meeting – the roads, the terrain, Anwar's demeanour and security. And I showed them the encryption software as an encore.

As a thank you for my efforts, the British had arranged for me to go on a bushcraft outdoors course in East Sussex. It was run by Woodlore, the company owned by Ray Mears, a survival expert who had turned bushcraft into a television series and a successful business.[2]

---

2 I later met Mears on a course that I signed up for in the Arctic Circle. He never knew of my work for the intelligence services.

As we sat around the campfire, exchanging introductions, I found out that the dozen or so participants were bankers, lawyers and accountants from high-profile firms in London. They described their day jobs with smug satisfaction.

'So what line of work are you in?' the instructor asked me when it was my turn.

'I'm a taxi driver in Birmingham,' I replied.

I caught some condescending glances. If only they knew that earlier that week I had been in a remote corner of Yemen on behalf of Western intelligence.

No sooner had I left the Sussex countryside than I was asked to a meeting in Copenhagen. Jed showed me satellite images of the village where I had met Anwar and Abdullah Mehdar. He asked me to pinpoint the compound where I had stayed. There were more images from a different angle and then a third.

I could clearly make out the compound and its high walls and was quietly astonished that a satellite photograph could provide such fine resolution.

'That is definitely the place,' I said.

'Thank you,' said Jed – his glacial eyes betraying no satisfaction but the smirk at the corner of his mouth directed at the British contingent.

I detected a growing tension between the Americans and the British, who had very different priorities for me. I began to wonder whether Usman had been an MI6 plant. Perhaps they wanted to sow confusion among Awlaki and the AQAP leadership. Perhaps they were testing my loyalties; perhaps they wanted their own man close to the action – rather than acquiesce to Jed and all his money as ringmaster? The spy business was all about 'perhaps'.

At the end of the meeting I took Emma aside and told her about the mysterious Usman.

'That's very interesting,' she said and asked a few more questions about him.

I tried to read her expression. She had been well trained.

'Come on – I know he's working for you. Don't play this game with me,' I said.

'No – you're mistaken, Morten. He's not.'

Perhaps it was fatigue or a budding paranoia that inevitably fed off this double life. I would never know for sure because Usman never resurfaced. But the incident made me edgy. I had always enjoyed a good relationship with my British handlers, but was apprehensive that they might be using me to develop their own exclusive sources.

My anxiety was fed by another episode when I returned home to Birmingham. As I climbed into my venerable Jaguar one morning, I noticed that the panels above the glove compartment had come loose. I thought they'd been tampered with and a bug had been hidden. I furiously ripped out the panels but found nothing.

I told Sunshine that I needed a meeting with the MI5 station chief in Birmingham. We met at a rundown local hotel, in a room which reeked of stale cigarette smoke. He looked like a middle-aged football hooligan.

He lit up a cigarette while he heard me out, and then took a long drag before responding.

'Morten, we trust you – we wouldn't do something like that.'

'Do you think I'm stupid?' I replied.

'I swear on my son's life.'

I doubted he even had a son, but didn't press the point further. From that point on I presumed my car, my phone and my home were bugged by MI5.

Perhaps the pressures were beginning to get to me. By now I realized that loyalty and trust were not exactly overflowing in this business; no one got results by fair play. I might be discarded or betrayed at any moment as priorities shifted and competition intensified. For my handlers, the first rule of the game seemed ruthlessly simple: the ends always justified the means.

Even if they were not playing me, maybe one of the agencies would get careless, or I would slip up – and be unmasked by the groups I had infiltrated. The first Nairobi mission had made it all seem so easy.

I had no one to confide in, no one to test my suspicions. Fadia still knew nothing, and as the deceit went on it became impossible to introduce her to this dark world. My mother knew vaguely what I was doing but had never been a sympathetic shoulder. The loneliness that came with being an agent began to gnaw at me.

In the autumn of 2009, the CIA was concerned by Awlaki's evolving role, but it was an event in Texas that transformed a figure of growing interest into a target of urgent necessity.

At 1.30 p.m. on 5 November, a 39-year-old US army major named Nidal Hasan entered the sprawling Fort Hood base, some sixty miles from Austin. A psychiatrist, Hasan was assigned to the Soldier Readiness Processing Center, where troops received medical evaluation before and after deployment.

Hasan was armed with an FN Five-seven pistol, a powerful handgun which he had fitted with two laser sights. In the space of a few minutes he shot dead thirteen people and injured thirty more. Some witnesses said they heard him exclaim: '*Allahu Akbar*' as he began shooting. There was so much blood at the scene that the first responders kept slipping as they tried to attend the wounded.

In Birmingham it was late evening when the news networks began reporting the story. I was at home with Fadia when I stumbled across the breathless breaking coverage. To begin with I had no idea there was some terrorist motive. When I heard the name of the suspect late that night, I sat up.

Hasan apparently picked out personnel in uniform during his brief rampage, which ended when he was shot and wounded outside the centre. As he was taken into military custody, an urgent investigation began into his background and contacts. But even before the horrendous carnage of that day, the FBI knew Hasan had been exchanging emails with Anwar al-Awlaki.

Between December 2008 and June 2009, Hasan had written some twenty emails to Awlaki – focusing on whether it was permissible for a Muslim to serve in a foreign army and the conditions for jihad. He had been troubled and radicalized by the accounts of combat he heard from soldiers who had returned from Iraq and Afghanistan. He was clearly in awe of the cleric, whom he had heard preach at the mosque in Falls Church, Virginia, in 2001.

In one email he said he could not wait to join Awlaki in the afterlife, where they could talk over non-alcoholic wine. Two FBI Task Forces had reviewed the intercepted emails and concluded there were no grounds for action against Hasan, because the communications were seen as within the scope of an army psychiatrist's legitimate area of interest and research.

By the morning of 6 November 2009, those communications were seen in a very different light. Federal agencies began a rushed review of communications that other Americans might have had with Awlaki, trawling through databases of intercepts.

I was not surprised that eventually someone in direct contact with Awlaki had committed an act of terror. That likelihood had increased as the cleric's views had become more incendiary. And Awlaki was quick to celebrate Hasan's attack. Within four days of Fort Hood, the cleric wrote on his website: 'Nidal Hasan is a hero. He is a man of conscience who could not bear living the contradiction of being a Muslim and serving in an army that is fighting against his own people.

'The US is leading the war against terrorism, which in reality is a war against Islam. Its army is directly invading two Muslim countries and indirectly occupying the rest through its stooges,' Awlaki added. And he encouraged other Muslims in America to follow Hasan's example.

'The heroic act of brother Nidal also shows the dilemma of the Muslim-American community. Increasingly they are being cornered into taking stances that would either make them betray Islam or betray their nation.'

It was an uncompromising clarion call to Muslims living in the West, urging them to violence.

I had seen at first hand Awlaki's hold over his followers in the West. In March that year I had organized a secret fundraising call via Skype with a group of British-Pakistani supporters in Rochdale. Among them were several doctors eager to contribute to jihad. They listened spellbound to Awlaki's assured answers on a variety of religious topics. MI5 had given its blessing to the event to bolster my credentials in militant circles, on the condition no funds raised reached the cleric.

I still have a recording of the event. Awlaki was as adept at fundraising as any American politician:

'The enemy is oppressing the Muslims. It becomes important for every brother and sister who knows the *Haq* [truth] to act upon it . . . if Allah has blessed you with wealth then you should support the Islamic causes, whether we are talking about Somalia, Afghanistan or Iraq . . . and not just sit on the sidelines and watch.

'When it comes to Yemen because it's not on the news, it's being forgotten and therefore I would encourage every brother who has the capability to assist.'

But now – in lionizing Nidal Hasan – Awlaki must have known that he was crossing a Rubicon. I suspected it would be a matter of hours before I was called to another meeting. I was looking forward to a weekend with my children, but would have to bow to the inevitable.

I told Fadia I might need to go to Denmark.

'My mum's not so well,' I said, at a loss for something more original.

Jed was a bundle of nervous energy when I arrived at the designated Copenhagen hotel.

'It's time to take Awlaki out,' he said bluntly.

'You mean to arrest him?' I asked, knowing otherwise.

'Nah, I don't think so.'

The CIA wanted to use the information I had gleaned to target the man who had both sanctioned and glorified an act of terrorism against American citizens. The gloves had come off.

I was not the only route to the cleric; other intelligence sources were being developed, and the Yemeni government was being heavily pressured into cooperating with a new drive against the militants. But no one had the sort of relationship with Awlaki that I did. As he realized that Western intelligence was stepping up its search for him, his trusted circle would shrink. I would most likely be one of the few on the inside.

Just six weeks after Fort Hood, US Navy warships in the Gulf of Aden fired cruise missiles at suspected al-Qaeda training camps in Yemen. The mission was claimed by the Yemeni government in an effort to mitigate a public backlash against American military action on Yemeni territory. It said that thirty-four al-Qaeda fighters had been killed, including some mid-level commanders.

But the intelligence behind that strike was flawed – again demonstrating the difficulty of accurate targeting where there were few informants on the ground. The cruise missiles destroyed a Bedouin hamlet where an al-Qaeda operative and around a dozen other militants were staying. Local officials said many women and children were among the nearly sixty killed in one strike.

'The Americans just scored a big own goal,' Awlaki wrote to me shortly after the attack.

That strike took place on 17 December, and exactly one week later came the first attempt to take out Awlaki, in another cruise missile strike.

He was presumed to be attending a meeting of senior al-Qaeda figures who had been discussing a response to the previous attack.[3]

First reports indicated Awlaki had been killed. I was watching the news the next day – Christmas Day, 2009 – while on a short vacation in Scotland when I received a text from Abdullah Mehdar, the tribal fighter close to Awlaki whom I had befriended three months earlier. 'The tall guy is fine,' it read.

On 28 December Awlaki himself confirmed his survival in an encrypted email. 'Phew. Maaaaaan – that was close,' he said. He also warned me not to get in touch with Mehdar, because he was a 'hot potato'.

At the very moment I was told 'the tall guy is fine', Northwest Airlines flight 253 to Detroit from Amsterdam was approaching the eastern seaboard of the United States. A young Nigerian – Umar Farouk Abdulmutallab – was in seat 19A, above the wing and close to the fuel tanks. As the flight descended through slate-grey skies to its destination he retired to the toilet for twenty minutes.

When he came back, he covered himself with a blanket and tried to detonate an explosive device hidden in his underwear. The main charge failed to explode and he was left with smoking underpants as several passengers – perhaps recalling Richard Reid or the heroics of the passengers on board United flight 93 on 9/11 – rushed at him.[4]

---

3 A statement from the Yemeni embassy in Washington said Awlaki was 'presumed' to have been at the site of an al-Qaeda meeting south of the capital city of Sana'a.
4 Bomb experts later theorized that the only reason the device didn't work was that Abdulmutallab's perspiration had desensitized the main charge: the result of wearing

The young Nigerian's mission had begun in Yemen four months earlier. He had been drawn there from his studies in Dubai, enticed by the velvet tones of Awlaki and the contemplation of martyrdom. In summer 2009 he had trawled the mosques of Sana'a, looking for someone who could put him in touch with the preacher. Eventually someone had taken his mobile-phone number and a few days later he received a text with a phone number. Abdulmutallab was surprised when the voice at the other end was that of his hero, who instructed him to make his case for joining jihad – in writing.

His essay written and his plea for guidance sent, Abdulmutallab was collected and driven to Shabwa to meet Awlaki – just a few days after I had left the cleric to travel in the opposite direction.

Abdulmutallab told the preacher that he was ready for any mission, including one that would take his own life. Awlaki arranged for and helped write a martyrdom video for Abdulmutallab to record. He told him not to fly directly from Yemen to Europe, aware that might provoke suspicion. And his final words, according to the young Nigerian, were chilling: be sure to wait until the plane was over the United States, and then bring it down.

In the hours after his arrest a badly burned Abdulmutallab began detailing these instructions to FBI agents by his hospital bedside. I would only discover the full extent of what he had confessed later, but my handlers made it clear that Awlaki had been both aware of and involved in the plot. Americans had only just been spared another attack on the homeland, and Awlaki was becoming almost as influential as Osama bin Laden himself.[5]

More disturbing still was Abdulmutallab's claim that Awlaki had consulted directly with the man emerging as AQAP's master bomb-maker – a young Saudi called Ibrahim al-Asiri. Al-Asiri had built the

---

the explosive underwear for three weeks as he travelled from Yemen through Africa to Nigeria. But all agreed he had come terrifyingly close to bringing down a US airliner over a major city.

5 Within weeks, lawyers at the US Department of Justice took the unprecedented step of writing up a short memorandum justifying the targeted killing of an American citizen overseas.

underwear device. Just months earlier he had built a bomb to be inserted into the rectum of his younger brother, Abdullah. The device contained around 100 grams of the high-explosive PETN, a difficult-to-detect white powder, also later used in the underwear device. Abdullah's target was Prince Mohammed bin Nayef, the head of Saudi counter-terrorism, whose security services had driven the brothers out of Saudi Arabia two years earlier.

Abdullah told the Saudis he wanted to become an informant and was granted an audience with bin Nayef. He went through security checks at the airport, but nothing was found. When he detonated the explosive, the force of the explosion was directed upwards. Abdullah's body parts were scraped from the ceiling of bin Nayef's office – but the Prince himself was only slightly injured. Despite the failure of the mission, al-Asiri's brother and comrades had been emboldened. Never had al-Qaeda come so close to killing a member of the Saudi royal family.

As the FBI's intense questioning of Abdulmutallab continued in Detroit, a few hundred miles to the south in Washington DC intelligence officials turned their attention to those satellite images of the compound that I had visited.

On 12 January 2010 Yemeni counter-terrorism commandos descended quietly on the compound in the al-Hota area of Shabwa, where the previous September I had been housed by the tribal leader Abdullah Mehdar. Their main target was undoubtedly Anwar al-Awlaki, whom I had identified as a frequent house guest. But the terrorist cleric was not there that day. Mehdar refused to surrender and fought to the bitter end, despite being urged by other fighters to flee.

I received the news a few days later from Awlaki himself, in an encrypted email:

'Remember the guy you stayed with? Its confirmed. He was killed. I had spoken to him a while back and requested from him if the gov attacks to retreat to the mountains. He said that he will fight until he is killed and will not retreat and that is what he did. There were 20 of them and they fought against the gov and killed over 6 soldiers and then they retreated in front of overwhelming forces. He refused and fought from his house until they killed him. May Allah curse them.' He added in a follow-up email that he had been with Mehdar just 'a few days' before he was killed.[6]

Later that day, Anders – the PET analyst who had recently joined the team – told me that the Americans had confirmed my information had led to the operation against Mehdar's compound.[7]

The news deeply unsettled me. My role in targeting Nabhan had not disturbed me in the slightest; he was a ruthless terrorist involved in the murder of dozens of civilians. Mehdar was different: an apparently honourable man prepared to fight for his beliefs and in defence of his territory. He had no dreams of global jihad, of bringing carnage to the streets of Europe or the skies above America.

Never before in my work as a double agent had I brought about the death of someone I knew. I recalled the last time we had met, when the tearful Sheikh had told me as he helped change the tyre on my hired car: 'If we don't meet again, we will see each other in paradise.'

For days I stayed at home in Birmingham, paralysed with guilt. Fadia must have thought I was having one of my dark moods. I found myself incapable of running even basic errands like going to the super-market. A grim realization haunted me, and I cursed my naivety in not expecting and preparing for it. My work as an informant – to put it coldly – was killing people. And I had no say in who should be a target. The Americans, helped by the Yemeni government, had cast a wide net – and no distinction was drawn between men like Mehdar and men like Nabhan.

But the stakes were now too high and the urgency too great for me to wallow for long. I remembered that one of the fighters who had

6 On 29 January 2010 Awlaki sent me this follow-up email: 'a few days [before] Shaykh Abdullah [Mehdar] died (btw he was the chief of his tribe) I was talking to him about you and remembering your visit to his house. He was a brave and sincere brother. A few weeks before his death I was advising him that if the government attacks him he should retreat to the mountains. He refused and said if they come to me I will not retreat but will fight until I am killed, and that is what he did. Alhamdulillah his family is doing well.'

7 Several weeks later AQAP released a short video eulogy claiming the raid on Meh-dar's compound was a joint US–Yemeni operation. US officials have not publicly acknowledged US special forces were involved.

attached himself to Mehdar had gone on to carry out a suicide bombing against South Korean tourists in Yemen. I never found out if
Mehdar had had any role in the attack, but it gave me some solace.

Several weeks after the death of Mehdar, Awlaki declared war on
the United States in a recorded audio message. 'We are not against
Americans for just being American, we are against evil. And America
as a whole has turned into a nation of evil,' he said calmly and
deliberately.

'Jihad against America is binding upon myself, just as it is binding on
every other able Muslim.'

CHAPTER EIGHTEEN
ANWAR'S BLONDE

Spring–Summer 2010

On 9 March 2010 I stood outside the international bus terminal on Erdbergstraße in Vienna, waiting for the 11 a.m. bus from Zagreb to arrive. It was cold and breezy, typical of March in the Austrian capital. A steady stream of tourists emerged from the buses and headed to see the palaces of the Habsburgs.

Jed had told me there would be a CIA team shadowing me. I looked at a man in a cowboy hat on the street corner checking his watch. Surely they would not be that obvious.

Then I saw her. She wore a long black skirt as I had anticipated, but instead of being fully veiled, she was wearing a simple headscarf. A few stray strands of blonde hair fluttered in the breeze.

'*As salaam aleikum.* I'm Aminah,' she said in soft-accented English, fixing me with her blue-green eyes.

Despite the fact that Awlaki had instructed me to wear Western clothes to avoid suspicion, I had to keep my distance from a woman who was not related to me. I didn't even shake her hand. But I was impressed; the photos had not done her justice. Aminah was strikingly pretty, with full lips, high cheekbones and an angular nose. She looked several years younger than her age, thirty-two. Gwyneth Paltrow, I thought – Anwar will love this girl.

I had come across her on a Facebook fan page for Awlaki in November 2009 – two months after he had repeated his request that I find him a wife in the West. I had left a message on the site requesting support and Aminah had replied.

'What kind of support and are you in direct contact with Shaikh?' she wrote in her first message on 28 November 2009.

Two days later, after we exchanged several messages, she wrote this:

'I have one question tho. Do you know personally AAA? And if it is so, may I be so liberal to ask you something?' AAA was our code for Anwar al-Awlaki.

'Yes I do know him. Feel free to ask,' I replied immediately. She had written back:

'I sent Shaikh a letter by mail, I am not sure if I had his correct email address, but actually I was wondering will he search for a second wife, I proposed him a marriage, and I do not know how silly it is. But I tried. Now, as I am in contact with you there is a possibility for you to get know me better in a way you can recommended me.

'I seek a way how to get out of this country, and I search a husband who will teach me and whom I can help a lot. I deeply respect him and the all things he do for this Ummah and I want to help him in any way.'

I wrote back:

'You will be wife number 3, as he already got two wives, however he don't stay with them because they are in the capital, and only see him now and then. But you will stay with him all the time, as you don't have a family there. You should expect hardship, and moving from place to place once in a while. Taking care of your duties in house as a wife. Be patience with all what you will see and face, as AAA may be expose to danger etc. and Allah is our protector. Can you accept this?'

She replied within ten minutes:

'I would go with him anywhere, I am 32 years old and I am ready for dangerous things, I am not afraid of death or to die in the sake of Allah. I didn't know he has 2 wife already. But I do not mind at all. I want to help him in his work . . . I am good in housekeeping job [and] I'm willing to be a very hardworking and active wife.'

Aminah's real name was Irena Horak. I would get to know her well. Dozens of emails and Facebook exchanges would follow. She sent many long notes about her life for me to pass on to Awlaki.

Irena came from Bjelovar, a small town surrounded by farmland east of Croatia's capital, Zagreb. In one of her subsequent messages for Awlaki, Aminah described coming from a loving home and being brought up, like most Croats, as a Catholic with 'family values and high moral standards'. She was particularly close to her twin sister, Helena, her only sibling.

As a teenager Irena excelled in athletics. Such was her dedication that she became a champion junior 100-metre sprinter. There were pictures of her in the local newspaper ducking at the finishing line, her arms flung out in victory. She was driven, throwing herself headlong into her sprinting in the hope she might one day represent Croatia in the Olympics.

The twin sisters both enrolled at the Faculty of Education and Rehabilitation Sciences at Zagreb University. Irena wanted to work with people with special needs. By then her dreams of athletic glory had faded. She devoted herself to her studies. By night, like many of her fellow students, she hit Zagreb's nightclubs, drinking and dancing till the early hours.

Much later I discovered that during this time she posted photos on social media showing herself in a variety of uninhibited poses in which she sported various figure-hugging outfits, low tops, knee-high lace-up boots, and even a sleeveless black-leather catsuit.

After graduating, Irena found work at a residential centre for children without parental care. The centre housed around fifty kids between the ages of seven and eighteen, many of them with behavioural problems.

Later, Aminah recognized the diffident streak in her own character. In one of her messages for Awlaki she wrote:

'People say about me I am strong character but actually this is my shield, I am strong but I am very emotional, sensitive and I hate injustice. I like to work, I am not lazy, people describe me as a empathic, kind, open to new people.'

She had found Islam by accident, at a wedding ceremony in Zagreb. One of the guests was Sage, a handsome lawyer with long dreadlocks and a broad smile. He was a Muslim and worked in London. A few days later she was on a plane to London, having unceremoniously dumped her boyfriend. The two started a long-distance relationship.

Sage saw himself as a believer and spoke to her fondly about Islam, but he wore his religion lightly. He enjoyed going out for drinks, and by all accounts she was thrilled to be on his arm in the bars of London and Zagreb. She told a friend she hoped they would get married.

Later, she would write to Awlaki about Sage:

'He talked about Islam so nicely and peacefully and he discovers to me a lot of different thing I didn't know before. I was curious . . . so I start to explore by myself.'

She connected with a group of Muslim women in Bosnia who in turn introduced her to others in Zagreb. She began to spend time with them in the mosque.

'When I saw description of God – Allah in Quran I said to myself – this is a God I always thought it should be,' she would tell Awlaki in one message.

'It was always a nonsense to me that God have a son, everything I discover in Islam was logical and simple, but yet very frustrated and hard to accept, in that period of my searching.'

I was reminded of my own sense of discovery in the library at Korsør.

After six months her relationship with Sage soured. It seemed Islam had become more important to Irena than the relationship. She began sending him hostile emails, criticizing him for not praying five times a day and for drinking alcohol.

Irena's faith may have been reinforced by a bout with cancer. She said she had treatment and made a recovery, but it ended her dream of having children. She threw herself into Islam, began learning Arabic, and changed her habits, the way she dressed – wrapping herself in long skirts and a headscarf. She lost touch with her former friends. Irena became Aminah.

She told Awlaki about this turbulent time in her life:

'After a period of ang[er] and frustration I find peace in my heart I never felt before . . . I was so happy for learning new things about Islam . . . I was very emotional about everything due to Islam, I crying during prayers, I cried when I heard Azan [the call to prayer].'

And just like me, she felt a surge of energy, a liberation, when she formally converted to Islam in May 2009 by saying the *Shahada* – the profession of faith.

One of Aminah's longtime friends would later describe how she was consumed by her new faith. All she could talk about was Islam and she tried repeatedly to get her friends to convert.

It was around this time that Aminah came across Awlaki's English-language sermons – by now all over the internet. His call for followers to live the simple life of the Prophet, uncorrupted by Western modernity, seduced her. He might not have movie-star good looks, but she came to admire his sincerity and intellect and his quiet charisma. And she began to daydream about being his wife; he could teach her a lot about Islam.

By the time we connected on Facebook, Aminah told me she was being ostracized in Zagreb. At work, her manager complained about the way she dressed. She felt cut off from society and even from Croatia's mainstream Muslim community.

'I live in a country of kuffar. I really want to get out of this place,' she later told Awlaki in one of her messages. Again I was able to recognize the sentiment, recalling that grim day I had washed the lifeless body of the old man who had collapsed outside Regent's Park's mosque.

'I was rejected a lot of proposal cause brothers weren't serious about marriage or they are not on the same ideology.'

Aminah could not bring herself to tell her father about her conversion, but her mother had reluctantly accepted it. By the time that first Facebook message reached me, she seemed shrouded in sadness. She felt she had few meaningful relationships beside her family. How familiar it was.

But I realized that in this lost, impressionable woman I had an opportunity.

'Aminah can lead us to Awlaki,' I told my MI5 handlers – Sunshine, Andy and Kevin – soon after our conversations started on Facebook.

'We understand your logic but we'll have to take this up the chain of command,' Andy said.

The British shared my concern that sending Aminah to the wilder parts of a volatile country might put her at risk. The Americans, supported by the Danes, were more enthusiastic.

'We like the idea,' Jed said when we met in Copenhagen. There was excitement in his eyes as he contemplated the mother of all honeytraps. The gloves had come off in the days since Fort Hood, and in Washington discussions had already begun on whether Awlaki – as an American citizen – could legally be targeted for assassination. Jed realized Aminah represented a golden opportunity to target the terrorist cleric.

The CIA was officially entering the matchmaking business.

At their bidding I sent word to Awlaki that I had found him a possible wife, and on 11 December 2009 he got in touch, asking that she write a brief description of herself.

She sent me this reply for the cleric:

'I am 32 years old, never married, no kids. I am tall (1,73cm) slim-athletic build, I am not sure is it permissible for me to describe my hair. Anyway, ppl say I am good looking, atractive, I look much younger, everybody giving me 23–25 year.'

On 15 December, Awlaki sent me another encrypted message to pass on to her:

'There are two things that I would like to stress. The first is that I do not live in a fixed location. Therefore my living conditions vary widely. Sometimes I even live in a tent. Second, because of my security situation I sometimes have to seclude myself which means me and my family would not meet with any persons for extended periods. If you can live in difficult conditions, do not mind loneliness and can live with restrictions on your communications with others then alhamdulillah that is great. I have no problems with both of my wives and we get along well. Nevertheless they both chose to live in a city because they could not handle village life with me. I do not want this to happen again with another wife. What I need is someone who could bear with me the difficulties of this path.

'One more thing. Can you please send me a photo of yours? Please send it as an attachment.'

With the 'underwear plot' in the pipeline, Anwar must have suspected he was about to shoot up the US wanted list; perhaps that is why he emphasized the hardships of life in hiding for any future Mrs Awlaki.

In mid-December Aminah asked me to pass a new message to Awlaki, laying down some ground rules.

'I do not want a husband just on paper, I want to be with him and live in Islam cause I can't do it here. I am not housewife type, I can cook and do all other house duties but this is not all with what I will be pleased. I started to translate your lectures on my native language so I can help brothers and sisters on this part of the world.'

She also asked Awlaki whether she would be able to travel in and out of Yemen. 'My biggest concern are my parents, I know it will be a great shock to them if I say I will go there,' she wrote. 'If I can't see them ever again I am afraid I can't accept that condition.'

Her naivety at times was worrying.

I encrypted her message through the Mujahideen Secrets software and sent it to Awlaki. He replied on 18 December:

'I forsee that if you come in the country you come in for good and if you leave the country you also leave for good . . . the country is heading towards war. Only Allah knows what implications that would bring,' he wrote.

And then he responded to her request for more personal details.

'I am a quiet person. I do not interfere alot in the affairs of my family but when i do it must go my way. I do not tolerate disobedience from my wives. With my kids its the opposite especially my girls. I am very flexible with them so it is the mother who needs to dicipline them because I don't. I love reading. I spend some time with my family when they are with me but my committments pull me away . . . My work takes priority over family therefore I would love to have a wife that is lightweight and part of my work. Having lived most of my life in the West I would like to be in company of a Muslim from the West.'

Awlaki asked for Aminah's email address so he could ask her some 'private questions' directly. Given his obsession with operational security, and the fact the 'underwear plot' was only days away, it was a remarkable risk to take. Lust had again got the better of him.

On Christmas Eve, after the missile strike against al-Qaeda in Shabwa province, Aminah again got in touch with me.

'Do you have news from brother, there is a rumour he is dead or prisoned? Is it true?' she asked.

As soon as I found out that Awlaki was unharmed, I wrote to her, using our agreed name of Sami for Awlaki.

'Sami is fine and well Alhamdolillah . . . just have some patience sister, he is under huge pressure, are you sure you can handle this huge test?'

Despite his brush with death, Anwar was still thinking of the Croatian blonde when he wrote to me just four days after his brush with mortality. I let her know this:

'Sami sends u his greetings, and cannot contact u directly again, however I will pass on his message to u and u can reply to him via me. he is fine and well. He is still interested and ask when we can arrange the travel etc.'

After the Christmas Eve missile strike, the disquiet of British intelligence became outright opposition. They wanted nothing to do with a plan that could send an innocent European woman to her death. I sympathized with their position. I wanted to be sure that Aminah would not be seen as expendable, 'collateral damage' in the pursuit of Awlaki.

The British bid to prise me away from the Americans began a few weeks earlier at a secret facility straight out of 007's playbook.

Fort Monckton had been built to protect the naval harbour of Portsmouth towards the end of the eighteenth century and retains its bastions, casemates and drawbridge. It also boasts high razor-wire fences, floodlighting and CCTV cameras and is nowadays referred to by the army as the No. 1 Training Establishment.

It is in fact the main field-training centre for the Secret Intelligence Services. For close to a century Britain's top agents have been trained there.

Emma, my MI6 handler, picked me up in London for the drive down to Fort Monckton. She was dressed all in black with her brunette hair tied tightly in a bun. As she weaved through traffic on the motorway she opened up about her background. She had attended Oxford

University but afterwards needed some quick cash and had become what might politely be described as an exotic dancer.

I was pleased that she felt she could confide in me. But later I wondered whether it was part of a routine, a confidence-building measure to make me feel closer to my British team.

When we neared the gates, Emma handed me a scarf.

'Put this on your head – we don't want the guards on the outer perimeter to see you,' she said.

Fort Monckton was old school in every sense. At dinner, elderly butlers in formal attire waited on the MI6 officers assembled in the wood-panelled banqueting hall. I stayed in the private quarters of Sir Mansfield Cumming, the legendary early-twentieth-century British intelligence chief who in signing his letters 'C' provided the inspiration for Ian Fleming's spymaster, 'M'.

'Who on earth are you?' I was asked by Steve, a veteran instructor. He was in his fifties and had led MI6 attempts to hunt down Uday Hussein, the sadistic son of the Iraqi dictator Saddam Hussein after the invasion of Iraq in 2003.

'They don't let civilians into this facility, period. And I've never been allowed to sleep in the Colonel's bedroom,' he added.

'Well, my name's Morten Storm . . .' I replied, immediately realizing my mistake. Emma had told me not to talk about myself during my stay.

'It's okay, don't worry,' she said.

During the day MI6 agents and I did role-playing games. I would be handed a scenario and given fifteen minutes to prepare. Cameras fed my responses to a team in another room. In the debrief Steve told me I was a natural problem-solver and had passed the tests. I couldn't be sure whether he was being serious or if it was part of a charm offensive.

The special treatment continued into the New Year.

I was invited to a course in counter-surveillance in Edinburgh run by Andy and Kevin from MI5.

In the morning, in my hotel room, they explained how I could detect that I was being followed and ways to shake a tail. One method involved finding an excuse to stop while walking and discreetly look around. Another way involved taking an apparently random zigzag route to see if the tail followed. But if your route was too random, professionals would know you were on to them. They said the same principles applied if I was driving. It made me recall my helter-skelter ride through the streets of Nairobi courtesy of Ikrimah's driver, Mohammed. Andy and Kevin also told me how to check whether a contact was being followed. I should tell them to pass through various locations and discreetly observe them.

My MI5 handlers told me that several agents I had never met had been assigned to follow me through the streets of Edinburgh. The first drill was for me to spot any pursuers and then shake them off. I set off up the hill from my hotel near the train station, admiring the turrets of Edinburgh Castle high above, gleaming in the winter sunshine. When I reached the castle I took a left and started walking down the Royal Mile. Despite a cold wind, the street was packed with tourists. It would be difficult to know who, if anyone, was on my tail.

I abruptly stopped at a cashmere store and checked the prices in the window. In the reflection I noticed a man in a black-and-blue jacket walk past me. When I set off again down the street he had stopped, and was looking at postcards on an outdoor stall. After I passed him I didn't look round. Instead I ducked into an alley. When I peered back from behind a wall I noticed he had taken the same route.

I increased my pace, taking as random a path as possible through the cobbled side streets. This was proving a very enjoyable exercise. Soon I had no idea where I was, but my tail had disappeared. When I recovered my bearings and got back to the hotel, I was told I'd passed the first test.

That evening, after several more drills, Kevin and Andy took me to a small shop specializing in haggis on the Royal Mile. I had no idea what it was.

'You need to taste this. It's a Scottish tradition,' Andy said.

As my face broke into a puzzled frown, they both began laughing. And then they told me exactly how haggis was made. But the fun was over. British intelligence were not investing so much valuable time in me for my own pleasure.

As we sat down in a quiet corner of a local restaurant, Kevin looked me in the eye and addressed me in a serious tone.

'We're not comfortable with what the Americans want to do with Aminah. Our job is to gather information. We don't participate in assassinations. We don't believe we should help get Aminah to Yemen. We fear she may get killed.'

But there was another element to Kevin's message which didn't exactly speak to the famous 'special relationship' between the British and US intelligence communities.

'Morten, we can't offer you anything like the money they can but one thing we can promise you is this. We won't fuck you over. You know we don't lie. We don't like this plan with Aminah and we don't want you to get fucked over.'

I turned over my options. The British seemed willing to invest in me for the long term. I liked my handlers and I too was concerned for Aminah's safety. But I had not so long ago harboured doubts about their endgame, and had suspected they were trying to manoeuvre their own informant into Awlaki's inner circle.

In the next few days both the Danes and the Americans pressed the mission hard, despite the fact that Danish law explicitly forbade PET from taking part in any assassination operation overseas.

Soon after my Edinburgh training, Klang called.

'We're going to Iceland – just us Danes, and Big Brother is paying.'

A few days later we were relaxing in the thermal waters of the blue lagoon in Reykjavik. There was a new addition to the team – an officer in his late forties called Jesper. He was Klang's opposite. Klang was a peacock, showing off his physique. There was nothing of the show-off in Jesper, who had a restrained dry wit. He had a receding hairline and plain features, and was thin to the point of looking frail. While Klang had cut his teeth in the hurly-burly of the drugs squad, Jesper was something of a desk jockey. Before joining PET he'd worked in banking and the financial crimes division of the police. I asked a fellow bather to take a picture of me and the PET agents. Surprisingly my handlers did not object.

Later in my suite in the five-star Radisson Blu hotel in Reykjavik I relayed to them what the British had told me.

'Morten, our view is that we should proceed with the Americans. It'll be more fun. And they have more money,' Klang said.

The money was a factor. They were offering to double my retainer. It was hardly a CEO's salary – some $4,000 a month. But to someone who had frequently been reduced to gathering the loose change trapped in the sofa, it felt like serious money.

I also felt I had an opportunity to influence the way the Aminah mission unfolded. Perhaps there was a way to cage Awlaki – rather than kill him.

In the first weeks of 2010 Awlaki and I continued to exchange emails, despite the intense pressure on him. He wanted Aminah to travel as soon as possible.

'Since things are getting stricter for foreigners over here with new laws . . . if you could try to speed up her travel into Yemen before she gets on the radar or is prevented from entering the country,' he wrote.

On the last day of January he strongly advised me against travelling to meet Aminah, concerned it might jeoparadize her chances of reaching Yemen.

'If you go there or inquire about her you may get her in trouble or yourself in trouble because the eyes are on you.

'There are millions of people around the world that listen to me but in the end it is a handful whom I can count upon. It's like looking for needles in a haystack. And since you are one of those brs that I can count on, I care about you, and your security, and your wellness, but I also care about your ideas and manhaj [methodology].'

For a few moments I was touched by his words. There was still a streak of humanity about him – he was a marked man but looking out for people he felt he could rely upon. I began to think how I might reel him in quietly and present him to the Yemeni authorities. He would no longer be free, but he would be alive.

Just two weeks later the CIA fast-tracked the Aminah mission. I was summoned to a meeting in Helsingør. Klang and Jesper picked me up at the railway station, a magnificent neo-Renaissance building with a towering triangular roof and an impressive array of turrets and spires.

'We've negotiated with the Americans,' Klang said as we drove out from the station. 'They are prepared to offer you $250,000. The deal is the moment Aminah lands in Sana'a and leaves the airport the money is yours.'

Jesper chimed in: 'But obviously you didn't hear this from us. One of the "masters of the universe" is here from Washington DC to make the offer in person.'

His delivery was acidic. The Danes might want to share a bed with the Americans, but they could be a jealous partner.

To our right the waters of the Øresund, the channel separating Sweden and Denmark, sparkled in the winter sunshine. After a few miles we reached Hornbaek, a holiday hamlet. Danish intelligence had rented a villa on the banks of a tree-lined lake, a setting of tranquillity in which to plot the elimination of one of America's enemies.

The third-highest-ranking official in Danish intelligence was in the reception room waiting for me in chinos and a blue open-neck shirt. He was tall and had cobalt-blue eyes and straw-coloured hair, which he combed neatly in a parting. Soren, the team leader, introduced him as 'Tommy' and from then on my handlers always referred to him as Tommy Chef because of his natural authority and his rank as PET's most senior covert officer. I was told he reported directly to PET's powerful director, Jakob Scharf. He gave me a firm handshake and thanked me for my efforts.

The remaining members of my PET team were assembled around a white dining table, on their best behaviour. The American delegation arrived a short time later. There was Jed in jeans and cowboy boots followed by a tall man with carefully parted salt-and-pepper hair. For a moment I thought he must be the man with the chequebook, but he was the CIA's Copenhagen station chief, 'George'. He held the door open for a short balding man. This was 'Alex', one of the masters of the universe, and one with a Napoleon complex.

Tommy Chef greeted him with a formal handshake, and then the American turned to me.

'We are really pleased with your results so far and thank you for them,' he said. His voice seemed to bounce off the walls.

'We see this as a big opportunity to stop Awlaki, which as you know is a high priority for my government. President Obama himself has been briefed on this. I know that because I report up to the White

House,' he said, unnecessarily. His two subordinates put on a show of being suitably impressed.

'So let's cut to the chase: my government is prepared to remunerate you a quarter-million dollars for your matchmaking services. Get Aminah to Yemen and we will transfer the money.'

Remunerate, I thought: how these guys love to play with the big words.

'You've got yourself a deal,' I replied.

'That's very good,' he said. 'I want to make one thing clear: you'll be mainly reporting to us now, not our British friends.'

The Danish agents brought in a collection of *smørrebrød* – sandwiches with smoked salmon, pickled herring and salami sausage.

Alex sat forward earnestly. 'We need a pretext for you to meet Aminah.'

Despite Awlaki's reservations about me travelling to meet her in Vienna, the Americans weren't about to let Aminah travel to Yemen without checking her out first.

I pulled out my laptop and began drafting an email to the cleric, writing:

'Regarding the sister, she insist me to meet her in Wienna, Austria, as she got questions which cannot be asked over the phone.'

Alex insisted on changing some of the language, no doubt so he could claim credit for its authorship.

I then opened up the Mujahideen Secrets software on my computer, entered my personal key and Awlaki's public key and hit 'encrypt'. I copied and pasted the resulting encoded text into my email browser, selected an anonymous email address Awlaki used, and hit 'send'.

Alex observed the process, fascinated.

'You know you're literally making hundreds of agents busy back Stateside,' he said.

Awlaki replied five days later.

'If you visit her I may upload for you a short clip from myself as an encrypted file and you can have her hear it to make sure it is myself.'

In offering up a video recording Awlaki was responding to Aminah's request for a private message on camera so she could be reassured that it really was Awlaki at the other end.

I told PET of Awlaki's email via the Norwegian email service provider Telenor. We used Telenor because it had better encryption safeguards than most providers. The Danes shared a great deal with the Americans, but like any intelligence service PET wanted the information first. It was a way of reminding the Americans that I was after all a Danish asset. But using Telenor's encryption safeguards was also symptomatic of the suspicions that every agency had about its communications being intercepted. MI5 had told me not to say anything of importance over the phone – in case the Russians or Mossad were listening in. And MI6 simply refused to use the phone at all.

Days later Awlaki wrote again, saying he was now living in a house rather than a tent.

'I personally prefer this arrangement over the tent in the mountains because it gives me a better setup for reading, writing and doing research.'

He attached a long private note for Aminah and asked me to instruct her how to use the Mujahideen Secrets software, adding: 'Most importantly she needs to setup a clean email that is not opened from home.'

Jed accompanied me to Vienna for the rendezvous, and over a beer the night before Aminah's arrival I was taken aback to find out we shared an appreciation of Metallica. I still knew so little about him. He was married and had several kids and a Dobermann dog. Where he was from, where he lived and worked – that was not my business and not my place to ask. But I did appreciate his determination to get results.

Alex's plan required me to bring Aminah past the way station of a designated bakery shop to the Lounge Gersthof, a nearby bar and restaurant where they had a surveillance team waiting. But at the last minute it dawned on me that it would be absurd to take her to a place that served alcohol. Instead I suggested a nearby McDonald's.

We slid into a booth. I showed her the note from Awlaki on my laptop.

'Sister the step you are about to make is a great one and I pray you are ready for it. However, let me share this with you from my personal experience . . .' his message stated.

'Overall for a while I had a very easy and comfortable life. On the other hand, I have lived in a tent with no running water and [been] stripped from my freedom of movement.

'But let me tell you that the pleasure Allah put in my heart and the tranquillity and peace that I felt going through difficulty for His sake made me despise going back to my former life. I would not exchange it for the world.

'[The months in prison] were the best days of my life. I never thought that I could handle that . . . but I did. Why? Because Allah helped me to . . .

'The problem [you'll face] is limitations on freedom of movement and communicating with others. Also being in a foreign country with no friends and the language barrier is an issue . . .'

Aminah read the letter slowly and without expression. She turned away from the screen and looked at me.

'Do you know the consequences?' I asked her.

'Yes, I'm ready, *Inshallah*,' Aminah replied. 'I want to devote myself to Islam and I want Sheikh Anwar to be my teacher.'

She asked me many questions about Yemen; her lack of overseas travel (her only visit to the Arab world had been to a resort in Tunisia) meant she had little idea about the life she would face. But there seemed little doubt about her devotion.

As Awlaki had requested, I showed her how to send encrypted email using the Mujahideen Secrets encryption software.

'Does this mean I'm part of the mujahideen?' she asked me with an intense look.

'Yes, sister, it does,' I replied.

She had tears in her eyes. 'I'm a mujahida,' she whispered, trembling.

I relayed details of the encounter that same evening in a hotel suite in Copenhagen.

George, the local CIA station chief, was delighted.

'We'll pass on the information to Washington and see what the next step will be.'

The British had still not given up hope of diverting me from the mission. In the second half of March I was invited to join my British contacts at the Ice Hotel in the far north of Sweden: a palace of wonders carved entirely out of ice and snow.

Several of my handlers came along: my MI5 handlers Andy and

Kevin, and Emma in her element, decked out in a chic ski outfit and moon boots. Klang, never one to miss a party, also came along. But no Americans were invited.

We went dog sledding through the powdery snow, zoomed around on the ice on four-wheel-drive cars and raced snowmobiles.

The British didn't discuss Aminah with me during the trip. Perhaps they thought it would have been too obvious and vulgar, perhaps they were wary of Klang. They knew Danish intelligence and the Americans had invested in the Aminah gambit. I think they hoped that after bonding with them in the northern snows I would reconsider.

But the Aminah mission had too much momentum now.

On a spring day in 2010 I was queuing at the check-in at Birmingham airport to catch a flight to Copenhagen for another Aminah planning mission, when I received a call.

It was Kevin, my MI5 handler. He knew where I was.

'Morten, if you travel now, you have to realize we are not going to see each other again,' he said.

I stepped away from the check-in counter. To the British, I had chosen the wrong side, and it was a terminal decision.

'I just want to say we had a fantastic time together,' Kevin continued with obvious sincerity. 'We've done such good work. It's really sad to see this happening but you know it's a bureaucracy and we can't do anything about it.'

MI5 and MI6 were cutting their ties to me.

I was restless on the flight to Copenhagen. I had grown close to Kevin, Andy, Emma, Sunshine and my other British handlers. The UK was my adopted homeland; and they seemed to understand me better than the Danes. But the break was complete. The Danes told me the Brits had mandated I could no longer open any emails from Awlaki on British soil. From then on I was forced to travel to Copenhagen to check for messages from the cleric.

I had little time to dwell on my divorce from MI5 and MI6. After reaching Copenhagen I was driven to a holiday villa on the southern shore of the Roskilde Fjord, some twenty-five miles west of Copenhagen.

Jed told me that I would need to purchase a suitcase for Aminah.

'Isn't that a bit risky – isn't she just going to think that's weird?' I asked.

I came up with an alternative. I would ask Awlaki what Aminah should bring. If she saw the request had come from him there was no way she would be suspicious.

Jed also showed me a wooden cosmetic case they wanted me to give Aminah. He didn't need to say there was a tracking device embedded somewhere. But it seemed to be inviting trouble.

Klang thought so too.

'There's no way we're going to let you hand her this; if someone drops it and discovers the transponder you'll be fucked,' he said. 'Sometimes I can't believe the Americans. They just don't think.'

On 21 April, just before flying to Vienna, I received a reply from Awlaki.

'She shouldn't have more than a medium-sized suitcase and a carry-on bag. She should also have on her some cash just in case . . . She should have with her at least $3k. Also the ticket needs to be round trip just in case she runs into any unexpected problems at the airport.'

Awlaki was expecting me to raise the money through mosques in the UK.

Awlaki's attention to the smallest detail was extraordinary, especially as just three weeks earlier it had been widely reported the Obama administration had designated him for what was known as 'targeted killing'. The *New York Times* had reported that the White House had taken 'the extremely rare if not unprecedented' step of approving the assassination of Awlaki despite his being an American citizen because he was now regarded as actively involved in terror plots.

Jed and George were pleased with Awlaki's reply. Another hurdle had been overcome, and their project might be the first to put the cleric in the crosshairs. They emailed me, using an encryption tool and referring to Awlaki as 'Hook' – one of his nicknames among jihadis.

'Our conversations about what the Hook might advise for her travel appears to have paid off! . . . We suggest you can use the Hook's guidance as a reason to give the sister the suitcase . . . pls tell the sister that the hook wants her to have 3000 dollars . . . this is perfect cover for your next trip to see her. have a safe trip and good luck, your brothers.'

It was one of the very few occasions the CIA left a paper trail, however coded the language.

On a breezy spring afternoon I met Aminah in a park in Vienna and strolled with her to a Turkish restaurant. I told her about Awlaki's suitcase requirements and that he had entrusted me with securing funds for her trip.

Alex flew in from Washington for the debriefing in Roskilde the next day. Apart from Soren, who sat with us, the Danish agents mostly hovered nearby, bringing us coffee and snacks from the kitchen: that said it all about the pecking order.

'It's time for the love messages,' Alex said. Awlaki had sent me a recording for Aminah several weeks previously and had requested Aminah record a video of herself before travelling. Jed fished out a camcorder from his bag and slid it across the table.

It was also time to buy a suitcase.

'We need to know the exact type, colour, everything,' Jed said. He suggested a Samsonite model. No doubt it would be substituted for an identical one with a tracking device at the airport when she left for Yemen.

There was a tension in the air. Gone were the attempts at camaraderie, the flashes of humour. There was a lot riding on this. Occasionally, Alex would slip out of the villa and down to the jetty – out of earshot. I could see him gesticulating as he barked into his mobile phone. Orders to be obeyed, no doubt. Jed seemed to be smoking more frequently. But I was worried that in their rush to see this mission through, the CIA would miss crucial details.

The Americans had been unhappy that – on my own initiative – on my previous trip to Vienna I had taken Aminah to a McDonald's rather than the bar/restaurant they had carefully staked out.

'This time when we ask you to do something we expect you to do it,' Alex snapped.

'I didn't think it was logical,' I retorted, annoyed by his arrogance. But I refused to get drawn into an argument.

I sat down to draft Awlaki an email, referring to the *New York Times* article about the approval of targeted killing.

'May Allah curse the Americans for this – the filthy Kuffar pigs,' I wrote, as a true jihadi might.

As Alex read the draft, a frown hardened on his oversized forehead.

'You can't say that – it's just not acceptable,' he said.

To my amazement, it was Anders who spoke next.

'You know what? That's the way we have always done it. We Danes like to do it our own way,' he said acidly.

Alex turned round to face the young Dane but Anders stared back. Without a word Alex got up and walked through the open French windows into the garden.

Later Klang beckoned me into the kitchen: 'Don't worry about it, Morten – we'll just change back the language when our friend leaves.'

But I had another dilemma – one that my handlers in their blissful ignorance of Salafist necessities had overlooked. I could not invite Aminah into some hotel room in Vienna and film her without a veil. It would seriously call into question my religious credentials. There was, however, one possibility.

By now, Fadia and I had moved from Birmingham to the nearby city of Coventry. Raleigh Road was considerably more appealing than Alum Rock in Birmingham, a street of neat pre-war terraced houses. I arrived home from Roskilde with money in my pocket, courtesy of another fictional stint on a Danish construction site, and began laying the foundations of my plan as we prepared dinner one evening.

'Darling, you remember Sheikh Anwar told me he was looking for a Western wife? Well, I found him one, on Facebook. She's from Croatia.'

She was surprised.

'A Western woman who wants to go to Shabwa? How would she survive?'

'She's really serious; she's mad about the Sheikh. So I need to tell you something. I had to go to Vienna to meet her. He asked me to.'

'Why didn't you tell me before?' Fadia asked. She was both hurt by the deceit and suspicious about my meeting a young Croatian woman in a far-off city.

'I didn't want you involved. Some Western governments think Anwar is a terrorist. And it happened very suddenly.'

Luckily, Fadia rarely followed the news and had no idea that Awlaki was now targeted for assassination by the US.

I looked at her. Those dark almond eyes were glistening with tears.

'Sometimes I feel I don't know you,' she said.

'I am sorry. But here's an idea. Anwar wants me to go back again to record a video of her, so he can see her. I can't go alone. You know it is forbidden by our religion that I should see a woman who is not related to me on my own in a private place. As the Prophet said: "Never is a man alone with a woman except that Satan is the third party with them."'

Fadia seemed relieved that my Salafist code excluded the possibility of extramarital misbehaviour.

'So,' I continued after a long pause, 'would you come with me? I would feel my honour preserved and you could help set her at ease. It would be a huge favour for Anwar. And then we can have some time in Vienna together.'

The sales pitch worked.

On 27 April we flew to Vienna. I had calculated that even with Awlaki's new profile, being involved in sending him a video of a prospective wife did not amount to 'material support for terrorism'. In any case, Fadia would – unwittingly – be assisting in tracking down a wanted man. We took a room in a modest hotel in central Vienna. Aminah arrived wearing large trendy sunglasses and a black hijab. I introduced her to Fadia and said that as a good Muslim I could not have met her alone in a private place. Thankfully they warmed to each other very quickly. Aminah even seemed reassured by Fadia's presence.

I asked her again whether she was sure she wanted to marry Awlaki. I needed this to be her call.

The promise of a quarter of a million dollars to act as matchmaker had given me qualms. What was my real motive now – to prevent terror or make money? I sensed the plan was to target Awlaki in a missile strike once he was united with his new wife, and it made me feel uneasy.

On my laptop I showed her the fifty-second video clip Awlaki had recorded. The cleric was dressed in a white tunic and wore around his head a copper-coloured scarf layered like a bandana over a traditional white *ghuthra*. He was sitting in front of a pink background with a floral motif. The trouble he had gone to was almost touching. He occasionally reached up to adjust his spectacles as he spoke. His tone was a seductive version of his video sermons.

'This recording is done specifically for Sister Aminah at her request and the brother who is carrying this recording is a trustworthy brother, the brother that is communicating with you.

'I pray that Allah guides you to that which is best for you . . . and guides you to choose what is better for you regarding this proposal.'

He also asked her to send him a recorded message.

At first Aminah smiled at these words, and then her eyes began to shine. She was overwhelmed by such familiarity with a man she revered.

Fadia stood behind the camera and told her gently to try to relax. Aminah, with only her face visible, addressed the cleric in a soft halting voice, swallowing her words nervously like a teenager with stagefright.

'I just want to tell you that right now I feel nervous and this is very awkward for me so I will just tape this just so you can see how I look and just to know I'm okay. I will accept everything what is needed to do now this way that I have chosen . . . I will send you another message, a private, private message – *Insha'Allah*.'

That was my cue to leave them and leave the room. On the second recording Aminah was a woman transformed. She took off her veil and her blonde hair tumbled down over her black blouse. A clip held back shorter layers – making her seem, not accidentally, much younger. She had coquettishly applied a little mascara and lip gloss. It was seduction by video.

'Brother, this is me without the headscarf so you can see my hair. I described it to you before. So now you've seen me without it and I hope you will be pleased with it – *Insha'Allah*,' she said, tilting her head to one side.

She ended with a halting Arabic salutation that she must have practised for days.

When she had finished recording the private message with Fadia, I handed Aminah the suitcase – a grey hard-top Samsonite. 'This is the one Sheikh Anwar recommended,' I said. She was trembling.

Fadia embraced her and said she should contact her through me if she needed anything or advice on being a wife in Yemen.

Three weeks later, I met Aminah in a McDonald's near the Yemeni embassy in Vienna. I gave her the $3,000 in cash which supposedly came from 'the brothers' in England but in fact was from the US Treasury.

I had shown her how to apply for a course at the Sana'a Institute for Arabic Language. At some point Awlaki's intermediaries would come to fetch his new bride. 'The Sheikh says you should take off your hijab before entering the embassy,' I told her.

Awlaki's instructions were for her to go to the embassy unveiled so as not to create suspicion. He also wanted her to put on Western clothing for her journey to Yemen. He had even issued a fatwa for me to pass on granting her permission. The need not to arouse suspicion trumped religious rules.

The embassy apparently thought there was nothing out of the ordinary in a Croatian blonde going to Yemen to learn Arabic and told her a visa would be ready the next day. Aminah was elated but nervous. She was leaving behind everything she knew and heading towards the unknown.

My CIA handlers had instructed me that Aminah should not take a direct flight to Yemen. I took her to the Turkish Airlines office in Vienna. I also gave her a new pair of all-weather sandals for Awlaki and an electronic Arabic pocket dictionary the CIA had provided me with, tracking device inserted.

We found a café that didn't serve alcohol and sat down outside. Every detail of her journey had been considered. Now, as we prepared to part, I realized that I was unlikely to see her again and suddenly felt tender towards her, a yearning to protect her from her own gullibility.

'I don't know how I will ever pay you back,' she said as I left. 'You've done so much for me. May Allah reward you.'

Her parting words lodged in my mind. She was so grateful but I knew I might be sending her into great danger. I could not know whether the American ploy would work, nor what would follow. I glanced back as I walked away. Her blonde hair was cocooned inside her hijab. She looked slight and vulnerable as she sipped her coffee and watched the elegant Viennese stroll by.

Allah wouldn't reward me, but Uncle Sam might.

The day of her flight I got together with my Danish and American handlers at the Hornbaek villa. It was the beginning of June and one of those endless Scandinavian summer evenings when dusk descends after II p.m.

Before Jed and George would let me open a beer they requested I draft Awlaki an encrypted email about Aminah's travels to send once we got confirmation she had arrived. He had indicated it could take one or two months before his couriers could organize her travel from Sana'a to wherever he happened to be. That had made the CIA jumpy.

I wrote the following:

'She is all by herself in Yemen, and a month or even two weeks is a very long time for her to wait, as she cannot be as a normal muslim, she constantly have to hide her reality . . . Try to arrange that she get picked up sooner, she will need support as she is alone.'

The entire Danish squad was present – Soren, Klang, Trailer, Jesper and the analyst Anders along with the spymaster, Tommy Chef. Buddha's back was better and he had been invited to join the party. He had gone on a diet; we inevitably called him 'Buddha-lite'. Jed was manning the barbecue, grilling steaks, and the atmosphere was better for Alex's absence.

Jed got text updates on his phone as Aminah took connecting flights: Zagreb, Vienna and Istanbul. Finally word came that she had landed in Sana'a. There were bear hugs and high-fives.

The next day Aminah sent me an encrypted message from Sana'a to tell me she had arrived. As planned she had bought a Yemeni SIM card for her phone and she provided me with the number. I emailed it to Awlaki later that day.

'Congratulations brother, you just got rich, very rich,' Klang texted me.

My reward followed a few days later at a suite in the Crowne Plaza Hotel near Copenhagen. Klang strode in with the CIA station chief, George, and beckoned me to follow them to the elevator. He looked self-important, holding a slim black briefcase tightly in his right hand.

When we reached the room, I discovered that the briefcase was handcuffed to Klang's wrist, and with good reason.

'Guess the code,' George said with a smile on his face.

I looked puzzled.

'Try 007,' George said with a smile on the corner of his lips. With a satisfying metallic click the case popped open. It was filled with thick bundles of $100 bills. Each of the twenty-five bundles contained $10,000.

'How am I going to exchange all this money?' I asked.

'That's your problem, not ours,' George replied, laughing.

My train ride home to my mother's house on Korsør was a strange experience. If only my fellow commuters had known what was inside the briefcase, wedged tightly between my knees.

'My goodness – is this from drugs?' my mother asked, laughing. In reality, she knew that I was now working for PET, but had no idea what I was doing – and no clue of the Aminah mission that had led to the jackpot. I took a photograph of the bill-filled briefcase. The kid from Korsør, outlawed, jailed, exiled – now standing in his mother's kitchen with $250,000 from the US government.

After what seemed like an endless wait in late June I received encrypted messages from Awlaki and Aminah. She had managed to join him in the tribal areas:

'Alhamdidullah I am fine and well,' she wrote. 'Everything went good and according to a plan.'

Then the bombshell.

'I couldn't take my suitcase from institute, so I need almost everything I left there.'

I stared at the screen, willing the words to change. No tracking device had made the journey with her into the tribal areas. Al-Qaeda had told her to repack her belongings in a plastic bag and leave behind all her electronics. The Americans verified this by sending an informant to her lodgings in Sana'a. They were furious that their carefully laid trap had been evaded by some conscientious al-Qaeda operative.

If the Americans were disappointed with the outcome of the Aminah mission, Anwar al-Awlaki was not.

'Alhamdulillah we got married. May Allah reward you for all what you have done. However, according to your description of her I expected something different. I am not saying you tricked me or anything. . . . I do not blame you or your wife because I believe you were sincere and you were doing your best . . .,' he wrote to me. 'So she turned out to be different then what you described. Masha'Allah she turned out to be better than I expected and better than you described:)'

While Awlaki was re-energized by my matchmaking, the CIA and especially the ambitions of Alex and Jed were frustrated that the investment in Aminah had come to naught.

Danish intelligence seemed less worried and planned a trip to Barcelona for what they described as a 'debriefing'. Soren, Klang and Jesper picked me up from Barcelona airport in a BMW hire car and drove me to a penthouse apartment overlooking the city's main avenue.

'I've organized some entertainment for the evening,' Soren announced with a glint in his eye as we sipped champagne. After a dinner at one of the city's best restaurants we drove through the automatic gates of a secluded villa. Soren handed over a thick wad of euros to a hostess and we were ushered into a low-lit bar. Girls in shimmering chiffon dresses and stilettos lounged on leather sofas. They bore no comparison with the escorts who had hung out at Underground in Korsør, but they had the same vacant look in their eyes.

This was clearly a different sort of debriefing to the one I anticipated.

As the others paired off, I was awoken from my reverie by a petite woman who announced she was 'Olea from Moldova'. But when I looked up in the gloom all I saw was Aminah. Unease came over me as I thought about how the blonde Croatian was now deep behind al-Qaeda lines, sleeping beside one of the world's most wanted men.

Olea took me by the hand and led me towards one of the bedrooms down the corridor. I told her that I couldn't sleep with her because I was married.

'So you want to talk?' she said with a sigh. She looked relieved when I asked if there was any way to get high instead. I needed to blow away my guilt about Aminah. Olea walked across the room and took down one of the oil paintings. From behind its frame she procured a vial of white powder.

I had started using cocaine again at the beginning of the year after learning that my work had resulted in the killing of the tribal leader Abdullah Mehdar. For a while his death had been all that I could think about; the guilt had paralysed me. But the first blinding high in my home in Birmingham had made it all go away for a few hours.

I was bending down next to Olea to snort a line when someone burst into the room. It was Klang.

'What the hell are you doing?' he protested. 'You can't do that!'

'Why not?'

'You can't do that with us.'

'Why the hell not?' I snapped back. 'First of all I'm only abusing myself. You are abusing women who are probably victims of human trafficking. And it's not like you're a police officer on duty here in Spain.'

The Barcelona visit increased the distance I felt from my Danish handlers. I asked myself whether their superiors had any idea of what was going on in far-off places, whether this was a rogue team, or whether PET was rotten.

The next few months would offer some answers.

CHAPTER NINETEEN

A NEW COVER

Summer–Winter 2010

The Americans froze contact with me after the failure of the Aminah mission.

'They aren't happy with you,' Klang told me. 'You got a quarter-million dollars, Awlaki got a beautiful blonde, and Big Brother got your charming letter,' he laughed.

I had written an angry email to Alex, criticizing the American way of doing things and reminding them that we Danes had invented my double life long before he knew of my existence.

For a time it seemed that double life would again be a solely Danish enterprise. The British had vanished; the Americans were smarting over an expensive failure. But I was undeterred. I knew the contacts I had in jihadist groups would soon have the agencies calling again.

I poured much of my energy into a new venture – Storm Bushcraft – an adventure travel company I had registered in the UK. A couple of Birmingham militants had begun questioning how I could travel back and forth to Yemen and East Africa with such ease. I had insinuated that I was making good money from selling drugs for the cause, but I badly needed a watertight cover story.[1]

---

1 Storm Buschcraft was not the only cover company I set up to justify my travel overseas. In October 2009 MI5 helped me register a company called 'HelpHandtoHand', which we described as an NGO providing aid for the needy in Africa and the Middle East. I even opened up a Twitter account to advertise the new venture. But I was eventually forced to abandon it after MI5 cut ties with me in April 2010.

Adventure travel was in my blood. I had always loved being outdoors and had made camps as a kid in the woods around Korsør. My
endurance training with the British in Aviemore had rekindled my
enthusiasm. And after my trip with British intelligence to the Ice Hotel
in northern Sweden in March 2010, I had gone further north for an
Arctic expedition course. The cold was so intense that it was difficult to
breathe. But I was in my element – learning how to survive in the Arctic by hunting, tracking and lighting fires.

The course was led by Toby Cowern, a member of the Royal
Marines Reserves. He was well regarded among fellow explorers, having trained the winning team for the 2006 Polar Challenge, a race to
the North Pole. Toby was one of life's enthusiasts and had extraordinary powers of endurance. While the rest of us lay exhausted in our
snow shelters at the end of each day he would be reading by
torchlight.

I sensed Toby yearned to do more than teach Arctic survival.
He had been frustrated that a back injury had prevented him from
deploying overseas when so many of the Royal Marines were sent to
Afghanistan.

I felt he was exactly the sort of person Western intelligence needed
to infiltrate jihadist circles overseas. He certainly knew how to deal
with extreme situations and his dark complexion meant he could be
mistaken for a Middle Easterner.

'Would you like to do something that makes a difference?' I asked
him as we trudged side by side through the snow.

'What do you mean?'

'Would you consider something related to intelligence?'

'Why? What do you do?'

I laid out the contours of my work without revealing any specifics.

'I think you could be a huge asset. Would you be interested in meeting some of my friends in the intelligence business?'

'Why not?' he replied.

In the midst of the Aminah mission I introduced Toby to Klang,
Soren and Anders, at the holiday villa on Roskilde Fjord. We made sure
the Americans were long gone. I was told I couldn't stay in the house
while my handlers spoke to him, so took a walk along the shore.

'We like this guy,' Klang said to me when I returned.

Soon Toby was working with me on Storm Bushcraft as I tried to build it into a vehicle for my intelligence work. I could persuade jihadis that it was a front to hide my work for the cause. In reality it would help me more deeply infiltrate their ranks.

I was meticulous in setting up the company, purchasing a camping vehicle and outdoor gear. I even approached Marek Samulski, the Australian-Polish convert I had met in militant circles in Sana'a, to design a website and Facebook page. After being deported from Yemen he had moved to South Africa, where he had found work as a web designer, but Danish intelligence still suspected he had ties to radicals. Salmulski agreed to design the site for $5,000, and so unwittingly helped me build the platform for my future work against al-Qaeda.

In order to get photographs and testimonials for the website I advertised expeditions in nature spots in northern Europe at below market rate, and employed two assistants.

My outdoor expeditions had the added benefit of attracting the attention of militants dreaming of jihad.

Earlier that year – before MI5 cut their ties to me – I had infiltrated a group of British-Pakistanis who used to work out at a gym in an immigrant area of Birmingham. As intended, word had spread like wildfire about the Awlaki call I had organized for the doctors in Rochdale, making it easier for me to gain the trust of young radicalized British-Pakistanis.

Tucked in an alleyway behind a fish and chip shop, the gym – known locally as 'Jimmy's' – was housed in a concrete and metal shed with a martial arts and boxing area on the ground floor and a weights room and prayer room above. The gym played Islamic chants on loudspeakers to pump up the young men working out. Fliers on the wall advertised paintballing trips. Many of the regulars looked like they were on steroids; some wore long Salafi beards.

'Jimmy' owned the gym. He was a British-Pakistani in his early forties with flecks of grey in his long beard. He saw it as his vocation to bring young British-Pakistanis who were deviating from their religion off the streets, away from drugs, and back to the true path. And there could not have been a better place than the gym for him to instil his world-view.

Jimmy and some of the young radicals who attended the gym were impressed that I knew Awlaki. After training sessions, we would sit and listen to his online sermons. Among their number were several radicals in their late twenties. Jewel Uddin was quietly spoken and collected money locally for 'religious' causes. By contrast Anzal Hussain could not have been more boisterous. He had been an overweight spiritual Sufi Muslim before a sudden and complete change in his beliefs turned him into a lean, intensely serious Salafi, with a suitably serious beard to match. He had heard about the training exercises I had run for al-Muhajiroun in Barton Hills, and implored me to do the same for his group.

So one weekend seven of us squeezed into a battered Mitsubishi Pagero to drive up to Wetherby in the Yorkshire countryside. For £2,000 a year I had rented a small patch of woodland among rolling fields from a local farmer.

It did not take long for me to find out that this group had watched too many YouTube videos. When we arrived at our destination, Anzal and two others jumped out of the car with walkie-talkies in their hands.

'*Allahu Akbar*,' they whispered urgently, glancing furtively around the woodland. I was dumbstruck.

Anzal then went into a frenzy and started hacking at saplings wildly with a machete. Another joined in with an axe.

'You can't cut trees like that – they are Allah's creation,' I shouted.

Anzal stopped, machete in mid-air. 'You got a point, bruv – *Subhan'Allah*, brother,' he said in his thick Birmingham accent.

Anzal and another of the party kept us all awake that night by exchanging jihadist supplications every few minutes by walkie-talkie from their hammocks. '*As salaam aleikum Allah all Mujahideen!*'

The following morning after dawn prayers Anzal grabbed an air-gun. He began moving stealthily about the woodland.

'I'm going to kill some rabbits,' he announced. I felt embarrassed for him.

Then Anzal froze and went pale. A man and a black dog were walking towards us through the trees. It was the farmer, Dr Mike, who lived just next to the woodland, coming to say hello. The dog was an amiable creature called Billy, wagging his tail at the prospect of meeting some new people. Dr Mike was rather surprised to see a gaggle of wild-eyed young men with long beards and put Billy on a leash. Anzal retreated like he had seen a demon: in some fundamentalist circles black dogs are synonymous with the Devil.

When I saw the movie *Four Lions* later that year I felt I had already witnessed one of its scenes.

Dr Mike ended up reporting what he'd seen to the local police. My MI5 handler Andy was furious the next time I saw him.

'What the fuck were you thinking – doing this without our prior approval?' he said. The last thing British intelligence needed was the newspapers finding out an MI5 agent was training would-be terrorists.

Despite all the information I provided on the group, MI5 dropped the ball. On 30 June 2012 – just days before the start of the London Olympic Games – several of them would head to Yorkshire once again.

This time they were travelling with an arsenal of home-made weaponry – including machetes, kitchen knives, sawn-off shotguns, a partially built pipe-bomb and an improvised explosive device built out of fireworks and shrapnel – very similar to those later used by the Boston bombers. As in that later attack, the group had built it by downloading instructions from Awlaki's *Inspire* magazine.

Their target was a rally by the English Defence League – an extremist anti-Muslim group – in Dewsbury, West Yorkshire. Fortuitously for the EDL, the rally ended before the British-Pakistanis arrived. Although I had alerted MI5 to the cell several years previously, police only discovered the weapons and the plot because their car was stopped on the way back to Birmingham by a traffic patrol and found to have no insurance.

Police found a message in the car addressed to the EDL. 'Today is the day for retaliation (especially) for your blasphemy of Allah and His blessed messenger Mohammed. We love death more than you love life.'

It later emerged that Uddin had also been on the fringes of a terrorist cell arrested in Birmingham in September 2011 which had been plotting a suicide-bombing campaign in the UK. Several of the plotters were familiar to me from Jimmy's gym and the militant scene in Birmingham, including two of the ringleaders of the cell who received training with al-Qaeda in Pakistan in the spring of 2011. Security services suspected Uddin may have raised money for the cell but had not arrested him.

The EDL plot raised some disturbing questions. Uddin had been under observation by agents just five days before the men drove to Dewsbury, but without someone on the inside MI5 failed to detect the plot. Agents had seen him enter a shop where he purchased the knives but had not followed him inside.

In June 2013 Anzal Hussain, Jewel Uddin and three others I knew were sentenced to lengthy prison terms for the EDL plot.

But by the time they were planning to attack the EDL, I had long ceased working for MI5 because of British distaste for the Aminah mission.

Back in 2010 adulthood and paternity had unfortunately not made me any smarter about my resources. Rather than stow away the $250,000 reward, I poured much of it into Storm Bushcraft and travel. PET were delighted; they wanted local eyes and ears in East Africa because of the number of Scandinavian Somalis who had joined al-Shabaab, and they were getting them for free.

Despite the Ethiopian intervention and the presence of an African Union force to protect the government, al-Shabaab had taken over much of central and southern Somalia. And a lot of ethnic Somalis from Europe and North America were fighting for the group. Some had already returned to northern Europe, including a young militant called Mohammed Geele. Danish investigators established that Geele had close ties to al-Shabaab and senior al-Qaeda leaders in East Africa, and had emerged as an important player in the group during time he spent in Kenya in the 2000s.

In January 2010 Geele took a taxi to the street in Aarhus where the cartoonist Kurt Westergaard lived. Westergaard was hated by radical Islamists because he had drawn cartoons of the Prophet Mohammed for a Danish newspaper in 2005. Geele approached the front door armed with an axe and a knife and shattered the glass, setting off an alarm. Westergaard rushed to a safe room before the killer could reach him.

When the police arrived minutes later Geele lunged at them with his weapons. They fired into his left hand and right leg and took him into custody.

I had come across Geele in the months before the attack. PET had asked me to pay a visit to Kenneth Sorensen, my former associate in Sana'a, who was now back in Denmark. The two of us ran into Geele in a Somali mosque in Copenhagen, and Sorensen suggested we have lunch. Nothing about Geele at that time indicated he was planning an attack, but had I developed a relationship with him I might have picked it up.[2]

To me the growing terrorism in East Africa – in both Somalia and Kenya – was an invitation. I calculated that an outdoor adventure business there would allow Toby and myself cover to maintain contact with al-Shabaab. But first I needed to provide Toby with a 'legend' – credentials to make him a plausible partner.

Toby had grown his beard long. I taught him everything I knew about Islam and the circles I frequented, and shelled out thousands of dollars to send him on training courses for leading expeditions. We started peppering our emails to each other with Arabic and Islamic expressions to create a digital record of his conversion to Islamic fundamentalism.

---

2 PET was also worried by the influence of Abu Musab al-Somali, a Somali refugee I knew from my radical days, who had returned to Somalia. Phone intercepts indicated a number of Somali extremists in Denmark were contacting him. Al-Somali had come to Denmark as a refugee in his youth, then moved to Yemen, and had been arrested in 2006 along with several other members of my Sana'a circle for his part in the plan to smuggle guns from Yemen to militants in Somalia. But he had only received a two-year sentence and when freed had crossed the Gulf of Aden to Somalia. Danish intelligence were now concerned he might be plotting attacks in Denmark.

I then spread the word to some of my radical circle in the UK that I had joined forces with a member of the Royal Marines Reserves who had converted to Islam. I introduced Cowern to Rasheed Laskar, one of my Sana'a circle, who was now back in the UK, and to a number of radicals in Luton. I won the backing of Awlaki for my plans.

'I am happy to hear the news of your NGO and insha Allah you are the right person for the job. It is a good long term idea and could serve many needs in the future,' he wrote to me.

But the critical breakthrough came from al-Shabaab itself. In encrypted emails I outlined to Warsame and Ikrimah how the business would make it easier for me to get money and supplies to the group in Somalia: tents, hammocks, solar panels, water purification units and GPS locators.

'The NGO'S is really good cover for everything on Business,' Warsame wrote to me.

Ikrimah, by now a rising star among al-Shabaab operatives, was equally enthusiastic about Storm Bushcraft, writing to me: 'how is shompole, is it a good place? how is the regestration and paper word going on? . . . this wil b a very good project to all muslims.'

And he ended: 'May Allah bless this project and keep it away from the eyes and suspicions of the kufar.'

Shompole – a reserve in the Great Rift Valley in the south of Kenya – was one site I was considering for Storm Bushcraft. It had the major advantage of being very remote; there would be no prying eyes.

Ikrimah's endorsement of the project was critical. His credentials within al-Shabaab had been burnished by the money and equipment I had provided, and his time in Europe had given him deep contacts in extremist circles there. He now supervised foreign and Western recruits joining the group, most of whom transited through Nairobi.

Ikrimah's status in the group had also been bolstered by his ties to AQAP. And for that I and my Western intelligence handlers were entirely responsible. Awlaki had told me in the Shabwa compound the previous September that AQAP now had an arsenal of anti-tank rockets thanks to the ambush of several military convoys. I relayed the news to Ikrimah and it piqued his interest.

'The anti-tank mine that brothers got will they be willing to sell them to us and do they have weapons that can hit a tank frm far like the ones hisbullah used to destroy israel merkeva tank? or rpg 29 etc?' he asked.

Ikrimah asked to be put in direct contact with Awlaki, whom he called 'Hook'. In early 2010 they started exchanging encrypted messages and began working on a plan by which al-Shabaab recruits would travel to Yemen for training before being sent back to fight – or more ominously dispatched to the West to launch attacks.

'And as for going to hooks place . . . then i was told by hook that they want to train brothers and then send them back or to the west,' Ikrimah wrote to me later that year.

As my visits multiplied and I became established in Kenya I met with al-Shabaab envoys. The local intelligence services seemed overwhelmed by the group's growing presence and unable to stem the recruitment of young Kenyan Muslims. I would email Warsame or Ikrimah and they would pass on a number to call. Then I would use a Safaricom SIM card to make the call.

A favourite rendezvous was the Paris Hotel in Nairobi; it was there that I met a short bespectacled Kenyan sent by my two al-Shabaab contacts. He wanted to speak Arabic but I insisted we speak in English to avoid attracting attention. I handed him $3,000 to give to Warsame, which Danish intelligence had given me to keep me in favour. Before he took his leave he asked me to hand over the mobile phone I had used to contact him.

'We need to check it out,' he said. Realizing I had used the same phone to contact Danish agents I had to think quickly.

'I never give my phone out – our mutual friend knows that,' I replied.

Anders in Danish intelligence later told me I was lucky; there were indications al-Shabaab had penetrated Safaricom, the East African mobile-phone company. If they'd obtained my SIM card they could have pulled up my phone records.

A few days after that meeting, suicide bombers affiliated with al-Shabaab blew themselves up at a restaurant and rugby club in Kampala, Uganda, where sports fans were watching the World Cup Final – killing more than seventy people. Many of those involved in the plot were

Kenyan. Ikrimah later told me his envoy was among those arrested in Kenya for helping plan the attack; the crackdown in Kenya meant it was no longer safe for him to travel from Somalia to meet me in Nairobi. I never found out whether he was involved in the Kampala attack but I got the sense he was taking on a greater operational role for the group. He had developed deep connections to Kenyan militants affiliated with al-Shabaab and told me of his regular trips to Uganda.

I had begun negotiating with the Kenyan authorities and the Masai tribe to establish an adventure camp. Beside Shompole, I was trying to lease a rundown resort at the Masinga Dam, built to harness hydro-electric power from the Tana River.

However, my expenses were beginning to overwhelm me. Money had a habit of running through my hands quickly, and I had not done much bookkeeping after my windfall from the CIA. I had ploughed more than a quarter of the proceeds into the Kenyan venture but it was like throwing money into a sinkhole. I still had no base from which to launch the next stage of my intelligence work. And while the Danes offered moral support, the British were less than delighted to find out that a UK national was involved in my scheme. If word leaked that a Royal Marine reservist had become a jihadist facilitator there would be explaining to do.

In late 2010 Toby Cowern was planning to relocate to Kenya from his Arctic Circle base in Sweden when he received a summons from the British embassy in Stockholm. An MI5 agent led him to a back room and told him it would be 'in his interest' to drop all plans involving me. The agent never spelled out why Toby should abandon the project; perhaps he didn't need to. The idea of a Royal Marine reservist consorting with al-Shabaab was just too much of a risk. Toby had no choice but to comply and my Kenyan venture began to unravel.

My confidence in my handlers was not enhanced when they asked me to take part in a sting operation that would have probably blown my cover.

Danish intelligence had learned that a group of radicals had bought a Kalashnikov from a Copenhagen drug dealer. The buyers were Swedes of Arab origin, and several of them had already travelled to jihadist battlegrounds.

A Tunisian in his mid-forties was the group's leader. He had recently returned from Pakistan, where he was suspected of having links with senior al-Qaeda operatives.

Klang asked me if I could travel to Copenhagen, where several of the group were staying.

'We believe they are doing target reconnaissance. We'd like you to befriend them and find out their plans,' he said.

The implication that I could sidle up to members of this group as they plotted a terrorist attack in Copenhagen was another disturbing sign of Klang's lack of tradecraft, or even basic common sense.

'Are you out of your mind?' I said. 'I don't know these guys from Adam – don't you think they're going to be just slightly suspicious?'

As it turned out the surveillance of both Swedish and Danish intelligence would be enough to thwart their plans. Several weeks later in the early morning of 29 December the four men crossed the Øresund bridge from Malmö to Copenhagen. They had a machine gun, ammunition, a silencer and dozens of plastic wrist straps. Wiretaps suggested that within days they planned to storm the offices of *Jyllands-Posten* in Copenhagen, the newspaper that had first published controversial cartoons of the Prophet Mohammed.[3]

All four were arrested later that day. The suspected Swedish-Yemeni mastermind of the plot went to ground and evaded capture. He soon headed to Yemen.

On a heavily overcast day early in December I arrived at Heathrow airport from Kenya to reassess my future. The skies matched my mood. Perhaps it was time to quit the spy game; I seemed to be running into opposition at every turn and was spending my own money to help the Danish government.

---

3 The men travelled to Denmark on 28 December 2010 and were arrested the next day. Mounir Dhahri was the Tunisian cell leader. Another member of the cell – Munir Awad, a Swede of Lebanese descent, whose curly, well-maintained long hair fell over his shoulders – had fought with the Islamic Courts Union in Somalia.

Western intelligence believed the plan was part of a wider conspiracy by al-Qaeda to launch 'Mumbai-style' attacks across Europe, which had triggered an unprecedented US State Department warning for Americans in Europe that October.

On the other hand I had moved in jihadist circles for more than ten years. I knew the networks and relationships among the groups, even though it was still difficult to predict who among the would-be jihadis would go operational.

I was reminded of just how difficult on 11 December 2010. A man plotting carnage on a huge scale drove into the centre of Stockholm with home-made explosive devices. Parking on a busy street amid hundreds of Christmas shoppers, he sent emails to Swedish intelligence and news outlets, saying his actions were in revenge for cartoons of the Prophet Mohammed published in the Swedish press and for the Swedish presence in Afghanistan. He then set fire to his car and walked away.

His plan was to wait until crowds converged on the burning vehicle, then set off a pressure-cooker device on the passenger seat by walkie-talkie. He had positioned himself so that those fleeing the scene would run towards him. He would then trigger devices in a backpack and waist belt.

The explosives in the car did not detonate. CCTV video showed that in a nearby street the man was trying to blow himself up. For ten minutes he walked through the area, trying to make the device attached to his stomach work. Finally part of the bomb exploded, killing the man instantly. No one else was hurt.

Later that day I discovered that the lone bomber was my former Luton friend Taimour Abdulwahab al-Abdaly. I had met him in a department store in the town and played football with him. Of all my circle in Luton I thought him the least likely to carry out an attack. In our discussions he had actually criticized me for my radical views. But that was more than five years ago.

Taimour had been operating on his own after training in Iraq. It seems no one else among the Luton set had any idea that he was preparing an act of terrorism, with the exception of Nasserdine Menni, an asylum seeker from Algeria who was subsequently convicted of sending funds to Taimour for the attack. It was possible that had I kept up my contacts in England I might at least have heard of Taimour's travel to Iraq, which in itself would have been warning enough. But after the falling-out of the intelligence services I was not allowed to work sources in the UK. So I laughed when Klang called me from Copenhagen.

'The Brits have asked us to get in touch with you about Taimour. Do you know his friends in Luton?'

'I don't think he was radicalized here, or at least if he was it was after I last saw him – and that was more than five years ago.'

The idea that the British could turn me on and off as a source was ridiculous. But I was soon to discover that they were not the only ones who wanted to reactivate me when it suited them.

CHAPTER TWENTY
TARGET AWLAKI

Early 2011–Summer 2011

There was a lull in my intelligence work in early 2011. The Danes were still paying my retainer but had no overseas missions. Instead I focused on developing Storm Bushcraft. I had begun to see the venture as a real business rather than as just a cover. After all I was sinking my own funds into it. I started thinking about a new life. My negotiations to buy the resort near the Masinga Dam in Kenya were finally coming to a head. Despite my dwindling bank balance, I had paid $20,000 for the option to buy the property outright within a year.

Most of the winter was spent brooding in my house in Coventry. Everyday life seemed so mundane. The gloomy skies and early darkness only added to my sense of restlessness. Although the British had cut ties to me, I was still on PET's books and had to keep up the pretence that I was Murad Storm, the zealous extremist. Living that lie had begun to gnaw at me. Was it really still worth it? From time to time the anxiety I felt about Abdullah Mehdar and Aminah would return, and I'd turn back to self-medicating with cocaine, snorting it joylessly alone at home.

In February I noticed on Facebook that my high school in Korsør was organizing a reunion. I signed up. I had lost contact with almost all the friends I had in Korsør as a teenager and it would be good to spend a weekend with them. But at the last minute I decided not to go – afraid that photographs of the occasion might appear online, showing me mixing with the *kuffar*. I was living in a prison of my own making.

Perhaps the most difficult aspect of that life was the constant need to deceive Fadia. I had managed to keep the cocaine a secret from her. But I had to explain my frequent absences overseas, where the money had come from for my investment in Storm Bushcraft, the negotiations in Kenya. I created a fiction that she seemed to believe. I told her that after I had recovered my faith, I had met some devout Muslims in Sana'a – from Yemen and Saudi Arabia – who wanted to build a retreat in the Kenyan bush for pious young men to attend. I claimed they knew of my Bushcraft experience and had raised the money to contract me to research the possibilities. It was a chance to build something valuable, I told her, and one that might open up other opportunities. There were one or two elements of truth in what I told her, but a big lie was at the heart of the story. Fadia had no idea that I had received $250,000 from the US Treasury – in cash – and no idea that it was quickly vanishing.

On the weekends that I had custody of my kids I longed to tell them that my Islamic robes, my beard, my prayers were all a sham, and I was secretly working against terrorists. But I never did. Such knowledge would only have put them in danger. And in any case even my eldest, Osama, was only turning nine.

It depressed me that the only people who knew my role, my real purpose, were my Danish handlers, but our contacts had become limited to phone calls. I felt redundant. The last thing I was expecting was another approach from the CIA. But, one morning in April, I received a text from PET. Big Brother had lost track of Anwar al-Awlaki and needed my help.

Klang said a 'very significant sum' was on the table from the Americans if I could lead them to the cleric. Perhaps the US government budget crisis was not as grave as I had thought, or perhaps they were that desperate. They had good reason to be.

Awlaki was rapidly becoming the face of al-Qaeda. Six months previously he had been involved in an ingenious AQAP plot to blow up US-bound cargo planes with explosives concealed in printer cartridges. Two bombs designed by master bomb-maker Ibrahim al-Asiri and inserted into laser printers had been dropped off at FedEx and UPS offices in Sana'a. They passed through airport security undetected and were then loaded on to the first leg of their journey towards the United States. Only an intelligence tip to Saudi authorities allowed authorities in Dubai and the UK to eventually intercept the deadly cargo.

Hours later President Obama addressed the American public, telling them that a dangerous plot had been averted.[1]

Al-Asiri had concealed the explosives so well that bomb disposal teams at both locations initially believed the printers were not bombs – even after examining them. It was the most sophisticated al-Qaeda device that Western counter-terrorism officials had ever seen and they said it had the potential to bring down a plane.

Awlaki had himself played a role in preparations for the attack. He had asked Rajib Karim, a British Airways employee in the UK, to provide technical details about X-ray scanning equipment deployed at airports and whether it was possible to get packages on board planes to the United States without their being scanned.

'Our highest priority is the US. Anything there, even on a smaller scale compared to what we may do in the UK, would be our choice,' he wrote in an encrypted email to Karim.

According to the US government, Awlaki 'not only helped plan and oversee the plot but was also directly involved in the details of its execution – to the point that he took part in the development and testing of the explosive devices that were placed on the planes'.

US officials spoke of Awlaki's involvement in 'numerous other plots against the US and Western interests'. And even when not involved, he inspired. Awlaki seemed the common denominator in almost every plot being uncovered in the West. Potentially the most dangerous was the plan by three young men in the US, including a naturalized Afghan called Najibullah Zazi, to blow up New York subway trains at rush hour in September 2009. Prior to connecting with al-Qaeda on a trip to Pakistan the trio had been radicalized by listening to Awlaki's sermons on their iPods. Another devotee was an American-Pakistani who tried to set off a car bomb in Times Square in May 2010.

---

1 Later British authorities revealed that one of the devices had been set to blow up over the eastern seaboard of the United States.

AQAP was also becoming the most sophisticated of the group's franchises in using the internet to rally supporters. In June 2010 it released the first issue of the online magazine *Inspire*. Awlaki was the driving force behind the magazine, which was edited by his protégé Samir Khan, an American Saudi-born extremist.

The first issue included a recipe 'How to Build a Bomb in Your Mom's Kitchen', which detailed how to make crude pressure-cooker bombs from gunpowder and shrapnel.[2]

So there were plenty of reasons for silencing Awlaki. And the Arab Spring that erupted in the first few months of 2011 would provide another. The unrest that had come to Yemen had provided jihadis with operational oxygen. And in the southern and eastern tribal areas, al-Qaeda began to take advantage of President Saleh's myopic focus on political survival and his growing unpopularity by recruiting fighters from sympathetic tribes.

Awlaki had an ever larger area in which to operate and growing resources with which to plot the next attack on the American home-land. In its publications AQAP promised it would only be a matter of time.

My Danish handlers knew me well enough by now to know that I would agree to rejoin the hunt for Awlaki – even as Yemen seemed to be imploding. They were aware of how frustrating the last several months had been for me.

At the beginning of May I was invited to a follow-up meeting in Copenhagen with them and my former CIA handler Jed. As I waited at Birmingham airport, the TV screens showed one face time and again: that of Osama bin Laden. Just a few hours earlier a team of US Navy SEALs had swooped on bin Laden's compound in Abbottabad, Paki-stan. The leader of al-Qaeda had been killed, his body whisked away by helicopter to an ignominious burial at sea. Normally, few travellers bother to watch the news channels at airports; on this day there were clusters of people gazing at the screens. The great bogeyman of the West had been vanquished.

---

2 In the following years the recipe would be downloaded and used by militants in multiple terrorism plots on both sides of the Atlantic, including the Boston bombing.

I thought of all the fighters bin Laden had encouraged to embrace martyrdom while he cowered behind the high walls of a comfortable house. He may have risen to fame in jihadist circles as a fighter, but I felt that the way he had lived his last few years and the way he died in a house full of women and children might cost him some of his lustre.

Even so, the man who had been an inspirational figure to a generation of jihadis was gone. The torch had been passed, but who would grasp it? Plenty of observers – within al-Qaeda and the intelligence agencies that were trying to eradicate it – regarded Anwar al-Awlaki as a candidate.

From Copenhagen I was driven to the holiday villa at Hornbaek where we had plotted the Aminah mission with the Americans. The mood this time was even more intense.

To my surprise Jed gave me a bear hug when I arrived. He seemed slightly embarrassed that I had been so unceremoniously put out to pasture after the Aminah mission.

'Congratulations on getting bin Laden,' I said.

'Thanks, man – this is a huge day for us.'

Klang interjected: 'You know what this means? Awlaki has just become US public enemy number one.'

It seemed to be the cue Jed was waiting for.

'We want you to find him. This has become a huge priority for my government.'

'Don't worry. I'll find him,' I replied. I was thrilled to be back in the game.

We agreed I would return to Sana'a to try to reconnect with Awlaki. Within days of our meeting, he showed yet again how difficult he would be to eliminate, even after suddenly appearing in the crosshairs.

On 5 May 2011, less than a week after bin Laden's death, US military drones over Yemen locked on to a pick-up truck leaving a trail of dust as it sped along a desert track some twenty miles from Ataq, the town where I had visited Awlaki three years previously. This was still his home turf.

US intelligence believed the cleric and several al-Qaeda associates were in the truck. But unlike the US Navy SEAL raid in Abbottabad, the Yemen operation had been hurriedly put together. Just a day previously, Yemeni intelligence had told US officials they had information indicating Awlaki was staying in a nearby village.

As US officials watched the satellite feed in real time three missiles were unleashed. Seconds later they slammed into the ground, sending up a cloud of debris and smoke. None scored a direct hit.

'We felt the wave of explosion near the car that shattered the windows,' Awlaki told a comrade the next day. 'We even saw a flash of light, so we thought that we were ambushed and under fire. We thought a rocket was fired on us.'

The car had accelerated away from the danger zone, making a mad dash along desert tracks. Despite the devastation outside nobody in the car had been injured. According to villagers, two brothers known for sheltering al-Qaeda fighters rushed to the scene of the attack and caught up with Awlaki's vehicle. With US drones still circling overhead they switched vehicles with Awlaki's group.

The swap saved the cleric's life. Minutes later the pick-up truck from which Awlaki had just tumbled exploded in an amber fireball, killing the two brothers instantly.

Awlaki was running for cover when he saw the explosion. The cleric's driver had sped to a nearby valley, where a few trees offered cover from the drones. Awlaki and his comrades had jumped out and scattered in different directions.

'Air strikes continued in the different areas, but I was directed by one of the brothers to one of the numerous cliffs in the mountains,' Awlaki told a comrade afterwards. He slept outside that night and was picked up by al-Qaeda fighters the following day.

'Something of fear befalls you, but the Almighty Allah sends down tranquility,' he told the comrade later. 'This time eleven missiles missed their target but the next time the first rocket may hit it.'

Prophetic words.

The preparations for this mission were more demanding than any before. PET sent me on a refresher weapons course because of the growing dangers of travelling into the tribal areas.

My instructors, Daniel and Frank, were men of few words, but put me through a punishing schedule of all-terrain driving and battlefield first aid. On the shooting range I fired live rounds from an MP-5 sub-machine gun, Magnum pump-action gun, a Kalashnikov assault rifle and a handgun. I was taught to shoot using left and right hands in case I was injured. I did drills where I raced towards a target, firing heavier weapons first before using the pistol at close range.

I was taught how to respond if my vehicle was ambushed – and how to shoot out of the windows while driving. If I came under sustained fire I should hide under the steering wheel because the engine block offered protection against incoming fire.

Daniel told me that if I felt my life was in danger at a checkpoint I should never wind down the window but shoot through the door with a handgun hidden in the folds of a newspaper. In one exercise I crouched on the tarmac beside the door and shot at a target on the other side of the car. The 9mm bullet pierced through both doors.

Finally I was taken into an abandoned complex, where I learned how to clear a building and respond to a hostage situation. I was given an MP-5 with ink bullets and each time I edged around a wall I had a split second to hit a target. As I cleared room after room my mind drifted back to the paintballing exercises I had joined with my militant 'brothers' in nearby Odense a decade previously. This felt rather more serious.

Frank laughed at the thought that he was training a former Bandido.

The Danes were teaching me these skills to protect me not only from al-Qaeda but from Yemeni government soldiers and tribal militias. In a volatile country where opening fire was a standard means of starting negotiations I could be the target of any number of well-armed groups. Klang told me that if my life was in danger it was permissible to shoot at Yemeni soldiers.

After the weapons training, a stern-looking psychologist working for PET conducted an evaluation on whether I was fit to proceed with the mission, asking me a battery of questions in a hotel suite north of Copenhagen.

'How do you feel about going back to Yemen?' he asked.

'I'm obviously a bit anxious.'

'It's good you feel that way. If you didn't I'd be worried,' he replied.

'I feel torn about going after Awlaki. He's been my friend, and I know he would give his life for me.' It felt good to talk.

'That's normal – it's only human to have a conscience,' he replied.

I told him that I'd been 'self-medicating' with cocaine to deal with the stress created by my intelligence work.

'That's just a temporary solution for a permanent problem,' he replied clinically.

The psychologist cleared me to return to Yemen. Nobody at PET ever suggested any treatment for my drug abuse. After the Barcelona trip I had told Klang that I was using cocaine to tackle bouts of anxiety but his only concern had been that I should not do it in his presence.

As preparations intensified agents were at my side every day – discussing travel arrangements, where I would live, the options for contacting Awlaki. Perhaps the best advice came from an outdoor specialist at PET whose name was Jacob. He looked at me earnestly as we discussed the mission ahead over coffee.

'You are the one doing the most dangerous job in the world and you shouldn't let them forget it,' he told me. 'Make sure you demand what you need. And when you are over there, don't sit with the terrorists because the Americans won't hesitate to kill you if you are with their target.'

I wasn't sure whether he spoke from experience or was exaggerating for effect. But it was chilling. I reminded myself that I was dispensable if a target of Awlaki's profile came into view.

Ultimately I could only rely on myself.

In mid-May I had a last pre-mission meeting with Jed and my Danish handlers, this time in a suite at the Marienlyst Hotel in Helsingør. From the windows there was a fabulous view of the Swedish coastline across the Øresund.

I opened up my laptop in front of Jed at the hotel and fired up the Mujahideen Secrets software. I typed out a message to the cleric, which I signed 'Polar Bear' – a private nickname Awlaki had given me. I then entered the public key supplied by *Inspire* magazine and hit 'encrypt' before sending it to an email address provided in *Inspire* magazine.

The Danes handed me an iPhone. It was configured so that everything I did was instantly uploaded to Danish intelligence. 'If you take a picture or video we'll see it in real time and we'll be alerted any time you send a message,' Klang explained. The phone had a Danish SIM card; I would end up running up a massive bill for the Danish taxpayer.

When Jed was gone the Danes also handed me an Acer notebook computer. They asked me to use the new computer when communicating with my al-Qaeda contacts instead of a Samsung laptop Jed had given me before the Aminah mission.

'We want to be one step ahead of the Americans,' Klang said. Danish intelligence were asserting their proprietorial rights.

On 23 May I flew into Sana'a. My cover story was that I was back in the country to set up a Yemeni branch of Storm Bushcraft. Fadia had travelled ahead of me. I had suggested to her she could reconnect with her family while I continued work on my Bushcraft venture. She was aware that I wanted to check on Awlaki's situation, but still had no idea why the cleric was so important to me.

The capital was in tumult with roiling protests, including a sit-in by students in the central square. The day I arrived clashes erupted between regime forces and an opposition faction after President Saleh backpedalled on a plan for peaceful transition. Al-Qaeda couldn't be happier, I thought.

I found a house on 50th Street. Its proximity to the Presidential Palace was problematic given Saleh's uncertain grip on power, but it was the most affluent neighbourhood in Sana'a. The Minister of Oil lived next door; almost all the properties had guards. It was – by Yemeni standards – an expensive rental. But I was hiding in plain sight. The Yemeni authorities would not expect a hardened jihadi to take up residence among cabinet ministers, and I could justify my extravagance to Awlaki and others on the same grounds – while boasting about the growth of my company Storm Bushcraft and my plans to bring it to Yemen one day.

I also thought there was a possibility that Awlaki might wilt under pressure and accept an offer to seek refuge with Aminah at our home, safe from drones and missile strikes. After all, bin Laden had done much the same – far from the killing grounds of Waziristan. Then I could turn the cleric over to the Yemeni authorities. He would live; Aminah would be free. And I would not have to glance anxiously at my withering bank balance every day.

Jed had said – grudgingly – that it was worth a try, but he really wanted to see Awlaki 'eliminated'.

When I returned to Sana'a the security situation was deteriorating. On the morning of Friday, 3 June, an explosion shook our building. My ears were ringing as I rushed to the roof. I trained my binoculars on a column of thick black smoke. It was coming from the Presidential Palace – and soon rumours swirled that President Saleh had been killed in a bomb attack. They were unfounded, but the ageing Yemeni leader was severely burned in the explosion, caused by a bomb that had been planted in a mosque in which he was praying.

As the President was flown to Saudi Arabia for emergency treatment, my mission took on extra urgency. Awlaki had not replied to my email to *Inspire* magazine and I feared he had gone into deep hiding after his recent close brush with US drones. If full-scale civil war erupted, I would not be able to stay in Yemen – let alone reach Awlaki. I turned to my old Yemeni jihadi contact, Abdul. He had a friend called Mujeeb who was a reliable go-between with al-Qaeda fighters in the southern tribal areas.

After reconnecting with Abdul, I bought thumb drives and set about writing a message to the cleric which I encrypted using Mujahideen Secrets. I asked Awlaki to send a messenger back with his reply. Polar Bear, I told him, would wait at a restaurant we both knew in Sana'a on three evenings I specified. I uploaded the message on to one of the thumb drives and gave it to Abdul.

'Tell Mujeeb to get this to Adil al-Abab,' I told him. Al-Abab, a Yemeni militant I had befriended in Sana'a in 2006, was now AQAP's religious emir in the tribal areas. I was confident he would be able to get the thumb drive to Awlaki.

'I'm using Abdul as a last resort because I don't totally trust him,' I wrote to Awlaki.

I was covering myself because of the doubts Awlaki had expressed about Abdul. At the same time I was taking a risk. If Abdul discovered the contents of my encrypted message, I would lose an intermediary at the very least and gain an enemy at worst.

The rendezvous restaurant was al-Shaibani, which served traditional meat dishes and was close to our home. I alerted my Danish handlers and they had in turn briefed the Americans. On the first of three designated evenings I waited at al-Shaibani, sipping tea. I had an eerie sensation that I was being watched. Two men dressed in Yemeni clothes were glancing my way a little too often. Perhaps I was worrying too much; after all I made an unusual sight in an Arab capital consumed by unrest. An hour ticked by and it was clear the courier was not coming. It was the same the second night, and I began to fear that Awlaki had not received my message.

On the third evening a slim, dark-skinned young man approached my table. He was wearing his scarf in the style of Marib, a province that was emerging as an al-Qaeda safe haven. He looked like he was in his late teens.

'Colour?' the young man asked me in Arabic. '*Akhdar*,' I replied, the Arabic word for green. It was the code word I had provided Awlaki. The messenger fished into his pocket and handed me a thumb drive, the same one I had given to Abdul. The young courier also handed me $300, gesturing at the thumb drive by way of explanation.

'Let me take a look at this. I'll meet you at the al-Hamra restaurant on al-Haddah Street in four hours, okay?' I told him.

Back in the house, my hands shaking, I inserted the thumb drive into my laptop, loaded the Mujahideen Secrets encryption software, and began reading.

'I did receive the flash you sent me,' he wrote, adding that it was 'fine if you don't want to use Abdul' for future messages.

Awlaki continued: '3 things: If you email me please write down the date on all your messages. Second, keep in mind that it takes a few days for emails to get to me so if you are setting an appointment then give me advance notice. Third: you do not need to write "to the sheikh" when you email Inspire. Anything from your email will be delivered to me.

'Please respond to this message with what you want to say and give it to the brother,' the cleric wrote.

'This brother may be the messenger between us for now. One IMPORTANT note: The brother does not know that he is delivering messages for me and he doesn't know where I am so do not mention that this message is for me. Just give it to him and he will deliver it where it needs to be delivered and will get to me insha Allah.'

Awlaki was employing a 'cut-out' to get his message to me. It was a classic technique. If the young Maribi were captured or followed he could not immediately lead the Americans to Awlaki. He was just one link in a chain and had no idea where the next courier would be going.

'For future correspondence I believe it would be better if your wife delivers the flash to the brother,' Awlaki wrote to me. 'It's up to you but I believe that you would definitely be watched and that might put you and the brother in jeopardy . . . The brother says it is not safe for him to enter sanaa frequently. So please mention all what you need to say in the message you send me.'

So much detailed guidance on security told me that Awlaki feared being betrayed and was aware just how important he had become. So he had insisted on several chains of custody.

'Please let me know what your program is and the latest news from the west,' he wrote. And he had this request: 'My wife needs some stuff from sanaa so can your wife buy it for her? We have sent other people before and nothing really suited her taste.'

The cleric had attached a message from Aminah for Fadia:

'I miss my family big time. Insha'Allah I hope one day I will see them. You probably wonder how I am doing here. I am fine alhamdid-ullah. Now after one year I did get used on condition we are living but restrictions we have just make our lives complicated . . . I am learning every day. I did learn to cook some Yemeni meals.'

Her shopping list had little to do with improving her Yemeni cooking.

'Please send us chocolate inside, Lindtt different flavor – 100g, Kinder Bueno 10 pc, Ferrero Roche. And I would like a parfume. It's Dolce&Gabbana – Light blue. Box is beautiful sky blue color.'

She really must miss home, I thought.

Then came a very different shopping list – one which must have been influenced by her husband. Taking Fadia to meet her in Vienna the previous year had turned out to be a useful move. Aminah had some detailed requests for her – clothes and other feminine requirements that I could not possibly have entertained as an upstanding Salafist. 'I give up of Yemeni clothes. All I have I don't like and it is too hot to wear it. Fabrics are not good, synthetic, it's just horrible.

'Please if you can find some European clothes. I miss it so much,' she wrote. 'Dresses should be long, without sleeves . . . fabric should be light, non-transparent . . . and if you can find denim mini skirt – tight and very short.

'Next I need 10 packages of feminine pads . . .'

And so the list went on.

I pulled out my Danish iPhone and called up Klang, my PET handler, who was thousands of miles away in Denmark. 'The Agriculture Minister has replied, and he has a message for me,' I said.

'Whaaaat?' Klang replied, not remembering our code name for the cleric. (Awlaki's father had been Yemen's Minister for Agriculture.)

'Holy shit! This is big,' he exclaimed. We continued the conversation in a Danish dialect we were sure no one in Yemen – or even the US National Security Agency – could understand.

'Listen, we should meet soon in a warm place,' Klang said at the end of the call.

I wrote a short reply for Awlaki, shut down my laptop and hurried to the stores. I did not buy everything the cleric and his wife had asked for; in any case the 'luxury' stores in Sana'a were a pitiful sight. It was also important that they (especially Aminah) should need to stay in touch for other items. I then went to the al-Hamra restaurant to give the bags and the message to the courier.

When I got there he was outside, chewing khat, addictive leaves consumed by the large majority of Yemeni men which produces a 'high' not dissimilar to amphetamines or a quadruple espresso laced with tequila.

'I couldn't find everything but I'm going back to Europe soon and will buy the other stuff there,' I told him. I placed the $300 into his hands. 'I can't accept this. Please make sure it gets back to where it needs to,' I said.

'I will,' he replied. He rushed off into the evening.

The next day I sent Awlaki an encrypted email through *Inspire* as he had instructed, to re-establish online communication.

'Please find a new courier,' I wrote to him: 'The guy you sent was chewing khat and this is not something I appreciate.'

Awlaki had previously expressed to me his frustration that so many of his compatriots were addicted to khat. My disapproval would please him as well as show that I was serious about operational security.

Al-Qaeda in Yemen generally frowned on the narcotic but tolerated its consumption in areas they controlled because there was no specific injunction in Islam against it – and because they knew stamping it out would be a fast ticket to losing support. Some of their suicide bombers had even died with khat-filled cheeks.

Shortly afterwards an encrypted email came back with a new request: hexamine briquettes and a fridge (most likely for storing explosives), a Leatherman knife and all-terrain sandals. In the same message Aminah suggested that when things were a little calmer my wife and I should come to visit them. Despite a year in Yemen, Aminah still suffered from chronic naivety.

As usual I immediately pasted the message into a draft email account I shared with Danish intelligence so they could read it straight away.

It was time for me to file an interim report. On 28 June I left Sana'a for Malaga in Spain – the 'warm place' Klang had promised. I had a renewed sense of purpose. My old tradecraft had not deserted me. I had arrived in the midst of an uprising and still, within a month, had established contact with Awlaki and confirmed his trust in me.

Against all expectations we now had one of the world's most dangerous men firmly in our sights, and for all the billions the Americans poured into their intelligence services, our tiny Danish outfit was leading the way. But I told myself not to get carried away. The Aminah mission had failed; and arrogance begets mistakes.

True to form, Klang had picked Malaga more for his own pleasure than my comfort.

'Akhi – what have you done? This is great!' he exclaimed as I came out of the arrivals hall. Akhi, which means 'brother' in Arabic, was the nickname that PET had recently given me. Klang was sporting mirrored sunglasses, chinos and a polo shirt with a giant Ralph Lauren logo. In contrast Jesper, the frail former banker, had rather worn jeans and a cotton shirt.

In a Costa del Sol hotel I sat down with the Danes in a quiet, shady corner of the poolside restaurant. Soren and Anders looked tanned.

'You've made Big Brother very happy – this is a huge deal for them,' Klang told me, after we ordered club sandwiches. Apparently I had also made Danish intelligence happy – to the extent that they had sent no fewer than four representatives to Malaga to greet me.

I quickly found out why.

'The Americans are willing to give you five million dollars if you lead them to Awlaki,' Jesper said.

'I understand,' I replied, scarcely believing.

They had not been lying about the 'very significant sum' and were clearly desperate to find Awlaki. I imagined the White House was now taking an active interest in the pursuit of the man who had become arguably the biggest threat to the West. The sum involved matched that offered by the FBI for some of the most dangerous men in the world.

'There's just one thing Jed needs you to help him with,' Klang said. 'His bosses are upset you told Awlaki you didn't trust Abdul as a courier and want you to explain.'

'It was my judgement call; I knew Awlaki didn't fully trust him.'

'Okay,' said Klang. 'Just use that language with Jed and we'll be fine.'

I was puzzled by this sudden anxiety over Abdul's role.

'Why the big song and dance?' I replied. 'Do you think Abdul's working for them?'

'Who knows,' Klang replied with a shrug, avoiding eye contact and refilling his glass. Carlsberg, I noticed – you can take a Dane out of Denmark . . .

I was intrigued that Abdul, of all the people I knew in Yemen, might also be a double agent. I had known him for ten years and he had always seemed a committed jihadi, deeply involved with al-Qaeda and hostile to pro-Western Arab governments and the US. But there were perhaps clues. During my most recent stay in Yemen, Abdul seemed over-enthusiastic in wanting information about Awlaki. He had more cash than ever; and had a new car with no obvious source of earnings. He had also started chewing khat.

Most significant, I thought, was that he now had the same model of phone – a Nokia N900 with a flip keyboard – which Jed had given me. Had the CIA developed Abdul as an informer during my ten months in the wilderness?

For two full days I was debriefed in a suite. Even MI6 had rejoined the fray, sending a young agent to observe the meeting.

Jed asked his question about Abdul and I gave the response we had choreographed. He grunted 'okay' and jotted in his notebook.

We went through the list of supplies Awlaki wanted – hexamine briquettes and the fridge.

'We can't agree to the hexamine,' Klang said. It could be adapted to make explosives.

'So I should just go back empty-handed?' I shot back at him. 'Isn't that going to make me look amateurish? Or worse, make him suspect I'm a Western agent?'

There was an awkward silence. Klang did not appreciate being shot down in front of the CIA.

'Why don't I just provide them with wooden briquettes?'

The agents exchanged looks. 'You know what? You're not just a pretty face,' Jesper said with a smirk.

I gave Jed the USB stick Awlaki had used so that it could be sent for analysis, and also handed over the remaining thumb drives I had bought and intended to use for future messages. I thought the Americans might want to install some sort of tracking device on them.

'Do you think you might be able to travel out to see Awlaki?' Jed asked me.

'Possibly, but the security situation has got a lot worse,' I replied, 'especially in the south. Al-Qaeda is beginning to take control in some areas, and it's impossible to know which units to trust in the army.'

In the evening I took a stroll with the Danes and the deferential MI6 agent. In the streets around the hotel stood expensive villas with lush gardens. Sprinkler systems shot a golden mist into the evening sunshine. A lot of Russian money had made it to this part of Spain.

'You'll be able to afford one of these properties soon, Akhi,' Klang said. 'And you'd better let us come stay.'

We even discussed a joint business venture funded out of my 'winnings' – a restaurant or bar on the beach. For the first time I sensed my Danish handlers had more than a professional interest in my success. But I was still a long way from delivering Awlaki to the CIA. And even as we walked among the scent of jasmine and lemon trees, I could not relish the prospect of becoming rich by sending a man who had once been my friend to his death.

Jed had stayed in the hotel: CIA rules dictated he could not be seen in public with me. After we left I caught sight of him at Malaga airport. He walked past pretending not to know me but smiling out of the corner of his mouth.

Days after I left Malaga, I discovered that the US had made an important breakthrough – at the expense of my old Birmingham acquaintance, Ahmed Abdulkadir Warsame. After my telephone call connecting him with Awlaki, he had begun regular contact with AQAP. He shared details on some of these communications with me, which allowed Western intelligence to track his plans. In 2009 he emailed to tell me he wanted to travel to Yemen to meet with AQAP's leadership and later informed me that Awlaki had invited him to train in Yemen.

Warsame took the offer. In 2010 he travelled to Yemen to broker a weapons deal between AQAP and al-Shabaab. During that visit he met Awlaki and received explosives training. Not yet twenty-five, he had become the main point of liaison between the two groups, funnelling money and communications gear from Somalia to Yemen in exchange for weapons for Somali fighters.

In April 2011, Warsame had boarded a fishing dhow in a small Yemeni harbour to travel back across the Gulf of Aden to Somalia. But the Americans were waiting for him and took him into custody on the high seas. Warsame would spend two months on a US Navy amphibious assault ship, the USS *Boxer*, where he proved a rich source.[3]

---

3 He was transferred to a New York courtroom, where he pleaded guilty to nine terror charges, among them conspiracy and providing material support to al-Shabaab and AQAP.

So now I had helped take two of al-Shabaab's most important operatives out of circulation, men who had no qualms about murdering and maiming civilians, or creating a tide of helpless refugees, if it advanced the cause of their ideology. While the Islamic Courts had at least brought a measure of peace, al-Shabaab had brought little more than terror and suffering.

Awlaki later told me Warsame had acted against all advice – always talking on his mobile phone. I wondered whether a phone I had supplied to Warsame had helped the Americans track his movements.

The next phase of the Awlaki operation was discussed at the Marienlyst Hotel in Helsingør. When I walked into the room there was a new face.

'Let me introduce you to one of my colleagues in Sana'a. You'll understand if I don't introduce him by name,' Jed said.

About 5 foot 10 inches, he might have passed himself off as a Yemeni but told me he was an American of Indian descent. We exchanged a few words in Arabic.

With Jed looking on, I wrote a new email to Awlaki providing venues and times where a courier could pick up the briquettes and sandals from me in Sana'a.

I was not going to heed his advice to have my wife deliver the package. I encrypted the email and hit 'send'.

Then Jed and Klang went shopping for the supplies Aminah had requested. I could only imagine what an odd couple they would have made in the ladies' sections of Copenhagen's department stores – picking out skirts, tops, bras and underwear. Klang later joked that he at least knew his way around the lingerie section. They also bought the shampoo, conditioner and hair colouring. The expenses department at Langley must be used to unusual purchases in the name of keeping America safe.

The two agents neatly folded everything into a sports bag which Klang kept until I was ready to travel. Remembering the CIA plots to poison Fidel Castro, I made a mental note to keep the toiletries well away from my wife in Yemen.

I would not yet be bringing Awlaki his fridge. Klang said the CIA were 'customizing' one for the cleric and it would take several weeks to build. I had no doubt CIA technicians were busily at work figuring out the best way to hide a satellite transponder in the freezer compartment.

Before I left, Jed bought me a gift: a Viking horn with an inscription in gold. I was their warrior again – readying for another battle.

CHAPTER TWENTY-ONE

A LONG HOT SUMMER

July–September 2011

I flew back to Yemen on 27 July 2011 into blinding heat. The operation to neutralize Awlaki was moving into high gear, but the country was a failing state, with most of the south beyond government control and paralysis among competing factions in and around Sana'a.

I wondered whether the chaos had prevented Awlaki from organizing a courier, because none showed up on either day I had appointed. Had Awlaki got my message? Did he still trust me?

The next day I sent Awlaki an encrypted email:

'I am back in Sana'a and got your shoppinglist. I have waited for the brother to meet me on thursday and saturday, he did not show up. I ask Allah that he is safe and fine insha'Allah.'

I provided three new times and places for the courier to pick up the supplies, telling Awlaki I would only wait fifteen minutes.

'I do stick out and people notice my presence. I will try to come down and join you in mid Sept insha'Allah. Take care habibi,' I wrote.

Despite the considerable risk of such a trip, it would undoubtedly make it easier for the Americans to track him. I had just about given up on the idea of luring him to the capital.

On 9 August I received a reply. I copied the seemingly random string of letters, numbers and symbols in the body of the email and pasted them into the Mujahideen Secrets software on my laptop. Then I entered my personal cipher key and pressed 'decrypt'.

Nothing happened.

Perhaps I had entered the wrong values? Or had someone got to my computer? I had to calm down.

I started again. A few seconds later the random text turned into prose. I breathed deeply.

'Assalamu alaykum, sorry man communication is a bit slow with me. I will insha'Allah send someone to meet you at one of the 3 appointments you set. It will be a different brother from first time so we will use the same codes as before: he says lawn [colour] you say akhdar [green],' the cleric wrote.

'Try to write down everything in a letter to me because it is not safe sending someone to meet you to[o] many times. You should open up a new account to use when you email me from Yemen so that the enemies do not know that this guy was emailing from Europe and then from Yemen. This way they may be able to figure out who you are,' Awlaki added.

I copied the message into the draft folder of the Telenor email account I shared with Danish intelligence so they could pass the details on to the CIA and their Sana'a field operative.

I was impressed by Awlaki's awareness of operational security and his concern that I not be suspected by Western security services. It was an important detail. I remembered how he had once said to me: 'It is better to have an enemy close to you than having a stupid friend,' a judgement he might have reversed if he had known which side I was really on.

The first rendezvous was at 10.30 p.m. on 12 August in the car park outside a KFC restaurant in the centre of Sana'a.

The drive in my Suzuki pick-up truck from my home would normally have taken about fifteen minutes but that night I went a round-about way. As my instructors had taught me in Edinburgh I weaved through the narrow streets, taking turns at random.

I had weapons in the car which I had borrowed from Abdul, including a pistol in the glove compartment and a Kalashnikov under a blanket on the back seat. Guns are ubiquitous in Yemen; none of the locals would have batted an eyelid. I had told Abdul I wanted to be able to defend myself if the Yemeni security services came after me.

At the KFC I waited nervously. Given my size and skin colour I was easy to identify. There was no sign of the CIA field officer I had met in Copenhagen, but if he knew what he was doing that was the way it should be.

I took in the scene. Colonel Sanders in his apron stared down at me from a brightly lit hoarding. Soaring above the Colonel, and lit up in the night sky, were the six towering minarets and monumental white domes of the al-Saleh mosque complex. Built by the beleaguered President, the mosque had recently been completed at a cost of nearly $100m, in the Arab world's poorest country.

Gaggles of well-dressed young Yemeni men were coming in and out of the restaurant. KFC is considered an expensive treat for most Yemenis. It seemed to be a busy evening, no surprise because it was the middle of Ramadan and the night hours were a time of feasting.

Perhaps I ought to pop in for some fried chicken, I thought. But then I caught sight of him, walking towards me across the car park, silhouetted against the lights of the mosque. He was older than the other messenger – perhaps in his mid-twenties – and shorter. But he too was dark-skinned and wore the unmistakable Marib headgear. We exchanged the code word and I gave the courier the sports bag with the wooden briquettes and other supplies, including the clothes for Aminah.

I also passed him a thumb drive with a Word document I had written for the cleric. I wanted him to approve my creation of an 'Islamic Defence Force' to protect Muslims in the West from Islamophobic attacks by training them in shooting, martial arts and survival skills. The idea had come to me following the deadly terrorist bombing and shooting in Norway by the anti-Muslim extremist Anders Breivik the previous month. If I could get Awlaki engaged in the project I would have another pretext for continuing my communications with him. I also knew the outfit would be a draw for Islamist extremists across Europe, which might help me identify new targets.

'Is this for Samir Khan?' the courier asked.

That surprised me. It was terrible tradecraft.

The editor of AQAP's online *Inspire* magazine, Khan had been born in Saudi Arabia but had lived in the US for much of his life. He moved to Yemen in 2009, where he aligned himself with al-Qaeda and connected with Awlaki. Khan met with the Nigerian underwear bomber, Abdulmutallab, and helped Awlaki research the air cargo system for the printer bomb plot.

'No, my brother – this is secret,' I reprimanded him. With a crest-fallen look he disappeared into the night.

I received an encrypted email from Awlaki three days later:

'Assalamu alaykum . . . I received all the stuff . . . except the flash! A brother who was delivering it got into a situation and had to destroy it. Things turned out to be fine but now I do not have the flash. The sandals are good. The tablets I was looking for are hexamine. The ones you sent are something else. If you are travelling again then see if you can get me hexamine tablets,' he wrote.

So they did want the tablets for detonating explosives.

Awlaki asked me for any new information on the arrest of Warsame. And he had a specific request: 'I heard on the news that the New York Times reported that al Qaeda in Yemen is buying a lot of castor beans to make ricin and attack the US. Find me what you can on that.'[1]

I found the *New York Times* article.

'For more than a year, according to classified intelligence reports, Al Qaeda's affiliate in Yemen has been making efforts to acquire large quantities of castor beans, which are required to produce ricin, a white, powdery toxin that is so deadly that just a speck can kill if it is inhaled or reaches the bloodstream. Intelligence officials say they have collected evidence that Qaeda operatives are trying to move castor beans and processing agents to a hideaway in Shabwa Province, in one of Yemen's rugged tribal areas controlled by insurgents.'

---

1 Although I did not know it at the time, Awlaki was then penning an Islamic justification for chemical and biological attacks on the United States and other Western countries. 'The use of poisons of chemical and biological weapons against population centers is allowed and strongly recommended due to its great effect on the enemy,' the cleric wrote in an article later that year in *Inspire* magazine.

I shuddered. It seemed like the cleric had something in the works and wanted to know what was being reported. For the first time, I thought that it did not matter any longer how he was stopped. He now seemed ready for any form of attack against the West, with civilians as the main target.

On 17 August I left Yemen again for Europe. Every summer my children spent a couple of weeks with me, camping, hiking, canoeing and fishing. That time was sacrosanct – even if it disrupted the mission to go after the most wanted terrorist in al-Qaeda. I also needed to get ready for a long-planned trip to the jungles of Borneo with a friend from the UK. I imagined my mission in Yemen might run many more months and I needed to recharge my batteries.

Just before leaving I sent an email to Awlaki that I would be overseas for my company, Storm Bushcraft. I knew that if he later checked its website he would see photographs of the expedition to Borneo. I told him I had left a USB stick with the media clippings on ricin with a contact in the capital and provided his address and telephone number.

When I returned to Europe I explained the situation to Jed and the Danes and gave Jed the number of my acquaintance in Sana'a so the US National Security Agency could monitor his calls.

At the end of the first week of September I received a text from my contact in Sana'a. 'The guy just called me and I'm waiting for him now at CityStar.' I called Klang so he could relay the message to the Americans.

'It's being picked up; be ready now,' I told him – explaining the rendezvous point was a shopping mall in the Yemeni capital. Less than an hour later my contact sent me a text telling me the pick-up had been successful. I imagined the Americans – by tracking the contact's calls – had monitored the handover. Maybe this time the USB stick would lead the CIA all the way to Anwar al-Awlaki – but hopefully not to Aminah.

The mission was going according to plan. Awlaki had confidence in me, and when I returned from the Far East I might be able to travel into Yemen's badlands to meet him. The next day I boarded a flight to Malaysia, on my way to the jungles of Borneo. It was a welcome escape. No one could reach me; and I had to survive on my own ingenuity.

★

But just days after my return reality intervened in the most brutal way. On a brisk late-September afternoon, I turned on the television and saw breaking news. I stared at the screen, mesmerized.

Early that day – 30 September – CIA drones had taken off from a base in the southern deserts of Saudi Arabia and spotted a group of pick-up trucks that had congregated in Yemen's north-west al-Jawf province. Hearing the faint whirring sound they had come to dread, several men who had just finished breakfast rushed back to their vehicles. One of them was Awlaki, who had come to the region because of the growing threat from drone strikes in Yemen's southern tribal areas.

Two Predator drones focused lasers at the trucks to pinpoint the targets while the bigger Reapers took aim. The Reaper 'pilots', operating their vehicles from thousands of miles away, unleashed a clutch of Hellfire missiles. Awlaki and six other al-Qaeda operatives were killed instantly, their vehicles reduced to skeletons. One of those killed was Samir Khan; the CIA had no idea he was travelling with Awlaki. He was just twenty-four.

As I watched, my phone vibrated in my pocket. It was a text message from Klang: 'Have you seen the news?'

'I don't believe it,' I replied.

'No – it's true.'

The US had finally liquidated the man it considered an urgent and present danger. Awlaki, US authorities subsequently alleged, had risen to become AQAP's chief plotter of attacks against the West and was plotting new attacks against the US and Western interests when he was killed.

'The death of Awlaki is a major blow to al-Qaeda's most active operational affiliate,' President Obama announced later that day at a speech in Fort Myer, Virginia. 'Awlaki was the leader of external operations for al-Qaeda in the Arabian Peninsula. In that role, he took the lead in planning and directing efforts to murder innocent Americans . . . and he repeatedly called on individuals in the United States and around the globe to kill innocent men, women and children to advance a murderous agenda.'

CHAPTER TWENTY-TWO

BREAKING WITH BIG BROTHER

Autumn 2011

'I'm so sorry but it wasn't us. We were so close but it wasn't us.'

The text stared at me, black on green. It was another from Klang, several hours after Awlaki's death had been confirmed.

'Tell Jed and the Americans: well done. Send them my greetings and congratulations. He's a terrorist and needed to be stopped,' I replied.

I had to be magnanimous, even if it meant giving up the prospect of $5m. As it was, I might get a nomination as Best Supporting Actor.

Even so I was irritated and disappointed that neither Jed nor any of my other US contacts reached out to me in the following days. I also felt, despite my best efforts, sad and not a little guilty that Anwar al-Awlaki, with whom I had sat and talked for so many hours, had been incinerated. Yet I knew how dangerous he was, and how much more dangerous he would have become.

I tried to focus on a brief trip with my kids, but I was restless. I needed to know what had happened.

Two days after Awlaki was killed, I picked up a copy of the *Sunday Telegraph*, the UK broadsheet.

'How America finally caught up with Anwar al-Awlaki' ran the headline on the front page. And below: 'The capture of a low-level errand-runner was the key breakthrough that led to the al-Qaeda leader's death.'

The sentence caught my attention.

'Details of how the US finally managed to track down al-Qaeda's chief mouthpiece to the West can be revealed today by the *Sunday Telegraph*, which has learned that the key breakthrough came when CIA officials caught a junior courier in Awlaki's inner circle. The man, who is understood to have been arrested three weeks ago by Yemeni agents acting for the Agency, volunteered key details about Awlaki's whereabouts which led to Friday's drone strike as his convoy drove through the remote province of Jawf, 100 miles east of the capital, Sana'a.'

I felt my throat tighten. '*Caught a junior courier . . . three weeks ago . . .*'

I read the passage again. Had the CIA tried to hoodwink me? I recalled Kevin's words in Edinburgh: 'We don't want you to get fucked over.'

I checked the date of the text message my contact had sent from Sana'a confirming the pick-up of the thumb drive. It was three weeks ago. I called him and asked him to describe the handover.[1] He said the phone call had come in at 9 p.m. They agreed a rendezvous point and half an hour later he parked outside the City Star mall. A few minutes later a dusty battered Toyota Hilux pick-up truck pulled up. Two men in tribal outfits were sitting up front: a lanky man in the driving seat and a short fat man sitting next to him. Both were chewing khat.

The driver had come over to him. He was young, according to my contact, probably in his late teens, tall, thin, dark-skinned and dressed in a light-green *thawb* and Maribi headgear.

He said the driver had been in a hurry.

'Can I have the flash stick Murad asked you to give me?' he had asked after a curt greeting. My contact handed it over.

'Thank you,' said the driver. 'We have a long way to travel so we must go now.'

The description closely resembled that of the courier who had delivered the first thumb drive message to me at the al-Shaibani taverna in Sana'a. It also fitted that of the junior errand runner described in the *Sunday Telegraph* article. I doubted whether the courier would have

---

1 I have a recording, which I provided to Paul Cruickshank and Tim Lister, of a phone conversation in which my contact confirmed the details of this handover.

been able to lead the CIA directly to Awlaki, but he would have certainly led them to the next messenger in the chain.[2]

Perhaps I was just looking for connections where none existed. I needed a second opinion.

'Do me a favour, look at the *Sunday Telegraph* article – and tell me your opinion,' I said to Klang on the phone. I was driving through heavy rain after dropping my kids off with Karima and my mood was darkening. I could cope with most things, but not with being cheated by people for whom I had risked my life.

Klang phoned back shortly afterwards.

'I cannot see why it's not ours. It really looks like our job,' he told me.

I ended the call. The wipers were struggling to keep pace with the rain. I was a kaleidoscope of emotions. I felt a grim satisfaction that I had been involved in a successful operation. But that satisfaction soon gave way to remorse – for Awlaki's family and Aminah – and then to anger that the Americans had discarded me without any acknowledgement for my role.

'I'm sorry I had to do this,' I said out loud several times, my voice breaking. I had met Awlaki's children and now I bore responsibility for the death of their father. Perversely, I suddenly felt he was the honourable one in this struggle. He would have given up his life for me, but my handlers would not have given me a second thought had I died in their governments' service.

The next day Klang and I spoke again. 'We've been trying again to ask the Americans about this, but we have no comment from them,' he told me.

By then fury had smothered sadness. 'Fuck them. I don't want to work with them any more. Actually, fuck all of you. If it wasn't my guy

---

2 There was recent precedent for such an operation. The CIA located Osama bin Laden through his most trusted messenger, Abu Ahmed al-Kuwaiti. The courier was used by al-Qaeda's leader as his single point of contact with his senior deputies. Bin Laden's way of operating was similar to that of Awlaki: he composed messages on a computer, uploaded them to a thumb drive and passed them to a courier.

who led to Anwar, then why was information leaked about him?' I shouted down the phone.

The next day I was eating dinner at a half-empty TGI Friday's restaurant in the English Midlands when two men installed themselves in a booth behind me. There was something unsettling about them. From their conversation, I could tell that one was British and the other American. The British man kept turning round. He did not look at me – that would be too obvious – but towards a couple sitting in the next booth in front.

I snapped. 'What are you looking at?' I blurted out. 'You're American, right?' I said, turning to the other man. 'Are you from the CIA or what? I'm going to expose your guys. I'm going to the media to tell them everything that your government did. I was behind that operation and your government fucked me over.'

It was not my most eloquent performance, but it was passionate, and it had the desired effect. The mask fell.

'If you say anything, it will be dangerous for you,' the American told me.

They got up and left. The family in the adjacent booth looked as if they had just seen an alien.

The next day I received a call from Klang, my Danish handler. 'What did you say in the restaurant?' he asked.

'How did you know about that?'

'The incident was reported at the local police station,' said Klang.

Bullshit, I thought.

'Listen, the Brits and Americans don't want to have anything to do with you right now,' Klang said.

The feeling was mutual.

But the Danes wanted to try to engineer some sort of reconciliation, not least because of my threat to go public. They implored me to come to Denmark for a meeting to clear the air. Reluctantly, I agreed.

It felt strange to be standing in the lobby of the Marienlyst Hotel in Helsingør again. It was where we had planned critical missions as a team. But this occasion seemed likely to be a post-mortem of recriminations. It was 7 October 2011 – a week after Awlaki's death.

My PET handlers had set this up with the Americans and told me I would be meeting an agent called Michael. Jed, I was later told, had left Copenhagen abruptly – though I was sceptical about that. The meeting would be in one of the hotel's holiday villas. Perhaps that was a sign; they wanted to avoid any public scene.

Two cars with tinted windows arrived outside the hotel. Klang and a tall, muscular man with dark-brown hair walked across to the cottages, while the 'desk-jockey' Jesper and Marianne, a thirty-something agent who occasionally attended debriefings, waited by the car.

Jesper beckoned me to join them in the car park.

Screw all of them, I thought. Without the Danes noticing I discreetly reached for my iPhone, set it to video mode, and hit 'record'. Then I strode out, trying to look as menacing as possible. It wasn't difficult.

My decision to record the meeting was spontaneous. If I was going to be duped by Western intelligence then I wanted to be able to prove my story. At the beginning of the recording there is a quick glimpse of the blue sofas and gleaming marble floors of the hotel lobby. After I tucked the phone back into my pocket the picture goes to black, but our voices are clearly audible.

We walked towards the villas. Seagulls cawed overhead. There were few people outside – the pretty blue-and-white deckchairs that adorned the beachfront in the summer months had been packed away for the season.

I took in the view. A car ferry was navigating the choppy waters on its way across to the Baltic.

'You'll have to talk to him. It's no good not to talk,' Jesper told me.[3]

'I have nothing to talk to him about,' I said. 'It's so clear what happened. They arrested a boy who went to meet my contact and pick up that USB stick. It's so clear and they have exposed themselves.'

'Yes, that's right but he needs to explain himself,' Jesper said.

'Yes,' Marianne chimed in. 'They need to have a chance to explain

---

3 The extracts from this conversation with the Danish agents are translated verbatim from my recording.

themselves.' Not for the first time I thought she looked and sounded just like a bookkeeper.

I recounted our success stories – in Somalia, Kenya and Yemen and here in Denmark. For five years I had been on the frontline; and now the CIA wanted to disown me.

When we reached the villa, Klang opened the door and made some pleasantries about the weather. He seemed apprehensive, as if he were about to witness what the professionals call a 'psychotic episode'.

'There's nothing to talk about,' I repeated.

'We are also searching for answers,' Klang said. I had rarely seen the playboy of PET so serious – as if the long and close relationship of the CIA and PET could hinge on the next half-hour.

'Michael' was all-American – square jaw, the picture of a 'GI Joe'. I gave him the curtest of nods and carried on talking to Klang in Danish.

Klang switched to English, keenly aware I was trying to be offensive, and offered to order coffee.

I looked at Michael.

'You are not going to convince me,' I said.

'Convince you? I guess I'm not here to convince you. I'm just here to talk to you,' he said.[4]

He spoke slowly and deliberately with an accent that came from somewhere between New York and Boston.

We walked upstairs to the living quarters on the top floor and sat down facing each other at a glass table. Light streamed in from the windows.

I thought I would hold out an olive branch.

'I want to congratulate you . . . Never mind what happened, but the good thing is that these evil guys have been removed, that's number one,' I said.

'That's right, that's right,' Michael interrupted. 'And it is number one for me too. I did not come here to argue with you. I came here

---

4 The extracts from this conversation with Michael are reproduced verbatim from my recording.

because I respect you, plain and simple. I know you feel upset – but I don't know why you feel upset,' he said – looking at me intently.

He gave a good impression of looking perplexed.

I continued: 'There are two reasons. First of all I will honour the guy who got killed, if you understand. We honour him for being an enemy.' But, I stressed again, he needed to be taken out.

'That's right,' Michael replied. 'He had to be taken out.'

'And that's fine. Because if *he* was not taken out a lot of innocent people would have been taken out,' I said.

'Yes,' said Michael. He was doing his best to soothe me. His words were all camomile.

'He was a good friend of mine. He was my mentor. He was my sheikh. He was a friend of mine but because of the evil in him I have done this . . . I felt it was a necessity to eliminate, to destroy this threat,' I said.

'Absolutely, and I'm gonna tell you something. These types of things happen, are necessary,' Michael interjected, emphasizing each syllable in the second sentence with outstretched hands in a slow chopping gesture. I noticed he had strong hands. He could have been a boxer, I thought. Klang told me later he was an ex-US Navy SEAL.

He then tried to sway me with flattery.

'This whole thing was a team effort – a team thing from my organization, from me being here with you guys, from Jed being here with you guys . . . We had our team, we had our whole project going forward – of which you played the highest role.'

The chopping motion again for the last three words.

'And it is because of that that there are a lot of people in my government – when I say lot of people I want you to understand a select few that . . .'

'Yeah, we know Alex, we know George and you know all the others,' I interjected – recalling my brief interactions with the senior intelligence official from Washington and the CIA Copenhagen station chief.

'Yeah, but I am not talking about Alex and George, you know. I am talking about . . .'

'Obama?'

'The President of the United States, okay? He knows you. The President of the United States doesn't know who I am, okay? But he knows about your work. So the right people know your contributions. And for that we are thankful,' Michael said with a degree of repetition that I thought overdone.

'I'm thankful too,' I replied.

Michael was now getting into his stride. Perhaps he thought he was ahead on points.

'I understand you might feel, and we'll get to this in a second, like we fucked you over, and I don't know why you would think that. You've got your own reasons and I'll listen to them, okay? But I'm telling you if we were fucking you over I wouldn't be sitting with you right now. I wouldn't need to be.'

He had a habit of saying 'okay' after each point he made, as if to seek my agreement for each step of his logic.

'You don't have a good reputation,' I replied, meaning the CIA as an institution.

'That's right. Unfortunately, because we're in the business of protecting people like you, okay?

'There is all this negative stuff we don't respond to because it doesn't do any good. People are going to read what they read and think what they think and you're not going to convince them otherwise.'

People could not understand, he said, what it meant to ask someone like me to put their 'balls on the line, day in day out', at great risk to their family.

'It's very stressful,' I replied, especially – I thought – when your commitment to a mission was overshadowed by the realization that your circus-masters had decided you were no longer essential.

Michael chose the moment to move on to the real business at hand. His voice dropped to a stage whisper.

'Look – Awlaki was a bad man and bad in a lot of ways. You know this more than me.'

'I told you even before the Americans were even interested in him. I told you guys: be careful – he's going to be a danger,' I replied.

'That's right,' Michael said. He continued: 'So, you, we had our project together to go forward – we were not the only ones, okay? There were a number of other projects that were going.'

'I agree,' I replied.

'We were very, very close,' he said. 'We were moving towards – and when I say we – I am talking about – you know – I want success.'

He paused to deliver the analogy he had clearly rehearsed.

'It's like being on the field at the World Cup, you're moving down the field and you're in the position to score, the other guy could have passed it to you but he didn't, he took the shot, he scores. And that's that. That's what happened.'

It was a polite way of saying sorry – but not one I would accept.

'Who was the boy you arrested in Sana'a? A boy between fifteen and seventeen years old?'

'I don't have any information a boy was arrested.'

I explained how an al-Qaeda courier had come to pick up the thumb drive three weeks before Awlaki was killed.

'How do you know he was arrested?' Michael asked.

'Isn't that a coincidence then – a very extreme coincidence?' I asked.

Michael clearly sensed this was an argument that was not going to be resolved.

'You either trust us or you don't. In this case I guess you don't.'

'I don't.'

Michael insisted he was briefed on the various plans to eliminate Awlaki.

'So don't you think that if a courier that was associated with your contact was arrested, I would know about it?' he said.

Listening to the recording afterwards, I was struck by how Michael seemed willing to say anything to placate me – except to concede that my work directly led the CIA to Awlaki.

Now it was my turn. The Americans, I told him with some relish, had failed in their previous attempts to track down and kill Anwar al-Awlaki. Sure, they had come close a few times, not always by design. But it was only when I had gone in, established contact with him, passed on equipment and exchanged messages through couriers that he had eventually been killed.

I began to catalogue the other breakthroughs that Michael might not know about. I had been the one who encouraged Ahmed Warsame to develop a relationship between al-Shabaab and Awlaki. I had encouraged him to go to Yemen. And, I reminded Michael, it was when he was returning from one of his visits that he was seized.

Then there was the case of Saleh Ali Nabhan, who by 2009 had become one of al-Qaeda's most dangerous operatives. He had even invited me into Somalia to see him. And it was the BlackBerry and laptop I had been given by Jed that had helped track him down.

'Boom! He was wiped out using our gear. So why don't you just say thank you?'

Michael let me carry on. Perhaps he thought the venting would do me good.

'We just want gratitude from your government, just to accept the fact. Obama can take the honour – that's fine. At least a 'thank you'; that's what we want from him.

'I've been honest with you guys all the time. I know you listen to my phone, all my house, cars, everything. It's fine. Every single [piece of] information you have from my side,' I said, striking the table, 'it's always been honest, you never find a lie in it.'

'And I've never accused you of lying,' Michael said.

'I even sent Anwar a wife. Did any of your agents manage to send him a wife?'

I realized that Michael's mission was to watch a volcano exhaust itself. He was never going to acknowledge my role in leading US intelligence to Awlaki. The job was done; it was an American victory against terrorism.

I stood up and shouted down the stairs to Klang and Jesper.

'He's just sitting there and lying.'

Denmark's initiative to make nice had aborted in spectacular fashion. Michael stood up and without looking at me or saying another word walked downstairs and out into the gardens. I would not see him again.

I faced Klang and Jesper.

'You know what? I recorded the whole conversation.'

'You can't do that,' said Klang, looking as though he was about to be physically sick. Were the tape to become public, his failure to search me before the meeting would not impress his seniors.

'But I did. And I quit,' I told him.

Later, I realized the reason the CIA would never acknowledge that I had led them to Awlaki was that to do so would expose Danish intelligence to allegations that they had participated in an assassination – which was illegal under Danish law.

The agencies had closed ranks.

CHAPTER TWENTY-THREE
BACK IN
THE RING

Late 2011

The weeks after Awlaki's death were a dark time. I could not help feeling guilty about his killing. I kept imagining the grief of his ageing father, who had tried so hard to protect him, of his wives and children, and especially of the woman I had sent to Yemen to be his partner.

My sadness was compounded by an encrypted message I received from Aminah several weeks after Awlaki had been killed.

'I am sending you this mail with great sorrow and sadness in my heart but again happiness for my husband Shuhada [martyrdom.] Alhamdidullah he is now in the Jannat [paradise] and do not feel anything but joy and happines.

'I wanted to contact you in case I will go back in Europe, but I have 4 months to decide what to do. My first option is shahada . . . May Allah give us all sabr [patience] and strenght to go through this severelly difficult moments in our life.

'I ask Allah to bless you for connecting me with my husband. Our marriage was blessing from Allah and I am so proud for being his wife.'

I thought of her predicament – alone and helpless. But then I read the email again.

'My first option is shahada.'

Shahada: martyrdom. To avenge her husband's death, the young star-struck woman I had left sipping coffee in Vienna was ready to blow herself up.

In my sleep Awlaki would come to me, reprimanding me for what I had done.

My days were equally restless. I brooded incessantly over the behaviour of the Americans. They had vanished from my life. I was damaged goods, a loose cannon. I could hear the clichés echoing round Langley. I wanted to prove them wrong, to dispel the notion that I was a bit player. I wanted them to take notice of me again.

I also wanted to retire from frontline intelligence work on a high. The frustration simmered. Fadia was by turns anxious and irritated with my behaviour. I could hardly blame her; I was erratic and easily angered, but still I could not bring myself to tell her anything that had happened.

On a misty November afternoon I had an idea – a way to reconnect with PET and show that I, and they, could still sit at the top table. I might have missed out on the payday promised by the Awlaki mission but PET still had me on a retainer, and I was never the type to accept money for doing nothing. It was time to get to work again.

My time in Yemen had introduced me to a network that was far wider than just Awlaki. I had – as it were – grown up with al-Qaeda in the Arabian Peninsula, by now the most active and lethal of the terrorist network's tentacles. Awlaki had been critically important – but there was another figure whose operational skills and leadership were even more crucial: Nasir al-Wuhayshi.

A confidant of Osama bin Laden who had played a senior administrative role at his pre-9/11 headquarters near Kandahar, Nasir al-Wuhayshi had fled to Iran after the US launched Operation Enduring Freedom in October 2001. The Iranians had arrested him and extradited him to Yemen but his escape from prison in 2006 had galvanized the cause of jihad in his native country. Al-Qaeda in Yemen had become al-Qaeda in the Arabian Peninsula and Wuhayshi had become the group's emir. In August 2010, bin Laden had sent a message from Abbottabad praising Wuhayshi for his 'qualified and capable' leadership of the group.

By late 2011 Wuhayshi, who was known by his fighters as Abu Basir, had built AQAP into a powerful force. The group had exploited President Saleh's unpopularity to recruit thousands of fighters from sympathetic tribes. In April it had spun off a new group called 'Ansar al-Sharia' – partisans of the Sharia – to attract as broad a base of support as possible.

Ansar al-Sharia fighters had taken advantage of political turmoil to seize control of territory in Abyan, Marib and Shabwa provinces, including the dusty town of Zinjibar on the south coast, just forty miles up the coastal road from Aden. It was the road I had driven along that September night to see Awlaki.

An al-Qaeda mini-state was in the making, with the town of Jaar, ten miles inland from Zinjibar, its cradle and Wuhayshi its undisputed leader. This burnished his credentials within the jihadist movement. He was beginning to be seen as a potential successor to bin Laden and Ayman al-Zawahiri as the paramount leader of al-Qaeda worldwide.

I called Klang in Copenhagen; I needed a meeting. No longer was I immediately given a plane ticket; this time it was a trek across England and a ferry from Harwich.

I was contrite when I met Klang and Jesper. I knew they were my last chance to leave the game with a gold medal. I nevertheless was quietly confident: I knew what I was doing and there was no other agent – anywhere – who could get close to Wuhayshi.

'I think I can get him within a year,' I told them. Klang looked sceptical, almost uncomfortable – as if he were the barman being asked for one last drink by the local alcoholic.

Klang said he was happy for me to try to rekindle some militant contacts in Yemen, if that's what I wanted to do, but his enthusiasm hardly overwhelmed me. PET would as usual adjust my retainer – they paid a premium when I was overseas – bringing it to some $7,500 a month. But I felt I was a nuisance to them, no longer the ticket to dine with Big Brother.

My obstinacy kicked in: I would show them what I could do. But effectively I was now freelance, setting my own priorities, and without my most valuable contact, Anwar al-Awlaki.

On 3 December I returned to Sana'a – and immediately felt vulnerable. Not only had I lost the backing of my handlers, but I would be reliant on Abdul to put out feelers on my behalf. And after Malaga I was not sure where his loyalties lay. That meant another layer of danger.

Abdul showed no trace of being anxious or hiding something when we met. If he was working for the CIA he was good at displaying an air of composure. He suggested I talk to Mujeeb, who had delivered my first thumb drive message for Awlaki to al-Qaeda's religious chief, Adil al-Abab, in the tribal areas the previous summer. Mujeeb, he said, regularly met with Wuhayshi.

The three of us met on the roof of the house in Sana'a where I was staying.

Mujeeb was short and chubby and had a long beard. He always wore a scarf around his head but not a tribal one. It was clear by the type of car he drove – a newish Mercedes – that he was not your standard Salafist. He was a show-off, proud of his connections. He boasted that he was acting as a mediator between Salafis in Dammaj, where I had studied more than a decade previously, and al-Qaeda.[1]

Mujeeb told me he had recently carried a letter from the Saudis to Wuhayshi proposing a deal. They said they would pardon Wuhayshi and his group and donate weapons and money if they stopped fighting the Saudis and the Americans and focused instead on fighting Shia rebels in northern Yemen. I thought it an unlikely offer, as well as an outrageous infringement of Yemeni sovereignty, but with Mujeeb you could never be sure.

I changed the subject to my reason for being in Yemen. I had rehearsed the presentation, but only now would I find out if it had any traction.

'There are brothers in Sweden who are ready to avenge the death of

---

1 AQAP had proposed providing the Dammaj students with weapons training so they could fight the Houthis – a Shia revivalist movement – in the surrounding area. The Houthis had taken advantage of political turmoil to seize territory in northern Yemen. It was yet another reason why Yemen, despite its grinding poverty and relative lack of oil, was critical to the entire Arabian Gulf. In 2009 Saudi Arabia had sent troops across the border to confront the Houthis out of concern for its own security and (as yet unproven) suspicions that the Houthis were being supported by Iran.

Sheikh Anwar. They are also ready to take an oath to AQAP, so I would like to find a way to contact Abu Basir [Wuhayshi],' I told them. My hope was that I might be able to establish an avenue of communication through couriers as I had with Awlaki. That would give me a chance to re-establish myself as the group's point man in Europe – a source of supplies and recruits.

I was telling the truth. Shortly before travelling to Yemen I had met with a group in the Swedish city of Malmö who were looking for an overseas destination to wage jihad. Again, I had encountered them because of the many militants I had met over the previous decade. Danish intelligence had asked me to call on Abu Arab, the Danish-Palestinian who had adopted me during my visit to Lebanon back in 2007.

Abu Arab – real name Ali al-Hajdib – had spent some time in a Lebanese prison because of his role in the extremist Fatah al-Islam group. He had been tortured. The Danish government had done its duty and sent a diplomat to check on him in jail. Instead of thanking her he told her that when he came out he would kill her.

Despite his record, al-Hajdib had been allowed to resettle in Denmark. When I told him I was planning to return to Yemen, he urged me to come with him to Malmö to meet one of his brothers who lived there, yet another member of the Hajdib jihadist dynasty. I had met one brother – Saddam – shortly before he blew himself up as Lebanese security forces prepared to storm his house. Another was still languishing in jail for placing bombs on passenger trains in Germany. Their mother had produced eleven sons altogether and – as far as I knew – no daughters.

Two of the younger generation were especially keen to travel to Yemen. One was Abu Arab's nephew – a nineteen-year-old IT student who was tall, slim and fair-skinned, and had a short, wispy beard. He wore Western clothes to blend in and keep off the radar screen of security services. His cousin, who lived in Gothenburg, also enthused about going to Yemen.

The Hajdibs were afraid their residence might be bugged so we went for a walk in one of Malmö's public parks. When I told them I was returning to Yemen to re-establish contact with AQAP after the death of Awlaki, the young IT student looked elated.

'If you do re-establish contact we would like to come and to make *bayat* [an oath of allegiance to Wuhayshi]. I could offer myself to work on *Inspire* magazine,' he said.

I saw the Hajdibs as my next 'Warsame' – a conduit through whom I could learn more about AQAP, build a better picture of its intentions and alliances. I put the idea to Klang.

'These guys are very dangerous – ticking time bombs. It might be a good idea to send them to Yemen so that we can establish a new connection to the group,' I said.

Klang warmed to the prospect: 'You'd be in email contact with them without putting yourself in danger.'

But we knew this depended on me establishing contact with Wuhayshi, which PET then regarded as a long shot.

So I began to tell Mujeeb about the Hajdibs. It may sound like an absurd contradiction but I always tried to tell the truth as often as possible in my undercover work. It was the only way I could keep my story straight. Lying was easy, but remembering lies was difficult. Besides, if AQAP did connect with the Swedish militants, it would be important that they endorsed what I had said.

I told Mujeeb that I too wanted to avenge Awlaki's death; he promised he would make contact with Wuhayshi. I handed him a letter I had typed out for AQAP's leader on my laptop. It included plenty of red meat to get Wuhayshi's attention.

'My eyes are filled with tears over the great loss of my friend, my brother and my teacher, Shaheed Sheikh Anwar al-Awlaki, may Allah accept him as a pious man . . . Ameen. His death must be revenged with the kuffar's bloodshed and fear insha'Allah . . .

'Brother Anwar have requested from me to find brothers in Europe who could come over and get training with the intensions to return to their countries and work for our Deen. I have found a few and they are now ready insha'Allah.'

I had another card to play. My Kenyan friend Ikrimah, the long-haired al-Shabaab operative, wanted to establish contact with Wuhayshi now that Awlaki was no more. If I could connect them it would be an opportunity to track connections between different al-Qaeda affiliates, always a challenge for Western intelligence.

Before Irena became Aminah (from her public social media page).

Aminah's veiled video recording for Awlaki.

Aminah's unveiled recording.

The $250,000 CIA reward for the Aminah mission — the combination for the lock was 007.

Hassan Tabbakh.
(Credit: Press Association)

Ikrimah in Norway. (Credit: TV2 Norway)

Ahmed Abdulkadir Warsame in court.

Abdullah Mehdar.

AQAP claimed this was what was left of Awlaki's vehicle after it was hit by a drone.

My tour guide in Jaar, AQAP emir and al-Qaeda global #2 Nasir al-Wuhayshi, taken from *Inspire* Magazine.

SEEKING
INFORMATION
Saleh Ali Saleh Nabhan

The FBI's most-wanted poster for Saleh Ali Nabhan, who masterminded the bombing of the US embassy in Nairobi in August 1998.

At the Masinga Dam.

Storm Bushcraft
in Kenya.

Bathing in a geothermal spa in
Reykjavik with my Danish handlers
in early 2010.

My CIA recruiter, Elizabeth Hanson.
(Credit: colby.edu)

Dog sledding with Western intelligence in northern Sweden, March 2010.

My Ice Hotel bedroom on trip organized by British intelligence.

Skiing in the Arctic Circle.

My Kenya visa stamp for mission to deliver supplies to Nabhan in May 2009.

On my way to deliver
equipment to Awlaki in
October 2008 ...

... I recorded the drive.

On the road in Shabwa, just after
meeting Awlaki, in September 2009.

Yemen visa stamps
during mission
targeting Awlaki i
the summer of 2011
On 28 June I left
Yemen for a
debriefing in Malag
and returned on
27 July.

Klang

I can confirm its picked
up. Tell our boy "good
job"
From:Klang
23/05/12 19:15

Options   Reply   Back

Soren used
Klang's phone
to forward a
message to
me from the
CIA after I
returned their
equipment in
a Sana'a car
park in May
2012.

3 things: If you email me please write down the date on all your messages. Second, keep in mind that it takes a few days for emails to get to me so if you are setting an appointment then give me advance notice. Third: you do not need to write "to the sheikh" when you email inspire. Anything from your email will be delivered to me.
Please respond to this message with what you want to say and give it to the brother. We cannot have our brother travel with a laptop plus it is suspicious for you guys to type out a message in a public place.
This brother may be the messenger between us for now. One IMPORTANT note: The brother does not know that he is delivering messages for me and he doesn't know where I am so do not mention that this message is for me. Just give it to him and he will deliver it where it needs to be delivered and will get to me insha Allah.
For future correspondence I believe it would be better if your wife delivers the flash to the brother. It's up to you but I believe that you would definitely be watched and that might put you and the brother in jeopardy. Agree with the brother on the place of meeting. Also we need to keep the meetings to a minimum. The brother says it is not safe for him to enter sanaa frequently. So please mention all what you need to say in the message you send me. Please let me know what your program is and the latest news from the west. Also please send the emails of ikrimah and this other brother with your message.
My wife needs some stuff from sanaa so can your wife buy it for her? We have sent other people before and nothing really suited her taste.

Awlaki's first thumb drive message to me.

The KFC in Sana'a
where I met one
of Awlaki's
couriers, summer
2011. (Credit:
Panoramio.com)

Set-up/start

Key generator

1. Keymanager 2. Type User name and code
3. Close Keygenerator.
4. Go back key manager/import.
5. Opens window with public/private key
6. Type password for my user Id/click ok
7. Go to import key - click public key -/close

8 create connection. Click on "friend"
and the my Pub/Priv.

Decrypt a message

1. click on friend user key.
2. click on my own key
3. Messages - copy message and paste
   In message
4. Type your password in order to decrypt
   click "decrypt" - Read and close.

My notes from Awlaki's
tutorial on Mujahideen Secrets
when I visited him in Shabwa
in September 2009.

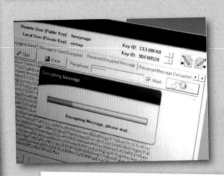

Decrypting an email from
Awlaki, received on 5 March
2010, using Mujahideen
Secrets.

My picture and others
pinned up against a wall
in Syria.

Al-Qaeda-linked
fighters fired at our
photographs.

After I went public my
story was picked up around
the world.

Drawing by my daughter
Sarah showing me
apologizing to former
Danish politician Naser
Khader.

On a recent trip to Korsør.

'Brother Ikrimah in Somalia has also found a few brothers with European and American citizenship, they too are clean and are ready to return after receiving the necessary skills,' I wrote. 'This brother got a special message for you from your own teacher from Afghanistan.'[2]

I also showed I was well aware of operational security.

'I cannot mention my name, my look or my nationality over this message, because it is not secure . . . Future communication should happen by a personal messenger, Adil [al-Abab] can receive my messages and forward them to you, and you can do the same in return. I do not accept any use of emails, mobiles, sms, phones etc'

A few days later Mujeeb and I met again. He told me he had just returned from meeting al-Qaeda figures in the tribal areas and had given them the letter.

'I might even be able to arrange a meeting for you with Abu Basir if you wish – perhaps in the New Year,' he said.

'Yes of course, definitely,' I said quickly, but with more than a tinge of apprehension. Such an encounter would be the most dangerous mission I had undertaken. Given the heavy fighting between government forces and al-Qaeda in the tribal areas, it also seemed very unlikely. Even as AQAP was taking on the Yemeni army in the south it had one eye on further attacks against America.

Mujeeb promised to provide me with sixteen gigabytes of unedited video footage from AQAP to circulate to their Western supporters. They had been unable to publish a new issue of *Inspire* since the deaths of Awlaki and Samir Khan and they were eager to advertise the territorial gains they were making in southern Yemen. Abdul showed me surveillance film shot recently of the US embassy in Sana'a and the Sheraton Hotel adjoining it. Unlike most top-class hotels, this one was surrounded by sandbags, and on the roof of the hotel were US soldiers, probably Marines. Abdul told me the group believed the Americans were running counter-terrorism operations from the hotel.

---

2 Ikrimah had recently emailed, asking me to deliver a long letter to Wuhayshi from an Islamic teacher who had taught the AQAP leader in Afghanistan many years previously. The teacher had recently been killed in Somalia.

Armed with the promises Mujeeb had made me, I returned to Denmark just before Christmas to brief PET. They seemed more interested than before – though we all knew a lot still hung on Mujeeb's word.

Klang suggested I travel across to Malmö again with Abu Arab to meet with the Hajdib clan. This was a risk for PET; they had no authority to send one of their agents on a fishing expedition in Sweden. PET and the Swedish intelligence agency, SAPO, cooperated in breaking up terrorist plots, but the Swedes would not be amused to find Danish intelligence running a freelance operation on their turf.

Even so the Danes saw an opportunity. The young English-speaking IT student would be the perfect candidate to succeed Samir Khan as the editor of *Inspire* magazine. I would have a key contact right at the heart of the group. The email address provided by *Inspire* was the portal through which supporters in the West could get in touch with the group. A year and a half after Aminah travelled to Yemen we were again plotting to send European extremists to join the terrorists.

The earnest IT student was still hungry. I met him and his father in a park in case SAPO were already eavesdropping.

'I've been to Yemen and passed on a message to Wuhayshi and am awaiting his reply. In the meantime you should prepare yourself,' I told him.

He was quietly jubilant, like a rookie player in the minor leagues suddenly called into the national team.

'I only wish I could go – but the *kuffar* are monitoring me too closely,' Abu Arab said. He was beaming with pride that a new generation of the Hajdib family were about to grasp the torch.

I returned to the UK for Christmas. It was not normally a time of year that I enjoyed. My childhood memories of what should have been a magical season were painful; as a father I rarely had my own children with me over the holidays. But this year Karima had agreed that they should stay with me and Fadia. Even though they had been brought up as Muslims, I spoiled them with gifts and every moment was precious. It was a bittersweet time. I knew I would soon have to return to Yemen and I found it hard to say goodbye.

I was always apprehensive before going on missions but this time I was especially uneasy. Finding Wuhayshi would truly take me into the lion's den. What troubled me most was that if I didn't come back alive, my kids might never know the truth about my life as a double agent. No doubt all they would see on the news was that another European jihadi had been killed overseas, and then my photograph would appear on the screen. Neither their mother nor their stepmother would be able to tell them that my life was not all it seemed.

Was I the veteran boxer extending his career one bout too far?

CHAPTER TWENTY-FOUR
THE LION'S DEN

January 2012

On 7 January 2012 I boarded a flight to Yemen. As I stared out from my window seat I listened to the band Metallica on my headphones. For five years their thumping tunes had helped pump me up before missions, but this time I turned up the volume extra loud.

Abdul was waiting at the airport for me, and we drove to his home, a comfortable three-storey brick building where I would stay for the next few days. Whatever businesses he had, they still appeared to be doing well.

Mujeeb visited but had neither news nor the video footage. It was time to exert some pressure.

'Do you know the brothers in different parts of Sweden collected the money for me to fly to Yemen so that I could gather this material and establish a connection with Abu Basir?' I said to Abdul angrily, channelling the role-playing lessons I had been given at the MI6 facility at Fort Monckton.

'Mujeeb is just wasting my time. I don't think he met with them. You know what – I'm going to travel down by myself to Abu Basir to tell him that Mujeeb is a liar.'

I had spoken without thinking. It was rash, committing me to a dangerous journey into the tribal areas. I checked myself. I could not let my determination to prove the CIA wrong make me do something stupid.

Abdul was anxious. He persuaded Mujeeb to call up a Yemeni militant who had connections to AQAP. His name was Hartaba. He had once worked as bin Laden's bodyguard in Afghanistan, and more recently he had been Awlaki's driver. He knew the safest – or the less treacherous – routes to territories controlled by AQAP. We could meet him on the road south from Sana'a.

The next day Abdul and I set out in his Toyota Corolla. My fears, felt so keenly in England, were not going away. Depending on whether he was a double or triple agent, Abdul could easily hand me over. What if the CIA had warned him about me?

But my immediate concern was to navigate the roadblocks out of Sana'a. I donned a Western business suit – for the first time in at least a decade – and held my iPhone to my ear, trying to make it look like I was taking calls. I was a businessman who had a meeting in Aden, and Abdul was my driver.

'Just look important,' he said.

I made my best impatient face at the soldiers. It worked.

After hours of driving, Abdul slowed down near a dusty settlement. The villagers eyed us suspiciously. This was bandit territory far from government control. My palms began to sweat; my toes curled.

A wiry young man climbed into the back of the car. I looked to see if he was armed, but tried to appear nonchalant.

'Do you know who that is?' Abdul asked me. 'It's Abu Basir's younger brother.'

He was the spitting image of Wuhayshi. I nearly hugged him with relief.

In the late afternoon we arrived at a small village just off the road from Sana'a to Aden that would not have been out of place in an Old Testament scene. Abdul pulled up outside what seemed a half-finished shack. 'This is Hartaba's house.'

Hartaba came to greet us. He was in his mid-forties but jihad had aged him. He was a caricature: a wiry frame and narrow face, big and slightly manic eyes, and a long beard. He tilted his head to hear because beatings in a Jordanian jail had left him almost deaf in one ear.[1]

Inside his bare home, Hartaba introduced us to two heavily armed Saudi fighters. We prayed together and then Hartaba told me to take

---

1 Hartaba had been captured by the Jordanians after fleeing Afghanistan at the end of 2001. He had been extradited to Yemen but escaped from jail in 2006 with Wuhayshi and other al-Qaeda members.

off my suit and put on traditional salwar kameez. He gave me tribal headgear to hide my face, though looking at my height and build he seemed to think I was beyond camouflage.

I noticed several of my new companions had mobile phones. I told them to take the batteries and SIM cards out so that US spy satellites could not fix our position. They seemed almost indifferent to the prospect of martyrdom but I was in no rush to become another victim of America's favourite weapon.

We set off in a Toyota Land Cruiser in the golden evening light for al-Qaeda's strongholds. Abdul and I sat up front next to Hartaba; the Saudi fighters and Wuhayshi's brother on the open-top cargo bed. The truck was full of weapons. I grasped a Kalashnikov which had been thrust into my hands along with an ammunition belt that was draped around me. The weapon was so long that I had to point the muzzle out of the window.

Abdul had a grenade launcher resting on his lap. 'Are you sure it's not going to go off?' he asked Hartaba after the car hit a large pothole and the top of the launcher banged against the roof. Abdul looked terrified, and I wondered again about his allegiance.

Hartaba got so annoyed that he stopped the car and explained that the weapon would only fire if levers were released. The same model had been used in an attack on the car of a senior British diplomat in Sana'a. He had been driving the getaway car used in the attack, he added, with a hint of pride.

'It missed by a few millimetres.'

Hartaba warmed to his theme and I could not help but admire the man for his sheer endurance. Hartaba said that on the day Awlaki died AQAP fighters had only been able to identify him by the skin on his forehead when they reached the carcass of the vehicle. Most of his body had been vaporized. Hartaba's eyes glistened as he told the story.[2]

He also talked about how AQAP was growing ever stronger in the southern tribal areas of Yemen. The group had raided military factories and taken machines to make their own ammunition.

---

2 Hartaba also said Awlaki had been devastated by the death of bin Laden. Hartaba had tried to cheer him up with practical jokes.

We passed through a checkpoint belonging to southern separatist fighters, who waved us on – another sign, I thought, of just how fast this country was falling apart. Villagers chanted 'al-Qaeda, al-Qaeda' as we clattered through dusty settlements. More than one policeman looked the other way. I glanced at Hartaba, who was miming along in a trance to the jihadist *nashids* blaring on a cassette player. To evade the last government checkpoint he went off-road and killed the headlights.

As the moon rose, we sped through the luminescent desert. Adrenalin surged through me and I felt a wave of exhilaration to be so deep behind enemy lines. For a few brief seconds on this perfect Arabian night I forgot all about my mission.

We reached the town of Jaar late that night. It had been transformed in the ten months since al-Qaeda fighters had seized control of it – renaming it the 'Emirate of Waqar' – or 'dignity'. It was now the capital of al-Qaeda's new statelet. The checkpoint we passed through was manned by Ansar al-Sharia fighters. The black banners of al-Qaeda were everywhere and fighters milled around the town. It was a new ground zero in the war on terrorism. Yemeni forces were positioned within firing range of the town and US, Saudi and Yemeni air power circled in the skies above. I realized that I was now in their crosshairs.

We pulled up at what passed for a restaurant and Hartaba went inside. He emerged with Adil al-Abab, AQAP's religious leader, whom I had befriended in Sana'a six years previously. His cheeks were even plumper. No wonder we had found him in one of Jaar's few functioning restaurants.

He had the same handlebar moustache above his pursed lips and still wore his beard short – probably because it wouldn't grow any longer.

'*Masha'Allah! As salaam aleikum* Abu Osama! How are you? How's your son, Osama?' al-Abab gushed.

'Fine. We are both fine.'

'We should go. You shouldn't be seen here if you want to come to meet Abu Basir. And I've got an old friend to introduce you to,' al-Abab said, with a broad smile.

We piled into al-Abab's white Toyota, a government vehicle the group had commandeered. He was a truly awful driver who had clearly taught himself after getting hold of the car. We juddered down pot-holed streets to a large house painted yellow and used for religious ceremonies. It was sparsely furnished but included a big chair with gold ornaments the militants had looted from the governor's headquarters.

The house had been requisitioned by Sheikh al-Hazmi, the nephew of the Muslim Brotherhood preacher Mohammed al-Hazmi. He had curly hair and unusually for a Yemeni green eyes. Al-Hazmi remembered me from my stay in Yemeni in 2001. He laughed to see me again after such a long time and we embraced. It was proof yet again of the value of the network I had built up over the years.

He, Abdul, al-Abab and I talked late into the night about the state of jihad in Yemen. Al-Abab said lots of Somalis had travelled to Yemen to fight with the group. Eventually Hazmi retired to join his family in their quarters upstairs, but al-Abab had one more question before he would let me go.

'Are you ready?' he asked, gravely.

'For what?' I asked.

'Will you take the oath? For al-Qaeda, for our emir Abu Basir?'

I replied I was prepared to take the oath but had certain conditions. 'I told Sheikh Anwar I don't accept civilian targets.'

'We already knew this – Abdul told me,' al-Abab replied.

I was left with no choice; I was about to become a signed-up member of al-Qaeda.

Taking his hand I made the oath: 'I will be true to Abu Basir, Leader of the Faithful, in all that obeys the will of Allah and His messenger. I will fight Allah's cause.'

'*Hamdulillah!*' al-Abab exclaimed.

I hardly slept that night – death might be around any corner. I even feared I might reveal myself to the brothers by talking in my sleep. I rose before dawn and walked out with al-Qaeda fighters to pray in the nearby mosque. As the first glimmer of dawn turned the eastern sky purple and then pink, the crack of distant mortar rounds interrupted the stillness. Yemeni military forces were bombarding the town, in one of their half-hearted attempts to retake Jaar.

The fighters hastened to the frontline, leaving me alone. Before departing they locked the heavy gates from the outside. I heard the clack of artillery fire and the roar of fighter jets overhead. Then there was the loud sucking sound of an explosion nearby, followed by a deafening roar. I could hear women and children screaming.

What if they're targeting this building? I suddenly thought. I went up to the roof but it was too high to jump. I was trapped.

I then had a sickening realization which made the aerial bombardment pale into insignificance.

I had left my North Face backpack in Sheikh al-Abab's car. Inside one of the pockets was a USB stick with the recording of my conversation with the CIA agent Michael back in Denmark.

I'd forgotten about it.

Game over.

I pictured my wife and kids back in Europe and wondered how they would take the news. I lay down on the floor and gazed up at the ceiling with a deep fatalism. I wished I hadn't watched so many of those brutal execution videos.

After several hours, Sheikh al-Abab returned to the house with fighters in tow and Abdul, who looked traumatized. I tried to appear relaxed but was ready to vomit. The Sheikh smiled.

'You forgot this in the car,' he said, handing me the bag. When I had a moment alone to look, I found the thumb drive still inside. I could have screamed with relief.

A few minutes later it was time to move on. I jumped into the back seat of a Toyota 4 × 4 next to Abdul and a young Saudi. Al-Abab rode shotgun with the driver. After a few minutes, he turned around and told us to lean forward and stare at the floor. We were on no account to look up until told to. We drove for a few more minutes.

The car stopped and a new passenger slid in next to me. I looked up and saw the unmistakable features of Nasir al-Wuhayshi – wispy beard, small, close-set eyes under his tribal scarf, and his trademark broad grin.

'*Salaam,*' he said cheerfully. He had a *miswak* – a Yemeni tooth-cleaning stick which the Prophet had recommended – in the corner of his mouth.

Somehow he was slighter than I had imagined.

'Murad, I know who you are. Anwar told me about you and I received your letter. I should tell you that Aminah is doing well. May Allah reward you for what you've done for her and Sheikh Anwar,' he said.

We set off with a car full of Wuhayshi's heavily armed bodyguards tailing us. We drove to a small farm outside Jaar, where we got out and walked across to a cornfield. Under the shade of some trees, we unpacked a meal of lamb and rice. The shade also provided some protection from drones, which could not be far away

I could not seem to eat everything in front of me. In an act of kindness, AQAP's leader was stealthily shovelling chunks of lamb towards me rather than eat them himself. No wonder he looked so thin.

At that point Sheikh al-Abab passed on a request to Wuhayshi from the young bearded Saudi fighter, who wanted to be put on a fast track for martyrdom. Wuhayshi considered for a few moments and then demurred; there were plenty who were ahead of him in the queue and he would have to wait his turn. The young Saudi looked crestfallen. I wanted to be sure I wasn't dreaming: a discussion over lunch of the suicide-bombing rota.

I was fascinated by Wuhayshi. He had the same softly spoken humility as his mentor, bin Laden, and exuded the same charisma. His fighters loved him and would do anything for him. No wonder people saw him as the leader-in-waiting of all al-Qaeda.

I had rolled up my sleeves to eat and Wuhayshi noticed one of my tattoos. It depicted the Norse god Thor's hammer but could easily be mistaken for a Christian symbol. 'Is that a cross?' asked Wuhayshi, one eyebrow raised.

'No,' I replied, laughing nervously, before telling the al-Qaeda emir that I had Thor tattooed on my forearm as a youngster. I gave Wuhayshi a quick lesson in Norse mythology. Thankfully he laughed too.

In fact the tattoo did not date back to my biker days. Late the previous year I had walked into a tattoo parlour in Copenhagen and had it inked on to my forearm. It was reckless. Had a militant noticed that I had suddenly acquired Thor's hammer I would have had some explaining to do. Perhaps at some level I was trying to escape the strait-jacket of my cover and reassert my identity.

Wuhayshi told the others to walk to the other side of the sandy field so we could talk in private.

'It is good you are here,' Wuhayshi said. 'I was about to head out of town, but I heard you were here so I delayed my trip.'

I told him I had sworn *bayat*, but as I had previously explained to Awlaki, I could not in good conscience be involved in targeting civilians.

'I know your position. But you should know: in Islam there is no such thing as civilians when it comes to the *kuffar*. They have chosen their states and governments,' Wuhayshi replied. That democracy thing again, I thought to myself.

There was a pause.

'But if I could choose I'd go after military targets,' Wuhayshi added.

Wuhayshi talked passionately about one day bringing the whole of Yemen under Islamic rule. 'The *Hadith* says Islam will be revived from Abyan,' he said, just as Awlaki had.

Wuhaysi confirmed the Saudi peace offer that Mujeeb had told me about, but said he had rejected it out of hand.

I told him about the letter my al-Shabaab contact Ikrimah wanted to send him from his former teacher, and offered to act as a bridge between AQAP and the Somali militant group. I needed to show him I could be useful.

'I was the one who sent Warsame to you,' I told him.

'Ah yes, the brother who got arrested on the sea. He was a very good brother and was always on the front. He was never scared. It is a shame the *kuffar* now have him.'

'We are actually in touch with some of the brothers in Somalia.'

I also told him about the militant group in Malmö, Sweden, and my own desire to get even for Awlaki's death.

He was particularly interested in the young IT student.

'Does he speak English?' he asked.

'Yes.'

'Then he can work on *Inspire* – we will arrange it,' he replied. We reminisced about Awlaki for a while. And then we talked about the cleric's sixteen-year-old son – Abdulrahman – who had been killed in a drone strike a month after his father. I remembered him that evening in 2006 as a young boy proudly presenting his homework to his father and looking after my son, Osama.

Although the strike was targeting other fighters it had provoked controversy in the US because of Abdulrahman's age and the fact he was an American citizen. Wuhayshi told me that Abulrahman had formally joined the group before he was killed.

I told Wuhayshi that, prior to Awlaki's death, the cleric had requested I bring him supplies. I was referring to the fridge and hexamine briquettes. The way he replied made it clear he knew what I was talking about.

'Should I carry on with this mission?' I asked.

'Yes, you should bring these things,' Wuhayshi said.

Wuhayshi wanted me to meet AQAP's chief bomb-maker, Ibrahim al-Asiri, who he said was some 150 miles away in Azzan, deep in Shabwa province.

Azzan was a desolate town halfway between the coast and Ataq, where Anwar al-Awlaki's son had died in the US drone attack some months previously. Al-Qaeda had seized the town a few weeks before the strike.

'Asiri's now the number three on the United States' most wanted list,' he added, with a note of satisfaction.

Al-Asiri was now in charge of overseeing the group's overseas attacks; he would be interested in the Swedish brothers who wanted to travel to Yemen.

The bomb-maker already had one Swedish operative working for him. Anders, the PET intelligence analyst, had told me that the suspected Swedish-Yemeni mastermind of the plot against *Jyllands-Posten* in December 2010 had escaped to Yemen and was now believed to be with al-Asiri.[3]

---

3 Al-Asiri was all the more dangerous for his knowledge of chemistry, which he had studied at King Saud University in Riyadh and was now passing on to apprentice bomb-makers. Like hundreds of other young Saudis, he had been determined to fight

Al-Asiri had sent his own brother to his death, built the underwear device that came close to bringing down flight 253 over Detroit on Christmas Day 2009, and constructed the so-called printer bombs. He was, put simply, among the most dangerous terrorists in the world.

To meet al-Asiri would surely reopen doors to the CIA, with a red carpet. But it would be tempting fate to travel to see him. The USB stick contained my only recording of the meeting with the CIA officer in Helsingør. If I threw it away I would also lose crucial corroborating evidence of my work for the intelligence services. But if I kept it I might not be around too much longer. I guessed the security around al-Asiri would be even tighter than that around Wuhayshi, and there was a real risk the USB would be discovered.

I had to think on my feet. 'Sheikh, that might not be possible. I told the soldiers at the checkpoints that I was on my way to Aden and if they don't see me there soon they may raise an alarm,' I told Wuhayshi.

It was a lame excuse but I knew the Yemeni government, under pressure from the Americans, was trying to keep tabs on the movements of Westerners.

'You will need to carry on to Aden, then. But when you get there you should set up email accounts with Abdul and Hartaba so we can communicate,' Wuhayshi replied.

We piled back into the vehicle and Wuhayshi gave me a tour of the al-Qaeda emirate. 'Make sure you keep your head wrapped up – we are worried about spies,' al-Abab told me.

The town was an alternative universe. Rusty old police cars patrolled the streets, driven by heavily bearded Islamist fighters. Strict Islamic law had been introduced and those who flouted it were punished.

Just a few days after my visit to Jaar, al-Qaeda's punishments reached a new level when an Islamic court ruled that a man suspected of spying for the Americans should be executed and crucified. According to residents his body was left hanging by a main road in Jaar for days. I would

---

in Iraq against the US occupation. He was arrested by Saudi security forces as he tried to cross the border into Iraq, but was released after a brief time in prison, which further radicalized him. After his militant cell in Riyadh was broken up by the Saudi security services, al-Asiri and his brother had fled to Yemen.

most likely have suffered the same fate had my true intent been uncovered.[4]

The code of laws imposed by al-Qaeda was called *Hudood*, a medieval form of justice long obsolete in most of the Muslim world. The al-Qaeda figure instrumental in setting up and overseeing *Hudood* courts in Yemen was none other than Sheikh Adil al-Abab, AQAP's amiable religious emir, whose portly frame was squeezed into the back seat next to me.

Wuhayshi would later depict AQAP's administration of justice as a model of restraint. A few months later, he wrote to the al-Qaeda group occupying part of Mali in West Africa, advising: 'Try to avoid enforcing Islamic punishments as much as possible, unless you are forced to do so . . . we used this approach with the people and came away with good results.'

As we drove around Jaar, Wuhayshi pointed out various public works projects. Al-Qaeda was handing out food, digging wells and storage tanks, driving water trucks around, bringing in free electricity to areas that had never known it, and providing other services that the central government in Sana'a had neglected for decades.

For Wuhayshi this was a means to an end. In his letter of advice to the jihadis occupying northern Mali he would write: 'Try to win them over through the conveniences of life and by taking care of their daily needs like food, electricity and water. Providing these necessities will have a great effect on people, and will make them sympathize with us.'

We stopped for a while at a cemetery for the martyrs of al-Qaeda in the semi-desert outside the town – row upon row of graves marked with little more than a stone. Their puritanical beliefs prohibited any sort of tombs. There were hundreds of fighters buried but you could walk right through it and never even know it was a graveyard.

---

4 Later that year fighters in the tribal areas beheaded a Yemeni woman they accused of sorcery and paraded her severed head. Her crime had been to work as a healer using natural herbs. In late 2012 Amnesty International documented the horrific human rights violations perpetrated by the group in Jaar on those it judged to have flouted 'Islamic law', including public summary killings, amputation and flogging.

Wuhayshi made a supplication – 'As salaam aleikum ya ahlul-qubur! . . .'
[Peace be upon you, O inhabitants of the grave] and we moved on.

I told Wuhayshi I planned to take a bodyguard course in the UK.
'Then you should become my personal bodyguard,' he replied. He told
me his own team of bodyguards had not followed them after the
picnic.

'They didn't notice me getting back in the car with you – you could
have kidnapped me,' he said. We laughed. It bordered on the absurd.

It was time for AQAP's leader to depart and he embraced me before
jumping into the car with Adil al-Abab. 'Wait here, I'll be back shortly,'
AQAP's religious emir told me and Abdul.

An hour later the sound of screeching wheels announced his return.
Al-Abab walked over to us with a grave expression on his face. Had
someone told him about the flash drive? But he addressed Abdul.

'*Alhamdulillah*, we think your brother has just been martyred – can
you come to see his body?' he blurted out.

Abdul, already affected by his exposure to the frontline in Jaar, could
not summon the courage to go. He asked me if I would view the body;
I had met his brother a few times in Sana'a. I was taken to a makeshift
morgue to see the corpse. The man had horrific injuries. A mortar
shell had entered through his cheek and blown out the left side of his
brain and there were shrapnel wounds all over the chest. But the right
side of his face was more or less intact, with his mouth curled up in a
smile. He definitely looked like Abdul's brother. I stared at him.

I went back to tell Abdul and this time he came with me to take a
look. 'It's him,' he said. He crouched beside him in a moment of silence
to pay his respects and then turned on his heels. But then he hesitated
and doubled back to inspect the dead man's teeth.

'This man has no fillings – it's not my brother,' he said, breaking into
the first smile I had seen from him since we arrived. It seemed a fitting
finale in what had been a surreal visit.

I was glad I would soon be travelling on to Aden. If a missile strike
or mortar round were to kill me here I would be buried in the anonymous strip of dirt with al-Qaeda's other martyrs, and the truth about
which side I was fighting for would surely be buried with me for ever.

We bade farewell to Adil al-Abab and the other fighters, including the would-be Saudi suicide bomber and Wuhayshi's younger brother. The Saudi kissed me on the forehead and then Wuhayshi's younger brother looked at me earnestly:

'Do you love the martyrs?'

'Yes,' I replied. I got the feeling he wanted to be one of them.

'May He whom you love, love me for loving you,' he said.

'*As salaam aleikum*,' I replied – peace be with you. He would never understand the irony.

I got in the car with Hartaba and Abdul for the dangerous drive to Hartaba's village, where we picked up Abdul's car. All the way to Aden, I pictured the look on Jesper's and Klang's faces at our future debriefing. I had enjoyed lunch and a few jokes with the leader of al-Qaeda in the Arabian Peninsula.

Wuhayshi's task for me in Aden was simple: create three email accounts for our future communications and hand them to Abdul, who would pass them on to Wuhayshi's men in the city.

After I created the accounts at an internet café, Abdul parked the car in a commercial street in Aden, just down the road from a call centre, the safest option for calling Wuhayshi's contacts. I watched dozens of customers walking in and out.

It shouldn't be taking this long, I thought, my suspicions about Abdul racing.

Across the street, something caught my eye. A car had pulled up and the driver was cleaning one of the side mirrors with a bucket of water and a sponge, glancing up occasionally. His surveillance training was good, except that he cleaned the same mirror time and again. And with all the dust and chaos of Aden, the exercise was pointless.

Was I about to become the victim of a set-up? I was relieved but also irritated when Abdul finally emerged.

'The emir's men will meet me here in an hour so that I can show them the email addresses – you should stay in the car.'

I had little option. When they came, Wuhayshi's emissaries did not look like jihadis. Both were clean-shaven, dark-skinned like many in Aden, and wore long *thawbs*. They greeted Abdul and disappeared inside a shop. The avid mirror cleaner was still across the street. He stared at them, his sponge dripping water.

I insisted on driving when Abdul got back in the car, and took a random route to shake off any tail. I ran through scenarios. Whose side was Abdul on? Had al-Qaeda sent somebody to monitor the pick-up? Or had Abdul spent so long in the call centre because he was calling a CIA handler to arrange for surveillance so the Americans could put a tail on Wuhayshi's representatives in Aden? As my mind raced I also wondered if this was all part of an American ploy for Abdul to take my place in Yemen. Might he have given Wuhayshi's men different email addresses so that he and not I would be in touch with Wuhayshi? He certainly had many jihadist contacts but given all the precautions taken by AQAP's leadership he was too low in the pecking order to get an audience with Wuhayshi. He had one ticket to the top table of al-Qaeda and that was through me. But that made me vulnerable.

I was relieved to leave Aden and escape Abdul's company. Maybe it was paranoia, but stranger things had happened. Back in Sana'a, I called Klang.

'I just met the big guy,' I told him in a thick Danish dialect.

CHAPTER TWENTY-FIVE

OPERATION AMANDA

January–May 2012

The one inevitable part of a successful mission was a debriefing invitation with PET. This time Klang chose Lisbon.

I was put up at the luxury Altis Avenida Hotel. Klang and Jesper had brought along a young analyst whose nickname was 'the Virgin'. It was obvious why. 'This is the biggest thing I've been part of,' he told me excitedly.

PET's spymaster, Tommy Chef, flew in later to join us, clearing his schedule. He handed me an envelope with 100,000 DKK – around $15,000. In the debriefing, I noticed how much the Danish team already knew about whom I had met in Jaar. Had they received word from the Americans courtesy of Abdul? If so, they were being very clumsy in tipping me off.

We all realized there was an opportunity to plant tracking devices in the fridge that Wuhayshi still wanted me to deliver. The fridge would most likely be sent on to Ibrahim al-Asiri, the bomb-maker, to store explosives, and thus could offer a unique chance to target him and also locate Wuhayshi. I told the agents I was willing to return to Yemen within two weeks.

'To be honest most people in the office thought you were done – finished,' Jesper told me on the balcony of our hotel after business was concluded that evening. 'Very few of us thought you could continue to work after what happened to Anwar.'

He paused. We watched the traffic drift past below on the Praça dos Restauradores.

'It's fucking good you are on our side – imagine the problems you would have caused us,' he added, slapping me on the back.

Of course, Klang organized a night out. We hit some of Lisbon's most exclusive bars and a gentlemen's club, champagne flowing freely, generating a bill of about $8,000 for the Danish taxpayer. The Danish agents all found 'companions' for the evening. Even Tommy Chef paired up with an East European woman. They were entangled on the couch when I left to return to the hotel.

Soon afterwards I travelled to Denmark to set up another meeting with the Hajdib clan, across the bridge in Malmö.

Oblivious to the raw cold of a February afternoon, Abu Arab and his nephew sat on a park bench enraptured as I recounted the details of my journey to and experiences in Jaar. It was as if I were Homer reciting the *Iliad* for the first time. The IT student wanted to know how soon they could travel. I told them I was awaiting instructions from the AQAP leadership.

What I did not know was that PET had finally come clean with Swedish intelligence about the Malmö ploy. The Swedes quashed it immediately. The idea of Swedish citizens being sent to join a terrorist group was beyond the pale.

On my return to Copenhagen I vented my frustrations with Klang: 'How the hell am I meant to maintain my networks if the rug is going to be pulled from beneath me like this?'

He had no answer; the decision had been taken higher up.

It turned out that we had missed a promising opportunity. A short while later AQAP released a new issue of *Inspire* magazine with a section entitled 'Rise Up and Board with Us'. From now on, it said, 'those who want to execute a slaughter to the enemies of Islam' should seek approval for their targets from AQAP's military committee. The magazine provided email addresses and details of how to download the Mujahideen Secrets software. It was essentially promoting itself as a clearing house for would-be terrorists in the West. Had our IT student been involved with *Inspire*, we could have had a window on AQAP's overseas recruitment drive and plots being hatched by its supporters in the West.

In any case, I had lost contact with Wuhayshi: no replies came back from the encrypted messages I sent to the three email accounts I had opened in Aden. Perhaps Abdul had deliberately passed on different email addresses to the ones I had created. I sent an encrypted email to Aminah telling her I needed to get in touch with Wuhayshi because I wanted to connect him to my contacts in al-Shabaab but received no reply. I wondered if she had already attained martyrdom.

For weeks I heard nothing from Danish intelligence, and the nightmares started to return, given fresh fuel by my eventful visit to Jaar. It was not until the beginning of March that PET finally summoned me. Klang arranged for us to meet in the same villa in the Marienlyst Hotel in which I had confronted the CIA agent months earlier.

It was good to be inside. An icy wind was blowing in from the Baltic, sending waves crashing on to the shore. Klang and I sat in the kitchen.

'We've been in touch with the Americans,' he said. 'They are prepared to offer you one million dollars if our mission leads to Wuhayshi and one million for al-Asiri.

'In addition they are offering one million dollars for Qasim al-Raymi. And if you later lead us to Ikrimah al-Muhajir they are offering a million kroner [around $180,000].'

I contemplated those on the hit list. Al-Raymi was a senior deputy to Wuhayshi. Klang would later tell me that the Americans suspected that Aminah had become betrothed to him after Awlaki's death.

Ikrimah, my long-haired Kenyan contact, had clearly climbed the ladder within al-Shabaab. His emails to me hinted he was in touch with Ahmed Abdi Godane – the shadowy and ruthless leader of al-Shabaab. The previous month Godane had formally merged the group into the global al-Qaeda network and appeared determined to transform it from an insurgent militia into a terror group ready to strike in Africa and beyond.

Ikrimah was now based in the Somali port city of Kismayo. The previous autumn Kenyan and African Union forces had launched an offensive against al-Shabaab, pushing the group out of Mogadishu and some of its strongholds in the south.

In response the group had vowed 'severe repercussions' in Kenya. In an email to me Ikrimah said he longed to take 'revenge' against the Kenyan government.

His emails had indicated he was still working closely with foreign operatives within al-Shabaab, including my American friend from Sana'a, Jehad Serwan Mostafa, known within al-Shabaab as 'Ahmed Gure'.[1]

Ikrimah was also working with perhaps the most wanted woman in the world – Samantha Lewthwaite, widow of one of the 7/7 London bombers, Germaine Lindsay. A mother of four who had been dubbed the 'White Widow' by the UK tabloids, she was on the run in East Africa after Kenyan police had come close to arresting her in Mombasa.[2]

'Kenya is getting really bad coz the kufar are doing all their effort to harm us,' Ikrimah emailed me. 'So you need to be extra carefull they dont get a single trace of anything coz they are now tracing a sister who was a window [sic] of one of the london 7/7 bomber (the jamecan brother) and they are accusing her of financing and organising terorisim.'[3]

Ikrimah was also friendly with an American who had become a prominent mouthpiece for al-Shabaab – Omar Hammami. Originally from Alabama, Hammami had won fame for posting jihadist rap songs on YouTube and calling on other foreigners to join al-Shabaab.

Hammami was eccentric and unpredictable and had recently fallen out with al-Shabaab's leader, Godane, over strategy, making Hammami fear for his life. In March he would release an extraordinary video claiming Shabaab's leadership was planning to assassinate him. Ikrimah had told me he feared his association with Hammami might place him in

---

1 Jehad Serwan Mostafa may have played a role in forging the February 2012 alliance between al-Qaeda and al-Shabaab. In October 2011 he had appeared in an al-Shabaab video stating he had been sent as an envoy by Zawahiri to Somalia to help distribute food aid to famine victims. It seems likely he would have carried messages between the two leaderships at the time they were negotiating the merger.

2 As of April 2014, Lewthwaite was still on the run.

3 Ikrimah added that money had grown tight after intelligence services increased their monitoring of the hawala money transfer system in Kenya, which had been used by jihadis there to transfer money to jihadis in Somalia.

danger too. In an email he had asked me to take care of his wife and daughters if he was killed.[4]

Shabaab was riven by internal conflicts and it seemed Ikrimah's climb up the hierarchy had created a new set of perils.

As Klang's words sank in, I realized I was not primarily motivated by the sums on offer for neutralizing the CIA's targets. I mainly wanted to hear that the Americans needed me again, driven on by wounded pride and the fear that Abdul might supplant me.

Klang's message about the rewards on offer came with strings attached. 'And on top of that we'd like ten per cent. Akhi, we also want to have some fun out of it. We can negotiate for you then.'

I nodded but said nothing. Now I had seen it all. A representative of Queen Margrethe's government was asking for a percentage of any reward I might receive from the US.

I wished my iPhone was recording the discussion, as it had the last time I'd sat in this villa. I wondered whether PET was altogether out of control or whether I had had the misfortune to be paired with its most dishonest officer.

Klang had sensed an opportunity and was ready to take a big personal risk.

'Big Brother doesn't want to deal directly with you any more so we would be the ones handling you from now on,' he said. I had little choice. I needed to earn the premium rate for overseas missions after spending so much to set up Storm Bushcraft.

The Americans clearly wanted to keep me at arm's length. Perhaps they didn't trust me; perhaps they thought I was high risk. Michael, sitting in the same cottage just a few months before, had surely drawn up a damning report. But I had already risked my life to meet Wuhayshi and I still wanted that heavyweight title.

'What guarantee do I have they won't screw me over this time?' I asked.

---

4 Ikrimah asked me whether he might be able to send his wife and children to Dammaj in Yemen or a similar religious institution. 'I am thinking of the future of the children i want them to have proper islamic education . . . anything can happen any time,' he wrote in an email in March 2012.

'You don't,' Klang replied, with a smugness that made me itch to punch him.

'I need to be sure that if I die my wife and kids will be taken care of,' I told him. My trip to Jaar had impressed on me the dangers that would lie ahead.

'They'd be in line to receive a million kroner ($180,000),' Klang promised.

'I'd be more comfortable if the Americans paid that up front,' I replied. I could hardly argue my family's corner from beyond the grave.

'We'll look into that.'

Klang promised that PET would also get my wife permanent residence status in Denmark before I travelled. I wanted to make sure she could continue to live in Europe if I was killed.

I went home to England to consider my options.

Against all the odds I had forced myself back into contention. As a freelancer I'd got on first-name terms with one of al-Qaeda's most important men. But still I was getting little support, and rather too many demands, from my handlers. And the situation in Yemen was far more treacherous than when I had made contact with Awlaki just a year earlier.

Two weeks later Jesper and Soren, the team leader, came to England. They had received permission from British intelligence to meet me on their patch. Klang was not with them; his security clearance had been suspended when he was arrested after a brawl at a pizzeria in Copenhagen. In another incident not likely to advance his career, he had been caught having sex with the mistress of PET's Director-General, Jakob Scharf,[5] in the toilets at the agency's Christmas party. Maybe Klang too was battling demons.

---

5 Scharf's tenure at the head of PET was to become embroiled in scandal. But at this stage he had been in the job nearly five years and was a powerful figure with deep connections throughout the Danish establishment. Before being appointed as Director-General of the Intelligence Service he had been Deputy Commissioner of Denmark's national police service.

Over breakfast in their hotel, Soren and Jesper conveyed to me the Americans' final word on the life insurance 'deposit' I had requested.

'We can get you fifty thousand dollars up front – they won't go a dollar higher,' Jesper said. The former banker had clearly been designated as the numbers guy.

It was not what I was hoping for, but I was working my way back to the summit and was still climbing in the foothills.

'I can live with that.'

Soren told me a plan was taking shape. I would drive down with Abdul as I had in January and deliver the supplies with the hidden tracking devices to Wuhayshi.

'When do I leave?'

'Soon,' Soren said.

They had brought my wife's Danish residence application and helped me fill in the paperwork.

'There won't be any difference between her and a Danish citizen,' Jesper declared.

Afterwards we drove into the countryside. I had promised to take them quad-biking. Soon we were racing along tracks, spattered in mud. It was the perfect pressure release valve. The only blemish was that Jesper broke his ankle after getting his foot caught in the track. I was stunned to see the insurance disclaimers they had signed. They had used their real names and Soren had listed an address in the vicinity of PET headquarters in Søborg as his home address. Had they been taught nothing?

Late in March, I was preparing for my most challenging and possibly final mission when an email dropped into my inbox. It was encrypted and it came from Aminah. She was still alive.

'Yes, yes,' I muttered to myself. The guilt of luring her to Yemen had never left me.

She said she had been divorced from the outside world for months and had only just received an email I had sent to her late the previous year. Her letter was long and rambling, peppered with Koranic references. Despite everything she had not lost the faith.

Aminah sent greetings to me and her 'dear sister' Fadia and talked about dreams she'd had that her husband would be killed – dreams which had continued after his death. I could empathize.

'Two weeks after his shuhadu I saw him in my dreams . . . We were talking and I told him I want to do martyrdom operation, and he said it is great idea, he was very happy about it. In my dream he was so close and yet so far away.

'He look so beautiful, in white dress, glowing and shining, he appeared above me . . . He was happy and smilling and he told me, Aminah – come to me, come to me.'

But she was still on this earth, thanks to none other than Nasir al-Wuhayshi.

'I wanted to do a martyrdom operation but Shaykh Basir [Wuhayshi] said that sisters so far will not do the operations because it would bring a lot of problems for them and then government would start to imprisoning Ansar sisters which would be very bad. So I cannot do the operation, I am praying for shuhada, I want to be killed like my husband was. Insha'Allah.'

Instead she was put to work – a blonde waif from the Balkans now committed to al-Qaeda.

'I am in contact with brothers now as I am started to work on Inspire [magazine], alhamdidullah.'

But – and here the guilt kicked in again – Aminah felt isolated and afraid.

'I didn't here from my family for a year and I do not know what is happening. I am sending letters to my sister but she doesn't responding. I do not know is she under the preassure of government or secret service . . . I ask Shaykh Basir can I come back after he didn't approve martyrdom operation, and he said I cannot. He said that my government wanted to put me in prison. I do not know that . . . And my husband told him in a case that he is killed he doesn't want me to come back.

'Is there any chance you can check am I on CIA wanted list or no fly list?' she asked.

Despite my sympathy, she was also a possible conduit for reaching Wuhayshi again and putting the second phase of the mission into gear. She clearly had a direct line to him.

'Insha'Allah you will receive a mail from Amir [Wuhayshi], I sent message to him. Insha'Allah you will manage to connect Somalia and Yemen.'

She ended with a note of fatalism:

'So I am here for now. Untill situation change insha'Allah. Shuhada would be the best solution for me.'

I had visions of a double triumph, rescuing Aminah and at the same time putting an electronic tag on Wuhayshi.

My orders to travel to Yemen finally came towards the end of April. It wasn't before time. I'd been ready to go for more than three months, and didn't understand why PET was holding back. Not knowing had further strained my relationship with Fadia, who could not understand why I was so agitated, constantly checking my phone for texts. I was so restless at night, muttering to myself in Danish, that she asked me to sleep on the sofa.

There was time for one last outing with my children. I took them to Waterworld, a theme park not far from Birmingham. They were in their element, slaloming down the water chutes and jumping in the pools and fountains. I tried to look as though I was enjoying it, but more than once felt tears welling.

I went to Copenhagen to discuss the final details of the mission and craft a response to Aminah. 'I am still not over the Sheikh . . .' I wrote to her, 'I have lost my friend brother teacher may Allah accept him as Shaheed.

'Regarding CIA then give me some time I cannot search their website from my town. I have also forgotten your name in your passport so you need to mail it to me again Inshallah. I don't think it's a crime if they find out you have been married to Sheikh. Just tell them you have been kept hostage and had no way of escaping. You have not committed any crime and they cannot prove your marriage to him.'

I felt treacherous using Aminah as a way to reach Wuhayshi, but justified it to myself by hoping that one day – if we remained in touch – I could help her.

'I agree with Sheikh Abu Basir don't do any actions without considering it carefully Inshallah. This is very important you give this message to Sheikh Abu Basir,' I wrote. 'Tell him I got the stuff for your husband and the stuff he asked me for. The stuff is ready and I should be at his place around the 10th [of May] Inshallah.'

I had another message for her to convey – one that would show Wuhayshi the importance of keeping lines open to me.

'Somalia . . . they are nagging me again for coming over to Yemen. Tell him that Abu Musab al-Somali and Ikrimah have intentions to come ASAP it seems like it's very important.'

I might well need her help: every avenue was precious.

'I have heard that Hartaba has been killed. Is this true? Then I ask Allah to accept him. He was my only way into Sheikh Abu Basir. Now how will I enter?'

I promised I would bring clothes for her and told her to take care of herself, signing off: 'Your brother Polar Bear.'

PET clearly liked Helsingør, the resort town on the coast near Copenhagen. They invited me to a summer house nearby to discuss next steps. The lashings of winter storms had given way to a mild spring and the Baltic was a placid blue-green.

Klang was back on the team because of the importance of the mission. We sat down in the reception room.

'We've discussed the Aminah situation,' Jesper told me. 'Our feeling is that it would be dangerous for her to come back to Europe. As you wrote in your email, there's no guarantee that she would be arrested and she could be a ticking time bomb.'

I wondered if he meant a time bomb for innocent civilians or for Danish intelligence. Perhaps they had calculated that her story would implicate them in a legally questionable operation.

I asked my handlers why there had been so much delay in sending me back to Yemen. Klang said implausibly that it was because the Americans were re-purposing spy satellites previously monitoring Afghanistan.

We discussed the mission. I was to meet Abdul in Sana'a and we would drive down to deliver the supplies.

'It's really important you stick with Abdul,' Klang said.

'Don't make a mockery of my intelligence,' I retorted. 'Don't you think I know he is working for the Americans?'

Klang threw up his arms. 'Fine, yes, he is working for them but as far as the Americans are concerned – you don't know this, okay?'

Finally my suspicions were confirmed. I had tried to flush Abdul out after the Lisbon meeting with a terse email in which I told him that I had been stopped by Danish security services at Copenhagen airport and warned that they knew about my visit to the south of Yemen. Someone had told them something, I wrote to Abdul, and my guess was that it was him.

Of course, nothing of the sort had happened, but I needed to lay the bait. I had received no reply, and that was confirmation enough for me.

'I have something for you,' Jesper said, changing the subject.

He came back clutching a make-up box. 'A present for Aminah from the Americans.'

It was a large oval box, plastic. When I opened the lid there was a mirror on the underside and beneath were rows of neatly packaged lipsticks, nail varnishes and eye shadow.

'Be careful how you handle it – it's a seriously expensive piece of kit,' Klang said.

Jesper said that if Aminah was engaged or already married to Qasim al-Raymi, one of Wuhayshi's senior deputies in AQAP and the second most powerful commander, a tracking device inside the make-up box might enable the Americans to target him.

'If Abu Basir decides to crush the make-up box in front of me and finds the device what am I going to say?' I asked. I felt uneasy. Two years previously the Danes had judged it too dangerous for me to supply Aminah a similarly modified cosmetics case. Had I become expendable?

'Just blame it on Abdul and let him be the fall guy,' Klang replied.

Not for the first time, Klang astonished me with his gall. It was never his problem, always someone else's. There was a blithe answer for everything.

'No, I'd never do that,' I replied. 'You have just told me he is working for us. We are on the same side.'

He had no answer but instead handed me a new iPhone the Americans had provided.

'This will allow us to follow your movements in real time. Leave it on all the time. If anything happens you can call us for assistance but only use it in emergencies.'

The Danes also gave me a sports bag with clothing for Aminah.

I caught the television news that night in my room in the summer house. Yemen was the lead: a new plot by AQAP against US-bound aeroplanes had been thwarted. It had involved the most sophisticated device yet designed by Ibrahim al-Asiri. But the man AQAP had selected for the attack – a Saudi recruit with a British passport – was a mole working for the intelligence services.[6]

The Saudi operation had culminated with the agent and another informant – most likely his handler – being whisked out of Yemen. Perhaps that's why my own mission had been delayed: Western intelligence already had a mole close to AQAP's senior leadership. But after he was extracted they had turned to me again.

Yemen was in a fog of war, which only complicated matters. It had a new president, Abd Rabbu Mansour Hadi. What he lacked in a power base he made up for with political manoeuvring and the promise of greater cooperation with Washington.

His focus was on reversing al-Qaeda's gains in the south. The group still controlled a stretch of coastline adjacent to some of the world's busiest shipping lanes, as well as several towns inland. Unless the Yemeni army – starved of supplies and leadership – acted quickly, even Aden might fall to the fundamentalists.

Government forces aided by tribal militia had embarked on a spring offensive. Wuhayshi's fighters were resisting fiercely, but air strikes were intensifying, aided no doubt by US intelligence, and regime forces were inching towards Jaar.

As I read an account of the battles, I asked myself one simple question.

'How the hell are Abdul and I going to be able to drive down there in the middle of a war?'

The next day I asked the Danish agents about the $50,000 payment they had promised my family.

---

6 The man had infiltrated the group in early 2012 after being recruited by Saudi counter-terrorism the previous year. Before switching sides he had lived in the UK for a long time and had moved in radical circles there – just like me. His background had given him credibility and his British passport had enhanced his appeal, because it allowed him to travel without a visa to the US.

'That's being processed – you should get it very soon after you return from Yemen,' Jesper replied.

If I return, I thought gloomily.

They had me on the hook. They knew I was hungry, focused – and were taking advantage.

Jesper handed over the immigration document for my wife, but rather than permanent status it conferred the right of residence for five years. I was furious. If I died there was no assurance my wife could stay beyond that and she would be in great danger in Yemen if word leaked that I had been an informant.

'We never promised her permanent resident status,' Jesper said.

I couldn't believe my ears. More than any reward, my wife's security was paramount.

I stormed out of the villa – shouting at Jesper as I left: 'You know what? I'm done.' As always, I'd quit first and negotiate later.

I spent that evening in my mother's house in Korsør. She had known about my work but had been the soul of discretion. I told her about my frustrations.

'I bet you Abdul is not even in Yemen. And if he's not there I have a feeling they'll want me to drive down myself and be killed in the fighting,' I told her.

It was all beyond her comprehension. Why should I even want to be involved in such a scheme? She looked at me in disbelief. It was far from the first time I had seen that expression.

I called a number Abdul had given me to use in Yemen. His wife answered. 'My husband is not here,' she said.

In a fit of pique I ignored calls from Danish intelligence but after two days finally took one from Klang. I told him I'd only meet them if the boss – Tommy Chef – was present. We agreed to meet at the Scandic Hotel in Ringsted, halfway between Korsør and Copenhagen. When I arrived, Tommy Chef was outside the lobby, checking messages on his phone.

'Hello, Morten. It's good to see you again. I'm sorry for these misunderstandings. Let's go inside to talk, just the two of us.'

In his suite he sat down opposite me on a sofa and looked me straight in the eye.

'I'm sorry for the mix-up. My agents had no authority to promise your wife these documents. There are steps that need to be taken; you can't just apply straight away for a permanent residence. But I've now taken charge of this and I can personally guarantee she will receive permanent residence status. As for the money I can also guarantee you will get it when you come back.'

His voice was calm and even, as if he were clearing up after some mischievous children.

'I'm glad to hear it,' I replied. 'Abdul is not in the country. How on earth am I supposed to get down to the tribal areas?' I asked.

'Yes, we know that. Believe it or not he's in China, but he'll get back the day after you arrive in Sana'a. It's all under control.'

He paused for effect.

'Morten, this is one of the most important missions in the history of Danish intelligence. Our director, Jakob Scharf, is closely following this. It's really vital you travel down to do this.'

The counsellor had just become a coach.

I had one more request. I wanted Klang and Jesper to come to Korsør and tell my mother about the mission. I wanted an insurance policy, some incentive for them to protect me. They would know that if something bad happened to me my mother could go to the media and explain what I was really doing in a remote corner of Yemen, hanging out with al-Qaeda's leadership. What they didn't know was that she had a copy of the photograph of the three of us in the pool in Reykjavik.

'Go and do what you need to do in Korsør and then let's meet for a nice dinner tonight,' Tommy Chef told me, charm personified. He smiled and placed his hand briefly on my shoulder in reassurance.

My mother lived on a quiet street in Korsør. The back garden was perfectly manicured, with a swing set and slide for the grandchildren who – sadly – rarely visited. She had at last found a gentle, honourable man to share her life with, a man I came to like. The inside of the house was an obstacle course for the clumsy: carefully placed china, cushions and ornaments meticulously arranged.

Klang and Jesper arrived wearing jeans and T-shirts and looking uncomfortable. I was sure this was the first time they had come to explain to an agent's mother what her son was doing, like schoolboys wanting permission to go for a bike ride. My mother greeted them with reserved Danish courtesy. Her husband was confined to the kitchen – not permitted to see officials of Denmark's secret service.

They moved to the living room, picking up the decorative cushions and holding them awkwardly. Light streamed in through the French windows. It was a picture of suburban orderliness.

Klang and Jesper were trying – not very successfully – to grapple with my family background. How could this hooligan have emerged from such genteel surroundings? They did not know the long and painful backstory.

We sat in silence as my mother made coffee. Klang took a sip from one of the delicate china cups and carefully replaced it on the saucer. I was amused to see that he was terrified of breaking something.

'Mrs Storm,' he began, with a synthetic cheeriness. 'You have to know Morten is a real one-off because he knows so many Muslims around the world.'

'Is it a dangerous job?' she asked.

'Yes – but he's doing this to fight terrorism,' Jesper said. 'It's important for the whole world.'

'It's why he got the $250,000 from the Americans,' Klang interjected.

'He brought the briefcase here,' my mother said. 'You know, even then it didn't seem real to me that he was working for the intelligence services.'

'We can't tell you much more than this but he's about to go back to Yemen,' Klang said.

'Will he be in danger?' she asked, more insistently.

'There's always some risk,' Klang replied carefully.

My mother looked at me as if to remind me that I had been trouble for as long as she could remember, and now I was thirty-six. But I felt reassured when we drove away at dusk. Both Klang and Jesper had taken a step out of the shadows.

There was a further bonus awaiting me. We joined Tommy Chef at a beach restaurant beside a pretty fishing marina. The house speciality was herring prepared several different ways. Washed down with Sancerre, it was an excellent dinner on the government's tab.

Tommy Chef dabbed his mouth with a white linen handkerchief.

'We've been doing some thinking, Morten. We're going to offer you something that has never been offered before to a civilian agent. Once you come back we are going to offer you a job. Because we don't want you just to stop working after this mission. We want you to continue – not on the frontline but on the cyber jihadi front – infiltrating these guys online.

'We also thought you could work with Anders to train agents.'

I was ecstatic at the prospect of a job that would put my address book to good use. Just days after I had quit, my future suddenly seemed to be opening up. Married life and approaching middle age were – just possibly – beginning to soften me.

As we left, Tommy Chef put his arm on my shoulder.

'You are doing all of us a great service.'

'You know what? We're going to do this for Amanda,' I said, referring to the code name of Elizabeth Hanson, the CIA agent who had recruited me and had been killed at Camp Chapman near Khost in Afghanistan in December 2009.

We called the mission 'Operation Amanda'.

CHAPTER TWENTY-SIX
CHINESE WHISPERS

May 2012

11 May 2012. A perfect late-spring dawn. Driving from Helsingør to Copenhagen, I watched the tractors rumbling up and down the immaculate fields. It was the picture of rural peace, at odds with my inner turmoil. My final field trip was underway. I had the 'modified' make-up box for Aminah (and Qasim al-Raymi) in my suitcase and a camping fridge for Wuhayshi to send on to Ibrahim al-Asiri, also fitted with a tracking device. I assumed it was the same fridge the CIA had been customizing for Awlaki.

The previous evening all the Danish agents, led by Tommy Chef, had attended a dinner in my honour. It felt awkwardly like a farewell and I was in a maudlin mood. Tommy Chef handed me $5,000 for expenses.

At Copenhagen airport there was one more piece of business. Jesper filled out an official notice stating that a package of hexamine had been confiscated from me. PET were still not comfortable with me providing hexamine to al-Qaeda, but at least Wuhayshi would see that I had tried.

By the time I boarded a connecting flight to Sana'a in Doha, my stress levels were rocketing. I began to second-guess everything: Tommy Chef's soothing words, the promise of Danish residency for my wife, Abdul's loyalties and his reaction on receiving my accusatory email. Why had he gone to China, of all places? Was he on the run? And if so from whom? I felt like I was facing a steep climb up a mountain lined with crevices and dotted with loose boulders. Any one of these hazards could finish me. But reaching the summit – leading Western intelligence to Wuhayshi and al-Asiri – would bring vindication. And – not incidentally – solvency.

At the customs hall in Sana'a nobody gave the fridge a second look; officials were used to foreigners bringing in appliances. I checked into a furnished apartment I had rented on 50th Street, the thoroughfare cutting through the southern part of the city. And I waited.

Tommy Chef had assured me that Abdul would return to Yemen from China the day after my arrival. I had no idea how he could be so confident, and in fact Abdul failed to arrive on the appointed day. I felt claustrophobic, holed up in an apartment on a mission I could not execute, my key intermediary thousands of miles away.

I got hold of the phone number Abdul was using in China from his anxious wife and sent him a text.

'Come and see me here,' he wrote.

'Why don't you come to Yemen?' I responded.

'I can't, brother, but I need to see you.'

A few seconds later my phone started ringing. It was Abdul. He was agitated.

'Murad, you must come here. I can't tell you what I need to tell you over the phone.'

'So you're telling me to come to China?'

'Yes, you must come, it's very important.'

'Let me figure this out,' I replied in disbelief.

I called Soren in Denmark, taking a calculated risk with security.

'Do you think you can persuade him to come back if you go?' he asked.

'Yes,' I replied.

'Then book your ticket,' he said. 'But don't take that iPhone we gave you.'

Perhaps Abdul picked China because he wanted to be sure he was beyond the eyes and the ears of the CIA.

Hardly had I arrived in Yemen than I was on the move again, connecting in Doha for the nine-hour flight to Hong Kong. I looked down at the vast cultivated heartland of India and the mystical green hills and jungles of Myanmar and could not help but be excited, despite the unpredictability of this mission. I always relished the prospect of arriving somewhere new. And the view on approach into Hong Kong was more spectacular than I could have imagined: soaring skyscrapers hugging steep hills, and wooden junks with their orange sails navigating between the islands.

From the airport I crossed on to the mainland and walked into Shenzhen railway station, a vast glass edifice. I thought of Yemen. Sana'a was nine hours and ninety years away. The Arab world was being left behind.

The new high-speed link between Shenzhen and Guangzhou had recently opened and covered the seventy miles in about thirty minutes.

Abdul had agreed to meet me at the railway station in Guangzhou, one of China's booming megacities. Amid the thousands of Chinese commuters hurrying to and from trains, he was not difficult to find, dark-skinned and slight. We embraced. He looked tense.

'What's going on?' I asked him.

'I can't tell you yet. We have our phones with us so it's not safe,' he replied.

I dropped my luggage and the cheap mobile phone I had brought in the apartment where he was staying. He told me he had come to Guangzhou because he knew some Yemeni businessmen in the city. We walked through thronging markets and squares where roller-skaters and acrobats performed. Skyscrapers lined the wide river flowing through the heart of the city.

Our destination was a spa. Before going into the jacuzzi room, we undressed in front of each other. Abdul clearly wanted to be sure that whatever he had to say could not be recorded. When we were alone in the gurgling water, Abdul turned to me with a worried look in his eyes.

'I have something to tell you.'

I cut him off. 'Remember the email I sent you about what they told me at Copenhagen airport. *I know* . . .'

I wanted to get ahead of him. I suppose it was part of the contest I felt between us.

'But the CIA, they're . . . they're going to kill you along with the terrorists if you travel down with me,' Abdul blurted.

'*Subhan'Allah* – what?'

'Murad, they don't want to kill you in Sana'a. They want to kill you when you are sitting with Abu Basir and the other brothers,' he continued.

He told me his CIA handlers had given him $25,000 to purchase a Toyota Prado SUV. He had taken the car to a workshop used by the Agency, where it had been fitted with a satellite transmitter connected to an electronic switch under the car seat. During a test run the equipment worked perfectly.

'One click would signal you had joined me in the car. Two clicks would signal we had left Sana'a. Three clicks would tell them we are in the same location as the target. And four clicks would mean I had left you alone with the target.'

He grabbed me by the shoulder. 'That's when you were going to be killed. They'll tell the world you were a terrorist like the others.'

Only my mother would know differently. It was plausible, but I was not convinced.

He climbed out of the jacuzzi. 'Murad, you can hit me now, you can hate me, but I couldn't bear it on my shoulders if you were hurt. I was scared about driving down with you, and that's why I left the country.'

I had not yet said a word. The CIA had been avoiding me, yet wanted me to return to Yemen. They knew that I had recorded one of their agents in Copenhagen the previous year and I had threatened to go public. There was also the iPhone which I had been told to leave on at all times.

I remembered the warning from Jacob, the outdoor instructor: '*Don't sit with the terrorists because the Americans won't hesitate to kill you.*'

Abdul was not exactly the most reliable of sources. But he did seem genuinely scared. Did he fear he would be killed with me?

'How long have you been working for the Americans?' I finally asked.

'You remember when years ago I told you I was arrested by intelligence services in Djibouti? That's when they recruited me. They left me no choice but to work for them. I am sorry that I lied to you.'

'Did you tell the CIA about me?' I asked.

'All I told the Americans was that you disagreed with the brothers about targeting civilians.'

Abdul was not an easy man to read, but he did not seem to have any inkling that I too might be working for Western intelligence. I fought back the urge to tell him.

'May Allah reward you for telling me this,' I told him.

He broke down. 'Murad – I am done working for the Americans. Do you think you can help me claim asylum in Denmark?' I promised to find out but told him it would be difficult.

When we got back to his residence I prayed with him. Now was not the time to drop my guard.

That night I had trouble getting to sleep. I didn't know whether to believe Abdul or not. I now knew he had lied to me just as much as I had lied to him. One idea kept coming back: could he be trying to scare me so he could return to Yemen and deliver the supplies himself? Just by being seen with me in Jaar he had boosted his credibility with Wuhayshi. And he could claim I had asked him to deliver the supplies. That would be one way for the Americans to tunnel directly into AQAP without needing me.

Then another thought: might Abdul have flipped back to the al-Qaeda side, like the Jordanian 'triple agent', Humam al-Balawi, who had killed Elizabeth Hanson and the other CIA agents in Afghanistan? Was he testing me on Wuhayshi's orders? If I returned to Yemen and didn't warn al-Qaeda of Abdul's treachery they would know I was a spy.

It was like trying to solve a Rubik's Cube blindfolded.

The next morning I was awoken by the buzzing of an incoming text. Jesper was asking me if I had persuaded Abdul to return.

I replied: 'I don't think he will travel or come down there while there is still fighting. He's convinced that I'm going to die and he will be taken with me.'

In a follow-up text I requested a meeting with my handlers in Doha on my way back to Yemen. Jesper said the Americans would be there too, but asked me to try to change Abdul's mind. Late that night, 19 May, I texted again: 'It doesn't look good . . . the boy doesn't want to travel right now.'

Jesper's reply came in a few minutes later: 'Can you ask for the car keys?'

I stared at the screen, startled. Did the Danes also want me to drive alone to the south? Were they in league with the CIA? Or did the Americans just want their high-tech car back?

There was no way I was going to ask Abdul for the keys. I texted: 'I tried with the car but unfortunately no he ready in one or two months. Right now he wants to have a break and to travel to the EU.'

At that moment Abdul's scenario, which seemed so outlandish at first, was beginning to look more than plausible.

Two days later I was checking in at the Mövenpick Hotel close to Doha airport. Jesper and Soren had already arrived and I met them for breakfast.

I related Abdul's warning, trying to sound sceptical but wanting to test their reaction. They both dismissed it out of hand.

'Where is Big Brother?' I asked.

'They're in the hotel but they don't want to meet directly with you,' Jesper replied.

'Fantastic,' I replied.

'Look, Akhi, this mission is very important to us. Do you think you might be ready to drive the supplies down to the south of Yemen yourself?' Soren said.

'You have to be joking,' I replied, reeling at such a rash proposition. Even if Abdul hadn't unnerved me with his warning, there was no way I was going alone into Yemen's war zone.

I asked them to put another idea to the Americans – that I should arrange a courier to pick up the camping fridge, cosmetic box and other items in Sana'a.

'That method is tried and trusted – it worked with Nabhan and Awlaki,' I said.

'That sounds like a good idea,' Jesper replied. He said they would ask.

When they were gone I sat in the lobby, staring vacantly at guests arriving and leaving, smiling and chatting, travelling the world in peace.

Eventually they returned.

'Big Brother says the courier idea is not an option,' Jesper said in a matter-of-fact tone. 'They insist you deliver it to Abu Basir in person.'

'I don't think I'm comfortable doing that,' I replied with what seemed masterful understatement.

I was staggered by the US insistence that I personally deliver the equipment. Time and time again I had successfully used couriers – with the Americans' encouragement – to supply Awlaki and through him AQAP. The ploy had also worked in Somalia. The Americans' refusal to even discuss this approach made me fear a trap. I wondered if they were even in the hotel.

'You don't need to give us your answer right away – sleep on it,' Jesper replied.

The next day – 22 May – Jesper, Soren and I went for lunch at L'wzaar, an expensive seafood restaurant in Doha. Decorated floor to ceiling with a mosaic of blue marble tiles, it brought cool to the oppressive heat of the Gulf. On one side were the still waters of the Gulf and on the other a row of chefs preparing fish.

'So, did you think about it?' Jesper asked me.

I allowed a moment to pass.

'I think I'm going to call an end to it,' I told them.

Jesper and Soren looked at each other.

'It's up to you – it's your call,' Soren replied.

And so, at a fish restaurant on the shores of the Persian Gulf, the curtain dropped on a journey that had begun, in the Islamist ferment at Dammaj on the other side of Arabia, fifteen years before.

It was an anti-climactic way to end more than five years on the frontline. And it was also – to me at least – inexplicable. The US, which had put the 'War on Terror' at the top of its agenda, had walked away from an opportunity to neutralize two of its most dangerous opponents – Nasir al-Wuhayshi and Ibrahim al-Asiri – and deal a blow to the most active of al-Qaeda's affiliates.

That decision would soon appear as a major error of judgement.

I flew back to Yemen the next day, 23 May, to fetch my belongings. After I landed I received a text message from Soren asking me to return the fridge and make-up box to CIA agents in Sana'a. The last thing the Americans wanted was tracking gear falling into the wrong hands.

I told them I would drive my silver Suzuki to the Sana'a trade centre – the closest thing in Yemen to a shopping mall – with the equipment inside.

'Place the small box in the large box and place it on the back seat just behind the driver's seat,' Soren's message read.

Even in these final moments, there was a change of plan. Another text from Soren asked me to leave the box on the tarmac of the car park. I did, but I was furious. There were security guards in the area. Had they noticed me leaving a large box unattended in the car park – in a country where plenty of bombs exploded – I could have been in deep trouble.

A few minutes later Soren forwarded a message from his CIA contact.

'I can confirm its picked up. Tell our boy "good job".'

I replied: 'Roger that, my pleasure.' If only phones had a key for irony.

CHAPTER TWENTY-SEVEN
A SPY IN
THE COLD

2012–2013

In July 2013, just over a year after my last mission in Yemen, an online message stream was intercepted by the US National Security Agency at its sprawling complex in Fort Meade, Maryland, and filtered through the most powerful supercomputers on the planet. Once the message was deciphered and translated it triggered a state of high alert.

We will carry out an attack that will change the face of history.

Within hours the entire US intelligence apparatus was mobilized to discover the scope of the attack being planned. It was clear an ambitious strike had been set in motion at the top level of al-Qaeda, but precious little was known about how, when or where. The US State Department took the unprecedented step of closing down more than twenty embassies and consulates across the Arab and Muslim world.

It soon became clear that the nexus of the threat was Yemen – with the US embassy in Sana'a one of the likeliest targets. The author of the message that triggered the alert was none other than my tour guide in Jaar – Nasir al-Wuhayshi, the leader of AQAP. In one of my last reports, I had told my handlers that Wuhayshi had ordered reconnaissance of the US embassy in Sana'a. Since then he had been appointed as Ayman al-Zawahiri's deputy – the number two of al-Qaeda globally. The man who had once been Osama bin Laden's protégé was now the annointed successor to Zawahiri.

Wuhayshi's creation of an Islamic emirate in the southern tribal areas of Yemen had enhanced his reputation in jihadist circles world-wide. His men had controlled Jaar and an expanse of southern Yemen for fifteen months. They had only retreated in the face of overwhelming firepower brought to bear by Yemeni government forces and loyalist tribal militias – supported by US drone strikes.

Even after being forced to retreat to more remote areas, AQAP had continued with suicide bombings against Yemeni security forces, assassinations of senior military personnel and ambushes of Yemeni troops. As Adil al-Abab noted in one of his last missives before he was killed by a drone, a new generation of jihadis had been blooded.

Less clear to Western intelligence were AQAP's priorities: whether Wuhayshi remained focused on carving out a state based on Islamic law and at the very least denying space to the Yemeni government, or whether, newly installed as al-Qaeda's number two, he now embraced global jihad as the pre-eminent mission. Perhaps I would have gained a sense of this with another visit or two. Equally, had I been given approval to organize the delivery of the fridge early in 2012, Zawahiri would most likely have been looking for a different deputy.

Since my final mission had been aborted I had turned to cocaine as my comfort blanket. For a few hours the frustration ebbed but as I came down from each high the jitters got worse. I was stressed about money, after sinking so much into Storm Bushcraft but losing both my business partner and a base in Kenya.

For half a decade I had moved back and forth between two worlds and two identities – when one misplaced sentence could have cost me my life. I had switched identity in airport departure and arrival halls around the world, travelling between atheism and hardline Islam, English and Arabic, T-shirts and *thawbs*, between being an agent for Western intelligence and a sworn member of al-Qaeda. As my fellow passengers reclined their seats and started the in-flight movies my brain was always running in fifth gear, focusing on the mission or trying to recall every detail of the one I had just endured.

My life depended on keeping sharp. Most recently my work had entailed maintaining layers of deception: the Western agent pretending to be an al-Qaeda operative pretending to be an outdoor travel entrepreneur.

Even at home – in England or Denmark – I was still on stage, as that well-known militant Islamist Murad Storm. In London or Copenhagen, Luton or Aarhus, Birmingham or Odense, there were enough radicals on the streets to mean I could not let the mask drop for a moment. It had been easy to play the role in the early days, but the further I travelled from my days as a radical fundamentalist, the more challenging it became to play the jihadi with any conviction.

Only when I was in the deep countryside or far-flung nightclubs could I become Morten Storm and knock back a beer. They were not the sorts of places that would attract serious jihadis, I reasoned. Even then I was on edge.

This lifestyle had brought me to the verge of a breakdown. For years I had been fuelled by the need to stop the next attack, by the rush of the spy game and camaraderie with my handlers. But their insistence that I travel alone down to Yemen's tribal areas unnerved me. Abdul's warning kept ringing in my ears and I was starting to doubt whether it was worth it. I had tracked down Wuhayshi, at a level of risk bordering on the insane, and Western intelligence had dropped the ball.

I had been lucky, but luck has a habit of running out. It was time to become a backroom boy, one of the analysts who did their best to divine the intentions of terrorists the world over.

On 12 July 2012 I flew from Manchester to Copenhagen to follow up on the offer made to me by Tommy Chef in that seafood restaurant. PET had booked a room at the airport Hilton for the meeting. I was apprehensive: the Danes had broken promises and my final divorce from the Americans had been ugly. It would be prudent, I thought, to have a record. I reached into my pocket to check my iPhone was primed.

Jesper was waiting for me, and told me Klang (restored to his job after a humiliating stint checking the records of would-be refugees) and Anders would arrive soon.

'Everyone is on vacation,' Jesper told me, with an eye on the coverage of the Tour de France on a TV in the corner of the room.

He reached for his laptop case and took out a large wad of $100 bills.

'Here's $10,000,' he said to me, handing me the cash, as if it were a perfectly normal thing to do in the middle of a conversation.

'Is this from the Americans?' I asked, conscious that I was recording his every word.

'This is for the trip – that's all I could do for you, Akhi. I hope it's good enough,' Jesper replied. He could see that the cash had not placated me.

'Akhi, what are we doing?' he asked.

'I don't know – we are on holiday until the Americans get back into it,' I replied sarcastically.

I still wanted an explanation for events in Doha.

'I was ready in January. I was down with Abu Basir and ready, and was ready two weeks later to return to Yemen. Why has everything been postponed? It's not my mistake.'

'Nobody's pointing a finger at you; that's why they gave you the $10,000.'

I made clear to Jesper it would be dangerous for me to return to Yemen.

'Abdul may be playing a double game. He could also be working for al-Qaeda, as well as the CIA,' I said. 'Maybe it's a test,' I continued. 'If I go back to Abu Basir and if he asks "Why did you never tell us about Abdul?". . .'

I let the consequences of failing such a test hang in the air.

'Do you really believe Abdul would save me if he's a traitor to his own brothers in al-Qaeda?'

'I don't think the Americans will ever work again with Abdul,' Jesper offered.

I didn't believe him but his response was useful nonetheless. The PET agent had just reconfirmed that Abdul had been recruited by the CIA, and I had it on tape.

I told him I thought it possible that Abdul's warning was an American ploy to remove me from the game and have him replace me as their key informant on al-Qaeda in Yemen.

Jesper said he could not understand why the Americans had rejected my plan to track Wuhayshi using couriers.

'Jesper, I'm not just talking about Abu Basir [Wuhayshi]. I'm talking about the bomb-maker too. They know I'm the one who would get into those two guys and yet they don't want to do anything about it. I'm frustrated. It must be something to do with me.'

'The reason why they stopped it with you is because they said it was too dangerous for you,' Jesper said.

In Qatar I had been the one who had expressed concern about the dangers in Yemen – not the Americans. Had Jesper simply forgotten that? Was he trying to rewrite history? Or was he just not very bright?

There was a knock. Anders and Klang had arrived.

We called up room service and ordered some sandwiches. Klang got a beer.

I decided to ask them about the position away from the frontline that Tommy Chef had offered.

'I'd like to take up the job,' I told them.

'I'm afraid that was conditional on you fulfilling your mission in Yemen. We can't provide it to you now,' Jesper replied.

Just as I had feared they were going to renege on a promise. I felt like I had fulfilled my end of the bargain, before having the rug pulled from under me. No one had ever told me that another actual meeting with Wuhayshi was the quid pro quo for a position.

'What about my wife? What about her papers?'

'We are still working on it,' Jesper said.

I did not believe them.

Klang had come forearmed. He had another proposal, though it was unclear whether his superiors had signed off on it. I should offer myself as the point-person for al-Shabaab in Europe. If I was the one arranging safe houses for militants in Europe, Danish intelligence could have eyes and ears on any terrorist plots being hatched.

I did not take the bait.

'If I retired now, what can I expect?' I said.

'If you quit then you should expect PET would be grateful,' Jesper said, as non-committal as possible.

'And then we probably would do some sort of agreement to step back, like retirement. Yeah, I think we would be able to do that,' he added, every inch the former banker.

He and Anders indicated they could get me a year's salary in severance pay. Anders seemed to be my only true ally, conscious of the value of intelligence from the frontline.

'You were just about to get hold of the ones who could carry out an attack against us,' Anders said – referring to Ibrahim al-Asiri and the AQAP operatives charged with planning attacks overseas.

'Isn't it just insane that the Americans stopped me?' I said.

He nodded.

We discussed other options, but with the possible exception of Anders they were only humouring me.

It was time to leave. The agents embraced me. Anders lingered longer. 'I know you got cheated over Awlaki,' he said with real emotion, shaking my hand.

My status with PET was in limbo for weeks. A Western Union wire transfer for £2,466 from Jesper came in on 30 July – my monthly retainer. But of the future there was no word until a call in mid-August.

It was Jesper. He began with some pleasantries about who was on vacation and the English summer.

'Now,' he said briskly. 'PET has decided you are eligible for six months' severance.'

'You said twelve,' I replied.

'That's all they are willing to approve,' he said.

I was being jettisoned. But I had some news for them.

'I've contacted the Danish newspaper *Jyllands-Posten* and they want to meet.'

For a few moments there was dead air.

'I'm going to need to call you back,' he finally said. He sounded disturbed, no doubt conjuring lurid headlines about lap-dancing clubs in Lisbon and champagne at the taxpayers' expense.

I had contacted *Jyllands-Posten* because I was fed up with PET's broken promises. I burned to set the record straight on Awlaki and knew I had the evidence to corroborate my side of the story. And I also thought that going public would offer me protection from any foul play. Abdul's warning haunted me.

There was another reason. Many of my acquaintances and some of my family still believed I was a radical extremist associated with terrorists who ought to be behind bars. It was time they knew otherwise. And I wanted to take a stand for other informants risking their lives for Western intelligence.

When Jesper called me back, it was to invite me to a meeting with Tommy Chef – troubleshooter-in-chief – at the Admiral Hotel, overlooking the Copenhagen waterfront.

The following day I flew to the Danish capital, unsure whether Tommy would find a solution or issue veiled threats. He greeted me warmly, but I wasn't in the mood for pleasantries.

'What about the job you promised me?' I asked.

'Oh, we can't do that,' he replied.

He looked out into the harbour at a wooden vessel bobbing gently in the water.

'That's a nice ship. Is that what you are going to do? Do you want to learn how to sail?'

I had mentioned that I might try to get work as a contractor in anti-piracy.

'No, I don't want to learn how to sail,' I replied curtly.

He continued staring at the boat, then turned to look at me.

'Let's just agree you will call the journalists and tell them not to come.'

'I'm not sure I can do that. You've cheated me and you've lied to me. We're done.'

The meeting had lasted ten minutes.

I walked through Copenhagen, feeling a sense of freedom tinged with apprehension. I was on my own now – and the Danish intelligence service would spare no effort to discredit me. They would certainly renege on the promise of permanent residency for my wife. With the sense that I had broken my chains came isolation and vulnerability.

At least I could take solace from the panic that had clearly set in on the top floor of PET's headquarters. In the hours before my scheduled meeting with *Jyllands-Posten* on 27 August, Jesper made a series of ever more desperate calls. I recorded them. They would offer me a year's severance. Rejected. Another call – two years' salary if I kept silent.

Rejected. And finally came an offer of $270,000 – 1.5 million DKK – that the Kingdom's long-suffering taxpayers would have to fund to save the agency from embarrassment and – worse – closer political scrutiny.

'The money you get from us you don't have to declare to anyone,' Jesper said.

They were offering me a payoff tax-free. I was no tax lawyer, but that seemed to me illegal under both Danish and UK law.

'But what really annoys me is the way you treated me last year with Anwar,' I replied.

'Yes, yes, but that's what we're trying to make up for now,' he said.

Then came the not so subtle threat about the consequences of my talking to the press.

'You don't have a lot of time to think about it because there are some people who are waiting to talk to you . . . The problem is once you have spoken to them there is no way back.'

Jesper tried his pitch once more.

'The offer they are coming up with now – I have never, never seen anything like it before. And this is a confession. It is a confession they make. And you can use that positively.'

I told him I needed to think about it. I badly needed the money – an informant's CV has plenty of gaps and whatever I could wring from them would need to sustain me and Fadia – and provide for a fresh start far from my former 'brothers'. Reinventing myself would not come cheap. This was my one shot.

I devised a proposal and called Jesper. In return for 4 million DKK ($700,000) I would hand them my computers and my file of corroborating emails and recordings and never speak of my work for Western intelligence. He called back, saying PET could not improve on their previous offer.

'I just can't accept that offer. I can only say thank you to you, Jesper, and I can only tell the leadership that they should feel ashamed,' I said.

'And the same from me to you. Sometimes you have been a bit difficult but you have never been boring,' he said with more than a hint of understatement.

Somehow, Danish intelligence must have been aware that I had begun to lay out my story to three journalists from *Jyllands-Posten*, because on 19 September Jesper called again. PET would give me the equivalent of five years' salary plus a cash payment of almost 700,000 DKK: a total of almost 2.2 million DKK or $400,000.

I asked Jesper if we could draw up a contract.

'It's very, very difficult to sign something. I don't know if it would make you feel more safe to go and speak to Jakob,' he said, referring to Jakob Scharf, the director of PET.

After some haggling over the details, I called Jesper one more time.

'Done deal,' I told Jesper when I called him back.

'Thank you – that was fucking difficult,' he replied.

Not as difficult as what was to follow. That same afternoon, the journalists at *Jyllands-Posten* told me that a Danish TV station was planning to break the story about my work for PET. It seems that the station had been approached by PET as part of a damage limitation exercise: throw enough mud and throw it first. I had no idea whether wires had been crossed at PET or whether they had planned this while trying to spin out negotiations. Whatever the case, a journalist at the station later confirmed to me that he had received a call from Danish intelligence offering their take on my story.

I felt it likely that PET would backtrack on the settlement. I suspected their offer was just a ploy while they figured out a way of separating me from the cache of electronic evidence I had built up. Incensed, I called Jesper back to say the deal was off the table.

Jesper made it clear PET would not protect me if I broke my cover.

'If you go public just to get revenge you have to think, was it worth it? You won't be able to travel around freely with your kids. They won't be able to see their grandparents freely. Just because you needed that satisfaction,' he told me in a rare burst of spite.

But his increasingly desperate arguments fell on deaf ears.

Just before the first article ran in *Jyllands-Posten* on 7 October 2012, I texted Jesper.

'Just wanted to let you know I recorded all our conversations,' I wrote.

'Why did you do that?' came his reply.

'Because I'm a spy – and that's what you taught me ☺.'

EPILOGUE

Undisclosed Location in the UK, Spring 2014

The first *Jyllands-Posten* article on 7 October 2012 caused a sensation in Denmark. The piece outlined the role I played in tracking down Awlaki for the CIA and PET so that he could be targeted with a drone strike: explosive allegations in Denmark, where the government is forbidden to take part in any such assassination. The *Jyllands-Posten* journalists were later awarded the inaugural European Press Prize for their stories.

The news was picked up around the world. In December 2012 I sat down with CBS's *60 Minutes*, the celebrated US news magazine show, for an interview which focused on my role in tracking down Awlaki.

After all the years operating in the shadows it felt surreal seeing my name in newspapers and on television and my work for Western intelligence made public. It was satisfying to go public with what I perceived to be both the achievements and the failings in my work with intelligence. But away from the cameras, I felt vulnerable. And my wife, Fadia, was still coming to terms with the fact that I had deceived her for so long with so many lies.

A couple of weeks before *Jyllands-Posten* published my story, I suggested to her that we go for a long country walk. I chose a beautiful late-summer's day; the air was fragrant with the harvest of barley and wheat. We sat at the edge of a field; I had even put together a picnic.

As we watched the skylarks above, I told her everything: my recruitment, my work in Yemen and Kenya, in Lebanon and Birmingham, Denmark and Sweden, my falling-out with the CIA and PET – my role in the assassination of Awlaki, the money, the cocaine and my mission to southern Yemen to see Wuhayshi. The strain had already affected our marriage; I warned Fadia that once my story was in the press the pressure would only grow. I could expect no protection from the intelligence agencies and plenty of people would want me dead. Our world would shrink; we would always be on our guard.

Fadia was traumatized.

'Why?' she asked. 'Could you not trust me? Five years of endless lies. And have you any idea how lonely I was? You were hardly ever there, and when you were it was in body only. Your mind was always somewhere else.'

I tried to explain that I wanted to protect her, that it was better she knew nothing, that in any case I could have told her so little.

'But I'm your wife,' she said – looking at me through eyes swollen with tears.

In the autumn of 2012, the pressures generated by my 'coming out' weighed heavily on both of us and we agreed to separate – at least for a while. I was diagnosed as suffering from post-traumatic stress disorder, unable to work, unable to get a new National Insurance number in Britain, where I still lived, for fear that a militant sympathizer working in a government office would uncover and locate me.

The moment *Jyllands-Posten* went on sale on 7 October, I was a marked man. On jihadist forums and Facebook pages, animosity and threats to me and my family poured out. Among militants Anwar al-Awlaki had been a beloved figure. To avenge his killing would be an honour, an act on which Allah would smile. My bitter fall-out with Danish intelligence meant, as Jesper had warned, that I could expect no help from my own government.

One of the Americans who had been at Dammaj with me, Khalid Green, took to YouTube to denounce me for pretending to love Allah but betraying Islam.

'Someone we considered a companion and a friend,' he intoned – sitting in front of shelves full of Islamic texts – 'who was with us in one of the most esteemed places of knowledge in the camp in Dammaj studying with Sheikh Muqbil . . . we find out that this person has worked for the CIA.'

Others among my circle were shocked and even grudgingly impressed. Rasheed Laskar, the young man from Britain whom I had known in Sana'a, wrote on an Islamist blog under the name Abu Mu'aadh:

'I knew Murad personally since 2005/6 & we lived together in Yemen . . . When I was first informed about the news from Danish friends I was in shock . . . his contacts with Sheikh Anwar raheemahullah are true.

'Believe me if his – whole ex-CIA-PET agent story – is true – & it really does go back to 2006 – then he was quite honestly – back in those days – brilliant at his job.

'Since 2005/6 I have had a lot of contact with Murad . . . and I never suspected him of being an agent. I know many brothers that have been in & out of Arab prisons, tortured, deported and hounded from country to country (and even assassinated) with one common element in our stories – knowing Murad Storm.

'From the bottom of my heart – I ask Allah to give him what he deserves both in this life & the hereafter.'

His tone suggested he didn't have seventy-two virgins in mind.

More seriously, in August 2013 a group of Danes who had travelled to Syria and joined forces with an al-Qaeda affliate released a video calling for my murder, along with several other high-profile Danes they considered enemies of Islam.

'It's important that we shoot with our Kalashnikovs at these *murtadeen* and those *kuffar* attacking Islam,' a Danish jihadi calling himself Abu Khattab said to the camera, overlooking a hilltop town in Syria. His face was familiar. I had seen him in Copenhagen. He was one of the followers of an al-Muhajiroun spin-off in Denmark.

The camera then scans along six pictures against a stone wall. My picture is the first that comes into view, followed by that of Naser Khader, a moderate Muslim politician in Denmark whose murder I had once called for, as well as Anders Fogh Rasmussen, the Danish Secretary General of NATO, and the cartoonist Kurt Westergaard. A caption comes on to the screen: 'Enemies of Islam'.

The fighters crouch and take aim – shouting *'Allahu Akbar!'* as they unleash a volley of gunfire at the posters. Another clip posted by the same band of jihadists in Syria featured Shiraz Tariq, a Pakistani extremist I had gone paintballing with a decade previously in Odense.

In a follow-up video Abu Khattab was asked why they chose to include me on the execution list.

'His task was to kill our beloved Sheikh Anwar al-Awlaki.'

Sure enough a threatening message appeared on my Facebook account. Its author was Abdallah Andersen, one of the Danes convicted in relation to the 2006 Vollsmose terrorist plot. He was now out of jail but his views had hardly softened; he now called himself 'Abu Taliban' on his Facebook profile.

'How's the family? Everyone hates you. Everyone wants you dead,' he said.

I passed the comment to Danish police. Everyone on the 'execution list' not already under police protection had been offered a round-the-clock guard by PET, except me. For weeks PET did not return my emails even when the story was all over the Danish media, and they never offered protection.

But there were compensations for going public, chief among them restoring my reputation among those who had been my friends before I vanished into the world of radical Islam. Many had cut ties with me, some just thought me a lunatic. Apart from my mother – and more recently Fadia – I had told nobody that I had become an agent.

Several of my friends and family didn't believe me when in the weeks before I went public I told them the truth. To them it must have seemed one twist too many in my already improbable story.

Jyllands-Posten's series of articles gave my story the stamp of credibility. Slowly I was able to rekindle some old friendships. I was given a chance to say sorry to a lot of people. Sorry for my behaviour. Sorry for disappearing. Sorry for the lies. But above all, sorry for hating you because you did not accede to my beliefs.

Many of my former friends, including Vibeke, my first love, were astonished by my story.

'I simply never guessed,' she said. 'I thought you had become this crazy guy always vanishing overseas and spending your life praying. I felt I didn't know you any more.'

It was also a relief to be able to escape the pretence of being a hard-line Salafist. Murad Storm was finally history, and gone with him were the Islamic robes, the long beard and the pretend prayers. It felt good to wear jeans and a T-shirt and grab a beer without worrying that my cover would be compromised.

In early 2014 I went on Danish television to apologize to Naser Khader, the moderate Muslim politician whose killing I had once called for. Now we were both literally in al-Qaeda's crosshairs, as the video from Syria had made clear. After the cartoon controversy had erupted Khader had attracted further ire from jihadis by bravely defending the cartoonists' right of free speech.

I handed him a drawing I had asked my daughter, Sarah, to do. It showed me apologizing to him. 'Dude Naser. I was wrong. I am sorry!!! Forgive me,' the speech bubble said. Underneath was written 'Free Speech is not negotiable. Long Live Democracy.'

He embraced me, saying all was forgiven. 'I am very touched and think it is extremely nice of you. I'll keep this in my home,' he said. We both had tears in our eyes; we had both been through a great deal and might yet face more.

Naser told me that PET had informed him more than ten years previously that I had threatened him. He had received many death threats since. He asked me to join him in an initiative to deradicalize Danish youngsters sucked into extremism. I readily accepted. If I could help just one person turn his back on al-Qaeda's murderous world-view, the shame I still felt would be slightly less.

From Danish, British and US intelligence there was a predictable wall of silence after I went public. PET had tried to cover their tracks by dissolving their front company, Mola Consult, after I told them I planned to go public.[1]

Jakob Scharf – the head of PET – limited himself to a carefully worded statement.

'Out of consideration for PET's operational work, the PET neither can nor will confirm publicly that specific persons have been used as sources by the PET . . . However, the PET does not participate in or

---

1 According to the Central Business Registry of Denmark, Mola Consult was dissolved on 31 August 2012.

support operations where the objective is to kill civilians. The PET did therefore not contribute to the military operation that led to the killing of al-Awlaki in Yemen.'

His denial of involvement in 'the military operation' was a very precise formulation. No one was accusing the Danes of actually firing the drones that killed Awlaki, but one of their agents had been leading the hunt for him. And it wasn't to inquire after his health.

The revelations led Danish parliamentarians to demand new oversight rules for PET. In January 2013 I met with several of them. At the same time Denmark's Ministry of Justice announced it would set up a supervisory board to oversee the Danish intelligence agency. The Justice Minister, Morten Bødskov, a close friend of Jakob Scharf, said the new board would strike 'the right balance that will ensure that we have an effective intelligence agency and a good rule of law'.

In March 2013 my account received heavyweight backing from Hans Jørgen Bonnichsen, Scharf's predecessor as head of PET. He told Danish television that the corroborating evidence confirmed to his satisfaction the agency had used me to track down terrorist operatives overseas to help the US target them for assassination. 'I now have no reason to doubt that they have participated,' he said.

The establishment closed ranks. Denmark's two main parties blocked a parliamentary inquiry. It was perhaps no accident that they had both been in power while I was working for PET.[2] They seemed to believe the story would eventually go away. For a while I thought perhaps they were right. Danes take pride in the transparency of their democratic institutions but I have long believed that in the process they have become too trustful of the state – almost complacent.

My time working for PET revealed an agency with some competent, decent people, but with too many others incapable of worthwhile intelligence work. Many were ex-cops who had spent most of their lives in vice or drug squads. Handling foreign intelligence and

---

2 On 3 October 2011, three days after Awlaki was killed in a drone strike, Helle Thorning-Schmidt of the Social Democrats took over as Prime Minister from Lars Løkke Rasmussen, of the Venstre party, who served from 2009 to 2011. Prior to that Anders Fogh Rasmussen of Venstre held the top job.

understanding terrorism seemed beyond them. Others seemed to see the agency as a gravy train – and me as a source of income or expensive trips.

In late 2013 stories of impropriety within PET exploded in the Danish media. The first centred on the previous year's riotous office Christmas party. It was revealed that Director Scharf, in a rare act of transparency, had drunkenly made out with a subordinate in a glass-walled corridor in full view of everybody. Klang had at least been more discreet in his choice of rendezvous with Scharf's mistress.

Revelations followed about discord and expensive trips Scharf and senior aides made overseas. According to internal complaints leaked to the media, Scharf was 'unprepared' and 'frivolous' during meetings in Washington DC and more interested in sightseeing, leading the CIA to lose confidence in his leadership. Government insiders revealed that this trust had already been eroded after I went public. The CIA expected friendly agencies to keep their informants under control.

Finally it emerged that Scharf had instructed subordinates to obtain information on the movements of a Danish MP. The scandal forced the resignations of both Scharf and his boss, the Justice Minister, Morten Bødskov. The revelations put my story back in the public spotlight. Scharf's predecessor, Bonnichsen, sharpened his criticism of the agency, asserting that my disclosures on Danish involvement in assassination plans overseas were so serious there was a basis for a criminal investigation.

The tide seemed to be turning. At the end of the year the beleaguered agency was put under more pressure when *Jyllands-Posten* disclosed PET's refusal to offer me protection after the Syrian death threat video.

'Is it really a satisfactory way for the security services to carry out their task in that it takes three weeks before you answer a former employee who – rightly – felt threatened by Islamists?' the chairman of the Danish People's Party said to the newspaper.

Such were my jihadist networks that hardly a month went by without a former associate being arrested, martyred in the service of jihad, or identified as an emerging leader in a terror group. Kenneth Sorensen, who had been part of my circle in Sana'a, was killed fighting alongside jihadis in Syria in March 2013, one of a staggering 2,000 European militants who would travel to fight there. Jihadis in Syria released a martyrdom video to honour his sacrifice to the cause. His mortal wounds were horrendous. The video showed the congealed blood streaked across his face and then fighters bulldozing dirt over his unmarked grave.

It was a fate I too could have shared, for I was led to believe by one of my handlers at PET that by 2013 Sorensen was working as a double agent.

Abu Khattab, the Danish jihadi who had called for my murder, was himself killed fighting in Syria; so too was my former paintballing buddy Shiraz Tariq.

In February 2014 Abdul Waheed Majeed, the British-Pakistani al-Muhajiroun follower who had so assiduously taken minutes during Omar Bakri's talks in Luton, became the first British suicide bomber in Syria. He had been recruited by Jabhat al-Nusra, al-Qaeda's affiliate in Syria. A video released by the group showed him in a white tunic and black Islamist bandana cheerily speaking to other fighters beside a heavily armoured truck before the attack. Fighters cheered '*Allah Akbar!*' as he set off towards the central prison in Aleppo, where he detonated the vehicle in a huge fireball.

Only a small number of my jihadist contacts paid their debt to society. Clifford Newman, the American convert who had assisted John Walker Lindh – 'the American Taliban' – in getting to Afghanistan served five years in prison in Dubai from 2004 to 2009 for attempted robbery. He then served a three-year sentence in the United States for child abduction.

Aminah, as far as I know, remained in Yemen – still committed to her deceased husband's cause. On 18 July 2012 – just before I left the intelligence fold – I received one last encrypted message from her.

She revealed she had spent several months under Wuhayshi's protection, but with the government retaking territory across the tribal areas she had relocated to Awlaki's village, and was hoping eventually to go to Sana'a.

'You are always in my *duas* [supplications]. Sometimes I cry when I remember all things you have done for me and my dear Anwar, may Allah have mercy on him.'

How she must hate me now.

As for Abdul, he eventually returned to Yemen, and I received a message from him in which he recanted his previous accusations that the Americans had wanted me to go to southern Yemen and planned to have me killed there.

'The yanks never ever, never ever, never ever mentioned harming you at any time, never said they will kill you, the car was not for you,' he wrote.

But he maintained the CIA had warned him that I was on my way back to Yemen – an extraordinary breach of faith if true.

'They told me Morten is coming, leave everything behind and stay with him because we think he is up to no good.'

Abdul appears never to have entertained the thought that I too was an informant.

'I did not want you to come to yemen and go back to the south and get deeper with the misguided, and therfore, you might be a target one day. I made up the story just to make you stay out of yemen and out of the trouble in this miserable country.'

Abdul said his CIA handlers had been furious that he had travelled to China and then met with me – and had cut ties with him afterwards.

I will never know what the CIA's plans for me were. It is conceivable that someone at the Agency wanted me out of the way, and that Abdul's final message to me was a desperate attempt to cover his and their tracks. Perhaps Abdul was a compulsive liar. Perhaps the Americans had originally wanted us both to return to southern Yemen and complete a mission that could have helped decapitate AQAP.

Looking back at the hectic events of 2011 and 2012, I think that to the CIA I had become expendable, worth sending on one last mission to southern Yemen on my own just in case it came off – even though they and the Danes knew the risk to my safety was exorbitant.

What is beyond dispute is that a real chance to track and eliminate Wuhayshi and other leaders of AQAP was lost in the mishandling of that final mission. Despite losing territory in the latter half of 2012, the group remained a potent threat well beyond Yemen.

In September 2012 three of its operatives took part in the terrorist attack on the US diplomatic compound in Benghazi. At a large gathering in Spring 2014 Wuhayshi made clear to fighters that attacking the West was a priority and made good on another pledge by greeting several operatives recently liberated from prison.

Intelligence agencies believed Ibrahim al-Asiri was developing a new generation of explosives that would be more difficult for scanners to detect. In February 2014 the US Department of Homeland Security sent out an alert to airlines after intelligence indicated he was developing a new shoe bomb design. With every year that passed the Saudi terrorist was becoming more ingenious – and instructing apprentices in the mechanics of terror. So high was concern over an emboldened AQAP that the US and Yemen carried out a large wave of strikes in April 2014. When this book went to press a week later no key figure had been confirmed killed.

The temporary closure of US embassies in the summer of 2013 – from Libya in the west to Madagascar in the south and Bangladesh in the east – illustrated how much of the world had become unsafe for Westerners. Al-Qaeda's black banners fluttered in the deserts of Mauritania, close to the Atlantic shore, in the Sinai desert, throughout Syria, in western Iraq and in southern Somalia. In many of these places, AQAP had a role, a presence or contacts. It was the first among equals of al-Qaeda's affiliates.

Al-Shabaab too shifted its centre of gravity from insurgency in Somalia to more 'classic' terrorism after formally becoming an affiliate of al-Qaeda. And I knew some of its most accomplished operatives.

On the morning of Saturday, 21 September 2013, at least four heavily armed gunmen in jeans and T-shirts marauded through the upscale Westgate shopping mall in Nairobi. In a siege that lasted four days and appeared to have been modelled on the Mumbai attacks in 2008, more than sixty men, women and children were killed.

Al-Shabaab claimed the attack was in retaliation for Kenya's 2011–12 military offensive in Somalia which had pushed the group out of the port city of Kismayo, an important source of income for the group.

The suspected mastermind was none other than my main point of contact in al-Shabaab – Ikrimah, the long-haired Kenyan who spoke Norwegian.

Unlike the American jihadi Omar Hammami, who was killed a week before the Westgate attack, Ikrimah had survived the infighting within al-Shabaab. Kenyan intelligence believed that he had emerged as the key figure plotting attacks in Kenya because of his militant contacts inside the country.[3] One of his previous schemes, disrupted by the Kenyan security services in late 2011, envisioned multiple attacks on the Kenyan parliament, United Nations offices in Nairobi and politicians, which Kenyan intelligence learned had been sanctioned by al-Qaeda in Pakistan.[4]

Two weeks to the day after the gunmen launched their assault on the Westgate Mall a team of US Navy SEALs from the same unit that had killed Osama bin Laden raced towards the Somali coastline in a high-speed boat. It was a moonless night. Their mission was to capture Ikrimah from an al-Shabaab compound south of Mogadishu. But this time the mission went wrong. Their approach was noticed and al-Shabaab fighters emerged from the compound, guns blazing.

Reports suggested several of the SEALs had seen Ikrimah through the windows of the compound, but could not get to him. The American commandos continued to take fire while trying to find a way to get closer to their target, but soon realized that women and children (not accidentally) were inside the house. They abandoned the mission.

Ikrimah escaped alive and became more dangerous as a result. Not only was he still free to plot terrorist attacks in East Africa but by

3 Ikrimah had worked to build up a network in Kenya to plot attacks. According to a 2013 Kenyan government report he dispatched an operative to Kenya in July 2013 'to train youth, lay down the infrastructure for a major attack and await instructions'.
4 Before Kenyan police made arrests in late 2011 the planners had trained the operatives designated to carry out the attack, acquired safe houses in Nairobi and Mombasa, transported explosives from Somalia and begun to construct bombs. The 'White Widow', Samantha Lewthwaite, was believed to be connected to the cell, but escaped capture in Mombasa. The green light for the plot from al-Qaeda in Pakistan may have been communicated to Ikrimah by our mutual American friend, Jehad Serwan Mostafa, if he did indeed meet with Zawahiri in Pakistan a few months before.

surviving a Navy SEAL attack his credentials had been burnished. In our communications between 2008 and 2012 Ikrimah made it clear that his ambitions stretched further than just Africa. His goal was to dispatch Western al-Shabaab recruits to launch attacks in their home countries. If he finally suceeded in his attempt to connect with Wuhayshi, the leader of al-Qaeda in Yemen, both men could pool resources in plots to attack the West and Western targets around the world.

To some degree Western intelligence created Ikrimah. The CIA, MI6 and PET helped him rise through the ranks in al-Shabaab because the supplies and contacts I provided him with impressed his superiors. But my contacts with Ikrimah netted valuable results, including the removal of one of the most dangerous al-Qaeda operatives in East Africa – Saleh Ali Nabhan – and gave us a window into the operations of al-Shabaab. Helping Ikrimah was the price paid for a greater gain.

After the Westgate attack I wondered if Ikrimah might have been apprehended or killed had I continued my relationship with him. Had I been able to build up Storm Bushcraft in Kenya, I might have had a better sense of his place in al-Shabaab, his plans and even some of the recruits he was training. Of course, it would have been difficult and hazardous to meet with him. By the middle of 2012 Ikrimah's emails suggested he rarely ventured beyond Somalia. But it would have been possible to deliver a tracking device to him hidden in equipment – as I had arranged for Nabhan.

In my view, Western intelligence would have found it easier to remove Ikrimah from the battlefield by taking advantage of the trust he had in me. And even if we had not been able to target him it is possible that he would have shared information with me, hinting at some of the deadly attacks he was planning.

My retirement also meant that Western intelligence lost a resource in one of its most arduous challenges: detecting small-scale 'lone-wolf' attacks. These are the most difficult for counter-terrorism agencies as there is often no trail of communication. Al-Qaeda had seen the advantage, releasing a video in 2011 entitled *You are Only Responsible for Yourself*, which called for solo attacks by followers in the West.

The Boston bombings of April 2013 and the murder and attempted beheading of a British soldier, Lee Rigby, on the streets of Woolwich in

South-East London the following month signalled that such attacks could be the wave of the future. In both cases militants based in the West had carried out the attacks independently of any group. I knew their motivation and their path to radicalization because I had made the same journey.

One of the two Woolwich killers – Michael Adebolajo, a British-Nigerian convert – had once been a follower of my former group, al-Muhajiroun, and I had come across him at a talk in Luton.

Such 'lone-wolf' attacks are virtually impossible to prevent unless there is someone on the 'inside' who detects a change of behaviour or appearance, is asked a strange question or confided in. Twice during my career I had informed Western intelligence of terrorist plots by radicalized zealots determined to bring carnage to the streets of Europe – because the plotters had told me of their plans.

Awlaki's sermons and writings, even from beyond the grave, had provided the inspiration for both the Boston and the Woolwich attacks. The Boston bombers built pressure-cooker bombs from a recipe in *Inspire* magazine.[5] Since his death Awlaki's sermons have only grown in popularity among radicalized Muslims in the West, their message as simple as it is spellbinding: the United States and its friends are at war with Islam and Allah commands that Muslims must fight back by any means necessary.[6]

It was a message that had appealed to so many who felt marginalized, discriminated against, rootless – or simply lonely.

After publication of the first story, *Jyllands-Posten* put me up in a country hotel in England, both for my own safety and to keep competing media away. But I felt obliged to go to the local police station.

The well-meaning sergeant behind the desk thought I was unhinged when I told him my story and said I needed protection.

---

5 The recipe entitled 'How to Build a Bomb in Your Mom's Kitchen' featured in the first issue of *Inspire* magazine, published in June 2010, and was found on one of the Boston bombers' computers.
6 Awlaki's death triggered a New York extremist, Jose Pimentel, to plot a bombing in the city in late 2011 to avenge the cleric's death.

'Just Google my name,' I said. 'Morten Storm.'

Up popped my face splashed across the front page of *Jyllands-Posten*.

In a place where disorderly drunks were the daily fare, I was an unusual subject.

'Just a moment, sir,' the sergeant said.

An hour later, two detectives arrived and admitted that they had no idea what to do with me.

'I've never met anyone like you, nor will I again,' one of them said with a wry smile. So I was passed up the food chain, to my old friends at MI5.

The following day, a middle-aged woman with a plain face and pursed lips, her hair cut in a no-nonsense bob, arrived at the police station. She was accompanied by a man who introduced himself as Keith, a tall and genial fifty-something officer. I spilled out as much of my story as I could, saying that I believed the Americans had tried to get me killed in Yemen. The pair of them took notes but said little.

Occasionally the sergeant would pop his head around the door to see if we needed refreshments. He was quite enjoying the small circus from the world of 007 in his shop.

Neither of the MI5 officers said much until the end of our meeting.

'You must understand,' the woman said, 'that we have no obligations towards you; you are no longer working with us. This is a problem between you, the Danish government and the Americans. I can't understand why you want to drag us into it.'

I recalled that phone conversation with my MI5 handler Kevin as I had prepared to leave Birmingham airport in April 2010: '*Morten – if you travel now, you have to realize we are not going to see each other again.*'

Even so, MI5's concern at the possible fall-out from further disclosures prompted them to invite me to a follow-up meeting in a nearby city. A large and voluble Londoner called Graham, who must have been close to retirement, joined the party.

MI5 wanted to explore the outlines of a possible deal. Several detectives lurked in the hotel car park and reception as we met in a conference room. This time I was relieved of my mobile phone. The nameless woman with the sensible shoes probed about future instalments of the *Jyllands-Posten* series. To date only one story had been published. If I would tell the newspaper I wanted nothing else published and refused other requests to talk – including the appearance on *60 Minutes* – British intelligence would consider relocating me to somewhere like Canada or Australia. Alternatively, we might discuss a role as a trainer for informants inside the Muslim community or helping former agents deal with the transition to retirement. They even asked me to write papers on both subjects.

But first there would be a probation period of six months, during which I would have to vanish from the radar. I might only have limited access to my kids, and MI5 would have no financial obligation to me. I recalled the fate of the Danish informant who had helped Klang bust the Vollsmose bomb plot but was then forced to flee into unhappy exile overseas.

There was talk of cosmetic surgery and a place in the witness protection programme. But the thought of changing my appearance – to the point where my children would not recognize me – was beyond the pale.

I said that I would think over their terms, but in the meantime wanted a meeting with the security services psychologist, whom I'd met in Scotland at the team-building exercise four years before.

A couple of weeks later I was invited to a hotel in Manchester. The psychologist I knew as Luke from Aviemore was there. He gave me a hug and seemed genuinely pleased to see me again. But concern was soon etched across his face as I recounted my experiences. I was on the verge of tears.

'Do you think I am insane to believe the Americans wanted me dead? Am I paranoid?' I asked.

'Look,' he said. 'You are in a very difficult situation. Fear is not paranoia; it's based on what could have happened and what still might happen. You may have done the right thing in not going to the south of Yemen. You might well have been killed, and, yes, the Americans might not have cared. And I understand why you decided to go to the media; it's a form of protection.'

Luke made it abundantly clear that I needed help. My struggle in processing what I had been through was only just beginning, he said; and while understandable my cocaine use had to stop. He was at pains to cast himself as independent of the security services but I noticed that on occasion the 'I' slipped into 'we'. And he clearly was not at liberty to counsel me or recommend a course of treatment.

It was a long and painful conversation. At least I had been able to talk. He hugged me again at the end.

I still had to give MI5 a response to their proposal. They were already unhappy with me for leaving hotel accommodation that neither *Jyllands-Posten* nor I could afford and returning home. My pervasive distrust of the agencies held me back. I could not spend six months underground, without work, income or protection, for the outside chance of acceptance into the fold.

At a final meeting in a bland hotel conference room, I told Graham that I couldn't accept MI5's scheme; there were too many risks and I had some trust issues.

He looked disappointed but not surprised. He shook my hand firmly and grasped my shoulder.

'That's okay,' he said. 'Take care of yourself; I think you know how to look after yourself.'

As I walked home through blustery, rain-swept streets, I began to absorb the scale of the challenge.

I had made the choice to be on my own. I would no longer suffer from false expectations or be deceived by false promises. I could speak freely but would always need to look over my shoulder. I could look at my children and feel I had made some small contribution towards making the world a better place.

In a school project, my son, Osama, decided to make me his subject. He scanned a photograph of me and wrote an essay entitled: 'My Dad, the Hero'. I had to make sure he deleted the essay from the school computer, but I was also proud. All those tearful farewells suddenly seemed worth it.

Now I would have to start again and deal with my demons. I would also have to adapt to a life without the rush of travelling into terrorist heartlands, and protect my obscurity while at the same time laying out a story that should have lessons for those charged with keeping Western societies safe.

Passers-by glance at me but can't know the role I played in protecting their way of life.

With a shrug or a raised eyebrow, I read media stories of individuals I knew and the threats they posed, the attacks they were planning (or indeed had carried out) and the millions of pounds and dollars being spent trying to stop them. A group I had known in Luton was convicted in 2013 of plotting to blow up a British army base with a bomb strapped to a toy car – one incident among many.

Occasionally I reach the checkout of a supermarket with my groceries, only to see a newspaper headline about one of my former 'brothers' who has finally crossed that Rubicon from talk to terror. As I scan the article for details, the cashier presses coins into my hand and says vacantly, 'Take care.'

I smile as I leave the shop, muttering to myself, 'Take care.'

DRAMATIS PERSONAE

Bødskov, Morten	Justice Minister of Denmark 2011–13
Bonnichsen, Hans Jørgen	Former Director of Danish intelligence agency PET
Butt, G. M.	British-Pakistani kiosk owner in Milton Keynes
Cindy	My girlfriend in Luton
Cowern, Toby	Royal Marines reservist I enlisted to help me run my cover company
Fadia	My Yemeni wife. A pseudonym
Hadi, Abd Rabbu Mansour	President of Yemen since 2012
Hulstrøm, Mark	My boxing coach and smuggling boss in Korsør
Karima	My Moroccan wife. A pseudonym
Khader, Naser	Danish Muslim politician
Lisbeth	My mother
Mears, Ray	Famous British outdoor survival instructor
Nagieb	Documentary maker who travelled with me to Yemen in 2006
Osama	My son
Rosenvold, Michael	Head of the Bandidos in Denmark
Sage	Aminah's fiancé
Saleh, Ali Abdullah	President of Yemen till 2012
Samar	My Palestinian-Christian girlfriend in Korsør
Sarah	My daughter
Scharf, Jakob	Director of Danish intelligence agency PET 2007–12

Mark Hulstrøm.

Awlaki's son was
killed a few months
after his father in a
drone strike.

Negotiating with
the Masai tribe in
Shompole, Kenya.

Toby Cowern in
northern Sweden,
March 2010.

Apologizing to
Naser Khader on TV.

PET director
Jakob Scharf
(Danish DR).

Stevens, Cat	The British singer now known as Yusuf Islam
Suleiman	Muslim friend I met in prison in Denmark in 1997
Tony	Head doorman at the Shades nightclub in Leighton Buzzard
Vibeke	My first serious girlfriend
Westergaard, Kurt	Danish cartoonist responsible for a controversial 2005 depiction of the Prophet Mohammed
Ymit	Turkish childhood friend in Korsør

Militants and Islamists

Abab, Sheikh Adil al-	Yemeni cleric who became religious guide of AQAP
Abdaly, Taimour Abdulwahab al-	2010 Stockholm suicide bomber I knew in Luton
Abdelghani	Islamist I knew from Denmark who sent me an invitation from the Islamic Courts Union
Abdul	Yemeni friend who worked as a courier for al-Qaeda
Abdulmutallab, Umar Farouk	Nigerian 'underwear bomber' who targeted Northwest flight 253 over Detroit
Abu Bilal	Swedish-Ghanaian room-mate in Dammaj
Abu Hamza	Radical Moroccan preacher in Aarhus
Adebolajo, Michael	Nigerian-British radical who killed British soldier in London in 2013.
Ahmed, Zohaib	British extremist convicted for plot to target the EDL in 2012
Ali	Danish convert and fellow member of Awlaki's Sana'a study circle

Aminah	Croatian convert seeking to marry Awlaki. Real name: Irena Horak
Andersen, Abdallah	Danish convert from Odense convicted for 2006 terrorism plot
Arab, Abu	Danish-Palestinian extremist I met in Lebanon. Real name: Ali al-Hajdib
Asiri, Abdullah al-	Brother of Ibrahim al-Asiri and so-called butt-bomber
Asiri, Ibrahim al-	AQAP master bomb-maker
Avdic, Adnan	Bosnian extremist friend in Denmark acquitted in terror case
Awlaki, Abdulrahman al-	Awlaki's son
Awlaki, Anwar al-	American-Yemeni terrorist cleric
Awlaki, Omar al-	Awlaki's brother
Bakri Mohammed, Omar	Syrian founder of British extremist group al-Muhajiroun
Balawi, Humam al-	Jordanian 'triple agent' responsible for suicide attack on CIA in Afghanistan
Barbi, Rashid	US army veteran who travelled to Dammaj with me
bin Laden, Osama	Al-Qaeda's founder and leader till 2011
Choudary, Anjem	Deputy to al-Muhajiroun's founder, Omar Bakri Mohammed
Geele, Mohammed	Somali convicted of axe attack on the Danish cartoonist Kurt Westergaard in 2010
Godane, Ahmed Abdi	The leader of al-Shabaab. Aka: Muktar al-Zubayr
Hajdib, Saddam al-	Brother of Abu Arab and senior member of Lebanese terrorist group Fatah al-Islam
Hajdib, Youssef al-	Brother of Abu Arab convicted of a 2006 plot to bomb a train in Germany
Hajuri, Shaikh Yahya al-	A teacher at Dammaj

Hammami, Omar	American al-Shabaab member from Alabama. Aka: Abu Mansoor al-Amriki
Hartaba	Awlaki's driver and a former bin Laden bodyguard
Hasan, Nidal	US army major responsible for 2009 Fort Hood shooting in Texas
Hazmi, Mohammed al-	Muslim Brotherhood cleric in Sana'a
Hazmi, Sheikh al-	Cleric with links to AQAP I met in Yemen in 2001; nephew of Mohammed al-Hazmi
Hussain, Anzal	British extremist convicted of plot to target EDL in 2012
Ibrahim	Algerian radical in Aarhus
Ikrimah	Somali-Kenyan al-Shabaab operative I met in Nairobi. Real name: Mohamed Abdikadir Mohamed
Ja'far Umar Thalib	Dammaj alumnus and leader of the Indonesian terrorist group Laskar Jihad
Jimmy	Owner of a gym popular with extremists in Birmingham
Khan, Samir	American editor of AQAP's *Inspire* magazine
Khurshid, Hammad	Danish-born Pakistani convicted of 2007 Denmark terror plot
Lewthwaite, Samantha	So-called 'White Widow' of a 7/7 bomber on the run in East Africa
Majeed, Abdul Waheed	Omar Bakri acolyte who became the first British suicide bomber in Syria
Masri, Hussein al-	Egyptian Islamic Jihad operative I met in Sana'a
Mehdar, Abullah	Yemeni tribal leader close to Anwar al-Awlaki

Menni, Nasserdine	Algerian friend from Luton convicted of providing funds to Stockholm suicide bomber Taimour Abdulwahab al-Abdaly
Misri, Abdullah	Yemeni AQAP financier and arms broker
Mostafa, Jehad Serwan	American member of Awlaki study circle in Yemen who became a senior al-Shabaab operative
Moussaoui, Zacarias	French-Moroccan I met in London who became the 'twentieth' 9/11 hijacker
Mujeeb	Yemeni Islamist who mediated between Salafists and AQAP
Mukhtar	French Muslim friend and flatmate of Zacarias Moussaoui in Brixton
Muqbil, Sheikh	Salafist founder of the Dammaj Institute
Nabhan, Saleh Ali	Kenyan al-Qaeda operative responsible for 1998 bombings of US embassies in East Africa
Newman, Clifford Allen	American convert I met in Dammaj along with his son, Abdullah. AKA: Amin
Ramadan, Mustapha Darwich	Fellow prisoner in Denmark who took part in the beheading of Nick Berg
Raymi, Qasim al-	Second most senior Yemeni in AQAP
Reid, Richard	So-called shoe-bomber who targeted a Paris–Miami flight in December 2001
Saheer	British-Pakistani Birmingham ex-con who plotted attack on Danish newspaper

Salim	British-Pakistani al-Muhajiroun follower whose father owned taxi company I worked for in Birmingham
Samulski, Marek	Australian-Polish fellow member of Awlaki's Sana'a study circle
Somali, Abu Musab al-	Somali terrorist operative I knew from Denmark
Sorensen, Kenneth	Danish convert to Islam who was in Sana'a with me in 2006
Sudani, Abu Talha al-	Sudanese senior al-Qaeda operative based in East Africa
Tabbakh, Hassan	Syrian refugee convicted of the 2007 UK terror plot
Tariq, Shiraz	Pakistani friend from Odense extremist circle
Tayyib, Mahmud al-	Saudi I met in Regent's Park mosque who suggested I study in Dammaj
Tokhi, Abdelghani	Danish resident of Afghan descent convicted of 2007 terror plot
Uddin, Jewel	British-Pakistani extremist convicted of 2012 plot to target the EDL
Uqla, Sheikh Humud bin	Saudi cleric who issued a fatwa in support of 9/11
Usman, Mohammed	British-Pakistani I met on the flight to Yemen in September 2009
Warsame, Ahmed Abdulkadir	Somali friend who became a senior operative in al-Shabaab
Wuhayshi, Nasir al-	Leader of AQAP and former senior bin Laden aide
Zaher, Mohammad	Palestinian from Odense convicted of 2006 terorrism plot
Zarqawi, Abu Musab al-	Jordanian founder of al-Qaeda in Iraq
Zawahiri, Ayman al-	Leader of al-Qaeda from 2011
Zindani, Abdul Majid al-	Head of Muslim Brotherhood in Yemen and founder of al-Iman University

Radicals from the West

Mohammad Zaher
(Danish DR).

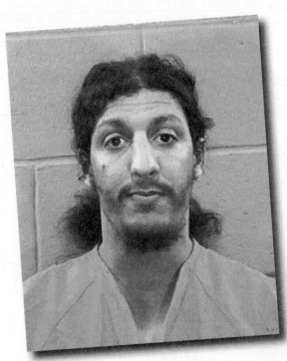

Richard Reid, my
one-time friend
in Brixton and
the so-called
shoe bomber.

Anzal Hussain
(police handout).

Abdallah Andersen
(BT.DK).

The Danish
militant Abu
Khattab (centre),
threatening my life
in 2013.

Radicals in Yemen

Mohammed al-Hazmi.

Adil al-Abab.

Abdul Majid
al-Zindani.

AQAP master
bomb-maker
Ibrahim al-Asiri.

Jehad Serwan
Mostafa
(*Guardian*).

My Intelligence Handlers

Alex	Senior US intelligence official who oversaw the 'Aminah mission'
Amanda	The CIA agent Elizabeth Hanson, who recruited me to work for the CIA
Anders	PET intelligence analyst specializing in Islamist extremism and terrorism
Andy	My senior MI5 handler; ex-British police
Buddha	One of the two PET agents who recruited me
Daniel	Weapons instructor in Denmark
Emma	My second MI6 handler
Frank	Weapons instructor in Denmark
George	CIA Copenhagen station chief
Graham	MI5 operative I met in 2012
Jed	My main CIA handler
Jesper	Danish intelligence handler who joined the team in 2010; former banker
Joshua	CIA agent I met at same time as Amanda in 2007
Kevin	MI5 handler reporting to Andy
Klang	My main PET handler who recruited me as an agent. He first introduced himself as Martin Jensen
Luke	Psychologist working for MI5
Matt	My first MI6 handler
Michael	CIA official I met in Denmark after killing of Awlaki

Dramatis Personae

Rob	SAS trainer at MI6 retreat near Loch Ness
Robert	MI5 official who approached me in Luton just before the London bombings
Soren	Team leader of the PET agents handling me
Steve	MI6 instructor at the Fort Monckton training facility
Sunshine	Female MI5 agent reporting to Andy. My main point-person at MI5
Tommy Chef	Director of Operations for PET
Trailer	One of my Danish intelligence handlers; former farmer

AGENT ARCHIVE

Jihadi Communications

Official Invitation
from the Islamic
Courts Union to move
to Somalia.

Awlaki email correspondence
in my Yahoo Account.

Mujahideen Secrets
Software Interface.
You can see Awlaki's
public key 'hereyougo'
which he used to
communicate with me.

Aminah's very
first Facebook
message to me.

Aminah on
Facebook broaches
the possibility of
marrying Awlaki.

20:54

Aminah Muslimah Fisabilillah

Assalamu alaykom

Eid Mubarak to you and your family. Can you tell me please what do you mean specifically when you type in your post on the wall of group od support Shaikh Anwar al-Awlaki? What kind of support and are you in direct contact with Shaikh?

Aminah Muslimah Fisabilillah

No problem, I think you mixed South East Europe with South Croatia

I have one question tho. Do you know personally AAA? And if it is so, may I be so liberal to ask you something?

11:23

Murad Al-Danimarki

Yes I do know him. Feel free to ask

11:32

Aminah Muslimah Fisabilillah

As I told you before I do not have mahram, and I sent Shaikh a letter by mail, I am not sure if I had his correct email address, but actually I was wondering will he search for a second wife, I proposed him a marriage, and I do not know how silly it is. But I tried. Now, as I am in contact with you there is a possibility for you to get know me better in a way you can recommended me to s Shaikh, if you are interested in it and if you want to help me, inshaallah. You can see I am a revert, convert on Islam alhamdidullah. I seek a way how to get out of this country, and I search a husband who will teach me and whom I can help a lot. I deeply respect him and the all things he do for this Ummah and I want to help him in any way.

What do you think about that?
JazzakAllah khayrun

11:38

Murad Al-Danimarki

Waleikum Salaam Warahmatullah

Sister, I was with him for 3 months ago, and he asked the same, if I could help him getting married to a revert sister. Subhan'Allah how Allah plans. But sister by getting married to him, means that you may never again come to croatia as you know his current situation. I can however travel with you to him, as there is no way for you otherwise to know his whereabout. Could I get your personal details to forward them to him today? I will write down his requirement for marriage, as he told me to search.

Regarding the sister first of all thanks for keeping me in mind:) so far I am interested. I just need a few clarifications from you and then I need you to pass on a message to her:
1. How did you get to know about her?
2. Are you communicating with her in a secure manner?
3. I want all my communications with her to pass through you. But just in case you got cut off the internet if you could pass on to me an email for her that I would only use if I am unable to communicate with you. My name in any on-line communications with her should be Sami
4. What do you suggest in terms of how to get her here?

Extract from
Awlaki's email
telling me he
is interested
in Aminah.

Awlaki tells me in an
encrypted message he
has attached a video
recording of him for me
to pass on to Aminah.

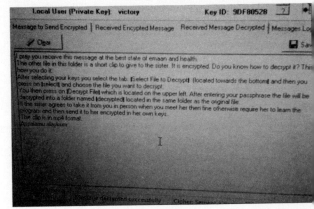

Local User (Private Key): victory   Key ID: 9DF80528   ?

Message to Send Encrypted | Received Encrypted Message   Received Message Decrypted | Messages Lo

Clear   Sav

I pray you receive this message at the best state of emaan and health.
The other file in this folder is a short clip to give to the sister. It is encrypted. Do you know how to decrypt it? This
how you do it:
After selecting your keys you select the tab: [Select File to Decrypt] (located towards the bottom) and then you
press on [select] and choose the file you want to decrypt.
You then press on [Decrypt File] which is located on the upper left. After entering your passphrase the file will be
decrypted into a folder named [decrypted] located in the same folder as the original file
If the sister agrees to take it from you in person when you meet her then fine otherwise require her to learn the
program and then send it to her encrypted in her own keys.
The clip is in mp4 format.
Assalamu alaykum

                                                 essage decrypted successfully   Cipher: Serpe

|Assalamu alaykum
Alhamdulillah we got married. May Allah reward you for all what you have done. However, according to your
description of her I expected something different. I am not saying that you tricked me or anything; I am just
saying that I expected something different.
I do not blame you or your wife because I believe you were sincere and you were doing your best.

.

.

.

So she turned out to be different then what you described. Masha Allah she turned out to be better than I
expected and better than you described:)

Awlaki's encrypted 28 June 2010 email giving
me the verdict on his new wife Aminah.

Sister, please can I ask you a favor. If it is possible for you to go and buy some stuff for me.
So far everybody who bought it, majority I didn't like. And it is hard for sisters here to buy
some western clothes. I give up of Yemeni clothes. All I have I don't like and it is too hot to
wear it. Fabrics are not good, synthetic, it's just horrible.
So please if you can find some European clothes. I miss it so much. I just need few dresses
(2) and skirts (2) and top (4). All simple without any glittering stuff and pleats, I hate it.
Dresses should be long, without sleeves - like top, wide but tight in top part and all in one
piece. Not 2 pieces like Yemeni dresses. Fabric should be light, non-transparent. Skirts also
should be long and light fabric, wide, solid. Tops whatever you find simple and nice. Colors
and patterns never mind, just please avoid pink and orange color. White, black, different
shades of blue and green. Floral pattern is nice, and solid is just fine. And if you can find
denim mini skirt, size 40 or L, tight and very short. ?
Next I need 10 packages of feminine pads; it's called FAM thin, regular with wings, made in
Lebanon. Package is white and green color with sunflower. I am sure you will find it.

Extract from the request
for clothes and beauty
products Awlaki attached
from Aminah for Fadia.

if some of hooks men r still interested to come here then let me know so that arrangements could be done ....
and as for going to hooks place ... then i was told by hook that they want to train brothers and then send them
back or to the west .... i told him i need advanced training so he told me its on and off so it could take long
and i have to be patient .. for me i can b patient and learn more of deen and improve arabic inshaAllah
question 1 ... if they gonna train brothers from here what kinda traing is it gonna be?
question 2 ... the anti tank mine that brothers got will they be willing to sell them to us and do they have
weapons that can hit a tank frm far like the ones hisbullah used to destroy israel merkeva tank? or rpg 29 etc?
question 3 .... regarding the project how is it coming so far? how is shompole, is it a good place? how is the
regestration and paper word going on? update me inshaAllah and inshaAllah this wil b a very good project to
all muslims inshaAllah
i checked the site and its really interesting for people who love nature and hicking and expedition may Allah
bless this project and keep it away from the eyes and suspicions of the kufar
akhii al habib take good care of yourself especially in yemen after wat happened in usa .. and the yemen
furniture business u told me abt .. check on it if it would b worth dealing with it but let it b like something for
mustaqbal inshaAllah

bro in iman
ik

Extract from an
encrypted email
Ikrimah sent to
me in November
2010 indicating
Awlaki and he were
hatching a plan to
send operatives to
attack the West.
He also praised my
Storm Bushcraft
Kenya venture.

The sandals are good. The tablets I was looking for are hexamine. The ones you sent are something else. If
you are traveling again then see if you can get me hexamine tablets.

Please send any messages from my wife's sister.
If you are going on-line please send me all what is available on the arrest of our Somali brother.
Also I heard on the news that the New York Times reported that al Qaeda in Yemen is buying a lot of castor
beans to make ricin and attack the US. Find me what you can on that. You could do a search for: Yemen +
ricin

Extract from an encrypted email from Awlaki
asking me about a *New York Times* report on ricin.

|Assalamu alaykom we rahmetullahi

I am sending you this mail with great sorrow and sadness in my heart but again happines for my husband
Shuhada. Alhamdidullah he is now in the Jannat and do not feel anything but joy and happines. Alhamdidullah,
Allah grant him Shuhada what he wanted and grant him the higest rank of Jannat.

My husband give me this in case something happend to him so I can contact you. Actually I wanted to contact
you in case I will go back in Europe, but I have 4 months to decide what to do.

My first option is shahada inshaAllah

Extract from an email
from Aminah telling
me she wanted to
carry out a suicide
attack to avenge the
death of Awlaki.

Kenya is getting really bad coz the kufar are doing all their effort
to harm us. And they monitor the hawala (dahabshil ,qaran etc)
accusing them of helping and financing mujahidin. So you need to
be extra carefull they dont get a single trace of anything coz they
are now tracing a sister who was a window of one of the london
7/7 bomber (the jamecan brother) and they are accusing her of
financing and organising "terorisim" so please watchout when
you are here coz they may put you in a case that you dont know.

Ikrimah encrypted email referencing the
White Widow, Samantha Lewthwaite, March 2012.

Spy Stuff

The Ascot Hotel in Copenhagen
where I had many of my meetings
with Western intelligence.

Business card for
Storm Bushcraft.

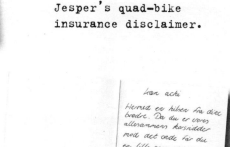

Jesper's quad-bike
insurance disclaimer.

Business card for Alum
Rock Cab Company, which
I worked for.

Greetings card from Klang
Trailer Buddha and Jed.

Jimmy's gym.

første mødested
① Gersthof S-Bahn Station
Anker bakery.

② Café "Segafredo" Gersthof Lounge
on Gersthof strasse 30, Wien 1180.

My mission notes for my
first meeting with Aminah
in Vienna. The CIA
wanted me to bring her
to a bar-restaurant, but
I changed the plan and
took her to McDonald's.

10:00 am meeting at McDonalds. Cover story, gifts, money.
embassy

meeting up after embassy, going to buy ticket, travel security
new emails, only use it until you arrive to X.
 hghxthg11@gmail.com - Send your public key - you get a number
buy a mobile phone in Y, you will get a new laptop.

Flight details to Sh. +385 92 28 666 76 - mobile
whiteblue2010
~~~~~~~~~~~ @gmail.com
islam 786 islam

africansunrise 2010@gmail
~~~~~~~~~~
islam 786 islam

Mission notes from
the last time I met
Aminah in Vienna.

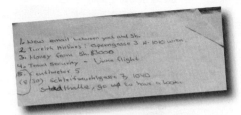

1. New email between you and Sh.
2. Turkish Airlines! Spenngasse 3 A-1010 wien
3. Money from Sh. 13000
4. Travel security - Vienna flight
5. Centimeter 5
(8/30) Schleifmuchlgasse 7 1040
   Stadthalle, go up to have a look.

Mission notes as Aminah neared
travelling to Yemen.

Text message from
Klang — 'You just got
very rich'.

'Place the small box in
the large box and place
it on the back seat just
behind the driver's
seat.' Soren texted me
in Yemen from Klang's
phone after my last
mission was aborted.

The $10 000 Jesper gave me
in my Hilton hotel room.

Paper Trail

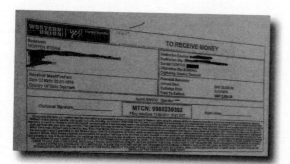

Western Union transfer from PET. Note that the sender lists their address as Soborg, the district in which PET HQ is located.

Invoice for a hotel paid by Klang. Note his invoice address is Mola Consult, the PET front company.

Invoice for one of the MI5-authorized money transfers to Somali terrorist Ahmed Abdulkadir Warsame.

Invoice for chemical gloves also purchased for Ahmed Abdulkadir Warsame.

Visa stamps for a Lebanon
Mission in 2007.

Hong Kong and China visa
stamps on my trip to see
Abdul there in May 2012.

Signing contract to
develop Masinga Dam.

regarding the money, pls tell the sister that the hook wants her to have 3000 dollars with her which you
will provide at the next meeting in vienna.   this is perfect cover for your next trip to see her.

have a safe trip and good luck,

your brothers

Email from my CIA handlers
Jed and George before one of
my trips to Vienna.

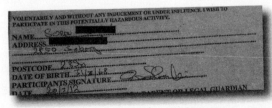

Confiscation notice for
Hexamine, signed by
Jesper ahead of the May
2012 mission to Yemen.

Soren's quad-bike
insurance disclaimer.

ACKNOWLEDGEMENTS

Morten Storm

I would like to thank all my family members and friends in Denmark, Sweden, Norway, Holland, the UK, Kenya and around the world for their support.

Thank you, Paul Cruickshank and Tim Lister, for masterfully making sense of it all during the many weeks we spent together and for the many months you spent investigating every last detail of my story and peeling back the layers of my memory. I will always be in your debt. I first met Paul during my 'radical years', when he came to Luton in 2005 to report on the extremist group al-Muhajiroun. He is now CNN's terrorism analyst and the editor of a recent five-volume collection of scholarship on al-Qaeda. It seems like a lifetime ago we met in Luton.

Paul and Tim have reported on al-Qaeda terrorism and international security for many years, and their expertise was invaluable in providing context to this story. Tim travelled across Yemen well before I did and unlike me made it to Afghanistan, where he reported on the US bombing of Osama bin Laden's redoubt in Tora Bora for CNN.

Thanks to the *Jyllands-Posten* reporters Carsten Ellegaard Christensen, Orla Borg, Morten Pihl and Michael Holbek Jensen who broke the story about my work for Western intelligence. You deservedly won the inaugural European Press Prize. Thanks also to all the Danish journalists who have believed in and supported me.

I'd also like to thank our literary agents, Richard Pine and Euan Thorneycroft, and our editors, Joel Rickett at Viking and Jamison Stoltz at Grove Atlantic, for giving me the chance to tell the world my story. If this book makes just one person think twice about following the path of violent extremism it will have been worth it.

Thanks to the Danish politician Irena Simonsen for her huge help and backing, and thanks too to my lawyer, Karoly Nemeth, in Denmark for all his guidance and support.

There are several others I would like to thank for their support, including Nic Robertson at CNN, Mark Stout at the Washington Spy Museum, Frederik Obermaier at *Süddeutsche Zeitung*, Howard Rosenberg at *60 Minutes* and Bent Skjaerstad at TV2 in Norway. Thank you also Joost in Holland. There are many others I can't thank for security reasons, but you know who you are.

Thanks to the bands Metallica, Slayer and Anthrax for your great music. You helped me wind up and wind down after missions.

Finally a massive thank you to all the lovely, kind and generous people and families I met in the Middle East and in North and East Africa. They enriched me with great knowledge and taught me how to live with honour and be a generous human being.

Paul Cruickshank and Tim Lister

Thank you, Morten Storm, for making it necessary and for allowing us to burrow deep into your life during stressful times for you and your family. We were staying with you when al-Qaeda types in Syria threatened your life in an online video and were struck by your humour and poise.

Thank you to your friends and family and ex-girlfriends we met in Denmark. Thanks to the Danish politician Irena Simonsen for inviting us into her home and helping us understand the political dynamics.

A giant thank you to Richard Pine, our literary agent at Inkwell in New York, for making it all possible. Huge thanks also to Euan Thorneycroft at A. M. Heath in London for working with Richard to bring this story to the world, and for your valuable feedback.

We have been blessed in having two of the best editors in the business: Joel Rickett at Penguin and Jamison Stoltz at Grove Atlantic. Thank you for working so seamlessly together and for your brilliant edits and ideas which immeasurably improved the book. Thanks also to the team of people working with you who helped put the book

Acknowledgements

together, including Ellie Smith, Allison Malecha, Ben Brusey, Sara Granger and the copy-editor, Mark Handsley.

Thank you Eliza Rothstein and Lyndsey Blessing at Inkwell for all your assistance and getting this book translated around the globe. Thanks to Taryn Eckstein for her legal advice.

Thanks to Carsten Ellegaard Christensen at *Jyllands-Posten*. You are a pro and it was Morten's good fortune to first approach you with his story. Thanks for the help you provided when we visited you in Copenhagen and keeping us in the loop on your investigations. You and your *Jyllands-Posten* colleagues deserve all the accolades for first breaking the story.

A special thanks to the Croatian journalist Sandra Veljkovic at the Croatian newspaper *Večeřnji List* for her help on the Aminah side of the story. Thanks to Bent Skjaerstad at Norway's TV2 for sharing information on Ikrimah's time in Norway.

Big thanks to Nic and Margaret Lowrie Robertson, as well as Ken Shiffman, for their counsel on the project. We are indebted to Magnus Ranstorp, one of Scandinavia's leading counter-terrorism academics, for casting his expert eye over the text and his smorgasbord of insights on the Danish context.

Thanks to those who read various iterations of the book and provided precious feedback. Some cannot be named because of the sensitivity of their positions, but you know who you are.

Thanks to our friends and family who indulged us while we disappeared off the map for a year to write this book.

And finally thanks to our wives for their love, support, feedback, ideas . . . and transcribing.

NOTES

1. Desert Road

2 **'Come to Yemen . . . see you':** This is my recollection. This is one of the few emails quoted in the book I did not save. Unless otherwise stated all emails, text messages and recorded conversations quoted in the book are reproduced verbatim, including spelling and grammatical errors.

4 **met two of the hijackers:** The 9/11 Commission said, in its final report, that it had 'been unable to learn enough about Aulaqi's relationship with Hazmi and Mihdhar [two of the 9/11 hijackers] to reach a conclusion' (p. 221), and that its attempts to locate and interview the cleric had been unsuccessful (footnote 35, p. 517).

9 **'The ballot . . . your ranks':** 'Salutations to al Shabaab of Somalia', Awlaki blog posting, 20 December 2008.

9 **'I pray . . . or not':** Brooks Egerton, 'Imam's emails to Fort Hood suspect tame compared with online rhetoric', *Dallas Morning News*, 28 November 2009.

10 **'the blame . . . a few dollars':** Ibid.

10 **suicide attack:** The four South Korean tourists were killed in the suicide bombing in Hadramaut on 15 March 2009; 'False Foundation? AQAP, Tribes and Ungoverned Spaces in Yemen', Combating Terrorism Center at West Point, October 2011.

10 **soliciting prostitutes:** Chitra Ragavan, 'The Imam's Very Curious Story', *US News and World Report*, 13 June 2004.

2. Gangs, Girls, God

19 **third-largest illegal business:** Klaus von Lampe, 'The Nicotine Racket. Trafficking in Untaxed Cigarettes: A Case Study of Organized Crime in

Germany': guest lecture given at the Institute of Criminology, University of Oslo, Norway, 6 May 1999.

22 **killing one:** Edward Winterhalder, *Out in Bad Standings: Inside the Bandidos Motorcycle Club*, Blockhead City, 2005, chap. 24.

25 **I learned . . . God's messenger:** For one of many accounts of this event, see John Miller and Aaron Kenedi, *Inside Islam: The Faith, the People, and the Conflicts of the World's Fastest-Growing Religion*, Da Capo Press, 2002.

25 **'Proclaim . . . blood':** Koran, al-Alaq, 96:1–2.

25 **'Allah is with us':** Koran, al-Tawba, 9:40.

25 **'Our Lord is God':** Koran, al-Haj, 22:39–40.

4. Arabia

39 **what was driving:** For more on Sheikh Muqbil and the Salafist world-view, see Bernard Haykel, 'The Salafis in Yemen at a Crossroads: An Obituary of Shaykh Muqbil al-Wadi'i of Dammaj (d. 1422/2001)', *Jemen-Report*, 2 (October 2002); Bernard Haykel, 'On the Nature of Salafi Thought and Action', in Roel Meijer et al., *Global Salafism*, Columbia University Press, 2009; Quintan Wiktorowicz, 'Anatomy of the Salafi Movement', *Studies in Conflict & Terrorism*, 29:3 (2006), 207–39.

43 **US authorities . . . year before:** *United States of America v. Clifford Allen Newman*, Appeal from the United States District Court for the Middle District of Florida, 17 August 2010.

5. Londonistan

47 **'Had it issued . . . many a contradiction':** Koran, An-Nisā', 4:82.

49 **Master's degree:** 'Profile: Zacarias Moussaoui', BBC, 25 April 2006.

49 **What he . . . Chechen war:** Richard Willing, 'Westernized kid grows into 9/11 suspect', *USA Today*, 25 June 2002; 'British have file on Moussaoui', *USA Today*, 13 June 2002.

49 **one of al-Qaeda's camps:** Indictment: *United States of America v. Zacarias Moussaoui*, US District Court for the Eastern District of Virginia, 11 December 2001.

50 **Russian rockets rained down:** Amelia Gentleman, 'Russian rockets hit Grozny market', *Guardian*, 21 October 1999.

51 **He had . . . 'twentieth hijacker':** Indictment: *United States of America v. Zacarias Moussaoui*, US District Court for the Eastern District of Virginia, 11 December 2001.

51 **'shoe-bomber':** *United States v. Richard Colvin Reid*, US District Court of Massachusetts, 16 January 2002.

6. Death to America

55 **issued a fatwa:** Noorhaidi Hasan, *Laskar Jihad: Islam, Militancy, and the Quest for Identity in Post-New Order Indonesia*, Cornell Southeast Asia Program Publications, 2006.

55 **'Fight in the cause . . . not aggressors':** Koran, al-Baqarah, 2:190.

56 **'must be fulfilled . . . their minds':** The words of Ahmad Yahya Ibn Muhammad al-Najm in response to requests for guidance from Salafis wanting to fight in the Moluccas. Al-Najm was a member of the Saudi senior Ulama committee. See Hasan, *Laskar Jihad*, p. 117.

56 **In September 2006 . . . the country:** Elisabeth Arnsdorf Haslund, 'Titalt: Mit TATP var ikke farligt', *Berlingske Tidende* (Denmark), 13 September 2007; 'Denmark convicts men in bomb plot', BBC, 23 November 2007.

58 **CALES:** The Centre for Arabic Language and Eastern Studies at the University of Science and Technology in Sana'a.

58 **USS Cole:** 'USS *Cole* fast facts', CNN, 18 September 2013; Michael Sniffen, 'FBI: Plastic Explosives Used in *Cole* Bombing', ABC News, 1 November 2000.

58 **jihadist network:** One of the men I got to know was a Yemeni-American called Abdul Rahman al-Yaf'i from a prominent tribal family, who several of my circle told me was Osama bin Laden's 'right-hand man' in Yemen. The previous year those alleged ties had prompted his extraordinary rendition by the United States during a family visit to Cairo. He was flown to Jordan for interrogation, where he was tortured and pressured to confess to a role in the 1998 bombings of US embassies in East Africa, which he denied. After his release he visited me several times – in secret – at my house, but never spoke of al-Qaeda.

59 **none of the al-Qaeda members:** Abdul told me he spent time with the Yemeni jihadi Adil al-Abab in Afghanistan. Al-Abab did not contradict this after I got to know him.

60 **women and children:** Tim Lister reported on the battle for CNN from a location near Tora Bora.

62 **a long fatwa:** The full text of bin Uqla's fatwa can be found at http://sunnahonline.com/ilm/contemporary/0017.htm.

62 **'When America attacked . . . terrorism?' the Sheikh asked:** Ibid.

62 **with us or with the terrorists:** President George W. Bush, Address to a Joint Session of Congress and the American People, 20 September 2001.

63 **He was referring . . . travel:** For more on John Walker Lindh's travelling to Afghanistan, see Mark Kukis, *My Heart Became Attached: The Strange Journey of John Walker Lindh*, Potomac Books, 2008.

65 **MV *Limburg*:** On 6 October 2002, in an attack allegedly endorsed by Osama bin Laden, a Yemeni terrorist cell blew up an explosive-laden boat beside the French oil tanker MV *Limburg*, near the port of Mukalla, killing the suicide bombers and one sailor: 'False Foundation? AQAP, Tribes and Ungoverned Spaces in Yemen', Combating Terrorism Center at West Point, October 2011; Sebastien Rotella and Esther Shrader, 'Tanker Blast Likely a Terror Attack, French Say', *Los Angeles Times*, 11 October 2002.

7. Family Feuds

67 **In September 2006 . . . sentence:** Elisabeth Arnsdorf Haslund, 'Titalt: Mit TATP var ikke farligt', *Berlingske Tidende* (Denmark), 13 September 2007; 'Denmark convicts men in bomb plot', BBC, 23 November 2007. For more, see Morten Skjoldager, *Truslen Indefra: De Danske Terrorista*, Lindardt og Ringhof, 2009, pp. 191–203.

71 **opened fire:** Dahr Jamail, 'Falluja's struggle after invasion,' Al Jazeera, 1 May 2008.

71 **an offensive . . . Sharia law:** Pepe Escobar, 'The Islamic emirate of Fallujah', *Asia Times*, 15 July 2004.

72 **'magnificent nineteen':** Dominic Casciani, 'Profile: Omar Bakri Mohammed', BBC, 12 August 2005.

72 **'The punishment . . . be imprisoned':** Koran, al-Ma'idah, 5:33.

72 **Several of his acolytes. . . in London:** The plot to target crowded spaces in London was broken up by 'Operation Crevice' in March 2004. For ties to al-Muhajiroun, see Peter Bergen and Paul Cruickshank, 'Clerical Error: The Dangers of Tolerance', *New Republic*, 7 August 2005.

73 **After two British men . . . their plot:** On 30 April 2003 two followers of al-Muhajiroun attacked a nightclub in Tel Aviv, killing three. See Bergen and Cruickshank, 'Clerical Error'.

73 **ultimate sacrifice:** Kiran Randhawa, Justin Davenport and David Churchill, 'Suicide bomber Brit worked as driver for hate cleric Omar Bakri', *Evening Standard*, 13 February 2014.

75 **demand for the training:** Training camps like the one I ran soon drew the attention of the security services and the UK media. See Ian Cobain and Richard Norton-Taylor, 'Training camps for terrorists in UK parks', *Guardian*, 13 August 2006.

75 **On 7 May . . . was filmed:** Maria Newman, 'Video Appears to Show Beheading of American Civilian', *The New York Times*, 11 May 2004.

76 **After his release . . . Ansar al-Islam:** Edward F. Mickolus, *The Terrorist List. Volume 1: A–K*, ABC-CLIO, 2009, p. 524.

76 **killed in Fallujah:** US Central Command statement, 8 October 2004; Hans Davidsen-Nielsen and Kjeld Hybel, 'Danmark i Krig: Krigens beskidte ansigt', *Politiken* (Denmark), 3 April 2007.

76 **'It is . . . Mighty, Wise':** Koran, al-Anfal, 8:67.

78 **'The woman . . . Last Day':** Koran, An Noor, 24:2.

79 **'Satan said: " . . . among them" ':** Koran, al-Hijra, 15:39–40.

79 **'Those are . . . forgives sins?':** Koran, Āli 'Imrān, 3:135.

8. MI5 Comes to Luton

80 **The magazine reported ' . . . detainee's lap':** Text of original article and retraction at John Barry, 'Gitmo: Southcom Showdown', Newsweek.com, 8 May 2005.

80 **used the story:** See, for example, Hendrik Hertzberg, 'Big News Week', *New Yorker*, 30 May 2005.

81 **still available online:** When this book went to press the footage was available here: http://www.youtube.com/watch?v=FG4fZNPLgWY.

9. Meeting the Sheikh

91 **designated a 'global terrorist':** The designation described the university as a training ground for terrorists. 'Al Iman students are suspected of being responsible, and were arrested, for recent terrorist attacks, including the assassination of three American missionaries,' it said in part: http://www.treasury.gov/press-center/press-releases/Pages/js1190. aspx.

93 **'44 Ways . . .':** '44 Ways of Supporting Jihad' was released in early 2009.

94 **He had been born . . . vocation:** Judicial Watch Awlaki FBI FOIA documents obtained in May 2013; Scott Shane and Souad Mekhennet, 'Imam's Path From Condemning Terror to Preaching Jihad', *The New York Times*, 8 May 2010.

94 **'more seriously':** See 'Spilling Out the Beans: Al Awlaki Revealing His Side of the Story', AQAP's *Inspire* magazine, issue 9, May 2012.

95 **he scored a 3.85:** Documents later obtained by the advocacy group Judicial Watch under the Freedom of Information Act provide fascinating detail into Awlaki's life in the US. A former teacher at San Diego State University wrote to the Doctoral Screening Committee at GWU to recommend Awlaki, ticking the 'Excellent' column for his maturity, self-confidence and analytical ability. His former professor said, 'Anwar brings a unique perspective to class discussions and the work he produces . . . His peers in the classes looked to Anwar as a leader . . . When Mr Al-Aulaqi completes his studies in the US he will become an educational leader in the higher education system in Yemen.' Awlaki's name was frequently spelled 'Aulaqi' while he was in the US. Judicial Watch obtained the documents in May 2013 and posted them online in July 2013.

95 **wrote Woodall:** Andrea Bruce Woodall, *Washington Post*, 12 September 2001.

95 **interview to *National Geographic*:** Brian Handwerk and Zain Habboo, 'Attack on America: An Islamic Scholar's Perspective', *National Geographic*, 28 September 2001.

97 **warrant for his arrest:** Investigators had sought the warrant as a way to detain Awlaki for further questioning on his links to the 9/11 hijackers. See ABC News, 'Investigators Blew an Opportunity to Arrest Awlaki', 1 December 2009.

97 **Tracing the . . . ' . . . coincidental':** Final Report of the 9/11 Commission, chap. 7, p. 221. Further suspicion about Awlaki's links to the hijackers is voiced on p. 230.

97 **'There is reporting . . . were terrorists':** National Commission on Terrorist Attacks upon the United States, 'Outline of the 9/11 Plot: Staff Statement No. 16', published 16 June 2004.

97 **There was . . . ' . . . group Hamas':** Final report of the 9/11 Commission, footnote 33, chap. 7.

98 **One article written:** Chitra Ragavan: 'The Imam's Very Curious Story', *US News and World Report*, 13 June 2004.

98 **character assassination:** Awlaki years later would put an elaborate spin on the police cautioning him for soliciting prositutes. He wrote in *Inspire* magazine, the online publication of al-Qaeda in the Arabian Peninsula: 'In 1996 while waiting at a traffic light in my minivan a middle aged woman knocked on the window of the passenger seat. By the time I rolled down the window and before even myself or the woman uttering a word I was surrounded by police officers who had me come out of my vehicle only to be handcuffed. I was accused of soliciting a prostitute and then released. They made it a point to make me know in no uncertain terms that the woman was an undercover cop. I didn't know what to make of the incident. However a few days later came the answer. I was visited by two men who introduced themselves as officials with the US government . . . and that they are interested in my cooperation with them . . . I never heard back from them again until in 1998 when I was approached by a woman, this time from my window and again I was surrounded by police officers who this time had go to court. This time I was told that this is a sting operation and you would not be able to get out of it.' See 'Spilling Out the Beans', *Inspire* magazine.

98 **Among the avid consumers:** Nic Robertson, Paul Cruickshank and Tim Lister, 'Documents give new details on al Qaeda's London bombings', CNN, 30 April 2012; Paul Cruickshank, 'Al Qaeda loses its English-language inspiration', CNN, 1 October 2011.

98 '. . . **revved up** . . .': Cruickshank, 'Al Qaeda loses its English-language inspiration'.

98 **favour of suicide bombings:** Ibid.

98 **'Constants on the Path of Jihad':** Anwar al-Awlaki, 'Constants on the Path of Jihad', 2005. The lecture was widely posted online.

99 **'Allah is Preparing Us for Victory':** By July 2006 the recording was circulating on online Islamist forums in the West. A good translation of the lecture, made when Awlaki was in prison in Sana'a, can be found at: https://docs. google.com/document/d/10SyzllD6ESWK9mUw18sOw5l2RK5QfRBAXxg pO5quKHY/edit.

100 **At morning prayers . . . in Afghanistan:** 'False Foundation? AQAP, Tribes and Ungoverned Spaces in Yemen', Combating Terrorism Center at West Point, October 2011.

100 **El Cajon Boulevard:** R. Stickney and Paul Krueger, 'Accused Terrorist Was "Kind, Peaceful Man": Friends', NBC News, San Diego, 6 August 2010.

100 **graduate to the FBI's Rewards:** http://www.fbi.gov/wanted/wanted_ terrorists/copy_of_jehad-serwan-mostafa/view.

103 **Abu Talha . . . most-wanted list:** His death was announced by al-Shabaab more than a year later. Bill Roggio, 'Senior al-Qaeda Operative Killed in Somalia', *Long War Journal*, 1 September 2008.

108 **sent troops into Somalia:** Mohamed Olad Hassan, 'Ethiopian Force Enters Somalia', Associated Press, 20 July 2006.

109 **The FBI . . . solitary confinement:** Judicial Watch Awlaki FBI FOIA documents obtained in May 2013.

10. *The Fall*

112 **push eastwards:** Jeffrey Gettleman and Mark Mazzetti, 'Somalia's Islamists and Ethiopia Gird for a War', *The New York Times*, 9 December 2006; 'Ethiopian Troops Seize Strategic Town in Somalia', *Somaliland Times*, 9 October 2006.

112 **Australians and my British friend:** The Australians arrested were my friend Mustafa Ayoub and his brother. For more on the arrests, see Cameron Stewart and Martin Chulov, 'Yemen ties terror's loose ends', *The Australian*, 4 November 2006; Abul Taher, 'UK Preacher in Secret Web Call for Jihad', *The Times*, 4 January 2007.

113 **released and deported:** Stewart and Chulov, 'Yemen ties terror's loose ends'; Taher, 'UK Preacher in Secret Web Call for Jihad'; 'Dansker Tortureret i Yemen', TV2 (Denmark), 27 December 2006; Janet Fife-Yeomans, 'Australians Placed on US Terror No-Fly List', *Daily Telegraph* (Australia), 31 August 2011.

117 **'Allah is ... due measurements':** Koran, Az-Zumar, 39:62, and al-Furqan, 25:2.

11. Switching Sides

128 **Egyptian al-Qaeda operative:** The senior Egyptian operative was Abu Ubaidah al-Masri. See Mitchell D. Silber, *The Al Qaeda Factor: Plots against the West*, University of Pennsylvania Press, 2011, pp. 142–52.

128 **discovered in his luggage:** Morten Skjoldager, *Truslen Indefra: De Danske Terrorista*, Lindardt og Ringhof, 2009, chaps. 15–16.

128 **used a front company:** A Western intelligence source provided the information on the Khurshid investigation to Paul Cruickshank in 2013.

128 **A short while later . . . in prison:** Silber, *Al Qaeda Factor*; Morten Skjoldager, 'Portræt: Trænet til terror mod sit fødeland: Portræt, Hammad Khürshid', *Politiken* (Denmark), 10 November 2009; Paul Cruickshank, personal communication with Elisabeth Haslund (a Danish reporter who covered the trial), New York, September 2009.

12. London Calling

129 **'Send him Bak!':** *Sun*, 20 July 2005.

129 **'. . . make it a long one':** Alan Travis and Duncan Campbell, 'Bakri to be banned from the UK', *Guardian*, 9 August 2005.

131 **terror dynasty:** For more on the al-Hajdib brothers, see Hassan M. Fatah, 'German Suspects from Opposite Sides of a Lebanese Town', *The New York Times*, 29 August 2006.

131 **Youssef, had been arrested:** 'A Terrorist Gets the Judicial Middle Finger', *Der Spiegel*, 10 December 2008; '9 arrested by Denmark in reported terror plot', *International Herald Tribune*, 5 September 2006.

134 **Not long after . . . were killed:** 'Slain Lebanese Militant was Suspect in Failed German Bombing', *The New York Times*, 21 May 2007, and Hassan M. Fattah, 'Lebanese Army and Islamists Battle for Second Day', *The New York Times*, 22 May 2007; 'Dozens killed in Lebanon gunbattle between Islamic militants, security forces', Associated Press, 20 May 2007; 'Nowhere to put us', BBC, 23 May 2007. For more on Fatah al-Islam in the Nahr al-Barid camp, see Muhammad Ali Khalidi and Diane Riskedahl, 'The Road to Nahr al Barid', Middle East Research and Information Project, no. 244.

136 **Hamid Elasmar:** James Orr, 'Guilty pleas over soldier beheading plot', *Guardian*, 28 January 2008.

138 **Tabbakh was arrested:** Duncan Gardham, 'Terrorist bomb maker Hassan Tabbakh jailed for seven years', *Daily Telegraph*, 30 July 2008; for more on Tabbakh's case, see Judgment: *Regina v. Hassan Tabbakh*, Court of Appeal, Royal Courts of Justice, 3 March 2009 [2009] EWCA Crim 464; Decision: Hassan Tabbakh against the United Kingdom, The European Court of Human Rights (Fourth Section), sitting on 21 February 2012; Judgment: On the Application of Hassan Tabbakh, High Court of Justice, Royal Courts of Justice, 9 August 2013 [2013] EWHC 2492 (Admin).

13. From Langley with Love

144 **arresting more than twenty men:** For more details on the arrests, see Michael Mugwang'a, Gitonga Marete and Tim Querengesser, 'Kenya: Scores Arrested in Terror Hunt', *The Nation* (Kenya), 15 December 2007; David Ochami and Mwangi Muiruri, 'Face to Face with Dangerous Terrorists', *East Africa Standard*, 6 August 2008.

144 **real name was Elizabeth Hanson:** For more on Hanson, see Joby Warrick, *The Triple Agent: The al-Qaeda Mole Who Infiltrated the CIA*, Vintage, 2012.

146 **'Because of the flowing style . . . me directly':** Moazzem Begg, interview with Imam Anwar al-Awlaki, Cageprisoners.com, 31 December 2007.

146 **Wuhayshi . . . upper echelons of al-Qaeda:** 'False Foundation? AQAP, Tribes and Ungoverned Spaces in Yemen', Combating Terrorism Center at West Point, October 2011.

149 **sixty email accounts:** Catherine Herridge, 'American cleric used more than 60 email accounts to reach followers, including Hasan', Fox News, 15 June 2012.

14. *Cocaine and Allah*

156 **acquitted in a terrorism case:** See 'Danish teenager sentenced to 7 years in Bosnia-linked plot', Associated Press, 16 February 2007.

15. *Clerical Terror*

165 **'. . . Hearts and Minds':** Anwar al-Awlaki, 'Battle of the Hearts and Minds', May 2008.

165 **The Dust Will Never Settle Down':** The lecture was released on 26 May 2008 and can be found in full on several Islamist websites, such as Kalamullah.com, which includes a wide range of Awlaki's lectures and sermons. Many of them have been removed from YouTube.

166 **as a dog:** 'Muslims protest Swedish newspaper's cartoon of Prophet Muhammad', Associated Press, 31 August 2007.

167 **'I have gifts':** This is my recollection. I do not have a saved copy of this email.

168 **gun and car attack:** Robert Worth, '10 are Killed in Bombings at Embassy in Yemen', *The New York Times*, 17 September 2008.

16. *Killing Mr John*

173 **In another email . . . deliver it:** I do not have a saved copy of this email. I have the invoice for the chemical gloves from Aspli Safety Limited dated 13 October 2008.

174 **moustache:** Paul Cruickshank and Tim Lister, 'U.S. target in Somalia: An inside story on an Al-Shabaab commander', CNN, 7 October 2013.

176 **now in command of hundreds:** Government Affirmation: *USA v. Ahmed Abdulkadir Warsame*, United States District Court, Southern District of New York, filed 26 March 2013.

176 **most dangerous operative:** 'Profile: Saleh Ali Saleh Nabhan', BBC, 15 September 2008.

178 **'Bad news . . .':** This is my recollection. I do not have a saved copy of this email.

179 **'Mr John says thanks':** This is my recollection. I do not have a saved copy of this email.

179 **On 14 September . . . at sea:** Jeffrey Gettleman and Eric Schmitt, 'U.S. Kills Top Qaeda Militant in Southern Somalia', *The New York Times*, 14 September 2009; Nicholas Schmidle, 'Getting bin Laden', *New Yorker*, 8 August 2011.

180 **'Mr John was killed . . .':** This is my recollection. I do not have a saved copy of this email.

17. Mujahideen Secrets

184 **'Fucking good':** This is my recollection. I do not have a saved copy of this text.

187 **Hasan was armed . . . the wounded:** Eric M. Johnson and Lisa Maria Garza, ' "Hell Broke Loose," Witness Says of Fort Hood Massacre', Reuters, 12 August 2013.

187 **Hasan had written . . . in 2001:** David Johnston and Scott Shane, 'US Knew of Suspect's Ties to Radical Cleric', *The New York Times*, 9 November 2009; Carol Craty, 'FBI official: Hasan should have been asked about emails with radical cleric', CNN, 2 August 2012; 'Anwar al Awlaki Email Exchange with Fort Hood Shooter Nidal Hasan', Intelwire, 19 July 2012.

188 **In one email . . . and research:** Ibid.; 'Fort Hood report shows FBI ignored warning signs on Hasan, lawmaker says', Associated Press, 19 July 2012.

188 **'Nidal Hisan is a hero . . .':** Awlaki's comments were posted on his now defunct blog. A summary of the posting can be found on the website of the Anti-Defamation League.

189 **thirty-four al-Qaeda fighters:** 'Yemen foils "al-Qaeda plot" killing 34', BBC, 17 December 2009.

189 **But the intelligence . . . one strike:** Amnesty International, 'Images of missile and cluster munitions point to US role in fatal attack in Yemen', 7 June 2010.

190 **destroyed a Bedouin hamlet:** Gregory D. Johnsen, *The Last Refuge: Yemen, Al-Qaeda, and America's War in Arabia*, W. W. Norton & Co., 2013, p. 253; Chris Woods, 'The civilian massacre the US neither confirms nor denies', Bureau of Investigative Journalism, 29 March 2012; Michael Isikoff, 'Yemen cable gives al-Qaida new "recruiting" tool', NBC News, 30 November 2010.

190 **' . . . scored a big own goal':** This is my recollection. I do not have a saved copy of this email.

190 **statement from the Yemeni embassy:** See Nasser Atta, Brian Ross and Matthew Cole, ' "I'm Alive," Says Yemeni Radical Anwar al-Awlaki Despite US Attack', ABC News, 31 December 2009.

190 **First reports . . . been killed:** Ibid.

190 **'The tall guy is fine':** This is my recollection. I do not have a saved copy of this text.

190 **several passengers:** On passengers' role in thwarting Abdulmutallab, see Peter Slevin, 'Fear and Heroism aboard Northwest Airlines Flight 253 after Attempted Bombing', *Washington Post*, 17 December 2009.

191 **collected and driven:** Details of Abdulmutallab's movements in Yemen are included in the US Government's Sentencing Memorandum, US District Court, Eastern District of Michigan, Southern Division, filed 10 February 2012. On the timing of Abdulmutallab's trip, see Steven Erlanger, 'Nigerian May Have Used Course in Yemen as Cover', *The New York Times*, 1 January 2010.

191 **Abdulmutallab told the preacher . . . to record:** Ibid.

191 **then bring it down:** Ibid.

191 **hospital bedside:** Trial transcript: *USA v. Umar Farouk Abdulmutallab*, United States District Court, Eastern District of Michigan, Southern Division, filed 11 October 2011.

191 **More disturbing still . . . Saudi royal family:** Paul Cruickshank, Nic Robertson and Tim Lister, 'Al Qaeda's biggest threat', CNN, 16 February 2012.

192 **commandos descended:** 'Yemen forces kill al-Qaeda chief', BBC, 13
January 2010; 'المحضار كان أميراً» «لولة شبوة» [al-Mehdar was emir of
Shabwa], Asharq-al-Awsat, 14 January 2010.

194 **Awlaki declared war:** Anwar al-Awlaki, 'A Call to Jihad', 17 March 2010,
transcribed by Al Ansar Mujahideen English Forum.

18. Anwar's Blonde

197 **As a teenager Irena . . .:** Details on Irena Horak's life in Croatia were
provided by Sandra Veljkovic, a journalist who broke exclusive details on
Irena Horak's story for the Croatian newspaper *Večeřnji List*. See also
Renata Rašović and Darko Marčinković, 'Teroristica: Irena Horak (35) iz
Bjelovara je Al-Qa'idina Amina', *Večeřnji List* (Croatia), 24 October 2012;
'Ekskluzivno: Kako je Hrvatica postala Al-Qaidina nevjesta?', RTL, 25
October 2012.

197 **posted photos:** These can still be viewed on one of her social media
profiles.

203 **spymaster, 'M':** Piers Brendon, 'The spymaster who was stranger than
fiction', *Independent*, 29 October 1999.

212 **approving the assassination:** Scott Shane, 'U.S. Approves Targeted Killing of American Cleric', *The New York Times*, 6 April 2010. Shane reported:
'"The danger Awlaki poses to this country is no longer confined to
words," said an American official, who like other current and former
officials interviewed for this article spoke of the classified counterterrorism measures on the condition of anonymity. "He's gotten involved in
plots."

'The official added: "The United States works, exactly as the American people expect, to overcome threats to their security, and this
individual – through his own actions – has become one. Awlaki knows
what he's done, and he knows he won't be met with handshakes and
flowers. None of this should surprise anyone."'

215 **'Never is a man alone . . . with them':** As narrated by the scholar
Muhammad ibn Isa al-Tirmidhi and classed as an authentic *hadith*
by Sheikh Muhammad Nasir ud deen al-Albaani in *Saheeh al-Tirmidhi*.

19. A New Cover

226 downloading instructions from *Inspire*: Vikram Dodd, 'Jihadist gang jailed for plot to bomb EDL rally', *Guardian*, 10 June 2013.

227 three others I knew: The others I knew convicted of the plot were Zohaib Ahmed, Mohammed Hasseen and Omar Khan. For details on the plot, see 'Six admit planning to bomb English Defence League Rally', BBC, 30 April 2013.

227 established that Geele: Paul Cruickshank, 'Al Shabaab: a looming threat', CNN, 5 October 2011.

228 In January 2010 . . . reach him: Ibid.; Marie Louise Sjølie, 'The Danish cartoonist who survived an axe attack', *Guardian*, 4 January 2010.

228 When the police . . . into custody: Ibid.

230 suicide bombers affiliated . . . seventy people: 'Somali militants "behind" Kampala World Cup blast', BBC, 12 July 2010.

231 Many . . . were Kenyan: Letter dated 18 July 2011 from the Chairman of the Security Council Committee pursuant to resolutions 751 (1992) and 1907 (2009) concerning Somalia and Eritrea addressed to the President of the Security Council.

231 received a summons: For more see Orla Borg, Carsten Ellegaard and Morten Pihl, 'Briten der skulle være Storms makker', *Jyllands-Posten*, 14 January 2013.

232 A Tunisian . . . al-Qaeda operatives: See Paul Cruickshank, 'Four convicted in Scandinavian "Mumbai-style" terror plot', CNN, 4 June 2012.

232 The suspected Swedish-Yemeni . . . headed to Yemen: Confirmed by Paul Cruickshank, conversation with European counter-terrorism source, 2013.

233 A man plotting carnage . . . No one else was hurt: Per Nyberg, 'Sweden bomb went off early, authorities say', CNN, 13 December 2010; Paul Cruickshank, Tim Lister and Per Nyberg, 'The last days of a suicide bomber', CNN, 9 December 2011.

233 exception of Nasserdine Menni: 'Nasserdine Menni jailed for seven years for funding Stockholm bomb attack', BBC, 27 August 2012.

20. *Target Awlaki*

236 Awlaki was rapidly . . . deadly cargo: Mark Mazetti and Robert F. Worth, 'U.S. Sees Complexity of Bombs as Linked to Al Qaeda', *The New York Times*, 30 October 2010; Paul Cruickshank, Nic Robertson and Ken Shiffman, 'How safe is the cargo on passenger flights?', CNN, 19 February 2012.

237 addressed the American public: 'At this stage, the American people should know that the counterterrorism professionals are taking this threat very seriously and are taking all necessary and prudent steps to ensure our security,' the President said. 'Going forward, we will continue to strengthen our cooperation with the Yemeni government to disrupt plotting by al Qaeda in the Arabian Peninsula and to destroy this al Qaeda affiliate': President Obama's Statement on Security Alert, 29 October 2010, 4.22 p.m. EDT, whitehouse.gov.

237 Al-Asiri had concealed . . . a plane: For a broader look at the growing sophistication of AQAP's bomb-making, see Paul Cruickshank, Tim Lister and Nic Robertson, 'Al Qaeda's bomb-makers evolve, adapt and continue to plot', CNN, 8 May 2012.

237 asked Rajib Karim: See Andrew Carey and Paul Cruickshank, '"Terror Planning" by Muslim cleric al Awlaki described in UK trial', CNN, 1 February 2011; Opening Note, *The Queen v. Rajib Karim*, Woolwich Crown Court.

237 'not only helped plan . . .': Letter from US Attorney General Eric H. Holder to US Senator Patrick Leahy, 22 May 2013, http://www.justice.gov/ag/AG-letter-5-22-13.pdf.

237 sermons on their iPods: See Kiran Khalid, 'Confessed bomb plotter takes stand in NYC subway terror trial', CNN, 17 April 2012.

237 Another devotee: Scott Shane and Mark Mazzetti, 'Time Sq. Suspect Drew Inspiration from Radical Cleric', *The New York Times*, 6 May 2010.

238 'How to Build a Bomb . . .': See Paul Cruickshank and Tim Lister, 'From the grave, the cleric inspiring a new generation of terrorists', CNN, 24 April 2013.

238 al-Qaeda began to take advantage: For an overview of AQAP's expansion in southern Yemen, see Andrew Michaels and Sakhr Ayyash,

'AQAP's Resilience in Yemen', Combating Terrorism Center at West Point, 24 September 2013.

239 **US military drones . . . locked on:** See Barbara Starr, 'Al-Awlaki targeted in Yemen', CNN, 6 May 2011.

239 **US intelligence believed . . . nearby village:** Margaret Coker, Adam Entous and Julian E. Barnes, 'Drone Targets Yemeni Cleric', *Wall Street Journal*, 7 May 2011.

240 **Awlaki told a comrade:** Shaykh Harith al Nadari recounted Awlaki describing the near miss to him and others in 'My Story with Al Alwaki', AQAP's *Inspire* magazine, issue 9, May 2012.

240 **The car had accelerated . . . Awlaki's group:** Coker, Entous and Barnes, 'Drone Targets Yemeni Cleric'.

240 **The swap . . . brothers instantly:** Ibid.

240 **'Something of fear befalls you . . .':** Shaykh Harith al Nadari, 'My Story with Al Alwaki'.

243 **clashes erupted:** Adam Barron, 'Chaos swirls in Yemen's capital as rivals clash', *Pittsburgh Post-Gazette*, 25 May 2011.

244 **planted in a mosque:** Robert F. Worth and Laura Kasinof, 'Yemeni President Wounded in Palace Attack', *The New York Times*, 3 June 2011.

248 **'Please find a new courier':** This is my recollection. I do not have a saved copy of this email.

248 **khat-filled cheeks:** On the importance of khat in Yemen, see Jeffrey Fleishman, 'In Yemen, chewing khat offers ritual and repose', *Los Angeles Times*, 5 January 2013.

251 **Warsame took . . . Somali fighters:** Indictment: *USA v. Ahmed Abdulkadir Warsame*, unsealed 30 June 2011; 'Guilty Plea Unsealed in New York Involving Ahmed Warsame', U.S. Attorney's Office, Southern District of New York, 25 March 2013.

251 **took him into custody:** Warsame was also accused of weapons offences; conspiracy to teach and demonstrate explosive-making; and receiving military training from AQAP. He pleaded guilty and cooperated with the authorities. See Benjamin Weiser, 'Terrorist Has Cooperated with US since Secret Guilty Plea in 2011, Papers Show', *The New York Times*, 25 March 2013.

21. A Long Hot Summer

257 **Khan had been born:** Khan was radicalized while living in Queens, New York, then moved to North Carolina, where from his parents' basement he ran a jihadist blog using catchy graphics that became a prototype for *Inspire*. See Paul Cruickshank, 'U.S. citizen believed to be writing for al Qaeda website', CNN, 19 July 2010.

257 **Khan met with the Nigerian . . . bomb plot:** US Government's Sentencing Memorandum, US District Court, Eastern District of Michigan, Southern Division, filed 10 February 2012; Paul Cruickshank interview with US intelligence source, 2013.

257 **'The use of poisons':** AQAP's *Inspire* magazine, issue 8, Fall 2011.

257 **found the *New York Times* article:** Eric Schmitt and Thom Shanker, 'Qaeda Trying to Harness Toxins for Bombs, U.S. Officials Fear', *The New York Times*, 12 August 2011

258 **text from my contact in Sana'a:** This is my recollection. I do not have a saved copy of this text exchange.

259 **Early that day . . . just twenty-four:** Mark Mazzetti, Charlie Savage and Scott Shane, 'How a U.S. Citizen Came to Be in America's Cross Hairs', *The New York Times*, 9 March 2013; 'U.S. officials warn of possible retaliation after al Qaeda cleric is killed', CNN, 30 September 2011.

259 **'I don't believe it' . . . 'No – it's true':** This is my recollection. I do not have a saved copy of this text exchange.

259 **leader of external operations:** Letter from the US Attorney General, Eric H. Holder, to US Senator Patrick Leahy, 22 May 2013, http://www.justice.gov/ag/AG-letter-5-22-13.pdf.

259 **President Obama announced:** Remarks by the President at the 'Change of Office', Chairman of the Joint Chiefs of Staff Ceremony, Office of the Press Secretary, White House, 30 September 2011.

22. Breaking with Big Brother

260 **'I'm so sorry . . .':** This is my recollection. I do not have a saved copy of this text.

260 'Tell Jed . . .': This is my recollection. I do not have a saved copy of this text.

260 *Sunday Telegraph:* Adam Baron, Majid al-Kibsi, Colin Freeman and Sean Rayment, 'How America finally caught up with Anwar al-Awlaki', *Sunday Telegraph*, 2 October 2011.

269 **'He's just sitting there and lying':** I do not have this on tape. I stopped the recording after the end of the conversation with Michael.

23. Back in the Ring

272 **Al-Qaeda in Yemen had become:** For details on the merger, see Thomas Hegghammer, 'Saudi and Yemeni Branches of al Qaeda Unite', 24 January 2009, at Jihadica, http://www.jihadica.com/saudi-and-yemeni-branches-of-al-qaida-unite/. On the group's expansion, see Sudarsan Raghavan 'Al Qaeda group in Yemen gaining prominence', *Washington Post*, 28 December 2009.

272 **A confidant of Osama bin Laden . . . leadership of the group:** Paul Cruickshank, 'Terror warning may be linked to choice of al Qaeda chief deputy', CNN, 3 August 2013; Eli Lake, 'Meet al Qaeda's New General Manager', *Daily Beast*, 9 August 2013; bin Laden letter to Atiyya Abdul Rahman, 27 August 2010, Combating Terrorism Center at West Point, Harmony Documents: SOCOM-2012-0000003 Trans.

272 **By late 2011 . . . as possible:** See Christopher Swift, 'Arc of Covergence: AQAP, Ansar al-Shari'a and the Struggle for Yemen', Combating Terrorism Center at West Point, 21 June 2012.

24. The Lion's Den

282 **attack on . . . a senior British diplomat:** This appears to have been the attack Hartaba was referring to: Richard Spencer, 'Britain's deputy ambassador to Yemen survives mortar attack', *Daily Telegraph*, 6 October 2010.

283 **reached the town of Jaar:** For a good description of Jaar at this time, see Casey L. Coombs, 'Land of the Black Flag', *Foreign Policy*, 9 March 2012, and Gaith Abdul-Ahad, 'Al Qaeda's wretched utopia and the battle for hearts and minds', *Guardian*, 30 April 2012.

288 **a month after his father:** Tom Finn and Noah Browning, 'An American Teenager in Yemen: Paying for the Sins of His Father?', *Time*, 27 October 2011.

288 **Al-Asiri was all the more dangerous:** For more, see Paul Cruickshank, Nic Robertson and Tim Lister, 'Al Qaeda's biggest threat', CNN, 16 February 2012.

289 **left hanging:** See 'Yemen In Conflict: Abyan's Darkest Hour', Amnesty International, 4 December 2012.

290 **Wuhayshi would later depict:** 'Letter from Abu Basir to Emir of Al-Qaida in the Islamic Magreb', 21 May 2012. This letter was discovered by the Associated Press in a house used by al-Qaeda fighters in Timbuktu, Mali, and was made available at http://www.longwarjournal.org/images/al-qaida-papers-how-to-run-a-state.pdf. See also Bill Roggio, 'Wuhayshi imparted lessons of AQAP operations in Yemen to AQIM', *Long War Journal*, 12 August 2013.

290 **'Try to win them over . . .':** Ibid.

25. Operation Amanda

295 **'Rise Up and Board with Us':** AQAP's *Inspire* magazine, issue 9, May 2012.

296 **Qasim al-Raymi:** For more on AQAP's senior figures at this time, see Gregory D. Johnsen, 'A Profile of AQAP's Upper Echelon', Combating Terrorism Center at West Point, 24 July 2012.

296 **Godane . . . determined to transform:** Tim Lister and Paul Cruickshank, 'Ruthless leader aims to extend reach of al-Shabaab, eyes the West', CNN, 24 September 2013.

297 **'severe repercussions' in Kenya:** Paul Cruickshank and Zain Verjee, 'Kenya's high stakes Shabaab offensive', CNN, 24 October 2011.

297 **longed to take 'revenge':** This is my recollection. I do not have a saved copy of the email.

297 **Lewthwaite . . . was on the run:** Jeremy Stern, 'Samantha Lewthwaite: Whereabouts of Kenya attack suspect a mystery', BBC, 3 February 2014.

297 **Hammami:** For more on Hammami, see Andrea Elliot, 'The Jihadist Next Door', *The New York Times*, 27 January 2010, and J. M. Berger, 'Omar and Me', *Foreign Policy*, 18 September 2013.

297 **extraordinary video:** Tim Lister, 'American fears fellow jihadists will kill him', CNN, 16 March 2012.

298 **internal conflicts:** For more on the divisions within al-Shabaab, see Raffaello Pantucci and A. R. Sayyid, 'Foreign Fighters in Somalia and al-Shabaab's Internal Purge', The Jamestown Foundation Terrorism Monitor, 3 December 2013.

305 **a new plot by AQAP . . . intelligence services:** See Nic Robertson, Paul Cruickshank and Brian Todd, 'Saudi agent in bomb plot held UK passport, source says', CNN, 11 May 2012.

305 **What he lacked in power . . . with Washington:** See Gregory D. Johnsen, *The Last Refuge: Yemen, al-Qaeda, and America's War in Arabia*, W. W. Norton & Co., 2013.

26. Chinese Whispers

311 **sent him a text:** This is my recollection. I do not have a saved copy of this text exchange with Abdul.

315 **'Can you ask for the car keys?':** This is my recollection. I do not have a saved copy of this text.

27. A Spy in the Cold

318 **In July 2013 . . . alert:** Barbara Starr, 'Details emerge about talk between al Qaeda leaders', CNN, 9 August 2013.

318 **change the face of history:** This was how the threatening message was reported by President Abd Rabbu Mansour Hadi of Yemen. In a speech he related: 'When I was in Washington, the Americans told us that they had intercepted a call between Ayman al-Zawahri and Wuhayshi, in which Wuhayshi told Zawahri that they would carry out an attack that would change the face of history.' Mohammed Ghobari, 'Al Qaeda plan to "change face of history" led to U.S. scare', Reuters, 23 August 2013.

318 **more than twenty embassies:** 'US embassy closures extended over militant threat fears', BBC, 5 August 2013.

318 **number two of al-Qaeda globally:** UK Foreign and Commonwealth Office: 'AQ Core is no more: the changing shape of al Qaida', October 2013; Paul Cruickshank, 'Analysts: Terror warning may be linked to choice of al Qaeda chief deputy', CNN, 3 August 2013.

319 **been blooded:** Adil al-Abab, 'Gains and Benefits of Ansar al Shariah Control of Parts of the Wiyalahs of Abyan and Shabwa', available at http://www.longwarjournal.org/images/al-qaida-papers-how-to-run-a-state.pdf; Bill Roggio, 'AQAP's top sharia official killed in recent drone strike', *Long War Journal*, 20 October 2012.

321 **'Here's $10,000':** I later took a film of the cash on a table in my hotel room.

322 **'I'd like to take up the job':** The discussion about the job offer took place during a break in my recording.

322 **He had another proposal:** Klang made this proposal after I resumed recording.

323 **He and Anders indicated . . . shaking my hand.** This part of the conversation occurred after I stopped recording.

323 **a call in mid-August:** I did not record this call.

326 **I called Jesper one more time:** I did not record this call.

326 **on 7 October 2012, I texted Jesper:** This is my recollection. I do not have a saved copy of this text.

Epilogue

328 **Khalid Green, took to YouTube:** Khalid Green, 'Darse Twelve: Nullifiers of Islam', uploaded to YouTube 17 October 2012.When the book went to press the video was available here: http://www.youtube.com/watch?v=POLWQogyEuo.

329 **wrote on an Islamist blog:** This was posted on the Islamic Awakening blog. When this book went to press the posting was available here: http://forums.islamicawakening.com/f18/morten-storm-had-undercover-company-61838/index4.html#post659177.

331 **apologize to Naser Khader:** 'Naser Khader til Morten Storm: PET sagde du ønskede at slå mig ihjel', DR, 7 January 2014.

331 **'Out of consideration . . . killing of al-Awlaki in Yemen':** Orla Borg, Morten Pihl and Carsten Ellegaard, 'Jeg kunne hjælpe CIA og PET til at

spore Anwar, så amerikanerne kunne sende en drone efter ham og få ham slået ihjel', *Jyllands-Posten*, 7 October 2012.

332 **'the right balance . . .':** Justin Cremer, 'New Controls Over PET Announced in Wake of Media Storm', *Copenhagen Post*, 11 January 2013.

332 **heavyweight backing from Hans Jørgen Bonnichsen:** Maria Malmdorf Laugesen, 'Beautyboks kæder PET sammen med drab', TV2 (Denmark), 31 March 2013. The video of Bonnichsen's remarks is available at: http:// nyhederne.tv2.dk/article.php/id-66670423:beautyboks-k%C3%A6der-pet-sammen-med-drab.html.

333 **made out with a subordinate:** Kristian Kornø and Thomas Gösta Svensson, 'PET-chef jokede med affære', *Ekstrabladet* (Denmark), 7 November 2013.

333 **CIA to lose confidence:** Thomas G. Svensson, Kristian Kornø and David Rebouh, 'PET-folk: CIA stoler ikke på Scharf', *Ekstrabladet* (Denmark), 4 December 2013.

333 **Government insiders revealed:** Paul Cruickshank, phone conversation with Carsten Ellegaard Christensen, a journalist with *Jyllands-Posten*, December 2013.

333 **Morten Bødskov:** Peter Stanners, 'Morten Bødskov out as justice minister', *Copenhagen Post*, 10 December 2013; 'Leader of intelligence agency quits', *Copenhagen Post*, 3 December 2013.

333 **Bonnichsen, sharpened his criticism:** Preben Lund, 'Tvivl om PET-chefens rolle i drab på terrorleder', DR, 9 December 2013.

333 **'Is it really a satisfactory way . . .':** Morten Pihl, Orla Borg and Carsten Ellegaard, 'PET sagde nej til at beskytte eks-agent', *Jyllands-Posten*, 19 December 2013.

333 **Kenneth Sorensen . . . was killed:** Bill Roggio, 'Danish jihadist killed while fighting for Muhajireen Brigade in Syria', *Long War Journal*, 7 May 2013.

334 **Abu Khattab . . . Shiraz Tariq:** Tariq was killed late in 2013 after releasing a video he recorded in Syria. See http://www.b.dk/nationalt/martyrvideo-dansk-emir-kaempede-for-al-qaeda. On death of Abu Khattab see 'Danish Jihadist reportedly killed in Syria', *Copenhagen Post*, 13 January 2014.

334 **first British suicide bomber:** 'Video "shows British Syria suicide bomber"', BBC, 14 February 2014; 'Crawley Suicide Bomb Suspect in YouTube Film', Sky News, 16 February 2014; Kiran Randhawa, Justin

Davenport and David Churchill, 'Suicide bomber Brit worked as driver for hate cleric Omar Bakri', *Evening Standard*, 13 February 2014.

334 **Clifford Newman . . . child abduction:** *US v. Clifford Allen Newman*, 11th Circuit Court of Appeal, 17 August 2010, #09-14557.

336 **three of its operatives took part . . . in Benghazi:** Paul Cruickshank, Tim Lister, Nic Robertson and Fran Townsend, 'Sources: 3 al Qaeda operatives took part in Benghazi attack', CNN, 4 May 2013. According to a US Senate committee, fighters 'affiliated' with AQAP participated in the attack. See U.S. Senate Select Committee on Intelligence: 'Review of the terrorist attacks on U.S. facilities in Benghazi, Libya', 15 January 2014.

336 **liberated:** '14 "mostly Qaeda" inmates flee Yemen jail after attack', Agence France Presse, 13 February 2014.

336 **new generation of explosives:** Rhonda Schwartz and James Gordon Meek, 'Al Qaeda Threat: Officials Fear "Ingenious" Liquid Explosive', ABC News, 5 August 2013.

336 **new shoe bomb design:** Robert Windrem, 'U.S. Terror Warning is about Yemen Bombmaker', NBC News, 20 February 2014.

336 **instructing apprentices:** Paul Cruickshank, Nic Robertson and Tim Lister, 'Al Qaeda's biggest threat', CNN, 16 February 2012.

336 **siege that lasted four days:** Daniel Howden, 'Terror in Westgate Mall: the full story of the attacks that devastated Kenya', *Guardian*, 4 October 2013.

337 **The suspected mastermind . . . Ikrimah:** Nima Elbagir and Laura Smith-Spark, 'Norwegian may be suspect in Kenya attack', CNN, 18 October 2013.

337 **Hammami . . . killed a week before:** Paul Cruickshank, 'American jihadi reportedly killed in Somalia', CNN, 12 September 2013.

337 **Kenyan government report:** Kenya Situation Report, 26 August 2013.

337 **acquired safe houses:** Ibid.

337 **Two weeks . . . abandoned the mission:** See, for example, Henry Austin, 'SEAL Somalia target named as "Ikrima" as questions remain about aborted mission', NBC News, 7 October 2013.

338 **releasing a video . . . called for solo attacks:** The video appeared on jihadist forums on 2 June 2011. The American al-Qaeda propagandist Adam Gadahn says that 'America is absolutely awash with easily

obtainable firearms.' Anyone can 'go down to a gun show at the local convention center and come away with a fully automatic assault rifle without a background check and most likely without having to show an identification card'. He concludes: 'So what are you waiting for?'

339 **Michael Adebolajo:** 'Two guilty of Lee Rigby murder', BBC, 19 December 2013.

339 **The Boston bombers built . . . *Inspire* magazine:** See Indictment: *US v. Dzokhar Tsarnaev*, 27 June 2013.

339 **avenge the cleric's death:** James McKinley Jnr, 'Man Pleads Guilty to Reduced Charge in Terrorism Case', *The New York Times*, 19 February 2014.

343 **A group I had known in Luton:** 'Four "planned to bomb Territorial Army base" with toy car', BBC, 15 April 2013.

INDEX

Small Dogs Can Save Your Life

BEL MOONEY

Small Dogs Can Save Your Life

A Story of
Survival

Collins

First published in 2010 by Collins,
an imprint of HarperCollins*Publishers*
77–85 Fulham Palace Road
London W6 8JB

www.harpercollins.co.uk

1 3 5 7 9 10 8 6 4 2

Text © Bel Mooney 2010

Bel Mooney asserts the moral right to
be identified as the author of this work.

A catalogue record for this book
is available from the British Library.

ISBN: 978-0-00-731870-4

Printed and bound in Great Britain by
Clays Ltd, St Ives plc

Mixed Sources
Product group from well-managed
forests and other controlled sources
www.fsc.org Cert no. SW-COC-001806
© 1996 Forest Stewardship Council

FSC

FSC is a non-profit international organisation established to promote the
responsible management of the world's forests. Products carrying the FSC
label are independently certified to assure consumers that they come
from forests that are managed to meet the social, economic and
ecological needs of present and future generations.

Find out more about HarperCollins and the environment at
www.harpercollins.co.uk/green

For Gaynor and Ernie

(and Bertie too)

I worry.
I have to because nobody else does.
Some strange car comes up the driveway –
They go right on talking. They trust,
I don't. Threat crosses my nose
Twenty times a day.
No wonder I bark and menace,
Who knows who it could be at the door
'Specially in these times.
Arthur Miller, 'Lola's Lament'

How to resist nothingness? What power
Preserves what once was, if memory does not last?
For I remember little. I remember so very little.
Indeed, moments restored would mean the Last Judgement
That is adjourned from day to day, by Mercy perhaps.
Czeslaw Milosz, 'On Parting With My Wife, Janina'

You were never masters, but friends. I was your friend.
I loved you well, and was loved. Deep love endures
To the end and far past the end. If this is my end,
I am not lonely. I am not afraid. I am still yours.
Robinson Jeffers, 'The Housedog's Grave'

CONTENTS

INTRODUCTION

*What counts is not necessarily the size of the dog in
the fight; it's the size of the fight in the dog.*
**Dwight D. Eisenhower, Address,
Republican National Committee,
USA, 31 January 1958**

*W*hen I look in the mirror I see quite a small person:
not tall and quite slight. My skin bruises easily and
as I grow older I notice more and more weaknesses, from wrinkles to stiff limbs to hair that is no longer thick and beautiful,
as it once was. This is, of course, all inevitable. I can do no
more about it than I can change all the experiences, good and
ill, which have shaped the mind and spirit within this vulnerable, mortal frame. In this respect I am exactly like you, the
über-reader I always imagine as a friend when writing. We can
(men and women alike) anoint ourselves with unguents in an
attempt to keep time at bay but the most useful exercise for
the soul is to square up to your life, no matter how much it

1

terrifies you, and try to make sense of it. That is the true business of self-preservation and it is what I try to do in this book – in the hope that this small, individual journey, one woman's personal experience of love, loss and survival, may (quite simply) be useful. Most of us have endured, or will endure, pain in our lives. If this book has any message it is that recovery and salvation can come from the most unexpected sources, and that largeness of spirit will most equip you for your personal fight.

Working in my study one summer day, writing the journalism which pays the bills but wondering if I would ever return to fiction and slightly desperate for something – anything – to break that block, I flexed a bare left foot which touched my Maltese dog, Bonnie. She sleeps on a small blue bed, patterned with roses, which sits beneath my home-made work surface. All day she waits for attention, rising to follow me wherever I go in the house, longing for the moment when, feeling guilty, I at last suggest a short walk. At which point she leaps up, races up the stairs from the basement and scrabbles wildly at the front door, like a prisoner incarcerated in the Bastille who hears the liberators outside and screams, 'I'm here! Save me!'

On that day in 2008 I suddenly realized how great a part my dog had played in my own salvation, and that I wanted to write about that process. I was encouraged by the experience of an artist I admire very much, David Hockney, whose paintings and drawings of his two dachshunds, Boodgie and Stanley, show the pets curled on cushions, lapping water, rolling on their backs. You don't have to be a lover of small dogs to be delighted by these works, and yet they should not be underestimated, despite their simplicity. What looks like a set of speedily executed

2

images of two faintly absurd, brown sausage dogs adds up to an idiosyncratic statement about love.

In the introduction to *Dog Days* (the 1998 book which collects this work) Hockney writes, 'I make no apologies for the apparent subject matter. These two dear little creatures are my friends. They are intelligent, loving, comical and often bored. They watch me work; I notice the warm shapes they make together, their sadness and their delights.'

What does he mean by 'apparent subject matter'? He's painting his funny tubular dogs, isn't he? End of story. Yet not so. In an online interview the artist explained, 'I think the real reason I did them was as a way of dealing with the recent deaths of a number of my friends … I was feeling very down. And I started painting the dogs and realized this was a marvellous subject for me at this time, because they were little innocent creatures like us, and they didn't know about much. It was just a marvellous, loving subject.' Asked (mad question!) if the dogs had any sense they were the subject of Hockney portraits, the artist replied, 'The dogs think nothing of them really. They'd just as soon pee on them. They don't care about art since they're simply on to higher things – the source of art, which is love. That's what the paintings are about – love, really.'

So, on an unconscious quest to deal with loss and celebrate love, one of the most popular artists of our time stayed at home and 'saw the nearest things to me, which was two little dogs on cushions'. Similarly, on my own quest to understand how love can survive even an ending, how a marriage can go on reverberating even after divorce and how the process of reinvention in a human life reflects the very movement of the universe and must be embraced, I stayed at home and stroked the nearest thing to me, which was a tiny white dog with a feathery tail who needs me as much as I need her. I had so much to learn from the force of devotion within that minuscule frame.

Dogs are patient with us; they have little choice. They continue with their dogged work of saving our lives, even if we don't know it's happening. Long before my foot reached out to rub her soft white fur that day, my lapdog was asking me to regard her as Muse. She was demanding proper attention, as well as instinctive affection. She was saying, 'I'm here!' And it worked. Since then my 'animal companion' (as the modern phrase insists, implying equality rather than ownership) has inspired my 'Bonnie' series of six books for children, which stars a small white dog from a rescue home who, as the saga progresses, helps to cheer and restore one unsure, unhappy boy and his family.

Now she is the beginning, middle and end of this book's story too – and, like Hockney, 'I make no apologies for the apparent subject matter.' I am writing about what happened to me between 2002 and 2009, using my dog as a way into a painful story, and a way out of it too. During that time my marriage ended and life was turned on its head. What do dogs know about marriage? Probably a lot – because they are in tune to our feelings and it's hard to hide things from your dog. As I get older I want to share more, hide less. That's why I'm willing to invite others to come along on a walk with my pet, in the hope that the activity might act as 'therapy' for them, as it has for me. Dogs are good at therapy – so mine will help me tell this story of a love (affair). Or, rather, a tale of many loves.

It's not easy to embark on anything resembling auto-biography, although bookshops are flooded with usually ghosted 'celebrity' tomes and there seems to exist an avid readership for the recollections of (say) a footballer or his wife who are not yet 30. Too often that sort of thing is little more than an extension of newspaper or magazine gossip. What is written will be inevitably full of half-truths and blurred 'fact' as the celebrity dictates the view he or she wishes to present. Even the finest biography will be hampered by unknowing.

If the biographer feels impelled to smooth over instead of flay (and much flaying goes on these days, both in books and column inches, which I doubt adds to the greater good), how much more will the writer of a personal memoir feel the need to evade? As I was working on this book I was entertained (as well as appalled) to read a prominent newspaper diary item about my work in progress which shrieked 'Revelation!' – although not in so few words. The journalist predicted that I would be blowing the lid off relationships within my ex-husband's family, and so on. Now I ask you, why would I want to do that? I agree with the nineteenth-century historian Thomas Carlyle that in writing biography sympathy must be the motivating force. I have no aptitude for slashing and burning, and am glad to say that I shall go happily to my grave never having learnt the arts of war.

A partial life is a slice of reality – a taste which leaves us wanting more. The multifaceted art of memoir suggests that even a few months within a life, when something extraordinary happened, can offer a story of almost mythic power. In the 'new' life writing (a fascinating topic now, especially in the United States) the freedoms of fiction have been introduced into auto-biography and obliqueness is allowed. The writer can say, in effect: 'This is what happened that summer, and afterwards. It's not the whole story by any means, because much must remain private. Still, I offer this as an act of mediation. If it happened to you, this might help you survive. This might well stand between you and your nightmare.' That is what I am trying to do in this book – although not without knowledge of the pitfalls.

At the end of 2003 I encountered a successful woman writer who had read in the newspapers about the end of my 35-year-long marriage. 'I hope you're going to write a book about it!' she said with glee. I shook my head. 'But you must!' she went on. 'Tell it like it was! And if you don't want to write it as a true story, just turn it into a novel. People will know it's the truth. You'll do really well.' When I protested that I hated the idea, she asked, 'But why shouldn't you?'

Maybe her counsel made commercial sense, but her avidity drove me further towards reticence. There is enough personal misery swilling around the shelves of bookshops without me adding to the woe, I thought. After all, any celebrity autobiography nowadays is required to take us on a turbulent ride from trouble to trouble – dodgy parents, colon cancer, mental illness, alcohol and drug abuse and the rest. The non-celebrity stories deal in poverty, ill-treatment, sickness and perversion to a degree that would astound even Dickens, who knew about the seamier sides of life. A publishing bandwagon rolls along fuelled by pain and suffering, with the word 'misery' going together with 'memoir' – like 'love and marriage' or 'horse and carriage'. Happy lives, it seems, don't make good 'stories'. But some of the stuff published is not so much gut wrenching as stomach churning.

So this is not a misery memoir. No, this is a happiness memoir, although it deals with unhappiness and recovery. It is just one portion of the narrative of a few years in my life and in the life of one other significant person – the man I married in 1968. Other people close to us have been left out; I do not intend to embarrass either his second wife or my second husband, or indeed to reveal what members of our respective families said, thought or did. Still, since I told that person that I had no intention of writing about the dramatic break-up of my first marriage, things have changed – although my rejection of the notion of 'telling it like it was' is the same. For there is always more than one Truth. Because the experience and its aftermath would not go away, I found myself keeping a 'quarry' notebook for the novel which will remain unwritten, as well as my essential diaries and notebooks, and realized that my own process of learning from them would go on. In the end the impulse to write became like a geyser inside. The aim must always be to find meaning in what happened, for what else can a writer do? I have to agree with the screenwriter Nora Ephron who was taught by her writer parents unapologetically to view her own life as a resource.

So, yes, a memoir of happiness of sorts, because the good times and the bad are indivisible in my memory and roll on forever in the mind's eye like a magic lantern show, or (to be more up-to-date) what Joan Didion calls 'a digital editing system on which ... I ... show you simultaneously all the frames of memory that come to me now ... the marginally different expressions, the variant readings of the same lines'. Writing about the deaths (within days) of her husband, John Gregory Dunne, and her daughter, Quintana, Didion explains (in *The Year of Magical Thinking*) that the book is her attempt to make sense of the period that followed the deaths, which forced her to reconsider so many of her ideas about life, luck, marriage and grief.

Like Joan Didion I was forced to confront not physical death but a different sort of bereavement: the end of a way of life I had thought (somewhat smugly) would continue into a cosy old age. The shattering of that conviction made me confront a myriad of other certainties and set me upon a strange path through the woods – which led, after a while, to the decision to write this book.

'No,' I said to people during that process, 'I'm not writing an autobiography – I'm writing a book about dogs.' The oddness of that statement was enough to stop questions. It came to me one day that all the qualities we associate with dogs, from fidelity to a sense of fun, are ones I admire most in human beings. I also know that small dogs display those qualities in a concentrated form – pure devotion distilled to fill the miniature vessel. Of course, anthropomorphism is dangerous. It pleases us to attribute virtues to canine creatures, who have no moral sense, and when the decision was taken to erect a magnificent monument in central London to all animals killed in war, I remember thinking it feeble-minded to use words like 'loyalty' and 'heroism' and 'courage' about creatures who had no knowledge of such abstracts.

There's a famous Second World War story about an American war dog called Chips who was led ashore by his master, Private John R. Rowell, when his outfit landed at a spot known as Blue Beach, on Sicily's southern coast. They were advancing on the enemy lines in darkness, when they came under machine-gun fire from a pillbox which had been disguised as a peasant's hut. The troops flung themselves to the ground, but the dog charged the machine-gun nest, despite the stream of bullets. Private Rowell said, 'There was an awful lot of noise and the firing stopped. Then I saw one Italian soldier come out of the door with Chips at his throat. I called him off before he could kill the man. Three others followed, holding their hands above their heads.'

I doubt Chips was a titchy Maltese, a Yorkshire terrier or a papillon, although a feisty little Jack Russell might have done some damage, despite his size. Still, the issue is: can you call a dog 'brave'? Was a contemporary writer accurate to assert that 'this American war dog single-handed and at great risk to his own life eliminated an enemy machinegun position and saved the lives of many of his comrades'? Even the most passionate dog lover must admit that the soldier who acts does so in full knowledge of the consequences, carrying within his heart and mind images of parents, wife or girlfriend, children – and risking life despite all. But the dog does not. Men and women act from courage; animals merely act.

Is that true? I do not know – and nowadays I don't really care. In her profound work *Animals and Why They Matter* the philosopher Mary Midgely points out that 'a flood of new and fascinating information about animals' in recent years has educated people who mentally place animal welfare 'at the end of the queue'. She states her belief in 'the vast range of sentient life, of the richness and variety found in even the simplest creatures', and believes it irrelevant that a dog's experience is very different from our own. Philosophers and writers alike have long suggested the idea of the dog as (yes) a moral teacher. This is not fanciful. Anyone who has (for example) studied the psychology of serial killers will recognize the 'flies to wanton boys' argument behind Kant's words: 'He who is cruel to animals becomes hard also in his dealings with men … The more we come into contact with animals, and observe their behaviour, the more we love them, for we see how great is their care of their young.'

Once I was an ignorant young woman who professed dislike of these animals. Now in my sixties, the more I read about dogs and learn what an influence they have had on their owners and the more I love my own small example of the genus, the more I understand Franz Kafka's statement: 'All knowledge, the totality of all questions and answers, is contained within the dog.'

This story asks questions and offers some answers about change and how we can deal with it, in order to survive. It is also about dogs in history, art and literature, dogs as therapy, dogs as everything they can be to humans, helping us in the process of living. The narrative is aided by those diaries and notebooks which were such a catharsis and by a few extracts from my published journalism. I choose to tell this slice of a life discursively, because I have never trodden a straight path and love the side turning which leads to a hidden shrine. During a long career which began in 1970 I have worn many hats – reporter, profile writer, columnist, children's author, commentator on women's issues, travel writer, critic, radio and television presenter, novelist – but it is my latest incarnation which provided the final driving impetus to write this book. In 2005, rebuilding my life, I became – quite by accident, as I will explain – an advice columnist on first one, then another national newspaper. The truth is that, although I have loved all aspects of my working life, I find this the most significantly *useful* role I have ever played, apart from those of wife, mother, daughter and friend.

But the work causes me much sorrow too. So many letters, so much heartbreak, all transferred and carried within me, with none of the safeguards in place for the qualified psychotherapist. This has opened my eyes, in a way impossible before, to the pain caused by the end of love and the destruction of marriage, although the two do not necessarily go together. Oh, I know about the other forms of loss as well. When widows or widowers write to me from their depths of grief and loneliness, it is very hard to know what to say. Death has to be faced, but no such glib statement of the truth of existence is any use to those in mourning. Still, I do my best. I have never been afraid of writing about bereavement. It's easier than addressing vindictiveness, selfishness and despair.

How do you advise people who are dealing with the end of love, or (especially) the 'death' of a long marriage? What resources can be drawn on to cope with the loss of all you were and all you think you might have gone on to be, with that person at your side? How do we make ourselves whole again? The entirely unexpected end of my long marriage confronted me with those questions, and I bring some of the knowledge gained to my job and to this book. Some people will think that all should remain private but I have never been able to shut myself away, and remain unconvinced that battening down the hatches is useful. For one thing, the act of remembering halts the rush of time, as well as being profoundly healing. Seamus Heaney expresses this idea in *Changes*: 'Remember this. It will be good for you to retrace this path when you have grown away and stand at last at the very centre of the empty city.'

Second, I know it is helpful to share stories. My work as an advice columnist has proved to me without doubt that there is valuable consolation for others in telling how it was for you. To hell with privacy, I say – though not with reticence. We *need* each other's stories, all of us, just as I need my small dog. We have to be courageous, just as my dog is brave, no matter how small. We can learn from each other and go on learning, as I have learnt from her. The poet and naturalist David Whyte perfectly encapsulates the motivation behind this evocation of life and dogs:

> *To be human*
> *Is to become visible*
> *While carrying*
> *What is hidden*
> *As a gift to others.*

One

FINDING

There is much to learn from these dogs.
And we must learn these things over and over.
Amy Hempel

I never knew where she came from and will never know. The central mystery will always be there when I look at her, reminding me that my mirror offers a similar puzzle: *who are you?* It is a Zen question, the one Gauguin must have been thinking when he painted *Where Do We Come From? What Are We? Where Are We Going?*, every vibrant brushstroke telling us that the answer can never be known and the central mystery has to be accepted in your journey towards the end. All this I knew. But the coming of my little dog was to herald a deeper awareness: that we cannot know what will happen to us. Not ever.

Yet I have always needed to control things. Spontaneity makes me uneasy. I like to know the history of a house, the provenance of a picture, the origin of a quotation, because such knowledge is a hedge against chaos. I plot and plan. My books are arranged alphabetically or (depending on the subject) chronologically, and my shoes and gloves have to be ordered according to the spectrum. Years ago, having children presented me with a philosophical shock to match the physical and emotional pain, because those outcomes I could not control. A stillborn son and a very sick daughter served only to increase my need for form and structure. Retreating within the four walls of the life I planned was the only security. This was Home. Everything therein could be organized, a perfect bastion created to face down the imperfections in the world outside.

Then, quite unexpectedly, there came from nowhere the smallest dog. She pitter-pattered into my life before I could think but, had I stopped to consider, she certainly would not have been let in. These are the moments when the universe smiles and plays a trick. You get up one morning with no inkling that the day will bring a life-changing moment. The face of a future lover seen across a room, a sudden stumble which leaves you with a black eye, a phone call which will seem to leave your career in tatters, at least for a while. There can be no knowing what will pop out from under the lid of the scary jack-in-a-box – so be ready for it all (I advise people), because then you won't be surprised. But Bonnie surprised me. She slipped in under the radar. My permanent high-alert system must have short-circuited, leaving me wide open. The small dog arrived with the unstoppable force of a Sherman tank, changing things for ever.

You should always share things with the people you love, and make decisions together, but I decided on this tiny creature on impulse. I told no one – not even the most beloved of my heart – that a 'toy' dog, an animal fit only for laps and satin cushions, would come to live on our farm. What did I think when I first saw her – apart from the obvious, '*Ahh*, how can a dog be so small?' As I said, I did not *think* at all. But looking back, with fanciful hindsight, surely I knew she was destined to share my life. *Hers* was the face of the lover seen across a room – the new person, the One. How could I have known that this dog spoke to an urgent need I had not identified, whilst her mixture of vulnerability and toughness would prove an exact match for my own? Bonnie the abandoned creature was to become my saviour during my own time of abandonment; she who was so small taught me most of what I was to learn about largeness of spirit. The lessons carried within the soul of my little dog go on and on. But that is to jump ahead …

This is how it happened.

On 13 June 2002 I drove to Bath's Royal United Hospital for a meeting of the art committee. Our task was to cheer the corridors of the hospital with artworks, and to commission an original work of sculpture with funds from the National Lottery to 'animate the aerial space'. I liked that phrase; it would be a sort of hanging, flying creation in the atrium. It might distract patients afraid of this part of their life journey, reinvigorate families who face so much waiting and generally cheer up everyone who passed that way, from the consultant to the cleaner. My own life is enriched by art every day; naturally I agree that hospitals should be too. So I said I would join the committee, and give time and enthusiasm to the 'unnecessary' decoration of a necessary place.

But I dislike meetings; my claustrophobia kicks in within minutes and I want to leave, do a runner, get the hell out of the 'good works' and go home to a glass of wine and Al Green blasting loudly in the kitchen. I feel a fraud: a 'public' figure who is really somebody disreputable, who wants to hang out and do nothing. Yet the desire to flee fights with my need to give something back – for if you lead a life full of blessings you need to keep them topped up. This is karma: the meals on wheels of a good life. That day it was taking me nearer to my soulmate dog.

The committee met in the hospital's charity office and we were all sitting around waiting to start when the door opened and Lisa (one of the younger committee members) came in, holding something in her hand. Because of the table, I couldn't see properly; she came further into the room and I realized it was a dog lead. With something on the end of it. I craned my head and glimpsed a flurry of white. It was the smallest dog I had ever seen.

Lisa was the head of fundraising for the RSPCA's Bath Cats and Dogs Home. Strangely, J and I had been there for the first time ever, just two days earlier. We went to recover his beautiful Labrador Billie, my fiftieth birthday present to the husband who had everything else and therefore needed a dog. Here I must explain that I was never a dog lover – not as a child when my grandmother got a snappy corgi called Whiskey, nor at any other time in my life. Yet when J and I first met in our second year at University College London and went to visit his mother, I was entranced by his way with the family Labradors, Bill and Ben.

That was the end of 1967; I was 21 and in love and all was new. Everything that the 23-year-old philosophy student did entranced me: the way he hunched his shoulders in his navy pea coat, strode out in his green corduroys and whistled to those sleek black animals, his voice dipping and elongating their names – 'Biiiiill-eee! Bennn-eee!' – with musical authority. I was awkward and nervous as I stroked their velvety ears, making up to the dogs because I wanted to impress *him* – the cleverest, funniest, sexiest, most grown-up man I'd ever met. Those 'real' dogs seemed an extension of his capability. But I was incapable of seeing the point of his mother's precious little dachshund.

Twenty-seven years later, in January 1994, I knew that if I chose to buy him a black Labrador for his July birthday I would have to learn to look after a dog, for the first time in my life. It was a serious decision, for since J was away a lot, the main care would fall to me. And so I, who had resolutely set my face against our son Daniel's pleas for a dog all through his school days, finally capitulated to the reality of dog hairs, dog smells and tins of disgusting mush. I chose Billie (named by me after Billie Holliday. A control freak will even name a man's birthday dog) and liked her, but I didn't know how to love her. Naturally J was delighted by the surprise, and equally happy when, 18 months later, I gave him Sam, a scruffy Border collie, for Christmas. Anyone might think that I had turned myself into a dog lover, but it wasn't true. I liked them, but that's not enough for dogs. They aren't satisfied with being *liked*. I was a dog *minder*, that's all.

This is partly a story of home, for dogs know their place in the pack, and the pack needs its lair, its fastness, its refuge. In 1995 we had moved to our farm, J's dream home, in about 60 rough acres of pasture which we would farm organically. It was a mile down a track, just outside Bath's city boundary, and hung on the edge of a valley like Wuthering Heights, with winter weather to suit.

J briefly employed a girl to exercise his horses and one day, somehow when she was riding with the dogs near the road, Sam came home with her but Billie did not. Nor did she come for supper.

She was missing.

This was June 2002. In the warm night, pierced by the sharp cries of foxes, J roamed the fields with a torch, calling her name, fearing her stolen – for Billie-of-the-velvet-ears was a beautiful bitch. He was in despair. The next day I wrote a round robin letter, got into the car and posted my note through every letter-box within a radius of about half a mile. An hour later the telephone rang and a couple living up on the main road along the top of Lansdown (the ridge which saw one of the decisive battles in the Civil War) told me they had found a collarless black Labrador on the main road and called the dog warden. Billie was safe.

We left the house at a run and went to the RSPCA home to collect her. One of the many glorious things about dogs is that you need no proof of ownership – not *really*. Of course the microchip is a failsafe – but the point is, your dog *knows* you. When she was brought from her holding pen, Billie's face showed relief and joy to match our own. This is something non-doggy people do not understand: the expressiveness of the canine countenance. Dogs' faces change, just like their barks and body language; they may not be as evolved as our primate cousins but human love serves to 'humanize' them in the most expressive way.

Holding tightly to her lead, we saw rows of cages and heard the mournful sounds of dogs wanting to be found homes – a desire of which they could not possibly be cognizant, in the sense that we know, all too painfully sometimes, our own innermost wishes and needs. Nevertheless the desperate wanting was there in those barks and yelps, in the lolling tongues and mournful eyes of the homeless dogs, the pets who were not petted, the working dogs with no jobs. The dogs who wanted to be *known* as much as Billie knew us.

'Let's have a quick look,' I said to J.

We wandered about, but it was too sad.

'Let's go home,' J said.

So we did. Sam welcomed Billie with bounds of joy and lolloping tongue, snuffling his welcome. Even the cats, Django, Ella, Thelonius (Theo for short) and Louis, looked faintly pleased, because cats like the world over which they rule to be complete.

Then, just two days later, Lisa is entering that office with a dog on a lead, but not just any dog. My dog.

'I have never seen such a small dog,' I said. 'What on earth is it?'

'I think she's a shih-tzu', Lisa replied. 'She's in the dogs' home. I'm keeping her with me tonight – that's why she's here, because I'll go home after the meeting. These very small dogs get quite distressed in the home overnight and so if one comes in all of us take turns.'

My first assumption was that the small white dog was lost, as Billie had just been lost, but that was not the case. Lisa explained, 'She was abandoned – left tied to a tree in Henrietta Park.'

Henrietta Park is a pleasant patch of green but very central in the city, and I simply could not believe anyone could abandon such a small dog in a place where – who knows? – drunken oafs might make a football of her.

'Impossible,' I said. 'No way! Somebody must have had to rush off for a dental appointment or something, and forgotten her for a while.'

Lisa explained that it had happened two days before, and nobody had telephoned, and if the dog remained unclaimed in seven days' time, 'We'll be looking for a new home for her.'

By now I had the anonymous shih-tzu on my lap, but she was eager to get off. She wriggled and looked for safety in the person who had brought her, but I was overwhelmed by a need for her to settle down – to *like* me. This was the magical moment of rescue.

'I'll give her a home,' I said.

'Are you sure?'

'Quite sure.'

Looking back, I know that moments of rescue cut two ways.

I gave no thought to the muddy farm (no place for a white lapdog), or the cats (one of which, Django, scourge of rats and rabbits, was certainly bigger than this miniature mutt), or to J, a lover of 'proper' dogs. Real dogs. Big dogs.

Couples should discuss decisions together – I knew that. But in that second of saying '*I'll* give her a home' – that spontaneous, expansive welcoming of the small white dog – I knew instinctively that the personal pronoun was all that mattered. This was to be *my* dog. If I were to mention the idea to my husband, son, daughter, parents or friends they would all shake heads, suck teeth, remind me of hideous yapping tendencies and say it was a Bad Idea. They would talk me out of it, and this small dog would be taken by somebody else, who couldn't possibly (I was sure) give her as good a home as I would. So I would stay silent. This was nobody else's business. I who had never had a dog of my own because I had never wanted a dog of my own was transformed, in that instant, into a lady with a lapdog.

I knew Chekhov's story 'The Lady with the Little Dog', described by Vladimir Nabokov as 'one of the greatest stories ever written'. This tale of an adulterous love affair tells us much about human beings – but once I grew to know and love my dog I felt it showed less insight into women and dogs than I had thought. Before I am accused of trivializing a great work of literature because it lacks dog knowledge, I should point out that the mighty art critic John Ruskin was no different when he wrote, 'My pleasure in the entire *Odyssey* is diminished because Ulysses gives not a word of kindness nor of regret to Argus' – the faithful dog who recognizes him after 20 years.

Chekhov tells how a chance love affair takes possession of two people and changes them against their will. The story closes with them far apart and rarely able to meet. Gurov and Anna are both married. He works in a bank in Moscow, Anna lives in a dead provincial town near St Petersburg. Each has gone on a stolen holiday to Yalta, a fashionable Crimean resort notorious for its casual love affairs. Gurov is an experienced 40-year-old philanderer with a stern wife; Anna is married to a dull provincial civil servant, ten years older than she. The opening sentence of the story dryly establishes the holiday gossip which leads to Gurov's interest: 'People said that a new person had appeared on the sea front: a lady with a little dog.'

The dog is key to Anna's identity; wherever she goes 'a white Pomeranian trotted after her'. The dog is clearly inseparable from his mistress. Gurov's hunting instinct is aroused. One day he sees Anna sitting near him in an open-air restaurant. Her dog growls and he shakes his finger at it. Blushing, she says, 'He doesn't bite.' Gurov asks if he may give the dog a bone ... and so the affair begins.

But here is also where the problems start for the lover of small dogs. A week later Anna and Gurov kiss and make love. *But where is that Pomeranian?* That's what I want to know. The affair goes on – lunches, dinners, carriage drives, evening walks, bedroom intimacy – with no mention of the creature who was so inseparable from his mistress, 'the lady with the little dog'. No dog. For all his great knowledge of human nature Chekhov understands little about ladies and their little dogs, or more specifically, the protective and possessive nature of the Pomeranian tribe. The dog would have been ever present. Those growls would certainly not have ceased, especially when this strange man became intimate with the human being the dog loved. Small dogs do not give themselves as easily as women. Easily bored Gurov would likely have been irritated by the yapping and surely suffered a nip. As a real-life lady with a lapdog, I know this. The dog could not have been written out of the narrative so easily by a man who understood.

Small dogs keep loneliness at bay for women on their own. Small dogs take you out along the promenade, because you must think of your dog, no matter how you are feeling. That Pomeranian would surely have consoled Anna when she reached out a hand in the night to curl her fingers in soft white fur, wondering perhaps if any man was worth so much pain. Or any affair.

Bonnie too was to growl at men. So great was her natural hostility to the faint whiff of testosterone, we speculated that it must have been a man who had tied her to that tree, or an unscrupulous puppy breeder who had decided her back legs were a touch too long for breed 'standard', or an unpleasant son whose elderly mother had succumbed to dementia and couldn't be bothered with her pet. The novelist in me made up stories, but never convincingly, since my imagination quailed at the image of anybody tying this vulnerable young dog to a tree and walking away. I pictured the small creature straining to follow, then being choked back by the lead. Or was it a rope? I never discovered the details.

Men she might not like, yet she was never hostile to J. He was in London on 20 June when I was telephoned by the rescue home and told that nobody had come forward and so the dog could be mine. I should explain that it is policy to make a home visit to be sure that the putative owner is responsible and the place is suitable – but Lisa knew our home, knew us well, and so there was no need. In the time between 'finding' my dog and collecting her I had researched and discovered the 'shih-tzu' was in fact a Maltese, and had already named her Bonnie, after Bonnie Raitt, the singer whose music I always played in my car. This habit of naming animals after musicians (Sam was Sam Cooke, Billie, Billie Holiday) was a foible of mine; it gave cohesion to the menagerie.

I left the house at a run, went to the supermarket for unfamiliar small-dog food and straight to the home to collect her, paying them a goodly sum for the privilege. They estimated her age at six months but, other than saying she was in good condition when found, still knew nothing about where she had come from. Bonnie would never give up her secrets; I looked into her jet-button eyes and wondered who she might be missing, what kind of house she knew, what damage had been done to her. Those who study dog psychology and behaviour know that dogs from rescue homes frequently display separation anxiety – but at the time I didn't know this. Bonnie and I were only just setting out on our journey together.

She was still my secret, not mentioned to anyone – neither daughter and confidante Kitty, nor close family friend Robin, a photographer who rented the cottage next door to our farmhouse (and with whom I occasionally worked on assignment), nor my parents – and certainly not the husband. I knew he would not want this silly scrap of a creature, and therefore need only know the *fait accompli*. But he was out when I called with the news, leaving me to recount my triumph to a disbelieving daughter, who was then living in our London house.

'*You*? *You've* got a little dog? No!'

A day later came J's voice on the phone – cool and faintly accusatory.

'What's this about a little dog? It hasn't got a bow in its hair, has it?'

'Not yet,' I replied.

He did not sound pleased.

Two days later J arrived home after his Sunday political programme on ITV, arriving at the farm after the two-hour drive from London, glad to be home. As always, Billie and Sam raced to meet his car – and right from the beginning Bonnie raced everywhere with the big dogs, who regarded her with puzzled amusement. With no practice, she became part of the welcome committee. Seeing her, J dropped on his knees in his Italian suit and, as the Labrador and collie pranced around their master, held out his arms to the small dog, who covered his face with licks. That, you see, is the point about *true* dog lovers – those in touch with the canine spirit. They can retain no sizeist prejudice when they realize that, although the eyes are tiny and the tail is an apology for a silk whisk, the potential for devotion which characterizes proto-dog abounds in the toy. J adored her – and it took just one week of us attempting to put her to bed in the 'dog room' with the other dogs and the four cats, one week of hearing her jump out through the dog flap into the darkness rich with smells of foxes, badgers, owls, stoats, rats, before she wangled her way on to our bed. And this is where comfort dogs belong.

Do you believe in signs? I do, for Billie going missing and taking us to the RSPCA home was one such. And less than a month before I first saw my small dog I had met two others, who had fascinated me. For some years I had been presenting a yearly series on BBC Radio 4 called *Devout Sceptics*, which took the form of a one-to-one interview about faith and doubt, a searching conversation between me and someone well known in fields of literature, politics, science and ideas. In May 2002, with my producer and friend Malcolm Love, I had been in California, to interview Dr Pamela Connolly in Los Angeles, Amy Tan in San Francisco and Isabel Allende in San Rafael. On 24 May we were up early to fly from LAX to San Francisco. Coming in to land I felt that old lifting of the heart with excitement, not just caused by the eternal promise and threat of travel, but because I love the United States and always feel truly myself there.

We took a cab to the Holiday Inn on Van Ness and California, and checked in, but had no time to change, because our appointment with Amy Tan loomed. I was looking forward to the interview; I loved Tan's novels and anticipated a good conversation about God and destiny. Having looked up our destination, in the smart, leafy Praesidio area of the city, Malcolm suggested that on such a fine morning it would be good to walk there. I agreed, but neither of us remembered that San Francisco is up hill and down dale – with the result that when we arrived at the address I was flustered and sweaty, which state seemed to increase as Tan's PA showed us into the huge, elegant condominium, furnished thickly with oriental furniture and fine *objets* which made you afraid to move. There was a crescendo of yapping from one corner; at the sight of us two miniature Yorkshire terriers created a tiny commotion behind a 10-inch barrier which penned them in. I gaped at the dogs – at that time, the smallest I had ever met. But they made me feel better, for when Amy Tan herself glided into the room, astonishingly beautiful in green pleated silk and soft leather ankle boots, I was able to disguise my discomfiture at being less than elegant by fussing over her pets. This much I knew – all people like to have their pets fussed over.

What I did not realize was that Bubba and Lilly were far more than dogs to Amy. We settled down for the interview and Malcolm fitted out microphones, noting with approval how quiet the condo was, the acoustic deadened by thick carpets, drapes and all that furniture. The little Yorkies nestled on her lap and Tan's slim fingers played with their ears as Malcolm took a sound level. Then he stopped.

'Er … Amy … I'm picking up noise from the dogs.'

'Oh really? Doing what?'

'Licking your hands – and snuffling. Er … do you think they could wait in another room while we do this?'

There was one of those moments of silence when the temperature drops a fraction and you know, as an interviewer, that this *faux pas* could spoil things. I caught the corner of Malcolm's gaze, knowing how much he (a man of great sensitivity, especially to women) wished he could recall the impertinent suggestion.

Then Amy Tan said coolly, 'The dogs have to *stay*. The *dogs* are *essential*.'

'Of course they are!' I cried.

Malcolm backtracked. 'Yes, I *absolutely* understand … Uh … but maybe they don't have to lick your hands?'

Pause.

'Sure.'

The novelist kept her hands out of reach of her pets' pink tongues, and the dogs settled down to sleep amidst the folds of her green silk, except for the occasional moment when I would intercept a beady gaze asking me what the hell I was doing there. Or perhaps sourcing that slight odour of perspiration. They yapped once during the next hour, but the interview was going so well by then it didn't matter. And when it was over Tan (more relaxed now) told me how she hates to travel in Europe since she can't take her dogs, how she loathes being in hotel rooms alone and how she dreads the thought of anything happening to her beloved pets. Her words intensified my impression of fragility wrapped in self-contained eccentricity.

As Malcolm and I walked to the restaurant she had recommended for lunch, I delivered myself – solemnly and with a certain degree of patronizing pity – of the opinion that those 'teacup' Yorkies were surrogate children for Amy Tan and her husband, Louis. Oh, statement of the obvious! What did I know? In the same way, years before when we were young, I had found some pathos in the fact that J's elderly aunts, who lived together, posted birthday cards to each other signed from their toy poodles, Lavinia and Amanda-Jane. Later I would shake my head in disbelief on reading, in a magazine profile, that the novelist Jilly Cooper kept a picture of her dead mongrel in a locket. I was smug in my refusal to acknowledge true value in that level of affection for an animal. How fitting it was that hubris would arrive on my horizon shaped as a small dog.

Malcolm was to tease me a few weeks later, when he was editing out those yaps and one or two small dog breaths for the finished programme, and I had already fallen in love with Bonnie. He laughed that the day in San Francisco had turned me into an aspirational copycat who realized that real literary ladies must have dogs. I huffed and puffed at the joke against myself – still resisting the notion that I could be perceived as one of those women with a handbag dog.

What matters is how profoundly I've come to understand what it meant to Amy Tan to have those comforting dogs on her lap as talismans and as inspiration. And now it is I who, with no irony, describe myself as my dog's 'Mummy'. She is as necessary to me now as Amy Tan's two were to her, and just as restricting of the impulse to travel, or even go to restaurants. I send cards from her and expect them back. Just three weeks after the encounter with Amy Tan and her dogs my diary entry reads, '*I adore Bonnie. She has transformed everything.*'

But even then I could not have known that the real transformation would be a work in progress. The dog would make me take myself less seriously – changing me into a foolish woman who would later buy a cushion saying 'Dogs Leave Paw Prints on your Heart' in Minnesota; a *petit point* of a Maltese in Portland, Maine, as well as a lobster-patterned macintosh, lead and collar set; a Navajo jacket and turquoise suede collar and lead complete with silver conchos in Santa Fe; a pink outfit in Brussels; a red set in Cape Town; cool Harley-Davidson accessories in Rapid City, South Dakota; 'bling' sparkles from a shop in Nice; and more. Not to mention purple mock-croc from an internet site for her bridesmaid's outfit ... but that was much later. Small-dog madness, I was to discover, is a worldwide phenomenon.

I concentrate on the trivial deliberately. These are necessarily small steps towards the big jump into that unknown which Bonnie brought with her but which was to drag me, too, into a pit of unknowing.

Smallness, I began to discover, fills some people with an irrational hatred, when they see a chihuahua, a Pekinese, a Yorkshire terrier, a Japanese chin, a shih-tzu, a pug. 'What's *that*?' asked a young man I know when I took Bonnie to his parents' house for lunch. Not to be outdone, his father joined in, suggesting with gentle mockery that Bonnie was 'not a proper dog'.

'Is the wren any less of a bird because he's small?' I demanded, drawing myself up to my full height (without heels) of 5 feet 3 inches.

'Aren't we allowed to tease you over your dog?' he asked, dryly.

I made a measured *so-so* movement with my hand and the subject was dropped.

One day in Bath a pierced and tattooed man in his late twenties said loudly to his big dog, who was pulling menacingly on its string towards Bonnie, 'Leave it! It's not a dog, it's a rat on a lead!' I was filled with a protective fury which took me by surprise. This new feeling was one of many signs that I too had entered into an ancient transaction, known to all owners of small dogs throughout the centuries. What else is this but an example of Darwinian survival? Survival, of course, will gradually unfold as the subject of this book – and so it is fitting to introduce it here, in the destiny of the small dog.

Of course Bonnie, like all canines large and small, is descended from wolves and somewhere – way, way back in her genetic blueprint – a part of her soul is roaming the forests and hills, filling the night with mournful howls to others of her kind. But I admit there is little of that behavioural memory evident in the animated powder puff on my lap. Now *I* am her kind, the leader of her small pack, and it is I to whom she calls, in those unmistakably shrill tones. She knows I will hear, swoop, soothe, hold fast. Out there in the wild the small dog would certainly perish, and therefore it has evolved an effective method of survival: being loveable. The transaction says, 'I will adore you and, in exchange, you – my very own human

– will protect me. Where you go I shall go, when you are full of sorrow I shall comfort you, and in return you will be my shield against the world.'

Or, as Elizabeth Barrett Browning put it when she fell in love with her small spaniel, Flush, who became her consolation and saviour: 'He & I are inseparable companions, and I have vowed him my perpetual society in exchange for his devotion.'

Those who dislike small dogs on principle sometimes ask, 'What are they *for?'* The acutely intelligent Border collie is bred to herd sheep and when not trained to do so it will neurotically round up anything it can, as if to be deprived of your function is to lose identity. Working dogs have a purpose. The veterinarian Bruce Fogle explains that the domestic dog (*Canis familiaris*) has the same number of chromosomes as the wolf, 78, and that over eons different canine cultures emerged. There were hunting dogs, herding dogs, guard dogs and, later, breeds to 'flush, point, corner, retrieve, or sit quietly on satin cushions'.

Later Fogle asserts that the chihuahua 'was bred to act as a hot water bottle', which contains some truth – and yet I suspect that two references to cushions in his book *The Mind of the Dog* indicate a man whose love of dogs grows in proportion to their size. Many men proclaim a dislike of small dogs. Is the opposite of a proper dog a fake dog? Or might it be an 'improper' dog, carrying with it a sense of scented, snuggling, sensual, stroking intimacy, such as would make any man jealous? In the sixteenth century a clergyman named William Harrison included in his *Description of England* a satirical assault on women and lapdogs:

They are little and prettie, proper and fine, and sought out far and neere to satisfie the nice delicacie of daintie dames, and wanton womens willes; instruments of follie to plaie and dallie withal, in trifling away the treasure of time, to withdraw their minds from more commendable exercises, and to content their corrupt concupiscences with vain disport, a sillie poore shift to shun their irksome idleness. These Sybariticall puppies, the smaller they be the better they are accepted, the more pleasure they provoke, as meet plaiefellows for minsing mistresses to beare in their bosoms, to keep companie in their chambers, to succour with sleepe in bed, and nourish with meet at bord, to lie in their laps, and lick their lips as they lie in their wagons and couches.

I wondered, from the tone of this, if the Canon of Windsor's wife had taken up with a toy spaniel. In fact, I find he was plagiarizing a scientific work published seven years earlier by John Caius, MD, court physician to Edward VI, Mary and Elizabeth I and President of the Royal College of Physicians. Our Western concept of breeds was first recorded in his *Short Treatise of English Dogges* in 1570. In this useful work I meet Bonnie:

There is, beside those which wee have already delivered, another sort of gentle dogge in this our Englishe soyle … the Dogges of this kind doth Callimachus call Melitoeos, *of the Island Melita, in the sea of Sicily, (which this day is named* Malta, *an Island in deede famous and reoumed …) where this kind of dogges had their principall beginning.*

He continues, 'These dogges are little, pretty, proper, and fine …' and so on, although the magnificent phrase 'Sybariticall puppies' is the Revd Harrison's own. Dr Caius goes on to make a perceptive point about lapdogs, which I would not have been able to understand in 2002, when Bonnie was so new, as I do now. Criticizing a female tendency to delight in dogs more than in children, he guesses at mitigating circumstances: 'But this abuse peradventure reigneth where there hath bene long lack of issue, or else where barrenness is the best blossom of bewty.' The small dog as child substitute? Of course – for there are many ways to save a life, and this is one to which I shall return.

That summer we took Bonnie to stay on our new boat, a Puget Sound cabin cruiser which was moored at Dittisham, on the river Dart in Devon. J bought the dog a tiny 'pet float' and each morning he would rise early, dress her in her red life jacket and row to the shore so that she could relieve herself. My lack of rowing skills was a good excuse, but in truth, he never once complained. I would stand on deck and watch him, remembering our honeymoon in that very village (so cold in February 1968, while this July gave us the hottest day of the year) and loving the fact that he was so at home on the water which scared me, a non-swimmer. By now he loved my dog; why else would he have agreed that she should come on holiday while Billie and Sam and all the cats remained behind on the farm, taken care of by my father? The dog came everywhere with us and when, after a few days, I developed an inexplicable pain in my right arm, my daughter suggested it must be a repetitive strain injury, caused by clutching Bonnie so tightly. Of course.

Bonnie was sitting between us as J and I heard *Devout Sceptics* broadcast at 9.00 a.m. on Radio 4, Amy Tan's voice filling the cabin as the waves made their soft slapping sound against the blue hull and J listening with his characteristic intensity. I imagined those tiny Yorkies on her knee, her long fingers held carefully out of reach of their tongues, as she talked about her belief that there is a benevolent spirit in the world, larger than any individual. 'That works with the concept of a god,' she said – and went on to link it with the idea of, not so much forgiveness in the Christian sense of the word, but compassion. Her voice was quietly firm as she told me that her aim was to learn about 'this notion of compassion', about empathy with her fellow human beings – which she defined as 'another way of saying Love'.

She added that of course you cannot measure love – it cannot be scientifically proven, no more than the idea of an afterlife. Yet she could say, 'Yes, I believe this,' because she finds 'intuitive emotional truth' in the idea each day of her life and in the writing of her novels.

As I re-read her words today (the interview was printed in my book, *Devout Sceptics*) I realize how much Amy Tan's philosophy informs my own life, and that the meeting with her and her small dogs was significant in more ways than one. Everything that has happened to me since Bonnie arrived from nowhere has at once tested and confirmed it. What's more, the entirely serious lessons my little dog has taught me confirm her optimism. There is no doubt in my mind what small dogs are 'for'.

But it was still so new. My diary entries record the process of dog intoxication – for that is indeed what it was. As the

American genius Amy Hempel wrote in her short story collection *The Dog in the Marriage*, '… you don't just love the dogs, you *fall* in love with them.' In the summer of 2002 I wrote in my diary:

> *27 June – Bonnie has transformed things. She is so sweet I want her to be with me all the time.*

> *3 July – I find it hard to concentrate on the novel because I spend too much time fussing over Bonnie.*

> *23 July – Bonnie continues to delight me. It is a strange feeling – to love a dog.*

Bonnie fitted easily into the Devon part of our life, although some of the old friends teased the lady with the lapdog. I suppose I can understand, because it was so unexpected to see me in that role; nevertheless we must all allow people to change. And I had changed. Instead of being impatient on the boat and feeling marooned I relaxed, strolling with the dog and gazing at the water, soothed by the ceaseless pinging of rigging in the breeze. Looking back, that summer seems idyllic. Robin had rumbled into the village on his Harley-Davidson, and joined us on the boat. Our son Daniel arrived, tense but liberated at the end of a long relationship. Kitty's boyfriend left early and she was upset. We spent time with the grandparents, I cooked meals in the boat's small galley, J took care of Bonnie's needs … and so family life went. From the time they were babies our children had loved that village, the scene of our many shared family holidays, not to mention our honeymoon.

The weather was hot, but a sudden squall disrupted J's birthday celebrations on the last day of July. No drinks on the boat for family and friends, but dinner in the local café for a pile of us. My diary records, '*The wine flowed and the noise rose and Bonnie sat on my lap and I thought how lucky we are to have all these talented, interesting and deeply kind Devon friends. It was a fabulous night.*' On another evening we joined friends for a beach barbecue. Suddenly fireworks from a celebration up the river filled the sky with falling flowers and stars and '*illuminated the evanescence of it all*'.

The year 2002 marked the jubilee of Her Majesty The Queen. The country which had in March confounded all republicans by mourning the death of Queen Elizabeth the Queen Mother joined in celebration of the fifty-year reign of her daughter. J and I had watched the London procession on television. We are both monarchists: my grandmother cleaned houses for a living and served lunches in a girls' school, yet the Royal Family was part of her sense of identity, like her quiet belief in God and love of her family. She liked to show me pictures of the young Prince Charles and Princess Anne, cutting them out of the *Daily Mirror*. She liked the smart woollen coats with velvet collars and buttons worn by the children of the upper classes.

In contrast, J's father, Richard Dimbleby, was an icon for my grandparents' and parents' generation: the most famous broadcaster the country had ever known, revered by the public first for his fearless war reporting, for his shocking, shattering dispatch as the first journalist into Belsen, and then for his commentaries on great events (the funerals of George VI, Sir

Winston Churchill and John F. Kennedy and the coronation of Elizabeth II) when the poetic dignity of his spoken prose expressed the deepest feelings of the majority of British people. When I first met the philosophy student (two years after his father had died) and told my parents I was dating 'Richard Dimbleby's son' they were awestruck. It was hard for me to believe too.

From different worlds we came, J and I, meeting in the second year of our respective courses and marrying after just three months, so much in love there was nothing else to do. It was just like fireworks – and naturally the years of married life would whoosh, crackle and bang too, sometimes so dangerously. Yet those first flames still had the power to warm, and the showers of stars still hung in the sky, even if sometimes behind clouds.

In 1994 he had published his much-admired biography of the Prince of Wales, a considerable achievement which came not without stress – largely due to the fact that J's simultaneous two-hour documentary about the Prince on ITV had included a short admission of adultery. The world seemed to go mad. J, a political journalist who was initially dubious about taking on the Royal project, knew that he had to ask the Prince about the state of his marriage to Princess Diana and his relationship with the then Camilla Parker-Bowles. He felt that the boil of sleazy gossip and tittle-tattle had to be lanced – and so, under firm but gentle questioning, the Prince revealed to the watching millions that once his marriage to Diana had irretrievably broken down he had started a relationship with Camilla. He would have been damned if he hadn't but was damned for telling the truth. At the same time, many people said that J ought not to have asked the question, although had he not he would have been pilloried for failing to do his journalistic job.

It was an exhausting time. Side by side we faced it all down but, seasoned journalists as we both are, we were unprepared for the tabloid feeding frenzy and the level of vitriol that was unleashed upon the heir to the throne – a much-misunderstood man whom J called in the closing words of his biography 'an individual of singular distinction and virtue'. I recall J standing in our garden or sitting in the library at the farm doing endless interviews with CNN, ABC, Sky, etc. and for a while it seemed as if he was almost the only one who would analyse and interpret not just the Prince of Wales but the British monarchy to the rest of the world. Although he did it with cool insight it was not a role he relished – not at all – but it was to be repeated after that terrible day at the end of August 1997 when Princess Diana died in a car crash in Paris with her lover, Dodi Fayed.

Looking back, the era of his biography and TV documentary seems oddly innocent. It is astonishing to remember that the Prince of Wales had wished to protect his estranged wife by *not* revealing all the detailed information J had in fact discreetly accumulated about Diana and her many problems. A few years later a slurry of cheap, gossipy books, prurient television programmes and mean memoirs by seedy staff would ensure no compassion or respect whatsoever for the dead Princess or for her living sons and ex-husband. Britain was turning into a pit bull of a nation.

The Prince loves dogs and in J's documentary one of his two Jack Russells appeared, jumping about in a Land-Rover as Jack

Russells will, and being told in no uncertain terms, 'Get *down*, Tigger!' Tigger had puppies; one went to Camilla Parker-Bowles and the Prince kept another, which he called Roo but Prince William renamed Pooh. In April 1995 Pooh vanished at Balmoral. This became an instant news story, the animal-loving British public responding with all the interest a beloved lost dog deserves. Jilly Cooper wrote a heartfelt piece about 'poor little Pooh' in the *Daily Mirror*, while the *Daily Mail* ran photos of the dog captioned 'Pooh: loved and lost by a prince'. The Jack Russell had been on a walk with her owner and her mother, when she ran off into the woods. Charles's whistles brought no response, and a three-day search by estate workers was fruitless. Neither an advertisement in the local paper nor the *Daily Mail*'s offer of a good reward brought forth anyone who had seen the dog. As a heartbroken Prince headed back to London on 21 April there was no shortage of theories about Pooh's fate. Some suggested that the dog had become stuck in a rabbit hole, as Jack Russells will, while a psychic asserted that she had 'a very clear picture' of Pooh stuck in a sewer. The *News of the World* gleefully theorized that she was devoured by a feral cat dubbed the Beast of Balmoral.

Such a fuss about a dog. Yet the true dog lover – the person I was metamorphosing into in 2002 – understands it. Once you love a dog you cannot bear the thought of losing your pet and you will torment yourself imagining your dog being kidnapped, or dying. No wonder the Prince of Wales put up a memorial to Tigger at Highgrove, when, in 2002, his beloved dog had to be euthanized because of old age.

That same year, Bonnie accidentally went to Highgrove and met the heir to the throne. For most human beings this would have been exciting, but it was quite an event for a nobody, a dog from nowhere who, just months earlier, had been left tied to a tree – a progression surely worthy of Eliza Doolittle. Yet like Eliza, she took it in her small stride.

Needless to say she had a royal welcome.

For centuries the Royal Family has embraced dogs as their favoured pets. Formal portraits from the seventeenth century onwards show kings, queens and their children happily posing with their beloved animals, from pugs to greyhounds, King Charles spaniels to corgis. Although we associate the British aristocracy with hunting dogs, big dogs with a serious role in life, the Royal Family has always loved smaller hounds too. Some pets have even merited their own portraits, and (as in many households) were considered members of the family. Photographs from the Royal Collection prove how much dogs were valued. A photograph of Queen Victoria's son, the Duke of York, shows him with his pug and is full of a playful humanity we can all recognize. The dog is wrapped in a greatcoat and its royal owner has tied a handkerchief around its head. The dog looks at the camera, the Prince looks down at the dog, full of mirth.

In 1854 the total cost of photographing the dogs in the Royal Kennels and mounting the prints in a special handsome album came to £25 19s. – the equivalent of around £1,650 today. When Queen Victoria's beloved collie Noble died at Balmoral in 1887, he was buried in the grounds of the castle and given his own gravestone, which reads:

> *Noble by name by nature noble too*
> *Faithful companion sympathetic true*
> *His remains are interred here.*

A terrier named Caesar belonging to Edward VII was given even greater status when, having outlived the King, he walked behind His Majesty's coffin in the funeral procession.

Elizabeth II favours the corgi. The breed was introduced to the Royal Family by her father, George VI, in 1933, when he bought a corgi called Dookie from a local kennels. The animal proved popular with his daughters, so a second corgi was acquired, called Jane, who had puppies, two of which, Crackers and Carol, were kept. For her eighteenth birthday, the Queen was given a corgi named Susan from whom numerous successive dogs were bred. Some corgis were mated with dachshunds (most notably Pipkin, who belonged to Princess Margaret) to create 'dorgis'. The Queen's corgis travel with her to the Royal residences, and Her Majesty looks after them herself as much as possible. Other members of the Royal Family own dogs of various breeds. The Duchess of Cornwall owns two Jack Russell terriers, Tosca and Rosie.

The day Bonnie went to a Royal residence the country was tossed by storms, with gales of up to 90 mph which screamed around our farm on the hill. Branches cracked from the beech wood and the trees groaned as if in agony. In my diary I wrote, '*I feel overwhelmed by all I have to do, but Bonnie is such a consolation*', but on that day it was hard to walk out with the three dogs and not be blown sideways by the power of the gale. Looking at Bonnie you would have thought she could be blown away, like a tuft of thistledown.

Earlier in the week we had been at the Booker Prize dinner, to see the outsider Yann Martel awarded the plum for *The Life of Pi* and to mingle with peers and swap gossip. When at such events I always feel two people: one at home within the glitz, the literary glamour, but the other detached, wanting to be at home – especially once the Maltese came to stay. The diary captures this feeling, recording, rather than a desire to be in London, '*I want to be home to see Bonnie. The little dog ties me to the farm emotionally more than ever.*' I also wrote, '*Home, home, home*', with no explanation, as if the repetition of what gave me security would fix it for ever. Now I see that scribble as a litany of faith. It was the only faith that possessed me completely.

On Sunday night J and I were due at Highgrove for dinner, and our friend and neighbour Robin offered to drive us. The journey is only 35 minutes' drive from where we lived, yet it would have been less than convivial for J to refuse a glass or three of wine, and even less wise to exit past the policemen having done so. So we left the dogs and barrelled along past fallen trees to arrive at the handsome Georgian house, just outside Tetbury, in Gloucestershire. I loved going there. The house is not overly grand; nor does it have an intimidating atmosphere. From the hats, boots and baskets at the entrance to the comfortable furniture which sometimes bears the marks of dogs (I remember an old chintz that had been shredded and was waiting repair) Highgrove is a genuine home, full of family photographs and treasured mementos.

Camilla was driving herself from her own home, and was late. The Prince fixed us drinks from the trolley, and as always I sensed a hunger within him to talk to someone like J about the issues he cares about: agriculture, the environment, educa-tion and so on. As on many previous visits he seemed strangely lonely: a good man marooned in a difficult role, frequently misunderstood and feeling it too keenly for his own good. At last Camilla blew in like a gust from a rather more robust world. My diary observed: '*She is warm and full of mirth – rejoicing that the* Panorama *programme about her is on TV tonight but she doesn't have to watch it because she is with us!*' While the men talked about serious things she and I perched on the leather fender and smoked a cheeky cigarette, puffing the smoke up the chimney as we chatted.

It was a good evening – and when the time came for Robin to pick us up, we were surprised to see Bonnie scamper into the room. With advance warning from the gate the staff had opened the front door and in she went – small dogs do not stand on ceremony. Robin told us later he hadn't had the heart to leave her behind, since she made such a pathetic fuss as he put on his coat. Astonished by her size (very small compared to a Jack Russell) the Prince and Camilla gave her maximum attention and were fascinated by her story of abandonment and rescue. Camilla's elderly, almost-blind terrier smelt the sweet young female and noticeably perked up, chasing her about. Bonnie responded flirtatiously and, vastly entertained, the Prince roared his contagious, bellowing laugh of which Falstaff would have been proud.

On the way home J and I agreed how much we liked 'doggy' people. At last I was including myself in their number.

The Royal Family's traditional affection for dogs might well be an antidote to the fuss that surrounds them. The Prince of Wales is, to his dog, just an owner, a human companion who offers treats and strokes and is always ready to stride out into the indescribably thrilling grass and trees. The dog is always there, always loyal. He will not sell his memoirs; nor will he bite the hand that feeds him. There are no complications; the dog does not have to say 'sir' or bow, and yet he will obey. I can imagine the Prince striding over the countryside he loves and telling a dog everything, knowing that whatever he says will never get back to the newspapers, nor be captured by any paparazzo's telephoto lens.

I would be telling lies if I told you that at this stage in my life I looked at my small white lapdog and saw in her a teacher. Yet I should have done, for the lessons were already beginning. For example, one day I hit her – for the first and last time. It was not a savage blow. The big dogs would not have noticed such a swat and the cats would have easily avoided it. But a padded envelope arrived containing a copy of my latest children's book – the first off the press. It is always an exciting moment for an author – that pause of satisfaction when you hold the fruit of your labour in your hand, look at it, admire your own name and think, I made this. That day I had put the book down on the futon in my study, gone to make coffee and returned to find that the young dog (less than one year old after all) was chewing the corner of my new book. And so I picked it up, swatted her and yelled, 'No!'

I did not know (neophyte that I was) that 'No!' is the cruellest word you can shout at a dog, even if sometimes you must. Nor could I have predicted that she would shrink back, raise just one paw as if for protection and shiver with terror. The lesson I learnt that day, as I cried with remorse and bent to cuddle her, was how quickly she could forgive. She licked me as if to say she was sorry, it was all her fault, it was all right, I shouldn't upset myself any more, all was well. There were no sulks. The tiny creature was bigger than I could have been –

and I was astonished. Much has always been written about the fidelity of the dog, and yet this quality of forgiveness should not be underestimated.

Saturday 12 October was beautiful. The sun glittered on the pond, where water spurted into the air from the spring swollen with autumn rain. The trees in the beech wood had crisped to russet, and the silver birch by the pond was weeping gold, like a metamorphosed princess in myth. J and Robin decided to go logging on our land, ready for winter. The big dogs raced, because they liked nothing else than to be down in the rough fields, smelling rabbits, foxes and badgers and rolling in mud. As always, the cats glided around on the perimeter of the action. But I had to leave the gang and drive the one hour to Cheltenham to take part in a discussion on marriage at the Literature Festival. As I backed my car from the car port I saw J scoop Bonnie up, then turn with her in his arms to tramp down to where the tractor waited in a gilded landscape.

I had contributed to a short book called *Maybe I Do: Marriage and Commitment in Singleton Society,* published by the Institute of Ideas. Over the years, as a prolific journalist, I have written many thousands of words on this subject, and in 1989 I compiled an anthology of poetry and prose about marriage. It had started as a silver wedding present for J, but ended by being published and dedicated to him. We had perfected a double act: reading a selection from the book at festivals and for charity. I liked being married and saw (as I still do) the institution as the bedrock of society – although with no illusions about how difficult it is. 'The greatest test of character any of us will have to face,' was how I described it in my anthology introduction.

Now a group of us were gathering to discuss marriage before a sold-out audience in the Town Hall in Cheltenham: the novelist Fay Weldon, journalist and novelist Yvonne Roberts, radical journalist Jennie Bristow, Claire Fox from the Institute of Ideas (my publisher) and me. It was a good, wide-ranging discussion and as usual I was the most conventional of all the speakers, banging a drum for what I truly believe in: the importance of stable marriage to the upbringing of children. That is, when it works. My chapter in the book was called 'For the Sake of the Children' and ended with these words – which sum up the essence of my platform contribution:

> *Of course marriages go wrong, but I do not believe anybody has the right to put their own needs/feelings/wants before those of their children. Most of us could have skipped out of our marriages at some time or other, in pursuit of romance – by which I mean, fresh sex. 'Staying together for the sake of the children' became a much derided mantra, but I see it as a potential source of good. Who knows – by putting Self on the back burner, many a married couple may find they weather the storms and ease themselves into the best of friendships, to share old age together, in married love.*

Now I regret the trite cynicism of that phrase 'fresh sex' but admit that the last sentence is pure autobiography, not theory. It was where I thought we both were, what I most wanted.

That night we went to a dinner party near Bath. Beautiful converted barn decorated with impeccable taste. Schubert floating through the scented air. Logs roaring in the wood burner. Excellent champagne, cold and biscuity in tall glasses. So many people; we didn't know them all. Such a buzz. Conversation about the arts amongst (mostly) practitioners. Delicious food cooked and served by our perfectionist writer-hostess and free-flowing wine to match its quality. The long, long table, lined with merry faces, as the laughter rose to the ceiling.

How many such evenings had we enjoyed, by the autumn of 2002? How many people had we met, talked to, flirted with, become friends with, forgotten in time? Both social beings, J and I always enjoyed gatherings where conversation was sparkling yet unstuffy – and this one was one of the best. He was sitting at the opposite end of the long table, between our hostess and a blonde woman whom I had not noticed during the pre-dinner drinks. I did not even notice her face in the candlelight; she was too far away. And why indeed would I notice? J and I had come too far together to fret that the person next to one or other of us at dinner might come to mean something.

Yes indeed, the moments do come when the universe smiles and plays a trick. Yes indeed, you get up one morning with no inkling that the day will bring a life-changing moment. The face of a future lover seen across a room, a sudden stumble which leaves you with a black eye … There can indeed be no knowing what will pop out from under the lid of the scary jack-in-a-box, to shake the foundations of the world you know. As we drove home, exchanging details of conversations and swapping gossip and opinion as we always did, J told me about his neighbour at dinner. He liked her a lot but was, he confessed, slightly bothered because it turned out she was a very well-known opera singer, just making her mark on the international stage, and yet he had not heard of her. Nor had I.

Her name was Susan Chilcott.

Two

LOSING

It is late last night the dog was speaking of you;
The snipe was speaking of you in the deep marsh.
It is you are the lonely bird through the woods;
And that you may be without a mate until you find me.
Lady Gregory, 'Poets and Dreamers'
(translating eighth-century Irish)

Our farm was J's dream from childhood, an echo of his happy family home with its barns and entourage of animals – to which ours bore a strange resemblance. An old, low, sprawling building protected from the worst winds by being tucked into a dip in the land, like the space a dog makes when it turns round and round to scoop out its bed. A house with barns and stables, a settlement whose ancient stones would become imprinted with our story, to add to all those it had known over three centuries. A home that could be created in our own image – the dank inner courtyard brought into the house, glazed and turned into an atrium, its weight supported

49

by Bath stone corbels which we had beautifully carved by an artist-craftsman *in situ* to my master design. They represented the four seasons, four elements, literary themes and so on. We wanted our house to *be* a work of art as well as to contain our collection.

But it needed to be made bigger, for we had moved there (following J's dream of farming organically) from a large rectory in a pretty village a few miles away and the existing farmhouse was too small for our needs. So a long, dilapidated animal shed at right angles to the main house was renovated to form a study for me, a spectacular double-height sitting room with windows on three sides and (best of all) a low, peaceful library with two window seats overlooking the valley. Across from the house was a small building which became a cottage for Robin (when he was around, as he worked a lot abroad) and our son Daniel, and (later) for J's groom and her family. There would be extra rooms for us over there too, and across the yard was the huge barn which would become, in time, a games room. We loved to have a house full of friends and family. At New Year for instance: space was necessary. The place was unusual and extraordinary, with a 145-degree view that was miraculous when the valley was full of mist but the surrounding hills and farms rose above it, like ships on a foaming sea. I find it almost impossible to describe the magical atmosphere of the home J and I created, or its wild beauty.

The summer we moved there (1994) had been the hottest in decades and the whole valley crisped to golden brown. These were the classic dog days of summer, when Sirius burned brightly in the night sky. This is the Dog Star, the faithful creature at the heels of Orion, the brightest star in Canis Major and called Canicula (little dog) by the Romans. Strangely, native American peoples associated it with dogs too – the Cherokee seeing it as a guardian of the 'Path of Souls', the Blackfoot calling it 'Dogface' and the Alaskan Inuit naming it 'Moon Dog'. Yes, it was right that the brightest star in the firmament should hang in the sultry night sky above our new home. But in the *Iliad* Homer describes this frozen firework as 'an evil portent, bringing heat/And fevers to suffering humanity'. That was to prove right.

We celebrated the two stages of the huge building project with parties for the carpenters, stonemasons, electricians and labourers who became as familiar as friends and gained nutty tans working shirtless on the site. But by the end of that first winter we had learned the measure of the place; the wind howled about the house like the ghosts of Cathy and Heathcliff and the north-facing position meant that frost and ice would remain in pockets and corners for weeks. Our flock of Lleyn sheep huddled below the library windows, coughing and grumbling under the ancient stone walls, just a couple of metres from my books. At night the brief, harsh yelps of foxes and screech owls would shatter the bitter air. Upper Langridge Farm justified its reputation as 'the coldest farm for miles around' – as a neighbour had helpfully mentioned while we were moving in and I was wondering what on earth we were doing. I had wept to leave our previous home, where the children had grown up and where the fifteen years had been (for the most part) contented. For a long time I would have a recurring dream of letting myself into the old, beloved rectory, walking through rooms that were empty and just as I had left them, then creeping into the attic to hide – for ever.

J and I were brave with each other, but at times I knew even he wondered if we had done the right thing. We made mistakes with the building, which was cold, cold, cold. The wind howled not just around it but through it. Poet Michael Longley captured both the good and the bad in these lines:

No insulation –
A house full of draughts,
Visitors, friends:
Its warmth escaping –
The snow on our roof
The first to melt.

The unlit yard was slate black. One night, having driven my daughter to a friend's (as the mothers of teenagers must), I stopped halfway down the track to the farm – because nobody was at home and I could not face its dark emptiness. I was starting to cry when, suddenly, I was startled by a flash of white and a muffled thud of paws. A badger charged across the rough track in front of my stationary car, and away into the darkness. Excited, I took it as a positive sign and went home.

The isolation could render your heart speechless in the face of the night and its sounds. This is not a fear of marauders, you must understand – although friends would ask me, 'Don't you get spooked – alone here?' It is the silence that underlies the harsh chatter of rooks in the susurrating stand of trees, as well as the sense of generations of struggle imprinted on the stones of that windy hillside. It is the exposure to such an immensity of sky you cannot but be brought face to face with your own inadequacy. And mortality. The strangest truth was this: in all

the years J and I lived at the farm I (who had previously written five novels, many more children's books and liked to paint
and make things) found it impossible to *create*. Once the home
itself was made, just living there and running our lives took
almost all my reserves of energy. Feng shui practitioners would
say the *chi* – the energy – could not stay in a house like that
because the front door and the back door were exactly aligned.
Whoosh – it goes, whirling through, and taking a part of your
soul with it. Tractors. Hedge planting. Infected sheep. Cows
getting out. People coming and going. Black ice matching the
hole of the farm finances. Feed delivered by lumbering lorries.
Lambing in a May frost. The track so bumpy taxis refused to
come down and so it had to be made up properly, at more cost.
The troughs frozen. Poisonous ragwort. Fences breaking.
Running out of oil. The fox leaving two headless chickens on
the track. A kitchen garden carved out of the hillside at great
cost. Dead sheep.

Ah, but on summer days, the light would spill over the
creamy stone floors of our hall and atrium and the homestead
had a Mediterranean air and everybody who came would
breathe in the scent of thyme planted in the courtyard,
exclaiming with admiration at what we had created for
ourselves. There was a meadow called the Aldermoor where
grew about twenty varieties of wild flower. The house appeared
in magazines. J said it was his favourite place in the whole
world and everyone who visited saw why – even if they might
not have chosen to live on the windy hill.

You have to allow places to change you, or else you will never
settle, let alone be happy. I confess (broken-hearted over the
move from *my* dream house, our rectory) that I was puzzled

that my husband should become so obsessed with the need to farm, at a time when farming was not in good health. Yet that need was rooted deep in his childhood. Despite myself I understood, even if I lacked sympathy. Not only had he been a champion show-jumper in his teens, but he had studied agriculture, worked on the Royal Farm at Windsor Castle, broken and trained champion horses professionally – and that all before going to University College London to read philosophy where (a brilliant student and student editor who took on the college authorities with late-sixties radicalism) he was to write a dissertation on 'Base and Superstructure in Marx'. There followed a distinguished career during which he reported from all over the world, made history in Ethiopia, risked his life working under cover in Pinochet's Chile, saw terrible sights and interviewed leaders, made countless documentary series (this in the much-lamented golden era of British television), wrote books, did sterling work for various charities … But through it all he never lost his yearning for a real country life: the deep desire to plant hedges, husband good soil, stride out on land that is your own.

Whenever I welcomed him back home to the farm from London, where he would have been interviewing politicians for his eponymous weekly television programme, he would throw off his suit to pull on old clothes and stride to the sheds to help with the lambing, like a true Renaissance man. When he bought a horse (then two, then three) and was still (in his fifties) able to vault straight up without even putting a foot in the stirrup, I knew that the most accomplished gaucho in Argentina would nod approval at his prowess. Women like men who straddle more than one world.

Gradually I became tougher, although my brother-in-law once said I was the least likely farmer's wife he had ever seen. I bought rubber boots – but rarely wore them. Learned to layer big sweaters over thick skirts. Even once drove the huge, ancient Land-Rover in the snow, because otherwise I would have been marooned. Alone on the farm (as I so often was), I learned independence. Once, with a coat over my nightdress, I even rounded up the escaped cows who were destroying the garden, placing Billie and Sam like troops on the flank and advancing fearlessly, shouting 'Garn!' and thwacking with my stick, driving them up to the barn, so that when the stockman and his wife arrived at last I was in charge. J was immensely (and disbelievingly) proud of me. The story of how the urban writer tamed the herd went up and down the valley. 'Field-cred' I called it.

One spring morning, not a year after we had moved, I experienced the epiphany which leads – in a way I can now see but could not possibly have known then – me back to the subject of this book.

It was late April and I was alone. The light woke me very early and from the window I glimpsed a morning of such limpid perfection it was impossible to remain indoors. I dressed quickly, afraid to miss the glitter of the dew, and released Billie and Sam from the laundry room where they had their beds. No need for leads. Out into the watery gold of the day with the dogs bounding and snapping at the air in exhilaration.

I walked past the well, across the wide circle of gravel, past the handsome barn and thence right into the fields. And then I saw them. The Herefords were crowding near the fence, their chestnut flanks gleaming in the sunlight as they bent their creamy topknots to tug at the grass. There is a sweetness about cows I had never noticed before: their gentle, wary eyes in big white moon faces. That heavy, grassy smell and the rhythmic, chomping sounds they make, between low, faintly protesting moos. Because it was still chilly their breaths came out in little clouds, like ectoplasm hanging in the air – the whispering spirits of their beefy herd. What had they witnessed since the seventeenth century, those pedigree Herefords, what breed memory looked out through those rolling eyes?

They ruminated and inspected me. I leaned on the fence and looked back and we were not afraid of each other. The air waited. And it was with a sudden leap of the spirit that I said aloud, 'Good morning, girls. You're looking so beautiful this morning! *Aren't* you gorgeous?'

To speak to them like that, to acknowledge their presence as I would a fellow human and admire their individual, curly-topped, four-square magnificence, was to put us on a level. To take my part in the wholeness of things. I now realize that it was at that precise point that I allowed myself to be affected by the *genius loci* – the spirit of the place. And it was the animals – rather than the trees or the distant sweep of the land, or the astonishing sense of worship I felt before the first primroses and the swathes of cowslips – which eased my heart finally into love. It was my humility before the universal beauty of which the animals were a part. In making me see the truth of their existence as on a par with my own within the greater Whole they were exerting a *moral* power over me which I had never experienced before.

This is not what you feel when you look at an animal in a zoo, even though you might marvel at the size of the giraffe or the intricacy of the markings on a snake. Nor is it what you feel when you take the lid off a tin and allow dried food to rattle down into your big dog's metal bowl, smiling fondly as he gobbles his supper. You may come near the sensation, though, when you watch your cat unfold its limbs and stretch – and realize that not in any universe could you ever hope to move with such indifferent grace.

I was learning from the cows.

The joy they gave me, in that brief exchange of looks and breaths that crystalline morning, when the brevity of the sunlight, the dew and all our lives, human and animal, made me catch my breath, was something I would never forget. It was as sustainable as J's method of farming. It set me on a journey. Lolloping Billie and Sam were on it too, but it was Bonnie who would – in a future I could not have then predicted – be the truest companion.

One of my favourite writers is Edith Wharton – she who, in late middle age, would so annoy her friends by the fuss she made over 'the damned Pekingese'. Her first biographer, Percy Lubbock, wrote: 'There is always a dog or two about Edith in her home, a small dog of the yapping kind, a still smaller of the fidgeting and whining breed – dogs that had to be called, caressed …' But writing an autobiography in her seventies Edith Wharton recalled the walk with her father in 1865 (when she was four), down Fifth Avenue in Manhatten, when a friend of her father's gave her a spitz-type puppy she called Foxy, the first of her cohorts of little dogs. Near the end of her life, after an unhappy marriage but a brilliant career, when many people she loved had died and many dogs too, Wharton located the beginning of her imaginative awareness: 'The owning of my first dog made me into a conscious, sentient person, fiercely possessive, anxiously watchful, and woke in me that long ache of pity for animals, and for all inarticulate beings, which nothing has ever stilled.'

The first couple of months of 2003 were (as always for J and me) extremely busy. What made us like that – both driving ourselves hard, always taking on extra projects, charity work and so on – and therefore unable to find much peace on our farm? The too-easy psychological answer might be that he was ever striving to emulate a famous father as well as an older brother who was himself a distinguished broadcaster. Yet the Protestant work ethic played an important role, over and above family history. I always thought that the last words of *The Woodlanders* summed J up, Marty South's passionate elegy over the grave of her beloved Giles Winterborne: '… you was a good man, and did good things!' Doing good things demands time and energy.

As for me, I was always striving to prove myself (girl from humble background makes good etc.) yet always worrying that I would be found out: the achievement of a distinguished degree, the marriage, the beautiful homes, the successful journalistic career, the careful glamour, the books, the programmes, the immense jollity of the parties we gave – all of it discounted when I was found out to be a fraud. To keep fear and boredom at bay, to prove myself as a multitasking, perfectionist alpha female, I – like so many women – took on too much. I also had to keep up with my husband. Had I not done so over the years of his success as an international reporter, writer and political journalist, I would have gone under. The key to our marriage was the meeting of minds in friendship. For all the flaws (what union does not have them?) I do not know what better can be said.

The pond was thickly iced, with a dusting of snow on top. In January and February 2003 I was struggling with the book of my radio series, *Devout Sceptics*, re-reading *Daniel Deronda* (because it was time to), brooding over structural problems in my sixth novel, *The Invasion of Sand*, taking on the chairmanship of a £2.2 million appeal to build a new children's theatre in Bath, moving our daughter into her first London flat and supporting her through the intimidating start of her new job at the *London Evening Standard* and arranging all the detail of a 30-minute programme for Radio 4 to mark the 100th anniversary of Harley-Davidson motorcycles. Kitty and I were writing a joint article for the *Daily Mail*, J was off to Iraq to interview the Prime Minister amidst ominous rumblings from the United States and in my diary I wrote, '*The world is such a terrible place at the moment – a cloud over all things.*'

Yet amidst all that, the diary also records consolations:

11 January: Bonnie and I return in the frost-bound midnight to the empty farmhouse. Her companionship is so precious to me, so essential now. Who would have thought that I would become so dependent on a little dog?

13 January: It's good to have J here again – so much cleverer than I could ever be – to sound ideas off. What would I be without him? This afternoon we go to the pet shop with Bonnie for new dog beds and the expedition is fun. We eat sausages, read and doze by the fire.

20 January: ... so good to be home again with Bonnie. She represents home now.

2 February: ... coming back home to be welcomed by an ecstatic, wriggling little dog.

Bonnie always cheered me, always inspired closeness and took both of us away from work.

The day before our thirty-fifth wedding anniversary was a normal Saturday, and so I listened to my husband on the radio, took the three dogs up through our wood for a walk and felt a great surge of happiness in the still, cold air. It was strange, I thought, to be happy when the news was full of the looming war in Iraq, but the sunlight glittered on a hard frost and I took my little dog to be groomed, and picked her up later, a fresh-smelling shorn lamb. How can one suppress natural joy? It was there every day in Bonnie's behaviour: the irrepressible *nowness* of each second, the perpetual readiness for action and adventure, even if that was only chasing a leaf. Each parting would be marked by the reproachful eyes and the drooping tail, even though she had two big dogs to stay with. I would return from shopping, one hour later, to be met with such an effusion of joy, such a frolicsome licking, that there was nothing to do but laugh.

On our anniversary, 23 February, J returned from presenting his usual Sunday television programme and presented me with his gift: a fine, chunky necklace of antique coral, since the thirty-fifth is the coral anniversary. In an imaginative touch he had also entered the bookmakers Joe Coral (for the first ever time) and placed a bet that Liverpool (my home team) would win their next away football match. He handed me the betting slip – and we laughed. That night we went to our favourite restaurant (not the grandest in Bath, but we ate out rarely, preferring to be in our blue and yellow kitchen) and my diary records: '*We ate well and drank better and talked best of all. Perfection. As I say so often, I am so lucky.*'

There it is.

Liverpool did not win.

As I explained in the Introduction, writing a memoir is to offer just a slice of a life, a section of truth – like a sample taken by an archaeologist, full of priceless shards which remain, nevertheless, mere parts, fragments shored against ruin. Sometimes when my dog is snoozing on my knee I trace her ribs with my fingertips, each one in turn, imagining the fragility of her skeleton laid in earth. Yet nowadays the computer can reassemble a whole head from fragments of bone, an image of what once was (a centuries-dead face reconstructed) turning and turning in cyberspace to awe us. So my dog's DNA will lie for ever in earth and so will mine and therefore the essence of what is true is unassailable.

That is how I feel about that last anniversary.

Whatever went before, and no matter what was to come after, what happened that day and is condensed into those few words, remains The Truth.

Yet in the end only he and I know that truth; therefore what is presented to the world remains as shards.

* * *

J was the Chairman of the Bath International Music Festival and worked tirelessly to promote it. It was he who had taken me to my first big classical concert at the Festival Hall in 1968, although in my late teens I did begin a small collection of budget classical LPs. When we met he was rather entertained that I could be so admiring of his piano playing, since I knew so little about technique. When I was 30 a friend took me for the first time to the Royal Opera House, Covent Garden, and my tears at the end of *La Bohème* began a craze for opera which took me to some of the great opera houses of the world and led me to study the famous Kobbé guide so that I knew all the stories. Yet by 2003 I had grown tired of the form, and returned to jazz and blues as my cooking music of choice, as well as classic pop tracks ('Leader of the Pack' etc.), cajun, country, not to mention urban grooves like Fishbelly Black. Our musical tastes had slightly diverged, although we shared a love of chamber music.

I remain unsure of exactly how it came about but this is what I know. Just after our anniversary J had been asked to interview Susan Chilcott where she lived, in a village called Blagdon, not far from Bath and Bristol. The article was to appear in the local evening paper, its purpose to promote the long-established Mid-Somerset Festival, invaluable for its encouragement of young performers each March. Later it was to amaze people that somebody as well known as J should agree to write for a local paper; at the time I hardly knew this was happening because I was planning a trip to Milwaukee as well as starting work on a public lecture at Bath University on the subject of pornography. Still, had it registered on my radar I would have attributed it to his good will. And I do know for certain that there was nothing suspicious about the meeting – on one level. Yet they had liked each other enormously at that dinner party four months before, and she told a mutual friend (I heard later) that she was excited to see him again.

In her case, I should probably have felt the same. Over the years she must have sat next to any number of self-centred men at dinner – you know the ones – who never ask a question yet, puffed up with needy masculine ego, assume you will uncover every achievement and interest in their lives. Sitting next to J she would have dazzled but been enchanted too, since he, the consummate interviewer, would always be sure to find out what made the most humble person tick, let alone a beautiful soprano.

He went to Blagdon that day.

They fell in love.

How can I know what happened? The novelist in me could write the scene and invest it with heady tension. But I never asked how it all came about, and speculation is irrelevant. What's more, in the days following I noticed no change. Our life was hurtling on in its normal way, and I had no inkling of any undercurrent tugging my husband into deeper water. But just as one reads a novel, listens to music or looks at a great painting differently once you know the circumstances of its composition or future, so it is impossible to look back without seeing clouds mass over our farm, our life.

So now I see everything we did after 23 February in the light of what was to come. Evenings with friends in London during which we argued about Iraq; me interviewing Ben Okri at the Bath Literature Festival; our children visiting for weekends to tell us how their jobs were progressing; one special evening when J and I ate caviar (a gift from a friend), blinis and sour cream helped down by shots of bison grass vodka, followed by pot-roasted pheasant and mashed potato with good red wine and then home-made rhubarb crumble and my own ice cream – all by candlelight in front of a crackling dining-room fire. Good times, all – yet now overshadowed.

My own days were made gloomy by work on my lecture for Bath University. Despite the *laisse-faire* attitude of so many of my peers, my attitude to pornography and the insidious 'pornogrification' of society – a subject I'd visited often in journalism – has remained constant over the years: I detested it for reasons that went beyond feminism and perhaps might be called humanist. And now the cruel hydra of internet porn is indestructible. I investigated, read – and became depressed. The dark world I uncovered revolted me even more than I expected. With hindsight it was a mistake to take it on; the task made me withdrawn, and perhaps less observant of what was going on in J's life than I might otherwise have been. A diary entry is very telling:

20 March: The farm is bathed in sunlight but I proceeded to make myself miserable by doing a trawl of porn sites to see what can be accessed freely and easily. It was far, far worse than expected and as I went on I became so overwhelmed by the scale of the horror that my mouth was dry – and at one point I had to walk out into the garden for air. The birds were singing, the crocuses pale gold in sunlight, and sweet little Bonnie rushed about at my feet – all white, all innocence. Yet not even she could make me feel better. That other world was 'in' my computer, 'in' the very air that I had breathed in my study. I felt polluted. Everything spoiled by it. The violence, the hatred against women defies description. This wretched lecture is a terrible black burden pressing down on me.

Meanwhile J was spending much time in London making extra programmes about the war in Iraq and besides writing the lecture I was planning a trip to Kenya for the charity Plan International, to visit my sponsored child and write about the trip for the *London Evening Standard*. I was also unwell; not in pain but afflicted by inconvenient female problems which grew worse and worse. And amidst the repetitive exhaustion of my diary I see one entry, laden now with irony. I went to visit a friend who had recently moved to Bath and wrote: *'What would it be like to be middle aged and alone, your husband having departed? I should realize, perhaps, just how lucky I am.'*

Two months later, I was in the Bath Clinic. My womb had gone, but my room was full of flowers. When the anaesthetist came to see me he admired them and I said, 'Yes, I'm lucky.' He was tall, middle-aged, South African. He smiled and said, 'You make your luck.'

In the silence after his departure I wondered if that was true. I had just learned that my husband was in love with somebody else – and yet that was not the worst thing. During the previous weeks he had seemed so weighed down. It was inevitable that he would have to share it with me – because, after all, we shared almost everything. When, after many years, a married couple become linked symbiotically, they may perhaps live as brother-sisterly best friends and soulmates rather than lovers, yet know what the other is thinking, before the thought has formed. As Judith Thurman puts it (writing about Colette), 'A marriage may be sustained by a deep complicity between two spouses, long after the extinction of desire.' You are attuned to nuances of mood – unless, that is, you allow work and other preoccupations to blind you. The lecture given, the programmes completed, everything else laid aside because of my physical health and the urgency of the hysterectomy, I became aware again, woke up to the real world. And the horizons all around our home filled with his unhappiness.

Dates and details do not matter. The simple truth was this: J and Susan Chilcott had fallen passionately in love, but their affair was not to last long – *as such*. For only about three months later she discovered that the breast cancer for which she had been treated two years earlier had returned, spread to her liver and would not let her live. The beautiful woman of 40, at the very height of her powers (although perhaps not, since opera singers grow in maturity), with a four-year-old son whom she adored and called the light of her life, had been given her sentence. She could expect perhaps another three months. I lay in my room at the clinic, minus my womb, looking at my flowers, full of sorrow for her, brooding hopelessly on the pitiless inevitability of it. Like J, I wondered how people could believe there is a god.

Morphine-induced imaginings chill the soul. I had a dream in that scented room. I am a woman who has lost many children, yet I am outside her, looking on. She goes with my husband to visit a certain church, running through the flowery graveyard as if for refuge. She is drawn to ascend the winding stair into the gallery and her husband follows. Up there is an elaborate monument, covered with dust and spider webs. It is black and grey marble, with skulls beneath. She is looking up and sees that the names of the dead on the tomb are those of her own children, and as she stares in disbelief something is rearing up, a carved figure come to life, arms stretching out towards her. And she is plucked, carried up into the air, then hurled forward over the balustrade, to smash down dead on the floor of the church below. In this short time her husband has been frozen by the stairwell. Now he darts forward to look over the balcony at the corpse lying broken. But even as he looks a form rises by it, a wraith, a personification of malevolence. It looks up; he cannot even cry – struck dumb by what he sees. And then there is a jump cut, as in a movie. A railway station, and a young girl waiting for a train. It chugs in, one of the old-fashioned type with compartments. The girl sees one with a woman in it – with her head shrouded in a scarf – and gets in because she feels safe. Oh no, but I *knew* – even in the dream, the watcher knew. That spirit would kill other people's children. Nowhere was safe.

('*Oh Lord*,' I wrote, '*what was all that about?*')

Our beautiful home awaited me, and it was sunny when I returned. Daniel and Kitty came to visit, as well as my parents – who lived near by. Because of the necessity for post-operative quiet I had no difficulty in keeping what I knew from everybody else. I had been looking forward to this time of rest and reading, with Bonnie on my knee playing the role perfected by Elizabeth Barrett Browning's Flush, 'in his eternal place on my bed'. She would be like the little dogs at the feet of the ladies on medieval tombs, eternally vigilant, devotion incarnate. The point is, at this stage I had no doubt whatsoever that what was happening in J's life would be endured, coped with and survived.

My journal records: *'There is a space inside me, where what we must think of as "womanhood" used to be. The loss of it seems less a source of regret than of celebration. Space in my body. Space in my mind. Space in my life. Vacuums are always filled, aren't they? So we shall wait and see what flows inwards.'*

I did not know that home would never be the same again.

Susan Chilcott sang for the last time in public in June 2003, at a concert in Brussels. She was accompanied by her friend, the pianist and Radio 3 presenter Iain Burnside, and the performance was with the actress Fiona Shaw, reading from Shakespeare. Susan wore white linen. She sang (among other things) the Willow aria from Verdi's *Otello*, when the doomed Desdemona, full of sorrow, remembers a song from her childhood:

> *The fresh streams ran between the flowery banks,*
> *She moaned in her grief,*
> *In bitter tears which through her eyelids sprang*
> *Her poor heart sought relief.*
> *Willow! Willow! Willow!*
> *Come sing! Come sing!*
> *The green willow shall be my garland.*

Later her voice would rise in a crescendo as she begged, *'Ch'io viva ancor, ch'io viva ancor!'* ('Let me live longer, let me live longer!') as death, in the form of her husband Othello, stands over her.

J was in the audience, with other friends. You would need a heart of granite not to see how unbearably poignant it must have been. The word 'heartbreaking' is overused, like 'tragic' and 'hero'. Anyone who watched Susan Chilcott's last performance, knowing that her life was already ebbing away, must surely have felt a breaking inside.

I wrote:

> I think of her and her son with numbness, because the horror of it is so hard to imagine. As for his feelings … well, my own knowledge of love is so far removed from narrow, tabloid newspaper notions, that I can only empathize. Do we have any choice about these coups de foudre? In this case, I don't think so. J is permanently upset – how can he not be? I don't know how he will be able to bear what is coming, but he has made a choice to involve himself and so he has no choice but to endure.

Stricken, J asked me if I understood that he would want to spend time with Susan in the three months of life she had left. I told him I did understand. Because I *did* – and it makes no difference to me that other women might think me mad. This was not something cheap or clandestine; he was going away from me (and I was regaining strength daily, with enormous reserves of inner fortitude, built up over the years) to take care of somebody very special whose strength was waning. Take care of her son too.

I wrote:

I cannot begrudge a dying woman the love of my husband. Can we choose who we love? To stand in a bookshop is to stand in the midst of a great, tumultuous, seething, writhing, coiling, heaving mass of complex human emotions, and to be deafened by the screams of passion and pain. Who am I to tell them all – all those writers and their creations – that they are wrong? I suppose my sadness is chiefly because I wish J and I could have been all-in-all to each other and yet – after that first intensity of passion – it was never to be. I wonder why? He is still the person I most like to talk to, and whose various roles in life I find the most fascinating. Looking back at us in our youth, falling in love, making a home, doing finals, starting our careers, I marvel at the sheer courage *of it all. Yet that swash-buckling love stepped sideways and lost itself among the alley-ways of other people, other lives, self-indulgence, guilt. And then we never quite managed to find the way back.*

The other day I was pierced by a pang that Dan and Kitty will never again live at home with me. Today this farm feels so empty … and yet, truthfully, I am all right. I will get through this. I know that J would not normally be here today, yet he would be here in spirit – but today he is not even here in spirit. But my little dog is at my feet. I reach forward and stroke her. I hear the fountain – and birds. I must begin to make again.

Bovine, I had watched him descend the stairs with a packed bag. What would have happened had I thrown myself down, clung to his leg, begged him not to go? I will never know because I didn't do so. 'I am dumb from human dignity' wrote Yeats, and I know what that means. Yes, I am proud – but perhaps foolish too. Later I began an unfinished novel like this:

She gave her husband away.

It wasn't that she didn't want him any more. Oh no, at that point she wanted him maybe more than she'd ever done before. But perhaps that was contrary of her – acting the child who clutches at an old toy because a friend suddenly wants to play with it, but gives it up all the same, in the end. Maybe if she'd clutched a little more fiercely it wouldn't have turned out as it did.

But I watched as blank passivity slid over her, and the woman who had been so deliciously bad in her past embraced a perverse form of sainthood. She became the kind of person friends described as 'so good', with that slight shake of the head which indicates disquiet, calling into question their own self-ishness, but also her common humanity. Good behaviour can sometimes seem intolerable, since we wish others to rage against the dying of the light, as we would ourselves.

I shook my head as she – so generously, so calmly – gave her husband away, and then turned to me as if to ask 'Why did this happen?', those great eyes filling, that generous mouth folded into a moue of sadness. You could strike a woman like that. You could shake her until the teeth rattled, and all her features fell apart, that beauty destroyed forever, with all the rest. But I was her friend and that defined my role – to witness all, to allow all, until the moment they both fell into the pit, at which point I would stretch out my hand to help.

Sometimes it is easier to tell a story in the third person. Yet I find these days I no longer want to make up characters (except for children) when each day, through my work as an advice columnist, I deal with reality and have to try to tell it as it is. When we were both young journalists J used to ask me if I ever thought of writing a novel. He thought it the way I should go. Excited as I was then by filing reports from every corner of Britain for magazines and newspapers, I said I had no wish to. Why would you want to make it up? I asked him. But he was to encourage me, patiently over the years, to write fiction. Without him, I doubt I would ever have done so. Without him, I doubt I will again.

On 20 June my parents came to lunch to celebrate my mother's birthday and the 'official birthday' of Bonnie, who had come to live with us on that day a year earlier. Lunch was outside in the courtyard, under the cream umbrella. I tied ribbons on Mum's chair, on Bonnie's basket, round her neck. J's absence was unremarked because it was unremarkable. He was a busy man. The dog's presence made it all much easier. By focusing on her and the meal I could deflect any anxiety my perceptive mother must have felt, looking at my face.

Here I reach the limit of what I can write about that summer. So much must remain unrecorded, although I will never forget. Too painful to recall the hope we shared that after it was over (it was not possible to utter the brutal words 'After she is dead') we could put it all back together. J and I had been through much in our long marriage but we recognized that this earthquake was truly terrifying, like nothing before. I wondered if, afterwards, we would find we had moved on a ratchet, making it impossible to go back. *Can* you go back? I asked myself if I would be able to live with a perfect ghost – my husband forever haunted by that amazing voice, like a mariner tied to a mast still hearing the fatal sirens' song. I wondered – when I finally told our children and the three of us talked obsessively about the subject, raging over bottles of white wine late into the night as moths slammed at the kitchen window – if I could recover the man I had known.

Susan Chilcott died in J's arms on 4 September. The obituaries were unanimous. The *Independent* noted: 'Her death came three months after she made her operatic debut at the Royal Opera House, in which her "radiant" and "glorious" performance outshone even that of her co-star, Placido Domingo.' The *Guardian* said:

> *Susan Chilcott, who has died of cancer aged 40, was one of the most compelling and intense English operatic stars to emerge in the last decade, with a wonderfully fresh, attractive and open personality and a rare commitment to her work. Her career was so distressingly short that too little of her best work has been captured on DVD or CD. But her singing had a purity and a forceful dramatic impact that made her a formidable operatic actor. Her last role on stage was Jenufa, which she sang in English for Welsh National Opera last March, with Sir Charles Mackerras conducting ... Sadly, when the run ended, Chilcott was too ill to record the work with Mackerras, as he had wanted. Her last performance, in Brussels in June, was ... with the pianist Iain Burnside and actor Fiona Shaw – and she was singing better than ever. Chilcott made an indelible impression on those who saw and heard her, or worked with her.*

On the day of her funeral at Wells Cathedral hundreds of people gathered to pay their respects. By this stage I had begun to feel enraged that – in the eyes of all those people – J was 'allowed' the role of widower. In fact Susan was married to her manager, although they were not living as man and wife and he was not the father of her son. But what do such details matter? I had packed my own bag, said goodbye to the dogs and cats, felt the (increasing) pang at leaving Bonnie – and was off to Heathrow. At the very hour of her funeral I was high above the Atlantic, en route for my beloved United States. I had work to do, but also needed to escape.

Snapshots in a family photograph album can come unstuck in time – adrift from captions which identify person, time and place. Will future generations know who they were, those faces caught faking smiles? Will *any* of it survive? Knowing all, remembering all, I can still only bear to offer small fragments of what Philip Larkin calls 'a past that now no one can share'.

In Port Reyes, Marin County, somebody has altered a sign on a wall from 'No Parking' to 'No Barking' and my laughter is over the top, hysterical. But when, not long afterwards, I see scrawled on a post overlooking San Francisco, 'I almost died here – but no such luck,' I become ridiculously upset. The view from the Marin headland – the Golden Gate Bridge, dwarfed sailboats, white caps on sparkling water – is perfect, and yet I feel my head is crumbling.

I talk obsessively about Bonnie to anyone who will listen (mercifully, Americans like dogs), miss her dreadfully and note, 'Who would have thought I would be so dependent on her?'

Pulling out her photograph to show to our lovely, kind niece, who shares a house with friends in Oakland, I think of Amy Tan and my last visit, when none of this misery could have been dreamt of. The point is, in talking about my love for my dog I'm really talking about my love of home, of J – just as Elizabeth Barrett Browning used Flush as displacement.

Ruefully I notice a hotel called Diva. Everything conspires to remind me. Not far away, just off Geary, in a jazz club called Biscuits and Blues, a guy called R.J. Mischo sings the blues. He reminds me of Snooks Eaglin. The mouth harp moans and the slide swoops and shimmies, mimicking my mood – while the passion he pours into his songs pierces my heart:

> *I wake up every night around midnight*
> *Cos I just can't sleep no more.*

Yes.

> *You have yourself to blame now baby*
> *For breaking up our happy home.*

Yes.

> *If you don't do right*
> *How you gonna be treated right yourself?*

Yes.

I turn up at a reception for the Sacred Dying Foundation, which was founded by a theologian author and deviser-of-ritual called Megory Anderson. One of the many purposes of this trip is a commission from *The Times Magazine*: a feature on the new American way of death – something I'd suggested months before, in a different era. I'd arranged a first meeting with Megory two days earlier but instead of talking about her work I angsted obsessively about my problems, like a skinny Ancient Mariner plucking the sleeve of any kind stranger. To make amends for that self-absorption I decide I must honour her invitation to the reception.

In the elegant house on Vallejo Street I sit on beige velvet under a high, panelled ceiling, determined to engage. There's a bishop here, four other priests over there, and a group of intelligent, lay people, all of whom look as if they have a calling. Their faces are sensitive. I know they would feel sorry for me if they knew what I was feeling. But I do not speak – and a round-room discussion which would normally fascinate me leaves me lost and panicky:

'It is not just our Ministry to the dying but their Ministry to us which matters.'

'The focus is not just on helping people to die with grace, but helping people to survive the death of loved ones with grace.'

'Prayer is placing yourself every day on the threshold of death. Because it is a way of living life to the full.'

No – I can't be doing with this. For years I have been writing articles and broadcasting on the subject of bereavement. I even won an award for this work from the charity Cruse, presented to me by the Queen, as patron. But what do I know? Back in

England my husband is (in his own words) 'broken by a grief that was more dreadful than I had ever imagined any pain could be'. I know he would want to tear down this gracious room and shout that there is no grace attached to dying, not for anybody. He would call these good people dishonest and tell them that to survive the trauma of witnessing a terrible death is beyond such gentle ministrations. He would stamp in fury on kind Megory's 'rituals for embracing the end of life'. In that room, desperate to break free from everything, I realize it is impossible for me to fulfil the bloody assignment.

Afterwards I walk three blocks to Union to meet beloved friends and confidantes, my producer Malcolm and photographer Robin, who have been having fun, cruising those switch-back streets on a rental Harley-Davidson, while I was listening to lofty talk of death. Now they're drinking white wine in a restaurant called Prego. They agree I'm right to ditch the commission and we drink and talk and eat and laugh as if there were no tomorrow. As never before, I sense the Mexican papier-mâché 'Day of the Dead' skulls in my study back home, all gibbering that there *is* no tomorrow. Ha!

Other work to be done, different days – Malcolm and I are making programmes with Armistead Maupin and Professor Jared Diamond. More *Devout Sceptics*, more talk about God, and doubt, and the end of the world. Which is surely at hand. There's a skull in Professor Diamond's office at UCLA and I feel the interviews slipping from my grasp. It's as if I can't do anything any more. My face, in Robin's publicity photographs taken on Maupin's terrace, grins horribly, like a lunatic.

In Grace Cathedral something happens – an epiphany which equals my encounter with the cows that sublime, golden morning. In the soaring miracle of concrete (finished in 1964 when I was just four years off meeting the man I was to share my life with) I find some peace.

In front of the great entrance is a vast carpet labyrinth woven in soft tones of lilac, purple, grey. The labyrinth (I read) is an ancient symbol worldwide. Prehistoric labyrinths served as traps for malevolent spirits, or as paths for ritual dances. In medieval times the labyrinth symbolized a hard path to God with one entrance (birth) leading to the endless winding, looping, puzzling path which leads to one centre (God). When people could not afford to travel on pilgrimages the symbol of the labyrinth substituted; you could walk it with your fingers if you were ill. Later labyrinths as religious symbols faded, to become maze-like entertainments. But now, in the New Age, they are used by people who want to walk in and escape the everyday and by mystics as an aid to medita-tion. Walking among the turns, passing where you have come and then turning off in a different direction, but always moving onwards, one loses track of direction and of the outside world. The mind is quietened. This (I read) is a form of meditation.

So I place my sandals neatly with the others, and step on the carpet. How strange it is to pace slowly, as if within narrow walls, when there are no partitions. In the stillness of that vast cathedral, I fold my hands behind my back and walk the labyrinth, turning and turning. And I am thinking of Susan Chilcott with such pity it is as if another weight is loosened from my back by invisible hands. I know that J had not intended to hurt me; nothing could have been farther from his mind or will. Yet he was overtaken by a *truth*: an intensity of feeling which could not be denied, or harnessed – not in those circumstances. Why, I think, should she *not* have been his soul-mate for that brief period? Who is to know the time or place of a meeting, or what form the soul's pilgrimage will take? Reaching the centre of the carpet labyrinth at last, standing in a beam of light, looking up at nothing, I give thanks for my life. Then, retracing my steps to walk that sinuous track, resisting the temptation to walk straight, I find myself amazed at just how much love there is in this story. Then I arrive back at the beginning, which is the end.

Two days later, at the entrance to the Mission San Carlos Borromeo at Carmel, a woman tries to give me something, pushing at my hand. It's like a playing card, small and laminated, and at first I shake my head, not wanting a religious tract. But she has a gentle face and I don't want to seem churlish, so I say 'Thank you'. Inside the church I look down and see on one side a picture of Father Junipero Serra, the founder of the California Missions in the seventeenth century. On the other side, an image of the Carmel Mission – and the words 'Always go forward and never turn back.' They shimmer. Standing in front of the ornately beautiful Gothic altar, staring at Father Serra's burial place, I wonder in what circumstances he said those words, which are now dancing around in my brain. A devout agnostic, I always light a candle in Catholic churches for the son who was stillborn in 1975. But now, within those adobe walls, I have no choice but to light one for somebody else.

No, for two people.

You may be thinking I have forgotten my small dog. Impossible. To say that I yearned for her, and for home, and

79

the husband, and the old life would be an understatement. In any case Bonnie was fulfilling a very important role back on the farm. J had moved back in my absence, and our daughter was taking care of him. At night, of course, Bonnie slept on the bed with him. 'She is such a *comfort*,' he told me on the telephone.

Thus my small dog fulfilled an ancient destiny, as a 'comforter dog'. Her breed is one of the most ancient in recorded history, about 8,000 years old. Very early on Maltese were believed to have healing powers: place one on the stomach or chest and you would feel better. It isn't hard to see why all lapdogs give comfort. A dog's body temperature is between 100.2 and 102.8°F and therefore, sitting on your lap in a draughty castle (for example), it kept you warm. This is where the vet Bruce Fogle's hot-water bottle idea comes in. Oriental emperors and their courtiers called their pets 'sleeve' dogs; a Pekinese popped in each capacious sleeve must have been invaluable in winter.

Myth has it that Marie Antoinette walked to the guillotine in 1793 clutching her papillon to give her strength. Another doomed queen, Mary Queen of Scots, was also repaid for her lifelong love of dogs by the last service of her faithful pet. Some say it was a Skye terrier, some a Maltese, some a toy spaniel – it doesn't matter. Mary was incarcerated at Fotheringhay Castle, about 80 miles north of London, by her cousin Elizabeth I, who is portrayed in a lovely small work by Marcus Gheeraerts the Elder with a Maltese at her feet, leading one reasonably to assume this was her own dog. Mary Stuart liked to dress her pets in blue velvet collars, and wrote from captivity to the Archbishop of Glasgow, begging for a couple of 'pretty little dogs' from Lyons, and explaining, '… my only pleasure is in all the little animals I can get. They must be sent in baskets, well stored so as to keep them warm.' She embroidered little, leaping dogs amongst flowers and leaves.

On the morning of 8 February 1587 Mary was led into the Great Hall to be executed. After the terrible, bungled hacking was over, an eyewitness records: 'Then one of the executioners noticed her little dog which had hidden under her clothes. Afterwards it would not leave the corpse but came and lay between her head and her shoulders.' The blood-spattered animal lay whimpering, refusing to leave its mistress, until dragged away by force to be washed. But afterwards the small dog pined, refused to eat and did not long survive its mistress.

If I had worn a voluminous gown on top of the multiple petticoats of that time, Bonnie (who sometimes seems tied to my heel by an invisible elastic) could have crept unseen with me to the scaffold. In a sense she did. Summer over, autumn tumbling down into winter, J continued to be absent, staying with friends and unable to shake off his grief, or pull himself back from what seemed like post-traumatic stress disorder. I would watch him on television, listen to him on the radio and marvel that he could still be professional, still be courteous to sometimes mendacious politicians. I thought he would come back, but he did not. Writing much later (in the introduction to his fine book *Russia*, published in 2008) he explained, with simple honesty, 'I was in no condition to repair the damage I had inflicted on my marriage.' So in that dark time, when I existed in a sort of limbo, I would reach out in the night to the space he used to fill – and my fingers would clutch the small, soft shape of my dog.

At this point I was still trying to keep his absence a secret, although close friends knew. For journalists we were both naïve. Susan Chilcott had many, many friends and admirers so it is no surprise their relationship had been the talk of musical London. Inevitably people talk, but I was so wrapped up in my own slow-burning shock that I was unaware how many people knew what was going on. As Chairman of the Children's Theatre Appeal (now flourishing and called The Egg) I had to make public appearances and be as British as possible, keeping a stuff upper lip. But one day I hosted a fundraising reception at the farm and in the middle of my socializing with the generous great and good of Bath, a reporter from the *Mail on Sunday* arrived on the doorstep, wanting to find out the state of my marriage. It happened more than once, and I would utter staccato lies about my own friendship with Susan Chilcott, still trying to conceal what everybody knew. At such moments you dream of a tall high window and the moment when you launch yourself through it into the blue vacancy, surrounded by bright splinters. Falling.

One night I had to go to a similar party, this one hosted by a friend and held at the great house St Catherine's Court, just outside Bath, which was then owned by the actress Jane Seymour. One of our appeal committee collected me at 7.30 p.m., and I remember thinking even then how strange it was that I – the independent and controlling one – was grateful to be looked after. The friend driving me was one of those I reluctantly chose to confide in, only to find he already knew. Of course people like to gossip, but it is not always malicious. The desire to be in the know, and the need to pass on fascinating scraps of information about our fellow men and women, is as old as humanity itself. It is malice that I loathe. Too many newspapers employ columnists whose sole function is to bitch, flinging vitriol around like a maniac on a bus with a bottle of acid, not caring who it burns and scars.

(Incidentally, it is a mystery to me that, for centuries, the term 'bitch' has been derogatory, and the verb 'to bitch' implies the nastiest qualities – traducing the reputation of the female dog. In the opinion of the great scientist Konrad Lorenz (awarded the Nobel prize for medicine and psychology in 1973) a bitch is more faithful than a dog as well as more intelligent. In *Man Meets Dog* (1949) he writes, 'I have known a great many dogs and can say with conviction that of all creatures the one nearest to man in the finest of its perceptions and its capacity to render true friendship, is a bitch. Strange that in English her name has become a term of abuse.')

That night my own little bitch proved her worth. The evening dragged on and I made small talk (as one must) and gazed on the actor Bill Nighy across the room, aware that my old self would have rocked up to meet him, but this new self did not have the mettle. When your marriage is cracking under strain (at that stage I did not yet consider it irretrievably broken) you look at the people around you as aliens, wondering how they can drink and talk and laugh when the world is falling apart. But of course, not *their* world. Yet people in pain subconsciously seek each other out; I met a woman unknown to me who was in a similar situation and we clinked glasses to wish each other strength. At last it was over, and at about 11.30 p.m. another friend drove a long way out of her route to take me home. It was icy and misty, and the half-mile track to the farm seemed longer than ever. As we clunked over the first cattle grid and swung down and round past the path up to the new barn where the cattle were wintering in, my spirits sank even lower, if that were possible. The games barn, the house, the cottage – all were empty. Sue was silent. I knew she didn't want to leave me, for this was something she had been through herself.

I saw the eyes first, chips of emerald in the headlights. There was a very large farm gate which we would close if going out, to keep the dogs enclosed. Bonnie's arrival had necessitated fine chicken wire along the bottom, for she could easily pass beneath. When I left that night at 7.30, climbing into my friend's car beyond the gate, she had been running around with Billie and Sam, all three hating the fact that they were going to be left for the evening. But for big dogs two bowls of food and a cosy bed is a big draw; they know that when they hear the car return they can bust out through the dog flap and set the yard echoing with their commotion. In contrast, small dogs keep watch. Small dogs wait.

'Look!' said Sue.

Bonnie was standing on her hind legs, paws resting on the wood, waiting. Seeing the car, she yapped frantically – and Billie and Sam came out on cue. But when I said goodnight to my friend, and opened the gate to take my dog, squirming rapturously, in my arms, I could tell by the iciness of her paws and the chill of her head that she had not left her vigil by the gate since I had left. Four hours in a bitter wind, 700 feet above sea level.

The American poet (and author of *Dog Years*, one of the best books ever written about the love of dogs) Mark Doty believes that dogs offer a 'cure' for the essential spiritual loneliness of humankind. When J and I had only just fallen in love we agreed one night that the conjoining of human souls is an impossibility: both the head and the body could love in passion and in friendship, yet that love is only possible 'if two keep souls apart' (as I wrote in a love poem to him). Such an idea was probably a product of the zeitgeist: that sixties radicalism which drew so much from Sartre and de Beauvoir (whom we admired) and was fed equally by reforming zeal and existential *angst*. Why did we start out by holding something back? Neither of us had ever been in love in the way we were at the end of 1967, and yet still we clung to something so aridly theoretical as the idea that there is no such thing as a soulmate. It was one of many things (I realize now) that we got wrong. To embrace the idea of the one mate for your soul, to cleave to another, giving and taking in equal measure, is surely the only cure for the loneliness that afflicts you when the umbilical cord is cut. That it is so hard to attain is no reason for not striving. For love, above all, demands great things of the self – including sacrifice.

Mark Doty maintains that animal presences are a door towards feeling and understanding. His account of his love for his dogs Arden and Beau and the agonizing death of his first partner Wally from AIDS demonstrates the profound truth that when you open your heart to such loves, different though they might be, you place yourself permanently on the interface between delight and heartbreak. He writes, 'You can only understand the world through what's at hand.' And if that is the 'intelligence and sensibility … complex of desires and memories, habits and expectations' which is a dog, then why should it not give insight into the human condition too?

The poet had bought the golden retriever Beau to please his partner. Yet generosity and love can bounce right back to reward you, as I too was to discover. Doty writes, 'I thought when I brought Beau home, I was giving a gift to Wally, but in truth the gift was his to me, or mine to myself, or both. If I'd planned it I couldn't have done a better thing to save my life.'

In the same way, Bonnie's vigil by the gate was another stage in my own education. To be adored so much was balm for the wounded spirit; to remain the centre of the world for this single, small breathing creature was solace for the soul. Some days I felt that if all else melted away it would still be me and Bonnie facing up to a universe of missing husbands, dead lovers, gossiping bystanders, curious friends and sorrowful loved ones. In needing me so very much she was throwing me a lifeline – although I did not know it. What's more, a dog (or cat, or horse) anchors you in reality. Even if each step is slow, and the face in the mirror is alien and full of shadows, each day the pets must be taken care of. For what did they know of change? It was not their fault. Mark Doty understands this well: 'A walk is a walk and must be taken; breakfast and dinner come when they are due. The routines of the living are inviolable, no hiatus called on account of misery, spiritual crisis, or awful weather.'

The year was falling towards Christmas, the feast that was always so important in our family – a festival of lights indeed. But J was not coming back; this would be the first Christmas for 35 years that we would spend apart. The situation was barely tolerable. My father had suffered a heart attack and (more or less) recovered. My daughter had been ill in hospital again and (more or less) recovered. In between all this, Malcolm Love and I had made radio programmes with the novelist Ian Rankin (in Edinburgh) and Professor Sir Robert Winston. Looking back, I don't know how I managed to string two words together, let alone ask good questions. My days felt as if I were stumbling across a field in darkness, only just managing to stay upright, hearing my own breath as the men with lamps and guns closed in. At night I would lie bolt awake and listen to the sounds outside – those sudden screeches and mysterious rustles of the countryside – and it was as if it was all happening inside my head, not out there: wildness scrabbling to be let out.

I'd had a few sessions with a local psychotherapist, in an attempt to make sense of what was happening, but when I entered her peaceful office and told the quiet woman my story, I could almost see her flinch. Oddly, I felt sorry for her, sensing she would be happier coping with a little local depression than this manic, self-analysing woman, whose savage determination to *cope* was a shield too strong for gentle therapy. In those days I knew little about such matters; since then I have wondered if J and I had been able to talk to somebody together we might have managed to save our marriage. Yet nobody suggested it – nobody he was speaking to, nobody around me – and so we continued in our private hells. By then, not long before Christmas, all the peace I had found in Grace Cathedral had ebbed away, all forgiveness forgotten. I felt enraged that he should remain so stricken with grief for a woman he had known such a short time, furious that he seemed to have fled from me, and everything we had created. The worst thought – in those bruised hours before the dawn, when the pills are not working and even the dog has lost her sense of duty and fallen asleep – was that the wrong person had gone. I could not banish the wretched thought that had I, his wife, died he would not have mourned so much.

(I now think that the comparison is as absurd as it is hypothetical. But it was how I felt at the time.)

How were we to cope with Christmas? I put up the usual tall tree at the end of our big sitting room and festooned it with the usual multicoloured fripperies, including a scrawny red garland which had adorned our trees in my Liverpool childhood, and some decorations Dan had made as a little boy. Our Christmas tree was always laden; it was impossible to find space for any more lights and ornaments. (I like what is extravagant and over the top; that was a difference between J and me.) Most cards were addressed to me, because enough people now knew what had happened, but those with 'Mr and Mrs' on the envelope seemed to make innocent mockery of tree, hanging stars, mistletoe, everything. Who would carve the turkey? What about the sweet, silly, private Christmas rituals?

Christmas had to be diluted. In 1987 I had met a Radio 4 producer called Gaynor Vaughan-Jones. We made a literary series called *American Authors* together, and became close friends. This was followed by a series, *Turning Points*, the high spot of which was an interview with Seamus Heaney about moving from the north to the south of Ireland, which was a political/cultural/spiritual upheaval. Gaynor was now married to Ernie Rea, the BBC Controller of Religious Broadcasting, who was the person to whom I had taken the original proposal for the long-running *Devout Sceptics*. They had shared an unhappy holiday with the kids and me back in the summer and been entirely supportive, as well as sad for us all. Now the children and I decided to invite them for Christmas. When they accepted I actually wept with relief, for the gap left by J was so shocking, so enormous it had to be filled.

So, in the event, Christmas 2003 saw a surprisingly convivial gathering at the farm. It was to be the last ever. With Daniel and Kitty, my parents, Gaynor and Ernie, and Robin and his best friend Lawrence, I even approached feeling happy. J's usual seasonal toast was raised by me instead, before the presents were unwrapped. My children did everything to take their father's place, literally and figuratively – whilst Ernie, just one year younger than J, was an essential father figure. We all tried so hard we actually succeeded. Gaynor's tough little Border terrier, Bentley, stared threateningly at Bonnie as if she were a white rabbit and when he began to salivate at the sight my friend realized she should keep her dog on a short leash. The cats kept out of his way. The big dogs were the same as ever – lolloping and lovely. I wondered if they missed their master, as we did.

Yet those feelings had to be kept in check. I opened J's gift to me in the privacy of my study. He opened mine somewhere else. We spoke on the phone. Nothing was as bad for me as it was for him.

Three

MOVING

A man and a dog descend their front steps
The dog says, Let's go downtown and get crazy drunk
Let's tip over all the trash cans we can find.
This is how dogs deal with the prospect of change.
Stephen Dobyns, 'How To Like It'

*I*magine a world where none of us has names. How much does a name shape your identity? Before I met Bonnie she had another name – or two other names. The small dog abandoned and left tied to a tree must have been named by whoever knew her for the first six months of life. Then the kind people at the RSPCA home gave her another name, for I remember being told, 'We call her–', but can't recall what it was. When she became Bonnie she was given a new identity. With her third and last name she became truly *mine*.

I agree with the dog-loving poet Mark Doty that the saddest dogs in the shelter are the ones without any names – because nobody cares enough about them to give them up accompanied by proper information. Like Bonnie, they have simply been abandoned, bereft of names and dates. I always feel touched by photographs of long-dead dogs (for example, the ones collected by Libby Hall and published in books like *These Were Our Dogs*) because you long to know the names, as if such knowledge would defy death by attaching importance. All of the people in old photographs rescued from junk shops once cared enough to be photographed with their pets, yet few recorded the names. But one photograph (in the book I mention) shows a moustachioed soldier sitting cross-legged with a St Bernard and a Jack Russell. On the front of the picture someone has written 'Hissy and Jack'. The reverse has more detail. It reads: 'France, August 1916. Our Corp pet St Bernard named Hissy 8 months old and the Terrier named Jack. Just after we came out here 16 months – and our Staff Sgt Farrier Len Nusse.'

The soldier who took the picture must have loved those dogs. In the carnage of France he took a photograph and recorded his affection by naming them both on the front and the back. Their identity is more important to him than that of his unit's farrier, who is mentioned as an afterthought. I like to imagine what comfort these pets gave the soldiers, their tails wagging despite the menacing *crump* of distant guns. What's more, there's something dependable and British about the solid name Jack, and equally odd and unexpectedly frivolous about the naming of the St Bernard. Perhaps Hissy was a diminutive for something more dignified – but she (surely a female?) remains Hissy for ever, a light caress contained within the word.

I wonder if a name plays any part in shaping destiny. Around three centuries before the birth of Christ, the Greek writer

Xenephon published a manual on hunting in which he gives advice on dog-rearing and also on choosing their 'short names – so we may call them easily', offering a selection, like Pylax (Keeper), Chara (Gladness), Bia (Force) and Horme (Eager). All the names have positive connotations. George Orwell called his poodle Marx, but was amused to keep it a secret whether his pet was named for Karl or Groucho. Surely you would look at a dog differently if he was named after the father of socialism and not a lovable clown?

The late Leona Helmsley, the wealthy hotel magnate, who served time in prison for tax evasion, left a fortune to her Maltese dog, Trouble. But who would give a small white dog such an unfortunate name? A difficult woman whom the newspapers called 'The Queen of Mean', of course. No wonder nobody liked the poor little rich dog who nipped anyone who came within reach of his tiny teeth. The Maltese received death threats, even when his bizarre inheritance was reduced by a judge from $12 million to $2 million. On one occasion Trouble even took flight through the traffic on Fifth Avenue as if making a bid for freedom – the event recorded on the internet. The dog who was so adored by his difficult and lonely mistress ended up living in Florida with an employee paid to take care of him. The nature of that care nobody can know. Poor dog: Trouble by name, troubled by nature. When I read about him I mused that if he were mine he would be renamed Toby and have a happier life.

In contrast, Bonnie is a name full of sunshine. In the northeast of England boys are greeted with 'bonny lad' and a girl is called 'bonny lass' – such benevolence there you feel nobody thus called could be mean-spirited or ugly. The Old English *boni* links to French *bon/bonne* meaning 'good' and Webster's *Dictionary* gives definitions: (1) handsome, pretty, beautiful and attractive and (2) merry, frolicsome, cheerful and blithe. A 'bonny baby' is rounded, rosy and full of health. The old rhyme about birthdays holds that 'The child who is born on the Sabbath Day/Is bonny and blithe and good and gay'. The name is full of positives, and so although I unthinkingly called my dog after one of my favourite singers, something more significant was happening. Subliminally, I was rewriting her destiny – transforming her from the unwanted thing tied to a tree to a well-beloved creature tied to a human heart.

At the beginning of 2004 I was transforming my own destiny too. I changed my name and I bought a house. Both were acts of almost aggressive self-assertion, although I did not realize it at the time because I was not thinking things through. I was reacting. No longer would I be tied to a home or to a married name; metaphorically I took flight along Fifth Avenue, making my bid for freedom.

I was born in Liverpool in 1946 and christened Beryl Ann Mooney. Ann was my father's mother's name, and I should have adopted it, for I thoroughly detested the name Beryl, once I was old enough to care. Like other names (Hilda, Pamela, Norma, Pearl …) it carries with it images of plain, struggling Britain in the forties and fifties, a world of low-wattage centre lights, smoky coal fires, the sound of the hand-operated sewing machine, the smell of frying and boiled cabbage – and the family clustered around the Bakelite radio to listen to *Two Way Family Favourites*. At primary school I was a thin, shy, bespectacled child, teased as 'Beryl the Peril' and 'Gooney-Mooney-Four-Eyes', and those names, those ugly personae, turned me in on myself, to take refuge in books. Beryl went to the library and read her way through all the shelves, while at home 'Our Belle' was grandfather's darling, sitting on his knees while he plaited my fair hair. She was the princess-shut-up-in-a-tower, whose identity was secret from everybody but who dreamed of being *known*, of being beautiful – *belle*.

Through the teenage years I went on being Belle at home and Beryl in school, but when the time came to leave home for university in October 1966 I decided to reinvent myself as Bel. I liked the economy of dropping two letters from my Christian name and disliked the spelling 'Belle' because of its too-flattering meaning. After all, I had only just got contact lenses, was able to see myself properly for the first time and realized that there was a way to go with the metamorphosis.

So at university I introduced myself with a variant of the pet name, and it did indeed coincide with a feeling of being hand-some – *bel*. The new persona fitted. But when I married J in February 1968 I took on yet another, changing my name to his. Henceforth my passport and everything else would belong to somebody called Beryl Ann Dimbleby, although I was always known as Bel. When I became a journalist I had no hesi-tation in keeping my maiden name for professional purposes, since my husband's surname was far too well known. Remember that the small, insignificant wedding of two univer-sity students in 1968 was covered in newspapers under head-lines like 'Dimbleby's son weds'. I was an ordinary girl, unused to this. There was no escaping it – not then, or ever.

Besides, I could not so easily lose my Liverpool-Mooney identity – which was, in the end, to prove more durable than the other. It is my essence, a source of pride which transcends academic, social or professional achievement, and I like to think there was something Liverpudlian-tough about my determination to survive. For by December 2003 I was possessed by rage at a level nobody could see. I am no saint, and nor have I ever been. Something J said on one of his visits prompted me to go online to see how easily I could change my name by deed poll. He implied that I (like my ex-sister-in-law) had been quite happy with the famous surname, a suggestion I thought unjust since I had never used it professionally. So, at a stroke (well, not quite so simply, since you have painstakingly to change all your legal documents, which can drag on for months) I became Bel Mooney in law, for the very first time. This was, in effect, a 'new' identity. I received my new passport on 13 January 2004 – all too aware of the powerful symbolism of what I had done. With this, my third name, I became truly my own person.

There was also to be a move to a new house. J and I had agreed that now, after six months without him on the farm, our beloved home had become my prison. The winds punished me, the dark was oppressive and despite the level of seasonal celebration we had achieved at Christmas, the sense of loss was pervasive. My husband knew it better than anyone; he could not return and acknowledged that I could not remain. Impasse. It was (I thought much later) as if we had been together in a little boat for 35 years, rowing strongly side by side. Sometimes the water had been choppy, sometimes the motion had made one of us seasick, yet we had kept going. Then suddenly one day we were caught up in a whirlpool and he fell overboard and I rowed in circles alone, looking for him, yet the current carried me onwards away from the danger. When his head finally broke the surface I was somewhere else, unable to row backwards to reach him. ('Always go forward and never turn back.') That is how it seemed.

My children had arrived just before that first Christmas without their father, driving down from London. They strode into the kitchen and asked what he and I had decided. By then they were resigned, on the surface at least. (Never below it, but that is another story.)

'He says I can look for a house.'

'Good – that's what you need, Mum.'

'I know.'

'So what kind of a house do you want?'

Without hesitation, it tumbled out: 'I want big windows and a walled garden and … I'd like a house with a door in the middle, like the houses I used to draw when I was a child.'

Our farm had small windows and endless landscape and a rambling shape, so I was constructing a diametrically opposite dream. They rushed off to do their Christmas shopping in Bath, and Kitty called me 30 minutes later in excitement. They had seen The House in an estate agent's window. A town house built in the Regency period, it had big windows, a walled garden and a door in the middle of the elegant frontage. What's more, she told me, in the picture of the sitting room there was a small white dog on the rug. That was surely a sign.

Next day I went to see the house with my mother and daughter, who enthused. It was spacious but compact, and the woman who owned it had installed every modern accoutrement without spoiling its period feel. All I would need to do was have bookshelves built and change one bathroom. It was all terrifying, but the presence of the owner's dog helped. A

West Highland terrier called Lily, she sat on a chaise longue in the window of the master bedroom, waiting for her mistress (a widow) to return. The dog stared fixedly at the road, ignoring (after the first barks) the estate agent and us: intruders on her territory. Her whole being was fixed on the possibility of reunion. That is what dogs want.

Humans want it too, but there is a limit to the amount of time you can stare, quivering with anticipation out of the window, or waiting in the graveyard. Looking back I sometimes feel sad that I, the enlightened human, did not match up to canine example and wait for ever – as dogs will do. For example, the famous Scottish story of 'Greyfriars Bobby' epitomizes a fidelity which touches humans who fall short. Bobby belonged to a night watchman called John Gray, and the two became a familiar sight in Edinburgh, out in all weathers. But John contracted tuberculosis, died of the disease in 1858 and was buried in Old Greyfriars burial ground. In rain and snow, Bobby refused to leave his master's grave and in the end the churchyard-keeper gave up trying to chase him off and laid sacking for the poor little dog next to his master's grave. The fame of the faithful terrier spread and each day crowds would gather at one o'clock when, hearing the gun signal, Bobby left the grave and went to the coffee house he had always visited with his master, where they still put down food for the dog. His vigil continued for 14 years, until he died in 1872, at the age of 16. There is a statue to Bobby now, and a pub named after him, and the long-dead emblem of loyalty even has his own website and sells souvenirs – proving that the story (like the similar one of Hachiko, a station dog, in Japan) goes on speaking to something deep within us.

After all, a woman's husband might leave her but her dog is there for its life. I once met a Canadian truck driver on the road in the States whose journeys were shared by the half-dingo (yes, in America) mutt he had found abandoned by the side of the road in Wyoming. He confessed that he had much more to say to the dog than to his wife – and thinking of his long months on the road I conjectured that perhaps his dog were the more faithful. The difficult truth is that some humans find it relatively easy to 'replace' people they have lost (both J and I were to do this) but the dogs hang in there. Since Susan Chilcott died I had waited for my husband to come back ('come to his senses' some said) and tell me, 'That madness is over, so let us pick up the threads of our life again.' But he did not – and I knew that unless I acted, I would go mad myself. Of course, I *could* have given J some more time to be healed and then return. But suppose that never happened? Never interested in gambling, I could not stop my highly developed instinct for self-preservation from kicking in.

I remember sitting one evening listening to Nina Simone singing Jacques Brel's beautiful song 'Ne Me Quitte Pas'. The track is long; I was listening acutely to the words and began in tears but ended feeling a powerful surge of rebellion. It bubbled up during the most abject stanza, at the end of the song, where the singer pleads (sounding beautiful in French): 'Don't leave me. I will cry no more, I will talk no more … Let me become the shadow of your shadow, the shadow of your hand, the shadow of your dog. Don't leave me.' And so on.

All those torch songs which fling themselves masochistically on the floor, waiting for the foot on the head ('He beats me too,' sings Billie Holliday), made for moody listening on tipsy nights when the cigarette smoke curled to the ceiling. But in real life? Your *own* life? No, no, no. I will *never* beg to be the shadow of any man's dog. I will pack up my own dog in her smart bag and make my own way now, thank you very much. Why should I play the victim and warble that other classic French ballad, '*J'attendrai*' – I will wait? My life was slipping by with each breath and I had no time to wait, not any more.

This is a refusal of underdog status. So many negative phrases attach themselves to dogginess. For example, a 'dog' is a plain woman. To call a man a 'dog' or a 'cur' is one of the worst insults. To be 'hangdog' is to epitomize ill-treated vulnerability, and an 'underdog' is … well, amongst other things, a woman whose husband has left her. That is, unless she leaves too. Walks in the opposite direction. 'Bends with the remover to remove,' to quote Shakespeare's sonnet 116. J had absented himself from our home first; now it was my turn to move. In the words of the philosopher Mark Rowlands, 'It is only our defiance which redeems us.' I cannot read that without imaging a clenched fist raised angrily, proudly to the sky. The truth is, there had developed, alongside the sorrow, something hard and unyielding in both of us. Grief and guilt render a man (or woman) immovable – but so does a sense of rectitude. It can be as difficult to forgive a person we have harmed as it is to forgive someone who has harmed us. Whatever the reasons, I simply could not bear to remain marooned, yet clinging to the wreckage.

These days, in my role as an advice columnist, I receive many letters from people whose marriages are at an end and do not know where to go – literally as well as figuratively. I always advise trying to take back some sort of control – even if it's changing the locks or your name. If you are the one who has been left you feel utterly demoralized. You forget to wash your hair and you take to your bed, only to remain sleepless. You go to your doctor and pour it all out until those professional eyes slide away, aware of the rows of patients waiting outside. Then you are given a prescription for amitryptilene to help you sleep, but feel like a zombie all day. You burst into tears when you hear somebody talking about love on the radio, and a scene in a film (as when Emma Thompson's character in *Love Actually* realizes her vain husband has bought a necklace for the sexy girl in the office, but knows she must put on a brave smile for her children ...) can leave you prostrated with grief.

So, as displacement, you spend an evening watching a Jackie Chan action movie or some tedious sport coverage, as if you were somebody else. And indeed, you *have* become somebody else now – the person who was left. You never thought you would meet this person in your mirror; you can stare at her in numb disbelief for ages. You pace your home and everything in it mocks you for having failed. Because you *have* failed, and nobody (not the well-meaning friends, nor the slightly inadequate therapist you find to burden with your woes) can tell you otherwise. You thought other people's marriages broke up but now you stare into the abyss of your own and believe with all your heart that *you* should have had the power to steer both of you in a different direction. The old house is falling down around your ears, but you don't blame the earthquake: you blame yourself.

22 January: I go to see SM – pretty, dark-haired solicitor in a businesslike trouser suit, taking the remnants of my marriage in hand. It will be the gentlest type of separation since we have decided a divorce is too brutal and I don't want it. She says, 'He's not only lost his wife, he's lost his best friend.' But he hasn't lost my friendship. That must continue. There are seconds when I think I could step across the gulf between us and beg, 'Come back.' Or he could say, 'It was all a mistake – I love you – take me back.' But it doesn't happen. And now I really do want to live in the new house and imagine its clean, empty spaces with delight. The farm is chilly. Cold weather forecast. The fields grey and muddy. A fence broken. Billie and Sam look sad and bored. Tonight I went to the American Museum for drinks and took Deirdre McS aside to tell her my melancholy news and her shock affected me. Yes, it is shocking and ought not to be happening. So I returned home even more melancholy, to pick at food, and cough, then fall asleep early by the sitting room fire. I feel silent and don't want to talk to anybody much. Even Bonnie palls.

'Taking in hand' is the key phrase there, although I could not have known it at the time. I realize how privileged I was to be able to think of buying a new property, because most people cannot. The London base we had bought in 1986 – which had been a happy family home at one stage, and which provided lodgings for various friends over the years, as well as being a working office for productions made under our company – would be sold to buy me this house. So I was lucky – in some ways. Still, it is vital for people who find themselves in a simi-lar situation to realize that taking even the smallest action to fight their own corner (a needlessly aggressive phrase, perhaps) will help. The key is not waiting for things to be done 'to' you, but to step forward and make autonomous decisions, even something as small as booking a new haircut and a facial. I know that some will think such counsel trivial; they do not understand that small decisions and undramatic actions form the bricks which, one by one, can build a new home where the self can learn its changed identity.

At the end of January my daughter left for a six-month back-packing trip with a friend; she had done what she could for both parents and now needed to escape. Her brother and I waved her goodbye, then drove back from Heathrow in silence, each knowing how much we would miss her. When she returned I would no longer be living in the family home. Dan and I wandered along Portobello Road, had lunch, talked quietly about all that had happened. I drove the 100 miles back to the empty farm and that night a blizzard raged about the house as I lit my wood stove and went through papers in my study, preparing to pack.

Messages come from the strangest quarters. Signs from the gods, I mean. A couple of weeks after Kitty left, in London to meet my agent I was very gloomy. There had been a hold-up with the mortgage and I was afraid I would lose the new house; J and I were in constant contact through melancholy emails, phone calls and meetings to discuss the division of property – at the end of which we would hold each other with wordless sorrow. Gradually we told acquaintances in a wider circle that we had separated, because it was still not generally known. Again and again I saw faces show shock – then sadness. I wondered if it is because the world holds up a long-married couple as a beacon – especially if, like J and me, they have always been honest about complex and difficult times. I could almost hear people thinking, But you've come so far, experienced so much together, survived it all – *don't give up now.* I went to a book launch and whispered the truth to a very distinguished historian, writer and art expert, many years older than J and me, with whom we'd enjoyed a warm relationship over many years. In a room crowded with people clutching glasses of champagne he actually shed tears. It was good for me to give comfort to someone else for the sad story which, I'm sure, seemed to call all marriages into question.

So there I was with an hour to kill before meeting my agent. And I wandered into the John Lewis department store on Oxford Street, feeling events bound round my heart like iron bands. With the new house in mind I wander to the basement where household and electrical goods are sold, and find The Message on a floor display. There is an iron, an ironing board and clothes drier, all in my favourite lilac and white, with a big sign suspended, proclaiming 'NEW START'. I blink and gaze around me, and it is as if everything is illuminated: glittering and surreal. There are signs everywhere: 'REFRESH', 'RESTORE', 'RENEW'. The spring colours lift me, despite myself, and I realize that nothing will ever prevent me from making a new start. No torch song in my brain, but the disco anthem, 'I will survive.'

12 February: I write sitting alone in the library. Good to be alone, even though I don't use my time well. Today I usefully terminated a lot of standing orders and direct debits. I'm overwhelmed by all the financial/organizational things I have to do on my own, for the first time. But then ridiculously pleased

*when I do them. J and I were so old-fashioned in the division
of our life: did it have to be that way? Will I ever regain my
confidence? Will I do any good work again? I feel tired and
bereft of energy and – yes – love. I read poems about love, all
alone in the library. Not – not alone. With Bonnie. And it was
all right. And will be.*

All this time I reviewed the occasional book for *The Times* and
tried to develop a book proposal but other work was impossible. I drifted through the days with the three dogs and the
cats, packing up those books, ornaments and pictures I would
take with me, and labelling the furniture which would fit my
new house. At night I curled up with Bonnie and my diary,
noting that '*the complete silence of the house and valley deafens
me. Yes, I can hear it like a muffled roar in my ears. If I put out
my hand I know I would be able to feel it, soft as cotton wool.*' I
missed J terribly. My diary spurts savage rage at Susan Chilcott
('*her selfish, greedy snatching at* our *life*') that stemmed, in part,
from the need to blame. I could not bear to resent the man I
had married and so I transferred all my rage to the woman he
had loved for such a short time. And still loved too.

One day when J was visiting I told him that if you can *love*
someone who's dead you can *hate* someone who's dead.

Bonnie and I went shopping. People in Bath always notice her.
Maybe it's the size, maybe the perpetual motion, maybe the
wardrobe of collars and leads that tend to match whatever the
foolish woman with her is wearing. The girls in the shoe shop
fussed over my little dog as I tried on heels higher than any I
had worn, savage shiny black things with Perspex sides. They

became mine. Three days later I bought some vintage red stilettos with lethal pointed toes, and wrote, '*I am overdrawn with no work and a new house looming and yet I buy high heels. The symbolism is obvious. I want shoes which have no place on his stupid, stupid farm …*'

Similarly, Valentine's Day found Bonnie and me hanging out with a dealer in vintage jukeboxes, about 20 miles south of Bath. I have always loved rock 'n' roll, and Americana, and the Beat poets, and girl groups with bouffant skirts and hair who sing and move in unison while their universal question joins the harmony of the stars: 'Baby, baby, where did our love go …?' In the basement of the house I was buying was a huge recess in the wall where an ancient kitchen range would once have been. On the first visit I had known that there, in the room that was to become office space, I would install the jukebox I'd always wanted. As a teenager in a small Wiltshire town I would hang around the cockroach-infested Milk Bar inexpertly puffing on cheap cigarettes and feeding the jukebox as I slurped milk shakes. I'd shimmy my shoulders to Little Richard and Roy Orbison (oh yes – 'Crying over you') and Jerry Lee Lewis. Such behaviour – then and now – was as remote from J's world as I was from his show-jumping or from Susan Chilcott's opera stages.

That is why I wanted a jukebox. It was another statement. The 1964 Wurlitzer with Cadillac lines, a sunburst etched on plastic and vertically loaded '45s became mine with a *click, whirr, hiss.* Although I did have to defer both delivery and payment, since I had no house and no money. Yet.

By March the press phone calls had begun in earnest. There had been some back in the summer/autumn of 2003 and the

Mail on Sunday's door-stepping visit while I was hosting a charity reception. I lied to all enquirers, saying that the soprano was much loved by everybody and a friend of 'ours'. But why, you might ask, did the end of one marriage merit such intrusion? For the same reason that we were snapped by strangers on our wedding day: there was no escape for the scion of a famous dynasty, or in turn for his family, when he became famous in his own right. J never came to terms with that. In his own eyes he was a professional writer and broadcaster, known for the seriousness of his work. He loathed the idea of 'celebrity', but in this he was out of tune with the times. In any case, Susan Chilcott was a beautiful performer in her own right, so whether he liked it or not, this was a 'story'.

I was packing up one house (the one in London sold now) and painfully extracting my own things from our proper home while being waylaid on doorsteps by junior gossip column writers who looked embarrassed ('Look, I'm just a hack, like you,' I protested) and telephoned by section editors I knew who said things like, 'The editor wants me to ask you to write about it all – this is awful, I feel like a vulture.' It was grim. Some days it was as if there were a door perpetually banging upstairs in my mind, deafening me, driving me crazy. Pathetically, I told myself that I didn't deserve this – but once you dare to raise the notion of just deserts you remember premature death, and ask yourself, 'Did *she* deserve *that*?'

For many people journalists rank very low in moral standing; certainly newspaper intrusion into private life and the lies spread by cheaper gossip magazines do damage and cause hurt. I am often amazed by the certainty with which colleagues will call a well-known person 'obnoxious' (just one example) when they have never met them. Over the years J and I were written about from time to time and I felt violent towards those who slighted him, but (perhaps because Liverpool people are bred tough in that bracing wind off the Mersey) did not care so much if people were rude about me. I was always reduced to rage at what I saw as any injustice to him, especially when he was working on the Prince of Wales project, indignant that people forgot all the serious achievements of a long career and reduced his journalism to one question about adultery.

But even at this, the worst stage, I could not hate the people who fed on gossip about us. To want to savour the most intimate detail of other people's relationships and to delight in seeing the mighty fallen are ancient human impulses; as someone who loves the classics I know that Roman poets like Martial, Catullus and Juvenal beat any modern writer in the nastiness stakes. In any case, I *like* journalists – hugely. I have worked for tabloids, broadsheets, a left-wing magazine, for colour supplements and women's magazines, and some of the most enjoyable times have been with my fellow scribblers. If I see one on my doorstep my instinct is to offer a cup of coffee – even though it is *our* flayed hearts which are the 'story'.

Nevertheless, the *Mail on Sunday* headline, across two pages, made my knees buckle, so that I had to sit down at the kitchen table. It said, 'Jonathan is in love with a ghost', and was illustrated by a press picture of the two of us arm in arm, handsome and happy, at some event or other, another a blurry snatched shot of him looking gaunt a few days before the piece appeared – and, in the middle, staring out at me, an enormous picture of Susan Chilcott, beautiful in a blue costume for one of her operatic roles. It filled me with horror, even though I knew the paper was planning an article. It was as if that face would stare at me for eternity, telling me that she had won.

On 10 March the new house became legally mine and it felt correct that I crossed the threshold with my son, who was seeing it for the first time. The two of them had spotted the place in the agents' window; Kitty had visited with me; now he was escorting me into my new home. With Kitty away, I leaned on Dan. I was consumed with a sensation of unreality which increased over the next two weeks. One day I was in London agreeing with a publisher to edit and contribute to a collection of stories on mothers and daughters, which would be published simultaneously in Britain and the USA; two days later the removal van was at the farm and the grim business began.

19 March: 'I wake at 7 knowing that this is the day I walk away from – not my marriage – but J's obsession with the ghost of the Soprano, because I will not live with her malevolent spectre. She possessed my oh-so-wonderful husband and has put a curse on his past and future. So. A morning of making coffee for removal men and watching my life (no longer our life) disappear into boxes, entering the van. I call Mum and Dad and as always they are there for me, going on to the house to unpack boxes. So. At 12.30 I look down and notice my left hand and scream. The large diamond in the ring my beloved J bought for our thirtieth anniversary is no longer there – torn from the setting. How to look? How could any search be possible? I was shocked and in tears. I called J to tell him and he was so sad, so sympathetic, so like the old J, before he met her.

He said, 'I'll buy you a new ring.' I had to overcome the loss of
the diamond (talk about symbolism) and of my marriage and
concentrate on leaving my home to J and the ghost of SC –
watching vanload after vanload depart, and rushing to the new
house to see mum and dad unpacking and unpacking, being so
'up' despite their age and despite this massive contradiction of
everything I have based my life upon. So overwhelmed by
contradictions: my new house is lovely yet so much smaller and
with traffic outside instead of the farm's peace. Fuck traffic! I
like it! Oh how strange it all is. What SC has achieved is a
geological shift. All is broken – and new. Tonight at 12.30 I feel
full of grief and bitterness. Why isn't one allowed to feel bitter?
Because that's too non-PC, or something. Yet everybody does, if
they are honest. It is late. I am tipsy. I love J.

The last thing I did before leaving my home was lay a fire in
the 'new' sitting room I had created for J (the old dining room)
so that when he retook possession of his home, alone now, he
would only have to strike a match to be warm. That action
came from the same place as his spontaneous 'I'll buy you a
new ring.' Although we were living apart we were to discover,
during the coming years, that we would never move far from
that place.

Bonnie was ever-present, the silent witness. But it was sad to
be leaving Billie and Sam and the cats. My own cat was Louis,
an impossibly elegant Burmilla, who was given to me by J when
I reached 50, together with a medieval manuscript and a
mother-and-child sculpture executed by an artist friend. (He
knew my tastes so well.) Naturally I imagined Louis moving

house with me and Bonnie – the smaller, less beautiful creature he regarded with indifference. But the reality of the main
road on which my new house was situated made me quail. The
cat had only ever known the freedom of the farm and I knew
(having moved with cats before) that he would inevitably seek
to return and, in all probability, meet his fate beneath the
wheels of a bus. So I would leave him with the other pets, to
be looked after by J's groom Fran, who had moved with her
family into the cottage Robin had vacated to house-share with
a friend in London. (In that sense Billie, Sam, Django, Louis
and Ella were fortunate. When Bonnie became mine I was told
at the Bath Dogs and Cats Home that increasing numbers of
pets come under their care because of broken relationships.)
But the truth is, Bonnie had triumphantly supplanted Louis
in my affections; the cat lover had fallen in love with one small
dog and there was no returning to the former state.

As long as my dog was with me, I would survive. One of the
most beautiful possessions of the British Museum is a medieval
manuscript called the Luttrell Psalter, an illuminated book of
psalms created between 1325 and 1340 for Sir Geoffrey
Luttrell of Lincolnshire, and world famous for its detailed
scenes of medieval village life. In one of the illustrations an
elaborate carriage (looking like a covered wagon) is setting off
on a journey. It carries four ladies of high birth. One of them,
dressed in gold with a blue veil from her coronet, is leaning
from the back of the carriage towards a squire riding close
behind. He is stretching over his horse's neck to hand a small
white dog, wearing a pretty collar, to the lady. The curve of her
body is tender as she leans forward to take the animal. The
precious lapdog is about to make a journey with her, wherever

it might take them, and you just know it is essential to her comfort.

That is how it felt when I moved house.

I was spending money wildly (a new TV and radio, mirrors and so on, for I had not removed such things from the farm) yet none was coming in. J and I had embarked on the complicated business of disentangling our finances. As usual I left everything to him, and payback came one day early in April when I went to the bank with just £3 in my purse, only to be refused money. With tears in my eyes, I begged the teller to increase my overdraft; clearly feeling sorry for me, she set the wheels in motion and said I would be able to get cash the next day – but the damage was done. I plunged into gloom, wanting my old safe life back.

Yet even then I had an underlying sense that this was *good* for me. While I found it lonely to register for council tax as a single occupant, after so many years as half of a pair, there was one part of me which thought it was time. For what? Coping with everyday reality, I suppose. When our baby son was still-born in November 1975 my grief was all-encompassing, but an epiphany came on the day when my cries of 'Why me?' were transformed into the quiet question, 'Why *not* me?' So it was now.

That query expresses an awareness that you are one tiny part of suffering humanity, and that it is your destiny, as it is the destiny of so many others, to endure without understanding why. Strange as it may seem, I knew that I must learn from (temporarily) not having any money for shopping. Even though I was not born into a wealthy family, I had never known want. That day, with £3 in my purse, I experienced the panic which afflicts the vast majority of humankind who are not as protected as I had been. And why should I be protected? Even when I felt so low, so bewildered, I could stand outside what was happening and see it as a source of future strength. The day before the bank incident I had written (after a visit by J during which I played him my jukebox): '*We hugged on the path when he left and the truth is – so much of my heart and soul stays with him, wherever he goes and whatever he does. Meeting him was the making of my life and the leaving of him re-makes it – because I know how strong I am.*'

I needed the absurdity of my dog at this time: her face all squashed when she had been lying down, her ridiculous frou-frou back view, the fearsome growls when she attacked a scrap of paper. Konrad Lorenz, great animal behaviourist that he was, had this to say about choosing a dog: 'I think that the great popularity enjoyed by some comical breeds of dog is largely attributable to our longing for gaiety. A Sealyham's love of fun and his fidelity to his master can prove a real moral support to a melancholy person. Who can help laughing when such an amusing little creature, bursting with the joys of life, comes bouncing along on his far-too-short legs …?' Any owner of a small dog will recognize that. Putting my books on the shelves in the new house and grieving for the old one, I felt dazed. It was torture to visualize J alone at the farm, just a couple of miles up the road, while I was sitting on one of a pair of old sofas (he had the other) wondering how I came to this strange place. That was the greatest absurdity, that we had come to this. So my little dog's antics were an essential antidote.

Five weeks after moving I left Bonnie behind with my parents and flew to Bangkok to meet my daughter. I hadn't seen her since 27 January, thirteen weeks earlier, and had arranged to write a travel piece about the spa resort Chiva Som, to give the backpacker a little luxury. To see Kitty waiting at the barrier and be given her welcome gifts, to wander through the night market with her and take a boat along the canals, then to be collected for the two-hour drive south to Hua Hin and a week of peaceful luxury … this was balm for the soul. At Chiva Som you have a daily massage, staring down through the table at a glass bowl, lit from underneath and filled with floating flowers. One day, in a reflexology session, the Thai therapist told me she detected a pain in my heart. Shocked, I whispered, 'My husband has gone,' and she simply bowed her head and laid a hand on my leg in sympathy.

But each day I relaxed more, and the unhappiness receded to a point where my marriage and family life on the farm seemed less real than the Golden Buddha on Monkey Mountain, which we reached by a 30-minute walk along the beach very early one morning, as the sun was rising in a mother-of-pearl sky. We lit joss sticks and I prayed that Kitty would be safe as she continued alone to Vietnam, Cambodia and Laos. That afternoon we left the resort, and the driver and I dropped her off in Bangkok on my way to the airport. I watched her small figure until it disappeared, weaving through hundreds of strangers on the Koh San Road in search of a cheap backpacker hotel. In the back of the car I snivelled, until the morose driver took pity on me and said, in his stumbling English, the only three words that matter, 'I am sorry.' Kitty and I had talked so much during the week and promised to be strong for each other. Now we were back on our different journeys, with a sense of new beginnings, as well as old loss.

At this point, returning from the holiday, I stopped keeping a daily journal (although I continued to keep notebooks). The recording of what seemed to be a mundane life (arranging furniture and books, sorting out the spare room and so on) became intolerable. The Bath International Music Festival began and when I took a friend called Stephen to a jazz concert I could sense people all round us staring, wondering if this was the new boyfriend perhaps? That's the problem with a small city. A couple I knew slightly asked me to dinner and I realized with astonishment that the spare man at the table was there for me. I felt withdrawn, although nobody could have detected it; naturally I was grateful that people should want me to find a new partner but the attempt to set me up embarrassed me. In any case, he wasn't my type.

The Bath Music Festival was one of the highlights of our year – and had been since 1981, when we had been living in Bath just six months. As Chairman, J was enthusiastic and innovative; he had forged a close friendship with the Chief Executive and Artistic Director, Tim Joss, whose wife, novelist Morag Joss, was a friend of Susan Chilcott. It was at their house that J and Susan had first met, at the fateful dinner party just 19 months earlier, and J had spent much time with them since her death. It must have been during the doleful months after Susan's death that it was decided that one of the highlights of the 2004 festival would be a special concert in her memory, from which all ticket sales would go to the hospital's on-going charitable appeal. When I saw this in the brochure I was deeply upset. It could not but feel like a slap in my face.

On 12 May Iain Burnside was on Radio 4's *Woman's Hour* to talk about Susan and publicize the concert. The presenter,

Jenni Murray, told listeners that Susan Chilcott had just been posthumously named Singer of the Year for her performance in *Jenufa*, and recalled the triumph of her 2002 debut as Lisa in Tchaikovsky's *Queen of Spades* opposite Placido Domingo. Iain Burnside extolled her talent and told of her courage, going on stage in 2002 between sessions of chemotherapy. In a soft Scottish voice, all the more impressive for its perfect control, he told how she was loved by her fellow singers, how fantastic she would have been in the next 10 years, how the cruelty of her premature death was already affecting a whole generation of singers.

Jenni Murray asked how, since Iain is gay, people viewed his guardianship of his best friend's child. His reply was memorable:

'When she gave me the choice that I should step up to the mark … I think … somewhere at the back of her mind, in the very black days before she died, there might have been some comfort in the thought that … I am unlikely to have more children, I am rather unlikely to marry, and that perhaps he would never be in a position where he could run to another woman with open arms saying 'Mummy.' She knows that Hugh will always be the sole focus of my love and attention and in that sense the choice of a gay Dad is perhaps not so strange as some people immediately presume.

On the night of the concert I was sitting in my new house on the green sofa with my little dog. Just a 10-minute walk away the beautiful ballroom of the Assembly Rooms was full of people (including my husband of course, making a short speech) celebrating the life and achievements of the gifted soprano whom, naturally, I blamed for the destruction of my marriage. I felt abandoned by everybody, except Bonnie. My new home was still. There was nobody to talk to about it all. The question in my mind was, is this what life comes down to, that I lose my precious diamond, and then someone, somewhere sings in celebration?

Journalist friends had rallied round and one of these, the editor of *The Times Magazine*, Gill Morgan, knew what leaving the farm had cost me and asked for a meditative essay on my idea of home. The article appeared in July, with a full-page portrait of me sitting on the pale Bath stone stairs with Bonnie – of course. She looks serene (because the photographer was dear, familiar Robin and she would have barked furiously at a stranger) but I look tense. Re-reading the article now, I realize how cathartic it was to write – to take a journey through the homes of my childhood and the homes of my marriage, attempting to make sense of the latest stage:

' … like many women, I have measured out my life with crowded rooms, until sometimes I felt like Alice grown too large, her head against the roof. Husband, children, parents, pets, parties, food, working at home, fitting it all in … the ceaseless struggle for perfection. Now, in these cool autonomous spaces, it's tempting to come out with the clichés of the independent, separated woman … 'I feel liberated … I can be myself …' and so on. But the truth is, I was myself in all our homes; it's just that I'm not sure whether I made them or they made me.

Walking down a street at dusk, the lamps lit, the curtains not yet drawn, you see rooms illuminated like stage sets for the comedies and tragedies of other lives. In just such a way I find myself looking back through lighted windows at my own life unfolding under different roofs, and ask myself – with due humility – how I got to be so lucky …

Now I wake to the sound of buses, the distant hum of a small city. There is nobody to consult over the colour scheme in the bedroom – which happens to be lilac and purple again, after all these years. If I want to festoon the place with butterflies and fairy lights, then so be it. I pay my own bills and turn the key in the door to a new world – awestruck by the generosity of its consolations. In the words of Sylvia Plath, 'I have a self to recover, a queen' …

For about three years I had been admiring a Chinese statue, for sale in a Bath gallery (since closed) which specialized in Asian art. She sat on a plinth opposite the entrance: a bodhisatva (enlightened being, follower of Buddha) carved from what looked like sandstone, and standing about a metre high. This was Kwan Yin, the goddess of compassion. The particular iconography of this statue had drawn me into the shop time after time, because Kwan Yin (often shown with a fish, or pouring a liquid from a gourd) was portrayed seated on a lotus and balancing, on one ample knee, a small manikin – a human child. His tiny hand clutched her large one; the echo of Christian iconography was haunting. When everything began to fall apart I continued to visit every few weeks to stroke Kwan Yin's cheek, while chatting to the owner about all the other beautiful works on display.

One summer day I was walking Bonnie down to the centre of Bath and went into the Lopburi gallery as usual to greet

Kwan Yin. The statue seemed to me to be a perfect representation of universal love – all the more appealing because of the small, crude areas of restoration and the discolorations of the stone. At some point, I think, she had lost her head but now she was put together again. The metaphor was unavoidable. Clumsy and flawed yet a thing of great beauty – that's how she seemed to me. Her downcast eyes, her glimmer of a smile spoke to me of acceptance in the face of time, loss, decay, death. Kwan Yin's serenity was what I most wished to attain, and had never even approached. Suddenly I realized that if the day came when I walked in only to find her no longer there – bought by a collector – I would be overwhelmed by sadness. At that moment I realized I *needed* her – as the icon of my new life. The gallery owner agreed to take three post-dated cheques and said with a smile, 'I knew she had to be yours.'

My goddess-protector soon had her first jobs, taking care of me and my small dog in equal measure. Exactly three weeks after she was installed at the end of my garden I heard that J was in a new relationship with a woman one year younger than our son. I do not intend to write any more about it; suffice it to say that I wandered blindly down the garden to put my arms around a statue. He and I were separated and yet the news was a bombshell. I had been worrying about his welfare all the time, but there was no need now. I had not expected this to happen so soon.

Three weeks after that Kwan Yin performed a miracle – yes, I do believe it, for how else to account for the extraordinary good fortune? Permit me to be fanciful; it is more consoling than trusting to random fate or chaos. I lie to think it was the benign influence of the goddess which saved the life of my small dog.

By now I was touting for work. That is all the freelance writer knows how to do, but marriage to J as well as my own success had lessened the need. Now Kwan Yin had to be paid for, and so I was back to selling ideas with additional purpose. To that end, I was due to have lunch with three editors (all women) from different sections of *The Times*. My parents always looked after Bonnie when I went to London but my father was in hospital once again, my mother would spend part of the day with him and could not cope with a dog as well. Therefore I would take her on the train, and Robin agreed to meet us at Paddington and take care of her while I headed east for my rendezvous.

At the beginning of lunch my phone sounded but I put it off without listening – still unused to carrying one and embarrassed by the intrusion. It was not until 3.30 p.m. that I checked my messages. To my horror, I heard an extremely rough London accent say, 'We got your dog …'

Now we must cut to West London, where at about 12.50 p.m. Robin (who was doing up a house with his friend Lawrence) turned his back for a few minutes to move a piece of wood across the terrace. Perhaps looking for me, perhaps fascinated by that distinctive West London scent of bus and burger with top notes of cannabis, Bonnie squeezed through a small gap beneath a gate and snuffled off alone into the mean streets. Distraught, Robin roamed around, sending Lawrence off in the opposite direction, calling her name. Then he telephoned the RSPCA, police, Blue Cross, Battersea Dogs' Home and another dogs' home in Kensal Rise. He was too afraid to call the council's cleaning department, as the police advised, because he couldn't bear to think of her being picked up dead off the road. He couldn't imagine how he could ever face me.

Back to the restaurant, at the sound of that recorded voice I naturally thought of the thieves who stole Elizabeth Barrett Browning's Flush, and their modern counterparts who hold dogs to ransom. Heart thumping I rang the number, heard the gruff voice answer and (oh joy!) it was telling me that he and his brother had found my dog on the street, telephoned the number engraved on her tag (my Bath home), picked up the mobile number from the message and tried that three times. Quickly (because his credit was running out) he told me the address where he and his mates had the dog. Rather shell-shocked, I called Robin, whose voice changed from despair to elation. He jumped into his car and collected Bonnie from a housing estate – and I was reunited with her in as much time as it takes the Underground to go from Aldgate East to Ladbroke Grove. Bonnie's own journey had been just over half a mile – which is quite a trek when your legs are only 5 inches long. The only evidence of her adventure was a reek of cigarettes on her silky fur.

That might have been the end of it. But, haunted by what might have happened, I wanted to meet Bonnie's rescuers and thank them in person. So after a couple of weeks, I rang the number, introduced myself to the man who answered ('Hi, Alan, I'm the lady whose dog you saved'), and arranged to meet him and the others, to hear their story. As estates go, Henry Dixon Court is quite pleasant, and the sun was shining when four men in their early thirties emerged from one of the blocks. There was Alan (the voice on the phone), his brother Richard (principal rescuer, it turned out) and two friends. One had 'LOVE' and 'HATE' tattoos on a fist, another bore a tattoo proudly proclaiming 'SKINS' and I was especially taken by the little cross tattoos on earlobes. These were tough-looking guys.

Richard told me he and his brother had seen her sniffing around the parked cars. He saw the traffic whizzing by, said to Alan, 'She's not a stray, she's too well kept,' and tried to catch her. He told me, 'When I got her she wriggled but I held her tight, and looked around, but there was nobody.' So they improvised a lead from some copper wire and string they found lying around, met their friends and took her back to their flat, where they tried to give her food and water, which she refused. That's when the phone calls were made. I asked Richard what they would have done if I hadn't made contact and they said there would have been no choice but to take her to Battersea Dogs & Cats Home. So Bonnie's life would have gone full circle. The thought was unbearable.

So that was it. Smiling at the unlikely vision of the tough guys mooching along with my lapdog, I said, 'She's not a very butch dog, is she?' Alan shrugged, 'Yeah, well, she's your dog, ain't she?' 'Oh yes,' I said, clutching her tightly. Then I pulled out my purse and gave them the reward they had not asked for. Off they went for several beers, looking as happy as I felt. Bonnie had survived her second experience of being alone in the wide world and I vowed it would never happen again.

I'm sure Bonnie never went looking for whoever tied her to that tree in 2002 because she knew she wasn't loved. But surely she must have been searching for me that day? She would have walked miles, hoping to find me. Whenever I drive into London and pass those streets she roamed, see the volume of traffic and all the strangers passing by, I know how close I came to losing her. The odds against a reunion were impossibly high. Four years later I included the tale of the dog loose in London and the unlikely rescue in one of my six 'Bonnie' books for children, which star a boy called Harry and his little Maltese dog with a big heart. And I allowed my characters to draw the quietly optimistic conclusion:

> *For a while Harry, Dad and Kim walked in silence. Harry had brought Bonnie's lead, and she just pulled ahead, sniffing at walls and gates, as she always did. Each of them was thinking of what might have happened to her – but none of them wanted to speak. Harry imagined a kidnapper's demands. Kim imagined a woman just stealing Bonnie because she was such a cute lap dog. Dad imagined the little creature getting run over – and couldn't bear it. He'd have been responsible, he thought, and would have found it hard to face Harry or his Mum ever again.*
>
> *But it was all right.*
>
> *At last Harry said, 'They were really good guys, Dad.'*
>
> *'They certainly didn't look it!' said Kim.*
>
> *'Just goes to show …' said Dad, thoughtfully.*
>
> *'Funny, isn't it?' said Harry. 'I mean, you see people like them walking along and you feel … you know … a bit scared. But they took care of Bonnie, Dad! Aren't we lucky?'*
>
> *'That's for sure,' said his dad, letting out a whoosh of breath.*

By the autumn of 2004 I was beginning to feel fortunate myself and could not help but attribute it to my superstitious purchase of Kwan Yin. Everything was falling into place, and that word 'lucky' chimed like a bell through my thoughts. Human beings will always search for an external reason for happiness, although perhaps I should have remembered that anaesthetist who had told me, at the darkest time, 'You make your luck.'

With the quiet approval of my parents and children, my life was changing. Robin returned to Bath that autumn to start his long-planned post-graduate course in website design at Bath Spa University and came to stay in one of my spare rooms until he decided whether he truly wanted to give up photography and forge a new career. The person I had first met in 1984 as a rather unprepossessing, bespectacled builder of 18 had now grown into a handsome 'walker' and best friend (apart from my women friends), and the woman he had first seen as a glamorous, achieving writer of 35, married to a famous man, was now single, which was something that could never have been predicted. Robin had changed, I had changed but little, and his absence in London (not to mention the dinner party with the designated 'spare man') had reinforced my need to have him in my life, a person who knew me well and who had always been there – notwithstanding the fact that he had led his own life, travelled widely, worked abroad, dated, started a business in France and so on. Robin had always been (as J himself was to write) 'a fixture and a fitting of our lives': supportive and loved, friend to our children. Robin told me that all he had ever wanted was to look after me, and I realized that all I wanted now was not romance – no, most definitely not that – but to be looked after. I've always believed that true friendship should be at the heart of any couple's relationship and been wary of destructive passion. Recent events had certainly reinforced my doubts about the wilder shores of love. So it was that Robin and I slipped into a new version of being, without knowing if it would work, or where it would lead, or whether I should take the step of changing the council tax registration to two.

Thanksgiving Day (25 November) 2004 saw us in Santa Fe, New Mexico on a travel assignment, the city glittering with snow and ice, chilli *ristras* hanging outside doorways and every rooftop outlined with *luminarias*, seasonal candles in weighted paper bags. The air was scented with pine and Thanksgiving turkeys. We had spent the previous night on the floor of chaotic O'Hare airport in Chicago, as vast jets of steam worked in vain to defrost all the grounded planes and people shrieked in frustration at ground staff because they wanted to get home to their families for the feast. The goddess and my dog were calling to me from home, saying they could give me a better day than this one.

I couldn't help thinking of our assignment to, or via, Chicago as ill fated. On 11 September 2001 Robin and I had been on a flight heading for O'Hare on assignment when (unbeknown to anyone) American air space was closed, the plane was diverted to Toronto and we learned of the unbeliev-able atrocity against civilization which happened that morn-ing in New York. That travel assignment was about the legendary Route 66 and we had completed it, united in a love of the United States. We had done so many jobs together over the years and made a perfect writer/photographer team. He would notice a freaky person's conversation in a bar and tell me; I would spot a good picture and point it out to him. He reminded me to make notes when I got lazy; I bossed him into trying shots when he just wanted a beer. We had seen each other at our worst, picked each other up when we had drunk too much and knew each other so well that even when we fell out it didn't matter – or last for very long.

This new commission was for *The Times Magazine* January travel special and had to be turned around quickly. Gill Morgan wanted me to convey something of the spirit of Santa Fe in the winter. It was a perfect job; I'd fallen in love with the place one blazing September – its energy, spirit, history and light – and was excited to end this year of extraordinary change with a return. In winter a place is stripped back to its true soul – and the end of a marriage does that to you too.

On my first trip there had been no time to make a literary pilgrimage to the D.H. Lawrence memorial, near Taos. Now I was determined to go. The Kiowa Ranch, which Lawrence's wealthy friend Mabel Dodge Luhan gave him in 1924 (in exchange for the manuscript of *Sons and Lovers*) lies about 15 miles north of Taos, 5 miles down a dirt road. To get there we had to hire a huge Chevrolet Trailblazer. The four-wheel drive crunched through a foot of snow as I scribbled a haiku in my notebook:

> *Steep silence beyond Taos*
> *Snow on the wind*
> *Clouds oppress coyotes.*

Apart from us, animal tracks were the only sign of life and heavy clouds above the dark trees were the outward symbols of my mood. It wasn't that I was dispirited – far from it. But some land-scapes force you to realize your essential loneliness, the hugeness of skies, trees and mountains compelling you to confront human vulnerability and the great cycles of living and dying.

The sky lightened but the pines wept snow. I thought of J and how much he would love this place of distant mountains and stillness. Robin is good with silence; he understood that I often brooded about J and if ever I apologized he just asked quietly, 'Why wouldn't you – after so long?' Knowing about Lawrence's own marriage I thought ruefully of how, back in the sixties, both J and I would have applauded his ideas of passion and individual freedom. Lawrence and his wife, Frieda, (especially Frieda) tried to live according to such wild notions but their restlessness was destructive. They loved each other, yet theirs was a quarrelsome, tempestuous love, founded on an extraordinary mutual dependency. As Lawrence's friend Aldous Huxley wrote of them, 'The mysteries of human relationships are impenetrably obscure.'

Trudging to the little shrine I brooded on their way of life, and thought too of Jean-Paul Sartre and Simone de Beauvoir, who also experimented recklessly with human emotions. J and I studied them when we were young and now, gripped by the cold, I pictured the head of my young husband bent over Sartre's great work *Being and Nothingness* as he took notes for one of his philosophy papers. A tender line of a song ran in my head: Paul Simon singing 'Still crazy after all these years'. Or, at least, not crazy any more, but still tender.

As we reached the small building which is Lawrence's shrine, I reflected that those notions of passionate individuality to which we had subscribed will always lead to pain, to many bitter quarrels and reconciliations, to much selfish sensuality. And how, in the end, all passion spent, it came down to this – a memorial to two people under trees burdened by purifying snow.

Lawrence's short life ended in the south of France in 1930. He was 44. Frieda was at his side. She wrote to a friend, 'He has left me his love without a grudge, we had our grudges out; and from the other side, that I did not know before his death, he gives me his strength and his love for life.' So despite all their problems, she honoured the love they had shared with words I find intensely moving. Oh yes, let people have their grudges out – let them forgive each other! Later Frieda went back to live in Taos with her Italian lover, Angelo Ravagli, 12 years her junior. He had left his wife and three children in Italy, moved in with Frieda in 1933 and married her in 1950. It was he who finally (with almost comic difficulty, in 1935) brought back Lawrence's ashes and built the humble little shrine in the hills, cementing the remains of the genius into place. It has yellow walls, a blue wooden roof and a round window painted crudely with a sunflower. Lawrence's symbol of the phoenix forms the altar, which is (sadly) an ugly thing cast from concrete. But at least Ravagli tried. Perhaps he had a guilty conscience.

In the absolute silence I laid my 'wreath' there – a tiny chilli *ristra* to symbolize the heat of the Lawrentian flame. In 1956 Ravagli buried the woman whom Native Americans called Angry Winter outside the door of the shrine, and after that he returned to Spotorno, near Genoa – where his patient first wife had waited 25 years for his return. He spent the rest of his days with her, until his death in 1976. Huxley was right. As I grow older I become more and more aware of the mysteries, and how impossible it is to assess what unexpected chemistry between this man and that woman will result in a lasting love. People will say, 'They don't go together,' or 'She's not bright enough for him,' or 'He's just not up to her,' but how do they know? When well-meaning friends occasionally intimated that they could not quite understand why I still felt so devoted to one man (and entirely defensive of him) whilst living with another, I just smiled and shrugged. But inside my head I retorted, 'So you don't understand? Well, that's *your* problem, not mine.'

Turning to flick through the visitors' book with numb fingers, I noticed that some anonymous sceptic (dragged there by whom?) had recently scrawled, 'This is the height of silliness.' I read it out to Robin, and we exclaimed in disbelief at such a failure of imagination. But there will always be those who will enter St Paul's Cathedral and see only religious excess, who are immune to the sound of a violin adagio, who view a tree as a green thing in the way of a development, who regard a visit to an ancient place as an excuse to search for tourist trinkets, who reduce human relationships to lowest common denominators like sex and pride, and who will travel to a literary shrine only to remain indifferent to the art (forged in what passionate fires) it commemorates. Yes – and Kwan Yin is only a lump of stone and Bonnie only a dog. So easy it is to beat a drum for reason and drown out the music of the stars.

Robin photographed me by Frieda's resting place, where I dropped a single chilli, scarlet against the grave's snowy quilt. Then we climbed back in the wagon and drove on to Taos to see D.H. Lawrence's crude paintings at the Hotel La Fonda de Taos. In 1929 these 'forbidden' works were confiscated by the police from the Dorothy Warren Gallery in London, on grounds of obscenity, and were in danger of being destroyed until Lawrence agreed to remove them from English soil. After Frieda died, Antonio Ravagli sold the nine oils to the owner of the hotel, who was a great admirer of Lawrence. To this day nobody knows how much money changed hands, but in any case the Italian would hardly have wanted to cart the daubs of bare-breasted women back to the first Mrs R. in Spotorno. I hope he spent some of the money from the paintings on some New Mexican turquoise jewellery for her, as a peace offering.

Lawrence summed up his first impressions of Taos thus: 'In the magnificent fierce morning of New Mexico, one sprang awake, a new part of the soul woke up suddenly and the old world gave way to the new.' When we flew back home to Bonnie (always so thrilled by reunion – as we were), I was aware that something like that had happened to me too. Twelve months earlier I had felt despair. In Santa Fe and Taos, and driving the empty, frozen high road between the two, Robin and I had shared a form of spiritual awakening. We knew we loved the same things: Mexican art, tin crosses, Catholic kitsch, cowboy boots, Danny Lyon photographs of bikers, the skulls of steers nailed to posts and the stacked brown adobe of the Taos pueblo in the fading light of a winter afternoon. We laughed a lot, and that was more important than anything. Frieda Lawrence's words about her Angelo were an echo of my feelings too: 'He is so human and nice with me and *real,* no high falute, but such a genuine warmth for me – I shall be all right … We have been fond of each other for years and that an old bird like me is still capable of passion and can inspire it too, seems a miracle.'

Settled in my new house and living more contentedly, more simply with this man and one small dog than would have seemed possible, I too felt the old world giving way to the new. I suppose it must – just as old leaves fall and mulch down to aid new growth, with no choice in the process. Another Christmas came, the first in the new home and therefore a huge step forward from the previous year. From now on the tree would be smaller, and the pile of presents too, and the old traditions would be remade to suit this new place. Of course, somebody was still missing, and I could not help wanting Daniel, not Robin, to sit in the important place at the head of the table. The greatest good fortune was to be loved by somebody who did not mind, who understood how complicated were my feelings. And that it is impossible to love two people in the same way.

Each night when I drew the cream curtains the previous owner had left behind in the sitting room, I lit candles to give thanks for hearth and home – and for the limitless resilience of the heart. The passage which closed my *Times Magazine* article inspired by the new house, earlier in the year, stands as a fitting summation of where I found myself as 2004 came to an end:

> This house is telling me the meaning. That all the joys and sorrows of the generations who lived in it are recorded since 1820 on its stone tapes. That the pleasures and pains of all the homes in my life were burnt on the CDs of their walls as well as on my spirit, and I carry it all with me, to dance to the old tunes here. I've already abandoned my plan to replace the 70s green 'dralon' covering my mother chose for the rosewood chaise longue with something more … well … *designer*. I can't be bothered. There may be smart skirting level lighting up those pale stairs, and brushed chrome plugs and switches, yet my Nan's brass hearth set and trivet stand by the marble fireplace, and will remain polished to a glimmer. Nothing demolished. Everything reclaimed. Now I can gaze back through those lighted

windows, glad of the bricks and mortar of what we all built together – grandparents, parents, Jonathan, Daniel, Kitty, all the dear friends who shared the good times.

And I know that moving is (after all) only a single letter away from loving.

Four

REBUILDING

I am I, because my little dog knows me.
Gertrude Stein, 'Identity a Poem'

J and I first saw Venice in 1972. In what was probably our
favourite city we had a special affection for the Scuola
de San Giorgio degli Schiavoni, and within that building we
especially loved one painting.

Between 1502 and 1509 Carpaccio decorated the small
guild (founded in 1451 by Slav merchants) with a sequence of
jewel-like paintings narrating the lives of Saints George,
Tryphone and Jerome. This one, the most enchanting picture,
shows St Augustine writing to his friend St Jerome, unaware
that he has recently died. Suddenly his elegant cell is flooded
with light as a voice from heaven gives him the sad news. The
saint sits, pen poised, transfixed by the vision. To his left, sitting
in the wide, pale space of the floor, is the little bichon-type dog,
ears alert, leaning slightly backwards, as if in wonder. Perhaps
my long-standing passion for this picture was prescient. Surely

even a non-doggy person could not resist those pricked-up ears?

I always used to think the animal was overwhelmed by awe. But now, in my enlightenment, I know that every fibre of his being – each curled white hair, those two bright, black eyes, the whole quivering *selfhood* of that animal – signifies eagerness. The dog is in the 'now'; the saint is in eternity. The animal concentrates on the man while the saint concentrates on heaven. The small dog is saying, 'Hey man, can't you leave those books alone now and take me for a *walk?*' And, 'Stuff God, master, don't you know it's *you* I love?'

That's what our dogs do: they bring us back to life, haul us into the present, make us get on with things instead of moping. They do not let us escape our humanity but save us from its worst aspects. In another Venetian museum hangs Carpaccio's *The Courtesans*. In it, two elaborately dressed and coiffed women sit on a balcony or loggia, lethargic and bored. Their faces are vacant – and yet at least the one in the front is teasing a big dog (head and paws just entering the frame) with the stick in her right hand, while her left hand holds the two front paws of the smooth-haired lapdog sitting up at her feet. Looking directly out at us, he is the one source of vivacity in the painting. You can almost hear the bells on his collar chiming to break the *ennui* as he begs his mistress for attention. I think he too is desperate for a walk – and hopes she will listen, forget satisfying the sexual needs of rich clients, slip on her pattens and stroll out into the grubby teeming streets to watch the gondolas crossing the grand canal, one of them containing a frisky, red-collared Maltese rather like mine (lovingly painted in another of Carpaccio's paintings, *The Miracle of the Relic of the Cross*, in the Accademia). I feel sure the artist loved the dogs that roamed the streets of Venice.

Yet maybe that is sentimental. Perhaps Carpaccio painted dogs simply because they assisted the composition. Perhaps the many dogs that appear in pictures by Veronese and Titian are not 'true' pets (which is to say, owned by somebody who cares, whether painter or subject) but merely exercises in painterly skills or props. How do you, as viewer (or, for that matter, reader), know what constitutes the truth? In an essay called 'Borrowed Dogs' the photographer Richard Avedon considers the carefully constructed falsehoods of portraiture. He remembers that when he was a child his parents used to borrow dogs to make the family portraits more stylish, posing the family with the dog on loan in front of smart houses that were also not their own. He says it was 'a necessary fiction that the Avedons owned dogs'. But why? It must have been because a dog conveyed a message of family stability as well as prosperity. Avedon believes that the images in their family album represented 'some kind of lie about who we were, and revealed a truth about who we wanted to be'.

Back in July 1994 when I had presented J with his fiftieth birthday present, the beautiful black Labrador puppy called Billie was not a borrowed dog, but one to be owned and loved, who would own and love right back. This animal would indeed put the seal on the kind of family we had become. There is certainly truth in the photographs which record that day: the children blindfolding J, me placing the beribboned puppy in his arms, his wide grin. I still carry, tucked in my address book, a later picture of J at the farm with Billie and Sam, on a summer evening, the valley spreading behind them. The one who is left with the family photograph albums becomes the custodian of all such truths (and some untruths too, like those smiles on days you know you were unhappy) and must fight the bleak feeling that subsequent history turns what was into an untruth. For a wedding photograph is not deprived of meaning because a marriage ends. Snaps of adorable young children should not be sullied by the frustration and disappointment caused by their evolution into difficult teenagers. Photographs inevitably make you sad, since they remind you of the time and of mortality. Yet the good can still be clung to – that this did happen.

It *was*. We existed.

At the beginning of February 2005 Robin and I went to Egypt. It was my first visit to Cairo but not his – and this was another travel commission. From our hotel we gazed through high-rise hotels and low-rise ugliness, to where the pyramids stood, their silence reaching across the cacophonous city.

'It smells so different to home,' he said, looking over our tenth-floor balcony.

'Yes, it does,' I said.

But in fact I could detect no smell – apart from traffic fumes. I agreed with him because most of us collude about the expectations of travel, the yearning for the Other which requires those aromas of spices and shisha, of different body smells, of donkey droppings, of alien and malfunctioning drains, which would have met intrepid travellers in earlier times. Safe within the international hotel we agreed on an imaginary Egyptian ambience which contradicted the polluted reality of the twenty-first century, because that is the way humans construct the truths they long for. Most of the time we live variations of a lie. Ask any married couple what happened and you will hear variations on the old 'Gigi' song 'I Remember it Well' – when he remembers being on time on the Friday and she says he was late on the Monday, he recalls her in a golden dress but she knows it was blue, and so on.

I was thinking about the visit J and I had made to Luxor just three years earlier, just after we had celebrated our daughter's twenty-first birthday with a big party. We were intensely excited by the glories of the Valley of the Kings and when we visited the Luxor Museum, we decided that a huge, battered king and queen (or god and goddess?) sitting side by side, just touching, were our alter egos. We invoked one of our favourite poems, Philip Larkin's 'An Arundel Tomb', and stood there amidst gods and grave goods, joyfully reciting the poem's last verse, word perfect, in unison:

> *Time has transfigured them into*
> *Untruth. The stone fidelity*
> *They hardly meant has come to be*
> *Their final blazon, and to prove*
> *Our almost-instinct almost true;*
> *What will survive of us is love.*

I wrote:

> *13 January 2001: … Tonight, another delicious dinner and talking about Egyptian culture. How well J and I get on! He said today he could not imagine re-marrying – being with anybody else. Let's hope the tiny 18c god Ankh he bought me today brings me the luck of many more years of life with him.*

I've put it on the gold chain with the 'Long Life' charm Kitty brought me back from Hong King when she was 12.

I only know such things because they were recorded in my diary – the chronicles of lost time.

So now I was back in Egypt, and life had changed utterly. Several times each day I would find myself wondering where J was, what he was doing, still amazed that now he had a new partner and so did I, but we went on missing each other so very much. Sometimes I felt guilty to be thinking of him; it was a strange turn-around to be secretly obsessed with the husband whilst travelling (and having a wonderful time) with the new partner. Even when we did something we liked (watching a belly dancer, for example) but I suspected he would not, I could not banish J from my thoughts. I wondered if he was followed around by a wraith shaped like me, whispering poems in his ear even when he was with his new lady.

Robin and I were looking at the Great Pyramid of Cheops, stung by a dusty wind (and soon to be stung by hucksters) when my mobile phone brought news which made us sad. Daniel telephoned to tell us that Billie had died. She of the velvet ears, the dependable paws, the thumping tail and melting expression had been ill and would salivate over her meals no more. 'Only a dog' some might say, and of little value in the great scheme of things – symbolized by those pyramids and the mysterious Sphinx, not to mention the everyday modern sorrows of East and West. But in Egypt of all places I knew differently. I could mourn Billie more truly far from home. Away from the added sentiment of familiar places, I could remember her as über-dog: beautiful and gentle in equal measure. She should be enshrined for ever on the wall of a tomb, I thought, to prove to future generations that she existed.

The Ancient Egyptians loved their pet dogs, and adorned them with fancy collars, just as we do. In the Cairo Museum we saw a Twelfth Dynasty coffin belonging to Khui, a man wealthy enough to have a decorated casket. On it he is painted with his dog Lupu (very like a Dalmatian, rather than the usual Egyptian Basenji) who trots along behind his master on a white lead. You can see the affection between them; it links dog lovers over centuries. On steles (grave markers), coffins and wall paintings their dogs are painted, and over seventy dog names are recorded, from ones referring to colour (Ebony, Blackie) to character (Reliable, Brave One) to qualities like speed (Antelope, North Wind). Apparently one Ancient Egyptian mutt was called Useless (unfortunate antecedent of Leona Hemsley's Trouble) but that could have been affectionate. So greatly were dogs valued that some were mummified to accompany their masters into the afterlife: faithful friends for eternity.

For the Egyptians, like all other dog owners throughout time, there was a distinction between the outside dog and the inside dog. They had their fighting dogs, their hunting dogs – and the dogs beneath the chair. But a Labrador like Billie makes the transition: the working dog turned into a pet. The Jack Russell is fierce in his pursuit of rats, but the Prince of Wales's Tigger had the status of Royal lapdog, even though the term is one all self-respecting Jack Russells would scorn. What interests me is the message the dog sends out about us. The savage youth with his pit bull is at one end of the scale; at the other is a symbiotic relationship which defies rational explanation.

Writing about his golden retriever Beau after the dog's death, Mark Doty recalls the golden, 'blonde shine' which is 'gone from the world forever' and yet '… something of it remains absolutely clear to me, the quality of him, the aspect of him most inscribed within me.' So for him the essence of the dog remains in the part which most correlates to its owner. In Cairo I laid Billie permanently to rest within my memory, with the realization that her quality – her absolute essence – of ever-hopeful love (no more, no less) was indeed a perfect correlation for her owner.

If dogs are held to look like their owners, what did a small white dog communicate about my own essence? It cannot be appearance, since I am assiduous in my mission to keep all white hairs disguised, and my eyes are blue. Yet I do move quickly – and so if I had to sum it up in one word I would choose 'eagerness' as the essence. It pleases me to think that I share at least one of Bonnie's best qualities and do not believe that anyone in the world (except Robin) has her true measure. Once a teasing friend said, 'Let's face it, Bel, your dog has a brain the size of a peanut.' And it was Robin who riposted, mildly, 'Well, surely a *walnut?*' Habitually we addressed her as '*silly* little dog', imbuing the adjective with honeyed affection. As a student of the English language, I know that the meaning of 'silly' has changed over the centuries, and choose to revert to the Old English meaning of 'happy' or 'blessed' when applying it to my dog. She is not foolish – no, not at all.

Yet widespread prejudice sees her as a 'handbag dog' – with all the connotations of leisure, style, money and ladies-who-lunch. I often see Maltese dogs used as props for photo shoots – as sweet and sick-making as cupcakes, but clearly viewed by marketing people as just as desirable. At one end of the scale of aspiration is the Paris Hilton syndrome, where it is as important to be photographed with your chi-chi pet as with your Prada handbag – but pity the creature if it pisses on your carelessly dropped Dior. At the other end are the people who choose a lapdog as an accessory because of all those smart associations, with no understanding of the particular neediness of the small breeds.

I met a young woman who worked in a dress shop in Bath. Her teenage sister had been clamouring for a chihuahua, was given the little dog by over-indulgent parents and then ordered a variety of 'designer' collars and leads online. Months later I found out that the girl had 'got rid of' the poor chihuahua. Why? 'It was so *naughty!*' explained the sister. The novelty of pink collars had worn off and the dog was left unsupervised in a field, where it was trodden on by a horse. The chihuahua's little leg was broken and so they had to find it another home – and all this was recounted to me as if the mishap were entirely the nuisance-animal's fault. Rescue homes worldwide give succour to thousands of dogs whose owners were just too hopeless, mean or stupid to take care of them. What other explanation can there be for the presence of Bonnie in my life? Especially at a time of economic hardship (like the one afflicting Europe and America as I write this), when dogs are abandoned in even larger numbers. I do not understand it, for I would share my last piece of meat with my dog. How else can we prove to our dogs that we are the people they think we are, other than by raising them beyond accessory status?

If artists in previous centuries used dogs as props (like the columns and aspidistras in later studio photographs) it was, after all, because the dog had *meaning*. People were attuned to symbolism in a way we are not now. When van Eyck painted the famous Arnolfini wedding portrait in 1434 he layered much symbolism within the frame – so much so that scholars are still debating whether this is a wedding or a memorial portrait (arguably commemorating the death of the wife, Giovanna) and what the single candle in the chandelier means. But at the right-hand front there is the dog, a Brussels gryphon, and surely nobody can argue what he signifies? The little dog communicates loyalty, faithfulness, trust. What else would you want a picture of a marriage to say? Contemplating this work of art in London's National Gallery I find myself thinking how much better are our dogs than we are. In general we don't do so well on the fidelity front – although how can we know the truth of the Arnolfini couple? Did they take care of that dog? Did they take care of each other?

In 2005 I was, by a strange turn of fate, to gain my first real, coal-face knowledge of the pervasiveness of aching romance, sexual passion and subsequent marital misery.

I needed more work. In archive boxes somewhere I still have records of what I earned as a young journalist: columns in the backs of diaries listing the article, the fee and whether it had been paid. Some of the amounts were pitifully small even in 1972; both J and I wrote for the *New Statesman* (then under the inspired editorship of Anthony Howard), which was not known for largesse. The years of having to keep such proudly independent (that was their importance to me) records had long gone; now I was in that position again. What's more, I believe in work as therapy. When married women give up *all* contact with the world of work (which may be voluntary or part-time) to keep house and raise a family they leave themselves so vulnerable. Your children will grow up and leave home and your husband may find himself a new love – and then what will you do? In my opinion, sorting clothes in the charity shop (when after all you can chat to fellow human beings) is better than sitting home alone. It was a jest of mine that in a terrible revolution, when the intellectuals were hunted out, I would survive – because, as a good seamstress, I could sew uniforms for the tyrants, and build a subversive *style* into each seam.

So – touting for work. For years I'd been contributing to *The Times*, under six different editors, but had never met the current assistant editor (Features) face to face, although we had spoken on the telephone. In the businesslike knowledge that you get more work if more people know you, I suggested a meeting. Sandra Parsons invited me to lunch at London's latest fashionable restaurant, The Wolseley, on Piccadilly – and, by quirk of fate, picked the date which would have been my thirty-seventh wedding anniversary. Looking back it seems 'meant' – that on that day I would shake hands with her as one person and rise from the table with a different direction, a new door opening in my career, for we were talking (as women will) about work and the problems and guilt of juggling a demanding job and a family, which I had been through and Sandra was still doing. I felt for her – and, without realizing it, gave some advice. Then I hit my own forehead and said, 'Listen to me! I sound like an agony aunt *manqué.*'

This was the first time I have ever *observed* what is called a light-bulb moment.

Her face lit up and she leaned forward. 'Have you ever thought of doing that?'

'Er – *no!*'

When a talented editor gets hold of an idea he or she will not let it go. Sandra persuaded me that I was just the person to write a problem page for *The Times*, and begged me to consider it. I was unsure – and went on feeling like that for a couple of weeks, although when I asked friends they all agreed it was something I would do well. But I was planning to write more fiction for adults and children, to continue with the radio work and get myself some regular 'proper' journalism to pay the bills. Becoming what is popularly known as an 'agony aunt' (a term I dislike, because it tends to be patronizing) could never have been part of my life plan.

But now, in an instant, it was.

Still, for a short while, I feared it might make me look … well … less than serious. This did not reflect (I must emphasize) my own judgement on the role, but an awareness of the snobbishness of those who sneer at all popular journalism (that slight curl of the lip, making the smirk look even uglier, and the tinkling question, 'Eeuw, you write for the *Daily Mail* …?'), wherever it may appear. Thinking hard about that, and feeling the old rush of irritation, was enough to make me say, 'What the hell!' As the iconoclastic Victorian writer Samuel Butler wrote, 'The great pleasure of a dog is that you may make a fool of yourself with him and not only will he not scold you, but he will make a fool of himself too.' Me – I've tended to rush at things with an uncool enthusiasm to match my dog's, as long as I could swiftly gain control over whatever it was I found. So at this point in my life I was prepared to head off down the side road suddenly presented to me, just to see what was there. To try, even if I might fail.

The canine readiness to breathe the whole of odiferous life up into its nostrils, to hurl adoration at you by the front door when you've only been absent for 30 minutes, to sense it is party time when you put down your pen and murmur, 'Right then …', to know that just around this next corner awaits something *so* exciting it must be raced towards immediately … This is a way of living – even a state of soul – that we should learn from our dogs. There is a certain level of British society which holds that to be enthusiastic, to bounce around wagging an imaginary tail, is deeply unsmart – and (worse) probably lower class. These are the snobbish people who use that tedious, tinkling little word 'agreeable' as high praise – so that to say that the evening was 'perfectly agreeable' means you had a superb, amazing time. Dogs do not find anything 'agreeable'; they are wild enthusiasts.

Still, as curious and excited as I was at the idea of a new start, it frightened me too. Even then I wasn't to know how hard I would find the transition. For one thing, *The Times* sent the feature writer Catherine O'Brien to interview me. The sensible thinking was that I could not possibly deal with other people's problems unless the readers knew I'd had plenty of my own. Readers will trust you if they think you know what you are talking about. Virgil understood this, 19 years before the birth of Jesus. It seems to me another strange trick of destiny that in 1963, aged 17 and a keen classicist, I copied into my commonplace book a line entirely relevant to this new branch of my career – almost predicting it. It is from the *Aeneid* (book 1, line 630) spoken by Dido, Queen of Carthage. The beautiful doomed Queen tells the visiting hero who will betray her, '*non ignara mali miseris succurrere disco*' – 'not unacquainted with grief do I learn to help the unhappy'.

Yes, I thought, I may not have any formal qualification to advise people on emotional issues, but it takes more than a piece of paper to understand pain.

There would be no choice but to answer questions about the end of our marriage, which until this point I had avoided. The journalist was intelligent and *sympathique*, and Sandra Parsons had promised me sight of the copy before it was published. But that didn't make it any easier. It was as if J was in the room with me – always – shaking his head. He had always been more conscious of personal privacy than I. Columnists are accustomed to drawing on their lives; even this book is an extension of that impulse to say, 'This is how it is for me.' Yet I hated answering questions about our life, about Susan Chilcott, about how I felt. It was still too recent. Although I knew that the price of the job was a degree of revelation, the interview set up a frisson of dread.

Then, unexpectedly, I was invited to the wedding of Prince Charles and Camilla Parker-Bowles, at Windsor on 9 April. The last time I'd seen J, I had asked if he had had an invitation – then joked that he should take me. After all, we had shared the gruelling experience of his writing of the biography of the Prince of Wales and the making of the television film which caused such sensation. No couple could have been more at one, at every level. We had sat side by side and watched in openmouthed horror when Princess Diana's brother, Charles Spencer, had made a funeral oration which, to us, lacked all taste. We shared disbelief at the rotting-flower stink of public sentimentality after Diana's shocking death, and support and affection for a Prince we thought much misunderstood and cruelly maligned. So it seemed to me fitting that we should witness his wedding together – even if fate had now set us off on separate paths.

J smiled somewhat sadly and shook his head – but in any case, I knew it would not have been protocol for him to telephone and ask to bring a guest. Things do not work that way.

Then my own invitation came. It says little for my confidence at that time that I was surprised to be treated as a person in my own right. Even though it was daunting to go alone, go alone I would. Every woman will understand that the worst problem was deciding what to wear. I trawled Bath and London seeking inspiration, when finally I saw a black silk dress, patterned with butterflies. Then I spent the day before the wedding, ill in bed, stitching feather butterflies on a straw hat. Obsessed with symbolism as I am, I knew that the early Christians saw butterflies as representing the soul, and therefore rebirth and transformation, whilst in Islamic stories the butterfly Sadaquah brings good news. For Native Americans the butterfly teaches that change may be painful but is necessary. Best of all, in ancient Chinese legend two butterflies symbolize the spirits of two lovers who find eternal married happiness together. Perfect. The Prince would like that, I thought, even though my symbolism, like the Arnolfini dog's, would be subliminal.

Robin drove me to Windsor and dropped me off. Inside the Chapel of St George I saw J, seated in the row in front of me, but about seven people to the left. It was impossible not to fix my eyes on him, not to think that we should have been there together, not to wish (with an ache) to be by his side. It must have been just as difficult for him. I gazed up at the great stone vault of the roof springing from stone pillars that look too delicate to bear it, and saw it as a metaphor for the survival of all that I believe in – from tradition, custom and ceremony to human optimism which somehow defies the gravity that always threatens to pull it down. The stone angels which run all round the interior of the chapel are resolutely facing upwards – winged like my butterflies. There is nothing to do but hope for better times, and that was the prayer I made for us both.

I found myself thinking of the sour people (especially in Cornwall) I had seen interviewed on the news the night before who mumbled that they weren't interested, that the wedding 'had nothing to do with me' … moan, groan, gripe, snipe. What a failure of imagination! You might as well say that the terrible tsunami which had begun the year with suffering on a vast scale, or the death of the Pope, or even your country's best athletes running their hearts out … all have nothing to do with you. I link those examples not carelessly but because I passionately believe we are all joined by ties of the spirit which enable us to reach out with compassion, grief, exhilaration, empathy or pride towards what goes on in the lives of others. That is why I felt, as we all made confession of our 'manifold sins and wickedness' in unison, 'Yes, this has *everything* to do with me.' And everything to do with the man on whose head I fixed my eyes once more. Conscious of imperfection, I reflected that all we can do is stumble along, like the Prince and the Duchess, hoping that after the darkness the light will shine.

And it did. At exactly the right moment in the service. The actor Timothy West had just finished reading the passage Prince Charles (very revealingly) had chosen from Wordsworth about the 'delight and liberty' in the human spirit, experienced naturally by children, but forgotten as we grow, when life gets so much more complicated. But the simple joy can be recaptured, the poet says, in maturity, through intense experiences of mind and heart. The Prince and his bride listened, then the orchestra and choir began a sublime Bach anthem, and the pale sun triumphed over those chilly April clouds and burst through the great east window. The day was telling us that all things go on, and can be made better. That, as the passage from Revelation read by Lord Carey says, ' ... there shall be ... neither sorrow nor crying ... for the former things are passed away ... Behold, I make all things new.' The smiles on the faces of Diana's sons banished the dark clouds of the past, and the pride in their father's expression boded well for the future. I always believed in his capacity for kingship – and now even more so with this wife by his side. That shared conviction was part of all our rejoicing.

On the way to Windsor I'd seen other people going to other weddings, and thought how the season kicks off now – each Saturday all the couples, of all ages, going forward in their finery to take their places in the ranks of the hopeful, toasted by their friends. And what is there to do but wish them well? Some marriages will fail, of course. Yet I realized – there in the chapel and later mingling at the reception – that being separated from J had in no way diminished my faith in the institution. Public statements of love will continue to be made because the need to affirm is a part of the human condition.

And here in the grandeur of Windsor Castle it was the same. After thanking his parents, family, staff and friends, and (very movingly) remembering his grandmother, the groom praised his bride. Adjective after adjective of love and gratitude, and finally his heartfelt thanks to her 'for having the courage to take me on'. His self-deprecating smile brought more cheers from the floor. But Camilla Parker-Bowles (now Duchess of Cornwall) is so English, so reticent. With nothing of the poser or smooth public figure about her, she shifted her feet and looked attractively embarrassed.

I felt elated for them and sad for myself. After the cruel criticism of her looks (mostly from other women, which is equally astonishing and loathsome) Camilla looked striking and elegant. And I thought how refreshing it was that here was a man in his fifties choosing a real friend one year older – not the cliché younger woman most men seem to want. As we raised our glasses my personal toast was to long-time love, to middle-aged marriages and to down-to-earth weddings – instead of stupid 'fairytales' which end in disappointment and disillusion.

When it was all over Robin collected me at the time we had arranged and drove me through the paparazzi and back to Bath. One of the truly amazing things about him was that he was (as he said) quite happy to play the driver. On our trip to Egypt I had walked through a hotel with the public relations manager, with Robin walking a few paces behind us, taking everything in, intensely interested but relieved that he was not required to play the PR game, as I had to. He joked that he was like the Duke of Edinburgh walking behind the Queen; his quiet sense of selfhood required no outward trappings of status. He and I were particularly delighted to discover a particular

Texas blues-rock number sung by Angela Strehli called 'A Stand By Your Woman Man'. Yes, that was it, and it was a source of celebration. I had told *The Times* journalist Catherine O'Brien that this practical man 'can fix anything including me'. He seemed increasingly like the intricate web of scaffolding which shores up a building and enables it to be renovated. He loved a poem I read to him one night, which uses this as a metaphor. By U.A. Fanthorpe, it is called 'Atlas' and begins:

> *There is a kind of love called maintenance*
> *Which stores the WD40 and knows when to use it …*

The poem celebrates 'the sensible side of love' and is a public tribute to the life partner who 'keeps/My suspect edifice upright in air' – just as Robin was doing for me.

J is a fourth-generation journalist who epitomizes what's finest about our trade. His trajectory began in local television but switched to mainstream political radio after one year, presenting Radio 4's flagship *The World This Weekend*. He then carved out an extraordinarily successful career on television both as an international reporter and as a political interviewer, tackling heads of state while still in his twenties and winning a BAFTA award for his epoch-making 1973 report on the terrible Ethiopian famine that had been hushed up by Hailie Selassie's regime. *The Unknown Famine* became a catalyst for the destabilization of the quasi-feudal regime. J was allowed to make an unprecedented appeal on both main television channels, which stimulated the largest amount of public generosity ever seen at that time. Treated as a hero of the

Ethiopian people, he was allowed unique access to the country – which led to films that excoriated the violence and oppression of Mengistu's Marxist-Leninist regime and J being banned from the country he loved. He was a brilliant reporter – working dangerously under cover in Pinochet's Chile, coming under fire in Cyprus when the Turks invaded in 1974, exposing outrages all around the world and so on. As well as those reports, he made a name for big documentary series analysing, with equal meticulousness and style, the ongoing stand-off between Russia and America and the plight of the Bolivian tin miner, to name but two.

In a meeting-of-minds-marriage your partner's achievements are as your own. I was very proud of him, searched the newspapers for reviews and once backed the now-distinguished novelist Julian Barnes against a wall at a party to berate him, then a humble television reviewer, for being flippant about one of J's films.

J began presenting the current affairs programme *Any Questions* on BBC Radio 4 in 1987, and the year afterwards *Any Answers* was reinvented as a phone-in, which was a perfect format for him. He went on to front BBC1's first Sunday lunchtime political programme *On the Record* from 1987 until 1992, and then, in 1995, started to present a similar programme on ITV, called *Jonathan Dimbleby* – which continued the ruin of family weekends. As ITV's most experienced political presenter he anchored general elections in 1997 and 2001 – and now, in 2005, he would do the same again.

The point is, I could not tolerate the prospect of *The Times* profile of me, heralding my new column, appearing days before his mammoth election-night endurance test. It made me feel frantic and so, torn between the prospect of perhaps destabilizing (and certainly upsetting) my separated husband and my new job, I chose him. I suppose this was my own version of canine loyalty. The column was postponed.

On 5 May I sat up, as I had always done, to watch him as the results came in, giving Tony Blair's New Labour win its third consecutive victory with a reduced overall majority of 66. In 1997 J and I, like so many people, had been elated by Labour's victory; the theme song 'Things Can Only Get Better' was genuinely inspiring. We all felt that the country needed change. Even with hindsight, that was right. But now all was changed, changed utterly. After supper out with friends, Robin went to bed and I watched J by myself in my own house, lying on the sofa with Bonnie, aware of our old home empty just up the road. We're all older and more bruised, and things rarely get better, I thought. In any case, I dislike change. That's why I could not kick my habit of staying with the exhausting election coverage through the night and into the morning, dozing fitfully to wake and see him on screen.

So his life was still my life too.

A new series of *Devout Sceptics* was in production. The general election over, I knew that *The Times* was planning to use Catherine O'Brien's profile on 18 May. This was the day Malcolm Love and I were to drive to Cornwall to stay overnight before recording an interview with Tim Smit, the charismatic founder of the Eden Project, one of the region's most beautiful and significant tourist attractions. I confess I was excited at the prospect of seeing *The Times* article – public sign of a 'new' life. A piece which (written with sympathy) said, 'Here I am, this is what I have experienced and this is what I have learned.' Robin had taken a beautiful set of photographs of me (and Bonnie) to accompany the profile, which would be the cover story.

But when I rose early to retrieve the newspapers from the front door I was shocked to see a small photograph of J and me on our wedding day on the newspaper's front page (trailing the profile) and then that same image blown up, covering the whole front of *The Times 2* features and arts section. Beneath was blazoned: 'MRS DIMBLEBY MOVES ON'. My knees buckled; I clutched my dog and wept into her fur. Pictures of our wedding are readily available; as I've explained, there were press photographers outside the registry office, which was the first shock for a girl from an ordinary background. Yet to me there was something thoughtless, even cruel, about this use of the photograph without consulting me. It seemed to me to be insensitive to hire an established writer to write a brand-new column for your newspaper – a column which would consider people's deepest feelings – and cause her real pain by splashing her wedding picture on the pages, with no warning. Did nobody think I might mind?

I hated them all and wanted to give it up – and this with the first advice column, called 'Life and Other Issues', ready for the following week and now thoroughly 'advertised'. I fired off an angry email to Sandra Parsons (who had wanted to use one of Robin's photographs on the cover, as well as inside, but had been over-ruled by the paper's editor) which concluded: 'I have no words for my shock (and misery) at the cover you have chosen. It makes me feel so terrible – as if I have been done over by the very people I trusted and I am supposed to be working for/with. It defines me as "Mrs

Dimbleby" and looks back to 1968 instead of forward and is terribly, terribly sad. In the words of Plath, I simply do not see where there is to go to.'

I was still very upset when Malcolm Love came to collect me. We had been working together for a very long time and had no secrets from each other. We had talked about his loss of the faith of his childhood, my seeking of spirituality, his deeply held beliefs, and our feelings about love and marriage. We had strolled the streets of San Francisco where women came up and told him he looked like Richard Gere (which is true) and he had managed to haul me back to the hotel one time after I had drunk too much on Fisherman's Wharf – and with an interview with Isabel Allende to do the next day. Now, like a true friend, he listened to my wailing and understood when I confided that the worst thing about the picture went far beyond what I had written to Sandra.

First, I simply could not bear to think of how it must have upset J – although I did not telephone him to explain that I had not known the picture would be used. Silence seemed the safer option.

Second, I felt overwhelmed – staring at the familiar monochrome image of that 21-year-old in a mini-dress and the 23-year-old in his kipper tie looking so happy, so in love – by the feeling that I wanted to rush back through time and *protect* them. I wanted to tell them not to get it wrong, for they were meant to be together and must not dilute that meaning with the prevailing 'anything goes' mores of the zeitgeist. I wanted to beg them to take *care,* to not be stupid, to not fail each other. Too late.

Malcolm heard me out.

But over dinner in the hotel that night it was my turn to listen. My producer and friend knew a lot about love and was wise to its glories as well as realistic about its limitations. He told me that you should never say that a marriage has 'failed'. You should see it as having run its course, like a journey which has reached its destination. Perhaps, he suggested, J and I were fated to be together for 35 years and then to take different paths, as now. There is no need to damn the outcome with the word 'failure', he said. And there was no need to be so angry about the picture in *The Times*. It had happened, people are careless, nobody could have realized the effect it would have on me and it was time for me to move forward, without looking back. Hearing this echo of the advice on the laminated card given to me at the door of the Carmel Mission, I knew he was right. Now I was to become an advice columnist I must learn to take advice. Malcolm and I would go on with our series, I would be brave and start *The Times* column and see where it would lead – and J and I would go on loving each other under separate roofs.

Which is what happened.

Nothing was said about the article by J or by me, then or ever afterwards. But a few weeks after it had appeared a flat parcel arrived for me from J. It contained, with no explanation, an embossed metal 'vintage' advertisement for the 1958 Harley-Davidson Duo-Glide. He knew my tastes so well.

There is no doubt that since leaving the farm, I had become more attached to Bonnie than ever. 'Just you and me against the world,' I used to murmur, and it felt true. I doted on my Maltese as much as the Roman Governor of Malta doted on his, in the first century. The poet Martial commemorated this military man's love of his *'deliciae catella'* ('darling little dog') in a gently mocking poem called 'Issa'. Almost certainly a Maltese, the lapdog Issa is described as naughty, pure, precious and seductive, and *'sentit tristitiamque gaudiumque'* ('feels sadness and joy'). There follow four lines which every one who lets an adored lapdog sleep on the bed will recognize:

> *et desiderio coacta ventris*
> *gutta pallia non fefellit ulla,*
> *sed blando pede suscitat toroque*
> *deponi monet and rogat levari.*

('And, compelled by the impulse of her bladder, not a single drop has dirtied the covers, but with her sweet paw she nudges you from the couch, warns you that she needs to be put down and asks to be lifted up.')

A dog on the bed, no matter how small, is not a good idea. But Bonnie had been sleeping with me for two years and since she had been my companion and consolation through the months alone, I was not about to banish her because there was another partner in my deliberately feminine (because not designed with a man in mind) boudoir. The dog and I were a unit. Fortunately the instruction 'Love me, love my dog' was one Robin found easy to obey. He genuinely loved Bonnie, even though a pair of beady black eyes watching everything you do hardly encourages intimacy. The husband of that medieval lady in the Luttrell Psalter would have had no need to furnish her with a chastity belt as long as she had her small white dog on the bed.

Re-reading Virginia Woolf's quirky, charming biography of Elizabeth Barrett Browning's spaniel Flush (a book I could not see the point of as a student), I was able to see parallels with my life with Bonnie. Woolf writes that Flush's life had been lived 'too close' to humans. He had 'lain upon human knees and heard men's voices. His flesh was veined with human passions; he knew all grades of jealousy, anger and despair.' You may think that fanciful, but to the owner of a small dog it makes perfect sense; there is no other way for a lapdog to be. Interestingly, Woolf invokes that idea of symbiosis: ' … made in the same mould, could it be that each, perhaps, complemented what was dormant in the other?' Whatever the truth, I suspect that had Flush not arrived the great woman poet would have slipped slowly into the greater darkness, where there are no poems and rebellion is pointless. That Virginia Woolf (who liked dogs and gave people she loved doggy nicknames) should devote a whole book to this literary dog demonstrates that she did not believe he had a mere walk-on role.

Elizabeth Barrett, already an invalid, was plunged into depression after the death of two of her brothers in 1840. Then her friend Miss Mitford offered the cocker spaniel puppy who was to transform her life – even within her gloomy, stifling sickroom. Everything the little dog did alleviated her depression. His excitement at a carriage ride (the eternal dog with its nose in the wind) made her smile; what's more, Flush strengthened her sense of self and somehow encouraged her to rebel against her fate. Her male doctor forbade the dog on the bed, so she hid him beneath the coverlet; her tyrannical father came to check on her meals, not knowing she had slipped food to her dog to clear the plate. And when she stood up unaided for the first time in two years it was with the help of her dog: 'Think of me standing alone, with only one hand upon Flush – he standing quietly on the sofa ... to steady me.' Yes, it was Elizabeth and Flush against the world.

Until Robert Browning came along. No wonder poor Flush was jealous. At least Bonnie *knew* Robin; poor Flush had to contend with a stranger who burst into the sickroom exuding equally powerful scents of poetry and testosterone. Elizabeth Barrett's first book of poetry (containing verses to her dog) was read by Browning who, six years younger than Elizabeth, was just making his name. They began to correspond, poet to poet, and at last he came on a first visit, carrying a bunch of flowers from his mother's garden.

Flush was used to total attention from his mistress and resented the interloper. No wonder he bit the secret suitor more than once. In love with the man, Elizabeth punished her pet, and wrote to tell Robert all the details.

> *I slapped his ears and told him that he should never be loved again, and he sat on the sofa ... with his eyes fixed on me ... with an expression of quiet despair on his face. At last I said, 'If you are good, Flush, you may come & say you are sorry' ... at which he dashed across the room & trembling all over kissed one of my hands & then another & put up his paws to be shaken & looked in my face with such great beseeching eyes, that you would certainly have forgiven him, just as I did.*

I can imagine Browning sitting in his club telling a friend, 'Good God, sir, if it were not enough to love a woman a man must offer his fingers to her lapdog!' But he wrote back that he loved Flush 'for his jealous supervision'. Next time it happened, the hitherto doting mistress threatened a muzzle. But the poet bribed the dog with cake instead.

Five months after their first meeting the poets were planning to elope, but Elizabeth could not think of going to Italy without Flush. Robert reassured her. But far less reassuring was his response when Flush was dog-napped for the third time by the notorious gang called 'The Fancy'. Miss Barrett was used to her father's indifference and the mockery of her brothers, but now her true love let her down as well. Browning wrote (sounding horribly like her father) to tell her that paying a ransom encouraged the crime, and that were the dog to be killed, 'God allows matters to happen.' Monstrous! He realized his mistake and wrote to apologize, but now the once-reclusive invalid took matters in her own hands. She jumped into a cab with her faithful servant and descended into the underworld of slums to find her dog. Even today her action would be brave; in 1846 the sights, sounds and smells would have been truly daunting. I find it incredible to think of this sheltered woman having the common sense to seek out the wife of the gang's ringleader and get her on side. Flush was returned that evening. Through her love for her dog Elizabeth Barrett had discovered she needed no brother, father or even husband-to-be to help her. She was *strong* – her courage channelled through the love of her pet. That strength, as well as her love for Browning, took her into her clandestine marriage on 12 September 1846, and a week later to France, with her loyal maid Wilson carrying the dog.

Two bronze relief portraits of Elizabeth and Robert (made by J's brother, the sculptor Nicholas Dimbleby) hang on the

red-brick garden wall of the house my children found for me
– beautiful talismans which remind me of this story each time
I see them. And I feel that the spirit of possessive, forgiving,
adoring Flush lives on in my dog – who was not kidnapped by
London ruffians, nor ransomed, and did not ever bite Robin,
nor could be bought with cake, but is brave in protectiveness
and savage with strangers and envelopes in equal measure. She
gives the amused postman no quarter.

Living with Bonnie and with Robin in a house that was far
more manageable than the farm, I began to feel new contentment. Virginia Woolf encapsulates this in a description of her
own life after she and her husband Leonard acquired Grizzle,
a mongrel fox terrier of dubious beauty. ('These shabby
mongrels are always the most loving, warm-hearted creatures',
she wrote to Vita Sackville-West, a dog lover herself). She
valued the dog as both companion and watchdog, but he
became more: a third presence who helped to create that everyday family life people take for granted. She wrote, 'The
immense success of our life is, I think, that our treasure is hid
… in such common things that nothing can touch it. That is,
if one enjoys a bus ride to Richmond, sitting on the green
smoking … combing Grizzle.'

In the same way Robin and I found immeasurable contentment in shopping and cooking together, wandering around our
garden to 'visit' Kwan Yin and the Brownings, and bathing
Bonnie – which is itself a sight of such rat-like pathos it would
make a sculpture laugh. 'Instant entertainment,' he would say,
about her waddle, the way her tongue stuck out like a stray
petal, the way she snuffled at the grass like a miniature rumi-
nant, the wholeness of the humour of the small white dog.

That was just as well, for there was little to laugh at in my new job. The role of advice columnist is old and honourable. The nineteenth century produced a number of books on how to live a happy life, but William Cobbett's *Advice to Young Men* (published in 1830 with the subtitle 'And (Incidentally) to Young Women') is perhaps the only one still read, albeit by very few people. Cobbett's classic work of socio-political reportage, *Rural Rides*, was one of J's favourite books; he had been working towards recreating the rides (as a superb horseman himself) and commenting on modern Britain but the project foundered because of the notorious inability of BBC television executives to make decisions. Now it was my turn to be inspired by the great radical; if giving advice was good enough for Cobbett (who, by the way, paid great attention to the welfare of his dog and was particular about its collars) it was certainly good enough for me.

'Happiness ought to be your great object,' says Cobbett near the start of the book, which takes the form of 'letters' written to 'a youth, a bachelor, a lover, a husband, a father and a citizen or subject'. Naturally this first advice manual is an old-fashioned read and yet at its core are some sensible values. The eccentric polymath addresses problems which affect the ability of people to live together, to make each other happy, and subjects like jealousy and fidelity. He counsels against frowns and advocates 'loving kindness' – although he believed that 'adultery in the wife is a greater offence than adultery in the husband'. Still, I cannot quarrel with him when he writes, 'Happiness, or misery, is in the mind. It is the mind that lives; and the length of life ought to be measured by the number and importance of our ideas, and not by the number of our days … Respect goodness, find it where you may.'

At 59, having written millions of words of journalism and six novels, I thought I knew quite a lot about human nature but becoming an advice columnist taught me how much I had to learn. Nothing could have prepared me for the depths of human unhappiness in readers' letters – and for the first two months I felt overwhelmed. It did not show on the page, just at home, when the would-be wise woman (for that is surely where the concept of the agony aunt began?) would cry helpless tears over the stories of sorrow, jealousy, infidelity, boredom, ineptitude and (worst of all) warring families that came with increasing regularity into my email inbox and through the letterbox. I knew that agony aunts with more experience, like psychologists, learn to remain detached. The neophyte could not.

So, after a month, when a woman wrote to me about her devastation at finding out about her husband's affair after 25 years of marriage, I wrote:

> Pain like yours is both universal and particular, and plenty of women reading your letter will cry out in sympathy and sisterhood. Your husband has done what many men in their fifties do, and although there is no gender monopoly on infidelity (after all, his lover has been unfaithful to her husband) it's strange that many middle-aged men choose to open themselves to this turmoil. Because it is a choice. All romantic indulgences about the *coup de foudre* will not persuade me that adults can't control their feelings, unless they will it otherwise.

Re-reading that reply now, I feel less sure of that point than I did then. But the ending of that article is revealing:

Your children will lead their own lives and you and your husband may or may not survive this ... Whatever happens, you will be left with your sense of self. I ask you to look in the mirror and contort your face in a silent scream of rage many times. Then let your features relax and study that face. Is it really broken and bitter? No. See it as the new self-portrait which is still a work in progress and which will bear your own name.

The readers knew about my own experience because they had read the profile weeks earlier. Many wrote to tell me that they could write to me precisely because they knew that I had not been born with a silver spoon in my mouth and had endured many of the painful experiences that were bothering them. As the weeks passed I cried less, read more – and knew that this was the job I had been waiting for all my life. I also knew that had my marriage not broken up it could never have come about. The paradox – that I could miss J so much and yet feel happy and even be grateful to him – was overwhelming.

13 July 2005 [written in pencil]
The ancient Persians said, 'If fate throws a knife at you, you can catch it by the blade or the handle.'

I write that on a day when I have my column in The Times, *a comment piece in the* Mail, *and I sit in the new white study Robin has built for me, sun pouring into the conservatory, Bonnie curled up on the old cane sofa and I'm asking myself if it is possible for things to be better. Wanting to be nowhere else but here. Heat and stillness folding together; the garden dense and green; distant hills like the background to a painting by Leonardo.*

I am holding the handle I have caught.

[in ink] To write in pencil is to be afraid, like a child first learning who will reach for the eraser to cancel mistakes.

Robin calls me from the Alps but I am embedded in solitude, greedy for the silence of the garden. Now 9.30 pm, pearly dusk, pink sky in the west, a chalked half moon, distant lulling of wood pigeons. You could live like this: efficient in the eyes of the world, existing through the telephone, the internet, your work – and yet all the while dropping below the horizon like the sitting sun, ready to make the long journey to the underworld.

These days I no longer think of The Soprano with compassion, and that in itself is cause for resentment, for she has taken away something from my core. It was a terrible death, I know; yet she toppled into the void and dragged the man who was mine with her.

Yet he of all people, how could he prove so vulnerable? Maybe this will be one of the many tasks I will set myself in the future: to understand.

The sculptor Henry Moore wrote, 'The secret of life is to have a task, something you devote your entire life to, something you bring everything to, every minute of the day for your whole life. And the most important thing is – it must be something you cannot possibly do.'

The white lobelia glimmering like thousands of fallen stars.

15 July
9.20am and a vapour trail lit up, like a snail track in the sky. A cloud shaped like a bird. Robin absent. Why am I content? I feel I will never truly need to be with a man again. Not after so many years. I read all the emails and letters from Times

readers and am over-awed by the unhappiness that they carry to me, evidence of the eternal human capacity to make a mess of things. But still, sitting here with Bonnie snuggled up to my side, watching the silver moon assert itself in a deep turquoise sky, knowing somebody who loves me is drinking beer in the French Alps, I catch my breath at my blessings. I work, I sleep … It's as if never before was life as simple and harmonious as this. Yet the act of writing those words feels like a betrayal of the past. Still … did I really get so stressed all the time? Did I usually feel very far away from the autonomous peace I feel now? Yes, it is true.

That summer brought a new shock. J was to sell the farm. I understood his reasons but had trusted he would live there for a while yet, as intended. But he had a new life to make and understandably no longer wanted to rattle around amidst the memories. Each time he drove into Bath he had to pass my new house; each time I drove out of the city towards the motorway I had to pass the track to our old home. He must have realized that the pulling at fresh stitches, re-opening the wound, would go on until one of us moved from the city. Now the next stage had been reached, and it was right – but we all dreaded it. More boxes. More lists. A final partition of things. Another ending.

It was just as well I was about to park Bonnie with my parents and escape to the USA – again. This was another job, but it was to provide a new, subversive perspective.

The week came when I had to write three advice columns because the page had to appear while I was away. Robin and I were commissioned to produce a piece for *The Times Magazine* on the growing phenomenon of women motorcyclists; I'd sold the idea because I was curious to see Sturgis, the small town in South Dakota which hosts the world's largest motorcycle rally every August. It meant that Robin could spend a week photographing semi-naked women straddling big bikes, which struck him as a fine assignment. Then, after six days at the rally, we would head off, travelling from Deadwood to the Badlands to produce a travel article for the *Mail on Sunday*. Friends groaned at the good luck of work like that. And as always, I experienced that sense of release when the plane took off for Minneapolis. From the Twin Cities we took an internal flight over the empty plains to Rapid City.

Sometimes, at the end of a long relationship, it's essential to try to do something – anything – to reinvent yourself and to realize that (no matter how the marriage ended) this may well be a liberation rather than a loss. Which is to say, it can be both at once, but the emphasis is placed (even if by the greatest effort of will and a degree of falsehood) on the new you, the new life, the new soul. It is one key to survival. Robin and I had worked together on many travel articles, and were used to gatherings of bikers too. J and I had always 'allowed' different sides of each other to develop over the years. His tennis and sailing interested me but little, my attempt to learn to ride horses was a failure and to the end I never fully understood why he wanted to farm. He did not share my penchant for jazz and blues (especially in the 'dark cafés' of Joni Mitchell's lyric), or jukeboxes, but he regarded my middle-aged fascination with biker culture with enough amused benevolence to buy me a Harley-Davidson which, in the end, frightened me too much to ride.

The point is, the whole week in Sturgis enabled me to enact a fantasy life a million miles away from the one I had described in *The Times Magazine* the year before. All the ingredients were there:

We were supplied with a Harley-Davidson Electra-Glide by the Milwaukee-based company.

We rented a trailer.

I was travelling light, with none of the things which normally give my life structure, like (for example) books or smart clothes.

For one week I could become the kind of woman who, wearing jeans and a singlet, swigs a cold beer sitting on the trailer steps, then puts on a cowboy hat or bandana (no helmets in South Dakota) and rides off with her man to join the deafening, throbbing rumble of 500,000 other iron horses on the streets of the small town. I could become the kind of woman who had never been Mrs Anybody, or sewed nametapes on school uniforms. Never owned a library in a fine house, surrounded by land. Never had to wear that woman-of-many-committees face at a charity event. Never known the lash of the work ethic or the dinner-party imperative. Anonymous, I could cut loose. Not give a damn. It was tempting to get a tattoo of a bird, with the word 'Freedom' on a ribbon in its beak. My T-shirts announced 'Badass Girls Need Badass Toys' and 'Good Girl Gone Bad'. What I needed was a small mongrel on a string who would guard the trailer (barking furiously at the world just as I often wanted to bark, but always restrained myself) until we roared back to unload the six-packs and the food and party on through the sweaty night, with biker universe grumbling in the distance, like a summer storm.

Another life.

Sitting in the trailer one hot afternoon, brooding about the (still 'our' in my mind) farm up for sale and strangers wandering round, looking up at those carved stone corbels to ask the unknowing estate agent what they meant, and peering at our furniture wondering what sort of people created a home so unusual, so beautiful ('Oh, and how could they *leave* such a place?' they'd ask), I felt miserable. Like the ghosts which haunt your childhood – slipping into your wardrobe and beneath the bed – you have to face the truth that your worries and your loves will follow you to South Dakota or the South Pole and even outstrip a motorcycle at speed. No choice. You carry it all with you, and always will. Still, many miles away and feeling free as I did, I was able to realize how wise J was to say, with sad pragmatism, 'Houses go on and on – they're just owned by different people.'

And Sturgis was full of different people. I walked up to women leaning against their parked bikes and found out all about them, cheered and inspired by people like 68-year-old Anita Feldman, a retired airline executive, who had ridden her H-D Fat Boy from St Louis – 1,000 miles in two days. Lolling over her yellow bike in a skinny blue camisole, with the face and body of a 50-year-old, she told me about her Drag Racing 'personal best' (for the uninitiated that means reaching a maximum speed over a quarter mile from a standing start) of 110 miles an hour – 'tho' I'm still just learnin', so I'm gonna beat that'. I met 80-year-old Gloria Struck from New Jersey, who joined the women's motorcycle club The Motor Maids in 1946 (the year I was born) and bought herself a new H-D Heritage Softail for her seventy-ninth birthday. On the back of her blue T-shirt was an image of herself on a motorcycle when she was young, with the caption 'A Living Legend'. She told me, 'Life is wonderful at 80. I've made a list of the things I want to do before I die and I'm working through them. I think next is a ride through China.'

There were so many more – women of all ages, all types, married, single, divorced, gay, glamorous, greasy, scary, mothers, grandmothers – all righteously sexy motorcycle mamas. I felt empowered by them, even though I had given up my own riding dream and settled for being the best pillion rider. (And by the way, my guidelines for being the best pillion are a reasonable guide to life in general:

1. Be prepared by reading the road.
2. Move with the bike, with what happens.
3. Never complain.)

Even in the throbbing hubbub of Sturgis I knew that back home in my white study this whole experience would inform everything I wrote. That I would be telling my readers that no matter what shit circumstances throw at you, no matter who hurts you, it's up to you to learn to grasp the handlebars of your own life, face the road ahead and crank up the speed before you die. I heard, *You can, you can, you can,* in the stuttering idle of every mean machine, telling me to catch life by the throat.

One day we rode out to the Full Throttle Saloon, 'America's No. 1 Biker Bar', just outside town, where cars are not allowed. Back home only our biker friends Al and Sue would have understood this wild place; everybody else I know would have deemed it another circle of hell – and that fact added to my feeling of a new identity. I felt a strange impulse to introduce myself as a biker lady called 'Bonnie Mooney', morphing into my dog. But I never did. The bar was in fact an enormous corral full of heat and dust and the endless roar of Harleys and thousands of bikers drinking beer and generally hanging out and having a good time. Old chairs and sofas to loll on. Stalls selling things like the purple zebra-striped cowboy hat I had to buy. Smell of burning rubber and fried food. Blue smoke drifting on hot air. Big men watching pretty women wearing underwear and leather chaps. A glamorous 40-year-old real estate agent called Jessica, wearing a black bra, mini skirt and white ankle socks rolling into the corral on her 8-foot long chopper, loving the stares. Everybody with attitude, and yet the sum total of attitude becomes camaraderie. We were a pack: an insanity of bikers.

On the stage a heavy band was led by a rock chick called Jasmine Cain: beautiful, talented and tough with bare midriff, jeans and long, flying hair. She played the mostly male crowd with that splayed-leg, come-on-and-try-me stance as she hit her guitar and they roared – dogs howling for the moon. And her lyrics cut through the scream of bikes and guitars and people, words that made me want to raise a fist in exultation. The song was called 'Not Gonna Turn Back' and Jasmine was singing just for me:

I never will give up
I've sacrificed too much
I'll stand and I'll face it I might get burned
but I'm not gonna turn back now
Push me down
And I'll get back up …

With a Budweiser cold against my hand, thinking of all that had happened, I was saying to myself, Yes! I would rather be here, listening to Jasmine in all this infernally cool chaos than in any of the great opera houses of the world. Yes! I want to ride down Bath's premier shopping street on a massive chopper, wearing cowboy boots and black leather.

This retrospective rebellion was changing me from the feminist who would disapprove of all the blatant sexism to somebody who didn't care. Nearby, a plump young girl with bare breasts was astride a slowly bucking pony-skin-covered bronco machine, trying to keep her seat while a bunch of men watched avidly, hot puppies with their tongues hanging out. Next to me, a woman in her thirties turned and shrugged, saying, 'I think of it as an anthropological study. I mean … *guys!* Show them tits and they're hooked. Can you imagine *us* standing around for hours in case we got a sight of cock?' We were convulsed with laughter.

A blonde girl called Kelly was serving beer at one of the rudimentary open-air bars, wearing white panties under leather chaps with a white T-shirt. When she bent to pick four cans of Miller-Lite from the tub of iced water she allowed the water to pour all down her chest, to reveal large, perfect breasts. The guy she was serving gave her a tip; I could almost see his tail wag. Next in line to be served was a woman. The two girls exchanged grins as Kelly murmured, 'It's easy!' She reminded me of a playful Bichon, all white curls and curves, who knows how beautiful she is and how readily men can be manipulated.

At last, somewhat relieved, we left the trailer, the Harley and the noise, to become different people yet again: tourists in a rental car admiring the sights and wildlife of South Dakota.

Wild burro, mustangs and Buffalo under Ponderosa pines. Silence of Wind Cave National Park, and a host of prairie dogs – who reminded us of Bonnie. The little creatures stood by their burrows, front paws dangling, giving out their strange cheeping squeak of warning as they rear up. (Sometimes Bonnie dances on her hind legs, paws in the air, attacking my playfully raised fists. Attagirl! I think, take it on! Attack that air!) Towards the end of the two weeks we were longing to return home. Robin pointed out that an additional plus of having a dog you love waiting is that you always want to go home. The dog creates the home. The dog represents that part of you which never really went away.

The last thing I did in Rapid City was buy Bonnie a Harley-Davidson collar, lead, T-shirt and peaked cap. Which was about as far away from the biker-cool of black leather and Sturgis, and equally as unacceptable to any English notions of style and dignity, as it was possible to be. But why should I care? A part of recovery is learning not to care what people think, to recover the true self. And if my true self was shaped by poetry, by motorcycles, by a lapdog, by rock 'n' roll, by chamber music, by family, by freedom and by countless complicated feelings including loving two very different men – so what?

J and I saw each other from time to time, of course. We had lunches in London, and sometimes in Bath, but not very often. Not as often as we thought we would. It was always unsettling to see each other because of the impossibility of ever saying what we felt. Yet we both knew – and so felt relieved to talk about broadcasting and writing as we had done for so many years. Then we would hug goodbye and stride off in our different directions. That's how it is.

All the things I was doing – from developing the style of *The Times* column (to the degree that soon strangers would stop me in the street to talk about it), to sitting in Bonham's auction house in Bond Street, wearing (I who had never given a damn about designer labels) a Missoni jacket and hat, and bidding for pictures – were still acts I observed from a distance as if carried out by an assured stranger. Sometimes I wondered where the persona I was accustomed to – the bespectacled, nervous child in Liverpool, the 21-year-old who did not know that the middle classes she was marrying into call the midday meal 'lunch' not 'dinner' and the evening meal 'dinner' not 'tea', the young wife, the mother of somebody's children – had gone.

Sometimes I wondered if this is a usual effect of separation. Yet I knew otherwise from my letters. Again and again I read about people stuck within their lives as a fly stuck on flypaper twirls helplessly over a void. Men and women wrote asking how to move forward, if indeed there is any place to go. Sometimes the letters caused me the same discomfort as lemon juice rubbed into a paper cut, or the sharp pain from a tooth you cannot help but touch. At the beginning of November, for example, a woman in her late fifties wrote a long letter, the nub of which was this: ' … How can one remain serene in the face of dead and dying family, offspring leaving the nest, the end of a long marriage (my husband left a few months ago) and the feeing that this is it? Everything I lived and worked for and made me happy seems to be disappearing in front of my eyes.' She felt empty, with no faith to console her. Her letter could have come from any one of thousands of people.

This reply shows how closely I was drawing on my own experience. I was talking to myself:

Like many people, you are overwhelmed by universal sadness. The trigger for these feelings was the departure of your husband, and most people reading would conclude that you have every right to feel sorry for yourself. Anybody would. Contemplating that void which was so recently filled by the whole rich, bright, multi-faceted construct that is married life, bewilderment is understandable. Some days it must seem that you are battered by a mocking snowstorm of symbolic birthday, anniversary and Christmas cards into which you stumble, cold and alone. And isn't the innocuous photograph album transformed overnight into an instrument of torture?

Most exhausting of all is the retracing of steps in memory, over and over, wondering if there was anything one could have done to pre-empt what happened. And at 4am, we are wakened by the distant laughter of the universe, that we – poor creatures – are doomed to attach so much desperate importance to monogamous personal relationships when they are so unstable.

Sometimes I think we are homesick for our own lives – for the fragrant land of imagining we mapped out when we were young, assuming the route would be clear, that we would claim the welcoming terrain as our own, and live happ— Oh, you know. Then in middle age we discover the limits of cartography – that those 'blue, remembered hills' are as far away as ever, though still close in dreams, still tantalizing us with what might have been. Of course, the trouble is that we usually think 'should' instead of 'might'. Whereas the genius of the poet A.E. Housman is to acknowledge that it is 'the land of lost content' itself which is our true inheritance.

I'm saying that because I want you first to release yourself from any sense of inadequacy or failure, and realize that your feelings are normal – so much so that there will be many reading this who will completely identify with you, whether they have a spouse or not. Loss is as central to life as growth; they are two sides of the coin. Graham Greene once referred to 'the madness, the melancholia, the panic fear which is inherent in the human situation'. His own faith did not save him from depression, and after all, the great theologian Teilhard de Chardin identified the things that beset us as fear, dread, sickness, old age and death. Religious belief does not necessarily protect you from sorrow; on the contrary it can intensify the feeling of being abandoned. I have to say that most of the questing agnostics I have interviewed over the years for Radio 4's *Devout Sceptics* are not 'stuck' but have worked hard to construct consolations (art, landscape, philosophy, children, a sense of being part of a whole, and so on) to light their way forward into the darkness. I see that imaginative reaching out towards the unattainable as a thrilling, creative act, and the defiant belief in the possible a world view as profound as any religion.

I want you to see your letter, this universal experience which you are sharing with the rest of us, as itself part of the solution. You are not asking, you are giving. It always fascinates me that people choose to go on living, even when they are suffering from depression. Where does that will come from? I suppose it's a simultaneous rejection of the darkness and an innate belief in the self. That is what your letter, sad though it is, already shows. You have already made progress, and your ability to be alone is a key part of this. But what seems to be bothering you most is the sense of being 'ill equipped' to deal with all the problems which beset you – all of which are made so much worse by a terrible sense of emptiness (and anger?) at the destruction of your marriage. You wonder how to repair the loss, fill the void. So if I were to assure you that such a task is actually impossible, would that make you feel less incompetent? You must not use up energy blaming yourself for a perceived inability to do something no one on earth can do.

I will not utter platitudes which seek to diminish the loss currently central to your life. Recently bereaved people feel (for differing lengths of time) that the world has become meaningless. It goes without saying that the end of a marriage is akin to a bereavement, since the structure and meaning of life were so bound up with that other person that a period of mourning is inevitable. Perhaps you might have lost one or two friends because of it (that happens) which adds to your feeling of abandonment. In addition you have endured death within your family, and know this is just the beginning. The knowledge that one's children are growing and moving away is hard enough for many women who are still married; for you (as for the widow) the prospect of the empty nest is made bleaker by the absence of the arm on which you might have learnt to share the experience.

There is absolutely nothing we can do about the changes which happen to us, except to strive to make them happen for us. You're on that path, and can have no inkling of where it will lead. I hazard a guess that your children will always view home as where you are, that when (with luck) there are grand-children you will be still be central to the whole family, that the baring of your soul to the mirror in solitude will make you grow – and that one day somebody new may well see how strong and utterly worthy of love you are. But you will have constructed a new life before then, for yourself, by yourself – knowing that without the perception of universal sadness, we would have no means to transform that burden into grace.

As always, on 26 November I lit a candle for our son Tom, who would have been 30. We attach to such milestone birthdays more importance than is reasonable, especially in mourning. What do the numbers matter: seven, 15 or 23 years? Each year you think about how old your child would have been and of the stages he or she would have reached: toddling, nursery, primary school, first love. When a child is stillborn the yearly imagining is all you have, since in 1975 there was no practice (as there is now) of helping parents to deal with the loss by allowing them to see and hold their baby. Our second son was taken away to be disposed of, in the way they did then. The Catholic Church used to consign these babies to limbo since they were born unbaptized (this is no longer the case) and a strange limbo-like stasis does indeed imprison the mother who did not actually view her dead child, as if it might all have been a dream. Many years later I wrote to the hospital to ask what had happened to him and somebody from obstetrics eventu-ally replied to tell me that stillborn babies were cremated in the hospital and their ashes 'scattered on the rose bushes'. I did not remember any rose bushes at St Thomas's. My mind quailed at the image of the furnace consuming detritus.

Still, the thirtieth anniversary did seem meaningful. It made me pause amidst the renewed activity (more travel pieces, giving talks on writing, a big interview with Salman Rushdie, book reviews, the column, the workaholism which usually kept contemplation at bay) to think about memory. I am the only person who *knew* the child I carried for eight months, and when I die that tiny memory of somebody who never drew breath will be gone for ever. I remembered how full of sorrow J was, and how supportive to me, how *good* – throughout an experience which is so hard for any couple that many marriages do not survive the shock, disappointment and grief. Nevertheless the actual date is not at the forefront of his mind as it is mine. I am the keeper of the flame, the candle is its symbol, and it occurs to me (strangely) that the loss was but a preparation for the much bigger conflagration which would set the house on the hillside alight.

I thought it ironic that I should be so full of sadness at the loss of the farm about which I was first so resentful. Night after night I found myself dreaming about the home J and I had created with so many hopes, but about which I complained so often. I grieved for the beautiful things we placed within it, in the sincere belief that we would be there for ever: rare antique tiles, a Victorian flowered lavatory, stained glass. At the same time I could hear J's voice in my mind telling me that, after all, these are *only* things, and no more. I felt anguish at the thought of the hedges he had planted which were growing tall and thick – even though I knew he was right to remind me that they would go on growing, to provide sanctuary for countless small creatures, whether we were there or not. Maybe all this had happened before in another life, and J and I were ghosts already haunting a house full of strangers.

But the trouble is I had placed my faith in the whole edifice, without acknowledging the cracks that had been in it all along. My natural tendency is to dissemble and call it honesty, to evade and pretend to be straight, to manipulate and then look surprised when what I wished for came about. But now I had lost all control. Thirty years earlier I believed that I had been punished for all my sins by the death of my baby. Now, deep down, I felt that our marriage would not have been destroyed, and our home sold, had it not somehow been my responsibility. There were times (let it be said) when I had hurt my husband just as much as he had recently hurt me.

The furniture and objects he did not want and I had no room for were stacked in the barn I had made into his games room – to be carted off to the sale room. Our children were summoned to remove some of their possessions. Knowing the rooms I knew so well (stone by stone, plank by plank) were being emptied made me weep afresh. Understanding why J was moving, I still railed against him in my heart for not wanting to preserve the precious relics. On the surface my life was good, but underneath the impending sale of the farm had a deep effect, which I kept hidden, because a brave face was my stock in trade. I was afflicted by a lack of trust in everybody and everything. One thing surprised me – I simply could not bear to listen to the soprano voice, whoever was singing. I would shiver and snap the radio off.

My notebook from this time is full of sorrow, with an obsession with home and with loss running through. My certainties had gone and it was lonely without them. Why would you place any trust in human love, I thought? Friends disappoint and work too will one day fade, your professional world not wanting you any more. How did I know Robin would stay with me? How did I know my children wouldn't abandon me when I am old? When you reach another ending in such a short space of time (the marriage, then the home) you glimpse, as if a curtain has parted on an empty stage, all the other endings which stretch ahead.

Still, this much I trusted, without consulting tea leaves or my own line of fate. The one thing you can always be sure of is that your dog will recognize you, no matter which mask you wear.

Your dog will know your voice, even when all you can utter is a cry.

Your dog will love you no matter what you have become.

No matter where you are, your dog will welcome you home.

Five

GROWING

It is a strange thing, love. Nothing but love has made the
dog lose his wild freedom, to become the servant of man.
D.H. Lawrence, 'Rex'

Robin, who is fascinated by the art of animation, particularly likes Betty Boop – but especially now, because of her small white dog, Pudgy. They remind him, he says, of his 'girls'. Betty and her pet sit atop our fridge in the guise of a salt and pepper set, by the kitchen sink holding washing-up tools, and also in my study as a funny resin ornament I bought in Brussels. Here Betty is wearing exactly the sort of glittery purple dress I might choose. Naturally Robin is correct to identify me with Ms Boop – a woman whose appearance (high heels, big earrings, tight clothes) belies dark, existential depths ('Ohhh, Pudgee, what shall we *dooo*?').

My dog is, of course, a ringer for Pudgy, if you discount the black markings which, in any case, the animators sometimes forgot. I love Betty's squeaky crooning over her little 'Pudgy-

Wudgy' in a language I understand, while Bonnie entirely sympathizes with Pudgy's aversion to baths and his jealousy of any interloper, even Betty's fox fur. What's more, when the little dog first appears in 1934 as 'Betty Boop's Little Pal' he is scooped up as a stray by the dog catcher and hauled off with other lost hounds. Naturally they make a break for it and he finds his way back to Betty, to lick her face in ecstatic reunion as the black screen circles in on them, signifying the end. And so I recognize my dog and me, prefigured seven decades before we met. Pudgy is lost, then found – and spends the rest of his cartoon life getting into scrapes of course, but watching out for Betty, attacking anything that might threaten her, and (of course) having fun.

Yet there is an intriguing puzzle at the heart of Betty Boop – another of those questions about identity. For Betty started life *as* a dog. Within that moon face beneath black wavy hair is a memory of the canine soul. In 1930 the Fleischer Studios (the only serious rival to Disney at the time) produced a 'talkartoon' called *Dizzy Dishes*. It contains a night-club cabaret scene packed with animals in which an unnamed female dog sings. It is only a walk-on role. The animator Grim Natwick who created her (and animated most of *Snow White* for Disney) explained that he just designed a little dog and put feminine legs on her, and long ears using a French poodle as the basic idea for the character. A year later this canine creation appears in another cartoon, as the abandoned wife of Bimbo the gun-totin' dog, a bandit who holds up a train full of oddball animals. Unfortunately for him, his wronged spouse turns out to be one of the passengers. Mad as hell, she whips out a photograph of his 17 kids and whups him into submission. I like that.

This virago is recognizable as Betty, but she still has dangling ears and a tiny button nose. Her jowls may have lessened slightly since *Dizzy Dishes* but she is still the humanoid dog, with a deep voice too. But the following year the Studios produced *Stopping the Show* as the first cartoon with the Betty Boop name on it, as well as the theme tune 'Sweet Betty', which was to introduce ever-single Boop animation. In *Stopping the Show* Betty has metamorphosed (who knows why?) into the iconic, oddly innocent sexpot familiar from a million dollars' worth of merchandise. The ears have become dangling earrings, she is a human cabaret artist performing impersonations to a huge audience of cheering animals – and a star is born, trilling 'Boo boop be doo'.

I am somewhat obsessed with the idea of transformation – and believe that each one of us is capable of reinvention. That's why I love the Betty story, because to *start* life as a dog (even an animated one) is surely to be a unique repository of metaphorical knowledge. Sometimes we look at our dogs and wonder what is going on in their heads, apart from devotion and desperation, of course. But, you see, Betty understands it all. Just as the legendary Greek seer Tiresias had the experience of living both as a male and as a female, thus giving him unique insight, I like to think that Betty's blend of sweetness and cunning derives from her half-doggy, half-human soul. The world of her early cartoons is populated mostly by jiving dudes in animal form – giraffes, rhinos, monkeys, cats and so on – but Betty is leader of the pack. Her habitual demeanour is surprise, she is always ready for an adventure, quickly forgets wrongs and works to put things right, is naughty and playful and appealing, and always entertains.

Yes, this is the essence of the dog in her.

Robin and I had begun to broadcast our obsession with Bonnie to the world by putting her on our Christmas card. The first one had her outside our garlanded front door, paws up against it, trying to get in (I was hiding inside, of course) but looking over her shoulder at the photographer – who was Robin, naturally. Beside her was a pair of scarlet high heels, as if kicked off by the lady of the house. The words inside said, 'Open up this Christmas – and in the coming year may you never lock the good things out.' It was a professional production, beautifully printed, but still, we half expected our friends and colleagues to mock our madness. Instead they loved the card – and one or two people even suggested we could go into business designing doggy cards. That was not a part of our life plan; nevertheless a different Bonnie card each year, complete with a meaningful message, was to become our trademark, looked forward to by friends. The cards are an outward symbol of how I have changed. The fun we have creating the concept and taking the photograph is obvious, and only a patient dog who loves her human companions would be such a long-suffering model. Yet I was the one who used to opine that the only cards sensible people should send are religious themes in aid of charity. With Robin and Bonnie to help, I could lighten up.

My first job for 2006 was an extended review for *The Times*, analysing memoir as 'the new novel'. There was a pile of books to wade through. Other people's lives. The reading snagged at the edge of my mind, as if I knew that one day I would embark on such an exercise of retrieval in the full knowledge that the truth is tenuous. How can you stop yourself cheating at Patience, and who will know if you do?

I might mistrust my own memories were it not for the diaries, which I cling to now as evidence of how the smallest things can bring light to days of unhappiness: a phone call from my daughter, getting to know her new soldier boyfriend, talking to my son, a shopping trip, a walk with my dog in cold sunshine. Diary entries which patiently state mundane things such as 'went to the supermarket' are as revealing of a life (especially, perhaps, a woman's life) than the angst-ridden musings of teen journals: 'Will I ever find love? What is the point of being alive?' And so on. In the memoirs I was reviewing, the pages of dialogue 'remembered' from childhood bothered me. How could the 'he said …' and 'she said …' have any validity after the passage of years? The writers might as well have been writing novels, or screenplays. The exponents of the 'new life writing' hold that this does not matter, but I remain unconvinced. It seems to me that it is the duty of the memoirist to leave out when necessary, but not to fictionalize.

Writing a diary is a chore, yet, having once abandoned the daily task, I took it up again because it grounded me in events. Otherwise, I sometimes felt, I might float off like an escaped balloon. So 2006 is set down in detail. Robin and I had wonderful holidays in Oman, St Petersburg, South Africa, yet what is far more significant is the record of daily life, delight, despair, divorce. And ageing, of course.

When your life changes radically you can't expect your personal growth to keep pace with events. Most of the time you feel left behind, wailing in the wake, wondering why this or that happened and (worse) why you continue to lack understanding. It astonished me, sometimes, that with the great good fortune of a pleasant house, a caring partner and a job I had grown into like a second skin, I still felt in mourning for the old house, the old marriage, the whole way of being we knew. As I passed the entrance to the farm (with the painted sign I'd commissioned for J, showing Herefords and Lleyns in silhouette), my hands would tingle, itching to flick the indicator and turn in, bumping over the cattle grids towards the 'home' that was now empty and awaiting its new inhabitants. Janus, Roman god of the first month, looks back and forward at once, back to the old year and forward to the new. So it was with me.

The idea that one can be still, yet still moving, is encapsulated in the 1912 Futurist painting which I love, *Dynamism of a Dog on a Leash* by Giacomo Balla. It depicts a dachshund on a silver chain walking beside his mistress. All you see of her are the feet (in heavy shoes and dark stockings beneath a long, dark coat) pounding briskly along. The dog trots to keep up, the chain leash swings with their motion – and each 'frame' of the action is captured in a blur, just as animation was later (paradoxically) to freeze time and create movement. The lady and her sausage dog are like Betty and Pudgy: motion in monochrome. Balla, like all the Futurists, wanted to reflect the spirit of the age by painting the movement of machines, the quantum essence of light, speed, motion. But this painting – of a woman and her small dog with somewhere to get to – represents even more: the forward movement of life itself, which we cannot escape. Small dogs (by virtue of their deficiency in leg length) *move*: they represent all energy, all life – and when I look at the Balla painting, the question I ask is, 'Who is leading whom?' Surely the dachshund has the edge on the lady? He is taking her into the future they will share, for ever linked by their silver chain. Although she may yearn for whatever she left behind, she is driven forward, impelled by the thrust of the universe, on her capable feet.

What choice is there in life? Sometimes unwanted change – and the deep unhappiness it causes – turns out to be the essential journey between two halves of your own soul. You have to make that journey (albeit running on the spot) in order to become more wholly yourself.

At first J and I had assured each other that divorce was not necessary, but things had shifted. Each of us had a new partner (although at the time still with no intention of remarrying) and therefore knew we needed to take a further step away from the past. In February, Robin and I went to Oman for five nights of peace and luxury, and when we returned to cold England the first divorce papers were waiting with the rest of my mail. I know that for some people this is a glorious relief, an essential step towards freedom from a detested marriage and a nightmare spouse. That was not the case with us. I wrote in my diary: '*How strange to think of J and me ending thus. But perhaps it never ends. No – of course not! Unless of course you hate each other, but even then it goes on ... all that you have been, for better, for worse.*'

A week later I walked by the River Thames to Tate Modern to meet him for lunch. It would have been our thirty-eighth wedding anniversary and I wondered if you go on having an anniversary when you are separated. And if so, for how long? Rain swept over the river, wrinkling the surface of the water like a worried brow, and the wind cut through my coat. Inside what is probably London's most popular gallery, a temple to

Modernism, the echoing spaces felt chilly too. I arrived deliberately early to have time to look around, but remembered too late that the last time I visited the few works of genius seemed lost amidst too much meretricious dross. Then I came across an installation by Susan Hiller, called *From The Freud Museum*, and all was redeemed. On each side of a dark room stood a long glass display case, containing about forty-eight boxes in two tiers. Each cardboard box contains a collection of objects, described by the artist as 'rubbish, discards, fragments and reproductions which seem to carry an aura of memory and hint at meaning'. It is not only a nod to Freud's collected objects (still on display in his north London home) but a representation of the many compartments of the human mind.

As you stare at the boxed collections you wonder why they were selected by the artist, knowing all the while that this is as random as archaeology: the shards, the fragments are there because they are there. You can see what you wish, make connections, remember what you wish. I imagine the boxes automatically shutting like eyelids at night, when the lights are switched off and the galleries given to darkness and emptiness. But even when a lid is closed, what lies within is permanently there, safe from dust. This installation fascinated me because I love both collecting and compartments, and used to create box constructions myself, to give to friends. I made one for J for our twenty-fifth wedding anniversary: a shallow lidded box which opened on to 25 little compartments behind glass, each containing miniature *objets* to evoke the year, and with an explanatory booklet hidden at the back. In the darkness of the Susan Hiller room I remembered it. The sudden recall was like a door thrown open on a pool you could drown in.

We met in the crowded restaurant. The windows framed foreboding, the weather getting worse. It is beyond strange to meet someone you have loved for so long, in a noisy public place, as you might meet a colleague. On the other hand, lovers meet that way too, the room disappearing as their eyes meet and they don't dare to touch because the brush of a finger would be too much to bear. It was strange that there was still something of that. We talked about work and our lives and our children and his Sunday programme on ITV and then I told him about the Susan Hiller boxes. I suggested that when we have loved somebody and endured great pain we can decide to put that person away into a box within us and then close it firmly. So we absorb the people we have loved, the things we have experienced, but we have to be safe from them. We have to bless the existence of lids. I even dared to mention Susan Chilcott's name.

I told him what he already knew, that it was 38 years since we had married. He replied that we had had 35 really good years – and I felt a strange exultation, because only we could ever know the depth of truth in that. Despite everything.

Lunch over, at the foot of the escalator we embraced and he walked away. I turned back, into the great Turbine Hall, to see the Rachel Whiteread installation *Embankment*. It was a mistake, because these boxes all but destroyed the good done by Susan Hiller and by the lunch, and plunged me into gloom. Whiteread's translucent polyethylene casts of cardboard boxes – 14,000 of them – stacked like mountains of giant sugar cubes, are about absence, about negatives, about time congealed. I felt something guarded and hostile about the whole piece; its coldness held me at bay. Whiteread maintains that her work is about memory, yet I saw nothing so human in the collection of shining white blanks. I visualized the time when I was leaving the farm and my cartons were stacked in the dining room, all containing precious things, like Susan Hiller's boxes. But this enormous installation seemed to me like nothingness incarnate and almost called into question everything I had ever loved. There seemed no way forward from this. How can you tuck something away when there is no container, simply emptiness made solid?

There was nothing to do but jump into a taxi, calling out, 'National Gallery!'

There I indulged a secret pastime – which is to walk through rooms of pictures in search of dogs, large and small. And I was rewarded. For in a fifteenth-century work called *The Mass of St Hubert* and in Catena's *A Warrior Adoring the Infant Christ and the Virgin* my eyes were delighted by Maltese dogs the image of Bonnie. As always, they made me smile.

Since my solution to all problems is always to keep moving on my silver chain, I had a new project to take my mind off anniversaries and memory. Although I had maintained that I would write no more children's books, there was now a contract for a new series, inspired (of course) by Bonnie. The first one was due in one month and I had not yet begun, but deadlines present no problems for a writer growing old in the trade. As I finished the 8,000-word story of a boy whose fantasy dog is big and rough, but who is forced to learn how to love the tiny Maltese his mother rescues from the dogs' home, I realized that (without thinking it through) I was writing out my life.

The series for which I became known as a children's author, and which took me to countless schools, libraries and festivals, starred a feisty little girl called Kitty who lived in a normal family with two parents and her older brother Daniel. Some of the stories were based on real things that had happened in our family. In time I gave them another baby, called Tom, as if constructing in fiction the life denied to us by our real Tom's stillbirth. In a sense, this merry nuclear family with their squabbles and jokes was old-fashioned; the prevalence of broken families brought a need in children's publishing for a more gritty realism, taking account of dysfunction and divorce.

I could not have predicted that such things would come to form my experience too. In the (implied) back story of the new series the mother has been left by her husband (whose new girlfriend we meet in a later book) and is struggling with the painfully altered life in a new home, with her son Harry. He is beset by conflicting emotions, worrying about his mother, missing their old life with Dad but gradually coming to terms with the new. The cute, small dog brings affection, entertainment and adventure. As each of the six books (written between 2006 and 2009) unfolds it becomes clear that Bonnie is the good angel: the catalyst who leads people to know each other and makes everything better. Most important, she is the means by which the humans relearn love. I knew that few seven-year-olds would interpret the books so overtly; they just need a good story about characters they like. But no matter: I like books which 'teach', no matter how subtly, and I knew that parents reading aloud to younger children would entirely 'get' the positive message of the stories my dog inspired.

* * *

One day I took Bonnie to visit my close friend Gaynor in the north of England. Robin was in France at the ski chalet he owned with two business partners. I hated him being away, and had grown used to him being there at my side, driving me places and generally being indispensable. I've always loved the song from *My Fair Lady* which celebrates (even if wistfully) the realization that becoming accustomed to somebody's face can indeed 'make the day begin'. Robin was certainly 'second nature to me now'. My much-vaunted independence was diminishing, and I was glad. At a service area I stopped to stretch my legs and let Bonnie pee on the grass verge. Suddenly the lead jerked from my hands and she hared away out of sight. I panicked, and ran in the direction she must have taken, horribly aware of all the cars and strangers who presented instant danger to a small white dog.

A couple walking towards me called out, 'Have you lost a dog?'

'Yes,' I panted.

'It's over there,' they said.

I turned to see a big motorcyclist undoing his helmet, clearly bemused to see a white fluffy thing jumping around excitedly at his feet, her lead trailing on the ground. I raced over, just as he revealed his face. Confused, Bonnie froze and shrank back, panting.

'She thought you were my partner,' I puffed, 'because he's got a bike.'

He grinned, perhaps thinking this was a novel way for a middle-aged lady to pick up strange men. But Bonnie's tail was down. She was disappointed not to see the man she loved. So I led her back to my car, and told her she really must learn to distinguish between the whine of a Japanese motorcycle and the sexy rumble of a Harley-Davidson.

People say we can learn a great deal about anxiety in humans from studying dogs. Of course we are very different species, and dogs do not feel emotions like ours, do they? Well, actually they do. They feel depressed and anxious and are usually miserable to be left alone; their lives are marked by disappointment and intense joy, as ours are. They experience jealousy, and grief too. All dog owners tell tales of how their pets anticipate the holiday before the suitcases come out of storage, as if they understood the word 'hotel' and saw the vision of a sun-lounger through your skull. Then there is the terrible anxiety about whether or not they will be taken with you, or to the kennels, or the minder … To hear the word 'stay' when the human companion is heading for the door is the worst disappointment. It strikes at the canine soul.

Bonnie always knows when I am going out; she reads it from my clothes, but how I cannot tell. The gym kit tells her I will be absent, but so does the smart dress. Perhaps her ability to read my wardrobe is one aspect of her femininity. Clothes apart, a sure sign of my intention is the application of make-up. Then her brow furrows and a terrible intensity possess her tiny frame and sets it quivering with anticipation. All I have to do is look at her sadly and shake my head for her to turn hers away sharply in reproach before allowing her whole body to droop. I always try to reassure her with 'I'm coming back' – just in case she remembers being tied to that tree. Dogs, like babies, suffer from the condition known as separation anxiety and it seems that psychological trauma in puppyhood is largely to blame. Often they are dogs who have been acquired, like mine, from a pound or dogs' home.

According to Dr Nicholas Dodman, professor of veterinary behavioural pharmacology, in his book *The Dog Who Loved Too Much*, anxious dogs usually have the canine equivalent of a dysfunctional human background. Many of them have been left too much alone, as well as, in some cases, suffering outright abuse. Dodman asserts that the relatively modern use of psychoactive drugs to alter animal behaviour 'seems to imply that animals have a psyche (which they do) and that they're prone to mental disturbances similar to the ones that affect people (which they are)'. He draws parallels between problem behaviour shown in dogs and equivalent behaviour exhibited by human beings, and points out that dogs' problems can be studied 'as relevant models of human psychiatric disease'.

Once I would have shaken my head in disbelief at such theories, snorting, 'Hey, come on, it's just a *dog*!' Now I read the experts, and marvel how their collective research experience is backed up by my own. It reminds me of what happened when I gave birth to Daniel in 1974. I knew nothing about babies beforehand and had shown no interest in them. Suddenly the world was full of them: other people's squirming, cooing, dribbling infants which fascinated and enchanted me almost as much as my own. Similarly I will now cross the road to ask about somebody's dog (huge or small) that has caught my eye, whilst encountering Maltese owners, whether in Florida or France, turns me into a babbling fool. If a single small white dog can thus enlarge one woman, is it not reasonable to acknowledge that there may just be a sum total of wisdom and feeling in the canine world, which has a greater potential for good in human terms? That learning from dogs can make us *better*?

The truth is that the more I was exposed to the woes of readers through my *Times* column and the more psychotherapy I studied in order better to equip myself for the task, the more I realized how hopelessly ill equipped most individuals are to deal with relationships. To put it simply, when (in that first summer) my six-month-old Maltese chewed my new children's book and I swatted her with it, making her tremble so piteously, the speed of her forgiveness was superior to any human response. Who, therefore, should I learn from – my dog or people who enmesh themselves in bitterness and recrimination until their souls starve to death? Whenever Bonnie saw J she covered him with joyful licks. Why should I not, metaphorically, do the same?

I often think that nobody should be allowed to have a baby until they have shown themselves fit to care for a pup and that a recognition of the importance of animal welfare should be a part of the moral education of all school children. For by learning more about how animal minds work and what they need, we gain insight into our own humanity. In his brilliant book *The Dog's Mind* the vet Bruce Fogle draws a parallel between the 'primal' need for touch (for example) in young animals and in humans. He describes how baby macaques who were deliberately isolated from their mothers at birth grew up to suffer from 'overwhelming and serious behaviour disturbances', banging their heads and sometimes mutilating themselves. It comes as no surprise to read that 'touch is the earliest and possibly the most important of all the canine senses' so that 'dogs that are deprived of touch will grow to become subordinate, fearful and withdrawn.' Anyone reading that who has had the distressing experience of visiting a children's home will recognize the description.

What's more, Fogle describes the mutual benefit possible when human and dog share this essential craving for physical reassurance. Touching is a two-way street: soothe your dog and it will soothe you. Learn to be soft, kind, giving, and your dog will help the world to send those qualities back to you in spades. All those who use dogs in therapy with old people, sick people and disturbed youngsters know that the truth goes even one step further than Fogle's observation: petting a dog which you do *not* know, but which is trained to respond therapeutically, can often be as rewarding as any session on the couch with a human shrink. Dogs can do this for us. Bred as hunters, guards and companions (to name but three roles), they are above all *helpers*. I suspect we are only just beginning to find out the extent of their capacities, but the important thing is: they respond to praise, example and affection, and the more we give it the more *we* will receive.

I can't separate this awareness from my (increasing) knowledge of how people can behave when a marriage ends. Sometimes it's hard to avoid seeing the humans who write to me as ill-treated dogs (and obviously no insult is intended from the terminology), backing into their lairs to lick their wounds and snarl at anyone who approaches. Some lick themselves so obsessively it becomes self-mutilation. Some display the greedy cunning of the sneaky Border collie who waits until the humans have gone and then jumps up on to the table, scattering the cats to steal their food – as Sam used to do at the farm. Some cower, beaten and whining. Others are angry because of what has been done to them, and never regain trust. Worst of all, some charge each other like savage dogs of war – and at the end of the battle their own children lie mangled and bleeding on the battlefield.

But some will always recall (and dogs have good memories) the best of times, the sublime moments when the air was full of the sweetest smells, the treats tasted delicious and every moment was full of possibility. They remember the mutual touch which gave such pleasure, and the loyalty which was (for a while) its reward. Some fortunate human hounds are locked into that primal 'training', and although they may feel disappointment when suddenly the present reality changes, still they choose to forget the tree they were left tied to – and instinctively summon up all the rest.

Yes, I am so glad to have learned from my dog.

The tail-sweeping, ear-drooping disappointment of the 'No' is something we humans have to get used to as well. Back in 2003, in the middle of the worst of times, when J had gone but few people knew, I had to fulfil an obligation to present the sixth-form prizes at a smart, academic girls' school and – very unhappy and nursing a (not unconnected) hangover – decided to talk to them about the forbidden subject of disappointment, instead of success. 'Girls, you will fail one day!' I said. I told them they should be prepared for it, because failure can help you grow – as in Samuel Beckett's staccato wisdom: 'No matter. Try again. Fail again. Fail better.' So get used to the real world, girls!

The unscripted talk was a hit; I could see the girls were relieved – even if their over-ambitious parents would have preferred a pep talk about university. Then three years after that day I had to come to terms with more disappointments of my own. First I faced the disheartening truth that adult fiction and I would probably part company. My sixth novel, *The Invasion of Sand* (set in Australia and the result of cumulative years of work), had only found a modest publisher and received just one major review (which was excellent). J had always been passionate about this book and could not understand why others did not feel the same; his belief in me had not changed, but now that seemed to me as sad as all my work on a novel into which I had poured my heart. It was tough.

Then Malcolm Love called me to say that the new Controller of BBC Radio 4 had decided not to recommission the interview series *Devout Sceptics*, which we had been making since 1995 and which had won an award for religious broadcasting. Even before it began, I had been a regular contributor to the station since the eighties: interview series, reportage, literary programmes, talks. People would stop me in the street to say they loved listening. Now it was over – and Malcolm and I would work together no more. These are the things you have to face as you get older in a competitive trade: the previous station boss takes you out to lunch and gives your series the prime 9.00 a.m. slot; the new man is not interested. It's tough too. But that's how it is in journalism and you have to face it.

More painful was watching J present his last eponymous Sunday programme on ITV on 7 May. Commissioned by the BBC to make a big documentary series on Russia, with a book deal too, he had to relinquish his political interviewer's chair. Naturally I watched. His guest was Charles Falconer QC, Lord

Chancellor, then Secretary of State for Constitutional Affairs, and close friend of Prime Minister Tony Blair. J was as good as ever, his unique blend of terrier tenacity and perfect manners as much in evidence as it ever had been. Still at the top of your game, I thought. But at the end Charles Falconer surprised him by turning the tables and doing a pre-arranged spoof interview with the presenter, after which the programme showed a montage of his 11-year tenure. Such high spots, such scoops … I felt the familiar surge of pride at his talent. But a second later I realized that was no longer 'mine' to feel. There would be a post-programme party and it was overwhelming to think that I would not be sharing it with him – I who had shared his whole career. He was with another partner now. In comparison with these still-new realities, ephemera like books and radio programmes dwindled to nothing.

Later that afternoon he telephoned to say he felt it all too. Of course.

The lesson of all these experiences is that jobs will come and go, creative work will have varying degrees of success, children will grow up and leave home, marriages may end, precious pets will inevitably die one day just as farm animals have to die … and that is how it is. Just as dogs have to get used to perpetual disappointment (the walks that don't happen, being left …), so do we. There's no escape – other than moving forward yourself with all the changes. Keeping pace. In the words of Rilke, you have to:

> *Want the change. Be inspired by the flame*
> *Where everything shines as it disappears …*

I will not deny the difficulty, but pain does lessen once you have learned to accept. What's more, there is an irony there – that to learn perpetual motion may bring you to a condition of Zen stillness. Like Betty Boop and Balla's dachshund you have to animate yourself in order to survive and, in surviving, you may learn how to 'be'.

There was nothing else to do, after J's last programme, but join Robin in the garden for three hours of punishing labour around Kwan Yin's temple. I slashed at grasses while Bonnie looked on in puzzlement, before retreating to search for the creatures who live beneath the lawn. The terrier in her always lives in hope that she will root them out – and the fruitless, grubby activity never ceases to make me laugh. Florence Nightingale was quite right when she noted the healing properties of dogs: 'A small dog is often an excellent companion for the sick, for long chronic cases, especially ...' Perhaps my ongoing obsession (for that's what it was) with my ex-husband made me a chronic case too.

Just four days later in Dorset I experienced one of those life-changing moments, which led me to realize yet again that you can go on remaking your life, and sometimes need a shock to force yourself to try something new. This was hardly one of those intense spiritual realizations. Instead it was rooted in an awareness of age and the realization that to indulge vanity can be the boldest affirmation, after which I decided that it was time I made myself 'better' in a very particular way.

Robin and I had taken Bonnie to Lulworth Cove for just one night and visited the famous beauty spot Durdle Door, which happened to be voted the best view in south-west England by the readers of a publication that would never be on my reading list, *Country Walking Magazine*. The giant rock archway juts out into the sea far below the cliffs; you descend from the ugly car park to the pebble beach on steep steps cut into the cliff. Bonnie hopped down like a small mountain goat, stopping to look back every few steps to make sure we were following. It was a very hot day. I sat with her on cushiony pebbles listening to the withdrawing roar of the sea, aware that it was shaping that Jurassic coast into strange caves even as I listened: the Portland stone eroded, the rocks crushed, the whole process happening in eons and eons of heartbeats. Although I cannot swim and dislike boats I love to look at water. Perfect contentment would have left me there all day, running smooth stones through my fingers and listening to the waves, with my little dog lying at my side.

Full of energy, Robin had gone to roam about and take photographs. After a while I looked about for him and spotted him on the clifftop, waving. He made a sign of pointing to his watch; we had planned to visit three ancient churches in the area before lunch in Weymouth. It was time to go. Reluctantly I hauled myself to my feet and walked across to where the steps began. I looked up. Bonnie scrambled ahead. The ascent looked impossibly exhausting and after about twelve steps I was puffing and had to stop. Hating all exercise, I had always turned laziness into attitude, and would rarely go for a country walk, even though we had lived amongst beautiful fields since 1980. Suddenly, at Durdle Door, I realized I had become a woman approaching her sixtieth birthday, in a relationship with a man 17 years younger – who was even then standing at the top of a cliff watching her huff and puff as she struggled to join him, carrying (at the end) her tired dog. I kept my head lowered, thinking, I look so old, I feel so old, I look so bloody, horribly, breathily, wretchedly, wrinklingly *old*, at every step. That was the turning point. Robin smiled affectionately at my state when I reached him, chest heaving, face hot and screwed up with effort. I said nothing but hated feeling and looking as I did. As we closed the car doors my thought was, You are a woman any man in his right mind would leave.

We drove to Osmington and walked to the church with Bonnie. Inside we found a 700-year-old font as well as a monument bearing a description of man's life in childlike letters: 'Man is a glass: Life is as water that's weakly walled about: Sinne brings Death; Death breaks the glass: So runs the water out: Finis.'

'Cheerful!' Robin said.

I said nothing. The message got to me.

After that, we went on to a little village called Chaldon Herring, on the edge of Winfrith Heath, called Egdon by Thomas Hardy. On a ridge above the village are the Bronze Age mounds called the Five Marys where, in excavations carried out before 1866, they found a deep chalk-cut grave in one of the tumuli, containing an adult male and female skeleton, buried sitting together, each with stag antlers on their shoulders. What was that about? I knew that stags' antlers have ancient associations with sexuality and fertility and that hundreds were found at the site of Stonehenge. But who were those people who had been buried up on the windy ridge? Was it a committed couple who were sacrificed? Or had they sinned against the tribe? Reading about them in the guidebook made me shiver, as though the spirits of the long-dead were all around, revenants dreaming of coming back to be christened in the church's two ancient fonts.

Our next destination was Winfrith Newburgh, where we intended to admire the gargoyles and stone corbels (we love such things) as well as the two Norman doors. But we found the church all prepared for an imminent funeral, while at the same time local ladies were getting ready for the weekend flower festival. I was intrigued by the twin spectacles of death and mourning, growth and celebration in one tiny church among trees. As we left the village I spotted people wearing black walking towards the church and it was then that the lessons of the whole morning burst like the 'Hallelujah' chorus in my head. I pinched my own arm, saw the signs of age like the rings on a tree or the branches of an antler and thought, *I am alive*.

Four days after that, for the first time in my life, I signed up with a personal trainer for two sessions a week in her ladies-only gym. No longer would I be that proudly indolent lady with flabby arms used only for pouring a glass of wine and turning the pages of a book. I would remake myself. And so it has been from that day until now. When the boxing gloves are donned or the 4-kilogram free weights lifted I know I am still a work in progress, becoming a person I never thought I would meet within my own mirror. My trainer, Debbie Robinson, smiles at how much I have changed – and I know that J would be amazed at this new person I've become. If I were back in the old life I would stride in our beautiful fields with him every single day, answering the perpetual doggy plea for walks. Too late. But that is the point about knowledge, change, regret. They whisper incessantly the message I learned at Carmel

Mission – that you can't go back. It will never come again as it was.

That indeed is what I wrote to J on the day in August when our divorce became absolutely final. It was (as I emailed him):

> … *a very strange feeling because I thought we would be married until one of us died and then probably afterwards too …*
>
> *But you can't run back through time. You can't change the bad things – but the wondrous side to that coin is, you can't un-write the good things either. And we – unlike so many sad, bitter couples – have not done that, and so we reach this point on our life journey taking different roads but waving to each other across the intervening grass verge. It's a proud testimony, isn't it? So we should always celebrate it. As Dolly Parton sings, 'I will always love you' – and with sweet memories.*

He wrote back immediately, in exactly the same vein.

I was alone in the house, thinking about the past and (as usual) being consoled by my dog. ('*Thank goodness for Bonnie*' is in the diary). Then an impulse made me do an unusual thing. I printed out the long emails we had exchanged and sent them to our son, with a covering letter. You know how it is: we have our children, watch them grow and wave them off into the world, but forget to engage with them as adults in all but the most easy, practical ways. The individual, faltering heartbeat is drowned by family chatter. We forget that you need to go on *showing* them and allowing them to understand you, adult to adult. It was that need to share important truths with one of my children which made me write:

Saturday night
12 August 2006

Dearest Dan

I'm going to scrawl this note and post the letter before I think about it. Enclosed is the email corresp. Dad and I exchanged today. I want you to see it, and keep it somewhere as a testimony to all that your parents had … and have. Because I know it's rare and I write this in tears, so I want you to KNOW.

I don't want you to be cynical about relationships. Read what Dad and I say to each other thirty-nine years after we first fell head over heels in love, and marvel at the miracle. You shouldn't say, 'Because they made mistakes and finally split up, it proves love can't last.' You should say, 'Because they love each other so much in parting, it proves that real, deep love can triumph over all. Even over death.'

Because that's what I believe. Nothing has changed it. And I so want you and Kitty to be proud of your parents – not for any worldly reasons but because we are two flawed human beings who had ideals, betrayed them and each other, yet some-how – as a result of the final, fatal betrayal – achieved some extraordinary private glory. A sort of ideal.

As for the road between Dad and me – the leaves may blow across it but it's as if I could walk that way in a dream and find the path back to our first home together and know that place as if for the first time.

But it's all OK, darling, because we will make it so. We aren't like other people; we never bought into petty possessiveness and corrosive jealousy and (although we got things wrong) we still don't. Your parents both love you and Kitty more than anything and anybody. And now, given that confidence, I want you to forgive us our transgressions and fly freely into your own *destiny.*

With all love
Mum
PS: You can show this to Kitty. I can't write it twice xxxx

So – it was done.

It made me very sad.

One of the most interesting memoirs I read (three-quarters through the writing of this book) was *The Philosopher and the Wolf* by the philosopher and academic Mark Rowlands. The subtitle is 'Lessons from the Wild on Love, Death and Happiness'. Rowlands analyses, in complex detail, his relationship with his 'pet' wolf Brenin, describes how he trained the destructive cub and reflects on how the lessons he learnt from his majestic animal companion served ultimately to transform his personal life – and to go on transforming it even after Brenin's death at the age of 11. If I had feared sometimes that readers might think me somewhat eccentric (or sentimental) to ascribe to small dogs an emotional significance and a moral purpose so much greater than their size, Rowlands has reassured me. He writes of his life with his lupine 'brother': 'Much of what I know about life and its meaning I learned from him. What it is to be human: I learned this from a wolf.'

One of the lessons Rowlands learnt from Brenin is defiance. The wolf bestowed on him the profound awareness that 'it is only our defiance that redeems us.' The epiphany came when he was still a cub, attacked by a pit bull terrier which pinned him to the ground. Instead of squealing in terror, the smaller animal let out a deep growl and the pit bull let him go. That defiance is, I realize, as much a part of my own being as my control freakery, vanity and love of books and art. When things go wrong my inner wolf growls, 'I'll *show* you!', not with malice, just resolve. The small girl from Liverpool still sticks her tongue out at the world, almost with no choice – just as my small dog's tongue lolls out like a scrap of pink felt, because the bottom front teeth have gone. (She is getting older whether I like it or not.) Rowlands takes his cue from the memory of a wolf cub; I take mine from the absurdly small dog who yaps her heart out in defiance of the man in black at the door, disguised as a postman but carrying a scythe.

Getting older too, whether I like it or not … I was approaching my sixtieth birthday, and my response to the strange sensation of divorcing someone I had never ceased to love – indeed to all that had happened in the past three years – was to celebrate. I planned two parties, one in London, one in Bath. The extravagance would say, 'I'm still here, still ready to party, no matter what happens. So there!' When I was 50 I had written two essays about ageing in *The Times* – and here I was again, asked to write about being 60. For the cover of *The Times 2* section Robin photographed me and Bonnie under a scudding sky, on top of Little Solsbury Hill at the edge of Bath. I wore my biker jacket, jeans and purple gloves; she looked like a small cloud briefly tethered to earth.

That evening we set up a second photo shoot at home, given a contrasting style by purple velvet and full make-up. I cooked pasta while Robin edited the pictures. Then, to my surprise, he invited me to go with him out into the garden. It was dark, dank, chilly. My dog and I peered dubiously out of the back door, only to see that he had already switched on the lights which illuminate Kwan Yin in her gazebo-temple at the end of our long garden.

'Come on.'

'Where are we going?'

'To Kwan Yin's house.'

'Why?'

'Just come!'

High heels in damp grass. The dog detests all wetness but will not be left behind. The Chinese goddess glows apricot, with no other lights around. I have no idea what we are doing, but fall silent for once, probably because I love our destination so much. (I have a habit of drifting out to Kwan Yin, stroking her stone face and telling her things.) I am guessing that Robin wants me to look back at the height of the house, where we have been busily preparing for my big birthday party four days away, because his inhabitance of it is so relatively recent and still gives him pleasure.

Instead, once we are in the gazebo beside the statue, he takes a box from his pocket and tells me that this is not a birthday present, and he knows that I have said I don't want to get married again and that (such a long preamble, this) it doesn't matter at all and he won't mind if we never actually get married, but still … 'Will you marry me?' He sounds so nervous. I am totally surprised; the control freak did not see this coming. Bonnie sits and looks up at us and Kwan Yin's smile is serene. I love my two witnesses, and I love the ring – an intensely dark blue opal (they call them black opals) flanked by two diamonds. I recognized it immediately as one I had admired a couple of weeks earlier, walking through Bath with Kitty and gazing in the windows of jewellers as we always do. So my daughter was a part of Robin's great plan. Now he stands looking at me and everything is quiet and I am so moved by this unexpected thing: this gift of steadfastness which (it seems in that moment) only my dog and my statue can match.

'Yes, I will,' I say, not knowing what I have done to deserve this.

'Phew,' he says, with that lop-sided grin.

We go inside to dance to the jukebox and I wonder if it is possible to feel happier. Yet human beings so have a tendency to stand outside the moment, don't we? As soon as it is there, greeted with joy, we consign it to memory and start to worry. For I knew that I had been happy once before, that Robin was 17 years my junior (with all the complications that implies) and that – in my deepest heart – I really didn't want to be called Mrs Anybody again. We were contented just as we were; therefore I saw no need for more change, in the form of an actual marriage. Let's just stay committed, I said, and he agreed. Still, at my birthday party on Saturday 7 October, to my great surprise, the hitherto rather reticent man jumped on the chaise longue in our sitting room and announced to the guests that he had asked me to marry him and I had accepted. Everybody applauded.

The next day was my actual birthday. When lunch was over, and even my children had left for London, and Robin and I had moved all the furniture back, J came to visit me. Robin opened the door, shook his hand and then disappeared to the basement office to give us privacy. J brought a perfect gift: a limited-edition volume of poetry published in 1970, containing work by some of my favourite poets. Bonnie greeted him with a flurry of ecstatic licks and twirls as if he had never gone away – or as if I had never gone away – and everything was the same. That is the beauty of dogs. They carry their old allegiances and affections right at the front of their minds, ready to prompt the always optimistic tail. (Once, I encountered J at Paddington Station – he off the train from Totnes, me from Bath – and he had Sam with him, that needy muzzle greyer now, his hearing failing. Sam remembered me, of course, and the old collie thrust his face into my hand as he had done when he was a puppy and I brought him home for J's Christmas present.)

There is, surely, a choice as to how you choose to view a dog's excitement at meeting one who is no longer part of the pack. It is easy to sigh and say how sad that the faithful animals retain their loves when their humans have hurt each other and the pack is rent asunder. But look at it from the opposite perspective and learn from the small dog – and the old one too. Why not defy human weakness and sentimentality, and rejoice with the dogs at all fleeting reunions? Why not wag our tails and take the past along with us, like an old scent a dog will pick up and recognize for ever?

There was much of the spirit of our shared past in the article which appeared in *The Times* the next day – celebrating becoming 60. In it I made a link between Paul Simon's 'Still crazy after all these years' and Bob Dylan singing 'Forever Young' on Planet Waves, suggesting that if you can achieve the former then the latter will follow. The article goes on:

If the miracle were possible, why wish to be forever young? Crazy indeed to be deluded – spending more and more money on face cream and clothes, to hide 'the skull beneath the skin'. So let me get the vanity stuff out of the way, because it's not what this is about. In the sixties I had Quant hair, in the seventies long hair; in the eighties it was Big, in the nineties scrunched – and now I have plughole hair. Not good. I've had botox twice, and 'filler' injected into my smile lines and cheeks – all to write about, I must add. I've never paid for the stuff, but I'm quite prepared to, because I like the difference it makes, and hate the way certain newspapers delight in 'exposing' women who have 'confessed' to a bit of help, as if they'd been caught out touching up teenage boys behind the bike shed. The extremes of cosmetic surgery are sad, but if women (and men) want to 'prepare a face to meet the faces that they meet' (to quote T.S. Eliot) – where's the harm? It's a statement about life, not mere terror about aging and death. It winks at the guy with the scythe, chuckling, 'Not yet, baby!'

Somebody asked recently, 'What's the secret of staying youthful?' and I mumbled something about always be ready to reinvent yourself. But that implies putting on masks, trying to switch your selfhood as you might redecorate a room. Of course, it's meaningless. What is important is to ADD all the time, opening yourself to new experiences, never allowing yourself to congeal, always topping up the sum total of who you are, surprising yourself. Instead of saying 'One door closes, another opens,' you fling open ALL the doors. The truth is, never before have I felt such a powerful passion for life. I relish the biker-hen look one day and boho chic the next – because it's all authentic: the multi-faced self ...

The universal story is of aging; what I can bring to it is my own narrative. We baby-boomers are surely the luckiest generation. Born in 1946, we imbibed post-war relief and optimism with our mothers' milk and experienced a safe and structured childhood during the undervalued fifties. I was brought up in a Liverpool Corporation flat by young parents who demonstrated by example that if you worked incredibly hard you might one day be (almost) as good as 'them' (meaning, the ones with class, money, power). You stuck with what you started, did your homework, never whined over knees grazed in a hopscotch tumble, and accepted rules and hierarchies just as our medieval forebears accepted the Great Chain of Being. We had serious public libraries (which fed me), ultra-clean hospitals ruled by fierce matrons, and rigorous schools like my crowded state primary, Northway, which saw a top class of 50 all pass the 11 plus. As a clever child, I had to listen to younger, very poor 'D' stream children read aloud. Smelling neglect and feeling instinctively that it wasn't fair, I realized I was lucky. My home wasn't wealthy, nor always harmonious, yet love sat on the table with the bottle of tomato ketchup. Each day now I give thanks for that upbringing, as much as for all I possess.

Idealism born of a sense of gratitude – did that fuel us baby-boomer protesters? Liberated by the late sixties and early seventies we preached tolerance and challenged the old structures in as many ways as we could. For me CND and Movement for Colonial Freedom at 17, then feminism, then anger at Vietnam, racism, then Labour Party member-ship – all seemed much more significant than the so-called 'Summer of Love', in a world that was changing more rapidly than our parents could have predicted. When I became a journalist it was because I believed that writing could improve the world – you would tell it like it is, write passionately about the disadvantages which weigh people down, and then somebody with power would say, 'Hey, we'd better change that.' It's easy to be cynical now and say, 'No such luck,' and since 1946 history does show that human beings can take the long, slow road to improvement; 'things can only get better' indeed. There's no space to list the acts of parliament and liberalization of attitudes, but no amount of disillusionment or despair should blind us to progress …

I confess I went through a period of quiescence and complacency, enjoying the ivory tower; but as Dylan sings, '… I was so much older then,/ I'm younger than that now.' For I've returned to feeling that things can – and must – be fought for. If you don't cherish, deep in your soul, the conviction that things ought to be made better, you die slowly inside. It can happen to people in their twenties; we all meet them sometimes – so much older than they should be. It may seem crazy to cling to idealism when proofs to the contrary come in every day, but don't forget that crazy can mean 'mad' too – and the things that make me mad as hell drive all fluffiness away. Bad parenting; indifference to the environment; all fanaticism, racism, tribalism; greed – in whatever corner of the globe it raises its ugly, bloated head; the assumption that people cannot be stretched; cruelty and cynicism; selfishness and defeatism … need I go on? 'Cry shame' said Martha Gellhorn – and never before has Yeats's famous line seemed more true: 'The best lack all conviction while the worst/Are full of passionate intensity.'

When I was fifty I wrote a piece for this newspaper which said 'I didn't plan it this way. I wasn't supposed to get old.' Well, the good news is – I didn't! Things didn't work out the way I thought they would, but I celebrate the fact that you can come through a divorce with mutual love and respect, and work out pain, sorrow and regret, murmuring 'That's the way it was fated to be – dammit – but now let's move on.' And I know that somewhere in a trailer park in Arizona, or a block of flats in Marseilles, or a village outside Kampala, or a cottage in the Highlands, a woman is weeping because she has lost what she thought would last – that whatever the differences in our lives, we are the same. I celebrate the will to challenge corruption and war-mongering, and Susan Sarandon's rebellious victory sign at the Oscars, and Bob Geldof's endless, mouthy championing of the poor in Africa. I celebrate 'love thy neighbour' as the only way to live, and admire those who preach it.

You see, somebody has to speak out, and up. Always. That faith keeps wrinkles on your mind at bay. You're rejuvenated by the absolute certainty (even after six decades of life and so much experience) that the good ones are always beavering away, never giving up – real heroes, people brave in body and soul, humans full of love and compassion, whose deeds outweigh the evil. It makes me throw back my head with joy – because I am young again.

Re-reading those extracts now I realize how much the spirit of my life with J shines in every sentence. Although we will not descend into querulous age as a couple we were young and passionate together, and that is all that matters. He – idealistic philosophy student and angry young journalist (inflamed by all injustice) – played such an important part in moulding the better side of me and nothing can alter that.

I was busier than ever: interviewed Gordon Brown twice for a 4,000-word *Times* profile, did events at literary festivals, reviewed books, was a guest presenter on Radio 4's *Something Understood*, answered people's problems, learned to feel slightly less depressed about them, took part in discussions for *Woman's Hour*, went to South Africa with Robin to write a travel piece, prepared and delivered a keynote address for PEN for the Day of the Imprisoned Writer inspired by our visit to Robben Island, wrote a piece on angels for *The Times* and various comment pieces for the *Daily Mail*, signed letters as President of an appeal for a new neonatal intensive care unit in Bath … and on, and on. Through the years of marriage I used to shake my head to friends at J's workaholism, and now it was as if I had learned it at his knee.

'*Friday December 8: It's exhausting, but how can I make 2007 different? Too busy for everything has become an unwelcome mantra. I had a pain in my chest when I went to the gym. Stress? I feel old and stiff and too tired to play with Bonnie.*'

As Christmas drew nearer and I made all the usual lists and preparations something happened which inevitably disturbed me. J wrote to tell me what I had already heard from our daughter: that he and his partner were expecting a child. His letter was short but beautiful – and loving. Which made the news it contained even harder to bear. I picked up my dog and stared out of the window at the wintry garden and took several deep breaths. Robin was away; there was only the dog to tell. It was the day of our local parish Christmas craft fair which I had planned to support, determined to spend money in aid of the church, even though at such events there is often little I really want to buy. But now I wanted to hide in my house with my dog and not see a soul. Yet my church-going (admittedly only about one a month) had become strangely important to the questing agnostic who had made so many *Devout Sceptics* programmes. Stepping out of our front door and looking to the right I see the Victorian church tower; during the strange months after moving to my new house alone I had found refuge in St Stephen's and its thriving congregation. It made me feel that I belonged somewhere again. So why should J's news stop me doing what I had intended to do, which was not to let the organizers of the craft fair down? Surely I was made of sterner stuff ...

Making yourself go out, you are forced to don a smiling mask, and when people ask, 'How are you?' you inevitably answer, 'Fine!' That lie can move, by degrees towards a truth. There is research which shows that if you make yourself smile a lot you will actually cheer yourself in the end. So I walked around greeting my neighbours and buying second-hand books I did not want. Then came the shock. In one corner of the basement community centre an elderly lady was selling her own old-fashioned, lacy hand-knits for babies, most of them in rather ugly colours – artificial pink, saccharine blue, screaming citrus. Nobody was buying the clothes and I felt sorry for her. I stood staring down at the tiny jackets and bootees and suddenly the room swam, and I didn't know what to do. The size of the garments, the memory of being pregnant with Dan, the thought of Tom, baby Kitty's ill health, my longing for a grandchild, the sense of how unfair it all is … all overwhelmed me on this the day of J's important piece of news. It was like a panic attack. I could not move.

Do so many men (I wondered) leave their wives for younger women because of their powerful, instinctive need to go on having babies? In one sense, who can blame them? With Robin away in France there was nobody to talk to about these things, nobody to wail with … that *we* could not be so blessed. But the truth is, gaining control as I stood there, surrounded by Christmas decorations, home-made cakes, cards and jam and the murmur of good people, I felt neither real sorrow nor anger, but just a flat, bedded-down *angst*.

What can be done?

Then I found the thing to do. I picked out a cardigan, unusual for being white and plain, and bought it for them. How pleased the old lady was to get a sale. And how pleased I was to go home to Bonnie, wrap the small garment immediately before I could change my mind, address the parcel – and by those actions begin the process of acceptance.

Six

UNDERSTANDING

A little Dog that wags his tail
And knows no other joy
Emily Dickinson, 'A Little Dog that Wags his Tail'

*C*ruising along the M4 at night, the moon low in the east like the end of a lit cigar, Ray LaMontagne's breathy agony filling the car, I wonder idly if all the words from all the centuries' sorrowful poems and songs of love, placed end to end, would reach to that indifferent, orange moon. Robin and I had just seen *Treats* at the Theatre Royal Bath, with Billie Piper starring in Christopher Hampton's bitter comedy about the eternal triangle, in which the good man is ditched for the bastard (as so often they are – or the good woman left for the siren) and you know it must end in tears.

More tears.

'Life is long, my love is gone away from me,' moans Ray – and for sure he will be listened to by a million lost souls who know what that is like. It is easy to immerse yourself in such a mood. On the other hand (as I often tell readers, since advice columnists must offer some encouragement, even when the individual case does sound pretty hopeless) love can possess an extraordinary, surprising resilience too – not so much a melancholy moon as a rubber ball, bright orange and still bouncing.

As an old-fashioned children's reading book might say:
    Here is the ball.
    Watch the small dog run after it.
    Watch the lady pick up the ball and jump.

Displacement works in many ways. Sometimes self-indulgent melancholy can be driven away by indignation. So it happened that, at the beginning of 2007, I was refusing to brood on J's impending marriage, mainly because those who sniped at the fact that he was marrying a very much younger woman enraged me so much I found myself entirely on his side. The incontinence of comment (on the web and in newspaper columns) is one of our age's most bizarre pollutants: everybody has an opinion, and the meaner the better. Who are they, these people who get out of bed only to log on to this website or that, or read newspapers online, in order to spew their ungenerous comments about anybody they might have read about, or heard on the radio or seen on television? Desultory venom and vitriol hold sway. Is it living a life, to use up your precious time thus? Even chat rooms set up to offer mutual help (for mothers at home, for example) too often degenerate into gossipy snippets about this celebrity or that, crowding out thoughtful responses to each other. Sometimes (especially reading BBC online comment) I'm reminded of packs of starving, snapping curs. Of course, I do understand that curs usually get nasty because they haven't been taught any other way.

It was the same when J's new daughter was born that summer, and again 18 months later, when he and his wife were expecting their second child. There seems to be a widely held assumption that there is something perverse and/or pitiable in (a) an older man fathering a child (b) a younger woman wanting to be with an older man and then conceiving a child, and (c) a child being born to such a mismatched couple, when Dad will look like a grandfather and all too soon pop off to meet his Maker – at which point he will be eternally damned for the sin of loving. Or so the critics would have it, rubbing their hands in glee and chortling all the way to the guillotine.

The confusing, painful, dazzling truth – that life is infinitely various and coloured in many shades of grey – passes such commentators by. I realize that Chaucer too made merry with the idea of 'January–May' marriages, but they happened then, as now, the world over, and were/are often successful. If any young woman is forced or cajoled into a reluctant marriage with *any* man of any age (and they so often are, in other cultures) that should spark indignation. On the other hand, observation tells us that young fathers all too often neglect and abuse their children, then move on to repeat the pattern, whereas a man in his fifties or sixties with a second chance at fatherhood usually makes the most tender, intelligent and attentive of parents. I like to imagine a world where all our birth certificates were lost and so we presented ourselves each to each unfettered by chronology – when some people in their twenties would come across as more mature than some born-again teenagers of fifty.

In any case, what can I – happy in a relationship with a younger man – say, but that the issue of age is a distraction from the complicated truth about love? Which is that you never know how or when it will strike. That's what Ray LaMontagne is singing about on all his albums. That is why Edith Wharton asked, '... how many of us could face each other in the calm consciousness of moral rectitude if our innermost desires were not hidden under a convenient garb of lawful observance?'

This was the point in my life when I realized how important it is to avoid ossification. Just a year earlier, with my sixtieth birthday beckoning, I had announced to my children that I was not interested in mobile phones (except to call an occasional taxi), would never text because it was something else to have to think of, and could not see the point of iPods. Anyway, how did such things *work?* Why would I *learn* all this stuff, I asked – not understanding that such attitudes are as ageing as out-of-date clothes. They are the dreaded wrinkles on your mind.

On the other hand, an important process had begun with the unlikely exercise regime, and my constant message to readers was (and is) that you *can* change yourself. There is no need to be stuck in the selfhood that used to own you.

So, halfway through 2007 I was crossing Regent Street in London, stranded on a traffic island in the middle of the two lanes, having just purchased my elegant white iPod (which of course I knew how to work, since by then I wrote listening to iTunes) from the Apple Store, when my mobile phone (now full of texts sent and received) played its jazz riff. It was a journalist from the *Daily Mirror*, asking me for a comment on the fact that my ex-husband's baby daughter had just been born. The buses roared, the taxis did their U-turns; no time to stop and think, just to speak truly: 'There's only one thing to say when a healthy baby is born to two loving parents and that's ... Wonderful.' I expect they wanted a terse rejection (what volumes are spoken by 'no comment'!) but to my surprise my quote was printed. That serves to confirm my innate optimism (one of the qualities I share with my small dog) that every now and then, a small voice bringing simple, good news will be allowed to be heard over the din.

Did I ever ask Robin if he was jealous that J and his wife could have a baby? No. But was I certain that he would have loved a child and would have made the most perfect of fathers and did that make me sad? Yes. Would I, in fantasyland, dream of having a child with him? Oh, a thousand times yes. Would we follow the example of desperate people who seek options like surrogacy or overseas adoption, at enormous financial, emotional and even moral cost? No.

Because, after all, we have Bonnie.

The American psychiatrist Aaron Katcher says that pet owners look upon their pet dogs as 'four-legged Peter Pans caught between nature and culture'. Their nature tells them that they are dogs, and they expect their human companions to act like dogs – play, hunt together, sleep in the same den and so on. Yet we expect our dogs to take the place we have allotted them within our human culture – to be biddable, decorative, loyal and so on. We need small dogs, especially, to be our dependents. John Steinbeck expresses his distaste for this human need in *Travels with Charley*, the quirky, charming book about a road trip with his dog:

I yield to no one in my distaste for the self-styled dog-lover, the kind who heaps up his frustrations and makes a dog carry them around. Such a dog-lover talks baby-talk to mature and thoughtful animals, and attributes his own sloppy characteristics to them until the dog becomes in his mind an alter ego. Such people, it seems to me, in what they imagine to be kindness, are capable of inflicting long and lasting tortures on an animal, denying it any of its natural desires and fulfilments until a dog of weak character breaks down and becomes the fat, asthmatic, befurred bundle of neuroses. When a stranger address Charley in baby-talk, Charley avoids him. For Charley is not a human: he's a dog and he likes it that way.

Reading that makes me guilty, because I talk baby language to my dog and swear she likes it. What else would I think? The smaller the dog the more we are likely to treat it like a surrogate child. This is not to infantilize, in the sense of treating them in such a way that it denies their dignity – because the very concept of such maturity is not relevant to a small dog. When Bonnie was six months and had just come to live with me, a friend picked her up and, feeling her featherweight fragility, exclaimed, 'Oh, she's a permanent puppy!' You cannot (easily) pick up a Labrador to cuddle, but the small dog always remains the right size, whilst our innate instinct is to make the same sounds to any small animal as we do to babies. That the small animal is in fact *old* has no bearing on the way it looks.

Neoteny is the existence of juvenile features in an adult animal, the word coined in the late nineteenth century from *neo* (new) and the Greek *teinein* (to stretch). So newness of youth is stretched out into adulthood, and it is thought that any lapdog breeds were bred specifically to retain puppy-like traits, like short legs and relatively large heads. They may also have traits which resemble human babies, like high foreheads, short muzzles and relatively large eyes. Some small breeds resemble the puppies of larger breeds, for example, a papillon, like some spitz-type breeds, possesses the facial characteristics of an infant wolf. There can be no doubt that *some* of these puppy-like traits are the result of selective breeding, and although such breeding is controversial my point is only that such characteristics contribute towards the particular relationship between the adult human and the small dog. To put it simply, the dog is permanently *cute*. Therefore you want to baby it.

Me and many others. In January 1920 the writer Katherine Mansfield wrote to her husband, literary critic John Middleton Murry, from Menton in the south of France, where she was convalescing from the tuberculosis that was to kill her. Mansfield's stories were the first in England to show the influence of Chekhov, whom she greatly admired. Her letter to Murry shows a keen observation of a lapdog in action which surpasses that of the author of the famous short story I quote in my first chapter:

> *Connie came yesterday to see me, carrying a baby Pekinese. Have you ever seen a really* baby *one about the size of a fur glove – covered with pale gold down with paws like miniature seal flappers – very large impudent eyes & ears like fried potatoes?*
>
> *Good God! What creatures they are … We must have one. They are not in the least pampered or fussy or spoilt. They are like fairy animals. This one sat on my lap, cleaned both my*

hands really very carefully … His partner in life when he is at home is a pale blue satin bedroom slipper. Please let us have one …

One stillbirth and two further miscarriages (or abortions) and a tempestuous private life did not equip Katherine Mansfield for motherhood. She desperately wanted Murry's child but couldn't achieve it and constantly grieved over the reality. She and Murry consoled themselves with fantasy children – which he went on to have with other wives after her death. He was woefully ill fitted for fatherhood; neither was he a husband any woman would want, not even (at times) Katherine. Into that innocent paragraph about someone else's baby dog I read so much unfulfilled longing it is hardly bearable.

Sometimes we pity those who turn their dogs into child substitutes, sometimes we mock them instead. That genius of the short story O. Henry wrote a hilarious first-dog narrative (*Memoirs of a Yellow Dog*) which gets inside the head of a 'babied' pooch: 'From that moment I was a pet – a mamma's own wootsey squidlums. Say, gentle reader, did you ever have a 100-pound woman breathing a flavour of Camembert cheese … pick you up and wallop her nose all over you, remarking all the time … "Oh, oo's um oodlum, doodlum, woodlum, tood-lum, bitsy-witsey skoodlums?"'

Because, in the pre-Bonnie era, I had shown no interest in matters canine, I was initially embarrassed that my dog inspired such nonsense-talk in me. I believed that lapdog mania, with all its attendant accessories, was a modern phenomenon. But my recent researches have brought me relief, as well as justification. The urge to pet small dogs is centuries old, and there is nothing new about turning a dog into a child substitute. In 1896, for example, *The Strand Magazine* (which first published Arthur Conan Doyle's Sherlock Holmes stories) ran a long article (uncredited, as was the norm) about an establishment called the Dogs' Toilet Club in New Bond Street, London. This canine beauty and fashion parlour was patronized by wealthy ladies who might buy a travelling leather kennel at 10 guineas or the latest dog's driving coat – the Lonsdale – made to measure, in fawn cloth, lined with dark red silk, finished off with two gold bells and a fur collar.

This makes Bonnie's wardrobe seem restrained.

The reporter documented that sometimes 'an aristocratic mistress' would say that she wished to see her precious pet bathed and throw herself on the dirty floor near the bath ('unmindful of her eighty guinea dress') and 'keep up a running fire of oral consolation – Now, it won't last long, Birdie. Ah, 'oo's all dripping wet, little darling, but 'oo'll soon be d'y. Don't pull Birdie so, naughty man!'

The article ends with a gently ironic paragraph, economical in its social satire yet as damning as any of the bludgeons used by some contemporary journalists: 'In conclusion, it may be said that pet dogs are treated by their mistresses almost precisely as though they were human members of the family; the only discrepancy in the analogy being that it is horribly bad form for a lady to drive in the park with her baby by her side, while the presence of a pompous pug or toy terrier is irreproachably correct.'

In July 1859 such a pug came into the life of my favourite novelist, George Eliot (born Mary Ann Evans, in 1819, and later calling herself Marian Lewes). The dog made the entirely serious woman laugh. She was so overcome with delight at the delivery of her new pet that she suffered a failure of grammar and wrote 'Pug is come!' to her publisher, who gave her the pet. And couldn't she who created so many living, breathing fictional characters (Silas Marner, Adam Bede and the rest) come up with something more imaginative as a name than 'Pug'?

George Eliot's novels are full of dogs. She uses them as subtle pointers to the character of human protagonists. For example, near the beginning of *Middlemarch*, over-serious Dorothea Brooke is being courted by the handsome Sir James Chettam – a catch in any woman's eyes. One day he appears 'with something white in his arms ... which was a tiny white Maltese puppy, one of nature's most naïve toys.' But Dorothea sniffs, 'It is painful for me to see these creatures that are bred merely as pets,' and goes on, 'I believe all the petting that is given them does not make them happy.' It gets worse: 'They're too helpless; their lives are too frail. A weasel or a mouse that gets is own living is more interesting. I like to think that the animals about us have souls something like our own, and either carry on our own little affairs or can be companions to us like Monk [a St Bernard]. Those creatures are parasitic.'

What can I say but foolish, deluded Dorothea! George Eliot uses the dog to highlight her lack of judgement, and condemns the young woman who dismisses the Maltese (with its infinite subtlety and generous soul) to a terrible marriage with the arid, pretentious, loveless old stick Casaubon, whom she thinks is a man of insight and intelligence. She who can't comprehend the companionship of small dogs is doomed to life with a man who mistakes a wife for a secretary. Whereas her sweet sister,

Celia, lover of tiny terriers, gets the handsome, rich, affable man as well as the rejected Maltese.

Dogs populate the pages of Victorian fiction – which is perhaps not surprising given the Queen's well-known love of dogs. Yet George Eliot has a uniquely strong sense of the relationship between animal and human, 'the glance of mutual understanding'. Her letters reveal how her relationship with her own pug ('transcendent in ugliness') developed. At first his presence promised an almost moral companionship of equals. He would 'fill up the void left by false and narrow-hearted friends. I see already that he is without envy, hatred or malice – that he will betray no secrets, and feel neither plain at my success nor pleasure in my chagrin.'

Then, just under a year after the pug arrived, comes the apotheosis of the dog baby. With her partner, the writer and polymath George Henry Lewes, she travelled Italy, leaving Pug in the care of a Mrs Bell. They always missed their dog 'terribly' – just as all dog lovers do. On 8 June 1860, GE wrote to Mrs Bell: 'You have never sent us a word of news about Pug! I hope no tragedy awaits us on our return. We have seen a pair of puppies – brother and sister – here at Venice that make us long to carry them home as companions for *our very slow child*' (my italics).

So when I call the two of us Daddy and Mummy to Bonnie, I remember the author of *The Mill on the Floss*, and smile. She proves to me that it is *allowed* – this silliness, this harmless projection of longing onto a dog, this infantile crooning.

And what of all the others – long-dead women, united with me in dog-loving sisterhood? The life of long-suffering, sweet-natured Jane Carlyle, wife of the irascible historian Thomas

Carlyle, was transformed by Nero, half Maltese, half mutt ('the chief comfort of my life'), whose loss after eleven years ('loyal until his last hour') devastated her so deeply she wrote, '… my little dog is buried at the top of our garden, and I grieve for him as if he had been my little human child.' Similarly, Peggy Guggenheim, the art collector, whose life was erratic, whose relationships were fraught with pain as well as appalling irresponsibility and who was a truly terrible mother, found consolation and uncomplicated love in a succession of Llasa apsos. In a corner of the garden of what is now the Guggenheim Museum in Venice there is a stone which marks the resting place of her 'beloved babies' – all 14 of them, all named. Next to it is another plaque which bears the words 'Here rests Peggy Guggenheim 1898–1975.'

Edith Wharton's dogs played the same role. In her French houses she sketched her sleeping Pekes, and doted on the gaggle of small dogs, led by her favourite Linky, who would survive them all. The dogs spent the mornings with her in bed and the fiercely intelligent, cosmopolitan author of *The House of Mirth* and *The Age of Innocence* dispatched photographs of her dogs to friends with inscriptions like 'Please come and see me soon – Linky.' But her friends grew irritated by the childless Wharton's excessive (in their view) doting on her little dogs. One wrote, 'Much as she loved conversation, we all complained bitterly that her frequent endearments to the dogs and expostulations on their behaviour ruined all consecutive talk.'

Most new parents will recognize that tendency. When you first have children you sit over dinner, obsessing over first words and adorable little habits, and agreeing that your baby possesses all charm, all intelligence. J and I were like that, of course; once, accidentally on purpose, we woke Daniel up because, besotted by his babblings, we needed to hear the musicality of his baby voice. (J took a photograph to mark the moment: it is 1975, Daniel is about fourteen months, held sleepy in my arms in his striped Babygro, and I'm in an old, lace Biba dress, hair permed to a fashionable curly mane.) It is a short step from this delicious, private collusion in gene worship to boring your friends too, just as Wharton bored hers with her little dogs.

J and I loved family life – even though the state of parenthood brought more anguish to us than it does to most, because our daughter spent the whole of her childhood through into university years afflicted by a condition known as Hirschprung's disease, which is (to simplify) a congenital malfunction of the bowel. This was, for J and me, intensely bonding; when those times came when I was too exhausted to ask a doctor a simple question, let alone an intelligent one, and cried that I couldn't cope, he stepped in, strong enough for us both. This was required of him, over all those years. Like most young couples we had not thought much about having children, but assumed that there would be no problems. Yet the physical mechanics of motherhood did not come easily to me. To set out the history baldly is a convenient shorthand for much stress, disappointment and grief: five pregnancies and three births allowed us to bring up two children. From time to time I would whisper miserably that I was 'no good' at having children, disappointed (like so many women) by destiny. Fortunately, as they grew, I could counter that old mood of self-blame with the unassailable fact that the emotions of motherhood came very easily, and I was indeed 'good' at loving the pair who were the centre of my being.

Assuming we would live on our farm for ever, J and I imagined that one day Daniel and Kitty would arrive for weekends accompanied by spouses and grandchildren. Life would evolve and quieten, or so we believed – although with our tendency to cram our days with work and outside obligations, the prospect was unlikely. All through Daniel's and Kitty's childhood and teenage years into their twenties, I was accustomed to their friends choosing to hang out in our home when they might not like to socialize with their own parents.

But that was the merry side. When Kitty left home I was, briefly, stricken by deep gloom and sought help from the doctor, who prescribed a type of antidepressant known as a selective serotonin reuptake inhibitor, which I took for a while, then threw away. (In the same way I had flushed the antidepressants away after Tom was stillborn, believing that I had to walk through the darkness to emerge on the other side.) Sitting in the silence of the farm where Kitty would never have her permanent home again, I realized that I was still a mother, naturally and perpetually maternal. The mothering days would never be over, but would just take a different form.

Therefore when Bonnie came along in 2002 it is no surprise that she was answering a primitive need. Her perpetually babylike characteristics were exactly what I (like so many other women *d'un certain age*) needed. Kitty was 22 and Daniel six years older; nature had made me ready to become a grandmother, but since that remained a distant prospect, I was primed and ready to love a little dog. The dependence of my very own dog reminded me of how my children were; I was *needed* once more. But this adorable creature would never grow up to stamp a foot and say 'No' at the age of two, or start smoking at 14, or suffer anguish over a girl, or weep over exams or boys, or defy the curfew and come home reeking of alcohol, or slam a door screaming, 'You don't understand anything!' or return miserable from university, ready to drop out – keeping you sleepless because you feel so helpless, knowing it's impossible to make everything all right. Instead, the small dog would curl in her basket at my feet, and follow me around with utter devotion, and greet me ecstatically after an absence of perhaps less than an hour – as if every slice of ham and cheese and roast chicken, as well as all other glories of the universe, were contained within my embrace.

Like George Eliot and George Henry Lewes, Robin and I are incessantly amused by Bonnie. Like Peggy Guggenheim I feel sometimes that she is far easier to deal with than people; like Edith Wharton I like to talk about her and show her photograph to those who show the slightest flicker of interest. And when I call her Baby-dawg and Babba and Baby-girlfriend and Mummy's Precious and Little Treasure and all the other sweet nothings that tumble from my lips as easily as when I used to blow raspberries on my first baby's stomach, I am not embarrassed, as John Steinbeck would wish me to be, for this is nothing more or less than acting in accordance with my essential nature.

What's more, in the daily exchange of love and mutual benefit between me and my dog, a covenant is enacted which transcends the obvious notion of child substitute. An ancient Mediterranean saying has the olive tree (essential to a whole culture) telling its 'owner': 'Care for me and I will nurture you.'

It's my passionate belief that we should thus listen to all the living things, plant, marine and animal alike, which share our planet. We do not 'own' them, any more than I 'own' my dog. If we learn the art of taking care, or respecting, of love, we will be repaid.

And that is why, when I stop to think (which happens infrequently, since I am not given to brooding) that life is unfair because I cannot have a baby whilst the unequal laws of gender mean that my first husband can go on having children with somebody else, I console myself with the ever-present reality of our little dog. Not 'mine', but ours. As we are hers.

Robin refuses to take Bonnie out for walks wearing pastel collars and leads, especially (horror) the pink set I bought in Brussels, but always selects the black, knowing that her long hair will obscure the diamante trims. A man has to try to keep up appearances. One day he was walking through Bath with the dog. They passed two women, who stopped to point.

'That's cute,' said one.

'The man or the dog?' asked the other.

A confident man has no problem being seen with a lapdog, as he doesn't believe it calls his manhood into question. Why should it?

That's why I think it sexist to assume that loving small dogs is intrinsically foolish and feminine – because many men dote on their pets just as Robin does. The list could be very long, but a few examples will do. The seventeenth-century statesman and poet Sir John Harington was so besotted with his clever spaniel Bungey that (uniquely) he put his portrait on the title page of his book. The diarist Samuel Pepys was inordinately fond of his 'little bitch' Fancy, the poet Robert Herrick wrote affectionately about his spaniel too, the historian Edward Gibbon adored his Pomeranian, the artist William Hogarth is pictured with his pug and the great French novelist Emile Zola grieved for Fanfan, 'a griffon of the smallest kind'. The emotions he expressed in memory of his little dog echo the theme of this book:

> *An animal, nothing but a little animal, and to suffer thus at its loss! To be haunted by its recollection to such an extent that I wished to write of my sorrow, certain of leaving the impression of my heart on the page! ... But then it seemed to me that I had so much to say ... upon this love of animals – so obscure and so powerful, at which I see people around me smile, and which pains me to the extent of troubling my life.*
>
> *And why was I attached so profoundly to this little mad dog? Why have I fraternized with it as one fraternizes with a human being? Why have I cried as one cries for a lost friend? Is it not that the unquenchable tenderness which I feel for everything that lives and feels is a brotherhood of suffering! A charity which inclines one towards the most humble and disinherited?*

With the help of his small dogs Mickey Rourke, the Hollywood actor and boxer, has endured the darker side of fame: a fall from grace followed by personal redemption. He came to rely on his most cherished pet, a chihuahua–terrier cross called Loki, flying her (at enormous cost) to be with him on film sets, because he simply couldn't do without her. In 2009 Loki died at 18 (120 in human years, according to some calculations, about 85 in others) just after accompanying

Rourke to the Golden Globes. In his acceptance speech for his role as 'The Wrestler' Rourke paid a touching tribute to his chihuahuas, living and dead, proclaiming to the world the saving power of dogs: 'It's been a long way back for me ... I'd like to thank all my dogs, the ones that are here and the ones not here any more, because sometimes, when a man's alone – that's all you got – your dog. And they've meant the world to me.'

When interviewed by Barbara Walters on television he credited another dog, Loki's father, with distracting him from dark thoughts of suicide. It seems that Rourke had taken an overdose but then he saw a pair of brown eyes fixed on him: 'I looked at my dog Beau Jack, and he made a sound, like a little almost-human sound. I don't have kids. The dogs became everything to me. And the dog was looking at me, going "Who's going to take care of me?"'

There we see the old transaction working: in making clear his dependence on his master, Beau Jack was saving his life. Yet nothing could protect Mickey Rourke from the loss of his favourite: Loki died just before the Oscars in 2009 and no piece of diamond jewellery received as much attention on the red carpet as the pendant bearing Loki's picture which the macho man proudly wore. In an interview he remembered his dog: 'She's the love of my life. She made it until six days ago. She left me at a time when, after 18 years, she knew I'd be all right.'

If anyone should deem that anthropomorphically saccharine, I can only cite the philosopher Mary Midgley, who argues that animals can be 'fellow sufferers and useful indicators of shared trouble'. Who knows enough to deny that one small dog might well have clung to life to a great age until she was certain her master was back in business, a player rather than a failure? That such unconditional love is an essential part of the treasured dog's medicine cabinet?

Not long ago, on a trip to a literary festival in Scotland to publicize my 'Bonnie' books, Robin and I were in the Lake District, visiting Dove Cottage, the home of William Wordsworth. We were delighted to be greeted near the entrance by a near-life-size oil painting of Pepper, a Norfolk terrier given to Wordsworth by the dog-loving Sir Walter Scott. That the poet hung it so prominently says much about his feeling for the animal companion of so many lengthy walks. More than one poem displays an acute empathy with dogs and an understanding of their interaction with humans and with other dogs, while 'Tribute to the Memory of a Dog' leaves us in no doubt that Wordsworth identified, in the lamented animal, the redemptive, moral force he perceived also in mountain and stream:

> *For love, that comes to all; the holy sense,*
> *Best gift of God, in thee was most intense.*

That same day we located a pub in Keswick we had been informed was dog friendly. One of the irritating things about travelling with your dog in England (unlike in France) is that the supposed nation of dog lovers bans the faithful friends almost everywhere, usually because of absurd rules of 'health and safety', but sometimes simply because the owner of the hotel or bar dislikes dogs, even tiny ones who nestle happily in a handbag. Once, on a visit to Oundle, I went into a chi-chi shop with my dog (as pretty and pristine as anything in the establishment) tucked under my arm, but was swiftly dispatched by the two ladies behind the counter. 'You can tie it up outside,' they said helpfully, clearly unaware of the phenomenon of dog-napping. I left speedily – and have kicked myself ever since for not retorting, '*Big* mistake! Ladies with little dogs spend *big* money.'

Anyway, the pub we found bore the appropriate name, the Dog and Gun, and was clearly a favourite of tough, outdoors-loving men – the kind who go ratting with terriers and would certainly regard the British Parliament's ban on hunting with hounds as a pernicious infringement of liberty. Robin and I sat in a corner with our drinks and sandwiches and Bonnie on my knee, her back straight with tension, as she watched two rather intimidating Norfolks rear and wrestle in the space in front of the bar – round and round, over and over, teeth drawn back in friendly play. A couple with an English bull terrier sat near us. The man was tall and burly with close-cropped hair and a tattoo on one arm: not a man to argue with, any more than his bruiser of a pet. Suddenly his blonde partner rose and walked across the room, out of sight. The dog watched intently, those tiny, sunken eyes fixed on the direction she had taken, the tension along the spine and down those powerful forelegs mirroring Bonnie's miniature stance. Moments passed. At last the dog quivered and his head jerked up. She was returning, packets of crisps in hand. And the big man reached down to stroke the butch creature, saying softly, 'There's yer Mam.'

In the early spring of 2007 I had to make a career choice, or rather, shift. For years I had contributed occasional freelance comment articles to the *Daily Mail*, and I knew well the way that newspaper worked. I had been told that the editor, Paul

Dacre (recognized, even by his critics, as the most influential, feared and admired editor in London), liked my advice column in *The Times* and wished me to switch allegiance, writing exactly the same column for the *Mail* and guaranteeing me autonomy. We met over lunch in February and established an immediate rapport, which surprised me. Yet the decision was very hard and I took over two months to make up my mind. I credited Sandra Parsons (then still in charge of features at *The Times* and now a friend) with the invention of my new, fulfilling persona as an advice columnist and was reluctant to show my appreciation by accepting the blandishments of a rival newspaper. I also liked writing essays and book reviews for *The Times*, whilst also being able to contribute to the *Mail*, sometimes appearing in both newspapers on the same day.

The then *Times* editor, Robert Thomson, took me to lunch and offered inducements, which could not, however, match up to those coming from Associated Newspapers. I even asked my dog what I should do – guilty that the fidelity we so admire in her kind is not matched by humanity. When you write regularly for a newspaper you come to care about the readers, and writing an advice column makes them all too real. To love a job yet be seduced into flitting after only two years? On the other hand, the Saturday edition of the *Daily Mail* (where I would be berthed) is a fine, fat and busy newspaper with a readership of over six million and I had always loved the paper's bruising swagger as well as its courage. It has its finger on the pulse of a middle England – which I understood.

My love affair with newspapers began in childhood. My parents read the *Liverpool Echo* and the *Daily Express*; my grandparents took the *Daily Mirror*, then in its mass-circulation, crusading heyday. Each Saturday night my brother and I would stay with Nan and Grandad, who would have saved the week's *Mirror*s for me. I don't know if anybody thought it unusual that a girl of eleven or twelve should be so absorbed by a pile of newsprint, but I would sit and work my way through the papers, sometimes cutting out a picture of Prince Charles and Princess Anne in their velvet-collared coats, because my grandmother and I loved such things, royalty and smart coats alike. (The bespectacled little girl furtively fascinated by the semi-naked strip-cartoon character Jane would have been astonished to learn that one day she would (a) sit down to dinner with the Prince of Wales and (b) write a column in the *Daily Mirror*.)

When I reached that stage (bizarrely called 'Britain's Brightest New Writer' on the masthead at the age of 32) I was somewhat disillusioned when the legendary advice columnist Marjorie Proops, doyenne of the *Mirror* (and the person who had recruited me), counselled me not to care so passionately about what I wrote because 'It just wraps tomorrow's chips.' Brought up on delicious, greasy, salty fish 'n' chips in newspaper, I recognized the truth of that, but rejected its spirit. Newspapers, I thought (and still think), matter, and we should be still proud of the wide-ranging quality of the British press, for all its faults.

Throughout 40 years, having written for every single national newspaper except the *Sun* and the *Daily Star*, and had columns in three papers and three magazines, I found my natural berth at *The Times*, but always admired the *Mail* for its professionalism and verve. The mixture of campaigning clout, acerbic comment, judiciously placed sentiment, wide-ranging coverage of women's issues and an entertaining habit of printing photographs you don't see anywhere else (if a tiger is born without stripes somewhere in the world they will run his picture) drew me to the *Mail*. Left-wing friends excoriate the paper (but often buy it secretly) and I myself feel uneasy about its tendency to encourage bitchiness and its occasional reversal to outdated sexism. But no one can argue that it is a newspaper which matters. In terms of 'reach' the *Daily Mail* is unequalled, and for somebody like me – who, after all, epitomizes social mobility – that is very appealing.

These media affairs are of interest only to those in our trade; the more general point is that being courted so assiduously and generously by two newspaper editors was heady for a woman of 60 and reminded me that the recent, testing changes in my life had brought me to this place. The paradox is expressed most memorably by Rainer Maria Rilke in one of his 'Sonnets to Orpheus':

> *Every happiness is the child of a separation*
> *It did not think it could survive.*

The irony was extraordinary. Had my marriage not been shattered by fate, I would still have been at the farm, coping with our life in the same way, trying to wind down, getting older, wondering what to write next. And (to be honest) always living somewhat in my husband's shadow, no matter what I achieved. Instead, I felt intoxicated by new opportunities. Sometimes I asked myself if I would turn the clock back, and the inner voice whispered a half-ashamed negative. The silver chain was (almost) broken.

Still, in my vacillation over the job decision, I retreated into old habit – and asked J's advice. To my surprise he thought I should move to the *Mail*. His grandfather had worked on the paper as Parliamentary Correspondent, but stormed out in May 1931 after a furious row with the editor over the proprietor Lord Rothermere's flirtation with fascism. Now J – who shared his grandfather's liberal values and his dislike of some of the attitudes widely associated with a right-of-centre paper – was telling me I'd be mad not to accept the *Mail*'s offer.

On the other hand, Robin, who tends to value contentment over worldly concerns, thought that the best course would be to stay with *The Times*, where I was happy. 'Stuff the money,' he said at first. In the middle of all this debate I tripped on a pavement, hit a wall, knocked myself out and injured my eye. With enforced time to think (although I never missed writing a single *Times* column) and looking in the mirror to see a gargoyle looking back, shocked once again by how quickly things happen and how in one second I could have lost the sight of one eye, I took the message of fate. Let it happen. You have to reach out, and go on reaching out, taking risks, allowing yourself to become excited rather than staying safe – until the moment when those reaching arms fall lifeless to your side.

I would change newspapers.

This was not the only shift of allegiance I was to make in 2007. Paul Dacre said to me when we finally reached our agreement that my new column would begin in June: 'So – you're getting married again and you have a marriage to a new paper … This is a good year for you.'

It would be dishonest not to confess that my capitulation to the idea of actual remarriage (rather than wearing a ring as a symbol of emotional commitment) was encouraged by J's own remarriage in March. This was not a matter of tit for tat – rather an acceptance that his life had moved on irrevocably, and therefore mine should too. I realized that my determination not to marry was much to do with clinging to the entirety of what we had had – the dream of home as well as the individual man. His new marriage would help me to let it go – but just as some people cling to bereavement, I did not really *want* that parting. The Nobel laureate Seamus Heaney expresses this idea with characteristic insight in his interviews with Dennis O'Driscoll: 'A wedding always has its moments of strangeness, sudden lancings or fissures in the fun, when parent or child have these intense intimations that the first circle is broken. It is in the literal sense an *unheimlich*, an unhoming.'

Another translation of that German word is 'uncanniness' and I recognize that etymological connection between the idea of being unhomed (or unsettled) and being spooked. In my imagination J and I were ghosts revisiting all the places we had known and trying to find our way home through the darkness. I dreamt of him constantly, which was very unsettling, yet I had started to accept it as a part of my new life too; the on-going journey within another dimension with somebody I had never ceased to love. It seemed miraculous to me that the unhomed love was not, in the end, homeless. It would live on as long as we did. So my strange dreams were written down in yet another notebook I had begun in 2004, jotting down passages from books, scraps of poetry and brief thoughts to help me make sense of things. Looking at it now (lying permanently on my desk) I realize how much of what I put down has to do with those ideas of home as well as of loss – the two inextricably bound, as when Philip Larkin writes: 'Home is so sad. It stays as it was left.' The mood of my notebook varies from elegiac, in Tennyson, from 'The Princess':

> *For when we came where lies the child*
> *We lost in other years,*
> *There above the little grave,*
> *O there above the little grave,*
> *We kiss'd again with tears.*

to furious Marina Tsvetaeva, in 'An Attempt at Jealousy':

> *… Tell me: are you happy?*
> *Not? In a shallow pit? How is*
> *Your life, my love? Is it as*
> *Hard as mine with another man?*

Robin and I were fine living as we were, and he would never have pushed the situation, but it was my daughter who suggested that marriage would make him very happy. So our decision to go ahead was relaxed, even light-hearted. For a while we thought of going to Las Vegas and rumbling along to the Elvis chapel on a big motorcycle, with only Daniel and Kitty as witnesses. But then, one night when he was away on a job and Bonnie was looking anxiously for his return, I realized that I did not want a joke wedding in a tacky place. Robin was my rock, the support which he had demonstrated over so many years crystallized into something more beautiful, more permanent. We decided to have a church wedding. Back in 1989 I had published a travel book called *Bel Mooney's Somerset* and had persuaded the publishers to pay Robin (then a young film and photography student as well as Kitty's babysitter) a very modest amount to take the black and white photographs. Through the project he became fascinated by piscinae and rood screens and Norman arches. Now it seemed to us sublime and fitting that we would choose to be married beneath one.

The decision made, we parked Bonnie with my ever-willing parents and went to Bali for another travel piece for *The Times*. We stayed at Ubud, at Jimburan and Candidasa. Much-travelled acquaintances had predicted how much I would love Bali, but their estimations fell short.

I was transfixed by the ubiquity of worship. Even the scruffiest motorbike on the streets of Kuta is made sacred by decorative hangings on handlebars. Similarly a car dashboard becomes a shrine, and an open drawer in a clothes shop is transformed into an altar – complete with an offering of food and flowers on a palm leaf plate and a joss stick, reverently lit by the beautiful salesgirl. You walk along a beach, careful not to tread on the palm-leaf plates, exquisitely arranged with food, flowers and incense, which are laid down with reverence, sanctifying tourist haunts. Nowhere else have I been where the smartest, international hotels have shrines in their gardens tended many times a day by staff lighting incense and murmuring ritual prayers. There is no self-consciousness about this, even if guests gawp. Everyday ceremonies keep the darkness at bay. I was prepared to be sceptical about claims made by Bali-high friends that it is a special, spiritual place. But that greenest of islands gave me more than a good holiday. It confirmed my belief in the essential wholeness of things.

On our second day we visited the great temple at Ubud, and noticed the ubiquitous black-and-white-checked textile wrapped around priests and shrines alike, and made into temple umbrellas. It reminded me of tablecloths in fifties Britain, and I wondered why it was everywhere when the vibrant colours of silk would have been more beautiful. I discovered that the cloths – called *poleng* – are designed for protection, warding off evil spirits. The white squares represent good, the gods and health. The black ones stand for evil, the underworld and disease. Yet in the traditional *poleng* (rather than cheap modern printed versions) the two are woven together, and the intersection of warp and weft, of black and white, forms the grey squares. This is the visible confirmation that you cannot have one without the other – the grey squares are, if you like, mitigation. The grey is emblematic of the pitiful and brave nuances of the human condition. In the dull neutral lies a simultaneous acceptance of darker realities and hope for redemption.

I was once given a box of grey pastels for monochrome artwork, and I had marvelled at the range of shades – about twenty – between the black and the white at either end. In Bali, on a day when disappointing rain fell, I looked up at the multihued clouds and remembered those pastels, then imagined the *poleng* wrapped around all of us, offering protection against the dangerous, fanatical certainty which sees life in black or white with no shades of grey in between. In Bali's capital, Kuta, the monument to the young victims of the Islamist terrorist outrage of October 2002 is a permanent reminder of what happens when men believe they are right and condemn the rest of humanity to death as 'infidel'. That is the blackness. But the flowers and shrine and messages all around represent the opposite: the white light of faith, hope and love, which cannot be extinguished. Bowing my head at the monument, and seeing the symbolic *poleng* cloth all over Bali, made me determined to fly the flag of blessed nuance all my life, even within the portals of the mighty *Daily Mail*.

Robin and I talked endlessly about our wedding, and drew up a guest list – which was very hard since we wanted only about thirty people. It grew to just over forty, but still, some had to be left out. We decided that only people from Bath should come, although that had to change. Yet – wedding plans? Lists? Worries about hurting some feelings by not inviting? A part of me still couldn't help wondering why I was *doing* this, but the other part (the larger part) simply relaxed into the quiet, philosophical feeling that what will be will surely be. At the same time, that is too passive, for you do indeed create your own destiny – rushing to meet it with the same speed as my little dog responds to the sound of the doorbell.

Each lazy day, at some point (or two points, or maybe three) we would find ourselves talking about Bonnie, just like doting parents. Her silly little habits, the inconvenience of her sleeping on the bed, her endless reassurance that we are wonderful people – and so on. This was a part of life now, the knowledge that the three of us formed a 'pack' that was mutually dependent. One day we were exploring the faded grandeur of the palace, Puri Agung Karangasem, in the small town of Amlapura. In truth, there's not much to see there, but we both exclaimed in glee when we spotted, as part of the design on a carved and painted balcony balustrade, a strange, small, white animal. Floppy ears, long hair, furry paws, funny little face, plumed tail … it was clearly a Maltese dog. A sign. At that moment I knew I was looking at my bridesmaid. Robin was delighted with the idea.

But not so other family members. 'You can't have your dog as your bridesmaid, Mother,' my daughter protested, and was careful to get her brother on her side as well. He suggested that surely I didn't want attention to be deflected from me? 'I don't care – I want them to look at my dog,' I replied. She said people would think it silly if I walked down the aisle with Bonnie.

'Well, if everybody in the church is grinning on my wedding day that's fine by me, ' I retorted.

'But it's a solemn occasion,' she said.

'No, it's a joyful occasion,' I replied, 'and as long the vicar approves that's fine!'

In any case, I have books of historical photographs which show dogs nestling at the feet of brides in Victorian and Edwardian times. They obviously knew what Amy Tan had told me, so long ago: 'The dogs are essential.'

On 8 September 2007, my second wedding day, an article appeared in the *Daily Mail* in place of my usual advice column. It was surely a testimony to one marriage that this (polemical as well as personal) could be written just before the second:

In February 1968, at the age of 21, I married in a registry office, wearing a purple mini dress. We had barely thought about what we were doing; the smallest, plainest wedding was less important than being madly, impulsively in love.

Today, at 60, I am getting married for the second time – in another purple dress. I have thought very deeply about it, and the beautiful church ceremony will be an important declaration of deep friendship and commitment. As it is for all those brave and lucky souls who choose to utter publicly the most important words they will ever say.

One or two friends have asked me, with affectionate curiosity, 'Why marry again?' After all, when my first marriage ended after 35 years, I believed I would never sign up for it again. I reverted to my maiden/professional name by deed poll, worked hard to develop a good relationship with my still-dear ex-husband, loving each other under different roofs – but saw no need to become 'Mrs' anybody else. In fact, I shall not take my new husband's name today, but that's an irrelevance.

My answer to the question, 'Why marry?' is that I believe – profoundly – in the importance of marriage as an institution. Or (perhaps a less stolid way of expressing it) as life-choice in which the well-being of society and personal happiness are uniquely united. This is the point at which the person blends into the political. It's easy for me to explain why *I* choose to tie the knot for the second time. I can say, simply, 'I want to belong to the one who says that all he wants is to look after me. And I want to look after him right back.' But more important is why marriage matters to us *all* – perhaps more than ever before …

It won't surprise anyone when I say that of all the categories which make up my postbag of questions on human relationships, the largest is marriage. Any day I can pluck a handful: cries for help from young women who long for their boyfriends to display commitment, from older women who chafe at the sexless sterility of their marriages, from wives tossed aside by husbands who started affairs or just got bored and went off in search of lost youth. Whatever problems women have, men have them too – although honesty compels me to point out that the bias of my letters is borne out by statistics, middle-aged men more likely to skip off than older women …

Some marriages end with a bang, others with the most pitiful of whimpers. Yet the other side of the story needs to be heard too. There are plenty of marriages which last, nurturing children in harmony and carrying the couple into a contented and loving old age. I could not do my job if I was cynical about wedlock – or rather, if I ever lost faith in the human ability to get it right, to sustain long-term love, 'till death us do part'. I believe it is natural for human beings to want to nest in pairs, to grow together, to share, to say 'we' instead of 'me.' I repeat, why would you *not* marry?

Caught between the sorrows of my postbag and the seemingly contradictory statistics which proclaim that the divorce rate is at its lowest for decades but also that fewer people are choosing to marry – I still say it's too soon to pronounce the funeral rites on the institution. How could something which does so much good die out? The subject is complex, involving an analysis of the role of women, of changing expectations, of fiscal policy, and so on. But to simplify, let me isolate two reasons to marry. One no longer affects my personal choice, the other does.

First, traditionally, you marry to procreate. But now that there is no shame attached to having children outside marriage this is only a 'reason' to marry if it is seen as best for those children, and therefore for the long-term values and stability of the society they inherit. Personally, I have no doubt that this is the case – an assertion confirmed by so many surveys. Children whose parents marry and stay married are more likely to have stable marriages themselves and to wait until marriage before becoming parents.

One study has shown that children brought up by two birth parents until the age of sixteen have higher levels of happiness and fewer psychological problems. Children bear the brunt of a no-commitment culture. Rates of mental disorder among children in lone parent families are double those amongst children living with both parents; they are more likely to live in poverty and harm or kill themselves. The shift is partly due to marriage breakdown, of course, but mostly to the big increase in mothers who have never married. Single people are turning their backs on the institution yet regarding singledom as no barrier to accessorising their lives (carelessly or deliberately) with kids …

Why not praise stable marriage as the ideal? Ideals are what give a culture cohesion; they must be enshrined equally within political and individual actions. Call me sentimental, but I believe that the old wedding photograph in its silver frame on the shelf possesses a symbolic value beyond anything contained within statistics.

What it stands for brings me to the second reason to marry, which has little or nothing to do with children. The exchanging of vows in a civil or religious ceremony tells the couple that they 'belong', proclaims to those who witness it that love and faith and commitment have lost none of their power – which positive message ripples out into the wider community. It's a universal affirmation …

A few weeks ago, in Bath, we were looking for a shirt for Robin and kept encountering the same, unprepossessing grey-haired couple in the same shops. They could have been retired teachers. Making a fuss of our little dog, the lady confided at last that they were looking for 'wedding clothes.' 'Ah, so are we!' I smiled – and what we shared in that moment was a secret delight that even when you are older, when maybe you have experienced much pain, it is still possible to be renewed. And to tell the world …

In the months since we decided to marry we have both been struck by how *happy* people are to hear. To a guy cold-calling me to sell solar panels I said, 'It's really not the time, 'cos I'm about to get married.' His 'Oh, sorry … of course … and many congratulations' was surely politeness, yet sounded so genuine. Why shouldn't I think he meant it? After all, people long for good news – and the word that this couple (or that) care enough for each other to articulate that love in front of others causes even strangers to share in the celebration.

Today, when I am listening to the vicar say 'It is given that as man and woman grow together in love and trust, they shall be united with one another in heart; body and mind,' and 'Marriage is a sign of unity and loyalty which all should uphold and honour' I shall be agreeing with all my heart. When we repeat, 'to have and to hold from this day forward, for better, for worse, for richer, for poorer, in sickness and in health …' my heart will overflow. And into the Christian service I have written a famous Apache blessing (often used at modern weddings), containing words which express why I, and so many people the world over, choose to make a shared declaration of love and faith and belonging:

Now there is no loneliness for you,
For there is no more loneliness.
Now you are two bodies,
But there is only one life before you.

On the morning of our wedding I lay in bed, somewhat dazed, reading my own words in the paper, looking at the large picture of Robin and me which accompanied it, as if (for a moment) I didn't know who we were. It all felt strange. Family and friends rampaged about the house, looking for cufflinks, the iron, shouting to use the shower and so on. During the morning J texted me from Russia, where he was filming his television series. Certain that he would do so, I had rushed around the house frantically amidst the chaos, to find my mobile phone, simply to be ready for his message. He wished us luck. My text back told him I would always carry him in my heart. Because even on this golden, happy day that remained the truth.

After the houseful of loved ones had dressed, there was no hot water remaining for me, and so the mature bride endured a cold bath, compelled to play the mother's old, self-sacrificial role even on her second wedding day. The house grew quiet as they all left for church. Bonnie was on my bed, watching me get ready, quivering with nervous anticipation, in case she was going to be left behind. 'Just you and me, girlfriend,' I told her, as I put on my purple and turquoise silk dress, then decked her out in her matching purple harness, collar and lead, fixing a purple feather to her harness with slightly shaking fingers.

'You look lovely,' I said, grateful for the comic relief of that feather waving over her back, just like her tail.

'Take me, oh, take me,' was all she had to say in reply.

At last, just before noon, Daniel returned from ferrying my parents and drove Bonnie and me to Charlcombe Church, the oldest ecclesiastical building in Bath still in use. Hidden up a lane in trees, about a mile from our house, it has literary associations which naturally delighted me. In 1799 Jane Austen wrote, 'We took a charming walk to Charlcombe, sweetly situated in a green valley.' Sixty-five years earlier, one of the great fathers of British fiction, Henry Fielding, married his beloved Charlotte Crawford in the church, and in *Tom Jones* he conveys something of the way I felt on my second wedding day. I even included the longer extract as a frontispiece to our Order of Service:

All were happy, but those the most who had been most unhappy before. Their former sufferings and fears gave such a relish to their felicity … Yet great joy, especially after a sudden change and revolution of circumstance, is apt to be silent and dwells rather in the heart than on the tongue …

Bonnie was excited and pulled on her lead. The purple feather slipped to one side. Outside the church we paused for a moment while the Reverend Jonathan Lloyd said a brief prayer, just for me. He strode ahead – and then I entered Charlcombe Church with my small dog leading me forward to the next stage of my life.

8 September: I walk in, smiling, not seeing any individual faces, just a blur of beaming all around me. R waiting at the front, looking happy, not at all nervous. Just a few steps down the tiny aisle. I hand Bonnie's lead to Gaynor, who gives her to Mum next to her. And then it unfolds, this beautiful, holy 'performance' of which we are a part – like actors who are also believers – in an ancient, sacred drama. I am aware of such a great joy in that ancient place: a sharing, a confirmation. And, so quickly, it is over, and the 'Ode to Joy' booms out and we float upon it, joined by Bonnie as we walk up the aisle out into bright sun and warmth and snapping cameras and petals thrown and so many smiles and kisses …

In his address, our friend Ernie Rea (a man of the cloth as well as former Controller of BBC Religion, and Radio 4 presenter) said words that meant much to us both:

… today marks a new beginning. It is you two who matter from this moment on. Now is the time to put the past behind; not of course, forgetting all that has happened; continuing to cherish all the good things life has handed you until now. But letting go too; focusing on the joy that you two share together and all the good times that lie ahead … At the heart of what Jesus taught is the message that there is always another chance. Grace and forgiveness always have the final word over rancour and bitterness … I firmly believe that love is at the heart of the universe. That is why I believe that there is rejoicing in a little part of heaven as you two come together as man and wife.

No wonder I chose to read the U.A. Fanthorpe poem 'Atlas' to everybody, as a public tribute to the man who 'insulates my faulty wiring'. Robin's own choice was Raymond Carver's 'Late Fragment' – six lines in which the poet, at the end of his life, answers the question about the only thing he ever desired: 'To call myself beloved, to feel myself/Beloved on the earth.'

All weddings are, in essence, the same – which is something easy to forget when you have to deal constantly with unhappy letters from the ones who lost the way, lost their love. Surely, no matter how different we are, we make our vows (civil or religious) in the hope that this will last? Even when you know too well the pitfalls of marriage, you must only choose to remarry if you can restore trust (in a partner, but in yourself as well) to its essential place in the centre of the household gods' (the Roman *penates*) shrine. And when, despite those pitfalls, you have also experienced the profound rewards of a long love, it is not so difficult to set hope up there, alongside trust. Through the rest of that day – champagne, long, delicious lunch in an elegant hotel, and affecting and accomplished speeches by Robin and Kitty, followed by a mad evening of wine and Indian takeaway for the small group back at our house – I felt, above all, grateful to have come through to quiet camaraderie.

On our honeymoon, in Sri Lanka and the Maldives, Robin and I talked incessantly about our dog – as always. We reminded each other of the entertaining things she does, and the smallest gesture – like sticking out the tip of a tongue for a second – was a secret, silly signal that would evoke our pet. And as always, we were perfectly happy for the holiday to end, so we could return to our dog and our life.

Two months later we strolled into the National Gallery to be confronted by a poster which made us laugh: 'Look – it's us!' The poster advertised an exhibition of German Renaissance stained glass, called *Art of Light*, and the object shown made us rush to the exhibition to see the original. It glowed on the wall – a special message which we interpreted in significantly different ways. *Tobias and Sarah on their Wedding*

Night (measuring just 56 x 66 cm) is an exquisite panel which shows a couple asleep in their fine bedchamber. The luxurious bed has rich red hangings and a vivid blue and green patterned coverlet. The floor is tiled yellow and black, and – sweet domestic touch – a pair of slippers lies by the bed. In the foreground is a table, expertly shaded to show its bulk but also the fine grain of the wood. On it stands the snuffed candle in a yellow ceramic or brass candlestick, which lit the married pair to bed.

And there they sleep chastely, because (according to the Old Testament story) Sarah's previous seven bridegrooms were strangled by a demon on their wedding night, but the Archangel Raphael briefed Tobias to avoid this terrible fate by not consummating his marriage until three nights had passed. Their pale heads in nightcaps are propped up against soft white pillows, and – certainly assisting the vow of chastity – a small white dog nestles in its own glass oval, on the bed at their feet. His eyes are firmly closed too, his ears flop down, his tail ties him into a small ball – and the stained-glass master has shown his skill in the minute depiction of curly hair.

It was like looking at ourselves through the wrong end of a telescope: a couple, frozen in endearing intimacy, at the beginning of their life together, with their little white dog asleep at their feet. One family. One small pack. In a second, centuries of devoted owners and their dogs were strung side by side like glass beads on a thread of time.

I said, 'Just shows – people have always been as soppy as us.'

Robin said, 'Oh, you should *never* allow a small dog on your bed.'

Seven

SEEKING

Side by side, their faces blurred,
The earl and countess lie in stone,
Their proper habits vaguely shown
As jointed armour, stiffened pleat,
And that faint hint of the absurd –
The little dogs under their feet.
Philip Larkin, 'An Arundel Tomb'

The snow has fallen. The trees on the top of Lansdown, where J and I used to live, are heavy with frosting, and the hard earth glitters. One bitter Friday night we drive over the hill to drop Bonnie with my parents for company, then crunch our way through the streets of Bath to meet friends in the pub next to the theatre, for drinks, a play, then dinner. The Garrick's Head is packed and very noisy; people call out greetings – with that merry sense of mutual congratulation which agrees that on a night like this we're all rather bold and stylish to be out. Then our friend Lucy beckons me over, shouting an introduction to man I've never seen before.

'I know you,' he says. 'You're the one with the little white dog!'

'That's right!' I smile.

He does not seek to know my name; nor do I offer it. Like Chekhov's heroine (though much happier than she) I am suddenly identified through the absent Bonnie, and that suits me. This is my new persona: the lady with the lapdog. When my children were at school I had the common habit of introducing myself not by name but through my relationship with them: 'Hello, I'm Daniel's/Kitty's mum.' Now it entertains me hugely that my various changes of name and shifts of persona and career developments boil down to this uncomplicated truth: I hang out with a Maltese.

After a very long marriage, after the pain of breaking and refusal to let go, after the confused efforts to form new life and the bittersweet acceptance of success and failure alike, you often ask yourself who you really are. The answer is, of course, you are *all* the people you became throughout all the experiences. Just as the philosophers tell us that we never step in the same river twice, so I maintain that you never view exactly the same face in the mirror. Acknowledging that challenging truth can transform even the unwelcome process of ageing into an adventure. Wondering who you are and whom you may become during the next twenty-four hours, let alone the next few years, turns each day into that staple of fairytale and myth – a quest.

I was reading Penelope Fitzgerald's last novel *The Blue Flower* when a sentence jumped out at me: 'If a story begins with finding, it must end with searching.' The meaning is not elaborated; Fitzgerald knew the value of the silence between words – since what is left unrevealed must surely make you curious. I firmly believe that the ongoing inner questions – the constant queries of 'Why?' and 'What might it have been like?' and 'What if?' and 'How does it all end?' – form the imaginative workout which builds strength for our human quest.

The child within us will always cry, 'Why did that happen to *me*?' when misfortune strikes. It is only when you reach the moment of epiphany and turn that round, to ask, 'Why not?' (as simple as an acorn containing an oak) that the door of the self can swing open, releasing you into questions more fundamental than your own *angst*. It happened to me when our second son was stillborn. It happened more than once during long years of hospital visits with our daughter – when I sat on National Health Service paediatric wards with mothers whose precious children were dying but who (some of them) still managed to don lipstick, the better to defy the vicious Reaper.

It happened when I tasted the ashes of our marriage in my mouth and wondered (like so many other separated people, especially in middle age) what to do. And nowadays, when I study readers' problem letters I often feel it too – but cannot tell them. Not in so many words. No counsellor can advise a person immured in misery that this particular grief may be the making of them, may lead them through a gate into a field they never knew. The bereaved are afflicted by well-meaning souls who say, 'You can have another baby' or 'You'll get over it', but the desperately unhappy are similarly punished by breezy advice. The statement 'When all this is over you'll look back and see what it taught you' may have an important truth at its core, but is rarely helpful.

No, you have to experience the meaning yourself.

That is the quest.

It must begin with the realization that no one is immune, and therefore anything can happen to you. The test is not what you will make of it, but what it will make of you.

This particular story began with finding. A small white dog, aged six months, was left tied to a tree in a park, found by somebody, then taken to the RSPCA Cats' and Dogs' Home, to be rescued by me. Who could have known that she was destined to make the transition from toy dog to muse? Because of that miraculous transformation I find myself (now, as she sleeps in her blue bed at my feet) imagining her death. This is because the universe rolls on and sooner or later we must all come back to the beginning. My journey began with finding and ends in this chapter with seeking, and yet that can never be the end, because I must lose again, and again. This is the price of that very humanity which all the words in my library, all the birds in my garden, each stamen and petal on the flowers on my desk and all the loves I have known urge me to celebrate. What you seek can take you right back to the start, and with ending, begin once again.

The search is for nothing more, or less, than a state of grace.

It was loss that transformed Bonnie into my muse. Love and loss which changed her role and set us both on our journey – my little dog and I, sniffing our way forward, step by small step, not knowing quite where we would arrive but being stout-hearted together. I love her expressive wordlessness. Even the people you most love will sometimes disappoint through not having the right words for the moment you need them, and besides, their truth may not match your own. But the dog watches you with a mute understanding which hovers on the edge of wisdom. There are no blandishments, no words brisk or comforting, no rationales, no promises, no arguments to complicate or halt our pattering steps – as human friends would give. There is only (and how easily the cliché springs forth, like a Doberman in a dewy dawn) that old dogged devotion. My dog and I stand, shoulder to ankle, every sense alert. Seeing what we shall find.

Outside a bank in Milsom Street, Bath, a man was clearly waiting for someone, his enormous red setter sitting peacefully at his feet. Bonnie and I drew level with them. In contrast to the big dog she was restless, pulling on her lead, (in truth) badly trained. When she saw the elegant gun dog she adopted her pose of maximum aggression: chest out, back legs splayed, head jutting forward with that very 'Don't mess with me' attitude which I tend to adopt myself in situations which rattle me. Then an ear-splitting rattle of hysterical yapping fell down on the other dog's astonished head, like hail. He shrank back. His owner laughed. The setter rose nervously and put the lamp-post between himself and the tiny pest. I could imagine him thinking, What on earth is *this?* Looks like a rabbit or a cat – but that smell? … *sniff* … Lordy, lordy, it's a mad *relation*. Take it *away*.

Passers-by, noticing the confrontation between the unlikely little aggressor and the enormous softie, stopped to point and smile.

'That's a tough little one,' said the red setter's owner.

'Too right,' I said, with pride.

I read a haiku somewhere and memorized it, to give me strength when my own life requires Bonnie's splayed-leg squaring up, and her burst of angry yaps:

Big Dog towering
Little Dog versus Big Dog
Little Dog stands tall.

An experienced clinical psychologist I turned to during the difficult process of writing this book told me, with absolute seriousness, that she was convinced Bonnie had come into my life for a 'reason'. To those imprisoned by reason itself, such a statement will be meaningless, even absurd. But to those who believe that 'The heart has reasons that reason cannot know' it will make perfect sense. Robin gave me those words engraved on a heart pendant. They were written by Blaise Pascal, the seventeenth-century French mathematician and philosopher, who (despite his grounding in science) recognized alternative universes longed for by the human soul. I believe that in one of those universes the small dog has a significance far greater than the sum of its parts, or the frequency of its cuddles, or its comforting charms. In one of those other worlds, full of mystery, the small dog is the guide, leading us on a search for grace – just as Emily Dickinson believed that a dog is the fitting companion for the soul's final journey, 'Attended by a single Hound ...'

She described her beloved Newfoundland Carlo (as far from a small dog as it is possible to be) as her 'Shaggy Ally' – an endearment which will resonate with anyone who sees a dog as a confederate and other self. She filtered the world through him, put his interests above her own, and when he died at the grand age of 16 her grief went beyond all expression, other than a brief, anguished note sent to her friend and literary mentor, Thomas Higginson, editor of the *Atlantic Monthly*:

> *Carlo died –*
> *E. Dickinson*
> *Would you instruct me now?*

It was to Higginson that she had confided her belief that her dog – like the hills they roamed together – was 'better than Beings', i.e. people. In the year following Carlo's death Emily wrote next to nothing, and she never replaced the dog who represented her connection to all creation, as well as her protector and guide. Many years before his death, looking ahead she had told a friend, ' … do you know that I believe that the first to come and greet me when I go to heaven will be this dear, faithful, old friend, Carlo?'

It seems to me that one of the functions of the dogs we love is to lead us towards an awareness of the inevitability of loss. From time to time we have to take Bonnie to the vet, to have her teeth seen to, her glands attended to, or for booster injections. She is always terrified, her tail sweeps the floor and she quakes, while we hate the whole experience just as much, wishing she would understand that it's for her own good.

One time a vet we didn't know asked bluntly, 'How old is she now?'

'Seven,' I said.

The response was casually blunt: 'OK, so she's about halfway through her life – with luck.'

Robin grimaced. Suddenly you are forced to contemplate your precious pet's mortality – those dog years that race to catch up with your own age, and then overtake. The thought fills you with a powerful, anticipatory sorrow which is yet another aspect of the dog's saving grace: knowing he/she must die (and most likely, before you), you are put into training.

I was interested to read the results of a survey with the veterinarian Bruce Fogle conducted into his British co-professionals' attitude to per death. It seems that one out of five practising veterinarians admitted a belief that a dog has a soul and an afterlife. Interestingly, two out of five believed that humans have a soul and an afterlife. When the same survey questions were put to practising veterinarians in Japan (where Buddhist and Shintoist traditions allow for an afterlife for all living things) every single veterinarian surveyed believed that dogs have a soul which is likely to survive death. Does that sound ridiculous? It doesn't matter. The poet Mark Doty remembers walking in the wood with his now-dead dog Beau, and 'hears' the sound of his paws. He writes,

> ... this is almost a physical sensation, the sound of those paws ... allied to the colour and heat of him, the smell of warm fur, the kinetic life of a being hardly still: what lives in me. And just as I'm feeling intensely grateful for that ... on the autumn path, scents and tones of leather, brass, resin, brandy, tobacco, leaf mold, mushrooms, wet bark – I think Paradise. Then I think, If there's a heaven and he's not there, I'm not going.

My octogenarian father, who delights in Bonnie's company, is convinced that she has a soul. He's in good company, for Elizabeth Barrett Browning wrote, 'If I leave off verse to write in prose, it shall be a dissertation on the Souls of Dogs.' Lord Byron was angry that his dog Boatswain, who saved him from drowning, was 'Denied in Heaven the soul he held on Earth'. Indeed it is hard to imagine any Elysian Fields deserving of the name, without dogs, large, small and middling, bounding through the grass – rewarded for their enthusiasm, joyfulness, readiness, absurdity, intelligence, unconditional acceptance, constancy and devotion by permission to romp for ever in the land of the blessed, a perpetual supply of good food and clear water and chewy treats at hand. It may be foolish, but if we thought it might be true, the promise might help alleviate the terrible grief at the loss of a beloved pet, which Rudyard Kipling warns against, in his anguished poem 'The Power of the Dog':

> *Brothers and sisters, I bid you beware*
> *Of giving your heart to a dog to tear.*

But you can't refuse to love because of the pain which may or may not ensue. New parents usually find themselves over-whelmed by the terrifying mixture of responsibility and adora-tion which places you for ever on the rack, imagining everything that may – or will – threaten the small humans you love beyond speech. Even when your children have long grown up (like mine) you may still wake at four in the morning, worrying because they are unsettled or unhappy, and dreading future difficulties which life is bound to roll into their path, tripping them when you are no longer there to break the fall. And, loving a dog, you dread the universe of germs and internal growths which could cut short the already short life of the animal who has come to mean so much.

It disappointed me to learn that one of my favourite poets, Rainer Maria Rilke, feared the emotional demands of dog ownership. Committed as he was to his art, he believed (correctly) that to live with a dog would require love and attention he could not give. He was afraid of his inner resources being used up. In a 1912 letter he makes a curious assertion: '… they touch me very closely, these beings who rely on us so utterly and in whom we have helped raise a soul for which there is no heaven.' Is he suggesting that the soul within the dog is a human construct, an imaginative projection, or alternatively a reality 'grown' through the human–canine bond? If the latter, why is he – who believed in angelic power – so very sure there is 'no heaven' for them? Rilke thought of dogs as a 'better' kind of creature than humankind, imagining them as such because they are simpler, more *real* than people. Quite apart from their capacity for devotion, they live closely in touch with the world because they read it through all their senses – which faculties lend a certain superiority ('Who among us can point to a smell?'). What's more, a letter Rilke sent from Spain describes an unsettling encounter with a stray in which he ascribes to the animal an insight (or 'in-seeing' – *einsehen*) equal to his own. He was having coffee when an 'ugly', pregnant bitch came up, pleading for attention. Her eyes 'implored my looking' and in them the poet saw 'into the future or that which passeth understanding'. He gave her a lump of sugar, 'yet the meaning and solemnity and our whole communion were boundless'.

To me, the 'meaning' within that encounter between poet and animal was the same as that I experienced that long ago morning, when I looked at a field full of Hereford cows, on our organic farm. The poet who was so sure there was no heaven for dogs could still ascribe to the animal a spiritual power 'which passeth understanding' and use the religious word 'communion' to convey what happened between them. No wonder the mysterious holy-rolling-gunslinger played by Clint Eastwood in *Pale Rider* described the patch where teenaged Megan buried her murdered Jack Russell as 'holy ground'. So Bonnie continues to teach me that I am a part of a community of animals, neither above nor separate. Sometimes I stare into her jet-bead eyes and wonder what it is she knows, that I do not. At night, when Robin is fast asleep and I am bolt awake, tormented by my usual demons of worry, I reach for her as I used to clutch my teddy bear as a child, curling my body around the ball of her on top of the duvet. Then, at the soft time before daybreak, I will see her eyes shine at me, as if to ask why rest eludes this person she worships? Then I bury my face in her back, inhaling the doggy scent which is sweet to me, and beg her not to go back to sleep, not to leave me 'alone'. But usually this encounter in the silence is itself enough to make me drowsy, as if unconsciously soothed by the beating of that small heart, as a foetus is within the womb.

There's an image in the photographer David Douglas Duncan's book *Picasso & Lump: A Dachshund's Odyssey* which expresses a moment rather like that. An experience of stillness with a small dog which is akin to worship. In the spring of 1957 Douglas paid a visit to his friend and photographic subject, Pablo Picasso, at the artist's home near Cannes. With him was his young dachshund, Lump, which means 'little rascal' in German. On that day Picasso and the small dog fell for each other, and the great man immediately painted his portrait on a plate, writing, 'Pour Lump, Picasso, Cannes 19.4.57' beneath the droll sketch of the sausage dog. Within days 'Lumpito' had established himself as the painter's muse and Jacqueline Roque's companion while her partner was absorbed in his art. Picasso was to immortalize Lump in his series *Las Meninas* – 54 canvases inspired by Velásquez's great work of that name. In the bottom right-hand corner of the original lies a giant hound; in Picasso's variations we see substituted the unmistakable elongated shape of the breed which would later enchant Andy Warhol and David Hockney too.

One day Picasso told Douglas, 'Lump has the best and the worst in us.' In the photograph I love, the artist is staring fixedly at the dog, as if to fathom his mysteries. The bare stone room is lit by two windows. Picasso and Jacqueline sit opposite each other, and with them are four others. The silence is palpable; all six humans are staring intently at Lump, who sits on the floor between them all, doing nothing, not even looking at the photographer but fixing his eyes on the middle distance. The casual composition is anchored by the dog. He is the focus, his trailing lead taking the eye back to the artist's fascinated contemplation and the whole image rendered somehow sacred by the Mediterranean light which gilds Picasso's head, and Lump's as well. 'What was his allure?' asks Douglas and he records that when the artist looked at Lump, 'a sweet gentleness glowed in his eyes'. Who can tell what the artist saw, or why he allowed this particular dog into his world as none before? Dachshund and master both died in 1973. Picasso was

92, and Lump equally venerable at seventeen, but immortalized for ever in art.

One Sunday afternoon in June 2009, Bonnie suddenly began to flip about, squealing like a rabbit wounded by a hunter's bullet, but not yet killed. Nobody was touching her, and this is not a dog who would accidentally ingest poison, since she often has to be persuaded to eat even her expensive small-dog meals. Yet the day before she had been off-colour and we had begun to worry. Now she looked at me piteously and one of her forelegs gave way. I was transfixed at the top of the staircase, so naturally she tried to ascend the first stair, only to fall back, tail low, paws flailing. When I rushed down to scoop her up, the tiny black eyes looked terrified, their whites moongleams of panic. Yet strangely reproachful too. What is this hurting-thing? Why doesn't my mother-goddess make it better? And all the time the high-pitched crying, tearing at the edges of my brain. Her straining ribs were like bird bones beneath my fingers; her heart beat a pitiful tattoo within a chest fragile as paper. I felt helpless.

At that moment I heard the rumble of the motorcycle outside, and Robin returned to take charge, phoning the emergency veterinary service again and again until we could get an appointment. Many times have I been the desperate, worried parent, cradling my child, dreading the worst news – so let nobody rebuke or patronize me with the obvious statement that there can be no comparison, because I *know*. Yet here I was again with all my being concentrated into an unspoken prayer: *Please don't let her die.* At such a moment you remember the grief of friends whose dogs have died, either naturally or after illness, and realize that although you made sympathetic noises, you did not understand. But now your dog is ill and the vet is puzzled and you have that presentiment that, even if this is not destined to be the end, she is halfway through her life – so it is coming. Sooner or later.

At the beginning of 2009, we were fascinated to read about new excavations at Saqqara in Egypt which revealed a burial chamber containing 22 mummies, in sandy niches in the tomb's walls. Amongst the mummies of children, archaeologists found the mummy of a pet dog, surely placed there to follow his owners into the afterlife. This was not uncommon. The dog would be embalmed with all the care given to a human corpse, and after it was wrapped in linen bandages, they would recreate eyes, nose, mouth and ears to make it look as lifelike as possible. What greater mark of value can be imagined? No wonder the long-dead dogs are immortalized on tomb paintings: the rangy basenjis and Dalmatian types with their jewelled collars, and (often under the master's chair) the small dogs with short legs, pricked up ears and curly tails. All acolytes of the dog-headed god Anubis – for eternity.

Other religions have always interested me – after all, I have a Buddhist goddess in my garden and little Hindu sculptures in the house: Ganesh and Lakshmi. Yet in the end I am part of a Christian culture and therefore it matters to me that while there is nothing in the Bible to suggest that any living creature apart from man has a soul, there is also nothing which denies such a premise. I like the Old Testament covenant between man, as steward of the earth and the animal kingdom: ' … every living creature that is with you, of the fowl, of the cattle, and of every beast of the earth'. (Genesis 9:8–7). Jewish law traditionally prohibited cruelty to animals, and promoted active concern for their welfare. The Old Testament is littered with texts containing this message. For example, in the book of Numbers we find the story of Balaam and his ass in which the man is rebuked by an angel for his cruelty to his beast. The rabbinic tradition preached compassion for the welfare of animals at all times. It is the moral requirement expressed by St Francis of Assisi: 'If you have men who will exclude any of God's creatures from the shelter of compassion and pity, you will have men who deal likewise with their fellow men.'

In the New Testament a remark by Jesus is comforting. He tells his disciples, 'Are not two sparrows sold for a farthing? And one of them shall not fall to the ground without your Father' (Matthew 10:29). So the smallest and most insignificant birds – so cheap you get two for next to nothing – are deemed to be so worthy of attention that the most powerful Being in the universe will notice the death of just one of them. With that in mind I see no reason why a person should not conduct a burial ritual for a mourned pet, perhaps using words from St Francis of Assisi, patron saint of ecology and of animals. He believed that we are all one, interrelated Creation, and all – from the smallest insect to the most noble human being, encompassed within the love of the Creator. On his feast day, 4 October, some Catholic and other Christian churches all over the world hold services where animals are blessed. Therefore, if the living creatures can be blessed, why not the dead? For it is a short step from such an honouring of valued animals to feeling that – since we know that dogs too have the capacity to 'love' (the human concept must serve) and since one idea of heaven is a state of pure love – there *could* be a spiritual dimension to our pet dogs about which we know nothing. In truth, I suspect this is not the case, but what does it matter, if believing gives comfort?

Myself, I still lean towards the words of wisdom which emanate from my statue of Kwan Yin, in her garden temple. She is telling me that we must understand that every single thing is in a state of flux; therefore struggling against it is a waste of spirit-energy. Sad we may feel – yet learning to be at peace with a loss begins with understanding that we must live in the moment, knowing that more moments will follow, each one begging to be experienced fully. Clinging to a grief traps the one grieving – and the one grieved for. It is no memorial to a person – or a beloved pet – to be rendered incapable of living because they have gone. Death is just one ending. If it is true that 'what will survive of us is love' then the only way to prove that is to *live*.

I can hear friends who have been plunged into terrible sadness by the deaths of their cherished dogs assuring me that it isn't so easy. At 2.30 p.m. on Wednesday 25 January 2005 (and how she remembers) my dear friend Gaynor's dog was put to sleep, after a long illness and more than one operation. Bentley was a Border terrier and she, a beautiful, vibrant woman, says truly, 'He was the only boy who broke my heart.' She is not making a jest; nor do such levels of grief result from modern sentimentality. Animal cemeteries – like the Cimetière des Chiens in a north-west suburb of Paris, and the one at Molesworth in Cambridgeshire – testify to the seriousness with which our forebears treated the deaths of pets. It was common for the owners of great houses to create pets' burial grounds and commission monumental sculptures of the animals. On a single lichen-covered stone in the woods at Overwater Hall Hotel in Cumbria Robin and I sympathized with a sorrow over a hundred years old, for 'Lyuth – sic a bonnie dog' and 'Brownie – too dearly loved'.

Around 1853 Giuseppe Verdi (whose operas have always thrilled me more than any others) bought a Maltese dog for his mistress (later wife), Giuseppina Strepponi, perhaps anticipating the long hours she would be left alone at their villa, San' Agata, in the province of Piacenza in northern Italy. The former soprano idolized the little dog, who followed her everywhere and slept on her bed. But in August 1862 Verdi wrote to the conductor Mariani: 'A very great misfortune for me has struck us and made us suffer atrociously. Loulou, poor Loulou is dead! Poor creature! The true friend, the faithful inseparable companion of almost six years of life! So affectionate! So beautiful! Poor Loulou. It is difficult to describe the sorrow of Peppina but you can imagine it … in my house there is desolation.' Giuseppina and Verdi buried the 'faithful and charming' Maltese under a willow in their garden – and visitors to what is now called the Villa Verdi can visit the handsome stone memorial by the lake, inscribed 'All memoria d'un Vero Amico', and see an oval portrait of the blue-ribboned dog, their 'true friend', still hanging in Giuseppina's room.

I find it easy to imagine Guiseppina's grief for Loulou, who looked so like my Bonnie. I understand about Flush and Carlo and reckon Byron's Boatswain did have a soul – because nobody can prove to me that he didn't. Their dogs, like my own, have a purpose. To pause for a moment in the neutral gloom of most days and allow yourself to plug in to the various sorrows of others, past and present, is to be reactivated by an electric current of understanding which can light the world.

The dogs are a way in. They are – in this particular story – the *portal*.

There proved to be nothing seriously wrong with Bonnie that time; anti-inflammatory and antibiotic drugs cleared up whatever it was, and the vets remained mystified. Robin and I were unable to take her out for a week while she recovered, but at last life returned to normal. Each day we take her for the same short walk: across the road, through a road of modern houses (like Wisteria Lane in *Desperate Housewives*), along to the allotments, and round and back through a small park. She likes the walk, but will refuse to come if one of us remains in the house. The whole pack must move as one. One day, when we were admiring the neat rows of cabbages and beans and Robin was saying how good it would be to be self-sufficient, we met a neighbour – a widow. Her steps were slow; she told us her old dog had died. 'The house is so empty,' she said. 'I hate going back there.' Her dog had given her comfort when her husband died suddenly a few years earlier, and through the dark days following. Now the basket was empty, and she found it insupportable. We murmured the right words of sympathy, aware of their inadequacy – knowing too that this is the point at which some people give up, because the pet dog is their last connection to life, or rather, to the will to live.

It's hard to read about the death of Edith Wharton's last dog without being moved. After 11 years together, Linky fell ill on 11 April 1937 and four days later Wharton had to take the decision to have her sick Peke ('the best and last of her race') euthanized. That night she imagined she saw the little dog's ghost by her bed. The day after, her diary says simply, 'Can't remember. Oh, my little dog,' and she tells a friend, 'I wish she could have outlasted me, for I feel, for the very first time in my life, quite utterly alone and lonely.' Then, for several days, Wharton does not mention her pet, but tries to write bravely of other things. At last, on 26 April, comes this cry of anguish: 'Oh, how shall I get used to not seeing Linky any more?' In May she was 'tired and depressed' and noted, 'Cannot forget my Linky.' Then, four months to the day after her dog became ill, Edith Wharton died of a stroke. She must have known that her great novels would give her immortality, but it is easy to understand why the childless woman of 75 had no wish to go on without that little heartbeat at her feet.

Fortunately our neighbour, though in her seventies, proved more robust. A few months later we met her again in the allotments, but this time her face was alight. She couldn't wait to tell us excitedly about her new puppy – a poodle: 'He's making *such* a difference.' Of course. The puppy brought life and movement back into her home. No wonder so many dogs are used successfully in therapeutic work – the best ones trained to respond positively to the most disturbed young people or to men and women suffering from Alzheimer's disease. My father was touched to observe how Bonnie – usually unfriendly to strangers and always restless – somehow knew that she must sit quietly on the lap of his 100-year-old neighbour, giving her such pleasure because she felt herself *liked* by the small dog. One of my readers wrote in response to a letter I published from a woman with multiple problems. Her considered advice? 'The best recipe – making you take long walks and giving you someone to tell everything to – is to get a dog! I've just got my second rescue dog and it really does change your life. Somebody who will love you unconditionally – always.'

Unfortunately it would not do for that to be my own standard response, although I agree that many lonely and depressed people would benefit from what we all call 'the Bonnie effect'.

My favourite evenings are at home, just with Robin and our dog: the pack in a pile on the sofa. Family and friends, though deeply loved, require attention; what's more, sometimes I can no longer face up to the demands of the books I love. After a day wrestling with words and meanings, I like nothing better than to curl up with the pack and watch a movie. But my taste in films becomes worse as I grow older. When J and I were in our twenties we used to queue at an art-house cinema in Chelsea to appreciate Fellini and Bergman. Now in my sixties, I am unashamed to enjoy Jennifer Aniston starring in *Marley and Me* and Sam Neill in *Dean Spanley*. Robin and I share a taste for romantic comedies and any movie which features Hugh Grant playing his own, floppy-haired English self. 'There's nothing wrong with wanting a story to end happily,' Robin says defensively, and although I argue that art does not always afford such a luxury, in my heart I agree. We were talking about Richard Curtis films one day when I pointed that, during the period covered by this book (spring 2002 to summer 2009), I had attended four funerals and a wedding.

'Whose wedding?' he asked, knowing about the funerals.

'Ours, of course!' I said.

I thought I'd not quite reached the age to meet acquaintances in the obituary columns, although, from time to time, there they are – transporting me back to a seventies party, with someone singing Persian love songs or blues to a sweet guitar, as wine flows, joss sticks burn and somebody across the room is falling in love and it will all end with sickness of head and heart. And then, years later, comes the obituary which tolls the knowledge that we are no longer 'Still crazy after all these years' but tired of living and scared of dying. Sometimes.

If imagining the death of your beloved pet puts you into training, it is also a way of avoiding the knowledge that your parents (for example) will die and you will feel bereft. But there was no avoiding those four funerals – and so I pause here to honour my friends, as a way through (yes, another portal) to the next surprising stage of my personal quest, when I'd be accompanied by my small dog alone. You must step with me into these shadows, because similar ones will have fallen across your own path – and there is no avoiding them, not with light-hearted movies nor wine nor sex, nor even laughter at the antics of a cavorting canine companion. The shadows must be embraced.

So, those four people, all of whom I first met in the eighties. First, the writer Bernard Levin died in August 2004. It was time he went, since by then the greatest journalist of his generation had mislaid language within the dense thickets of his mind. We had shared opera, meals and many jokes as well as confidences; I rejoiced in the happiness his last love brought him and, like all those who loved him, watched with despair and horror as Alzheimer's disease pulled him into the pit. We grieved for his lost wit, his bonhomie, his enthusiasms, his passion for wine, women and song, and that great, boundless kindness which piled up glittering Rheingold against the door into the dark. Speaking at his funeral, and then writing his entry for the *Dictionary of National Biography*, were among the hardest things I have ever done, because of the struggle to find words that could leap high enough to reach him.

Then, at the beginning of January 2005 one of Britain's most talented architects, Richard Feilden, died at his home just outside Bath, when a tree he was felling in the woodland he loved crushed him. He was 54 and at the height of his career. The day before his death two of his three adult children were at my home, celebrating my daughter's birthday. Then came the phone call from J, telling me the shocking news. Richard's talent and energy, his idealism, his firm opinions, his quizzical challenges, his hospitality and humour – all gone. He was the one who had once irritated me by teasing my lapdog, but how I wished to hear his banter again. Just a few days before his death the world had been shaken by news of the devastating tsunami which followed the Indian Ocean earthquake, killing over 230,000 people in 11 countries and shattering the existence of their families and communities. Such universal suffering and grief – and yet still one individual death makes the heart contract as you witness the devastation it causes to family and friends. At his funeral, Bath Abbey erupted with Richard's favourite motto, 'Onwards and upwards', and we all took his message of hope out into the cold day.

In November the same year I heard that the editor I had worked with on my children's fiction since 1985 was dead. I had last seen Miriam Hodgson at the end of 2003 when I wept in her arms, telling her about the end of my marriage. After that we had exchanged the odd affectionate note and postcard as usual, but she had retired and I was no longer writing the 'Kitty' stories, so there was no real need to meet. I assumed there would always be a Christmas party where we would slip into our old confidences surrounded by children's authors gossiping and quaffing wine. Now she too was gone. No more little ticks in the margins of a manuscript, no more little pencilled comments like 'Lovely!' and occasional plaintive protests because a character was meaner than she thought strictly necessary. The mournful task of writing Miriam's obituary for *The Times* fell to me and I took it as an honour. The article ended, 'She always said that children "deserve to keep a belief in good defeating evil." That spirit of optimism survives her, both in the books she edited and within those as yet unwritten, where her influence will live.'

A journalist, an architect, a children's book editor ... and then another writer. The prolific journalist Miles Kington died in February 2008. Like most people in our trade I had marvelled at his ability to write daily columns which floated above the common run on their airy wit, like cumulus in a summer sky. No wonder people laughed as well as cried at his funeral. An old school friend told the gathering how Miles had been persuaded to judge a dog show during a Highland Games. He knew little about dogs but compensated by dreaming up new categories of canine champion – like 'the most disobedient dog', and the one which looked most like a certain acerbic female television presenter. His wife had to persuade him not to give first prize to the dog which hadn't won any other prizes.

Oh, the poignant humour of non-achieving dogs! No wonder Miles Kington's last book is called *How Shall I Tell the*

Dog? It is a series of witty letters to his agent, putting up increasingly mad ideas for books – because now he is terminally ill he needs a best-seller all the more. Along the way he plays with all sorts of notions, like how to break the news to your dog that now – against all expectations – it will outlive you: 'He might not realize I am going to die, for a start. He doesn't know about death. As I lie expiring ... how do I know that as I open my mouth and prepare to utter my carefully prepared and rehearsed last words, he may not burst in and demand to be taken for a walk? And that my last words, after all that, will turn out to be: "Oh, for God's sake, not now, Berry!"' There was a man who understood the bounding, irrepressible nature of dogs – which could lead him towards jokes, even in the face of his own death.

All the deaths we endure have something to teach us, in the end, and the process is infinite. Thirty-four years on, I have just commissioned the artist and letter-cutter Iain Cotton to create a memorial in slate to the baby son who never drew breath. It will say, 'LOVE'S STILLNESS FOREVER MOVES', acknowledging the permanence of loss, but its transforming power too. And all these thoughts lead me to this point in my story. For how could I ever forget? During those years, the soprano Susan Chilcott died too – and her death was a source of great grief to those who loved her, but a tsunami to J and to me.

One Sunday morning, early in January 2009, I am listening to J talk about her on the radio. The series (on BBC Radio 3) *Private Passions* invites a different well-known person each week to choose music they love and explain why. Presented by the composer Michael Berkeley, the programmes place serious emphasis on the chosen music, as befits the station's remit. I cannot lose my long habit of listening intently when J broadcasts, wishing him to be excellent and admiring when he is, yet at the same time deflated by the realization that it no longer really matters what I think. As the programme's theme tune begins I am guessing what he will pick: some Mozart certainly (probably piano) and definitely some Beethoven (I predict a sonata for piano and violin, the 'Spring'), and of course – I know this – he will select Susan Chilcott singing one of the great arias, even though she recorded but little. I am prepared.

What I am unprepared for is the gradual discovery that the choices form, in a sense, a soundtrack to much of our life together. He does not intend it, but as the programme unfolds, they open gates of memory as not even words can do. He talks about his father, and about his chairmanship of the Bath International Music Festival, and then begins his selection. Benjamin Britten's *St Nicholas* reminds me how, when we were first married, he used to spoof-sing the line 'St Nicholas was born in answer to prayer', telling me how, as a teenager, he loved singing it in his school choir. Every Christmas morning the very first thing we would do was put on his old LP of Britten's *Ceremony of Carols*. He introduced me to such things.

Choosing Beethoven's Seventh he recalls going to Berlin not long after the Wall was torn down, and imagining what it must have been like when the Potsdamer Platz was opened and the Berlin Philharmonic played the mighty Seventh. And I remember his euphoria, his optimism as he brought me home a couple of fragments of the Wall, lurid with graffiti paint. These were *our* times. Then his choice of some wild, mad, hypnotic music from the highlands of Ethiopia rings out harshly on Radio 3, but is no surprise to me because only I know fully how much Ethiopia meant to him, through all the years of making documentaries there. I was the one he came home to, the one he talked to about it all. Does he, in a box in the attic, still have the record *Musiques Ethiopiennes* I bought him?

I was right about the Mozart; he is rueful about his limited skills as a pianist, but says he used to enjoy playing certain slow movements to passable effect – good enough to deceive those who did not know that much about music. As the first bars of the Piano Sonata in A major fill my ears I am transported back to his mother's long, low, beamed drawing room in Cranleigh, Surrey. Polished oak side tables, family photographs in silver frames, deep sofas, blue and gold velvet chairs, little pleated wall lights, a scent of logs and home. It is spring 1968, we are just married, and house-sitting for a week, looking after the Labradors Bill and Ben and catching up with our neglected university studies. J sits at the baby grand piano and plays me this very same sonata – and I lean to watch him, in surroundings more beautiful than any I have ever known, thinking that this man I love playing Mozart (*so* well – to me) is the most exquisite sound I have heard in my 21 years.

His final choice, number six, is introduced with some reflections on the wonders he saw over 30 years as a television reporter and documentary maker – and suddenly a sixth sense makes me say 'Thomaskirche!' to myself. I am right, of course – because I remember what it meant to him to hear the St John Passion in Bach's great church in Leipzig at Easter, when East Germany was still held in the grip of the communist Honneker regime, and the music of Bach was a sublime form of protest. He carefully carried home a simple poster for the concert, which we had framed – rendering due significance to the piece of ephemera. J tells how he sat in the glorious church, thinking how wonderful it would be for that oppressed society to be free, all the while transported (even though he describes himself as 'without faith really') 'by one of the great pieces of Christian art'. Which can transform even the sound of a crowd/chorus calling for the crucifixion of Jesus into a cascade of grace.

I take the lesson. This is a part of the seeking – to realize that the very worst can be so transformed.

But I must retrace, returning to his third music choice, introduced by way of his love of opera. There is Susan Chilcott, between Beethoven and the Ethiopians, between his memories of the Berlin Wall and of famine, bringing the first note of sadness into a programme full of enthusiasm. How could it be helped? How could he not choose her? Michael Berkeley is gracious in his lead-in to this choice, commenting that when events in life are heightened we often say, 'It's like an opera.' J agrees. He says that he always thought his life would go steadily along and that big dramas would happen to other people. But then, 'I fell in love with a glorious singer, the soprano Sue Chilcott, and she with me, and I spent the last three months of her life with her.' He talks about her greatness as a singer, how Placido Domingo described her as a genius, how beautiful she was, how suited for the great, lyric tragic roles – and at last, voice full of controlled emotion, chooses (from a newly released CD, *Susan Chilcott in Brussels*) a piece of music I know very well indeed: Desdemona's poignant final aria, 'Ave Maria'.

When the final 'Amen' has faded, J manages to say, 'You just think when you hear that voice, what the world of music and opera has lost.'

There is no gainsaying it. The beauty of her voice is over-whelming, but so is the message of the words, as the doomed Desdemona prays to Mary for sinner and innocent alike, and for those who are weak and oppressed. She prays for the man who bows beneath injustice and also beneath the blows of cruel destiny. She prays for the powerful man who also grieves. Finally, in her last benediction, Desdemona begs the Virgin to pray for all of us (*'prega per noi!'*), and there, miraculously, in Boito's words and Verdi's music, the separate parts of this whole programme are united into one whole: Beethoven's deafness, Mozart's suffering and early death, the people of East Berlin and of Ethiopia and the other beknighted countries J reported from, Shakespeare's tragedies, all Britten's lost and lonely 'outsiders' – and J himself, a powerful man who also grieves.

'Thy sweet compassion show' (*'tua pieta dimostra'*) begs Desdemona.

But what, I think, of *me*?

'I spent the last three months of her life with her,' he said, but there was no mention of that other woman to whom he was married for all those years. Not even in passing. Not even a nod. For a few moments I feel full of sadness and anger, even indignation, because I seem to have become like one of the 'disappeared' of Argentina whose grieving relatives could never discover what had happened to them, or like those airbrushed from history in communist regimes. But the feeling does not last. After all, he made no mention of his new wife either – and I know he would have made such decisions after careful

284

thought, because this programme is about *music*. The music comes first. And Susan Chilcott *is* her music now.

Thus reasoning, I quickly recover – because, in any case, what does it matter? There is permanent solace in what I know: the sharing of a whole, rich life behind the music he chose, the shaping of us both from when we were young, the suitcases packed and unpacked, the phone calls from distant places, the children, the Christmases and anniversaries, the silly names and splendid gifts, the farm, the three dogs and four cats … and so on, even up until the end, and her final, heartbreaking 'Amen'. It was ours – and so it remains. Just as the earlier writing on a palimpsest can always be read by the ones who know it is there, even though new words have been written over it. And just as when, after a note of music ends, its spirit still vibrates within the air.

Without fully understanding why, I bought the new CD J mentioned on the programme, and also the recording of Aaron Copland songs Susan Chilcott recorded with Iain Burnside in September 2002, one month before J first met her at that fateful dinner party. There was something almost furtive about my purchase. I told nobody, but squirrelled the CDs away as if I had done something wrong. Wanting to own them, I nevertheless could not summon the courage to hear them. So a month went by, and I began to write this book with my small dog nestling at my feet. Thinking I might listen in the privacy of my study, I loaded the music on to iTunes on my computer. But each time I went to select one or other – I changed my mind. It was impossible for me to expose myself to that.

Then, one day, a strange thing happened.

When writing, I sometimes have classical music playing quietly all day, relegating (I'm afraid) the glories of Hildegarde of Bingen, Mozart and Haydn to a background accompaniment. I will start somewhere randomly in the category and then just leave it playing. So it is on this particular cold March day, when suddenly I look at my watch and realize I have an appointment at the hairdresser's and must leave immediately. My hair is cut and coloured, then I wander into my favourite clothes shop next to the salon, then into another shop to pick up bracelets and put them down again. At last, after the contented time wasting which I rarely allow myself, I return home. Coat off, gaze critically at the hair in the mirror, make an espresso – and then comes the moment all writers dread. Restarting work that can be put off no longer. I go downstairs to my office, where iTunes has been playing to the empty air all the while.

And – What is *that*? I think.

Wind instruments like birdsong – oboe, flute and clarinet rising and falling cleanly, as if in the stillness of a perfect summer morning.

I stand still, then hear the soprano's first words, 'How beautiful it is!'

The shadowy butterflies fluttering on my screensaver are dispelled as I click to determine what track this is. But perhaps in my heart I already know. Methodically working its way down through the digitized albums, fate has delivered to me, at the precise second I enter my study, Susan Chilcott performing an aria from Britten's *The Turn of the Screw*. It is the very first track on the *Brussels* CD. What would be the odds on such a piece of timing?

She is singing the role of the governess who has arrived at a country house to take care of two seemingly innocent children, Miles and Flora. What she cannot possibly know is that they have been corrupted (in ways unspecified, which adds to the dreadful mystery) by a former valet and governess, Peter Quint and Miss Jessel, who are now dead. Yet they visit the children still. Within moments the mood shifts. In the background you still hear the sweetness of the wind instruments but now they form an ironic, almost cruel contrast to the singer's unease, then fear. She sings: 'Only one thing that I wish/that I could see him …' – but why would you want to see a ghost? The young woman glimpses a man (Quint's evil spirit) and you hear panic rise as she asks, 'Who is it? Who? Who can it be?' in her first intimation of the horror that is to come.

This music is full of ghosts. When the track finishes I press Stop, not wanting to hear her Desdemona and that rending 'Ave Maria'. Or unable to face it.

Do you believe in signs? I asked the question before and still ask. Two weeks after that strange occurrence, the coincidence happened again. This time I had hurried out to the gym, once again leaving the music playing in my study. After exercising I went shopping for food, indulged in more time wasting in clothes shops and at last returned home. Only this time I entered my study in the middle of a track, her voice in full flood once again, asking finally:

Why do they shut me out of heaven?
Did I sing too loud?

The crescendo on the final note seems to defy the forbidding angels ('the gentlemen in white robes') with its defiant volume. This is the recording of songs by Aaron Copland, and happenstance has entered me into track eight of his setting of poems by my beloved Emily Dickinson, who trusted she would be led across into heaven by her dog. There is hardly a pause before the next song begins:

> *The world feels dusty when we stop to die*
> *We want the dew then*
> *Honours taste dry.*

The poem/song tells us what anyone who has been very ill knows: that when you are dying, achievements mean nothing and all you want is a 'fan stirred by a friend's hand' which 'cools like the rain'.

This would be enough – but it is the next song which hits me like a message from another world. (I print this with Dickinson's distinctive punctuation, not the tidied-up version Copland had to work with in 1950):

> *Heart, we will forget him!*
> *You and I – tonight!*
> *You may forget the warmth he gave –*
> *I will forget the light!*
>
> *When you have done, pray tell me*
> *That I may straight begin!*
> *Haste! Lest while you're lagging*
> *I remember him!*

How can I shut this off? Press the Stop key and return to where I was – before the voice begged me to listen? There is no Pause button for the unfolding of pain. So I will not seek to escape it now – even in the safety of my white room. Because I believe that the random selection of Susan Chilcott singing, out of so many hours of music, not once but twice, has happened for a reason. And I must listen – as an act not of masochism but of meditation. This has little to do with forgiveness, for that is not my prerogative. I am just another flawed soul, muddling along, attempting to understand.

It was impossible to embark upon the next stage of my strange meeting with Susan Chilcott then, not with Robin elsewhere in the house. He would not wish me to do anything which might upset me, and therefore I must keep my intention secret. What's more, I did not want anybody to interrupt and find me out. So I waited. At last, four months after I had listened to *Private Passions*, Robin went away to France and so I could be quite alone, apart from Bonnie, lying in my lap. My room was illuminated only by a candle and the light from the computer screen, where the iTunes visualizer turned the music into magical abstract patterns. With a glass of Sauvignon in my hand I listened to Susan singing Britten (Ellen in *Peter Grimes* as well as the governess in *The Turn of the Screw*), and Verdi, and Strauss and Boesmans. It lasted almost an hour, followed by over an hour of Copland, with more wine. With my dog warming my legs and heart, I heard fear, love, wonder and resignation, as the piano notes were transformed into whirling fragments on my screen, showers of coloured sparks in a night sky. Purple shading to blue to red to green. And in the centre of it all, was the recurring black disc – now large, now small, now bounced away by light, now rolling back to the dark centre – burning on the retina the unmistakable message of mortality.

I thought, How unutterably gorgeous, that voice.

I thought, How could any man resist such beauty?

I thought, How I wish *I* had learned to sing.

But most of all, listening to that glorious sound, encompassing so much universal emotion, I thought of the singer, not the song. Once again, as in 2003, I imagined what it must have been like to know you were going to die at the age of 40, to look at your little son knowing you would never see him grow up and to try to explain that enormity to him. Oh, the pity of it. Glimpsing death, would you not cry out in terror at the spectre, 'Who is it? Who?'? And would you not hold out both hands to grasp those which stretched out in love to help you? Understanding that, I am suddenly filled with an inexpressible serenity, within that dark room. It comes from the knowledge that my husband left me, not to drink champagne with a mistress in a Mediterranean hotel, but to be the friend wielding the cooling fan. To take upon himself the burden of somebody's suffering, in all its ugliness. To face the real human drama – far beyond those artificially heightened emotions of opera – where there can be no resolution, nor catharsis, before the final curtain.

And what if it was bewildering – such an excess of love – to both of us, to our children, to everyone else? No matter. This is the end of this particular quest – just to accept. All I need to know, six years on, is the truth expressed in one of the Copland songs, which now, in the peace of my room and the comforting presence of my dog, I choose to play again and again, loving it more than anything else she sang. It is a setting of a poem by E.E. Cummings – whose work J gave me for Christmas 1968, with a loving inscription of course. There is no irony in such inscriptions. They tell an incontrovertible truth, one which is now echoed in this elegy, which Copland's music renders curiously inconclusive, as if to say, 'Nothing ends, the music continues in silence':

> *in spite of everything*
> *which breathes and moves,since Doom*
> *(with white longest hands*
> *neatening each crease)*
> *will smooth entirely our minds*
>
> *— before leaving my room*
> *i turn,and(stooping*
> *through the morning)kiss*
> *this pillow,dear*
> *where our heads lived and were.*

That is grace.

So now – since I am the one who is fortunate enough to be alive – I have to ask myself what I will do with the life that is left. This is the question which, as often as possible, I bat outwards too, towards my readers. You who are 30 and you who are 60 – think on it, with me. Each of us will have ways of working it out, but there should be no doubt about the urgency. My way begins with stretching out my foot to the small dog beneath my desk, who patiently waits for any crumb of attention to fall from the preoccupied human companion. Knowing her has taught me that there are more ways of loving than are dreamt of in your romantic novels.

As I grow older I find I detest romance. The Penelope Fitzgerald novel *The Blue Flower*, which sparked thoughts about finding and searching, echoes my mistrust of its blandishments. It tells the true story of how, in eighteenth-century Saxony young Fritz von Hardenberg falls in love with 12-year-old Sophie – an absurdly romantic attachment to a frivolous, ordinary girl he calls his 'true Philosophy' and 'spirit's guide' with no understanding of her real self. The otherworldly Hardenberg will later become the great romantic poet and philosopher 'Novalis', and the Blue Flower was an important symbol for him and for the German Romantic Movement – representing the metaphysical striving for the infinite and unreachable. In one of his novels the hero dreams about blue flowers and becomes obsessed by them, as if they only exist, unattainable, in the world of the mind ...

But wait a minute – in my own garden I see forget-me-nots, cornflowers, hydrangeas, delphiniums, veronicas, wild geraniums. Ordinary blue flowers abound, so why would you search for the Blue Flower? Oh, why does the stupid, agonized romantic perpetually scan the horizon, failing to see the beauty in the lowly, crushed petals at his feet? Why the fevered seeking, without understanding what is already found?

Fritz becomes engaged to Sophie when she is 13, but she falls terminally ill. There are unspeakable operations without anaesthetic; the prognosis is grim. She is destined to die days after her fifteenth birthday, when her fiancé (in the manner of romantics, unable to bear witness) has departed to his own home. But before that, there is a telling moment with the small dogs who run in the margins of the whole novel. Sophie's sick-room is bedlam, full of step-siblings, caged birds and lapdogs, and when the schoolmaster arrives he protests, asking, 'Kindly remove the five dogs, at least, from the room.' The sick girl should be quiet. But other people arrive, witless, blundering, and 'Sophie held her arms out to them all. In the racket her laughter and coughing could scarcely be heard. The little dogs, all desperate to be first, bounded back, with flattened ears, onto the bed to lick her face.'

No one, in the heat and odour of an eighteenth-century room, would have bothered about hygiene. Nor do people nowadays who love their dogs. In any case, the dogs' kisses are healing, even if only temporarily. (I believe Bonnie's licks keep my wrinkles under control.) As the pets bound about on the sick girl's bed, delighting her with their enthusiasm, the old schoolmaster closes his book and thinks, 'After all, these people were born for joy.'

Of course, what happens at the end of that particular story gives the lie to that statement of simple optimism. They loved, were deluded and died young. But the mad, loving licking of the dogs is indiscriminately generous. On a bumper sticker in Charleston, South Carolina, I saw the message 'DON'T POSTPONE JOY'. That is why I offer the lesson of dogs, who are incapable of postponement. Who *must* race, *must* bound, *must* wag, *must* lick, *must* play, *must* be petted – as if their lives, so much shorter than our own, depend on it. They do not seek the Blue Flower, but know instinctively that you have to keep digging in the ordinary little patch that you have, finding new things to sniff at all the time, right here, *now*. The dog says, 'Go for it!'

The messages are everywhere. In steamy Georgia, we stayed at an inn where a miniature Yorkshire terrier ran to greet every guest. Joey was exactly like the two tiny dogs I had met in Amy Tan's San Francisco condo in 2002 – and being reminded of that encounter made me realize how much I had changed. I had learned how to read the beseeching yet frolicsome intelligence in the eyes of the small dog. Cuddling this little stranger on my lap (unfaithful to Bonnie most days in Savannah) I whispered to him that only I of all the guests knew how very busy he was. How meaningful his very small life.

Charles Baudelaire understood. He wrote, 'Where do dogs go? … They go about their business. Business meetings, love meetings. Through fog, through snow, through mud, during biting dog-days, in streaming rain, they go, they come, they trot, they slip under carriages, urged on by fleas, passion, need, or duty. Like us, they get up early in the morning, and they seek out their livelihood or pursue their pleasures.' His contemporary, Alphonse Toussenel, saw further, identifying the point behind most of canine activity: 'In the beginning, God created man, but seeing him so feeble, He gave him the dog.'

Everywhere I see them, and know that they are quietly going about their business of doing good – saving lives as Bonnie saves mine. They tell us to enjoy the simple pleasures of clean water and simple food and a walk and a caress and just sitting right up close to someone you love. They know that to be apart is intolerable. They lead by example – following instincts, loving unconditionally, accepting treats with enthusiasm, being loyal and faithful and quick to forgive. They know that you can show defiance with a short growl, and should have no need to bite. Not able to dissemble, they throw themselves with adoration at the beloved person coming through the door. In their blood runs the knowledge that when you are small, you survive by being lovable – and that is the lesson which matters most of all. It is as if they know that life is but a few pants and wags and therefore all of the above, all those talents, must be crammed in, without stint, in the moments between breakfast, supper and the long dreaming of an eternal chase.

And that is why, determined now to rush at life as Bonnie rushes at the postman's trousers ... whilst she can ... whilst I can ... I listen to the cohorts of small dogs. They tell me I must always 'Go seek it out!' until no longer capable of doing so, because within that urging is promise, adventure, courage. And change. For the process of writing this has led me to another stage, and as I reach the end of one story, I begin a new one.

It sometimes made me uncomfortable that I invariably describe this elegant town house in the city of Bath as 'my' house. Mine. In my name. My children found it for me, it enabled me to make my final escape from the farm and I created it in my own image. Yet how could I have known that I would remarry? One rainy day in August, as we sat talking in the conservatory wondering what happened to summer, and Bonnie snoozed between us, I suddenly realized what Robin had not said, that this perfect home for a writer who likes high heels does not suit a man who longs to grow vegetables and mend fences. To stride over meadows and devise ways of living 'greenly'. To clear undergrowth, chop wood and remake things that have broken down. Sometimes he longs to push out these Regency walls with his elbows and plant a greenhouse in the formal garden. The man brought up on thousands of acres of Kenyan farmland needs space.

And me? I want to slow time down by learning to watch things grow.

It was time to go house-hunting together. As I reach this ending (before yet another beginning) we have fallen in love with a rambling old farmhouse in the countryside outside Bath, a home even older than this one, with beams and crannies, as well as outbuildings which are begging to be restored by a man who can fix anything. We plan to live in a different way, more simply, more peacefully. To listen to stillness at night, broken by the cries of owls and foxes. There will be chickens and perhaps even some sheep. Maybe in time we will rescue another dog – a shaggy mutt who will concede Bonnie's superiority, and tear across those few acres with the lolloping joy of being alive.

As we stood and looked back at the ancient house, frantically doing sums to see if it might be possible, Bonnie leapt through meadow grass and lapped from the river which runs through the garden. Her impractical paws were already muddy; there was a burr stuck to her ear. The lapdog with the jewelled collar looked in her element at the thrilling prospect of coming full circle, and being a country dog again.

EPILOGUE

I am booked for a children's event at the Oundle Literary Festival, to talk about my 'Bonnie' books. Robin, the dog and I make the three-hour drive north-eastwards from Bath to Northamptonshire, a part of England new to us. We're always reluctant to leave our garden, where daffodils and crocuses have already pushed their way through, and the branches of the neighbours' magnificent magnolia, tipped with candles of palest rose, hang over our ancient red-brick wall. After an unusually cold winter, this spring has promise. And I don't much like going away from home.

We are to be given a bed for the night by a generous festival committee member. All over the United Kingdom there are people like this – putting energy into good things and opening their homes to strangers. It reinforces my faith in human nature – sometimes tested by people as well as the news in general. The other week a dear friend predicted 'civil unrest' because of the worsening economy and there are many days when there seems little to celebrate. Yet these small arts festivals all over the land tell a different story. People gather to hear writers and musicians and to talk about ideas. You have to cling to such delights as you notice (and *always* notice) the piercing beauty of flowers or the warmth in somebody's welcome. The wine is sloshing into glasses as we walk through the door. Stuart and Jennifer are going out to a literary dinner but have left supper and tell us their house is ours. The fact that our dog is with us makes us feel at home.

In a way that is hard to explain, she *is* 'home'.

Next morning we have time to explore the area for a while, before the 1.30 p.m. event – and our hostess suggests a visit to Fotheringhay, 'just up the road'. I had not realized (ever too busy to examine a map) that we would be staying so near to the place (surely special to lovers of small dogs?) where Mary Queen of Scots went to her death, accompanied by her hidden Skye terrier. How fitting an accident to find ourselves so near while I am writing this book.

We say our thanks and goodbyes and set off under a lowering sky. The village of Fotheringhay is indeed just five minutes away by car, but there is little to see. Home of a royal line, birthplace of Richard III, the village was of national standing in the fifteen and sixteenth centuries, but now there are just a few attractive houses built from golden stone, a church and the site of the once great castle.

For there is nothing left. The wind blows straight from the Fens in the east, where the river Nene meets the sea. There is nobody around. Church lovers both, we are disconsolate to find St Mary and All Saints closed and even sadder to discover nothing but the green 'motte' where the keep of Fotheringhay once stood, on the broad green banks of the river. A part of my imagination had hoped for picturesque ruins – romantic stones tumbled to earth yet still reminding the visitor of a history which began in 1100. There we might sit and commune with the spirit of the unfortunate queen ... But no, that is fanciful, because I knew (from the leaflet our hostess had given me) that it would indeed take much imagination to conjure up an image of the Great Hall where Mary went to the scaffold. But I had hoped for more than what looks like an enormous burial mound on a wide curve of the waterway.

Still, the idea of the burial mound is fitting too, given the desolation of this site beneath the wide, grey sky. They've put shallow wooden steps on one side, to help the visitor climb. I say to Bonnie, 'Come on, you have to honour the spirit of Mary's faithful little dog.' Eternally responsive, she bounds up steps tall to her, until we are standing on the top, looking down over the wide, flat area where the Great Hall would have been. I find I'm humming a poignant tune from distant 1969, the year J and I graduated and began our careers. Sandy Denny of Fairport Convention was inspired by Mary Stuart's story to write the song 'Fotheringay' (an alternative historical spelling) for the LP *What We Did On Our Holidays*. I know the lyrics by heart and can hear those plangent guitar melodies inside my brain:

How often she has gazed from castle windows all
And watched the daylight passing within her captive wall
With no one to heed her call ...

Yet I can't help thinking that Denny got it wrong, since Mary was surrounded by servants who adored her, as well as that famous lapdog, the last in a long line of Mary's dogs. They *all* heeded her call, and it's important not to forget the strength of human love and of animal devotion – the contrasting side to a legend of failure, of victimhood, of loss.

As Bonnie races about like a tiny, ruffled cloud I stand still to read the historical leaflet, learning that Mary died with dignity and style, a marked contrast to the churlishness of her judges who withheld from her the last rites and persisted to the end with a battery of puritanical exhortation and abuse. As typical as any was the Earl of Kent, who rebutted Mary's request that her servants could be present at her death.

Aha, I think, but the bastards didn't know about the dog! They would deny the doomed Queen the comfort of people who loved her, but they could not ban her loyal pet. What must it have been like for the doomed woman, to feel his rough coat tickling beneath her shift? I know that he (or she?) would have given Mary courage … 'You're there, *cherie*, you're there.'

Mary Stuart had more soul than those who murdered her. She was a poet who wrote, with both wit and heartbreaking faith, in French, Italian and Latin, and she was writing until the day before she died. A sonnet to her cousin Elizabeth I contains the lines:

> *One thought that is my torment and my delight*
> *Ebbs and flows bittersweet within my heart*

She was begging Elizabeth ('dear sister') to see her, but it was not to be. Mary made so many mistakes in her life; she loved unwisely (like so many) and became a prey to politics and religion and circumstance, yet at the end she conducted herself with absolute dignity. How many people can say that? It is that dignity which remains, when her mighty prison is no more. And the honesty and humility which prompted her to tell her maid, Jane Kennedy, who on her last night read aloud the story of the good thief, 'In truth he was a great sinner, but not so great as I have been.' And at her end she prayed for the forgiveness of sins.

What else is there to pray for?

To be haunted perpetually by one thought, 'bittersweet within my heart' ('*amaro at dolce al mia cor ...*'), is something I understand. And the absolute necessity for dignity and forgiveness. And the love of a small dog. Standing in that bleak place on top of Mary's tumbled prison, all of this has meaning, and I feel grateful.

The wind attacks me and Bonnie. Robin takes a photograph of 'his girls', capturing a windblown moment of – yes – pilgrimage. I bend to pick up a stone and toss it from hand to hand, fantasizing that this could be a fragment from the castle itself, since stones do remain and huge emotions and great wrongs are imprinted on the earth and nothing is ever finished. But it's time to go, and suddenly I fling the stone down. What is the point in carrying stones away? I am already freighted with too much history.

We are alive and cheerful and have an important job to do.

At 1.30 p.m. around 220 schoolchildren aged six to eight file into the Great Hall of Oundle School, which looks as if it could have been graced by Mary Stuart but was in fact built in 1908 in Renaissance style. I'm waiting at the front with piles of my books – and a bejewelled dog bowl. Hidden beneath the table is Bonnie's bright (embarrassingly so, to Robin) pink dog bag, to be revealed at the right moment.

I have the 'performance' off pat; after all I have been talking to children about my work since my first children's book was published in 1985. With the new series, inspired by Bonnie, Robin and I have devised a little bit of *schtik*. After talking about how writers get their ideas, and asking the children lots of questions, and reading an extract from *Big Dog Bonnie* which tells how my character Harry's mother got the small dog from a rescue home … at last I ask if they would like to meet 'the real Bonnie', tell them she is shy and doesn't want to come – but say I will call her. So I fish the phone out of her pink bag and call Robin's number. He is, of course, waiting elsewhere with the dog. After the pretend conversation with Bonnie the children are motionless and silent with excitement. Then Robin appears at the back of the hall, puts her on the floor, whispers, 'Go find Mummy' – and the dog races down the middle aisle space, to be swept up, licking and wriggling, by the visiting author, as the children let out collective squeaks and sighs of pleasure.

As any theatre director would see, this works beautifully, and to great effect – a forest of hands in the air, and questions answered, and laughter, and children wanting to ask Bonnie questions (favourite food?) and all the time my dog is in my arms, unbothered by the Great Hall or the children and all their teachers, because she is with me. One little girl has her hand up for ages, frantically waving it for attention. When the teacher finally gestures for her to ask her question she squirms with pleasure and sighs, 'Oh, your dog's so *cute*.'

'She certainly is,' I smile.

Does life get much better than this – with the kids so happy and my dog in my arms and my man smiling at the back of the hall?

When it's over, after the long line of children clutching books to sign has been dispersed, and we walk out past the groups waiting to go back to their respective schools (young voices calling 'Goodbye Bonnie! ...') we head for Stamford. This famous Lincolnshire town is about a 20-minute drive north from Oundle and we'd been told it is worth a visit – 'the finest stone town in England', guidebooks say. Its great house, Burghley, was the home of Sir William Cecil, wily Secretary of State to Elizabeth I and one of the agents of Mary Stuart's downfall.

We should have made a better plan – for the great house is as closed as the church at Fotheringhay. Still, we walk a little in the grounds with Bonnie, looking at a miracle of Tudor architecture. 'We'll come back to this area,' we promise ourselves, for there is Peterborough Cathedral to see, and each year we say we must do a motoring tour of our own country, as John Steinbeck did with his dog, and call it 'Travels with Bonnie'. For now, aware that the journey home beckons, we drive into Stamford, park the car and wander around.

So many churches, so many good buildings, starting from the thirteenth century, and no time to do them justice. That optimistic 'We'll come back' is the promise all of us make to ourselves, in the hope that things won't change too much, that our luck will hold, that our loves will last, that we will walk our lovely, lolloping dogs through plenty more springs yet and go on noticing beauty (in the words of Mary, '*O Seigneur Dieu, recevez ma prière*') until the end.

In the meantime, Stamford's shops are good so I abandon all thoughts of visiting churches and ancient buildings today and spot a scarf in a window. It's cold, which is as good an excuse as any for darting in to buy the two-tone-purple accessory. As I am paying for it, while Robin is waiting patiently with Bonnie, an elderly couple enter the shop. Seeing the dog they coo and fuss – as people generally do.

The husband asks what breed she is.

'A Maltese,' says Robin, and then, after more compliments from the couple, he adds conversationally, 'She's a rescue dog.'

There is a tiny pause; the man looks puzzled. He doesn't understand. 'What does she rescue?' he asks.

Surreal images flash in the mind's eye:

– the small dog plunging into a boiling sea with a rope between her teeth –

– the small dog pinning the villain up against the wall, to protect her police handler –

– the small dog roaming the Alps, a barrel of brandy around her neck –

– the small dog sniffing through earthquake wreckage, looking for survivors –

The moment is too good to miss.

I turn and answer, 'Us!'

ACKNOWLEDGEMENTS

*M*any friends and colleagues understood why I wanted to write this book, but I must single out my children, Dan and Kitty, who, while not at all enjoying the prospect of old wounds being opened, nevertheless understood their mother's overwhelming need for catharsis, as well as my search for a creative form in which to frame it. My husband Robin gave the usual rock-like support which is central to my life, publisher Jenny Heller is a kindred spirit I am delighted to find, and my agent Patrick Walsh came up with the perfect title – which achievement he has forgotten and denies. The psychologist Linda Blair provided me with invaluable professional bolstering at a time of mini-crisis when I really did not know if I was doing the right thing.

Lastly I wish to thank Jonathan Dimbleby for his forbearance. A person who values privacy more than I do, he is at the same time Chair of that important organisation Index on Censorship, which may perhaps have a small bearing on his dignified silence about what I might or might not write. It is not the only debt I owe him.

Copyright Acknowledgements

The author is most grateful to the editors of the *Daily Mail* and *The Times* for permission to reprint extracts from her articles; also for permission to include the following extracts from copyright material:

'Not Gonna Turn Back' from *The Inside* by Jasmine Cain © Jasmine Cain.

'Late Fragment' from *All of Us: The Collected Poems* by Raymond Carver, published by Harvill Press. Reprinted by permission of The Random House Group Ltd.

'in spite of everything' from *Complete Poems 1904–1962* by E.E. Cummings, edited by George J. Firmage, by permission of W.W. Norton & Company. Copyright © 1991 by the Trustees for the E.E. Cummings Trust and George James Firmage.

'Fotheringay' by Sandy Denny from *What We Did On Our Holidays*, published by Kobalt Music.

'Atlas' from *New and Collected Poems* by U.A. Fanthorpe, published by Enitharmon Press.

'The Housedog's Grave' from *The Collected Poetry of Robinson Jeffers, Volume 3, 1939–1962*, copyright © Jeffers Literary Properties. All rights reserved. Used with the permission of Stanford University Press, www.sup.org.

ACKNOWLEDGEMENTS

'An Arundel Tomb' from *Collected Poems* by Philip Larkin, published by Faber & Faber.

'For Becky, Dan and Sarah' from *Collected Poems* by Michael Longley, published by Jonathan Cape. Reprinted by permission of The Random House Group Ltd.

'On Parting with My Wife, Janina' from *New and Collected Poems (1931–2001)* by Czeslaw Milosz, published by Penguin Books Ltd.

Susan Chilcott obituary by Tom Sutcliffe, *Guardian*, 6 September 2003.

'An Attempt at Jealousy' from *Selected Poems* by Marina Tsvetaeva, translated by Elaine Feinstein, published by Carcanet Press Ltd.

'What to Remember when Waking' from *The House of Belonging* by David Whyte, published by Many Rivers Press.

While every effort has been made to trace the owners of copyright material reproduced herein, the author and publishers would like to apologise for any omissions and will be pleased to incorporate missing acknowledgements in any future editions.